Graphis Inc. is committed to presenting exceptional work in international Design, Advertising, Illustration & Photography.

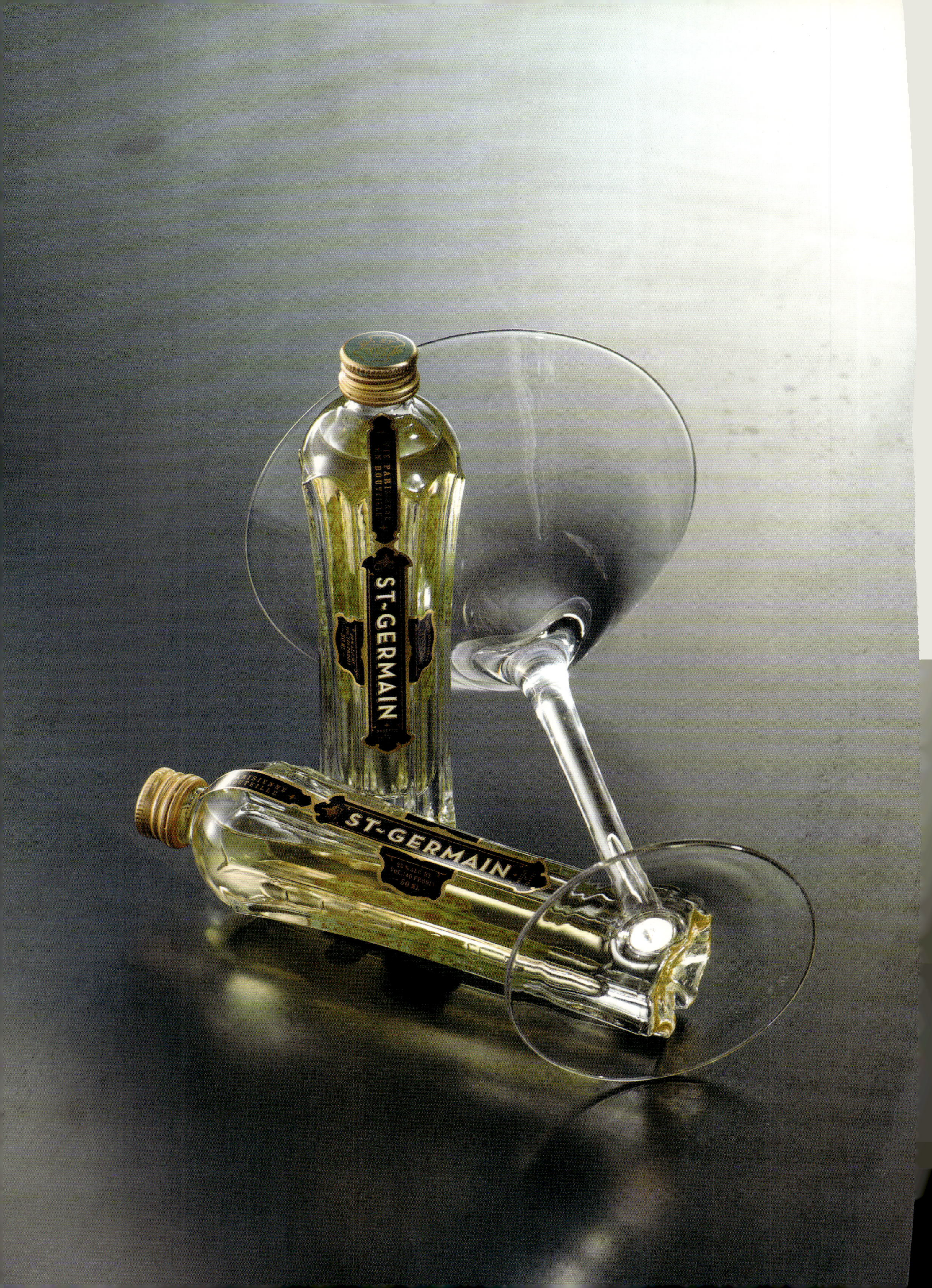
ST-GERMAIN
ST-GERMAIN

Branding5

Published by Graphis | Publisher & Creative Director: B. Martin Pedersen | Design: Yon Joo Choi, JiEun Lee | Editorial: Ariel Davis, Melanie Madden, Eby Gagel | Production: Jennifer Berlingeri, Abigail Newman | Interns: Jarrod Barretto, Natalie Davis, Jae Kyung Kim, Joseph Lee, Kimberly Lennex

Remarks: We extend our heartfelt thanks to contributors throughout the world who have made it possible to publish a wide and international spectrum of the best work in this field. Entry instructions for all Graphis Books may be requested from: Graphis Inc., 307 Fifth Avenue, Tenth Floor, New York, New York 10016, or visit our web site at www.graphis.com.

Anmerkungen: Unser Dank gilt den Einsendern aus aller Welt, die es uns ermöglicht haben, ein breites, internationales. Spektrum der besten Arbeiten zu veröffentlichen. Teilnahmebedingungen für die Graphis-Bücher sind erhältlich bei: Graphis, Inc., 307 Fifth Avenue, Tenth Floor, New York, New York 10016. Besuchen Sie uns im World Wide Web, www.graphis.com.

Remerciements: Nous remercions les participants du monde entier qui ont rendu possible la publication de cet ouvrage offrant un panorama complet des meilleurs travaux. Les modalités d'inscription peuvent être obtenues auprès de: Graphis, Inc., 307 Fifth Avenue, Tenth Floor, New York, New York 10016. Rendez-nous visite sur notre site web: www.graphis.com.

 ISBN: 1- 932026-20-7. Printed in China.

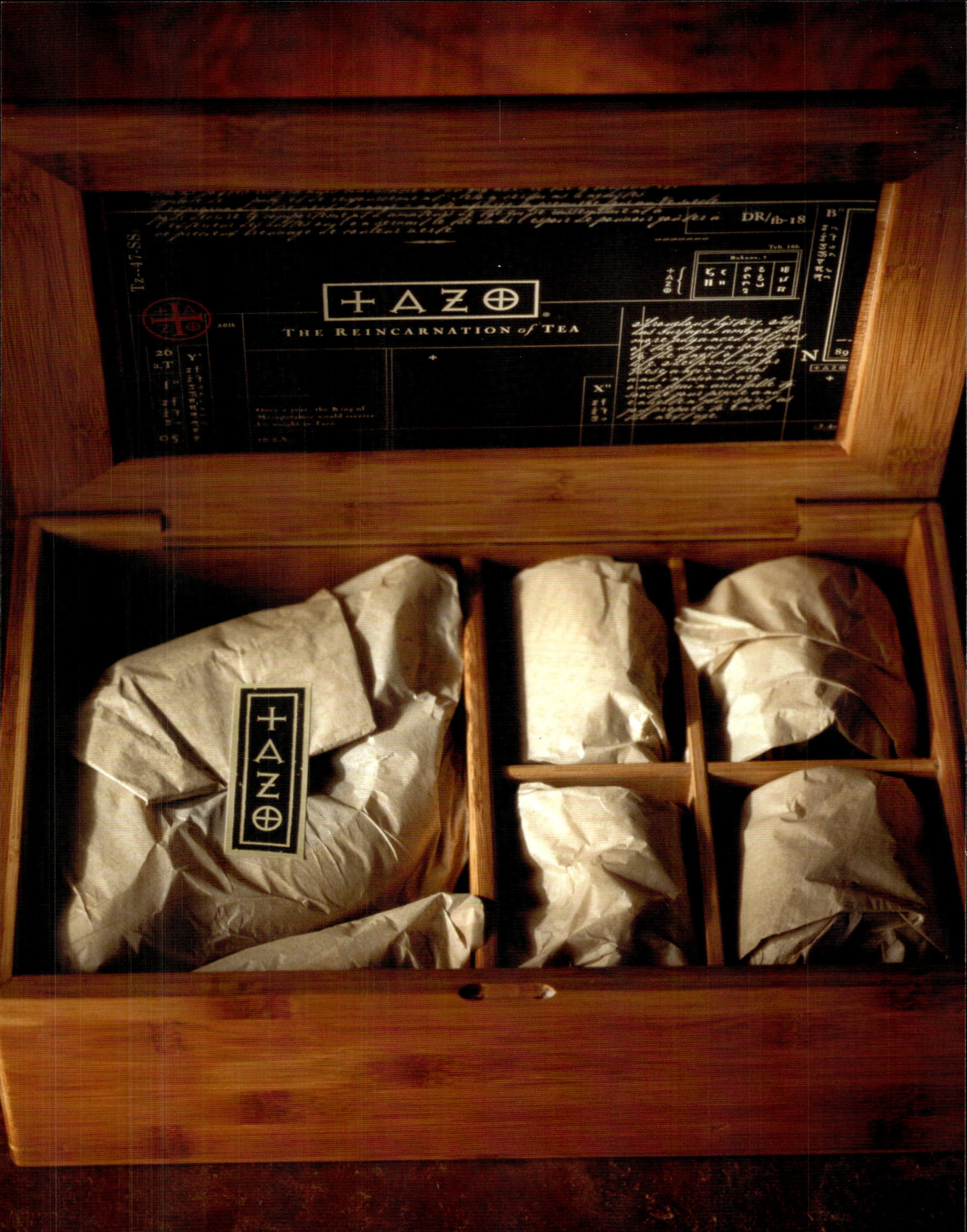
TAZO
THE REINCARNATION of TEA
DR/fb-18
TAZO

Contents

The 10 branding successes presented here are from a variety of international industries. An ad agency, a corporation, and four design firms emerged through the final selection. The results were chosen from entries to the Branding 5 book, as well as candidates from the past 5 years of the Graphis Design Annual.

Knut Maierhofer, of KMS in Germany, drove Canyon Bikes in Germany to success, and also in the most daunting of tasks, decided to do something most of us would have failed at, the successful identity for his own design firm.

Landor emerged with a real estate branding project for the Burj Dubai tower, as well as beautifully executed packaging and branding for Wolfgang Puck.

Vespa is also represented with a continued heritage of classic Italian good taste in both their products and branding.

Turner Duckworth, experts in branding, gave their talent to a very small bottling division of the Click Wine Group and gave success to Root 1. They went on to successfully deal with Coca-Cola, the soft drink giant.

Steve Sandstrom far exceeded his client's expectations. When the Tazo founders first saw his presentation, they were stunned. They decided to to go back and improve their product to match the quality of Sandstrom's design. Unheard of in this business. Steve also created another success story with St-Germain.

There are lessons here. Lessons of devoted commitment to the client, dedication to quality, and a continued focus for the project's financial success.

B.Martin Pedersen

Previous spread: St-Germain Small Bottle by Sandstrom Partners | *Opposite page:* Tazo Bamboc Box by Sandstrom Partners | *Following spread:* Burj Dubai by Landor Associates

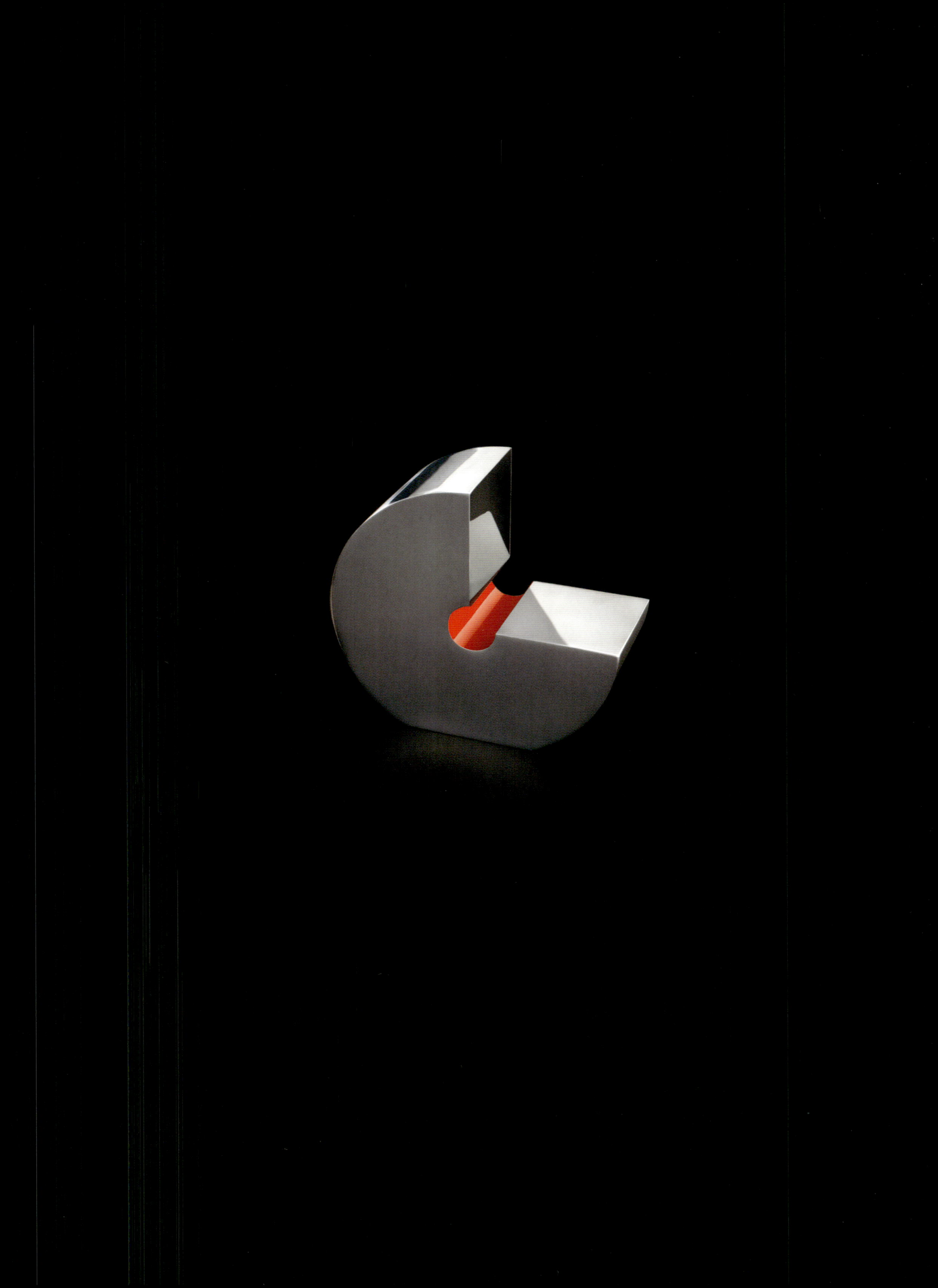

GraphisPlatinum&GoldAwardWinners

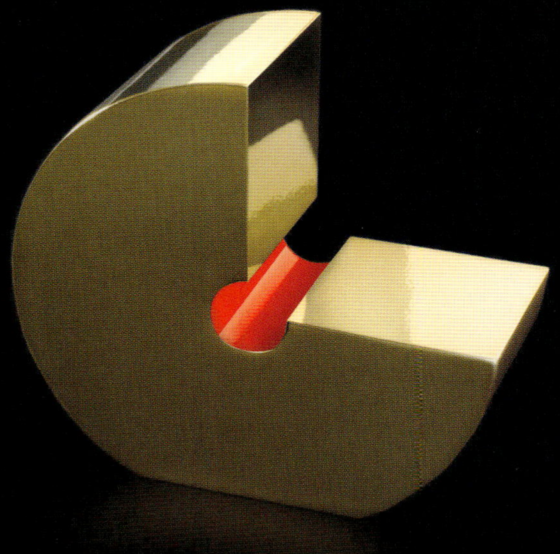

Award photographs by Henry Leutwyler

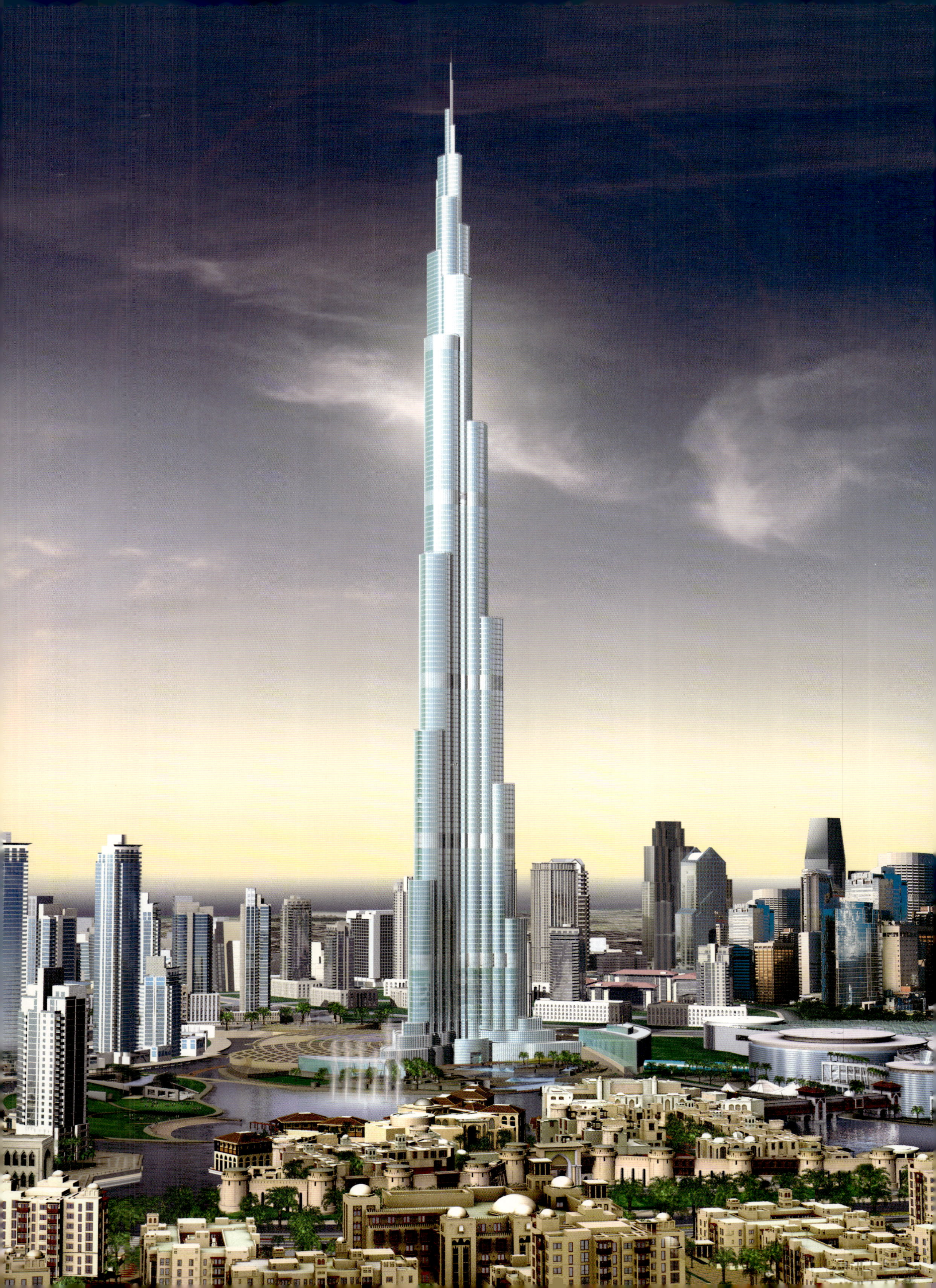

10BrandingCaseStudies:

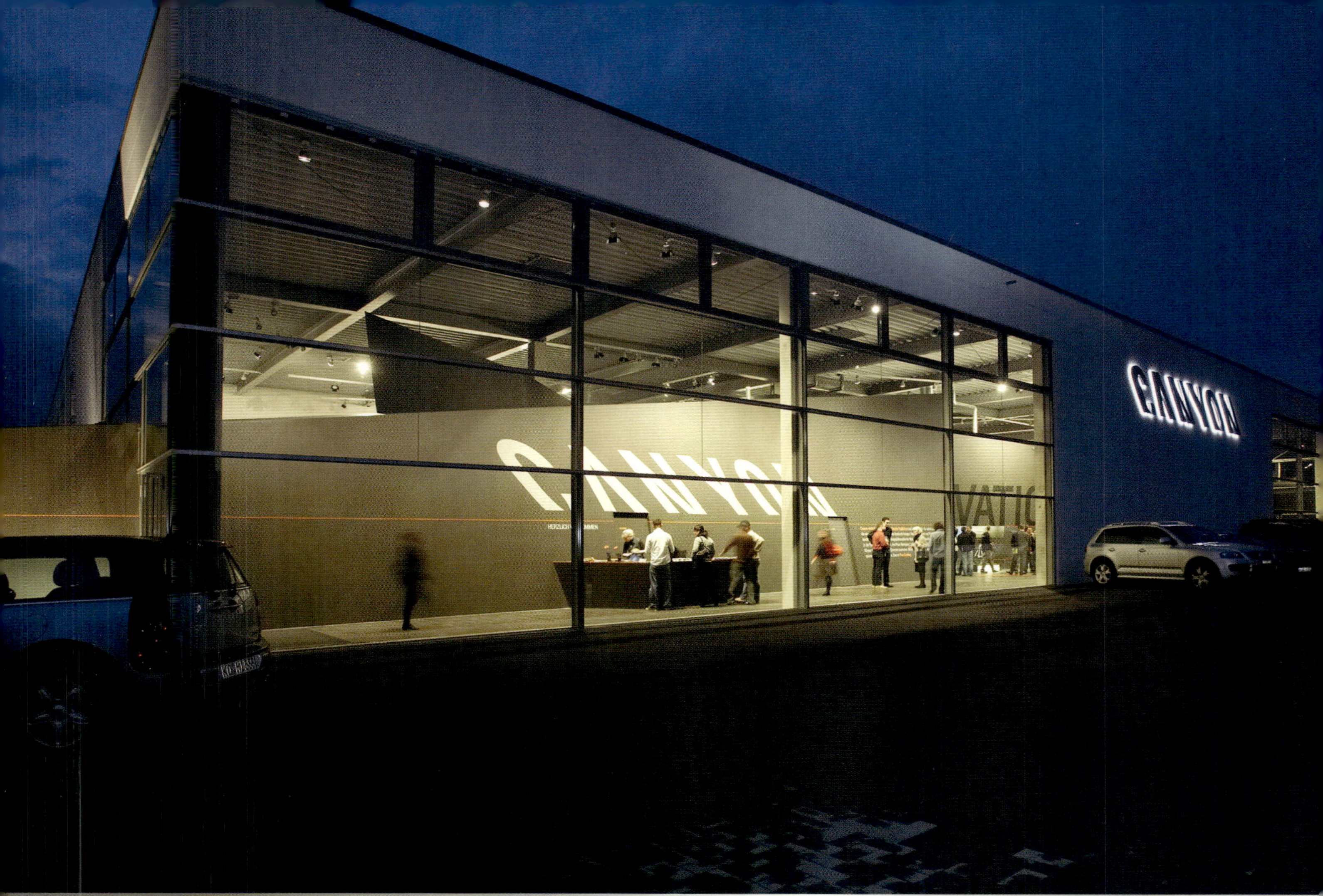
CANYON

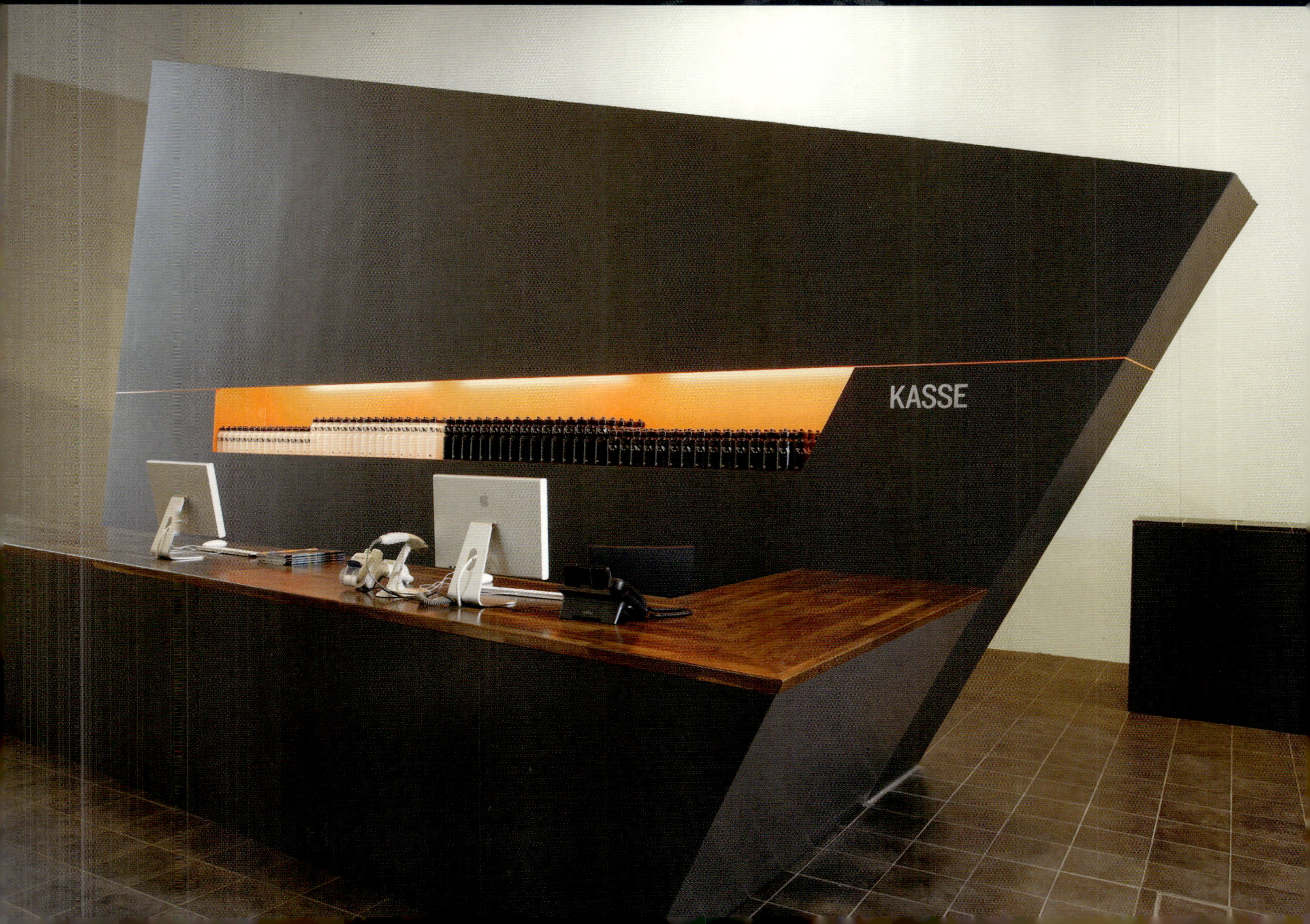
KASSE

Since 2005, Germany's KMS TEAM has handled branding and identity for Canyon Bicycles. Their innovative creative work for the bike company runs the gamut from typography to environmental design, including the Canyon showroom that opened in March 2008. For their efforts, KMS TEAM has earned a DDC Award, a Red Dot Communication Design Award, an iF communication design award, a European Design Award, and a Corporate Design Prize. KMS TEAM's Creative Director and Managing Partner, Knut Maierhofer, spoke to Graphis about branding the company that's changing the bike industry.

Q&A with KMS TEAM's Knut Maierhofer

Why was Canyon ripe for rebranding ?

First, Canyon's major challenge was that the traditional bike market has established an expectation that high-end bicycles are to be sold exclusively by bikeshops, which provide better products and the extra benefits of expert, personal advice. Customers were not used to the idea of buying bicycles via the Internet and catalogues. Second, before we started working with Canyon, the brand was a mixture of different styles. It was quite ambivalent in terms of design, story and media coverage. Canyon didn't realize the potential they had to build up a rich, powerful brand with a concise brand image. They did know, however, that they needed exactly this to succeed in directly distributing their bikes and convincing their customers of their high-end cycling technology.

What was the KMS TEAM's solution?

We approached the task simultaneously from design and content perspectives. 'Pure Cycling' was our key concept, an idea which encapsulated the brand's themes of perfect bikes, clear communication, and passionate bikers. The design went back to the brand's roots, considering the canyon motif, cracked rocks and the bikes' engineering appeal. We ended up with a formal language set, described best by pureness, precision and linear dynamics. These two aspects—the defined content and the new visual language—were then combined as an overall brand experience through all media applications, including product branding, packaging, fair booths, and more.

What was your main goal with this campaign?

To help Canyon best communicate their potential. To help them understand who they are, what they can credibly talk about, and what this looks like in a holistic branding concept.

Tell us about the typography you developed for this campaign. How does it reflect Canyon's identity?

The Canyon logotype is derived from the product. The angle of the letters corresponds exactly to the angle of the forward bar of the bike (in respect to the ground). Thanks to this design, the beholder always sees the Canyon type in a horizontal or a vertical position. While it is quite common to see logotypes using an italic type—i.e. letters inclined in forward direction (because this conventionally expresses speed and so on)—the canyon logotype does the opposite. Its inclination to the rear is a very special feature. It expresses dynamism, and at the same time it is associated with climbing (or descending). The cut-off letters also contribute to a dynamic, modern look. The Canyon typeface developed thereof is highly distinctive, and is an efficient branding tool that works even when the logo or signature is not shown.

How were you able to translate the designs from the Web store to the actual Canyon Bike store?

For us, the question was not how to translate from Internet to real space, but how to develop a global design which was applicable to each of the different spaces, be it the (physical) shop, the website, the product or the advertisements. Each of these aspects represents a tangible brand experience.

Other than the store, Web store and typography, what other elements were part of the Canyon campaign?

We developed the whole brand appearance. We believe a brand will only succeed when all media are aligned to to tell the holistic brand story. Therefore, we support Canyon in all areas of brand communications such as the catalogue, product branding, packaging, events, trade fair booth, etc.

Describe the creative process behind your design and typography.

One of the keys to success was close cooperation with those responsible on Canyon's side. Connecting design with strategy and ideas with marketing experience led to results that fit very well with the goals of the company and the expectations of its customers.

What else makes this branding campaign unique?

Definitely the imagery style and the visual language in the store, but also more subtle details like the oblique lines that are part of the layouts.

Is there anything else we haven't covered that you think is important to include?

Canyon is an extraordinary bicycle company. It has a unique approach, selling high-end cycling technology via direct distribution channels and staying in touch with its customers. This approach is changing the bike industry, and the Canyon brand underlines this approach of being direct, without compromise. They're straight, precise—and different.

To learn more about Canyon Bicycles, visit www.canyonbikes.com.
For more information on KMS TEAM and Knut Maierhofer, see page 23, or visit www.kms-team.de. *All photos courtesy of Canyon Bicycles.*

Creative Director & Managing partner of KMS TEAM: Knut Maierhofer | *Design Director: Patrick Märki* | *Brand Consultant: Simon Betsch* | *Designers: May Kato, Christian Hartig, Grace Chou* | *Account Director: Sandra Ehm* | *Junior Project Manager: Daniel Jacobi* | *Art Director: Helena Fruehauf* | *All photos courtesy of Canyon Bicycles.*

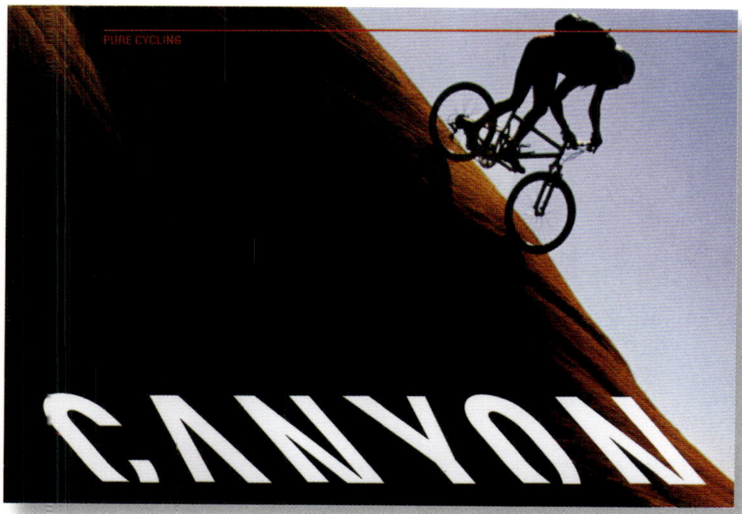

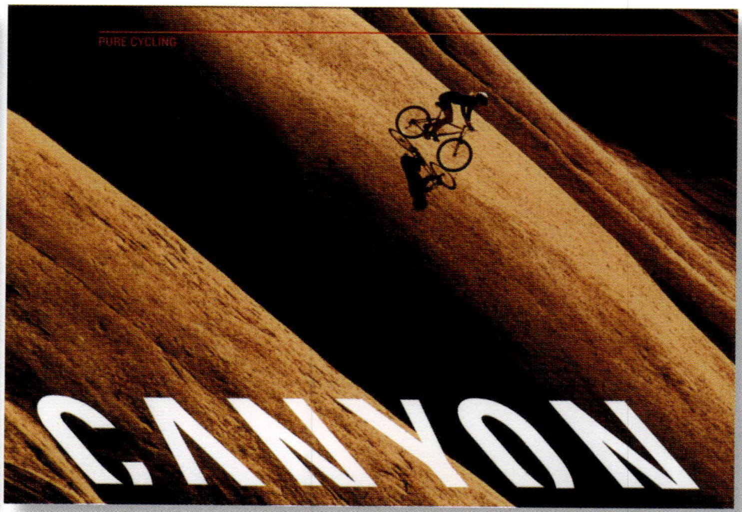

"The brand-building project with KMS TEAM (still in progress) has been an important investment for us to stabilize growth and to raise the Canyon Brand experience to a new level."

Roman Arnold, *CEO, Canyon Bicycles*

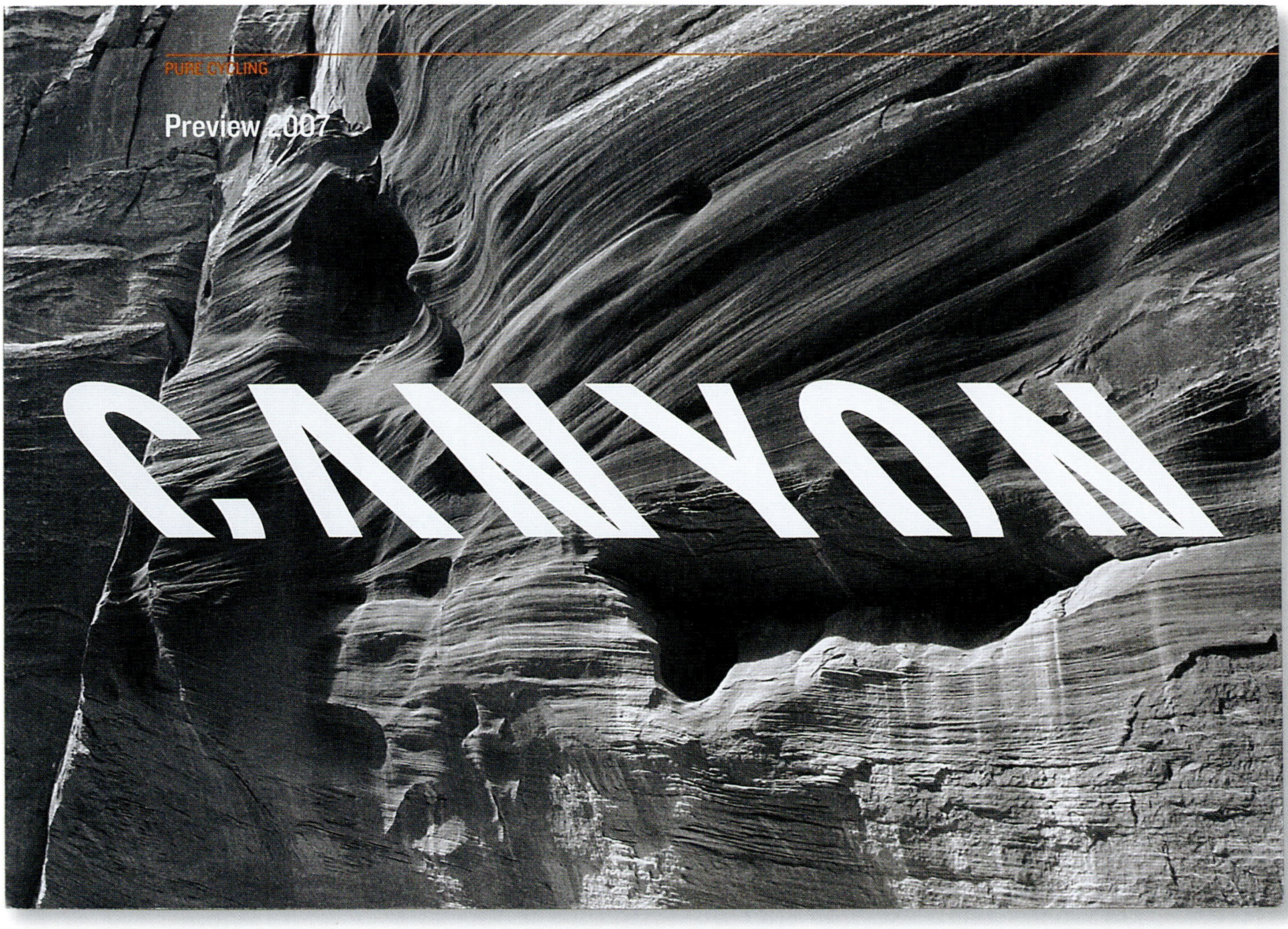
PURE CYCLING
Preview 2007
CANYON

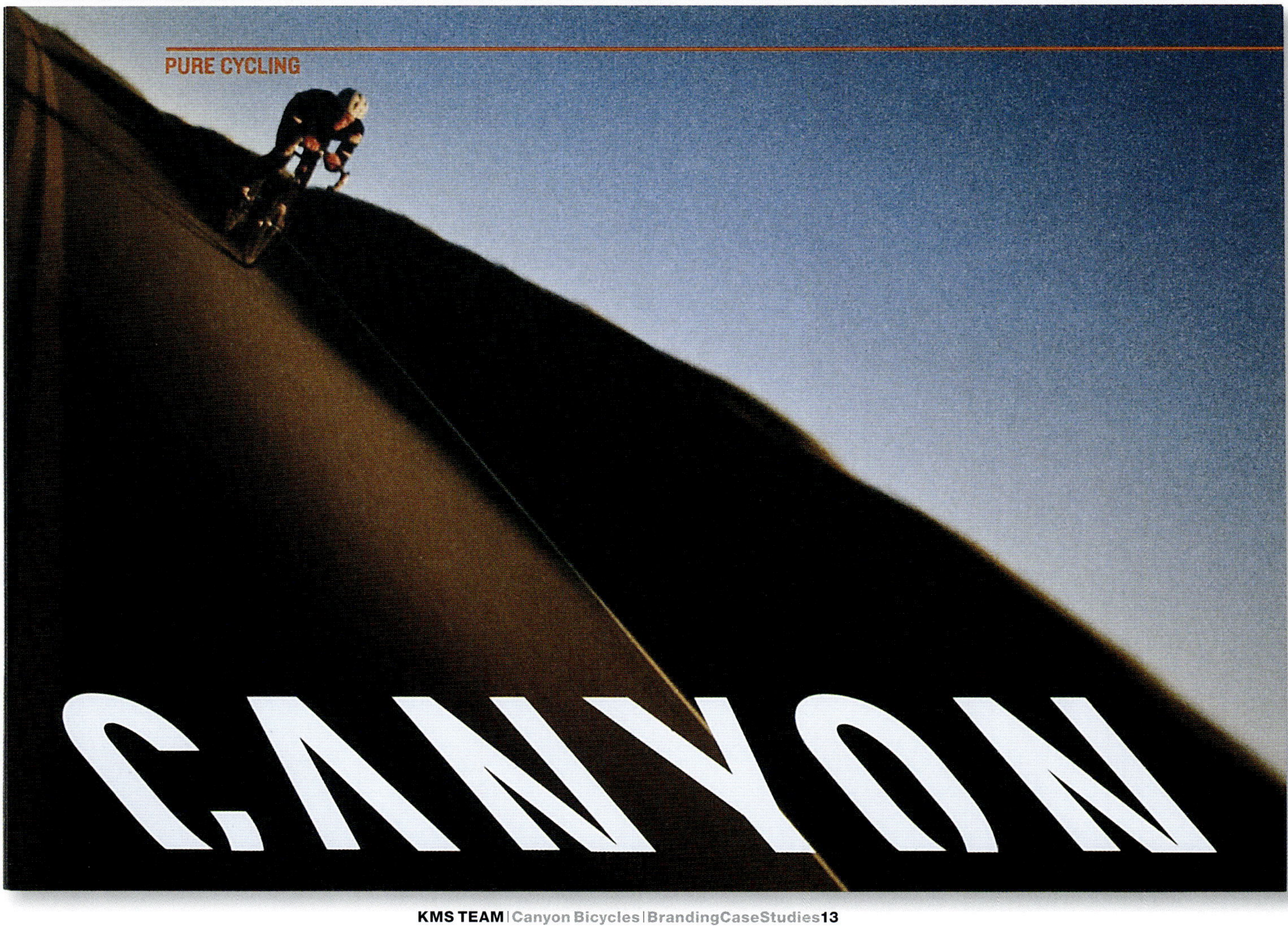
PURE CYCLING
CANYON

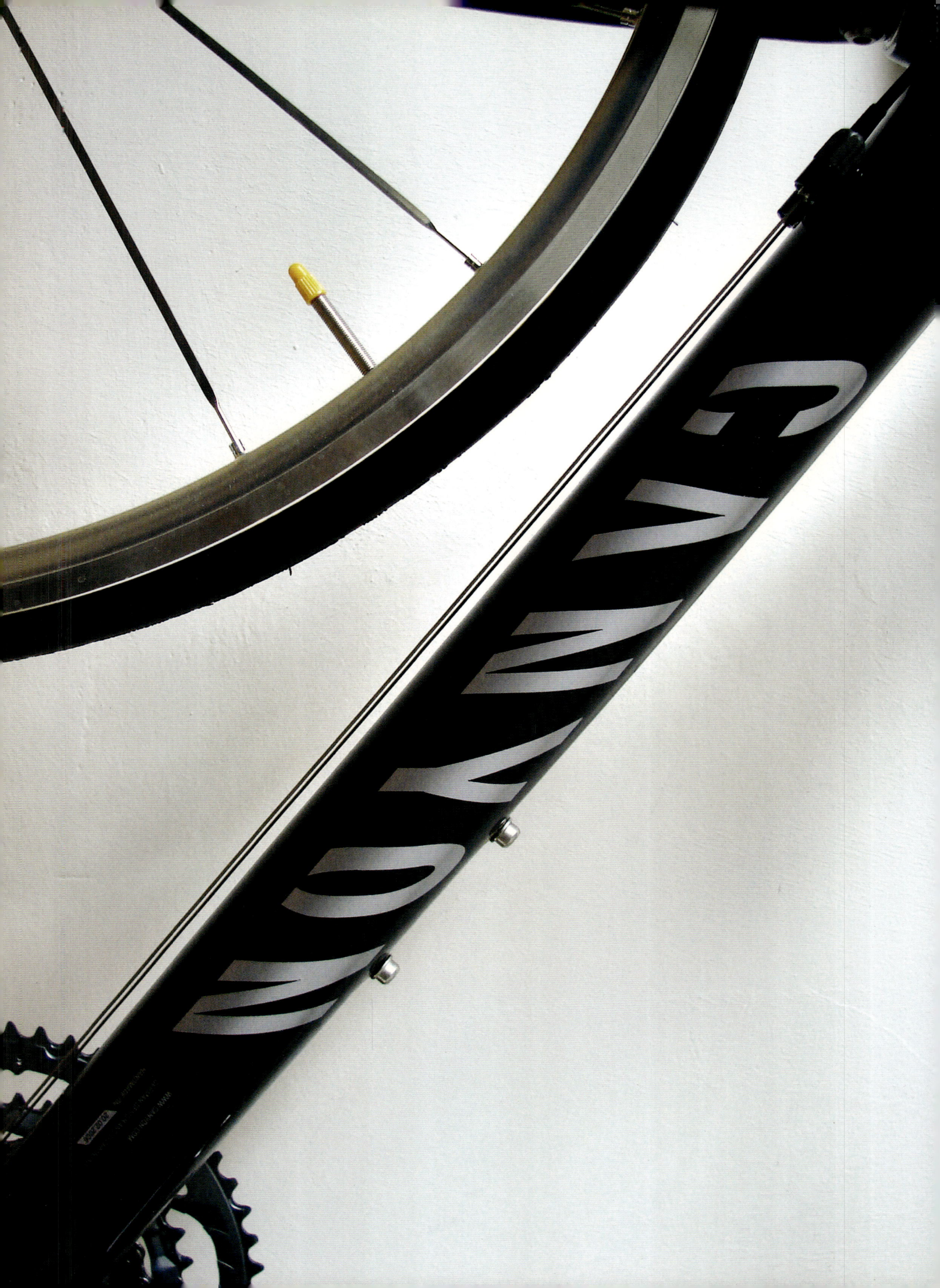

A ABCDEFGHIJKLMNOPQ

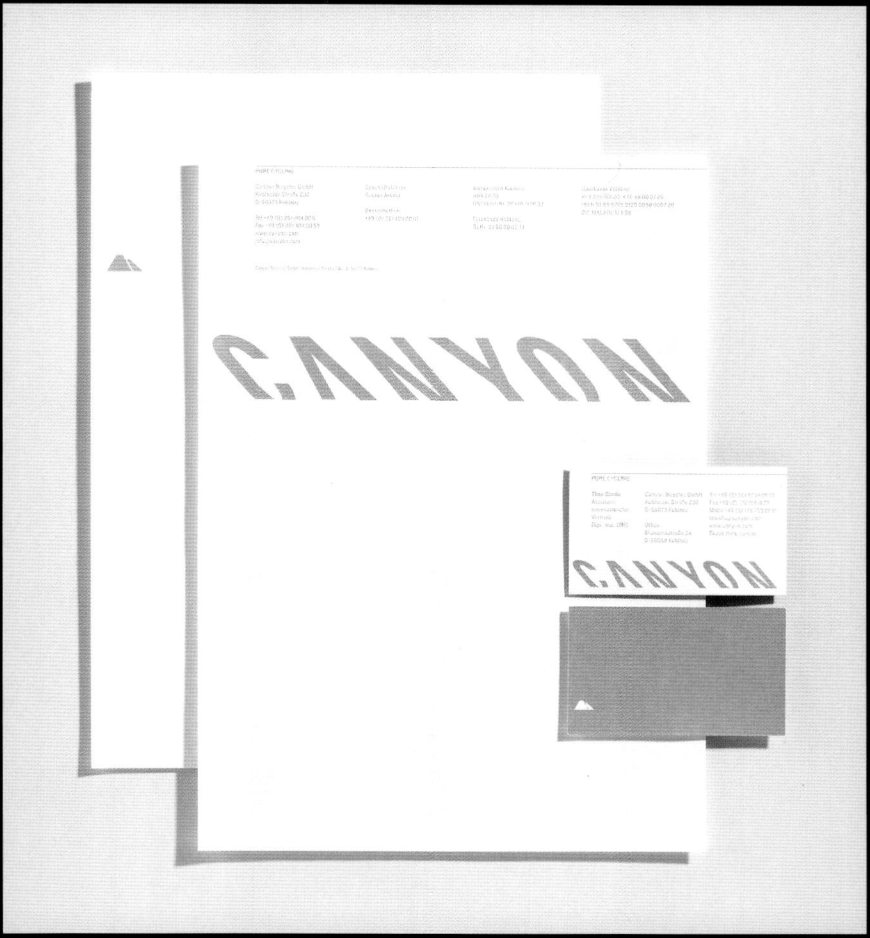

RSTUVWXYZ 0123456789

"The Canyon project is an excellent example of how our design approach works. We call it *Tiefendesign* (depth design)."

Knut Maierhofer, *Managing Partner, KMS TEAM*

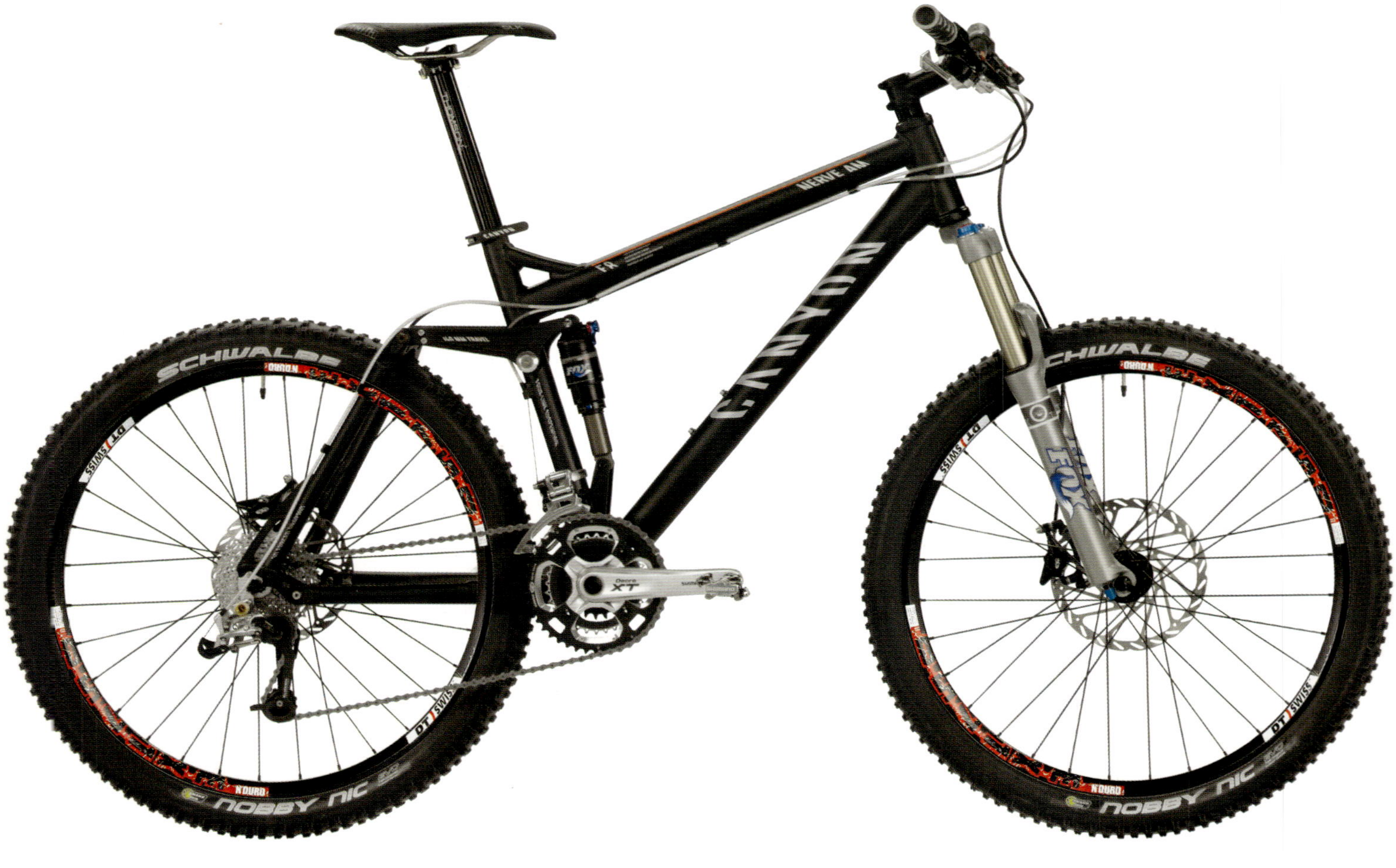

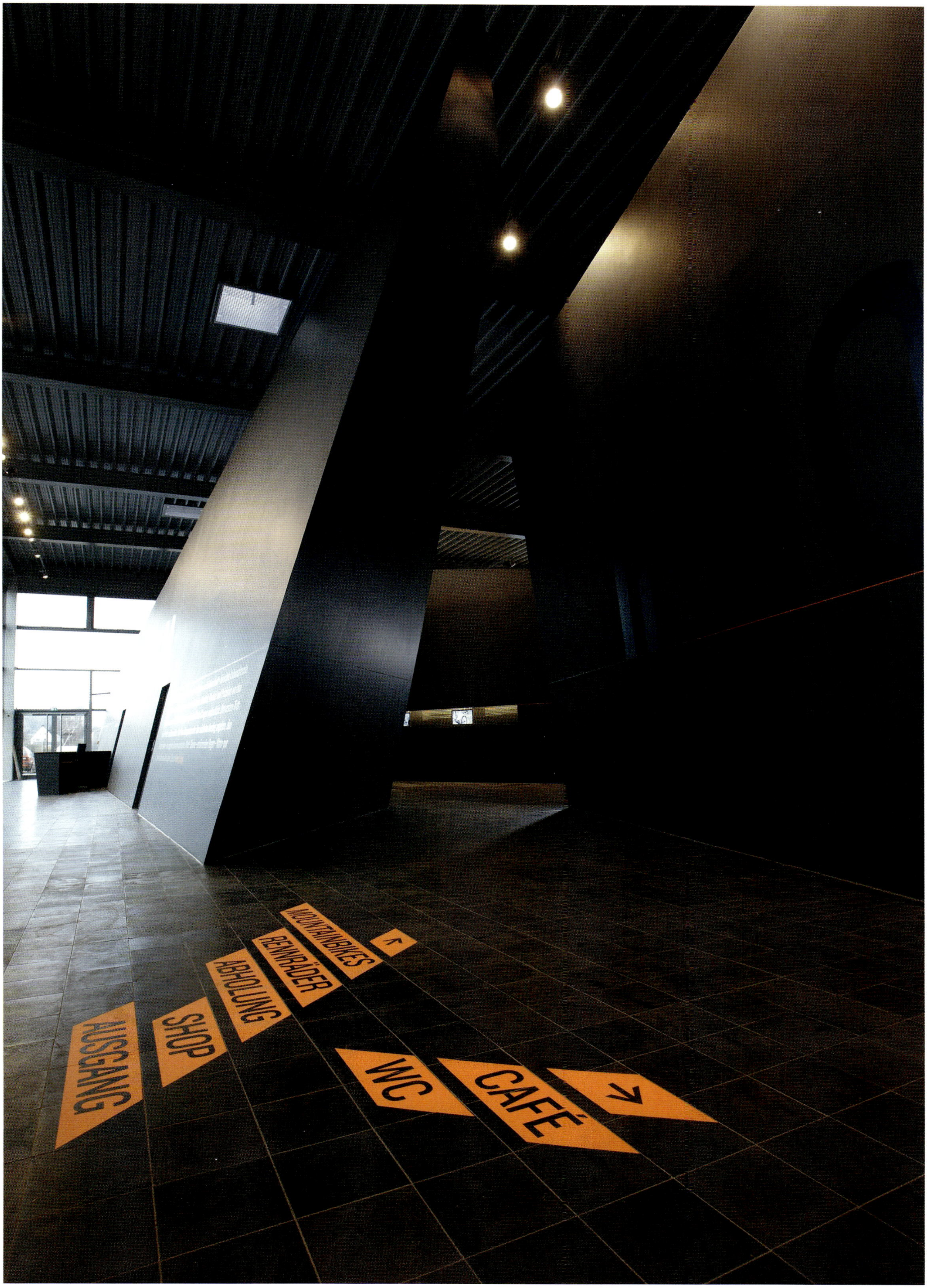
MOUNTAINBIKES
RENNRÄDER
ABHOLUNG
SHOP
AUSGANG
WC
CAFÉ

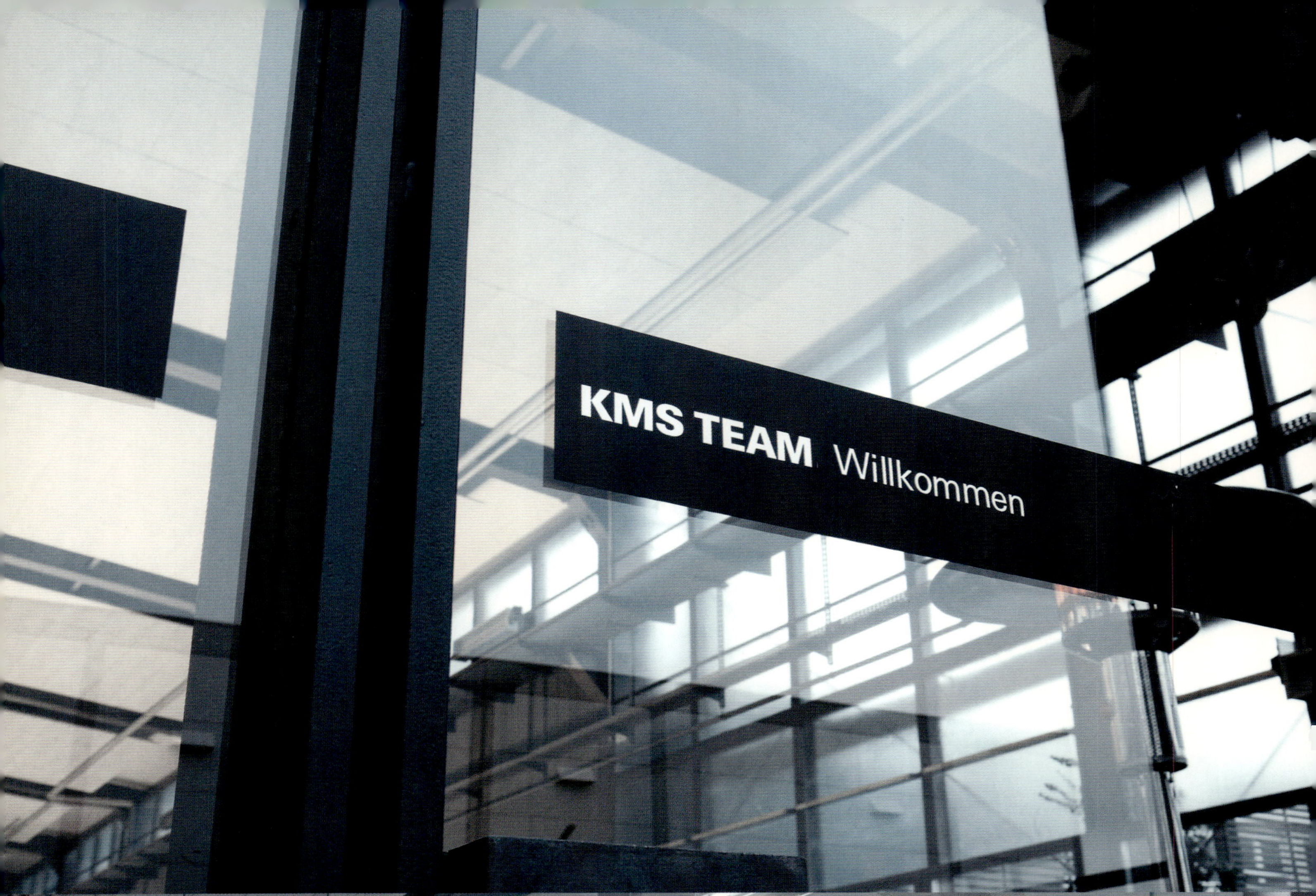
KMS TEAM Willkommen

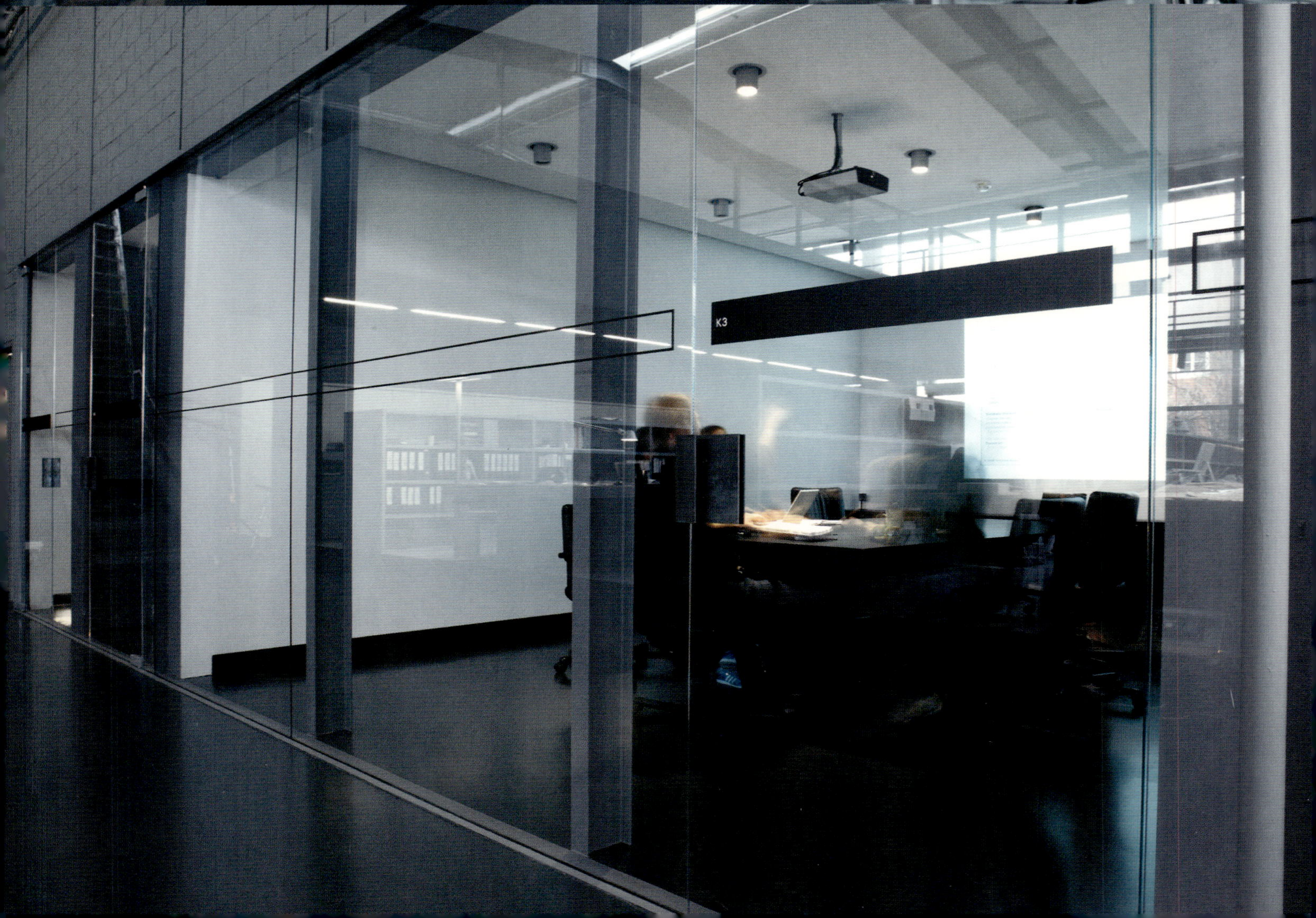
K3

In some ways, rebranding one's own design firm seems like an easier project than most. Who knows your company better than you? But that proximity can make objectivity nearly impossible. This awareness makes KMS TEAM's successful rebranding all the more impressive. ■ Their new corporate design highlights their position as Germany's largest independent design studio and visually reflects the operational method that helped get them there. The new design's goals were twofold: first, place KMS TEAM in public view in an assertive, concise manner; and second, simultaneously maintain neutrality with respect to their clients' corporate designs, illustrating the objectivity at the center of their consulting services. ■ The rebranding efforts center around the concept of a "cloud of ideas," depicting thoughts and questions as fields circling one's head, reflecting the diverse activities which occur at the studio and the multiple disciplines involved in the creative process. The "cloud of ideas" concept was implemented as a rotating bar animation in KMS TEAM's interactive applications, which gave rise to the visual core of the rebranding design: the individual black bar. This element is visible in all of the firm's branding applications. At the same time, it behaves as a playful, stylistic device and defines graphic organizational structure.

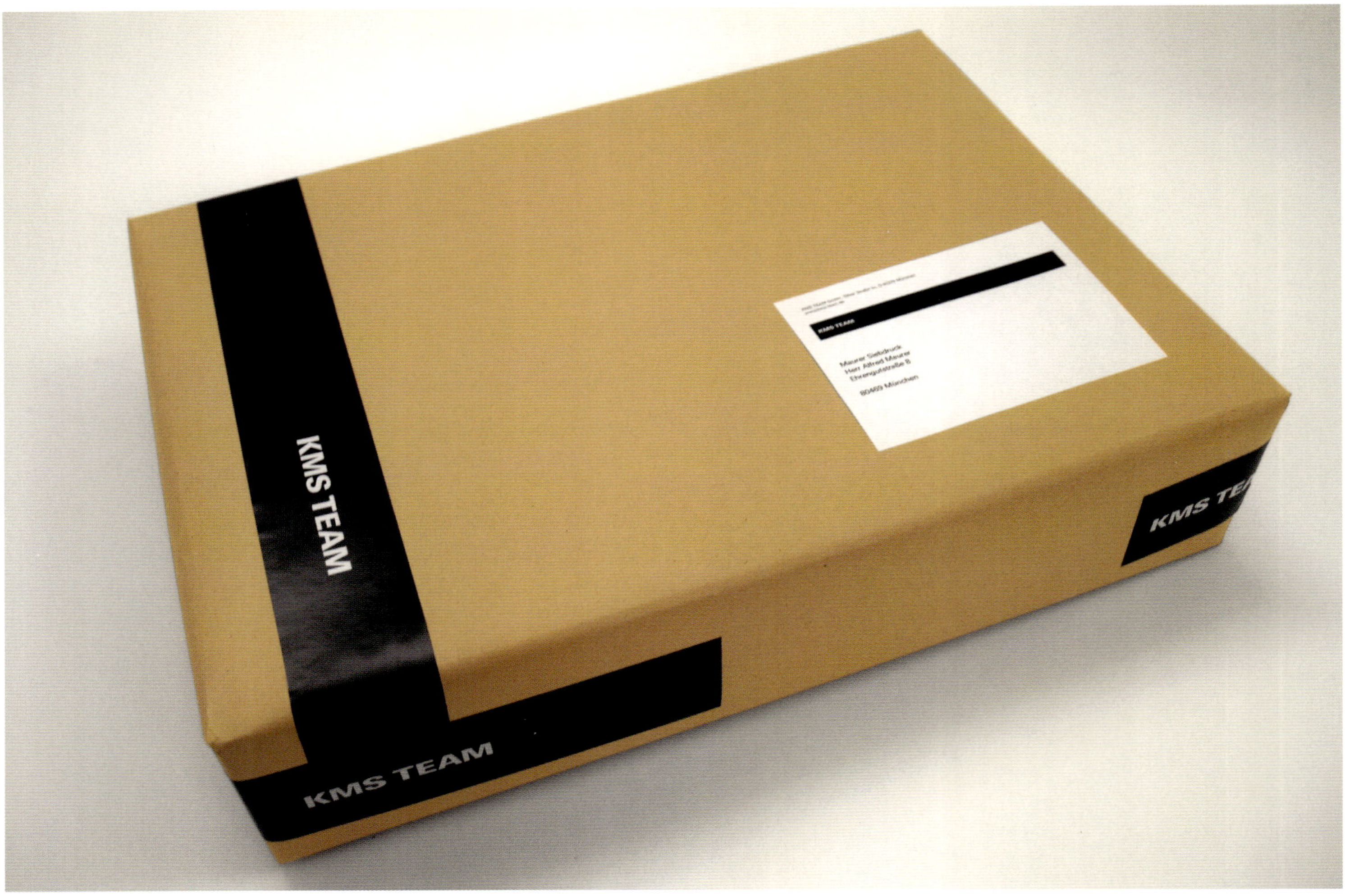

Limiting the color scheme to black and white further conveyed the firm's neutrality and objectivity with respect to its clients, and KMS TEAM uses it as a contrasting background in all communications. They chose Univers Black font for its precise, clear style. The capitalization of the appendage "TEAM" alludes to the importance of their staff members. ■ *Turn the page to read KMS TEAM founder Knut Maierhofer's take on the project.*

According to the German business magazines *Page* and *Horizont*, KMS TEAM is the largest independent German design studio, and the second largest design studio overall, following LBI International AB owned Meta Design.

KMS TEAM, Corporate Design
Internetauftritt

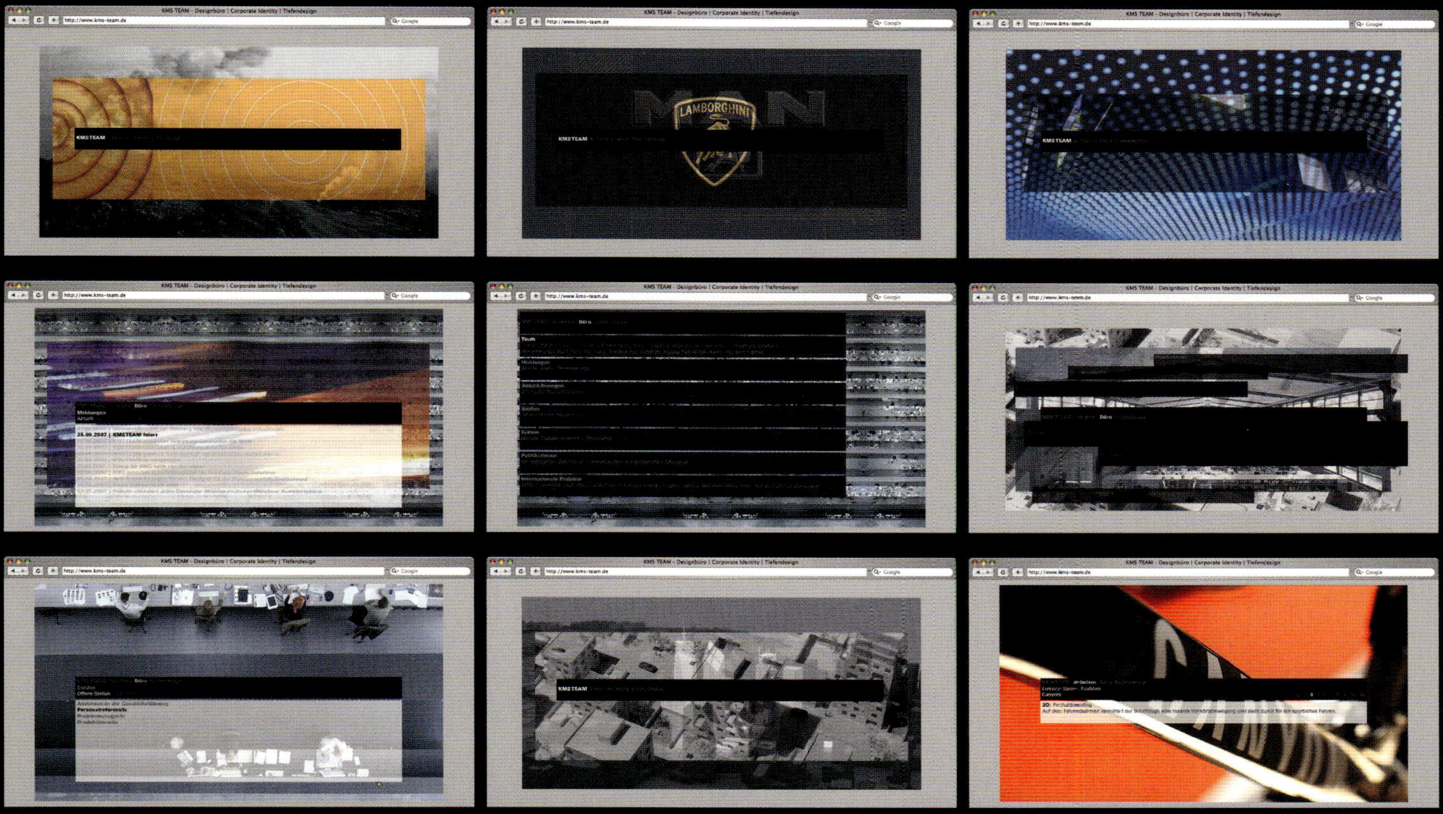

KMS TEAM, Corporate Design
Showreel

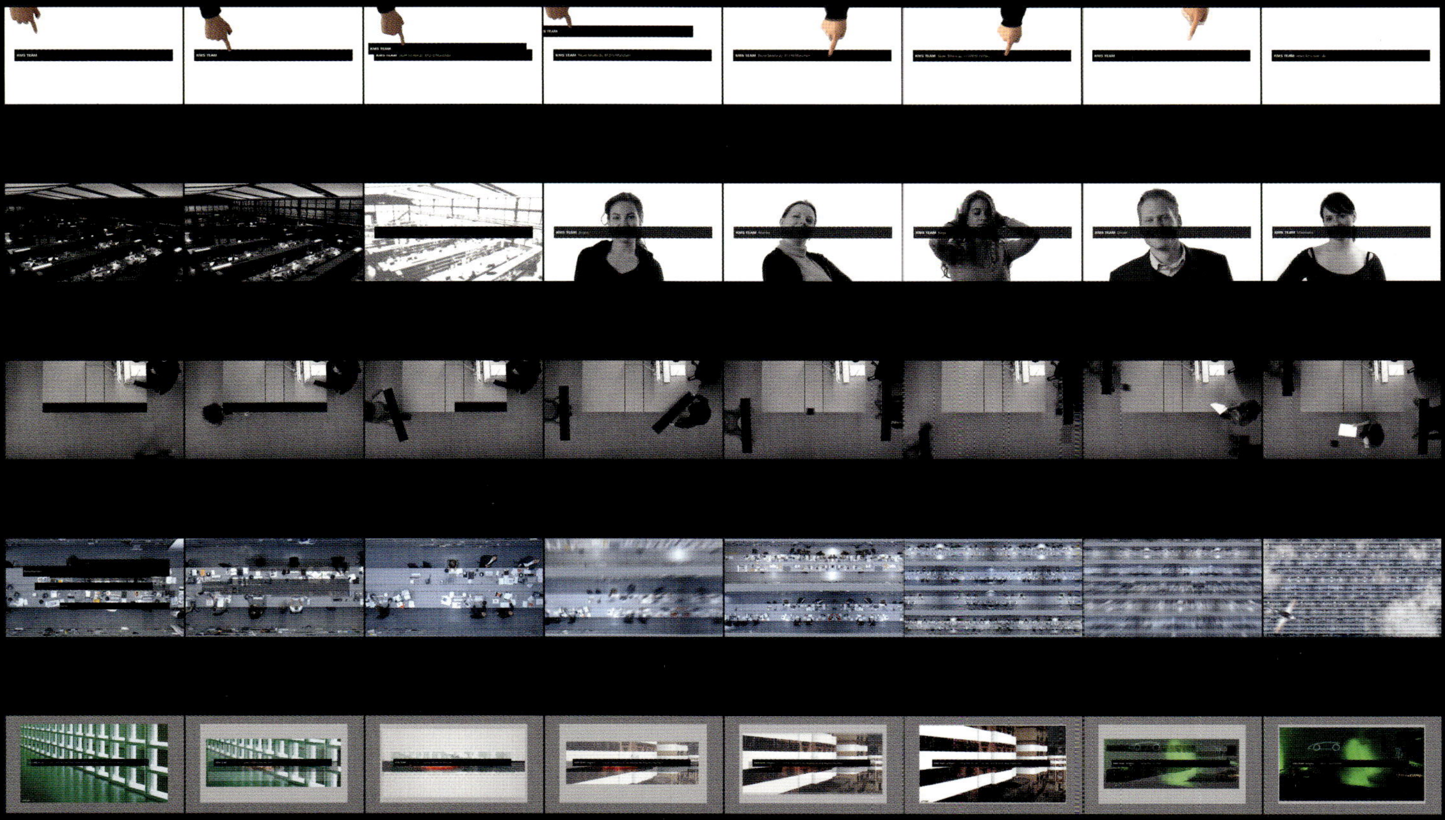

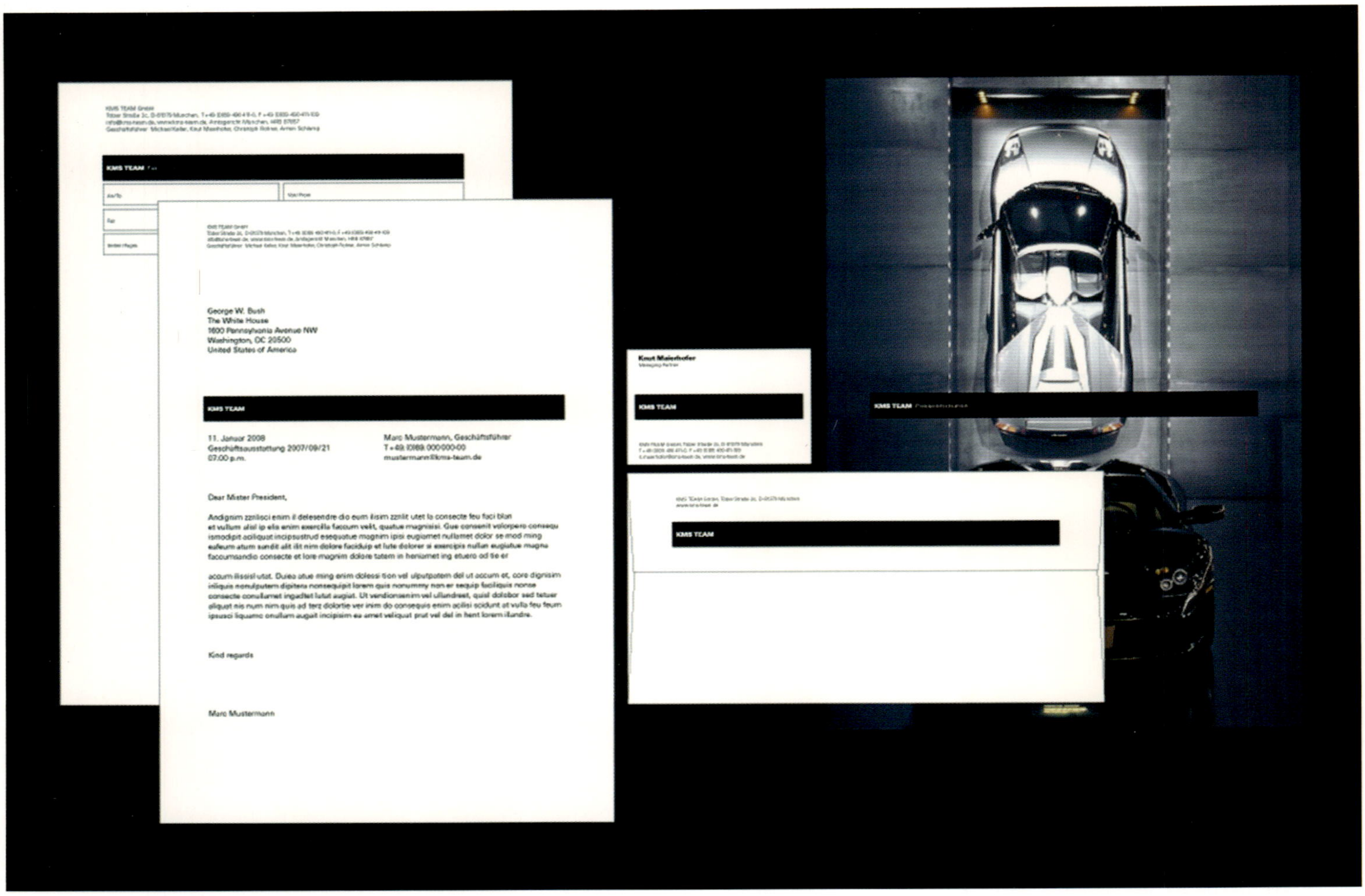

KMS TEAM Michael Keller

KMS TEAM Michael Keller

KMS TEAM Michael Keller

KMS TEAM Michael Keller

KMS TEAM Michael Keller

KMS TEAM Michael Keller

KMS TEAM Michael Keller

KMS TEAM Michael Keller

KMS TEAM Michael Keller

"We believe that design is more than just one, or two, or seven disciplines. It is the combination and their interaction that generates powerful design."

Knut Maierhofer, *Managing Partner, KMS TEAM*

Q&A with KMS TEAM's Knut Maierhofer

Why did you choose to handle your branding yourself?

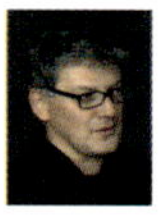

We knew that developing one's own corporate design is one of the most difficult tasks for a design company. But keeping in mind our work method, we thought it was no use trying to be objective. We always choose the subjective way, as it were—the way that begins with understanding the individual and unique perspective of the client in order to create a tool with symbolic and emotional power, that is also adequate for day-to-day business. And this time, we were the client.

How did you approach this project?

Our general approach (not only for this project) is called *Tiefendesign* (i.e., depth design), which is a holistic design method we have developed. Its core thesis is that you have to treat a brand like a personality. You have to look for the individual traits of the brand's personality and you have to understand the underlying (often hidden) structures in order to develop adequate expressions.

For this purpose, you cannot separate rationality from emotionality. That's why we always regard the entity we are working for as an undivisible whole. An enterprise always has to be able to tell a convincing story that is recognizable in the different utterances of the brand. Our story begins with the core of creativity, the idea. In its origin, it is an abstract term, and that's why we have chosen the beams or bars. They represent the ideas level, which is superposed to the reality.

How did you go about identifying your strengths and weaknesses as a company?

As we are regularly concerned with our clients' evaluation processes, we are able to draw parallels to our own work. We did the same analytical work we would have done for anyone else, and we defined a regular team that acted the same as if commissioned with an external project (actually, they were working on other projects at the same time, too, as that's the norm for every team).

The most important point is that in our regular work for clients, we very carefully identify their aims, their way of thinking and their company cultures, and that's key to finding the right formal solutions. We had to approach our own project the same way.

Looking back, is there anything you would have done differently?

No.

What makes your firm unique?

It's a combination of our *Tiefendesign* approach and our internal culture. We still look for adventures, and happily, as an independent office, we get the chance to live them. And we approach every project from a global point of view.

What type of clients do you work with most often?

International companies have come to dominate our list of references. The diversity of industries represented by our clients continues to be a clear indication of the broad spectrum of our activities. Thus we work for culturally or socially oriented institutions with the same professional passion as for automakers or manufacturers of sporting goods—whether they are midsize companies or global corporations.

Describe the culture of the KMS TEAM.

It's a very special mixture of openness and clearly defined targets, of freedom and discipline, of individuality and teamwork. We feel like a big family, we have a very organic structure, and we are a well-functioning organization. We always try to do high-quality work that is emotionally appealing, that gives goosebumps. We know we can only achieve that working as a team. We know that emotionality is not a simple ingredient, and that it has to emerge from an authentic, lively source.

How many employees make up the KMS TEAM?

At the moment, 97.

Tell us more about the designs behind your branding. What else did you develop besides signs and the other typical branding materials?

That's a very good question. It's characteristic of our work to develop features that do not match with conventional notions of graphic design, corporate design, internet design, environmental design, etc., although we actually work in all of these fields. Doing so for our clients, it's just natural that we have invented a lot of para-branding measures for ourselves, beginning with a common breakfast once a week and ending with uncommon Christmas greetings for clients.

One thing that may best express our attitude beyond graphics is the concept of our office. It's a former industrial building, which could easily accomodate over 200 people. It would take too long to describe the single features of the interior architecture (for instance, an extra hall of over 1,000 square meters for informal meeting, resting and occasional celebrations). The result is that we have created a space that represents our own brand, both for clients and employees, not via signs or metaphors, but through a direct experience.

We believe that design is more than just one or two or seven disciplines. It is the combination of them all and their interactions that generates powerful design. This comprises being concerned with fields that conventionally do not belong to classical communication design or brand consulting—like architecture or event planning, writing or film. I am convinced that one of our most important achievements is that we have avoided becoming too specialized.

What financial impact has your rebranding made?

We know it is crucial to make clearly perceptible the values one stands for. It's the best way to communicate one's position and to highlight one's business model. That's what we've done. From our work for clients, we know that corporate design can be an important factor for financial success, so we were not surprised that the launch of our new corporate design has enhanced our business results considerably.

For more examples of KMS TEAM's work, visit www.kms-team.de. All images courtesy of KMS TEAM. Knut Maierhofer headshot by Knut Koops.

KMS TEAM

KMS TEAM was established in Munich in 1984, and with its 97 employees, it is Germany's largest independent design studio today. We call our work depth design, which means that we find authentic forms and expressions that reflect the identity of a company, institution, or event. Because our starting point implies a holistic approach, we must naturally master all of the relevant media of communication and be able to design in these media on all levels of perception.

Guided by this idea of design, our role has increasingly transformed from that of "mere" designer and consultant to that of a director who arranges and coordinates, who promotes the growth of networks and manages relationships. In this role, we design not only the visual appearance of a brand—we discover the brand, develop it, accompany it and guide it actively to a strong and sustainable presence in its respective environment. Our core expertise in this process lies in the areas of brand consulting, brand design and brand implementation.

Tölzer Straße 2c, D-81379, Munich, Germany
Tel: +49.(0)89.490411-0 / Fax: +49.(0)89.490411-49
www.kms-team.de

Knut Maierhofer: Knut Maierhofer was born in 1962. He studied graphic design in Munich and graduated with a diploma. In 1984, he founded the design studio KMS TEAM, which concentrates on graphic design, business and financial communication as well as trade fair and exhibition design. Since the mid-90s, it has been focusing on corporate identity. Furthermore, the studio also works in the fields of strategy, branding, naming, corporate wording, 3D design and Web concepts. Maierhofer manages KMS TEAM together with Michael Keller, Christoph Rohrer and Armin Schlamp.

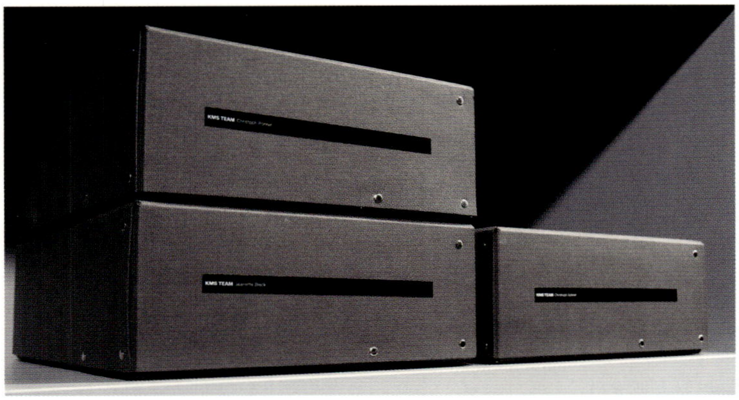

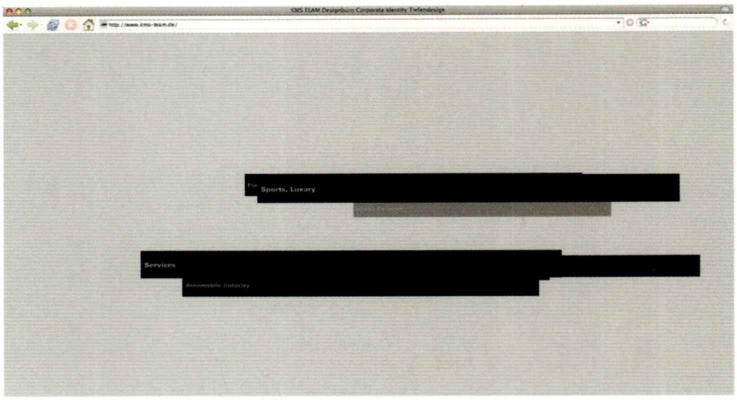
Sports, Luxury
Services

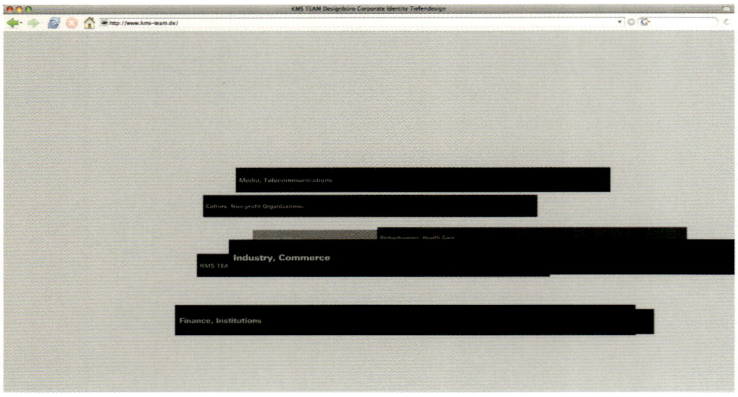
Industry, Commerce
Finance, Institutions

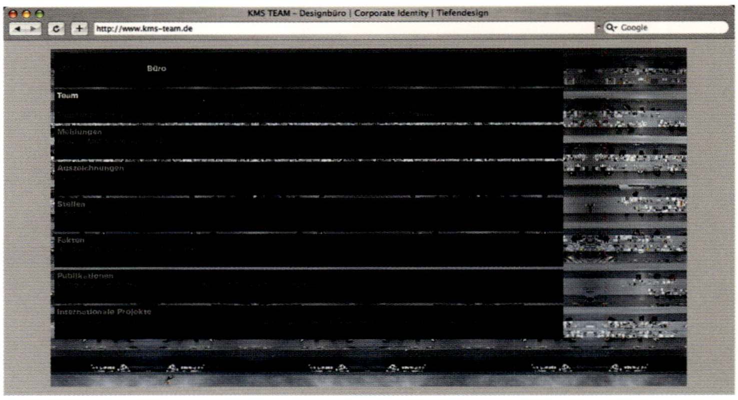
KMS TEAM - Designbüro | Corporate Identity | Tiefendesign
http://www.kms-team.de
Google
Büro
Team
Auszeichnungen
Stellen
Internationale Projekte

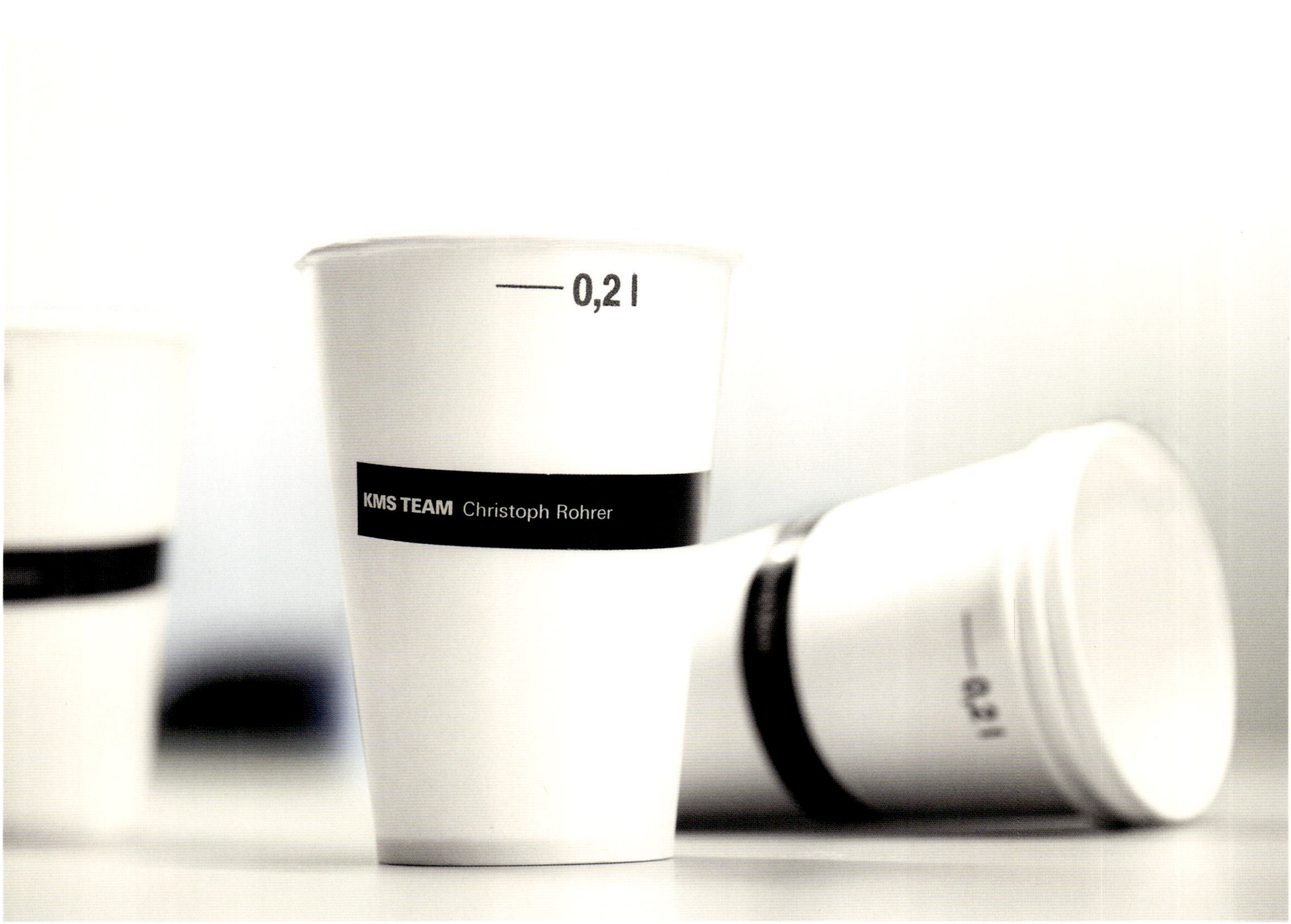
0,2 l
KMS TEAM Christoph Rohrer

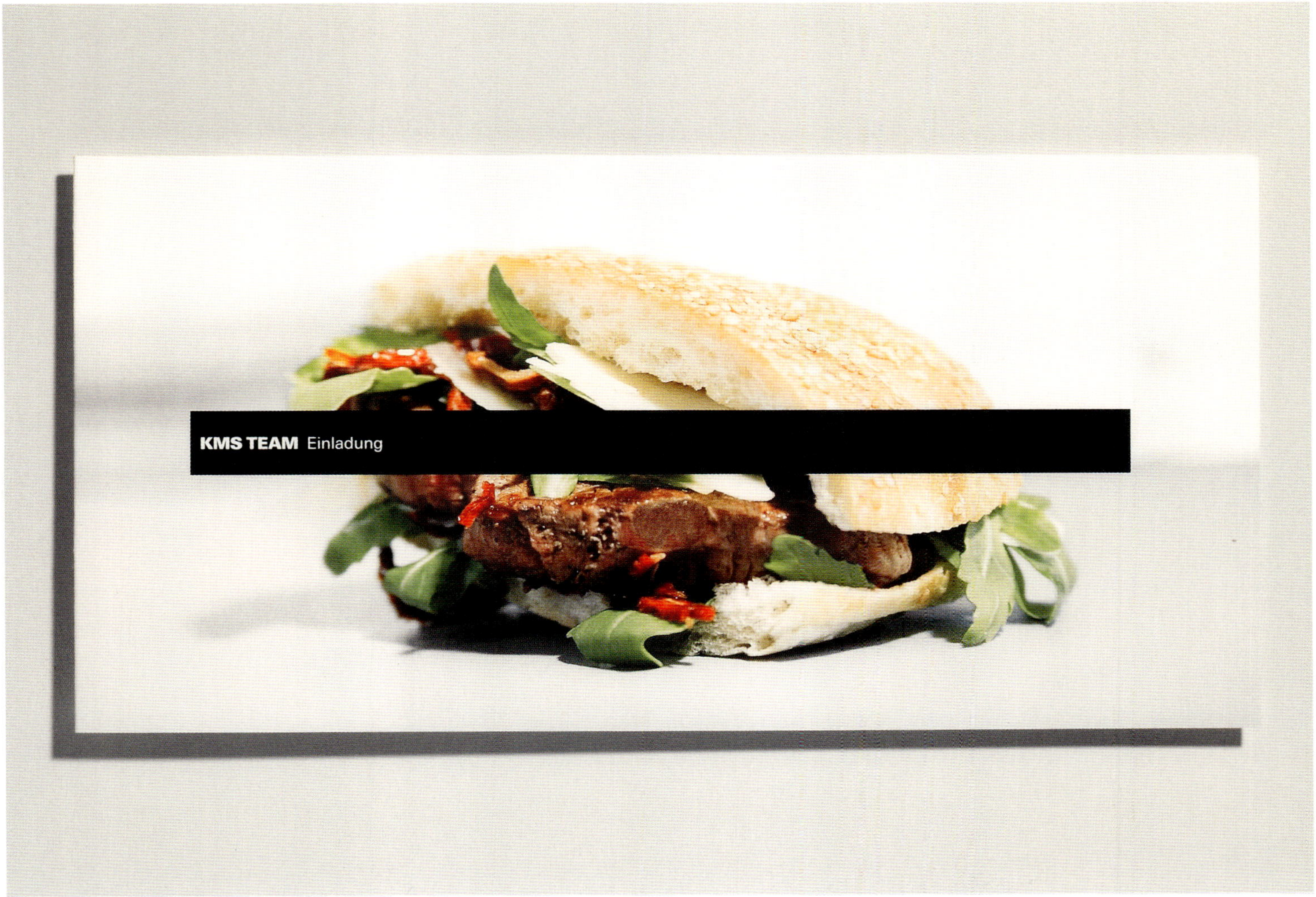
KMS TEAM Einladung

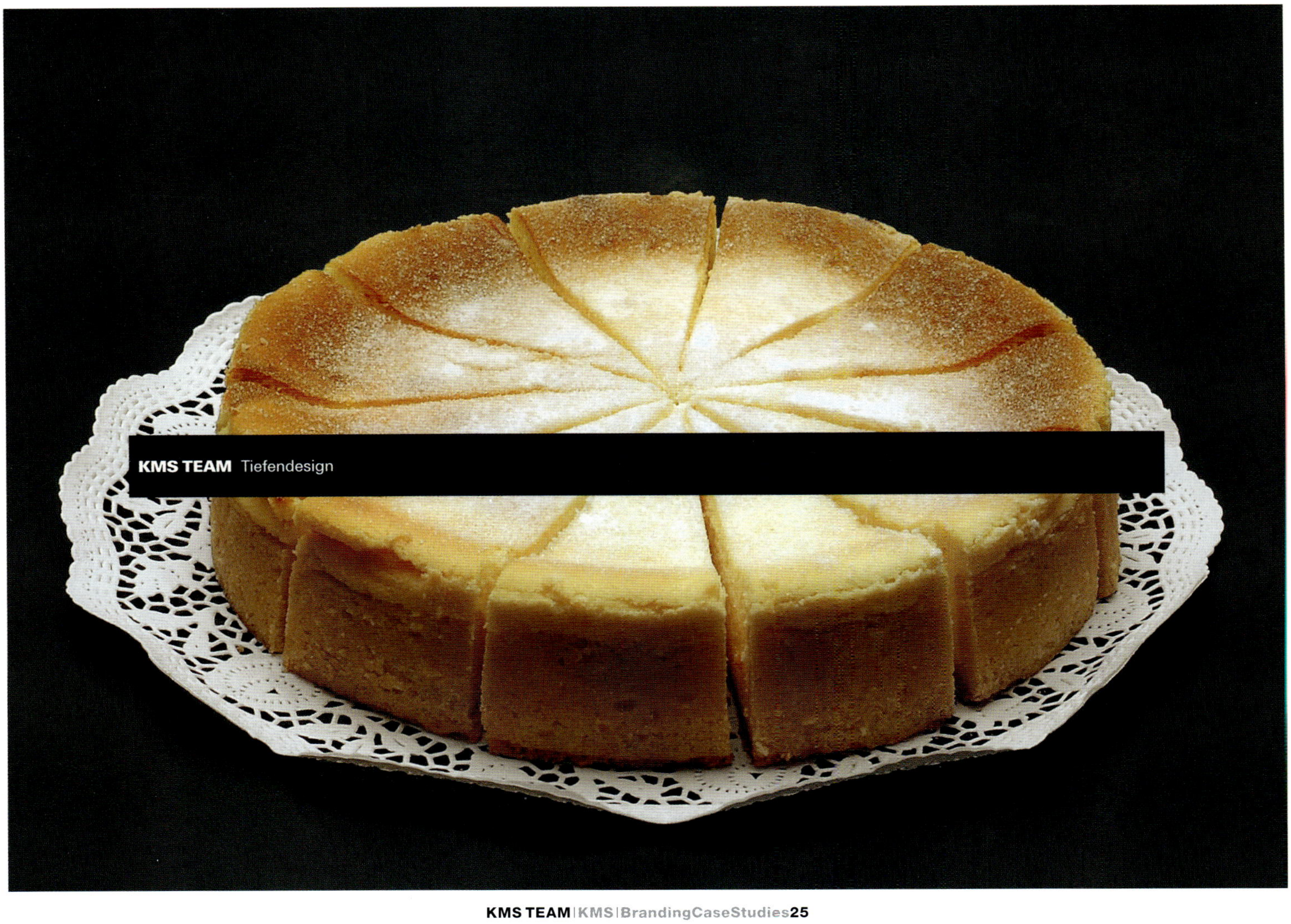
KMS TEAM Tiefendesign

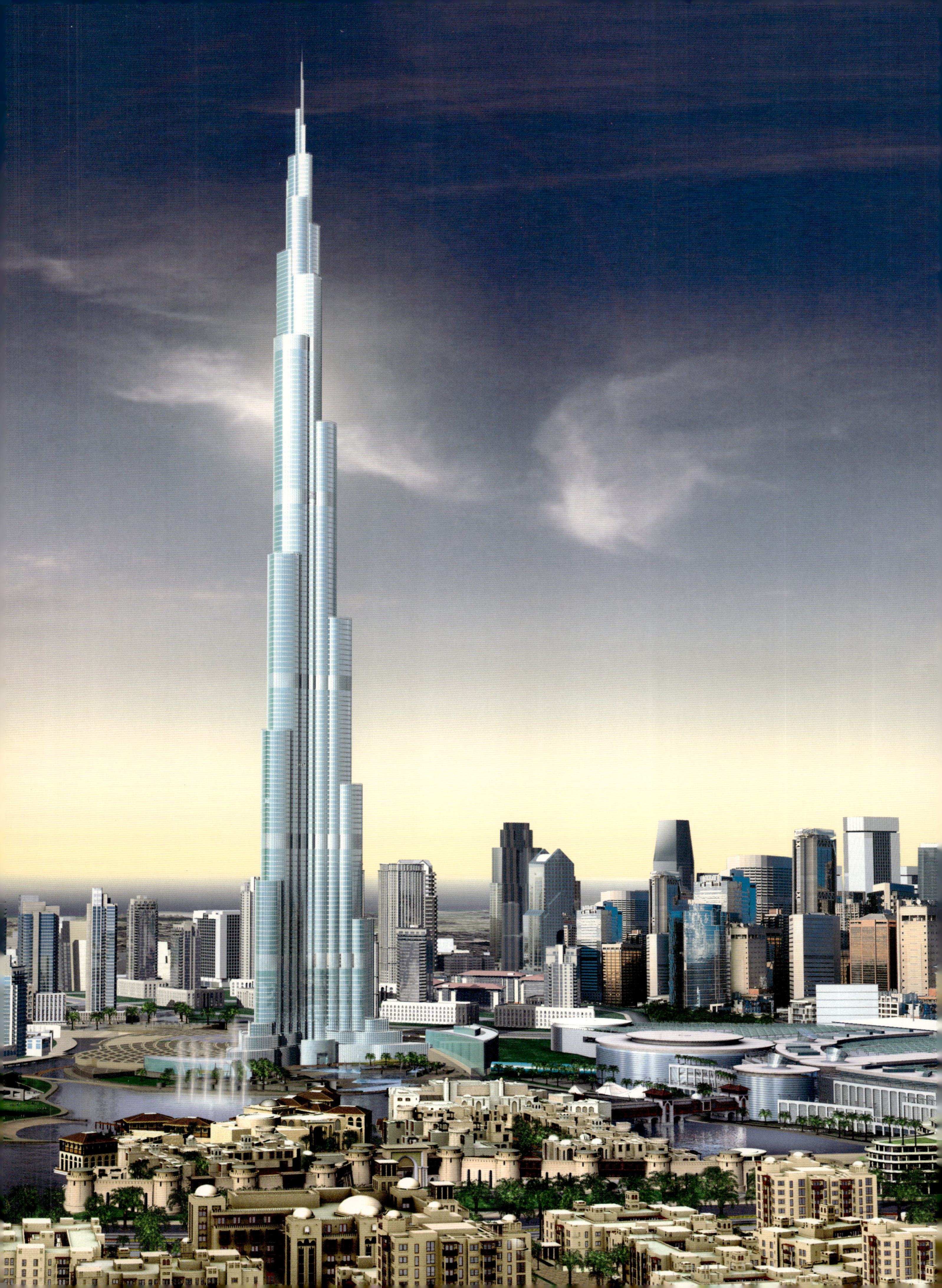

Internationally respected developer Emaar Properties hired Landor Associates to brand the Burj Dubai, currently the world's tallest building, situated in downtown Dubai. Skidmore, Owings and Merrill, the same company who created the Sears Tower in Chicago and the Freedom Tower in New York, designed the structure. Construction began on the tower in 2004, and is scheduled for completion in September 2009. □ *By focusing not just on its record-breaking heights, but also on what the tower represents, the Landor/Emaar branding campaign has taken the building's reputation even higher. The Burj Dubai brand is not so much about the title of world's highest structure, which will eventually be taken by another, but rather the world's highest aspirations. Focusing on preeminence—the best the world has to offer in terms of luxury, international teamwork, world-class design, and skilled craftsmanship—the branding work (a visitors' center, lobby and elevator design, as well as all relevant visitors' print materials) has had dramatic results. Helped in part by the strength of the iconic brand, Emaar continues to achieve substantial profit and expansion, most recently reporting 25 % revenue growth for 2007.*

Q&A with Landor's Bengt Eriksson and Olivier Auroy

What was the assignment?

Emaar, arguably the largest real estate developer in the world, was planning the Burj Dubai—the tallest structure ever built—as the centerpiece of a 500-acre, $20 billion mixed-use development. As radical as it was to design on this scale at the time, Emaar knew that eventually the building would be surpassed. So, Landor proposed building something that could not be surpassed: the Burj Dubai brand.

Working closely with Emaar, it became clear that Burj Dubai had the potential to be the centerpiece for the entire region, not only Dubai. It could showcase a Middle East often overlooked by the world audience. The Burj Dubai brand was not so much about the world's highest structure, but rather the world's highest aspirations. The brand needed to focus on preeminence – the best the world had to offer in terms of luxury, international teamwork, world-class design, and skilled craftsmanship.

What was Landor's solution?

Landor created a distinctive brand identity—a minimalist wordmark that emphasizes Burj Dubai's uncommon elegance and ambition. The design solution was almost shockingly simple: two fine lines juxtaposed, meeting near one corner of the brandmark. The two lines metaphorically add a crucial latitude and longitude pair to the world map. Burj Dubai stands for nothing less than a new standard and a new orientation, hence a set of coordinates that pinpoint the new centre of the world. Today, the Burj Dubai area is one of the most iconic and sought after real estate locations in the world, thanks to a unique identity, look and feel created by Landor.

What were Landor's goals?

To transcend history by creating a brand that was not merely representative of the world's highest building, but the world's highest aspirations. Our goal was to see that the concept of preeminence would set the standard, not just in terms of luxury, but also in terms of design, craftsmanship, and international teamwork.

What difficulties arise when branding for a structure, as opposed to a product? What additional elements did you have to consider?

Landor was chosen in part because of our success with comprehensive branding programs. Even so, the scope of this project presented novel challenges. The sheer range of applications required in a very short time was daunting. So was the requirement for an identity system that could work at almost any scale and with any media. It had to communicate the brand idea instantly on building fronts, signs, vehicles, ads, and uniforms, and appear equally elegant whether on hand-delivered event invitations or on hard hats at the construction site. Web presentation and other digital media had to be groundbreaking yet refined. The sales center and print materials needed to stand apart from anything the over-saturated Dubai market had yet witnessed.

Above all, it was essential that the superhuman scale of this project still communicate on human terms. For prospective visitors, workers, residents, and a growing worldwide audience, all the various pieces needed to come together as a single, differentiating Burj Dubai experience.

How did you maintain design cohesiveness across so many different mediums—a lobby, signage, ads, uniforms, elevators, print materials, etc.?

The Burj Dubai brand identity is the tissue that connects all the different touch points. It stands for nothing less than a new set of coordinates on the globe, a new standard and orientation not just for Dubai, but for the Middle East. Metaphorically, the two lines redraw local longitude and latitude, establishing a new Greenwich or a contemporary point of reference for understanding this part of the world. Launch materials put it this way: 'Throughout history, only a few structures have had the power to change history. And the horizon.'

This sophisticated linear approach was extended into a comprehensive design style to reinforce the brand's concept of preeminence. The wordmark, typography, look and feel, voice and imagery, and even color palette reflect prestige. In contrast to the over-the-top golds and bright colors prevalent in other Dubai premier developments, Landor chose understated tones echoing the building's finishes of stainless steel and aluminum and set them off with a sharp green accent inspired by the carpenters' levels found in the hands of hundreds of architects, engineers, and craftspeople building the tower.

Landor was both selling tower space and enticing visitors to the tower. How did you tackle both tasks?

To communicate life inside an as-yet-built icon, Landor was asked to create a showpiece sales center. Designing this environment posed many unusual challenges. Chief among them was how to use a two-story building to convey Sky Living—a new standard of international luxury that the Burj Dubai sought to define at a height as yet unattained by man-made structures. Landor's solution was to create a multisensory, multimedia journey, immersing visitors in an alluring brand experience. Black granite dominates the exterior and entrance, with sharp green architectural accents. After passing through a hushed, darkened entry, visitors come to a wonder wall—a towering display that places this project in a historical context with other icons.

Next, an elevator creates the sensation of lifting residents to their homes high above the city. The doors open to the future: a fully furnished apartment with panoramic renderings of the Dubai skyline in surrounding windows and a wall of sensual amenities.

Then, around a corner, visitors look up in surprise. In front of them, in a double-height gallery, an 11-meter replica of the Burj Dubai tower literally pushes through the ceiling of the first floor. Viewers are invited to climb to the second level to get a full view of this dramatic display, bringing them discreetly to understated sales offices. In line with the project's exclusivity, the presentation center is open only by invitation.

What elements of the campaign were the most effective?

The multimedia journey was extremely effective. Visitors were surprised and astonished every step of the way and most importantly, we were able to follow through with our brand promise, and literally took visitors to new heights.

Final thoughts?

I think it is important to mention that it is not by chance that the Burj Dubai is being built in Dubai. In the last 30 years, this city transformed itself from a regional center to a global one. The success was not based on oil reserves, but on the reserves of human talent and ingenuity.

For more information on Burj Dubai, please visit www.burjdubai.com.

Burj Dubai Facts

- At over 650 meters, Burj Dubai is already the world's tallest building and structure. Currently at 160 storeys, the tower also has the largest number of floors in any building. Burj Dubai has surpassed the height of the KVLY-TV mast in North Dakota, USA - 628.8 meters (2,063 feet) and taller than Taipei 101 (508 metres; 1667 feet) in Taiwan and CN Tower (553.33 meters; 1815.5 feet) in Toronto, Canada. Cladding work is currently being executed at an accelerated pace and Burj Dubai set another record for the highest glass panel installation at a height of 512 meters (1,679.76 feet) on Level 141.
- Burj Dubai will have over 160 storeys and be over 700 meters. When completed, the tower will hold the record in all four categories as recognized by the Council on Tall Buildings and Urban Habitats – namely, highest structure, roof, antenna and occupied floor—and have the highest publicly accessible observation deck.
- The tip of the spire will be visible 60 miles away.
- The curtain wall (external service) of the Burj Dubai will be equivalent to 17 football fields.
- An observatory 442 meters above ground on the 124th floor will be open to the public.
- A mixed-use tower, Burj Dubai will have the Armani Hotel Dubai and Armani Residences Dubai in addition to residences and commercial spaces.
- There will be recreational facilities and entertainment venues including four luxurious pools and a cigar club, a library, an exclusive residents' lounge, serviced residences, 15,000 sq. feet of fitness facilities and an observatory.
- The tower will be built of glass, aluminum, concrete and steel.
- At the peek of construction, over 8,000 workers are anticipated on site.
- The concrete used is equivalent to the weight of 100,000 elephants.
- Designer Adrian Smith based the tower design on the desert flower, the Hymenocallis, and patterning systems embodied in Islamic architecture.

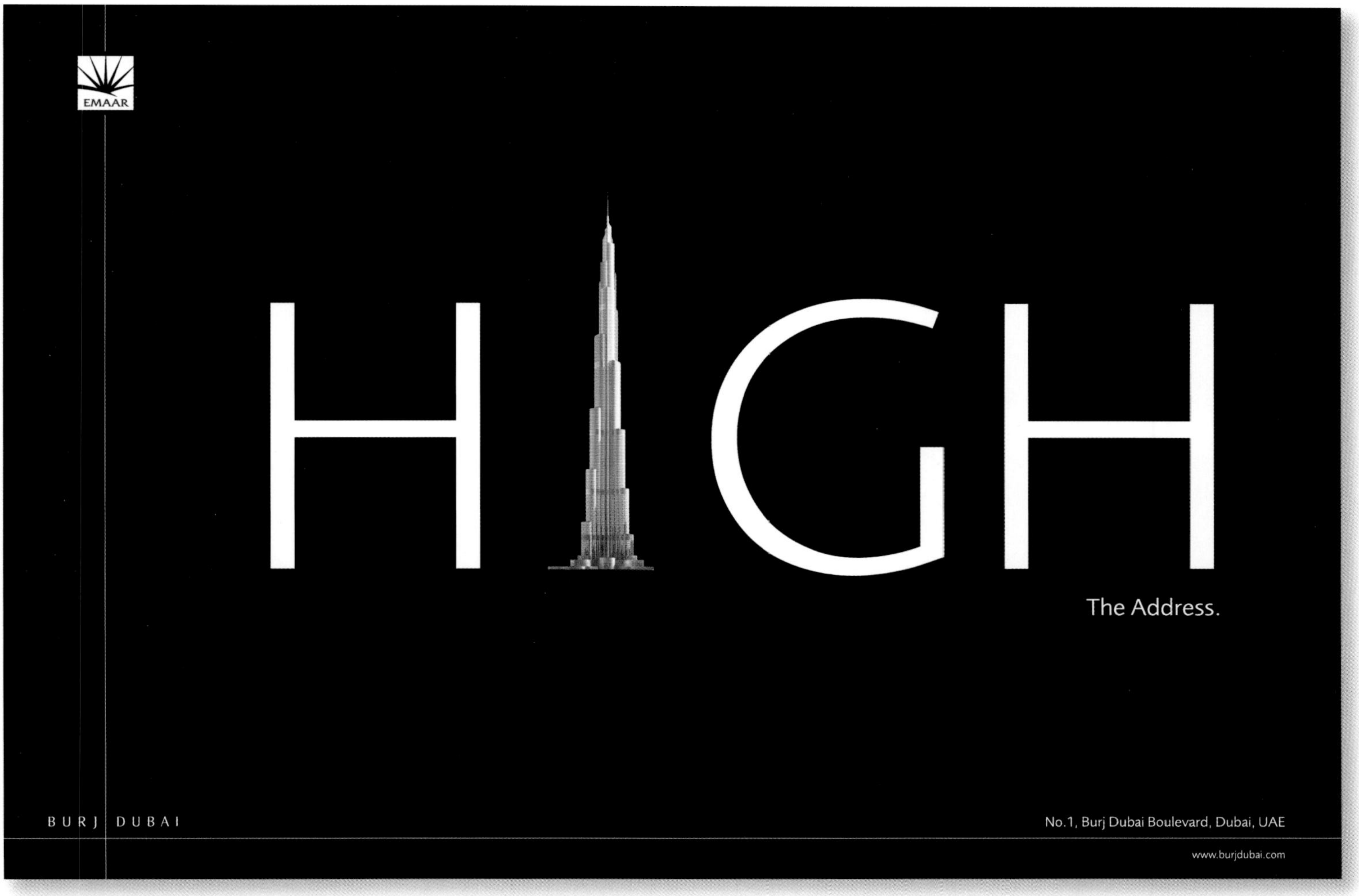
EMAAR
HIGH
The Address.
BURJ DUBAI
No.1, Burj Dubai Boulevard, Dubai, UAE
www.burjdubai.com

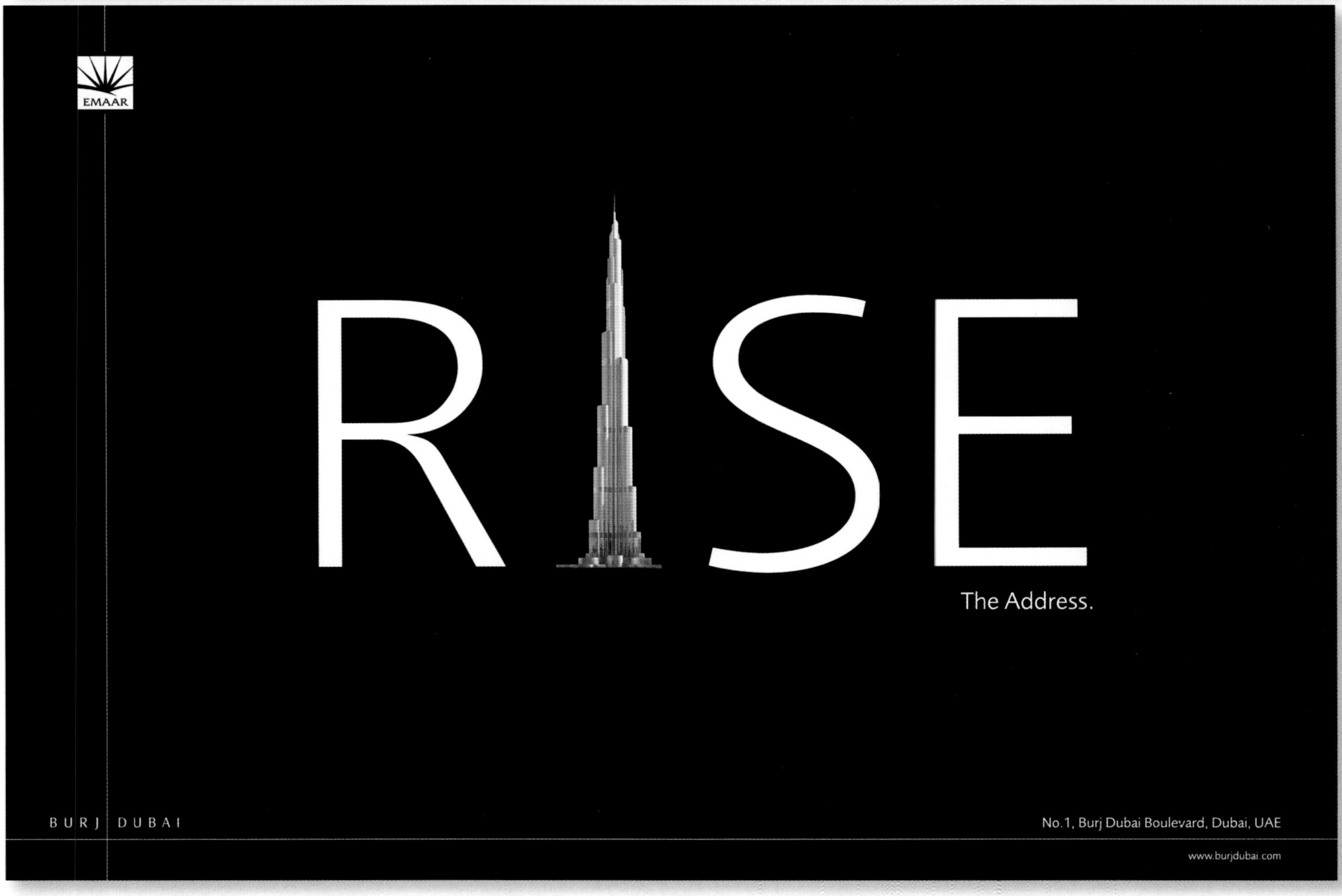
EMAAR
RISE
The Address.
BURJ DUBAI
No.1, Burj Dubai Boulevard, Dubai, UAE
www.burjdubai.com

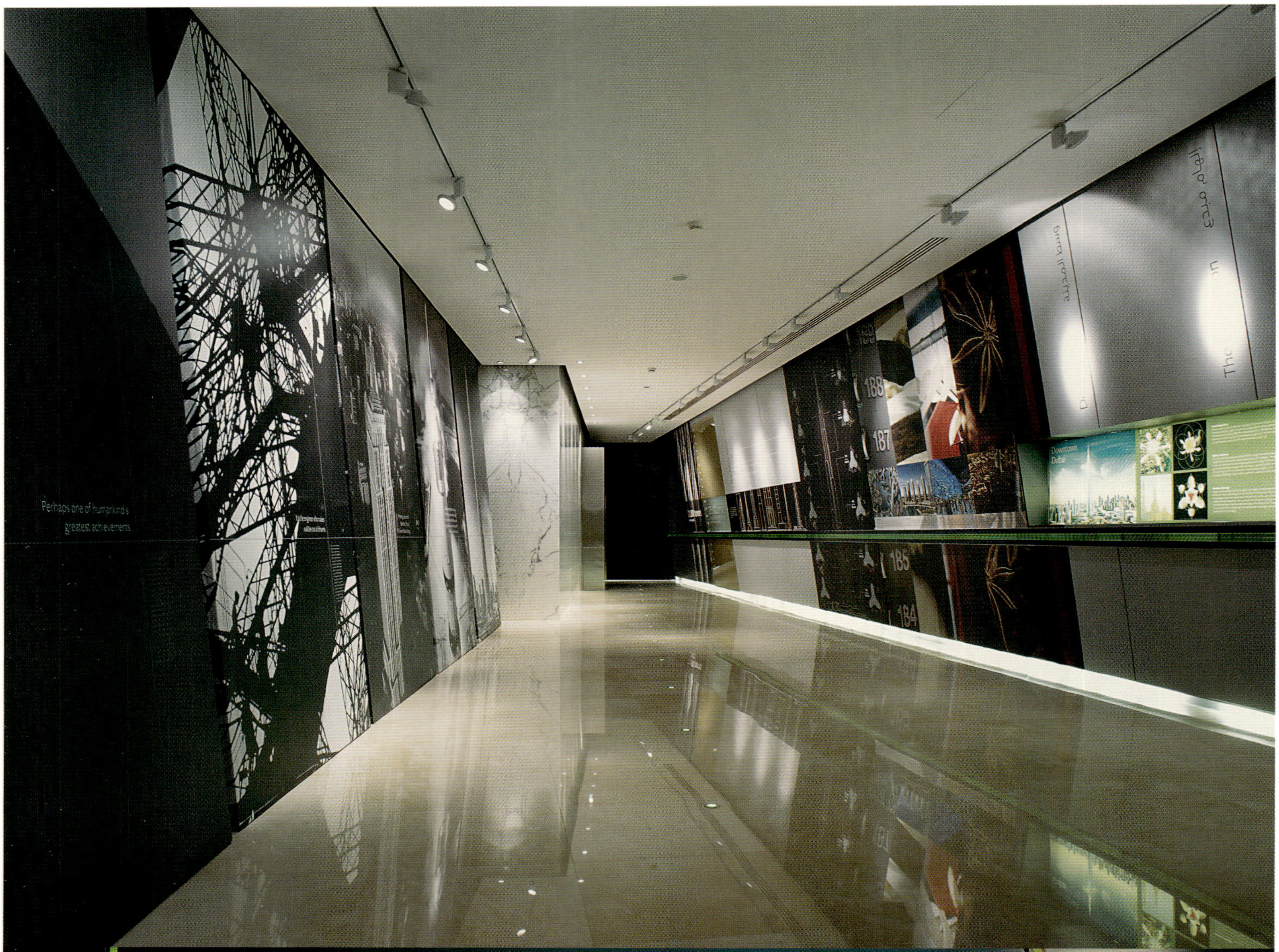
Perhaps one of humankind's
greatest achievements

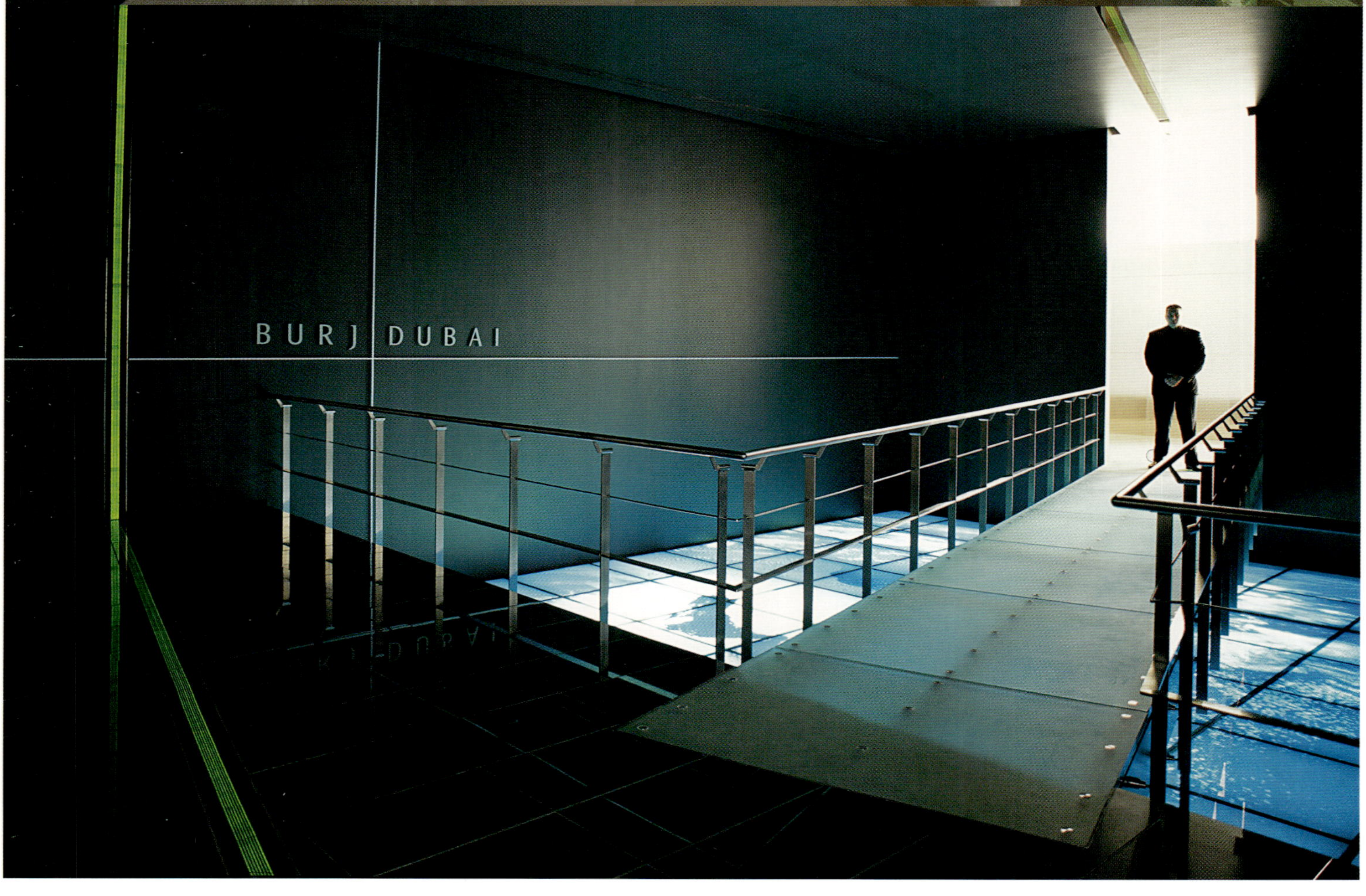
BURJ DUBAI

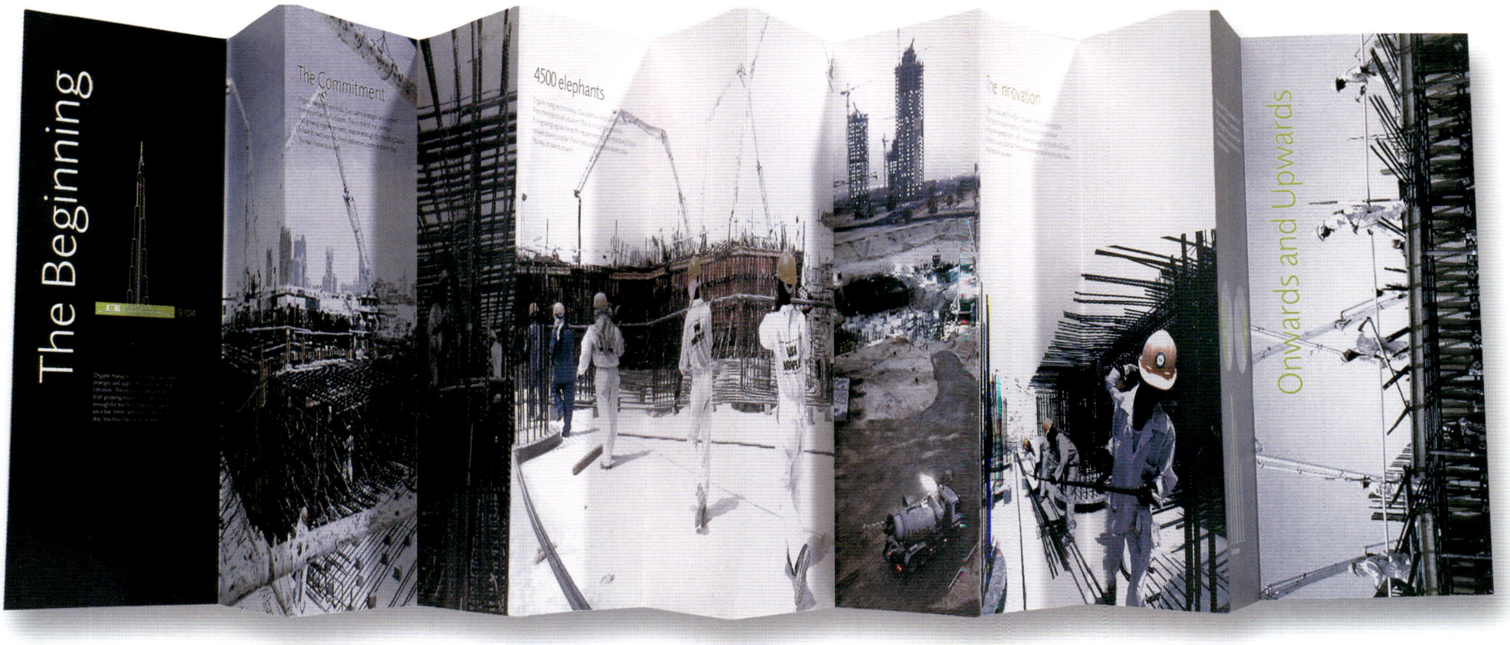

"Throughout history, only a few structures have had the power to change history. And the horizon."

A statement from Burj Dubai's launch materials

The Landor Creative Team

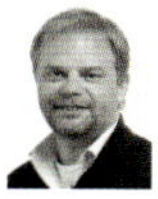

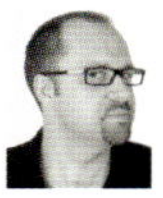

Bengt Eriksson (pictured left): Bengt Eriksson is Managing Director for the Dubai office of Landor Associates, responsible for the company's operations in the Middle East and North Africa. Eriksson has been with Landor for ten years, first in Europe and since 2002 in Dubai. He has led branding projects in financial services, real estate, telecoms, petroleum, airlines and fast-moving consumer goods (FMCG). He has extensive experience developing brands for places: countries, cities and tourism destinations.

Before joining Landor, Eriksson worked as a journalist and in advertising, specialising in travel and hospitality. Additionally, he has worked as a consultant on strategy development and internal marketing.

Olivier Auroy (pictured right): Olivier Auroy is Deputy General Manager of the Dubai office of Landor Associates where he manages a portfolio of International clients including Emaar Properties, Nestle Waters and Pakistan International Airlines.

He is Landor's naming leader for Europe, the Middle East and Africa, and drives new business and sound design expertise for the Dubai office. Auroy has managed brand identity and corporate identity programs in Saudi Arabia, Jordan, Morocco, Kuwait, Iran, the United Arab Emirates and Bahrain.

He has directed international corporate programs for France Télécom, the World Anti-Doping Agency, Degussa (Maxens aroma brand), Dentsply, BFGoodrich, Sélecta, HEC Business School, Sodexho, The American University of Paris, NextiraOne and Travelocity.

Auroy is regularly quoted in Gulf Marketing Review and *brownbook*, a lifestyle magazine in the United Arab Emirates. Before joining Landor in 2000, Auroy successfully launched and ran the Name Research Department of the design agency Carré Noir. From 1996 to 1999, he was Creative Director at one of France's leading naming companies, Kaos. While there he supervised and created more than 80 brands and trade names, including Egoïste Platinum (Chanel) and L'Atelier (Renault). Previous to this he was a product manager for utilitarian vehicles at Renault Italia (Rome-Italy) and worked for the Human Resources Department of Johnson Controls (Michigan-USA). Auroy graduated from the Sciences Po Paris, Institute of Political Studies in 1991. He also received a DESS (equivalent to an MA) in marketing and advertising from Paris Celsa-La Sorbonne in 1993. He is fluent in English and Italian.

For more information on Landor Associates, please see page 37 or visit www.landor.com.

Campaign Credits
Bengt Eriksson, Managing Director
Olivier Auroy, General Manager

Headshots and Burj Dubai images courtesy of Landor Associates.
Burj Dubai facts courtesy of Emaar.

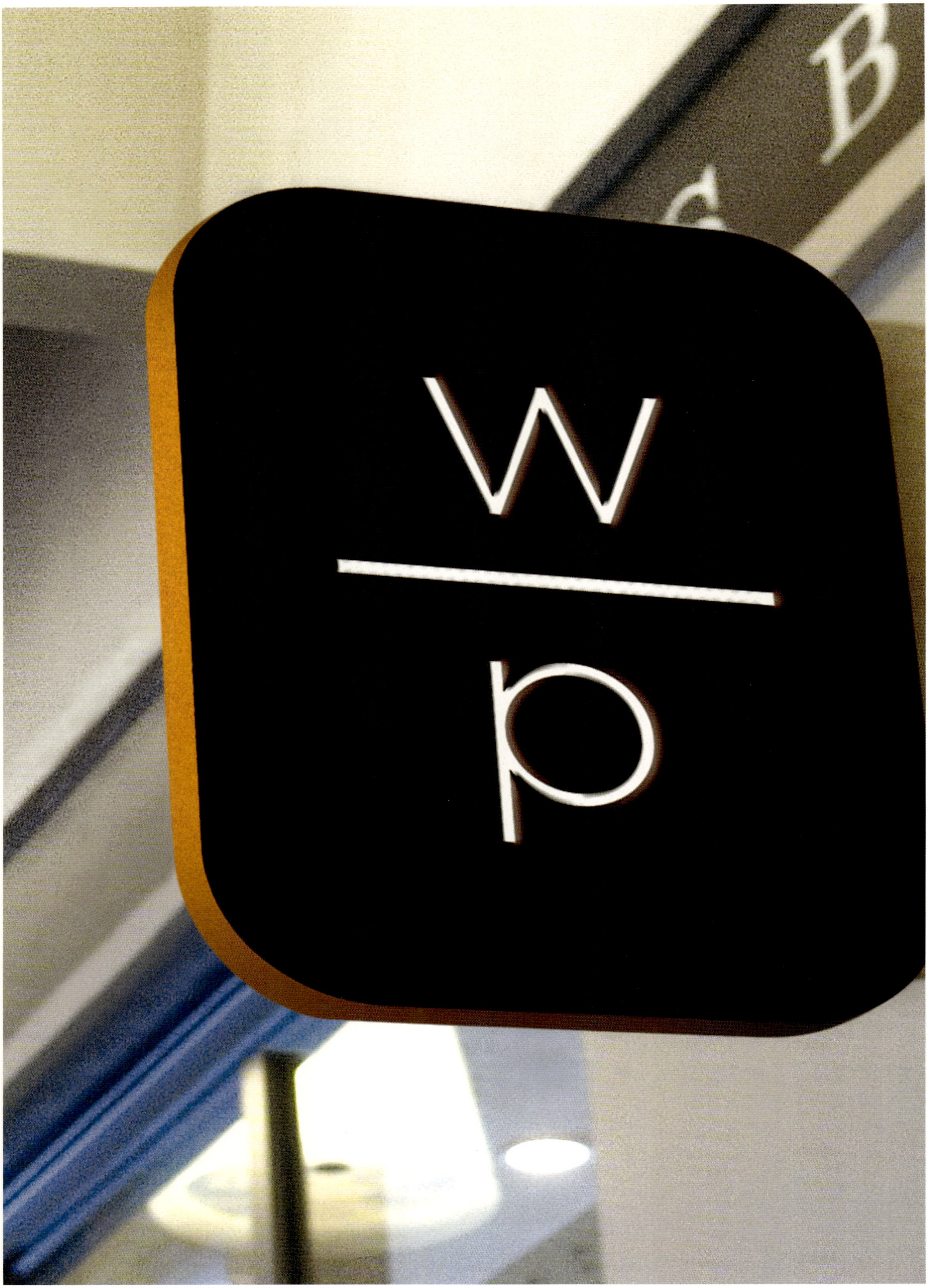
w
p

In 1982, Austrian-born chef Wolfgang Puck opened his first restaurant, Spago, in L.A. Since then, he's enjoyed remarkable success, opening over a dozen restaurants, launching Wolfgang Puck Catering, releasing extensive food and cookware product lines, television shows, cookbooks, and creating Wolfgang Puck Worldwide, which manages almost 70 quick-service kiosks and fast-casual restaurants. □ *In 2005, Wolfgang Puck approached Landor Associates with the following directive: create a cohesive brand identity applicable to a variety of enterprises, and one that could effectively live on after Wolfgang Puck's retirement. The Landor solution? Define one of the world's most well-known culinary brands by its origins, applying Puck's own charisma and personality to every element across the board.* □ *Executive Creative Director Nicolas Aparicio and Executive Director Deborah Chae-Crudo give their take on the Puck project.*

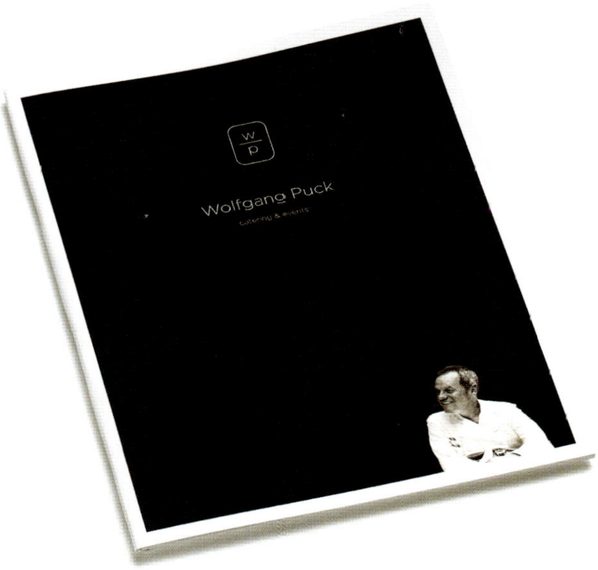

"Landor initiated the process of bringing our 3 companies: Wolfgang Puck Fine Dining Group, Wolfgang Puck Catering and Wolfgang Puck Worldwide, Inc. together with one cohesive look and feel."

Joe Essa, *Executive Vice President, Wolfgang Puck Worldwide, Inc.*

"Wolfgang Puck is an icon. Landor helped make his brand iconic."

Nicolas Aparicio & Michelle Gee, *Landor*

Q&A with Landor's Nicolas Aparicio & Deborah Chae-Crudo

Tell us a little about Wolfgang Puck, the company, and why this project appealed to you so much.

Wolfgang Puck is an icon. Landor helped make his brand iconic. We are fortunate at Landor to have the opportunity to work with some of the most influential brands in the world, so when Wolfgang Puck, the chef to the stars, came to Landor seeking our counsel on how to bring his brand to the next level, we jumped at the opportunity to work with him.

What problem were you asked to solve?

Mired in more than a decade of unmanaged license and franchise proliferation, Wolfgang Puck, master chef of the 1980s, wanted to create a legacy he was proud of. He hired Landor to help define the Wolfgang Puck brand strategy, identity and executional platforms for the brand to live on well after he plans to retire.

Additionally, Landor was tasked with helping the brand build consistency across product categories. Landor's work allowed Wolfgang Puck to examine the consumer holistically as a brand consumer, rather than a single-category consumer, and leveraged cross-category offerings to maximize brand impact and, potentially, revenues.

What was the Landor solution, and how was it applied?

Landor harnessed key consumer and business insights to define those elements unique to a personal encounter with Wolfgang Puck, and potentially ownable in the business categories Wolfgang was in. Through rigorous analysis of best practices in- and out-of-category, founder brands and an understanding of the business dynamics Wolfgang Puck faced, we developed a brand platform that served not only as a filter for strategic business imperatives and creative direction, but also as an inspiration and tool for engaging Wolfgang Puck employees and chefs.

Brand positioning, architecture and nomenclature formed the basis for clarifying existing offerings and identifying new areas of opportunity for the Wolfgang Puck business, including Wolfgang Puck's portfolio and market entry strategies. The framework developed even identified new areas of business opportunity, like a Wolfgang Puck signature line of consumer products, that Wolfgang could capitalize on.

Additionally, Landor used the brand platform and subsequent insights to unveil how to best communicate the brand to the right consumer audiences for maximum impact. Previously, any examination of the consumer had been done in departmental silos. Our work allowed Wolfgang Puck to examine the consumer holistically as a brand consumer, and leveraged cross-category offerings to maximize brand impact and, theoretically, revenues.

The identity system that was developed built upon the idea that these products/dining venues were personally offered to the consumer by Master Chef Wolfgang Puck, not a corporate food processing brand—that he alone could bring such innovative, freshly prepared food to you. The system was designed to be flexible enough to apply to 3-star fine dining venues, casual dining venues, consumer products and catering elements like kiosks, uniforms and trucks—ultimately wherever Wolfgang himself might be. The system impacted decisions not just about graphics and imagery, but of environmental and spatial relationships, packaging materials used, display formats, livery design, signage, billboard advertisements, corporate communications, training and guidelines materials, and other elements that defined the Wolfgang Puck experience beyond just packaging.

Did you encounter any obstacles?

One of the most difficult challenges was internal alignment. Business units and licensing agreements had been structured so that any centralized initiative (as brand often is) was very difficult to carry forward and ensure consistent implementation of.

How did the company respond to your initial efforts?

All, including Wolfgang Puck himself, were very pleased with how the strategy and the creative work made sense for where Wolfgang Puck wanted his brand to go. All were equally astonished at the resources that would be required to implement the change, and therefore the transition has been much slower than originally anticipated.

What was the most interesting aspect of the Wolfgang Puck project?

Being able to crystallize the essence of a person—the most charismatic and differentiating aspects of a person—into a brand that is meant to live on was a fascinating part of the project. One always had to step back and say, yes, we're talking about a brand, but we're also talking about a person here, and be able to ensure that the solutions we developed would be as true today as in the future when Wolfgang Puck was himself no longer involved with the brand.

How would you describe your personal experience on this project?

We found this to be a challenging yet invigorating program.

Talk to us about results. For example, what sort of financial impact did your branding have on Wolfgang Puck?

As alluded to earlier, some of the internal alignment challenges made broad-based adoption of our recommendations difficult to implement and gauge, but through various anecdotal reports we understand in those places where the new brand has been applied, it's been received very positively.

To learn more about Wolfgang Puck, visit www.wolfgangpuck.com.

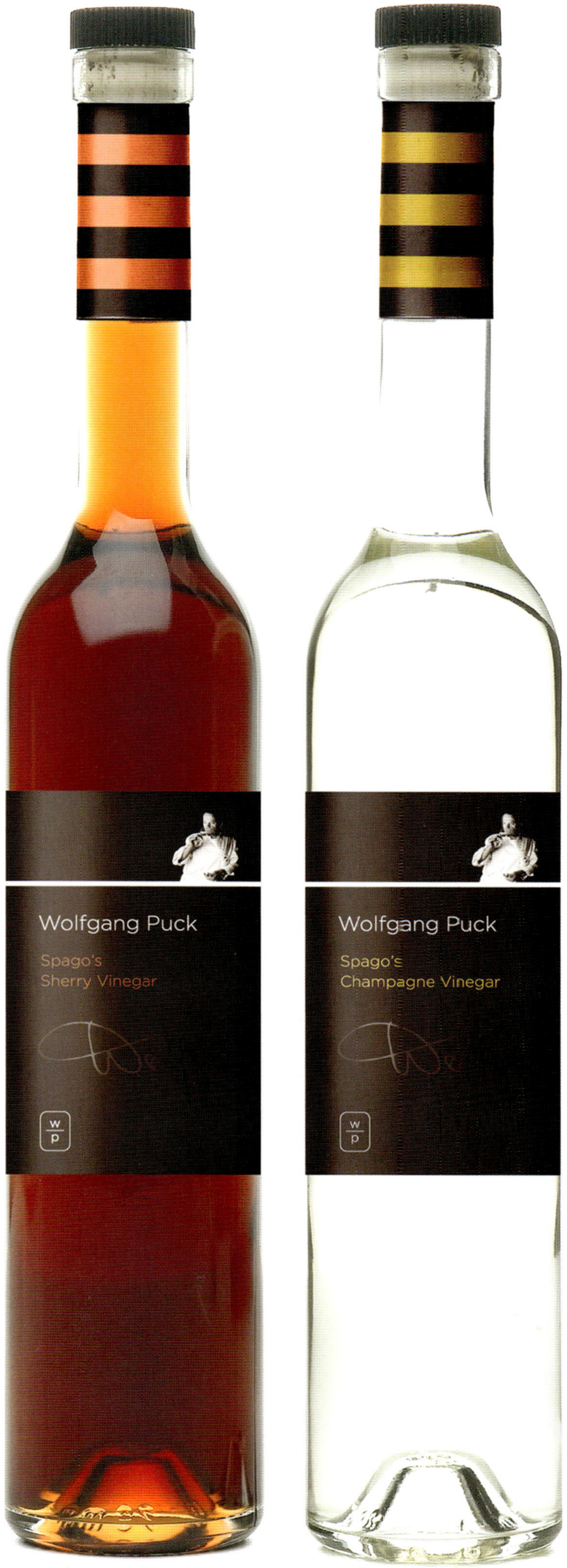
Wolfgang Puck
Spago's
Sherry Vinegar
Wolfgang Puck
Spago's
Champagne Vinegar

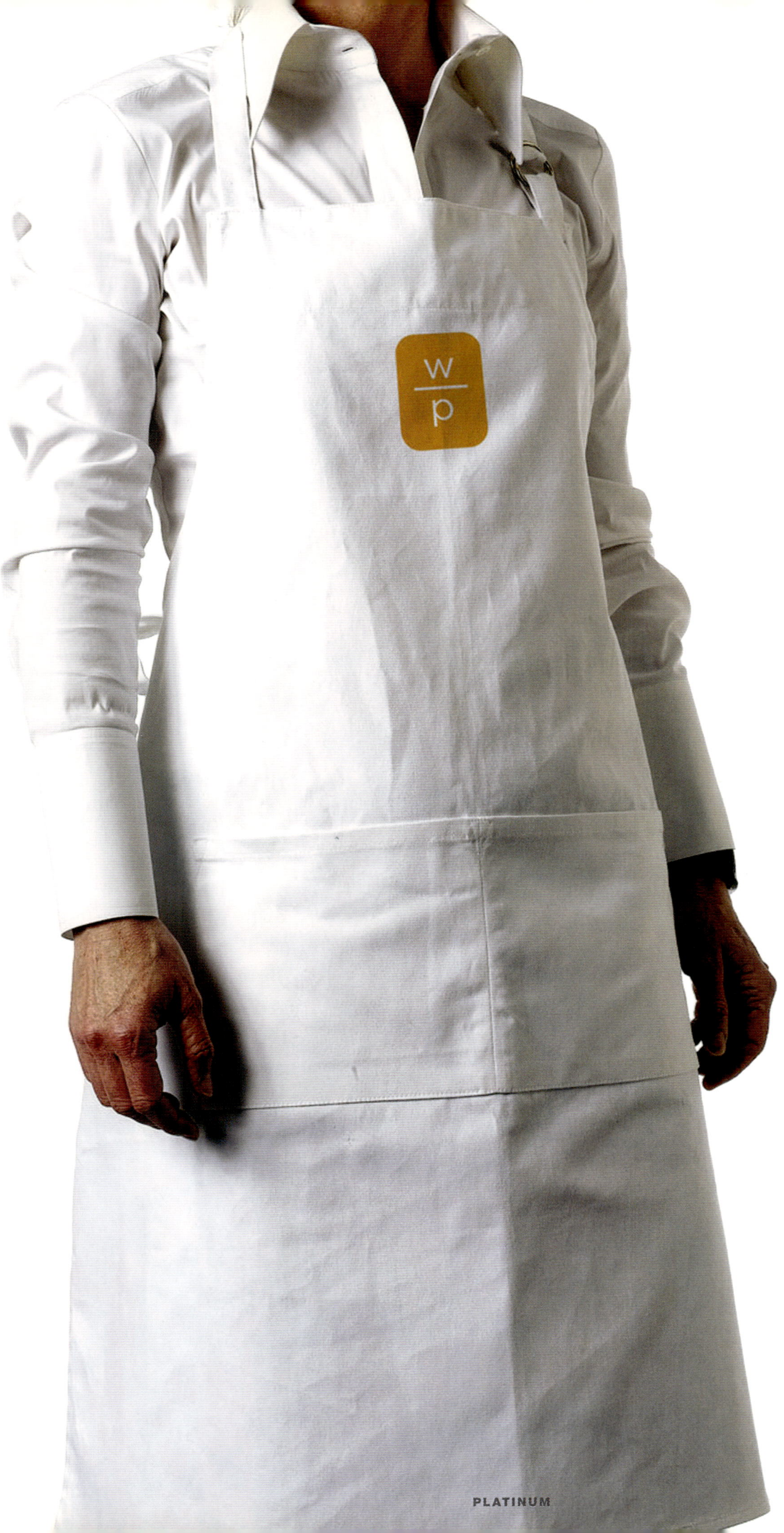

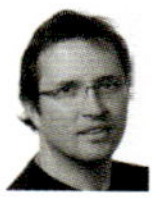

Landor Associates is one of the world's leading strategic brand consulting and design firms. Founded by Walter Landor in 1941, Landor pioneered many of the research, design and consulting methods that are now standard in the branding industry. Partnering with clients, Landor drives business transformation and performance by creating brands that are more innovative, progressive and dynamic than their competitors. Landor's holistic approach to branding is a balance of rigorous, business-driven thinking and exceptional creativity. Its work spans the full breadth of branding services, including brand research and valuation, brand positioning and architecture, naming and writing, corporate identity and consumer packaging design, branded experience, brand equity management, brand engagement and digital branding. With 24 offices in 18 countries, Landor's current and past clients include some of the world's most powerful brands, including BP, Cathay Pacific, Citi, Danone, Delta, Diageo, Emaar Properties, FedEx, Frito-Lay, the City of Hong Kong, HSBC, LG Group, Marriott Hotels & Resorts, Microsoft, Procter & Gamble and PepsiCo. Landor is part of WPP, one of the world's largest global communications services companies.

For more information, please visit www.landor.com.

Landor Associates Headquarters: 1001 Front Street San Francisco, CA 94111, United States / Tel: +1 415 365 1700 / Fax: +1 415 365 3190

Nicolas Aparicio (pictured left): Nicolas Aparicio is Executive Creative Director at the San Francisco office of Landor Associates, where he is responsible for establishing and maintaining its overall creative vision. Working closely with clients and the creative team, he oversees every aspect of the creative process to ensure excellence. Since joining Landor in 1986, Aparicio has been a key factor in the successful development of identity programs for a wide range of clients, including Coors Brewing Company, Hewlett-Packard, Seagate Technology, SKYY Vodka, Allied Domecq, Chandon, Microsoft, Dr. Pepper/7-Up, Coleman, Benjamin Moore, Brown Forman, Del Monte, Tropicana, Intuit, M&M/Mars, Sears Roebuck & Co., Kellogg's, Rand McNally, Taco Bell, A.G. Ferrari Foods and others. From his Colombian heritage, Aparicio possesses a

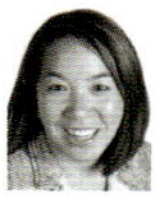

great understanding of the Latin-American market, which has been a tremendous asset in the development and implementation of global programs. He is fluent in Spanish and English. Aparicio has been quoted in the *San Francisco Chronicle* and *Brand Packaging* magazine.

His work has received numerous awards from *Graphis*, *Communication Arts*, the San Francisco Art Directors Club, *Print*, the AIGA, *Beverage World* and the Brand Design Association.

Prior to Landor, Aparicio was employed at Luckasiewicz Design in New York, where he was involved in the development and implementation of identity programs for Estée Lauder, Avon and Max Factor.

Aparicio holds a BFA in Communication Arts from Pratt Institute.

Deborah Chae-Crudo (pictured right): Deborah Chae Crudo is an Executive Director, Client Services and Technology Branding at the San Francisco office of Landor Associates. She leads an integrated team of strategists, designers and client directors in developing powerful branding strategy and identity programs. Crudo has 17 years of traditional brand strategy experience, as well as an extensive background in e-branding for both corporate and consumer brands. Her client roster includes eBay, 3Com, Intel, Symantec, Wireless Retail, E-Trade, Media One, Seagate RSS and Sierra Wireless. She has worked with consumer brand clients such as Chesebrough-Ponds, Levi Strauss & Co., IKEA, Lipton, Sutter Home, Oroweat, Uncle Ben's and Williams-Sonoma. Crudo has been quoted on MSNBC regarding technology companies and branding. Prior to joining Landor, Crudo served as the Managing Director of Interbrand's Western Region and global practice leader for e-branding. She also co-founded Novo, an ebranding agency, and grew the company from 5 to 300 people, successfully selling it to a public holding company in 2000. Crudo is a graduate of the University of California, Berkeley, where she double majored in Business and Art.

Creative Team
Deborah Chae-Crudo, Executive Director (strategy)
Michelle Gee, Strategy Director
Nicolas Aparicio, Executive Creative Director
Anastasia Laksmi, Senior Designer
Aparicio and Gee headshots by Landor.
All Wolfgang Puck images courtesy of Landor Associates.

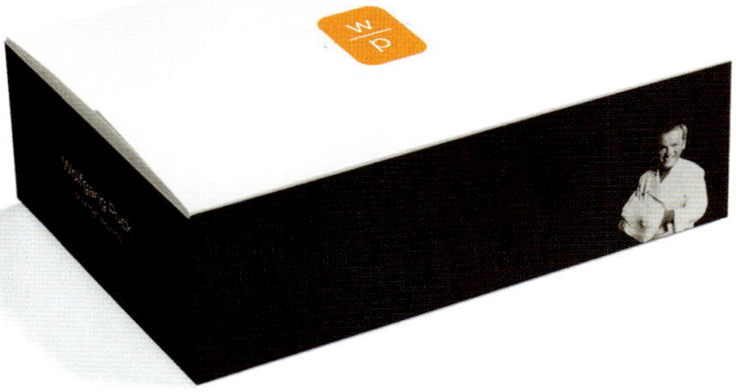

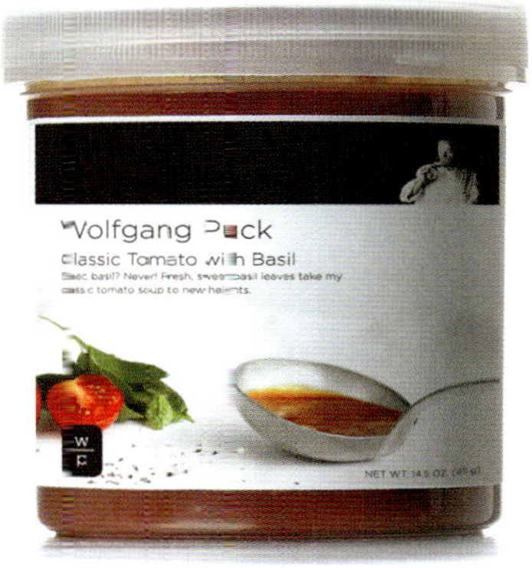

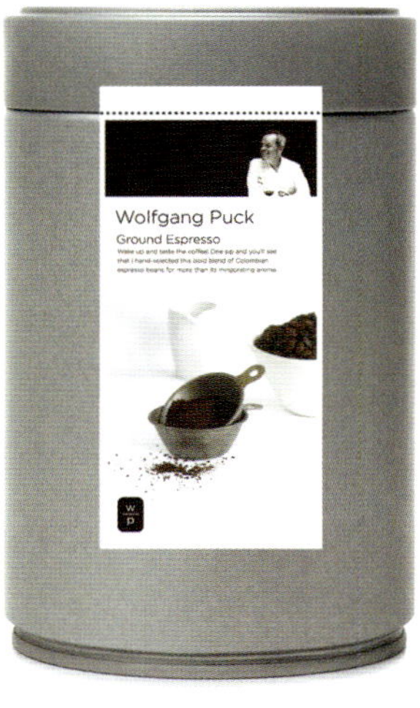

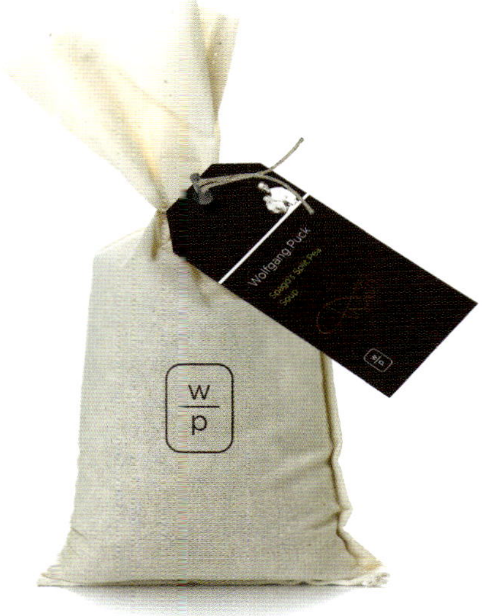

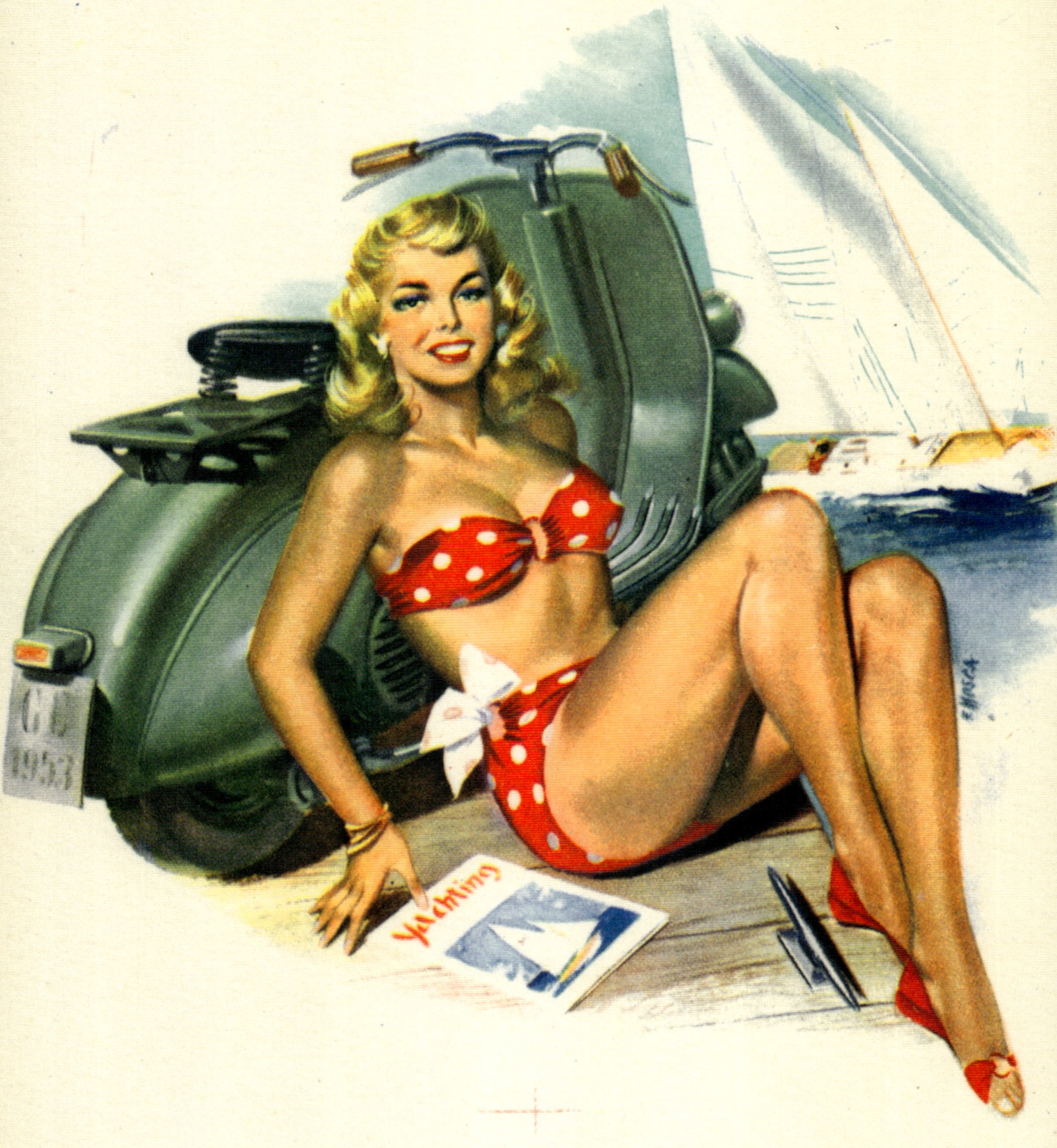

GE
1953
Yachting

Vespa Rolls On

In the 1940s, Enrico Piaggio created a scooter for the masses, and named it Vespa, or "wasp," in Italian. Since then, Vespa's unique brand identity has set it miles apart from other motorized two-wheel bikes. While their overall campaign has evolved in concert with the introduction of new motorbike styles, Vespa's innovative logo has remained consistent throughout. Perhaps The New York Times *put it best, describing Vespa as a "completely Italian product, such as we have not seen since the Roman chariot." As part of a special Graphis visual history, we showcase the brand's growth from its beginning through today.*

Vespa Advertising 1949~2006

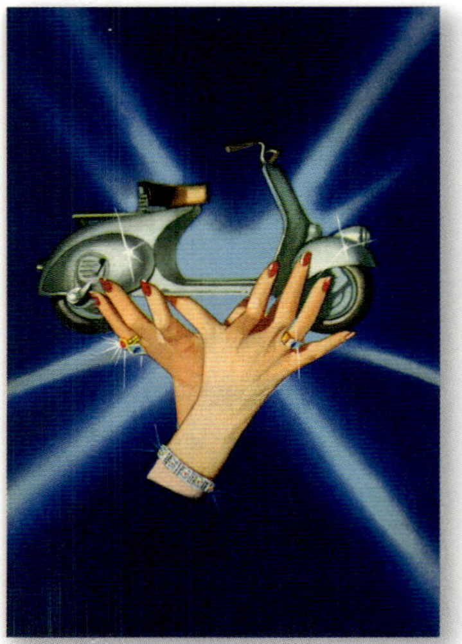

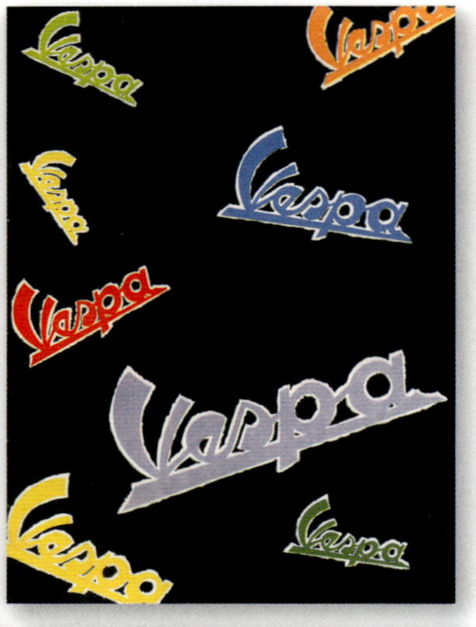

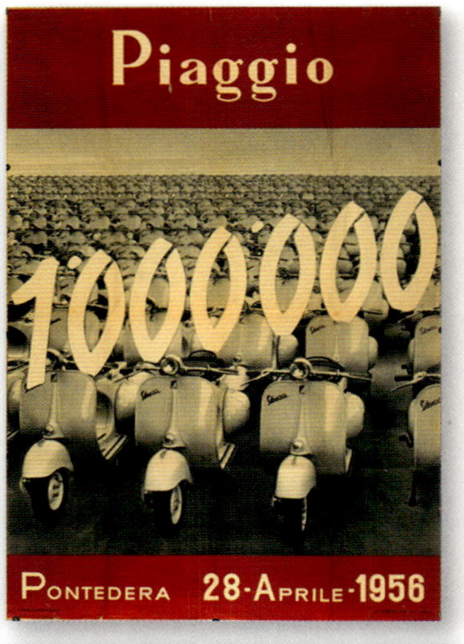

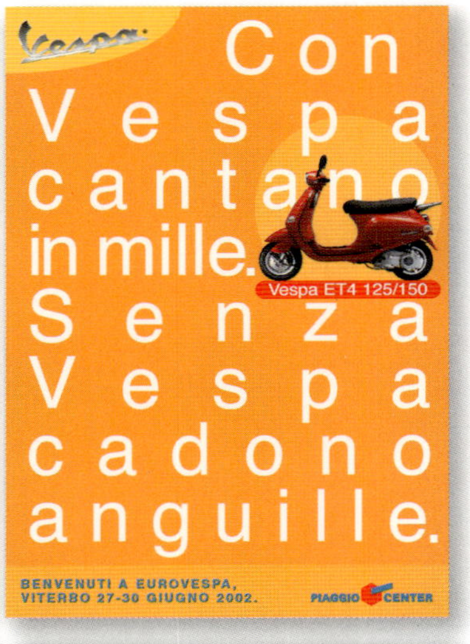

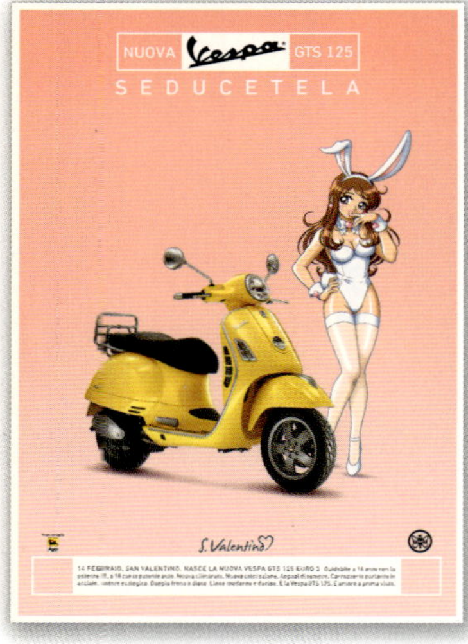

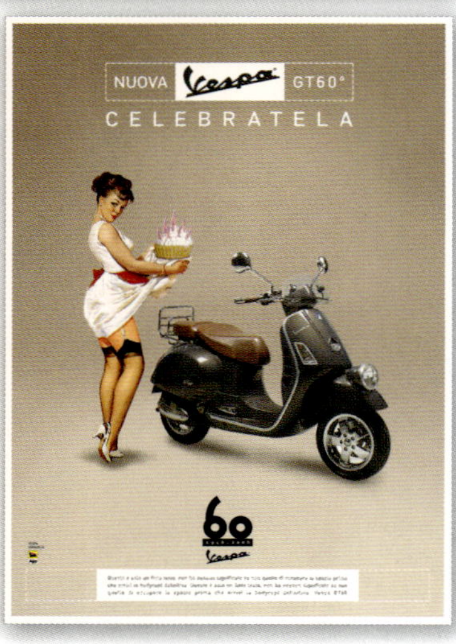

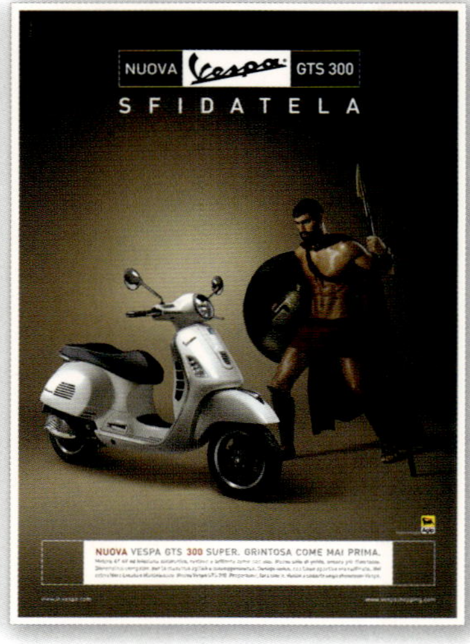

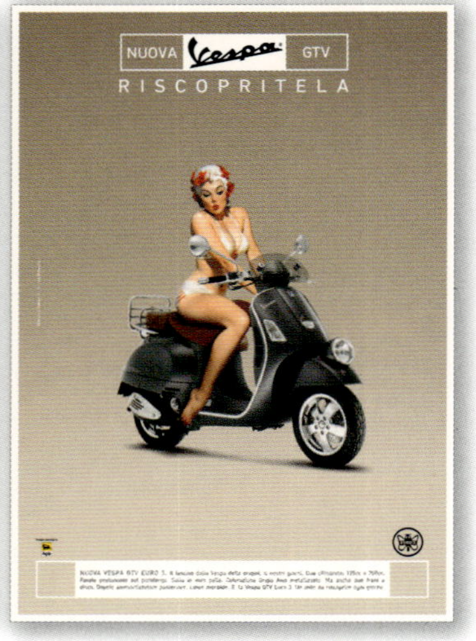

Image Credits

(page 38) 1953 Vespa Calendar, designed by Franco Mosca. Courtesy of the Piaggio Historical Archives. (page 39) Vespa cromata logo. (page 40 top row, left to right) 1949 brochure; 1955 "Vespa...the progress of technology" brochure designed by Zambelli; "100,000 Vespas" poster from April 28, 1956; "Urban ABC" Vespa advertising campaign from 2002. All photos courtesy of the Piaggio Historical Archives. (page 40 bottom row, left to right) 2005 Vespa advertisements by TBWA agency in Milan. Gina Ridenti (copy), Cristina Baccelli (art), Fabrizio Russo (art director). (page 41) "Their happiness only lacks a Vespa" advertising campaign from 1961 to 1962. Photo courtesy of the Piaggio Historical Archives. (page 42) Left, Rocco Sabelli, former Piaggio managing director from 2004 to 2006, and seated right, Roberto Colaninno Piaggio Group chairman and managing director. (page 43) Vespa GT 60, photo courtesy of the Piaggio Group. (page 44 top) Vespa Pontadera Factory in 1950, photo courtesy of the Piaggio Historical Archives. (page 44 middle row, left to right) Vespa M6 Protot created in 1945; Vespa Seigiorni created in 1952; Vespa 150 GS created in 1955; Vespa 90 SS created in 1966; and vthe Vespa PK created in 1983. (page 44 bottom) Vespa Siluro created in 1951. (page 45) Vespa 125, created in 1948. (page 46 from top to bottom) Vespa LX 50-125-150 created in 2005; Vespa GTS 250 created in 2005, Vespa GTS 300 Super; 30 Vespa GTV, and Vespa GT 60 limited edition created in 2006. (page 47 top & bottom) Piaggio museum. All photos copyrighted by the Piaggio Group. www.piaggio.com.

The New York Times **called the Vespa a "completely Italian product, such as we have not seen since the Roman chariot."**

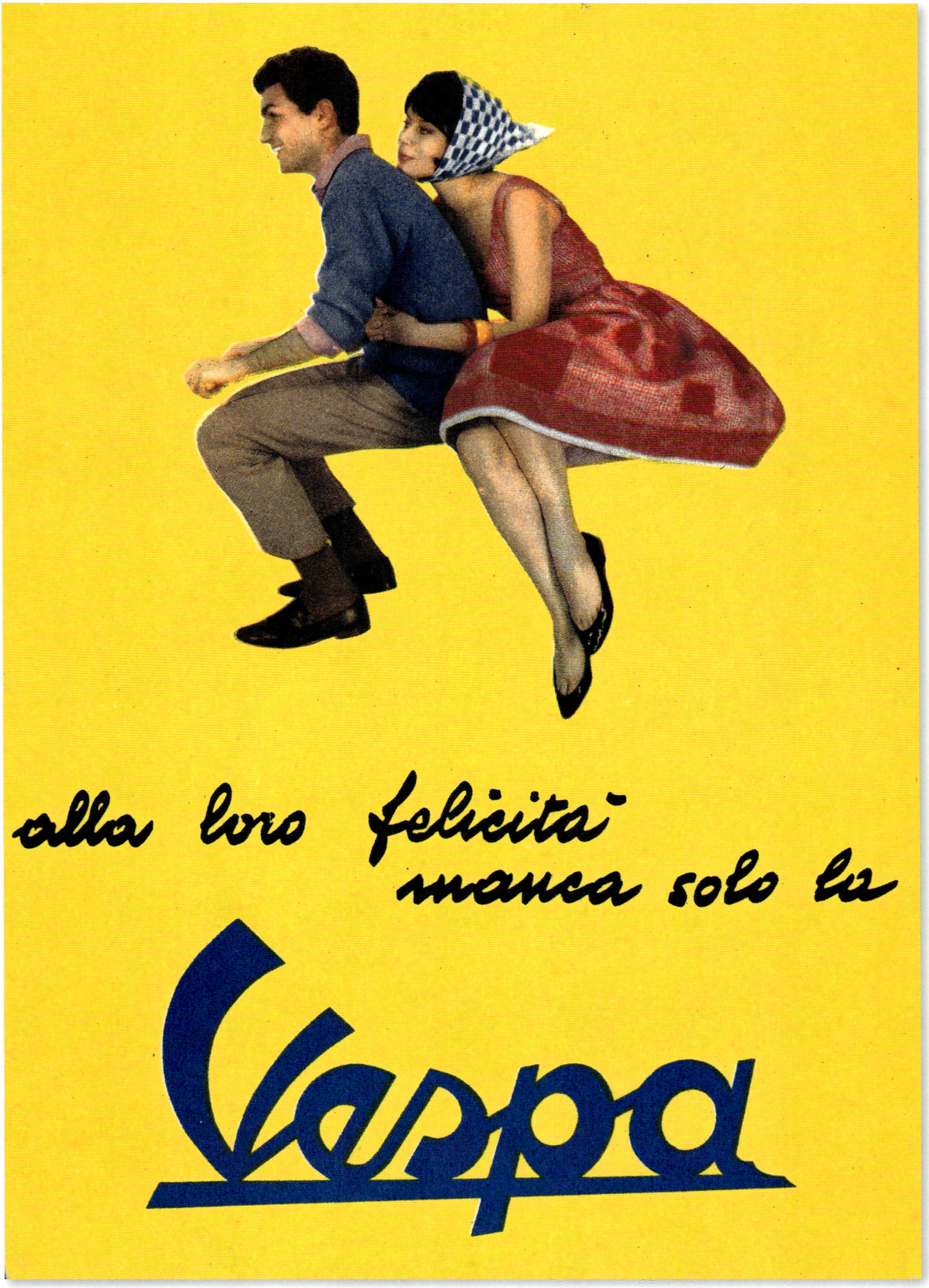
alla loro felicità
manca solo la
Vespa

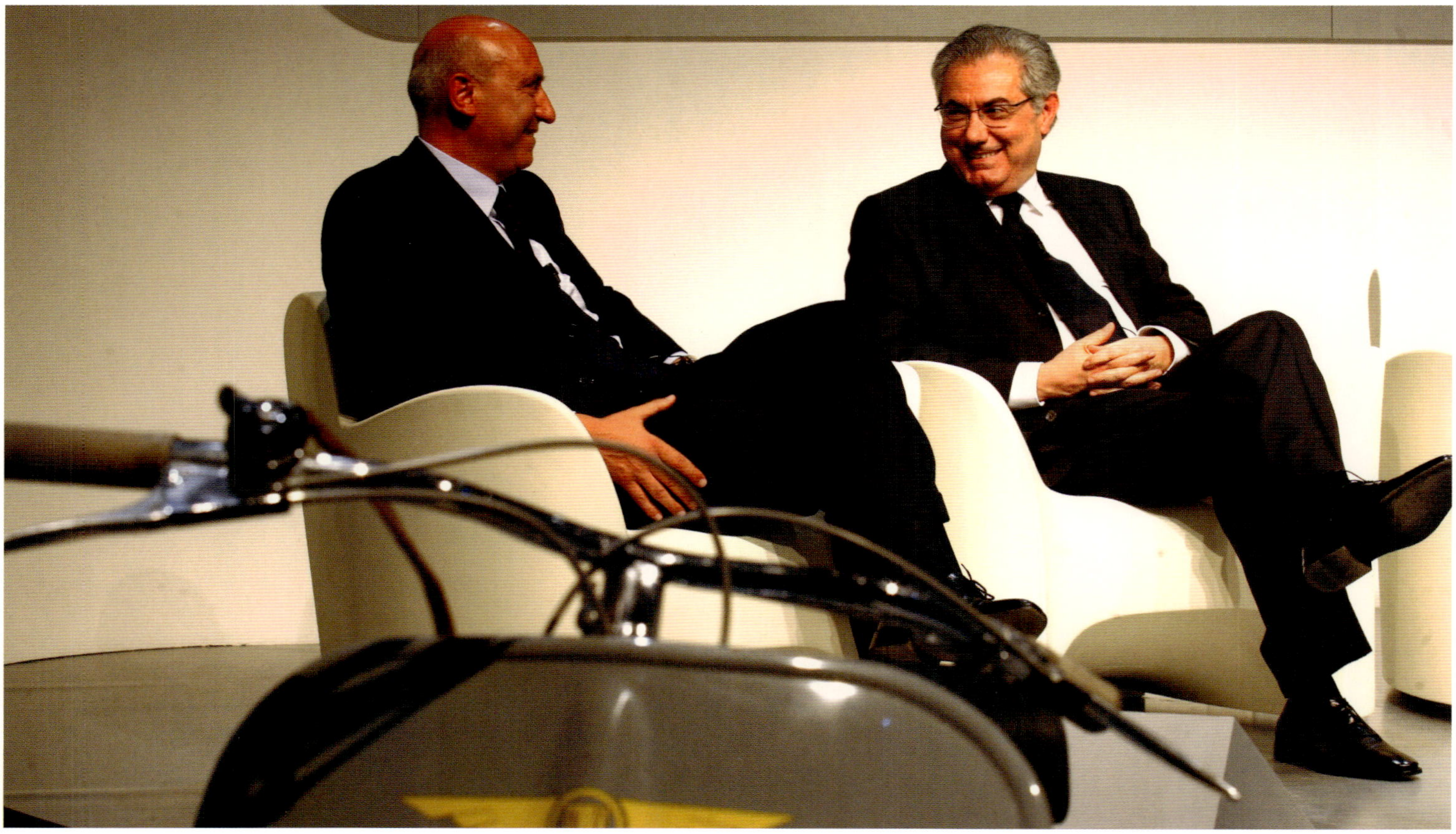

Vespa Company History

In 1884, Rinaldo Piaggio founded Piaggio & C., which specialized in luxury ship fitting, trains, airplanes and seaplanes. During World War II, Piaggio was one of the top aircraft manufacturers, but his plants were damaged after the war. Rinaldo's son, Enrico Piaggio, was responsible for rebuilding the plants, and he was also interested in creating a low-cost bike. Frustrated with the uncomfortable design of a motorcycle, he enlisted the help of Corradino D'Ascanio, an aeronautical engineer and designer. Together, they developed the first scooter to allow a driver to sit upright. In 1946, they applied to patent Vespa, describing it as "a motor cycle with a rational complex of organs and elements with body combined with the mudguards and bonnet covering all the mechanical parts." Four years after its start the company expanded beyond Italy, opening plants throughout Europe.

In the late 1940s, the first Vespa hit the marketplace, and since then the company has enjoyed extraordinary growth. From 1946 to 1965, 3,350,000 Vespas were manufactured in Italy, one for every 50 residents. In 1953, Piaggio & C. had service facilities in 10,000 locations, and in 1951, at least 20,000 Vespa fans attended "Vespa Day" in Italy. Even the Italian army was swept up in the excitement in 1963, requesting motorbikes specifically for parachuting soldiers, so that they could ride immediately upon landing. The Vespa PX, created in 1977 and known for its "original vintage" design, was the most popular bike in their history, and sold over two million units. Subsequent bike designs utilized technology to increase their power and speed capabilities. Case in point, the 1996 E4 model was the first with a four-stroke engine. Later, in 2000, Vespa unveiled their ET4 50, which can reach over 500 km on a full tank of gas.

Even more recently, Vespa has experienced another growth surge, with Piaggio & C. S.p.A. posting its best U.S. sales in June of this year, a 146 percent increase over June 2007. Sales are up 24 percent in 2008 overall in the scooter market. This can be attributed to rising gas prices, increasing traffic, and the appeal of scooters and bikes for city lifestyles. And with the release of the 146th Vespa model this summer – the sporty GTS 300 Super (which still uses the traditional steel frame introduced in 1946) there's no sign of slowing down anytime soon. And who'd want to, when the ride is so much fun?

"Vespa is an icon of Italian design where form was carefully defined to maximize every aspect of product functionality. When form follows function, design becomes timeless."

Paolo Timoni, *President & CEO, Piaggio Group Americas, Inc.*

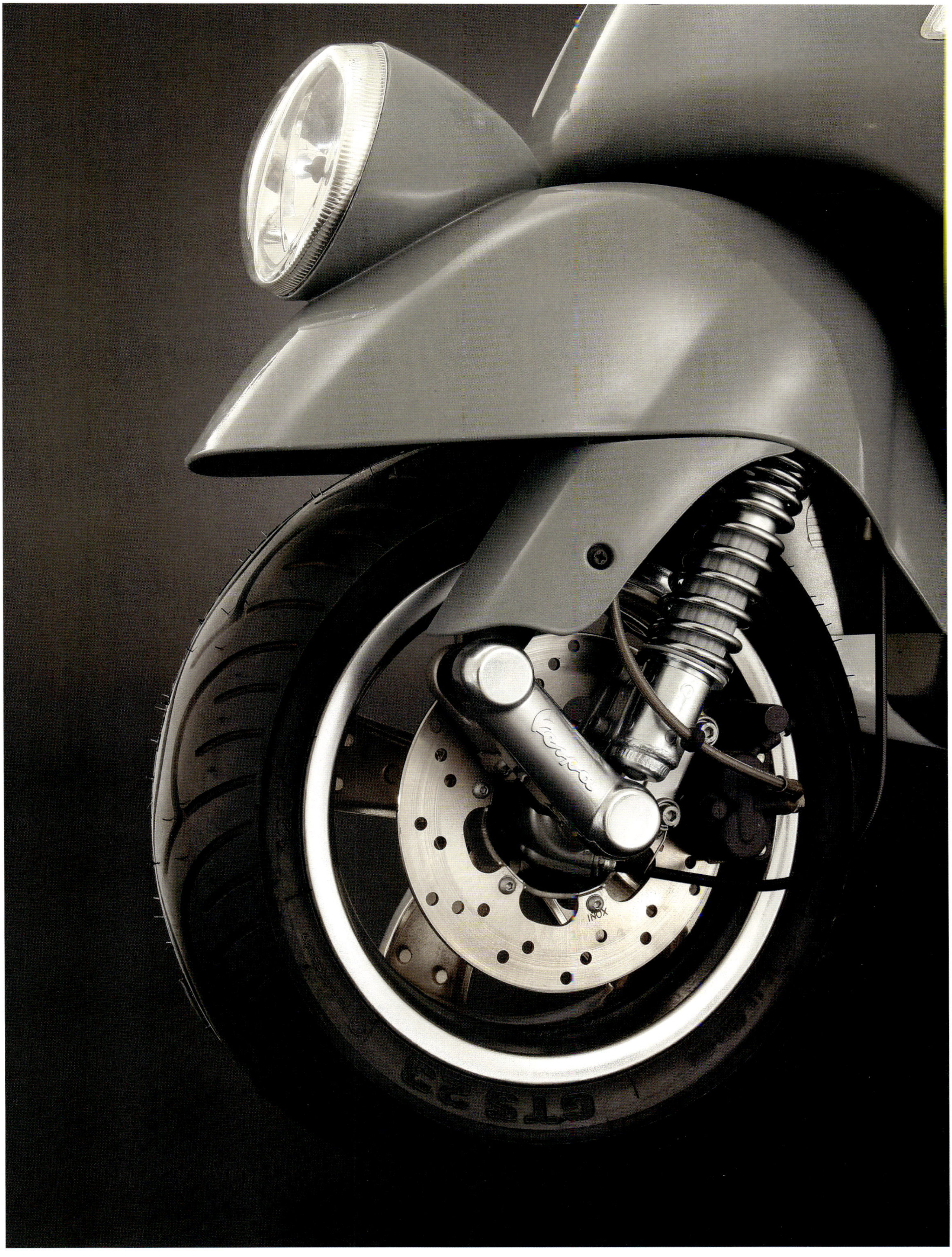

Vespa Potendera Factory 1950

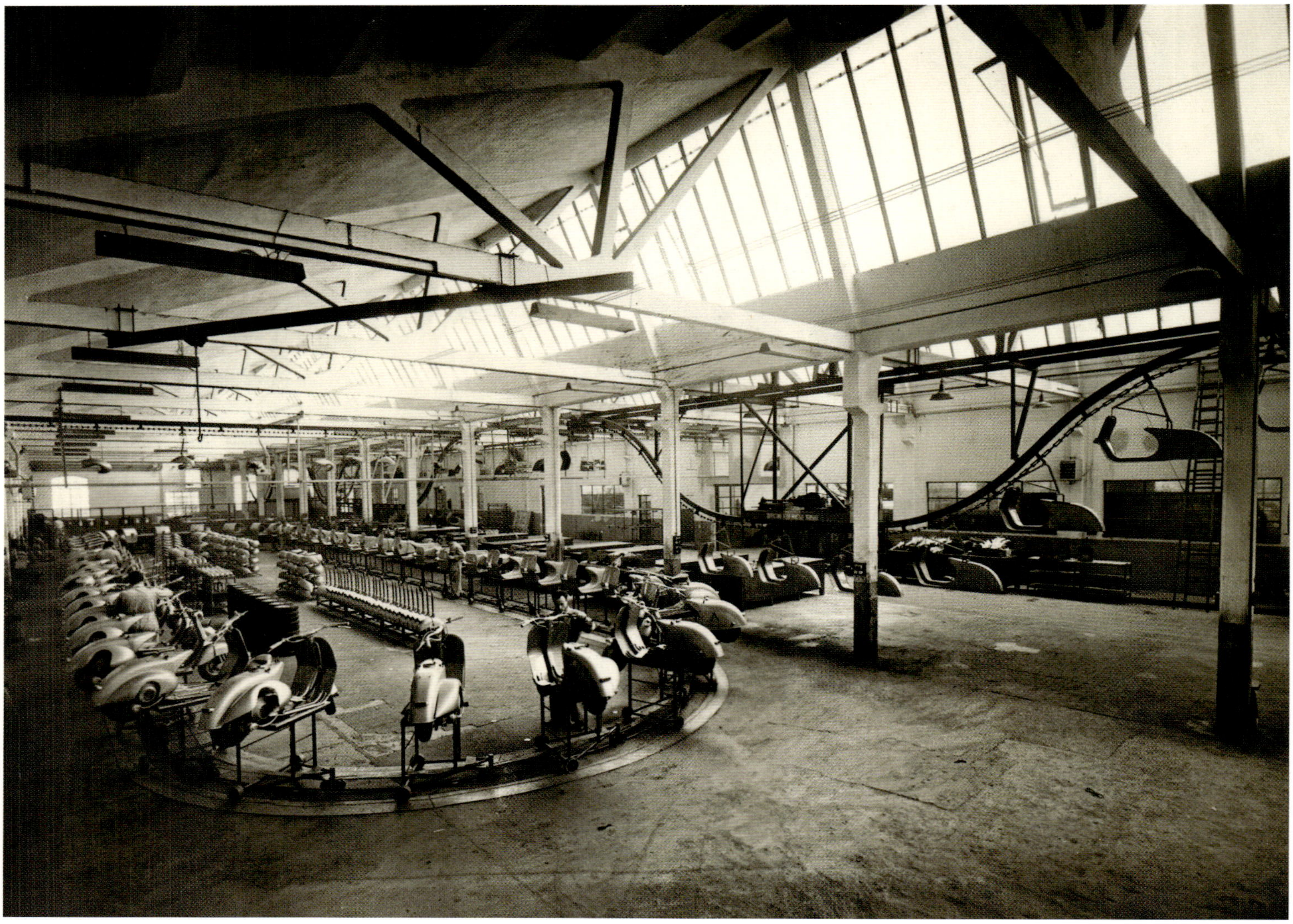

Vespa models 1945~2006

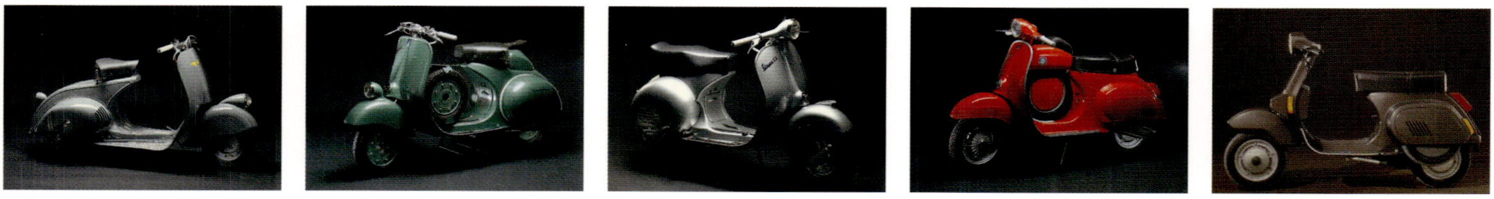

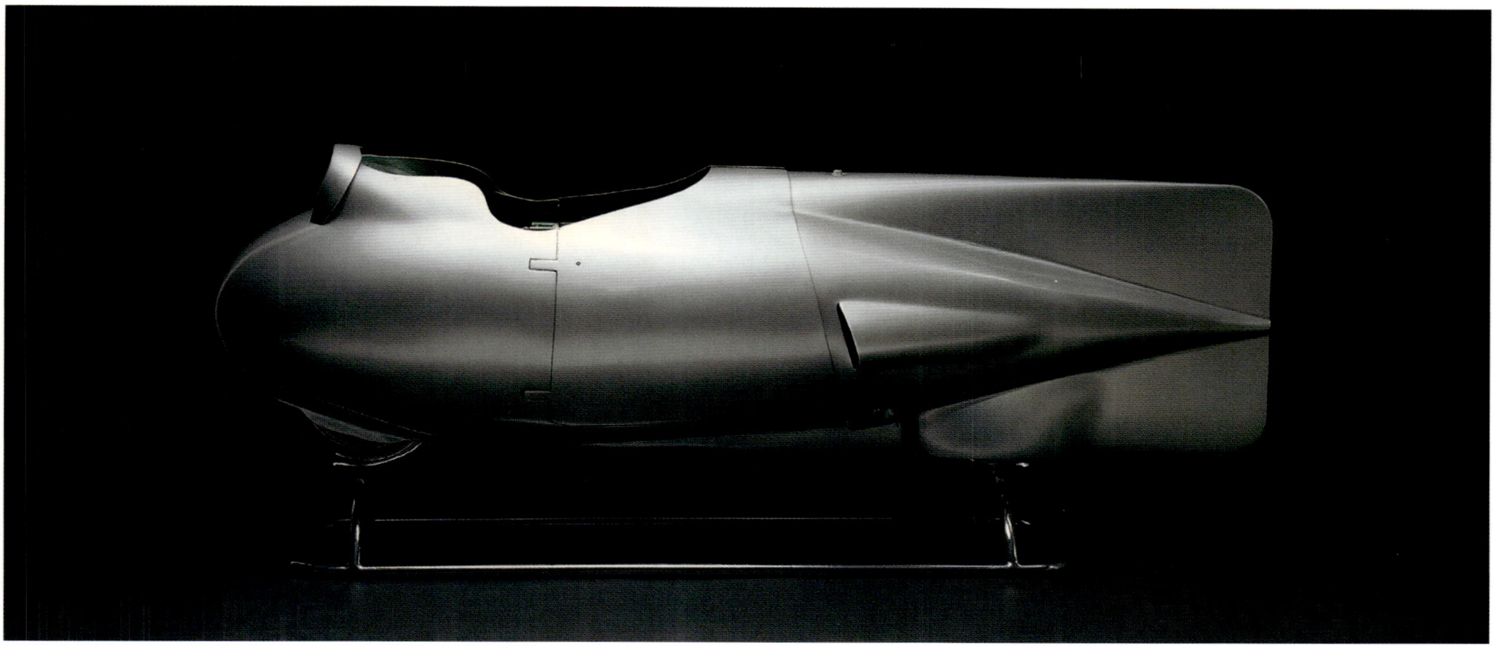

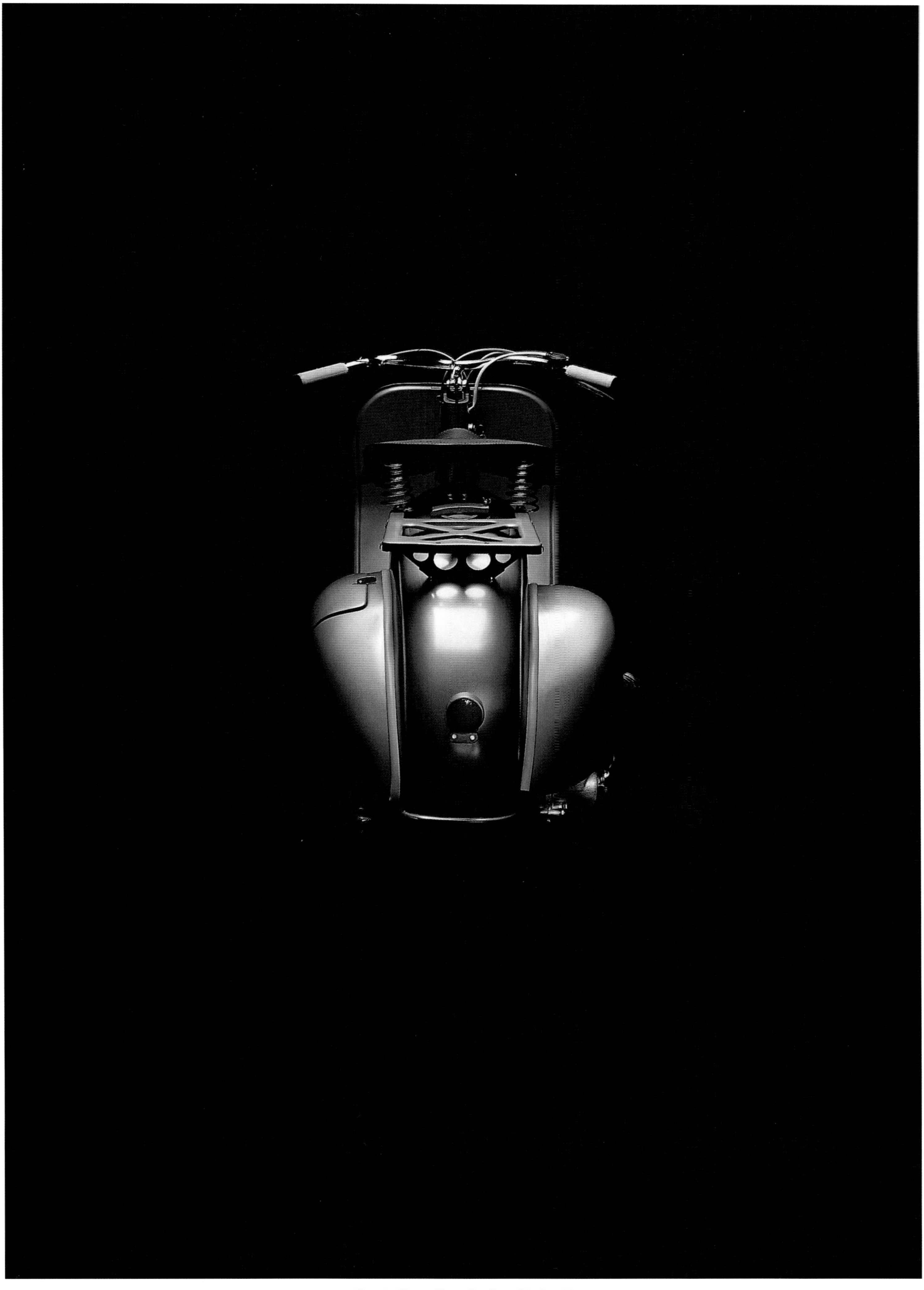

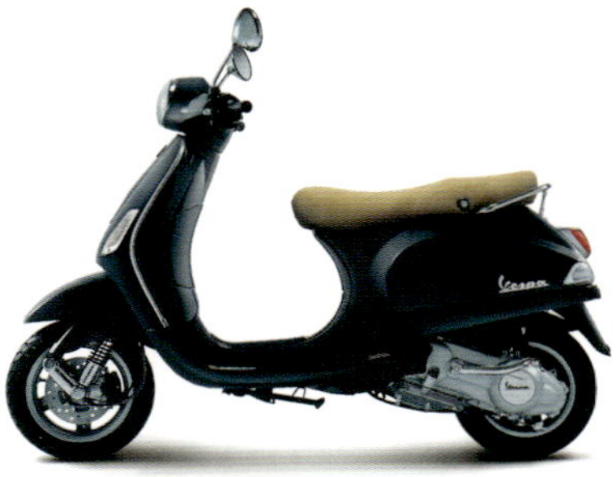

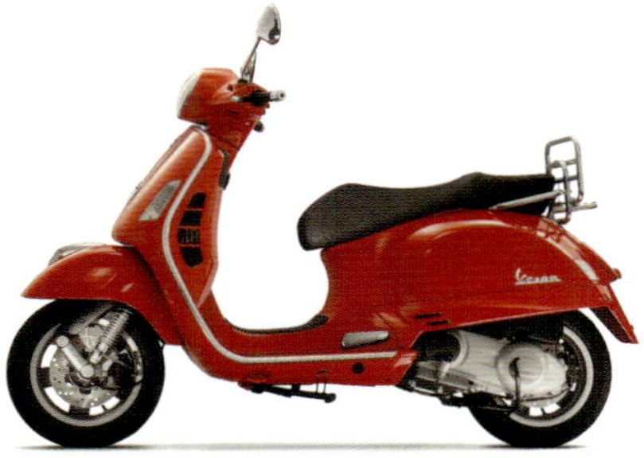

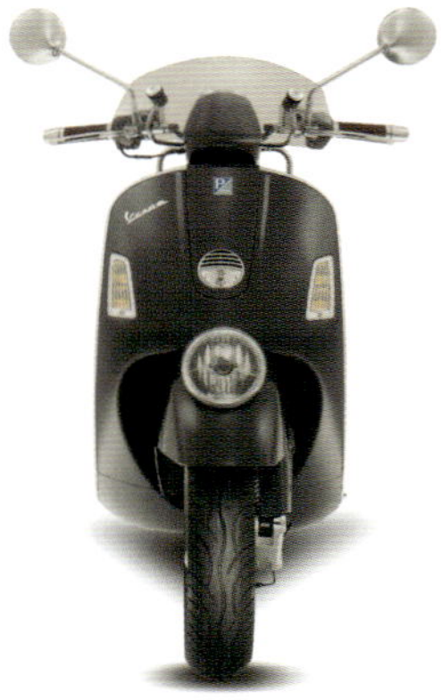

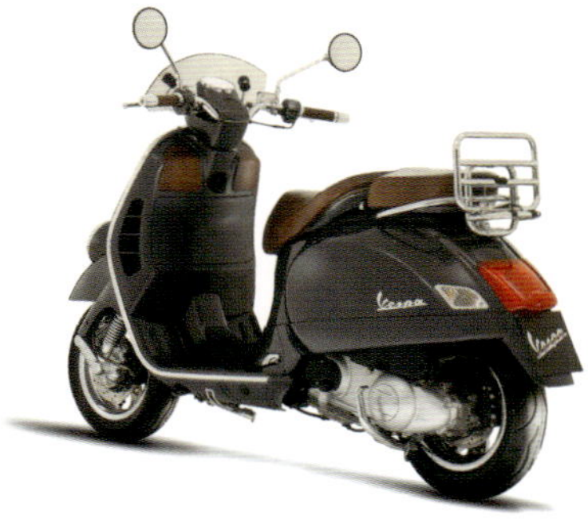

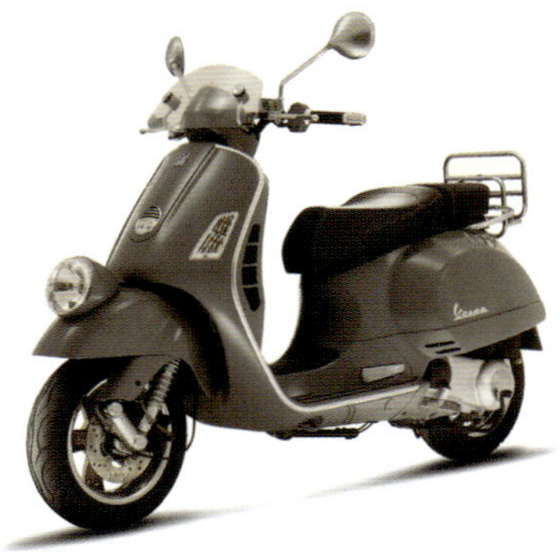

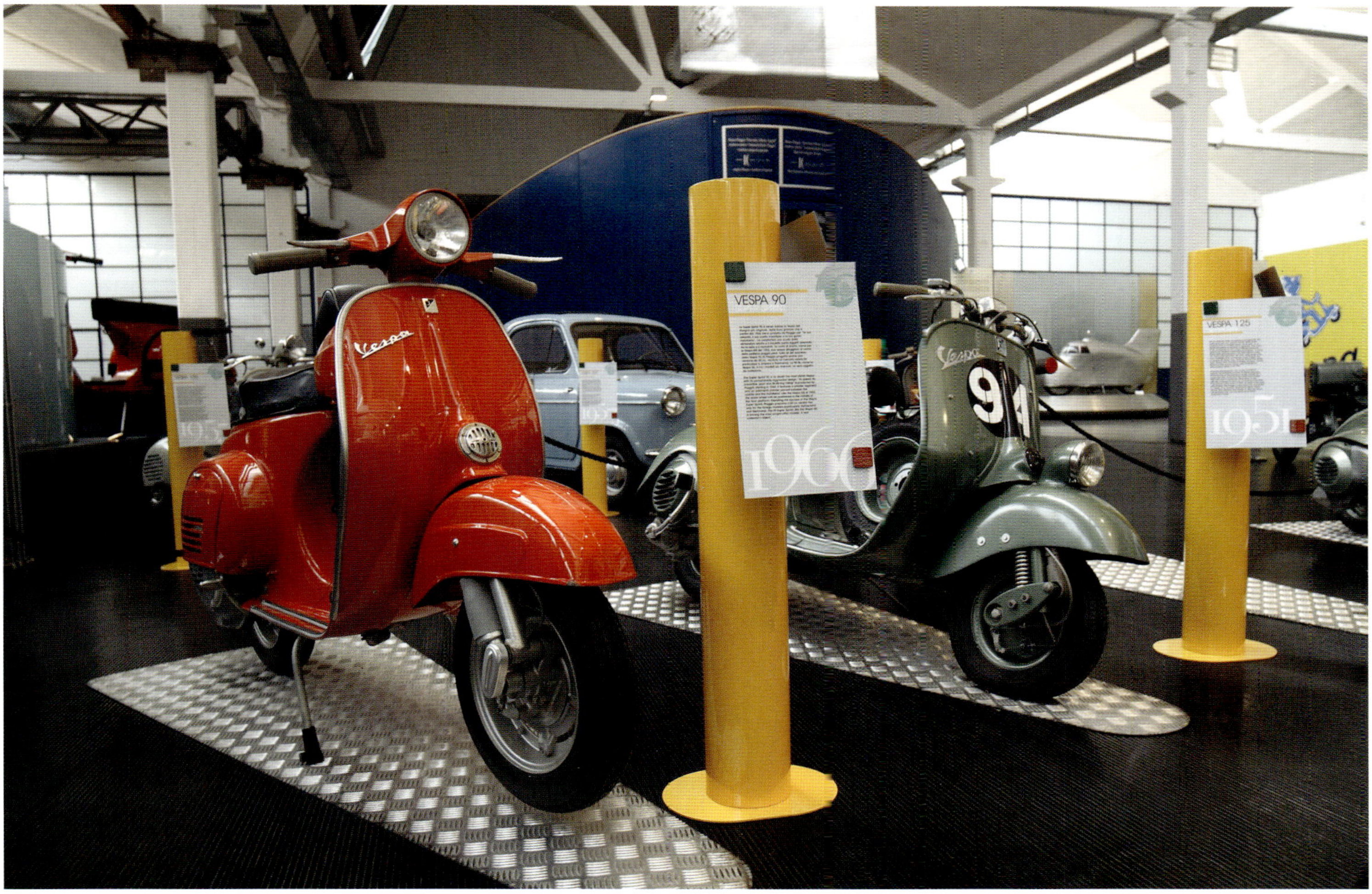
VESPA 90
1966
VESPA 125
1951
91

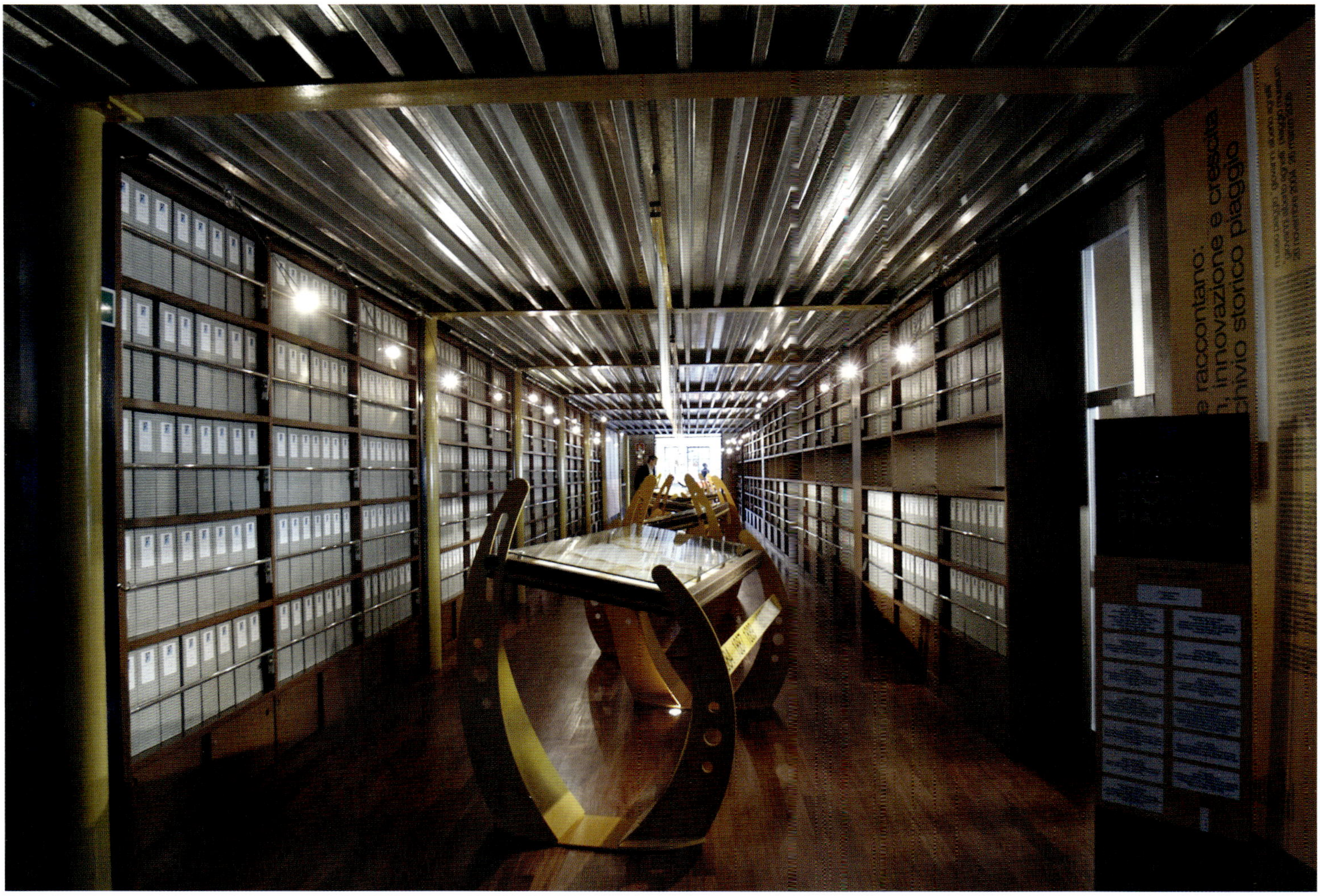

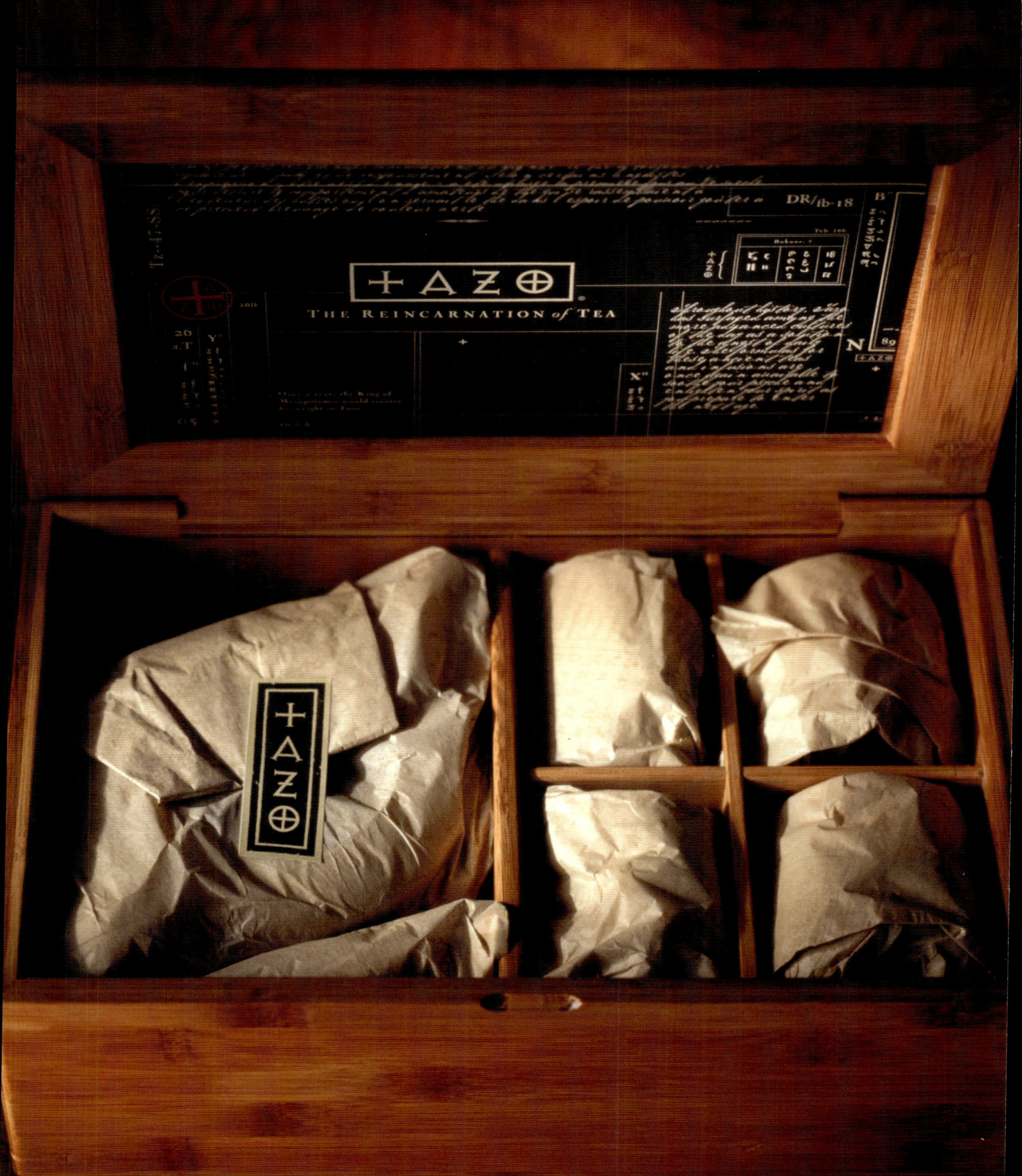

TAZO
THE REINCARNATION of TEA
DR/fb-18
TAZO

According to Sandstrom Partners: "One day, two gentlemen walked into our offices smelliwng faintly of herbs. It turned out to be tea. What they wanted to do was build a new premium tea brand from scratch and were looking for a design partner who could help them build the brand from the inside out. For lack of a better place, we started at the beginning—the ancient beginnings of tea. The name was developed to fit the strategy, and even the logo vaguely reflected some ancient civilization. Themed 'The Reincarnation of Tea,' packaging included copy that further built the mystique of the brand. We developed a fully integrated identity system, applying it to packaging, retail merchandising, collateral, website and apparel. This was the beginning of Tazo Tea. Four years later, in 1999, Starbucks purchased Tazo, and now sells it in more than 7,500 stores internationally. Interestingly enough, now these two gentlemen smell vaguely of money."

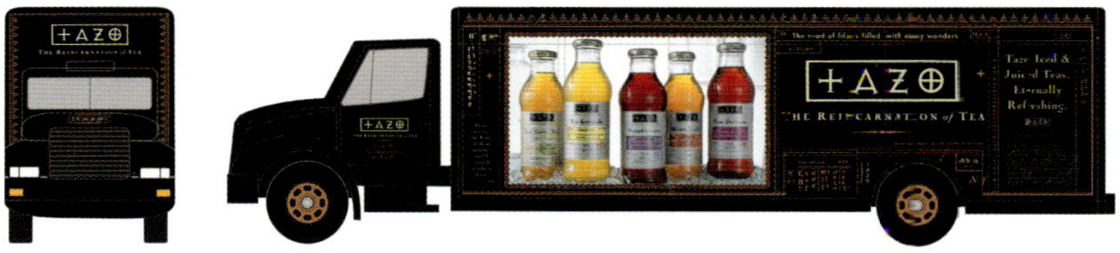

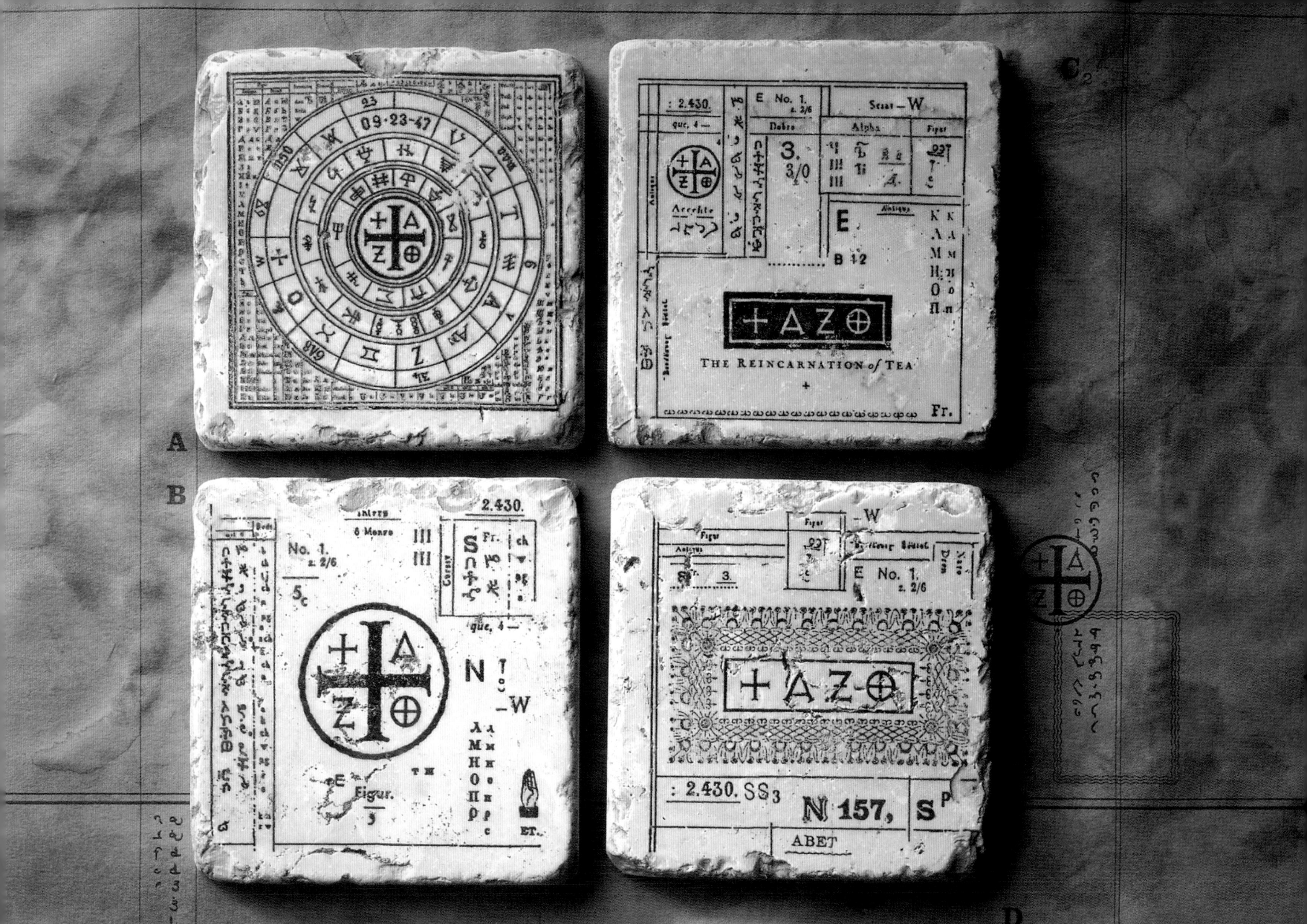

File No. T47-002a: TAZO COASTERS

Q&A with Steve Sandstrom

How was this campaign born? What problem were you presented—or shall we say opportunity?

Steve Smith and Steve Lee started Tazo in 1994. Both had worked together at Stash Tea, a company that Steve Lee started in the 70s. Stash is still around. Smith was the tea master and creator of the tea blends and infusions. He had established great relationships with some of the finest tea estates in the world. Lee was the entrepreneur.

Yet another Steve—a friend of mine who worked as a creative director and writer at Wieden+Kennedy advertising—referred these two Steves to us. His name was Steve Sandoz. I worked frequently on projects with Sandoz (who did so on a freelance basis apart from his job at the agency). Sandoz recommended that Smith and Lee come talk with me about a new tea company they wanted to start up. So the four Steves gathered in my office. Smith wanted this new tea company to be more engaging and interesting to Americans. While tea is the most consumed beverage in the world after water, it had no real culture in the U.S. He wanted to change that. Tea is the oldest known beverage, having often been used for remedies, and has recently been proven to have healthful benefits.

We all believed there was an opportunity to create something different in the tea category, even though there were plenty of tea brands filling up the shelves in grocery stores. The original plan was to launch a line of bottled teas blended with various fruit juices and infused with various herbs. This was to compete with Snapple and other so-called tea products that were promoted as alternative beverages to soda pop, even though they contained the same key ingredient—high fructose corn syrup. Smith knew he could produce tea products that not only tasted better, but also were actually made from much better ingredients. Smith's initial conceptual brief to us was 'Marco Polo meets Merlin.' He wanted to create a feeling of discovery, a sense of history, and to evoke some mysterious and mystical qualities around their tea-based concoctions. At that time, they had not fully developed any tea products, and the company had no name. It was a start-from-scratch deal.

What was your solution?

Sandoz created the name Tazo. He wanted a made-up name that had only four letters, one of them more memorable (like a Z), and something foreign sounding to Americans. He also came up with the positioning line, The Reincarnation of Tea. Our goal was to reinvent tea in an American consumer's mind. And referring to it as reincarnated gave reference to one of the world's greatest tea producing regions—India.

Marco Polo meets Merlin was a good starting point to create the visual approach. I liked the idea of old alchemist symbols, elixirs and potions. I thought it should appear multicultural (since tea is), with perceived influences of ancient Asia, Egypt, and Phoenicia, or to include remnants of Sanskrit or some forgotten language. I wanted to create something that felt ancient or historical, yet ironically still had a contemporary sense. When I found the typeface Exocet, created by English designer Jonathan Barnbrook, I thought it had many of the qualities I wanted. I made a few modifications and then distressed the art to create the look of a stone rubbing. The result was something like an archaeologist would create by rubbing graphite over a stone inscription or hieroglyph. This helped create the logo as a piece of art and not just a typographic solution.

The letter forms look more like symbols than letters, which is why I used the Exocet lowercase t. It created some tension and a distinct point of difference. Much of the attitude of the brand came from creating the logo.

What challenges did you face in branding a company that had yet to enter the marketplace?

The original concept of bottled beverages took longer to develop, and producing a line of hot teas (in filter bags) was an easier path to get product out on shelves. The downside of that direction was that those shelves were already crowded with tea brands, and there really wasn't any evident reason to create another one. We also had limited funds for production, so we were left with the most basic of packaging options to design. That's why I believed that stepping outside the comfort zone was necessary to get attention. We stepped outside, but not in a way that wasn't relevant. In fact, we made most of the other tea brands appear irrelevant.

What goals did you have initially for this campaign?

Being different was imperative to change perceptions about tea and what it could be for a new consumer—especially a design savvy and smart consumer. We weren't aiming to please everyone. We wanted distinction because you can't develop a very powerful relationship with consumers without that. We weren't creating products for the masses, initially. We wanted the discerning taste leaders to buy Tazo as a badge brand—one that they would be identified with. Organic and natural was to be expressed in visual ways.

We set out to create fans, not customers. Taking some risks had to be apparent in the design. People had to see that there were interesting and smart and talented people behind these products. And the products were developed to live up to this visual promise of something better. It could have just been great marketing, but because the products were great, the brand delivered in every aspect.

Within a few years, Tazo became the largest brand in the natural foods channel. It was used as props in upscale magazines, décor in windows or tabletop displays in high-end lifestyle retailers in SoHo, and the copy from the packaging was quoted in best-selling self-help books. It became something of a cultural lighthouse. Those who loved anything New Age took it to heart, and cynics and skeptics loved its irreverent attitude and the way we rewrote history to our own advantage. (The great pyramid at Giza was originally built as a warehouse to stockpile Tazo as a hedge against inflation.)

When the makers of Tazo tea approached you about their branding, did you imagine that the company would be as popular as it has become?

There is always a certain amount of luck in the timing of the market, and cultural sensitivities and trends that one can't always predict. You can do research and prepare a great business plan, but you can never really know if success will happen and to what degree. Awareness is a critical tool for a strategic designer, and sometimes your instincts are very much in tune with what needs to happen next. I do believe that it is important to step outside the comfort zones to connect with people in a way that they can't describe in a focus group. I believe Tazo was a hit because people could see the risk taken and could feel the presence of the people behind the brand—people you'd like to know and learn more about. Its opacity was very cool at the time.

You mentioned that one of Tazo's goals was to make tea fun and interesting. Do you think you achieved that?

Certainly all the copy written around the brand (and in every place possible) was an entertaining experience. Simply naming an English Breakfast tea 'Awake' and a chamomile infusion 'Calm' changed up the way one was going to interact with this brand. Everything on the packaging was worth reading, and every joke was either sillier than you could imagine or more brilliant than you could have expected. A popular author, admittedly jealous of the words, had actually stenciled a Tazo quotation about passion on her bedroom wall. But again, we need to talk about the products and how they also introduced a variety of unexpected flavors and creative blends to make the experience of the tea also so enjoyable.

Describe your personal experience with this project.

Creating Tazo and developing the brand over eleven years was joyful work and pretty close to my soul as I think back. There was a lot of my own visual aesthetic at play in the look of things, but also my own interests in the humanities, calligraphy, the fine arts and craft. I designed in some inconsistencies and irregularities to throw the perfectionist out of the room. But it was the collaboration of fellow creative partners Steve Sandoz and Palmer Pettersen, along with our very creative client, Steve Smith, that made the work a little magical. Maybe Merlin was involved and we just didn't realize it.

Talk about your experiences with Starbucks. How has the brand or your work changed since Starbucks bought the brand?

Tazo was at a point where they needed more investment dollars to keep up with their growth, and at the same time they found out that Starbucks was building a tea team internally. At several thousand stores, even if the tea was terrible by Tazo standards, Starbucks could make a move to dominate the tea market in the U.S.

So Tazo met with Starbucks management to let them know that building a Starbucks tea brand didn't make sense when there was a brand that met their consumer profile and was already the leader in the natural foods category. Starbucks agreed, but instead of selling Tazo at Starbucks, they decided they should buy the brand and bring it into their portfolio.

Tazo did better than expected after the Starbucks purchase, which led management to increase the financial goals for the brand significantly. That created a concern within Starbucks that the people who had built the Tazo brand were not necessarily right for achieving the new goals.

The new Tazo leadership believed that the brand needed to become more appealing to the mass consumer to achieve enough scale to meet these goals. A business relationship was formed with Kraft to secure greater national grocery distribution. Research and efforts to figure out how to alter the brand personality and packaging were put in motion, while innovative concepts and new products were typically put aside

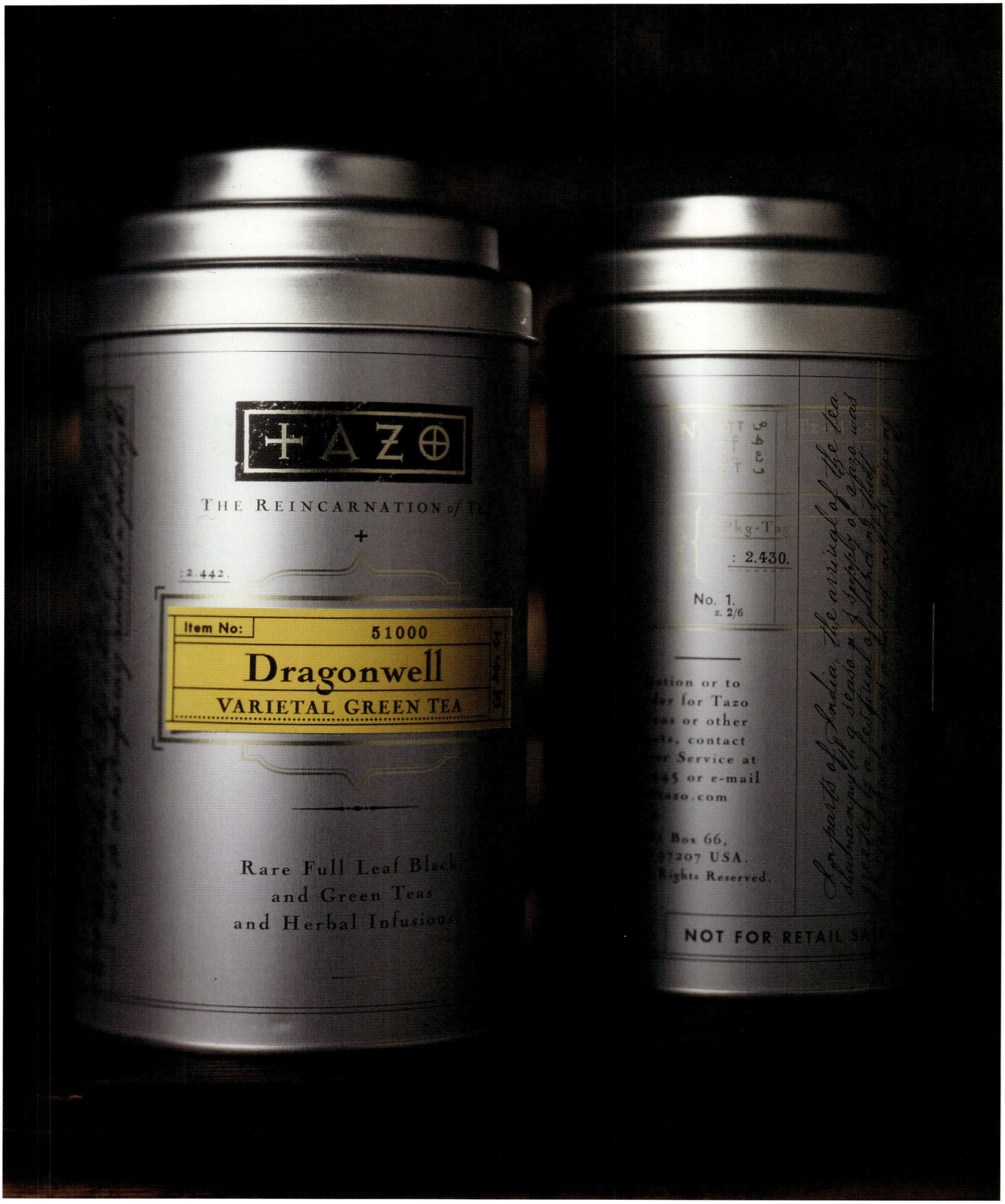

"The new Starbucks version of Tazo is on the shelves today. It is stripped clean of the personality and edge that created fans of consumers."

Steve Sandstrom, *Creative Director & Partner, Sandstrom Partners*

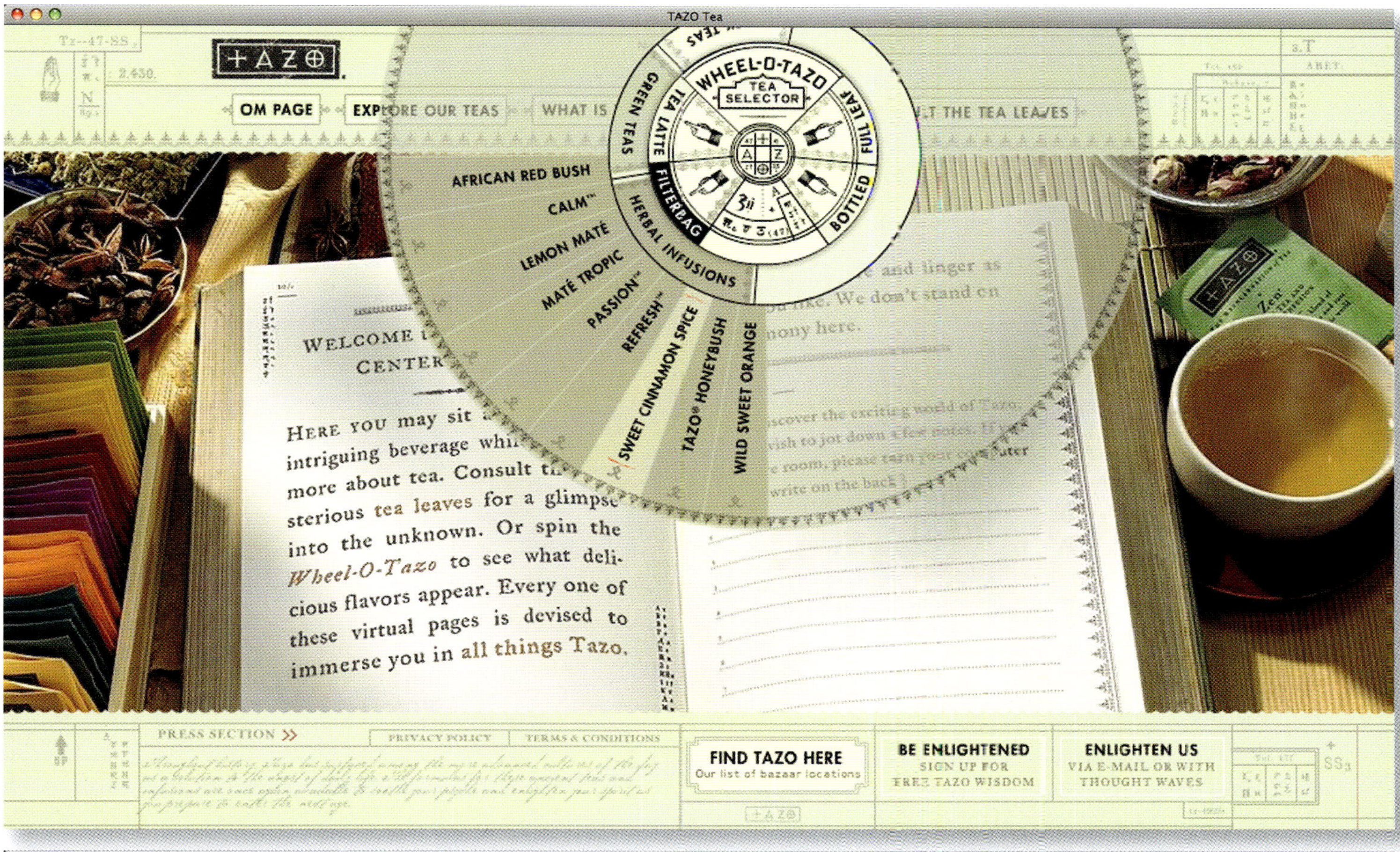

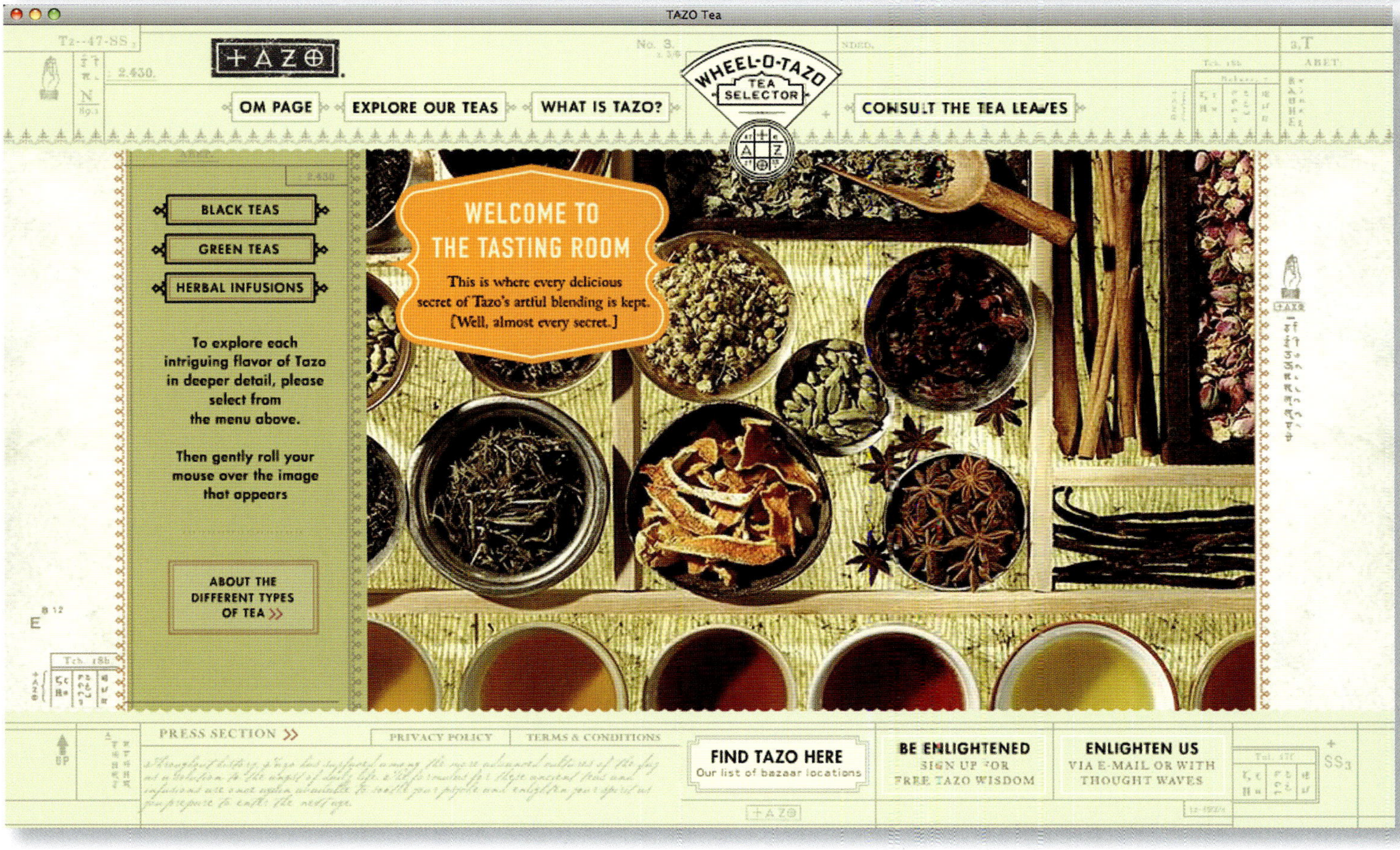

Sandstrom's initial packaging concept was so strong, it inspired Tazo's founders to go back and improve their product.

“The initial conceptual brief was ‘Marco Polo meets Merlin’... Within a few years, Tazo became the largest brand in the natural foods channel.”

Steve Sandstrom, *Creative Director & Partner, Sandstrom Partners*

and labeled as ‘not scalable.’ Full-leaf tea in filter bags was one of these ideas. This is an innovative concept that Mighty Leaf is known for today, but it is also an old idea of Steve Smith’s that was never supported or allowed to advance.

When Tazo was created in 1994, anyone who did yoga was strange. Very strange. By the time Starbucks had decided that Tazo needed to be more mainstream, yoga had become a widely popular form of fitness and wellness—even in the red states. Appealing to a mass consumer was, in effect, looking backward and not forward. Most consumers willing to spend more for a premium priced tea had already caught up to Tazo, and the brand was not nearly as unusual as it had been. There were also plenty of copycat brands diluting the market as well. What had been held back was Tazo’s (Smith’s) ability to create new, innovative products and interesting packaging executions, which would have allowed the brand to continue its path of surprising and delighting the expanding number of tea consumers in America.

It is also important to note that the natural foods movement was and still is growing nationwide, and has been putting pressure on mainstream grocery to get more ‘natural.’ I believe that Tazo was an early leader and significant brand in influencing the growth of the natural foods sector. But without innovation, Tazo was losing its energy and favor in the natural foods and specialty category.

The new Starbucks version of Tazo is on the shelves today. It is stripped clean of the personality and edge that created fans of consumers. The logo has been cleaned up and contemporized. The T is now a standard letterform. ‘The Reincarnation of Tea’ has been removed in case it might be offensive to those who don’t believe in the concept of reincarnation or any possible religious conflicts (even if it was referring to tea and not people). Starbucks’s research concluded that no one read the packaging and that it was a waste of space to fill it with our humorous stories and myths of Tazo, which were considered over the head of a mainstream consumer.

Yet in the Tazo warehouse were boxes full of thousands of letters from avid fans of the brand. These people weren’t writing because they were excited about the net weight or the brief flavor description on the front of the box. The new leadership chose to believe the research even with mounds of physical evidence to the contrary stored in their warehouse. An eye-tracking study was conducted to test the shelf presence of Tazo, using a projected image of a fully merchandised grocery aisle filled with tea products. Those tested wore special eyewear. It revealed that Tazo was so difficult to find that it registered in the bottom 5 percent. I asked how Tazo could have achieved the success it had if this were a realistic test. Wouldn’t the brand have died years ago if no one could find it, especially when you consider that it never had any advertising to support it?

I have no information on the performance of the new Tazo packaging. It appears to us that they aimed at and hit the middle, which isn’t a position of leadership. (At this writing, Starbucks stock has fallen from $60 to $15 per share.) It is, in my opinion, a sad example of how to turn a great brand into a mediocre product. Or how a parent company lacks the understanding or vision of how to leverage and support a subsidiary’s full potential. This wasn’t a direction that we could be associated with. It led us to resign from our relationship with the brand after eleven years and after having achieved some of the most influential and award-winning work ever done in the overall categories of packaging and branding. Our ideas for Tazo’s growth far exceeded the Starbucks plan, but the window of opportunity (and commitment) has passed. We envisioned an engaging lifestyle brand well beyond tea products, with design and humor and multi-cultural twists as core elements. It’s a huge concept left only in our imagination.

To learn more about Tazo Tea, visit www.tazo.com.

For more information on Sandstrom Partners and Steve Sandstrom, see *page 64* *or visit www.sandstrompartners.com.*

A Word from the Client: Steve Smith, Tazo Founder

“I presented Steve a concept that I believed would change the way people perceived tea. The existing tea category was stuffy and boring, and we needed to reach a younger audience with a better, more interesting product than was currently in the market. I had been discussing the notion of the brand and tea experience as ‘Merlin meets Marco Polo.’ Sandstrom and Sandoz suggested ‘a touch of Raiders of the Lost Ark,’ which would root the brand in history and have it appear to be from another time.

“Steve and his group were able to create a rich tapestry of color and texture working with fairly common packaging types. The voice and personality of Tazo evolved in the process as we (the three Steves) collaborated. Sandstrom was willing to listen and respond to my creative ideas and adjust his approach when necessary, or explain to me why my ideas did not fit. Most importantly, Sandstrom was willing to take risks, and present different design ideas that were not based upon what was in the market in the tea category at the time, taking his influences from other categories and applying them to Tazo. One of Sandstrom’s talents is his use of restraint—limiting color and graphics in a very noisy, crowded tea category made Tazo stand out.”

Image Credits

(page 48) Tazo Ceremonial Tea Set with bamboo box
Creative Director & Lead Designer: Steve Sandstrom
Writer: Palmer Pettersen
Support & Production Designer: Kristen Andersen
Project Manager: Kristen Cassidy
Photo by Polara Studio

(pages 49, 54) Tazo truck
Creative Director & Lead Designer: Steve Sandstrom
Writer: Palmer Pettersen
Support & Production Designer: Kristen Andersen
Project Manager: Kristen Cassidy
Photo by Todd Eckelman

(page 51):Tazo Stone Coasters
Creative Director: Steve Sandstrom/ Steve Sandoz
Lead Designer: Steve Sandstrom
Writer: Steve Sandoz
Support & Production Designer: Andrew Randall
Project Manager: Carol Johnson
Photography: Mark Hooper
Client: Tazo, Steve Smith

(page 52): Tazo Full Leaf Food Service Tins
Creative Director & Lead Designer: Steve Sandstrom
Writer: Palmer Pettersen
Support & Production Designer: Kristen Anderson
Project Manager: Kirsten Cassidy
Photography: Mark Hooper
Client: Tazo, Steve Smith

(page 53): Tazo.com website
Web Design & Development Firm: Zaaz
Creative Directors: Steve Sandstrom (Sandstrom Design) & John McVey (Zaaz)
Art Directors: Steve Sandstrom & Tom Klauda (Zaaz)
Writer: Palmer Pettersen
Developers: Jud Holiday, Cole Peterson, J.C. Vieth
Information Architect: Susan Campbell
Project Managers: Jill Raleigh (Sandstrom Design) & Whitney Zaring (Zaaz)

(page 55 top):Tazo Tea Tin
Creative Director: Steve Sandstrom/ Steve Smith
Art Designer: Steve Sandstrom
Writer: Palmer Pettersen
Project Manager: Kirsten Cassidy
Photography: Mark Hooper
Client: Tazo, Steve Smith

(page 55 bottom): Tazo Iced & Juiced Tea Bottles
Creative Director & Lead Designer: Steve Sandstrom
Writer: Palmer Pettersen
Support & Production Designers: Shanin Andrews
Project Manager: Kirsten Cassidy
Photography: Mark Hooper
Client: Tazo, Steve Smith

(page 56): Tazo Filterbags
Brand Design Firm: Sandstrom Design
Creative Director: Steve Sandstrom
Lead Designer: Steve Sandstrom
Writer: Palmer Pettersen
Support & Production Designer: Kristen Anderson
Project Manager: Kirsten Cassidy
Photography: Polara Studio
Client: Tazo, Steve Smith

(page 57): Tazo Mood Wheel
Brand Design Firm: Sandstrom Design
Creative Director: Steve Sandstrom
Lead Designer: Steve Sandstrom
Writer: Palmer Pettersen
Support & Production Designer: Kristen Anderson
Project Manager: Kirsten Cassidy
Photography: Mark Hooper
Client: Tazo, Steve Smith

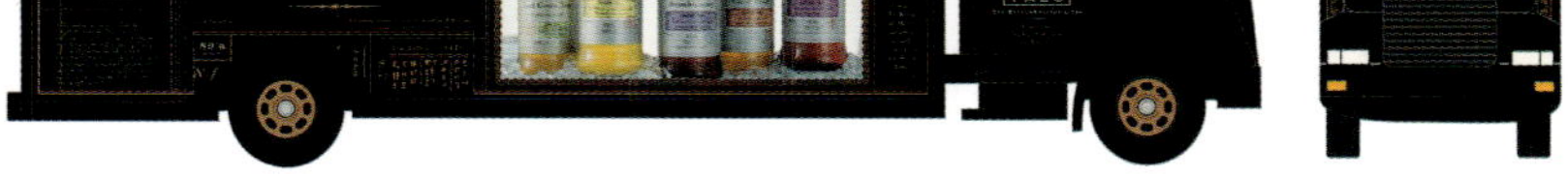

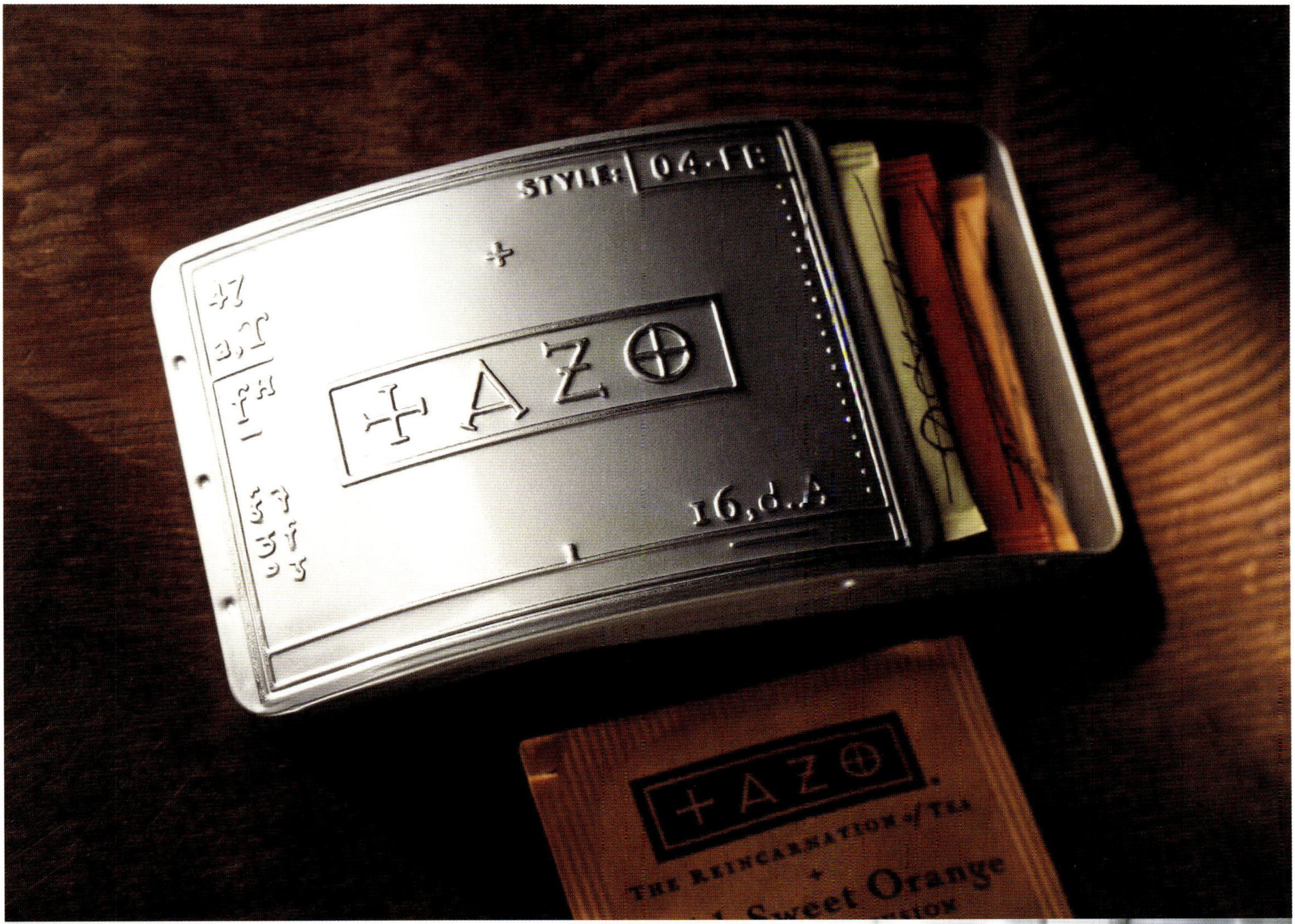
STYLE: 04·FE
TAZO
16,d.A
TAZO
THE REINCARNATION of TEA

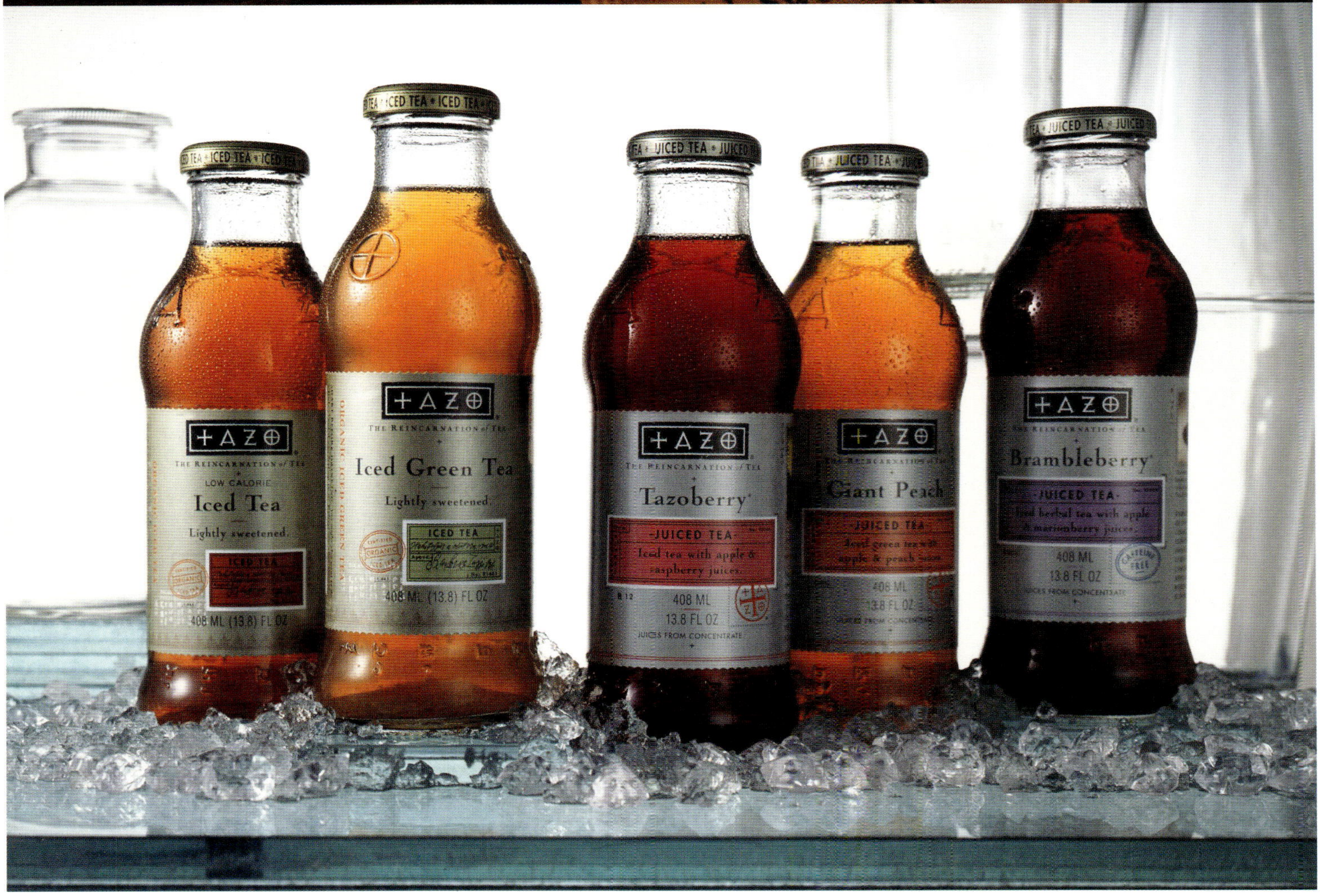
TAZO
THE REINCARNATION of TEA
LOW CALORIE
Iced Tea
Lightly sweetened.
408 ML (13.8) FL OZ
TAZO
THE REINCARNATION of TEA
Iced Green Tea
Lightly sweetened.
ICED TEA
408 ML (13.8) FL OZ
TAZO
THE REINCARNATION of TEA
Tazoberry
JUICED TEA
Iced tea with apple & raspberry juices.
408 ML
13.8 FL OZ
JUICES FROM CONCENTRATE
TAZO
Giant Peach
JUICED TEA
408 ML
13.8 FL OZ
TAZO
THE REINCARNATION of TEA
Brambleberry
JUICED TEA
408 ML
13.8 FL OZ
JUICES FROM CONCENTRATE

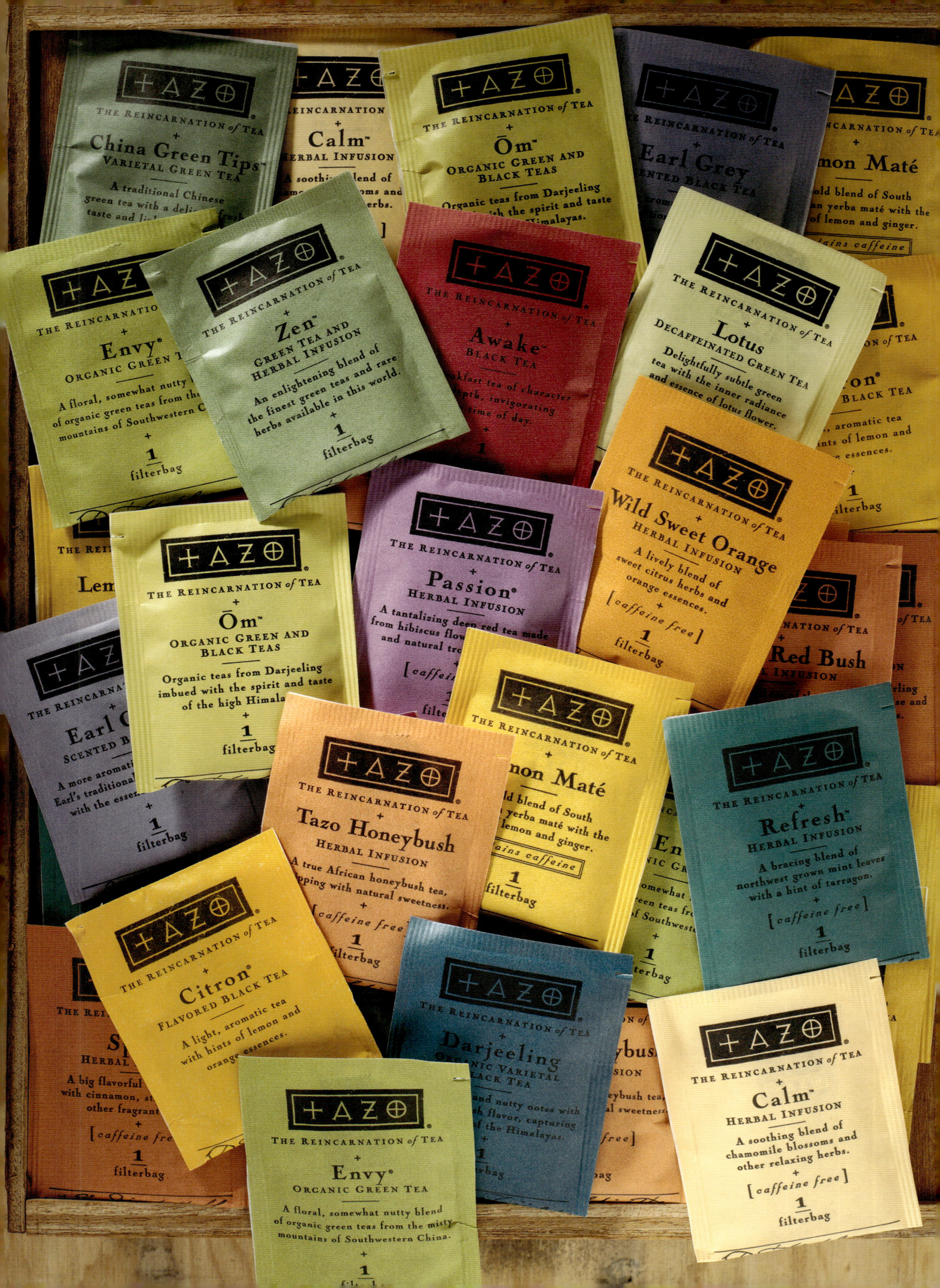
TAZO
THE REINCARNATION of TEA
China Green Tips
VARIETAL GREEN TEA
Calm
HERBAL INFUSION
Om
ORGANIC GREEN AND BLACK TEAS
Organic teas from Darjeeling imbued with the spirit and taste of the high Himalayas.
Earl Grey
Zen
GREEN TEA AND HERBAL INFUSION
An enlightening blend of the finest green teas and rare herbs available in this world.
1 filterbag
Envy
ORGANIC GREEN TEA
Awake
BLACK TEA
Lotus
DECAFFEINATED GREEN TEA
Delightfully subtle green tea with the inner radiance and essence of lotus flower.
Wild Sweet Orange
HERBAL INFUSION
A lively blend of sweet citrus herbs and orange essences.
[caffeine free]
Passion
HERBAL INFUSION
Red Bush
Lemon Maté
Tazo Honeybush
HERBAL INFUSION
Refresh
HERBAL INFUSION
A bracing blend of northwest grown mint leaves with a hint of tarragon.
Citron
FLAVORED BLACK TEA
A light, aromatic tea with hints of lemon and orange essences.
Darjeeling
Envy
ORGANIC GREEN TEA
A floral, somewhat nutty blend of organic green teas from the misty mountains of Southwestern China.
Calm
HERBAL INFUSION
A soothing blend of chamomile blossoms and other relaxing herbs.
[caffeine free]
1 filterbag

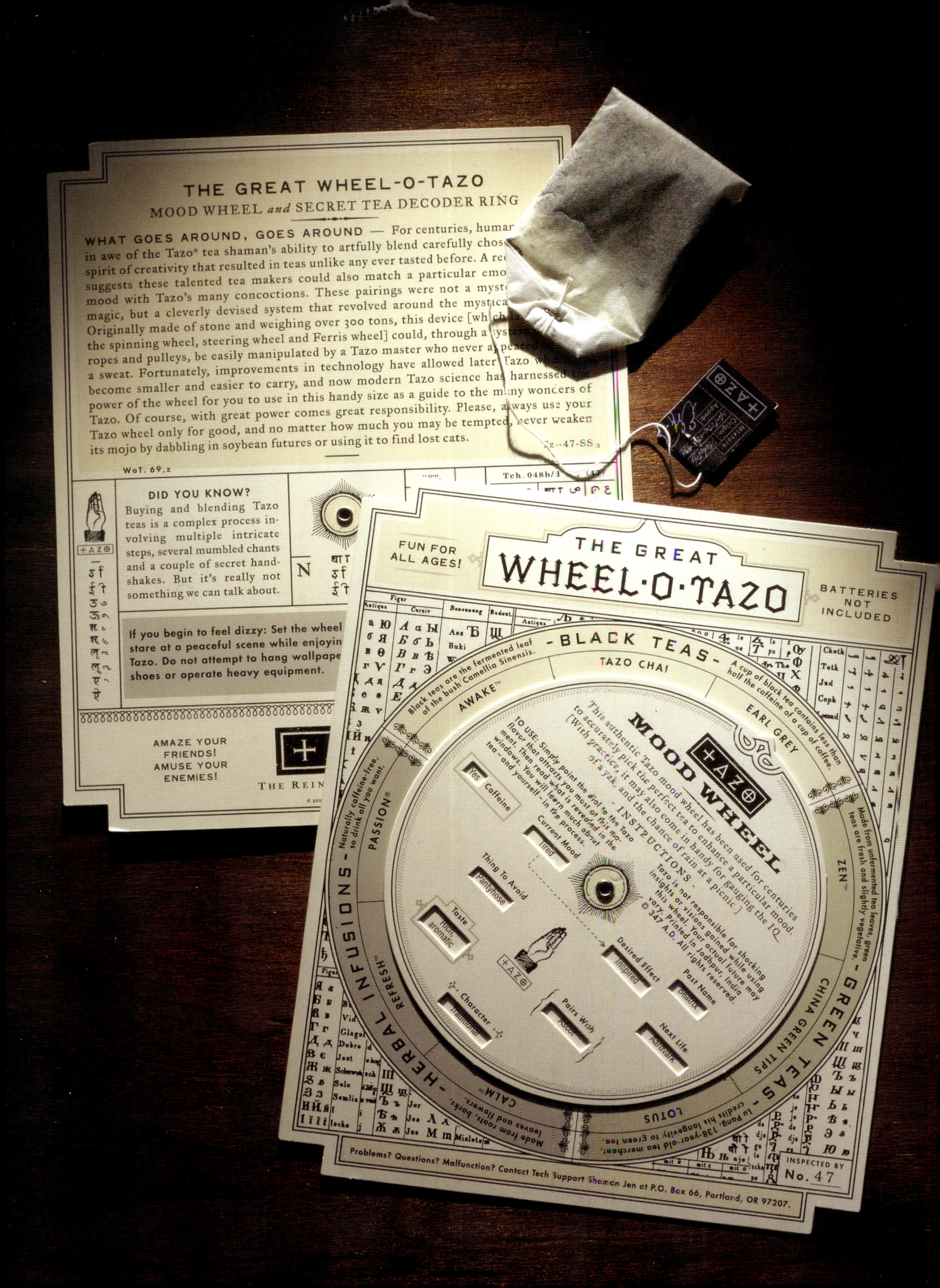
THE GREAT WHEEL-O-TAZO
MOOD WHEEL and SECRET TEA DECODER RING
WHAT GOES AROUND, GOES AROUND — For centuries, human
in awe of the Tazo® tea shaman's ability to artfully blend carefully chos
spirit of creativity that resulted in teas unlike any ever tasted before. A re
suggests these talented tea makers could also match a particular emo
mood with Tazo's many concoctions. These pairings were not a myst
magic, but a cleverly devised system that revolved around the mystica
Originally made of stone and weighing over 300 tons, this device [wh
the spinning wheel, steering wheel and Ferris wheel] could, through a syste
ropes and pulleys, be easily manipulated by a Tazo master who never a
a sweat. Fortunately, improvements in technology have allowed later Tazo wh
become smaller and easier to carry, and now modern Tazo science has harnessed
power of the wheel for you to use in this handy size as a guide to the many wonders of
Tazo. Of course, with great power comes great responsibility. Please, always use your
Tazo wheel only for good, and no matter how much you may be tempted, never weaken
its mojo by dabbling in soybean futures or using it to find lost cats.
WoT. 69,z
DID YOU KNOW?
Buying and blending Tazo teas is a complex process involving multiple intricate steps, several mumbled chants and a couple of secret handshakes. But it's really not something we can talk about.
If you begin to feel dizzy: Set the wheel
stare at a peaceful scene while enjoyin
Tazo. Do not attempt to hang wallpape
shoes or operate heavy equipment.
AMAZE YOUR FRIENDS! AMUSE YOUR ENEMIES!
FUN FOR ALL AGES!
THE GREAT WHEEL·O·TAZO
BATTERIES NOT INCLUDED
- BLACK TEAS -
Black teas are the fermented leaf of the bush Camellia Sinensis.
AWAKE™
TAZO CHAI
EARL GREY
A cup of black tea contains less than half the caffeine of a cup of coffee.
MOOD WHEEL
This authentic Tazo mood wheel has been used for centuries to accurately pick the perfect tea to enhance a particular mood. [With practice, it may also come in handy for gauging the IQ of a yak, and the chance of rain at a picnic.]
TO USE: Simply point the dial to the flavor that attracts you most of this moment. Then read what is revealed in the windows. You will learn much about tea – and yourself – in the process.
Tazo is not responsible for shocking insights or visions gained while using this wheel. Your actual future may vary. Printed in Jodhpur, India © 347 A.D. All rights reserved.
Caffeine
Yes
Current Mood
Tired
Thing To Avoid
Pantyhose
Taste
Rich, aromatic
Desired Effect
Inspired
Past Name
Character
Traditional
Pairs With
Ascot
Next Life
Aardvark
Made from unfermented tea leaves, green teas are fresh and slightly vegetative.
ZEN™
CHINA GREEN TIPS
- GREEN TEAS -
LOTUS
CALM™
Made from roots, barks, leaves and flowers.
- HERBAL INFUSIONS -
REFRESH™
PASSION®
Naturally caffeine-free, so drink all you want.
Problems? Questions? Malfunction? Contact Tech Support Shaman Jen at P.O. Box 66, Portland, OR 97207.
INSPECTED BY No. 47

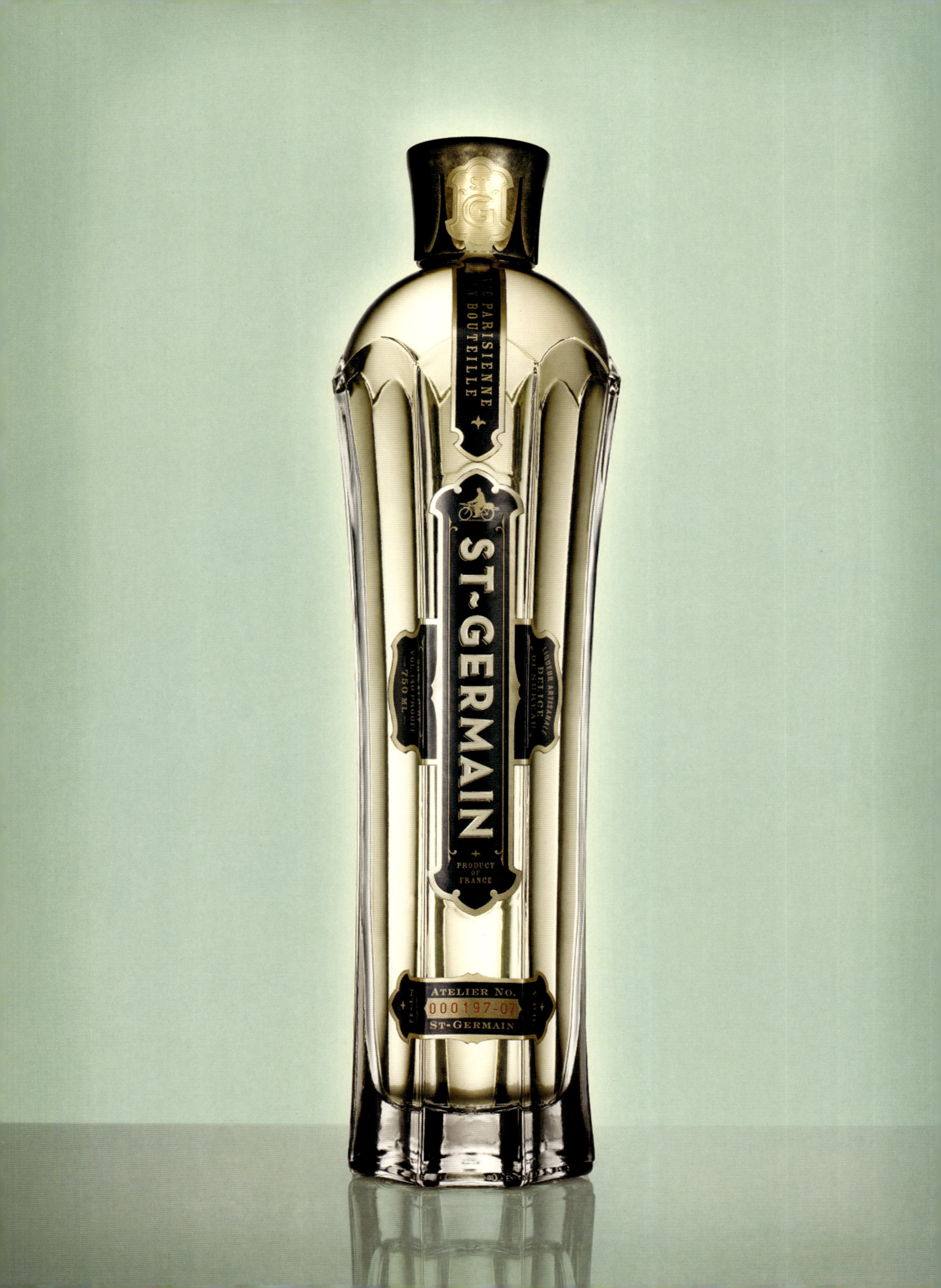
ST-GERMAIN
PRODUCT OF FRANCE
ATELIER No.
000197-07
ST-GERMAIN

In 2004, Sandstrom Partners was given the opportunity to develop branding for St-Germain, a one-of-a-kind French liqueur by Robert Cooper. Inspired by vintage postcards and art-deco, Sandstrom's work for the company has garnered accolades from London's FAB Awards and won first place in Dynamic's Advertising and Promotion Awards. The combination of a quality product and exceptional branding has also been good for the client, with St-Germain reporting a 50% growth each year. Steve Sandstrom, the Creative Director and Founder of Sandstrom Partners, offered us his insights on the project.

Steve Sandstrom & St-Germain

What was the problem?

Four years ago in London, our client, Rob Cooper, experienced a remarkable tasting cocktail and inquired about the ingredients. Elderflower syrup, he learned, was responsible for the mélange of flavors with notes of grapefruit, pear and passionfruit. The syrup was one of several available in Europe, but all were cloying and inconsistent, creating frustration for the best bartenders.

Rob grew up in the spirits business, and had spent some time marketing Chambord, a fine French liqueur his father created. He was excited by the opportunity to create a brand of his own, and spent the next few years diligently developing a truly artisan liqueur made in France from only fresh, wild elderflower blossoms. The process was complicated and required ingenuity and sweat. Also, while elderflowers grow abundantly in the foothills of the Alps, they bloom for only a couple of weeks each spring. Collecting the blossoms required getting to know the relatively small band of farmers and 'bohemians' who pluck them by hand and ride them to market on makeshift bicycles. It took a couple seasons to figure out the logistics of collecting the blossoms and getting them to the distillery a few hours away. Only fresh elderflowers would be used.

The result is a liqueur that has the consistency and integrity of the finest spirits and serves as a bartender's dream ingredient for creating interesting and new cocktails. It is the first and only one of its kind.

Rob secured the name St-Germain and asked us to help him create the identity and packaging. He had already experimented with art deco bottle shapes and brought us a Lucite model of a bottle with elaborate facets and a domed top that he felt captured the authentic French style he wanted to project.

The bottle was beautiful and complex in its design—almost like cut crystal instead of a spirits bottle. The sharp facets and multi-directional curves made labeling a challenge beyond what one could have imagined.

What was your solution?

The label design utilizes the bottle's best features while having unique, consistent elements that are drawn upon as consistent details used in display and various marketing materials. I did learn early on that the adhesive side of the labels needed to be printed because they reflect on every panel of the vessel. Since the bottle had a period feel, it was necessary to take a non-contemporary approach. It couldn't look like it was designed with the sensibilities of someone working in 2007. The labels have a mix of art deco, Gothic and classical touches that represent the interesting mixture of influences and styles in Paris. And since the quantities have a limit, we number every bottle.

Our client wanted the brand to have the elements of famous French luxury brands like Hermès and Louis Vuitton. We agreed on a color palette consisting of navy, deco green and gold. We created art deco–influenced typography for the St-Germain wordmark, and we illustrated one of the 'bohemians' on a bicycle taking a stash of flowers to market as the brand's icon. This is done as both silhouette and engraving. We designed an elderflower pattern that can be reproduced in a variety of color options using our palette. A circular seal was designed as a formal mark that became the top of the bottle cap. And we designed additional bistro-style typography to add to the brand's visual toolbox. We developed everything from our experiences of Paris, our love for French style, and the detailed world of spirits branding.

Describe your personal experience on this campaign.

About four months prior to my initial meeting with Rob Cooper, my wife and I had spent a few days in and around Saint-Germain-des-Prés on a vacation to Paris. Saint-Germain (the 6th Arrondissement) is one of the most historically rich and interesting districts in Paris. It has been the gathering place of some of the greatest artists, writers, musicians and philosophers of the 20th century—a cultural blender of sorts. Working on the St-Germain liqueur brand has fostered a deeper appreciation of that cultural and historic significance. It's made my Parisian experiences even more meaningful.

It has been a difficult design assignment on many levels. And our client has struggled as well with actually producing the product. But perhaps those difficulties are part of what is driving the award-winning results in both product and brand design. I feel like the cocktail of artists and intellectuals that made St-Germain their hangout deserve something that at least attempts to represent their cultural contributions in some small way, even if it is only a liqueur.

What message were you trying to convey in your advertisements for St-Germain?

St-Germain is a start-up, and the advertising and promotions budget has its limits. If what you create is really good, you'll get more attention and more talk for your dollars. The product is exceptional and it deserves to be represented in interesting ways, and we always like to bring a sense of style and humor to the consumer. There isn't a big company behind this brand and we don't want it to appear so. Like the original intention with Tazo, we want some risk-taking to be visible to the audience. We want people to be curious about the product and the people behind it.

The goal was to make it seem well established, not trendy-new. Too many alcoholic beverages appear to be novelties, and their life expectancy is therefore low. This is a product and a brand being built for the long haul, and it deserves whatever respect and appreciation we can muster up.

How were you able to create such a rich looking brand on a start-up budget?

As with most alcohol, the packaging is key to the brand experience, so every detail must be figured out. Rob Cooper had a collection of thoughts around the brand he wanted to have developed. He's a student of the spirits category and of French luxury brands, so developing the list of parts was an ongoing objective when he began thinking about creating the brand and what he hoped to achieve through packaging. He would probably say that he's spent a lot, and we would certainly say that he got a deal! And if you look at our timesheets, we'd be unquestionably right.

St-Germain's identity is very detailed in scope. Is that what you were aiming for?

Because St-Germain is a liqueur, its primary use is as an ingredient in a cocktail. And since it is a new type of liqueur, a variety of cocktail recipes are needed to illustrate how to use it. A collection of recipes along with the story of gathering blossoms and the process of creating the liqueur was developed into a 28-page hangtag. It might be the most pages ever created for a hangtag, spirits or otherwise. There is an elaborately produced brochure and set of sales materials to present the brand to the trade and bar owners. Even cocktail coasters were die-cut into the shape of the bottom of the bottle with a series of recipes printed on the backs. The website (*www.stgermain.fr*) also contains a collection of recipes and a little more in-depth account of the process. Its features include tips on making cocktails.

There is also a vintage Citroën delivery truck custom painted in London, which St-Germain uses for trade and promotional events.

Among the hundreds of pieces of inspiration Rob Cooper had collected over the years, an old postcard of a French prostitute sitting on a bar stool and exposing her breast made us laugh and gave us the idea behind an advertising direction for St-Germain. It's like soft pornography from way out of time. However naughty it was then, it is somewhat comical now. Our client appreciates the fact that the postcard is authentic. And that a postcard is a nice way to physically insert the brand into a magazine is also an interesting concept. It solved the problem of figuring out how to include a recipe in an ad without looking like Betty Crocker. We include a recipe as the note on the mailing side of the card. We also buy the adjacent page in the publication and cover it with our elderflower pattern to create a branded background for the postcard. It's a stylish way to deliver an ad that doesn't look like an ad.

The postcard image and flower pattern have been enlarged to poster size and used as wild postings around New York.

I flew to Paris with Rob Cooper last winter to rummage the flea markets for additional postcards. We are creating the next round of ads and wild postings from these, and the first round of these has been posted in New York. Because there are other brands using the same media—and even using very similar approaches—our visuals are getting more involved and the details more elaborate to keep some creative distance.

Rob Cooper is a creative guy, and there have been a number of events and promotions that he and his marketing team have conducted very well.

What sort of financial and overall impact has your branding made?

A recent article featuring St-Germain in *Brandweek* reported that first year sales were triple what our client had anticipated, and growth was at 50 pecent per year for the first three years. *Imbibe* magazine noted St-Germain as a rock-star brand among bartenders. It has been featured in *The New York Times*, *O, The Oprah Magazine*, and several other publications. All have either featured the packaging or mentioned its appeal.

To learn more about St-Germain, check out www.stgermain.fr.

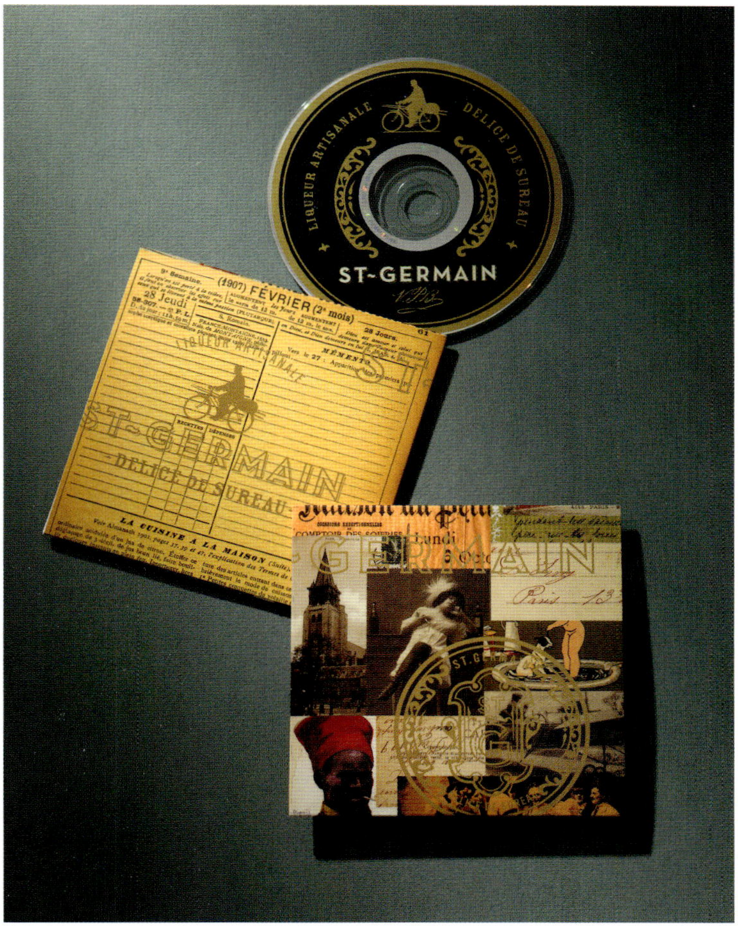

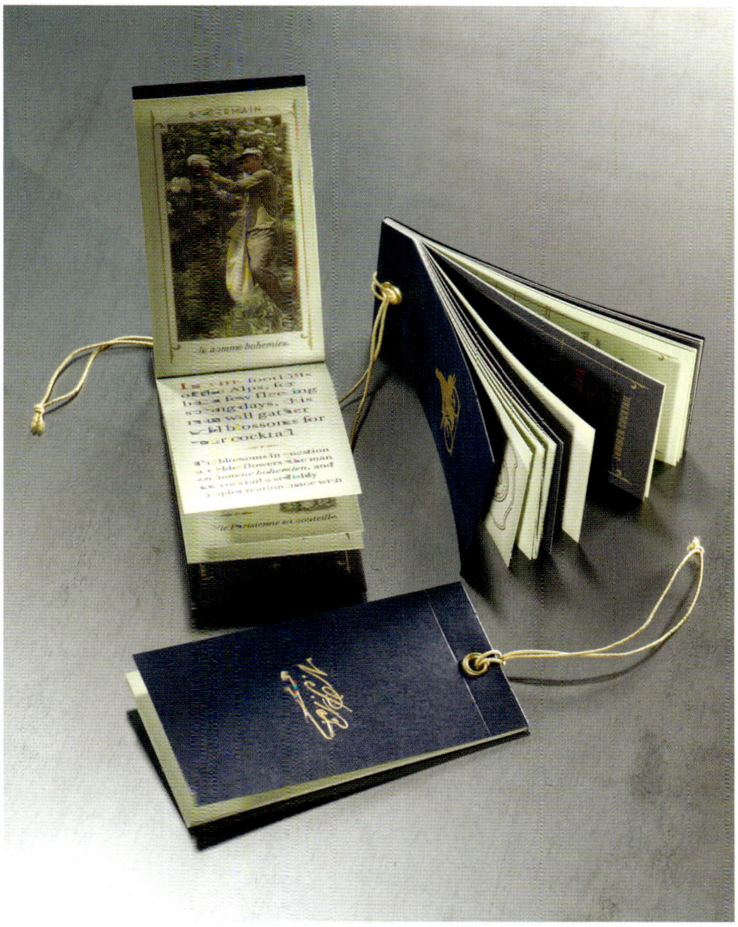

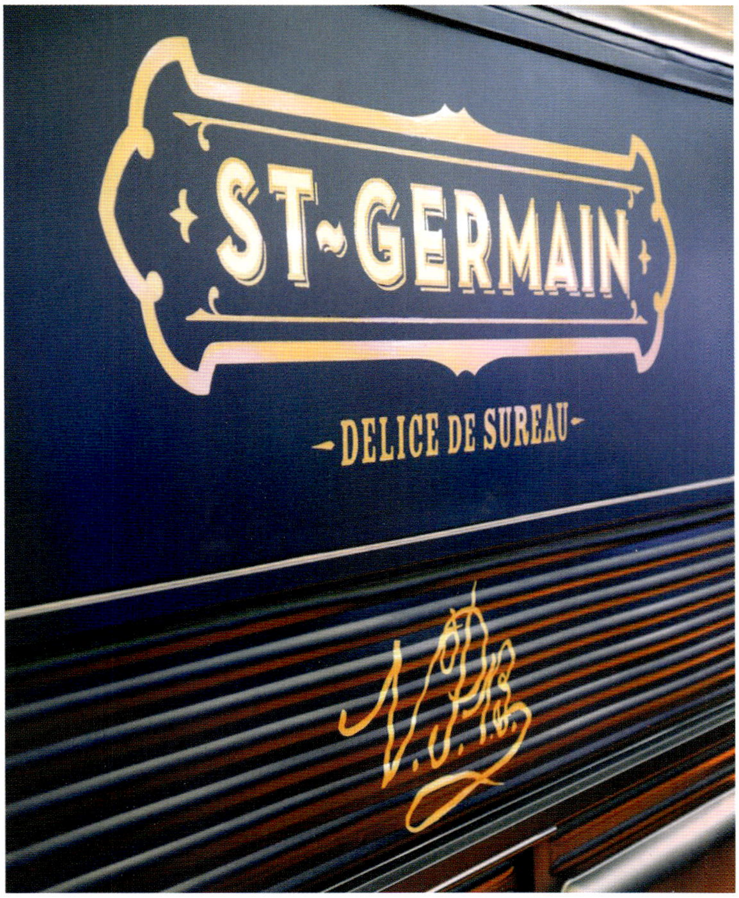

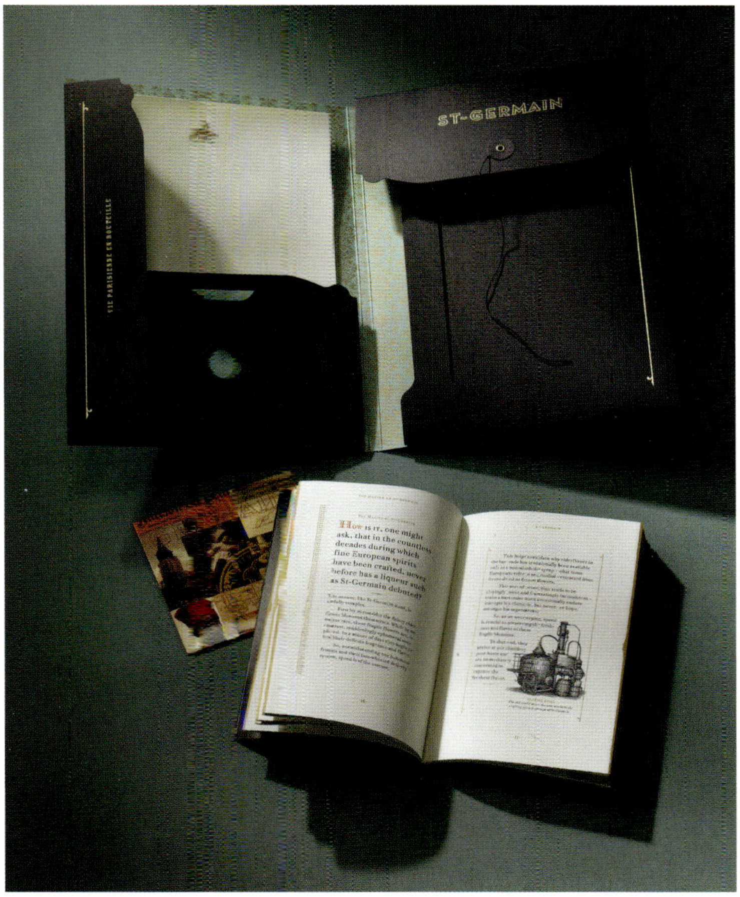

"We developed everything from our experiences in Paris, our love of French style, and the detailed world of spirits branding."

Steve Sandstrom, *Creative Director & Partner, Sandstrom Partners*

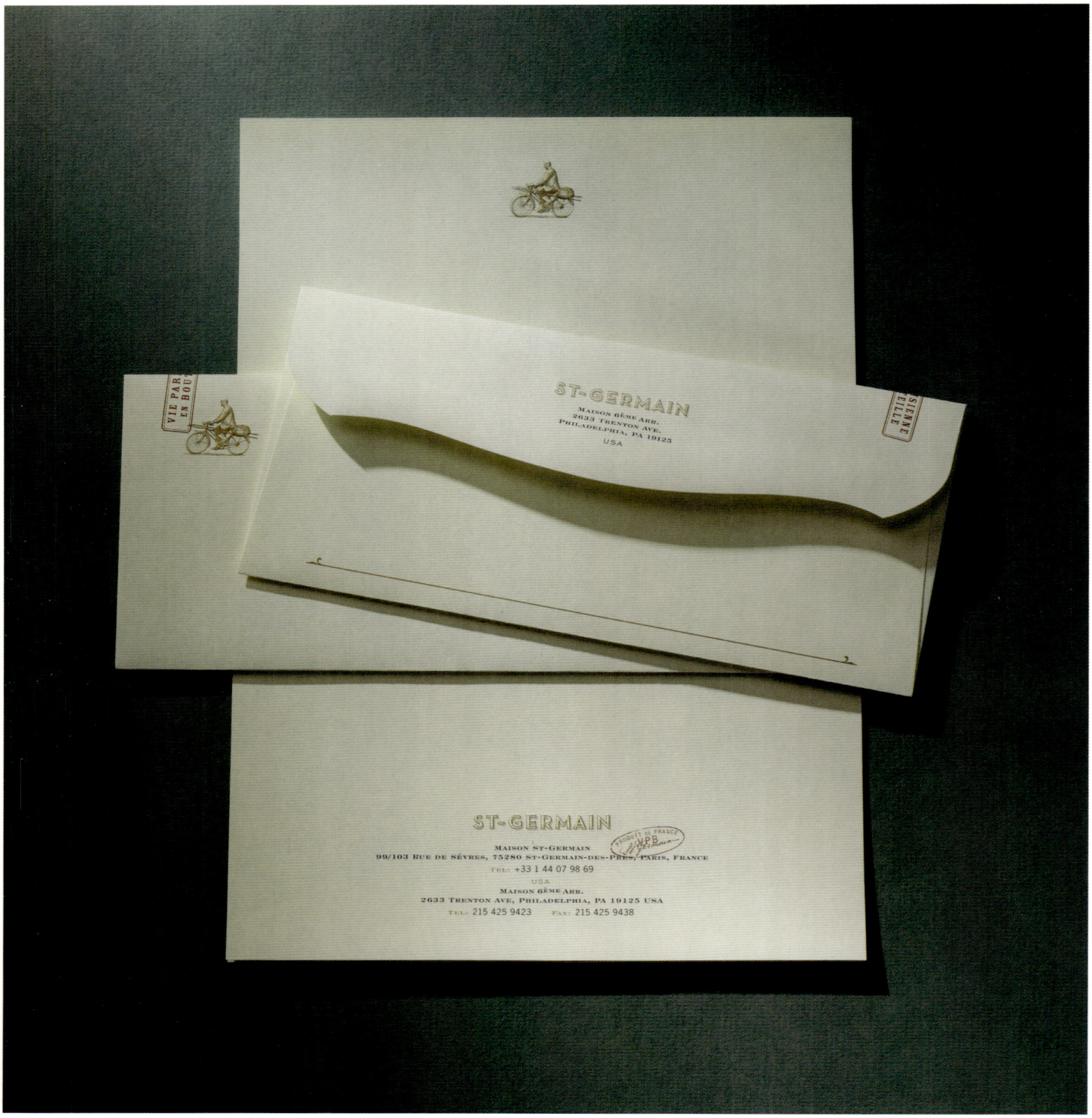
ST-GERMAIN
Maison 6ème Arr.
2633 Trenton Ave.
Philadelphia, PA 19125
USA
ST-GERMAIN
Maison St-Germain
99/103 Rue de Sèvres, 75280 St-Germain-des-Prés, Paris, France
Tel: +33 1 44 07 98 69
USA
Maison 6ème Arr.
2633 Trenton Ave, Philadelphia, PA 19125 USA
Tel: 215 425 9423 Fax: 215 425 9438

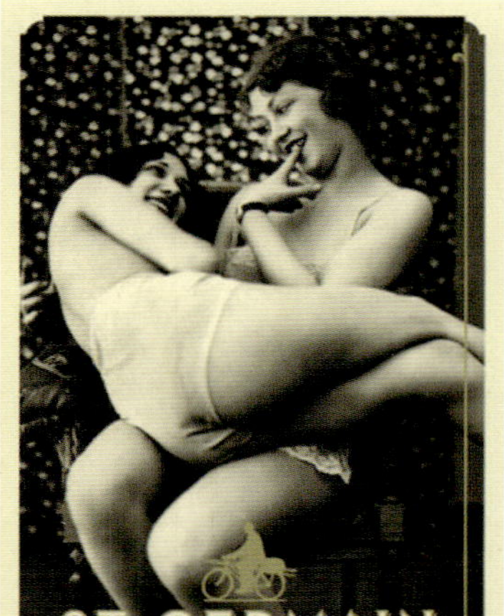
ST-GERMAIN

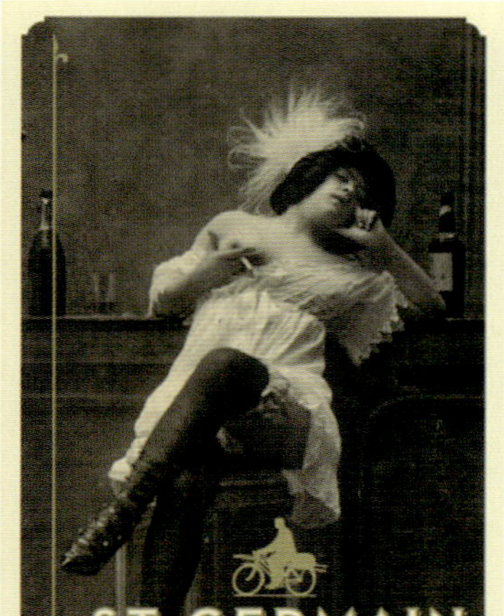
ST-GERMAIN
DELICE DE SUREAU

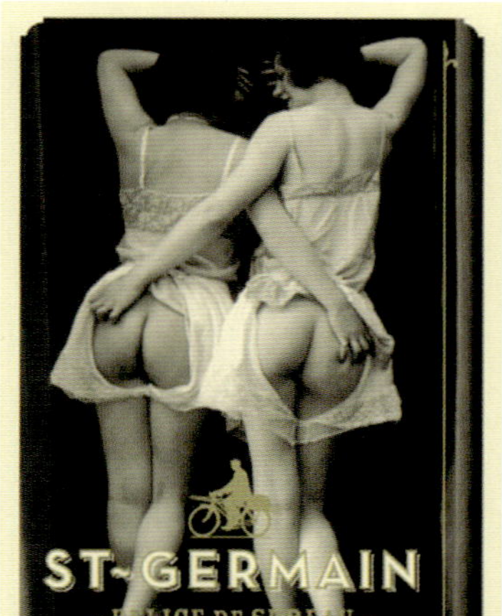
ST-GERMAIN

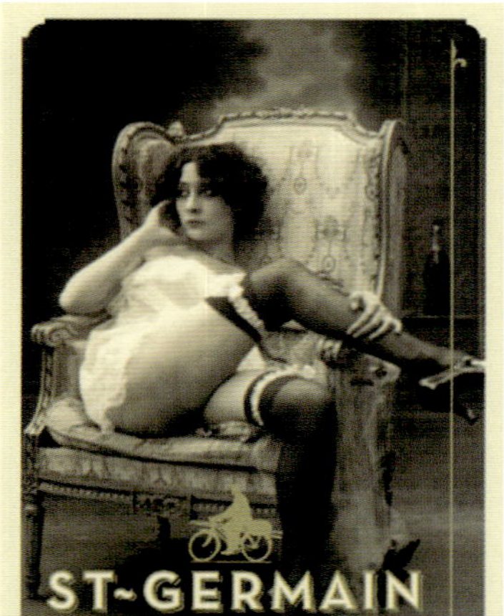
ST-GERMAIN
DELICE DE SUREAU

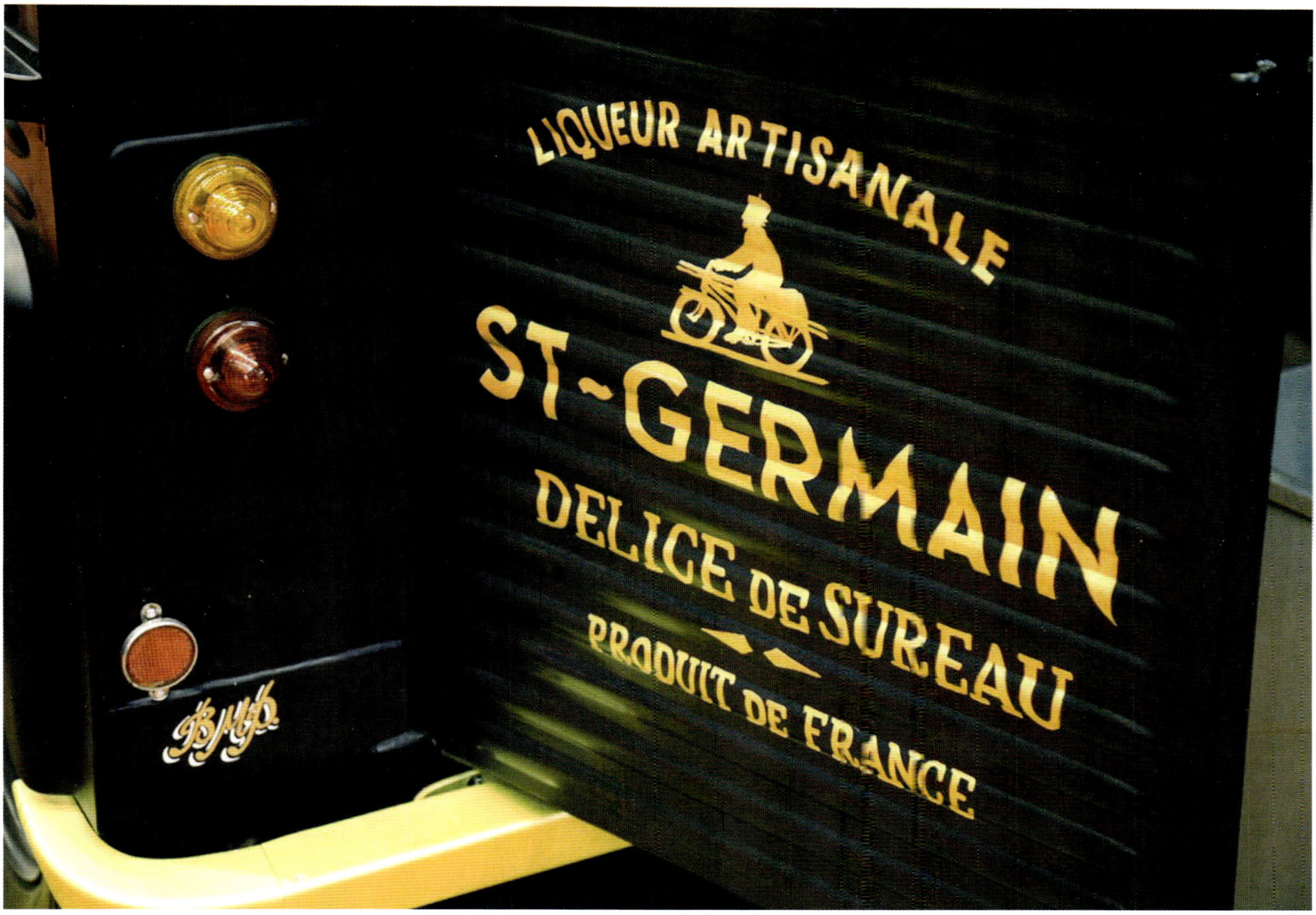
LIQUEUR ARTISANALE
ST-GERMAIN
DELICE DE SUREAU
PRODUIT DE FRANCE

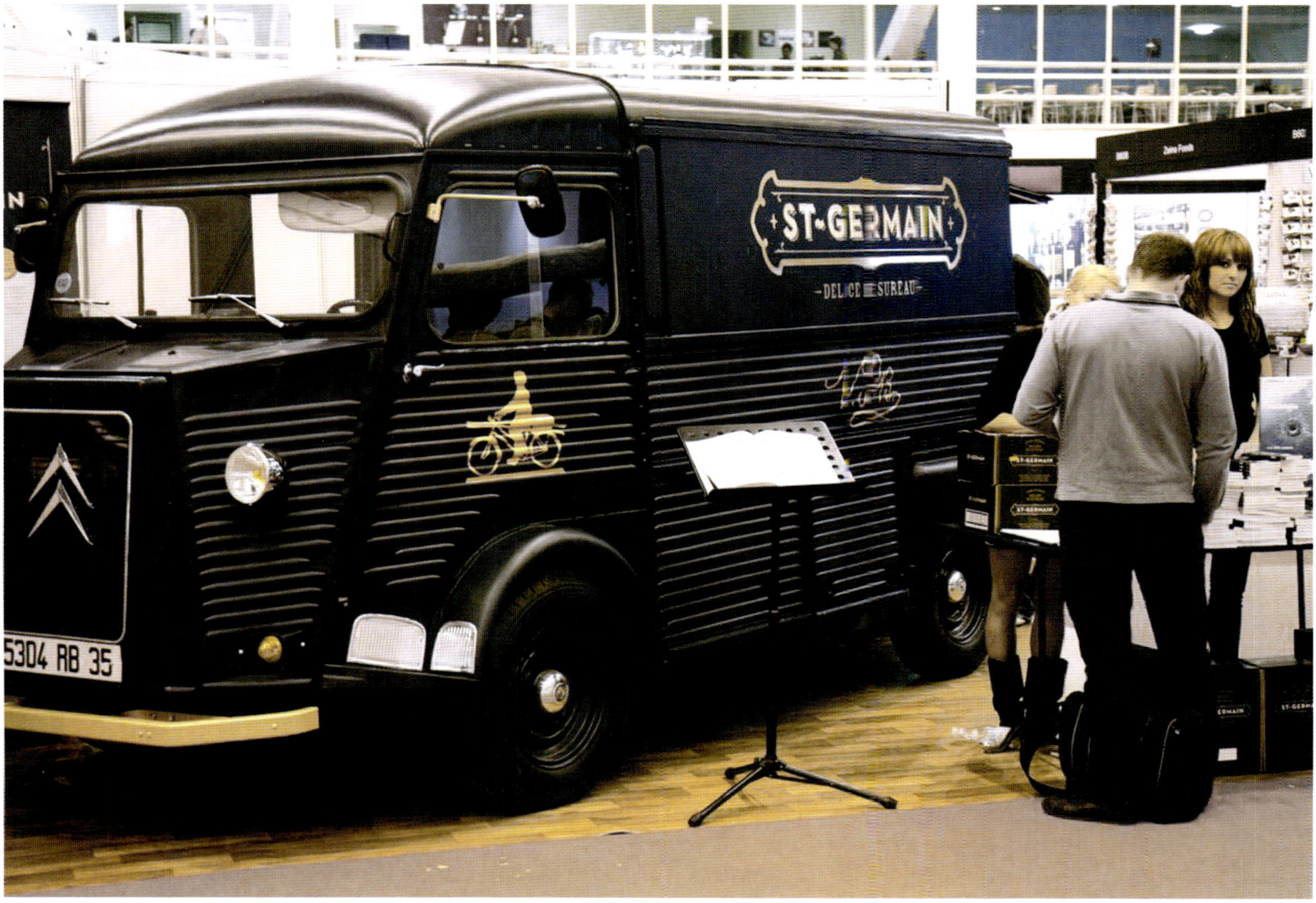
ST-GERMAIN
DELICE SUREAU
5304 RB 35

"A recent article featuring St-Germain in *Brandweek* reported that first year sales were triple what our client had anticipated; growth continued at 50% a year for 3 years."

Steve Sandstrom, *Creative Director & Partner, Sandstrom Partners*

The Client's Perspective

Robert Cooper, President of Cooper Spirits International, Shares His Thoughts on Sandstrom Partners

What was it like working with Sandstrom?

Great design results from a designer and a client joining together with genuinely open minds and collaborating. Without this willingness to work together, an inordinate amount of friction ensues and the design process gives way to ego. If the ultimate objective is to create great design that leads to a successful brand, then pride of authorship becomes secondary. I am most proud of the truly positive collaborative relationship I have with Steve, and this has allowed some amazing design work to rise to the surface.

Steve is a unique individual, in that he has remarkable, world-class talent, experience, and a strong opinion, but these traits are distinctly overlaid with a sense of humility, and an open-minded approach. He does not have the 'my idea or nothing' attitude that many designers have. I never could have asked for a better design partner, and I view Steve as much as a friend as a business associate.

How did Sandstrom Partners impact your brand?

Steve and his team (Prue Ruby is a vital player, as is Trevor, Jack, Mark Waggonner, and the rest of the Sandstrom crew) have made an impact on the brand in two important ways: 1. They are as particular about the design as I am about the liqueur itself—and not just the package, but every little piece of collateral. Perfection is not good enough, and this is what we always strive for, whether it's a brand book, an ad creative, or a little menu card—it all is done with the same degree of dedication and passion. 2. Sandstrom is deeply committed to the brand and therefore produces a large body of work for me. Without the Sandstrom design machine, St-Germain would not be where it is today. We are clearly the underdog in the industry, but we are winning the battle through the breakthrough, 'attention getting' design we churn out constantly.

Sandstrom Partners

Sandstrom Partners maintains a curious culture. We want to know everything about a company and their category. We subscribe to the notion that, "To every answer there is at least one question, usually more than one." We like questions, because they lead to strategies, and strategies lead to clarity, and clarity leads to innovation.

We think. Ponder. Wonder. Explore. We make unexpected connections. We think about what came before and what has never been, and while we invariably come to a conclusion, we know we can never stop thinking. The culmination of all this is what you see in the work, but it's based on a much deeper core. Message, voice, form—everything is considered. Every touch point is critical. We know that for a brand to come to life, it has to be believable and holistic. All points communicate, and all messages are important. And while our success ratio is extraordinary, we learn from every stumble. The more we absorb, the more we can add to the equation. So we keep looking for adventure and the unknown. It's where the great new ideas can be found.

808 SW 3rd Avenue, Suite 610, Portland, Oregon 97204
503.248.9466 / www.sandstrompartners.com

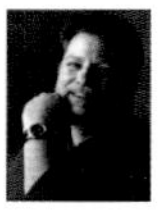

Steve Sandstrom: Steve Sandstrom is Creative Director and Partner of Sandstrom Partners in Portland, Oregon. Clients have included Tazo, Levi's, Converse, ESPN, Miller Brewing, Nike, Seagram's, Steppenwolf Theatre, adidas, Nissan, Coca-Cola, Virgin, Full Sail Brewing, Microsoft, Brown-Forman, St-Germain, Bossa Nova, Kettle Chips and G-Diapers. Advertising agency relationships have included Wieden+Kennedy, TBWA/ChiatDay, Ogilvy & Mather, JWT, Young & Rubicam and Butler Shine & Stern. The firm has been featured in several publications, including *Graphis*, *Adweek*, *Novum* (Germany), *Critique*, *How*, *ID*, *The New York Times Magazine*, *Metropolis*, *Creativity*, *@Issue* and numerous books about design, packaging, posters and corporate identity. Prior to founding Sandstrom Design (now Sandstrom Partners) in November 1988, Steve was a Senior Art Director at Nike, primarily responsible for brand image and collateral materials for the apparel division. He has won numerous design and advertising awards, The Graphis Top Ten in Design, D&AD (London), CA, The One Show, ID, Clio's, Andy's, Kelly's, Belding's, Type Director's, New York Art Director's, FAB (London), London International Advertising and American Advertising Federation Competitions.

In 1994, he was honored as Advertising Professional of the Year by the Portland Advertising Federation, and he received a lifetime achievement award from the organization in 2007. He also won a Blue Ribbon at the 1961 Oregon State Fair for a crayon drawing of a cow.

Steve is one of the first two designers elected to the Board of Directors of The One Club, the nation's most prestigious organization supporting creative advertising. He is also on the Board of Visitors for the University of Oregon School of Architecture and Allied Arts, and is past President of the Portland Advertising Federation, the first and only designer elected to that position in its 102-year history.

Image Credits
(page 58) St-Germain 750 ml bottle Designer: Steve Sandstrom Project Manager: Prue Ruby Photo by Mark Hopper. (page 61 top left) St-Germain presentation CD sleeve Creative Director & Designer: Steve Sandstrom Production Designer: Sarah Hollowood Project Manager: Prue Ruby Illustration: Antar Dayal. Photograph by Polara Studio (page 61 top right): St-Germain 750 ml hang tag Creative Director & Designer: Steve Sandstrom Writer: Mark Waggoner Production Designer: Sarah Hollowood Project Manager: Prue Ruby Illustration Antar Dayal Photograph by Polara Studio (page 61 bottom left) St-Germain Vintage Citroen Delivery Truck Creative Director & Designer: Steve Sandstrom Project Manager: Prue Ruby Photograph supplied by Cooper Spirits International. (page 61 bottom right) St-Germain sales and media kit Creative Director & Designer: Steve Sandstrom Writer: Mike Waggoner Production Designer: Sarah Hollowood & Trevor Thrap Project Manager: Prue Ruby Photograph by Polara Studio. (page 62 top) St-Germain letterhead. Creative Director & Designer: Steve Sandstrom Production Designer: Sarah Hollowood Project Manager: Prue Ruby Illustration: Antar Dayal Photograph by Polara Studio (page 62 bottom) St-Germain postcards. Creative Director & Designer: Steve Sandstrom Writer: Mark Waggoner Production Designer: Trevor Thrap Project Manager: Prue Ruby. Vintage stock photo. (page 63 top & bottom) St-Germain Vintage Citroen Delivery Truck Creative Director and Designer: Steve Sandstrom Project Manager: Prue Ruby Photograph supplied by Cooper Spirits International (page 64) Steve Sandstrom's headshot by Polara Studio. (page 65) St-Germain 50 ml bottle Creative Director & Designer: Steve Sandstrom Project Manager: Prue Ruby Photograph by Polara Studio All photos courtesy of Cooper Spirits International and Sandstrom Partners.

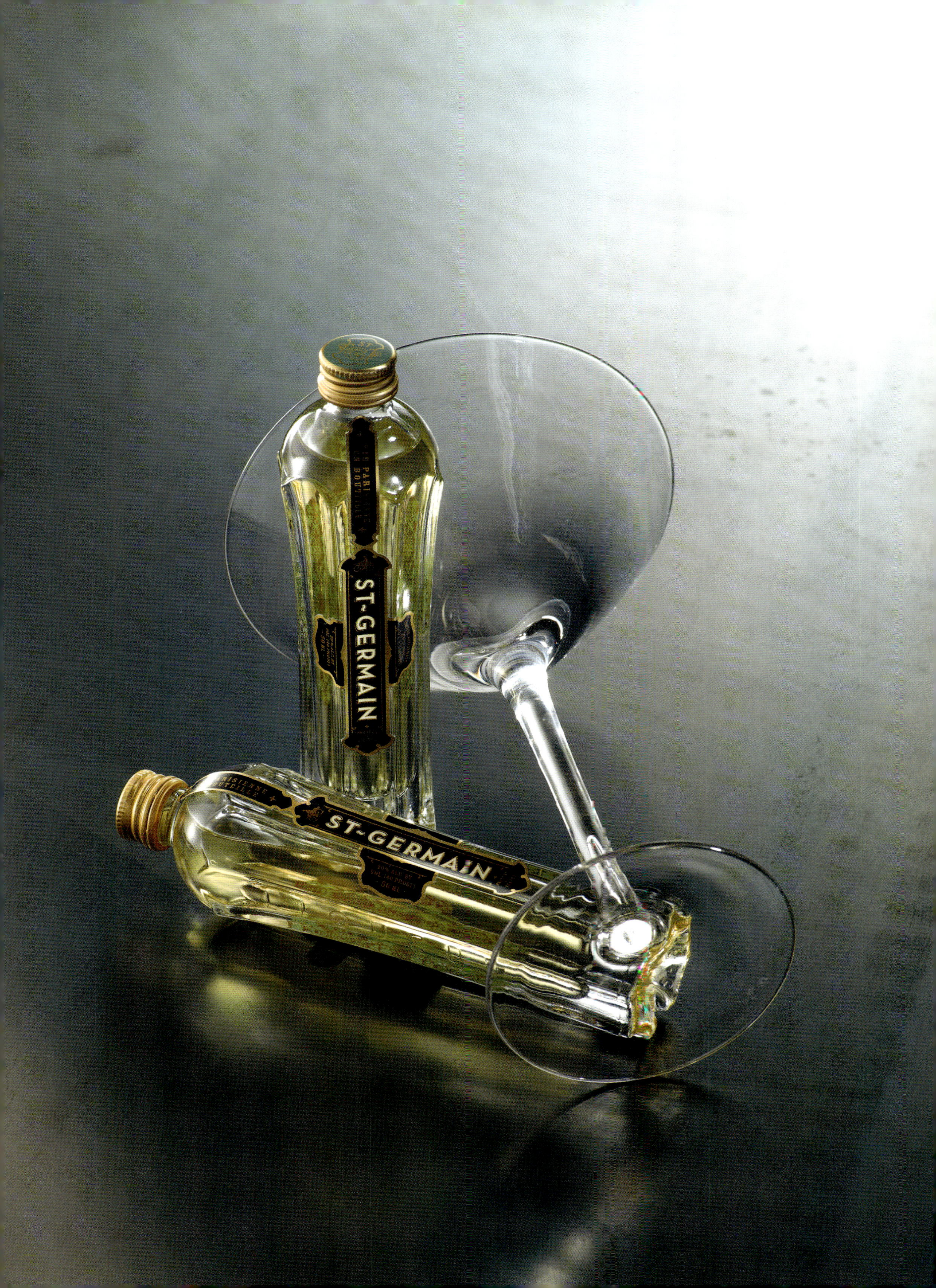
ST-GERMAIN
ST-GERMAIN

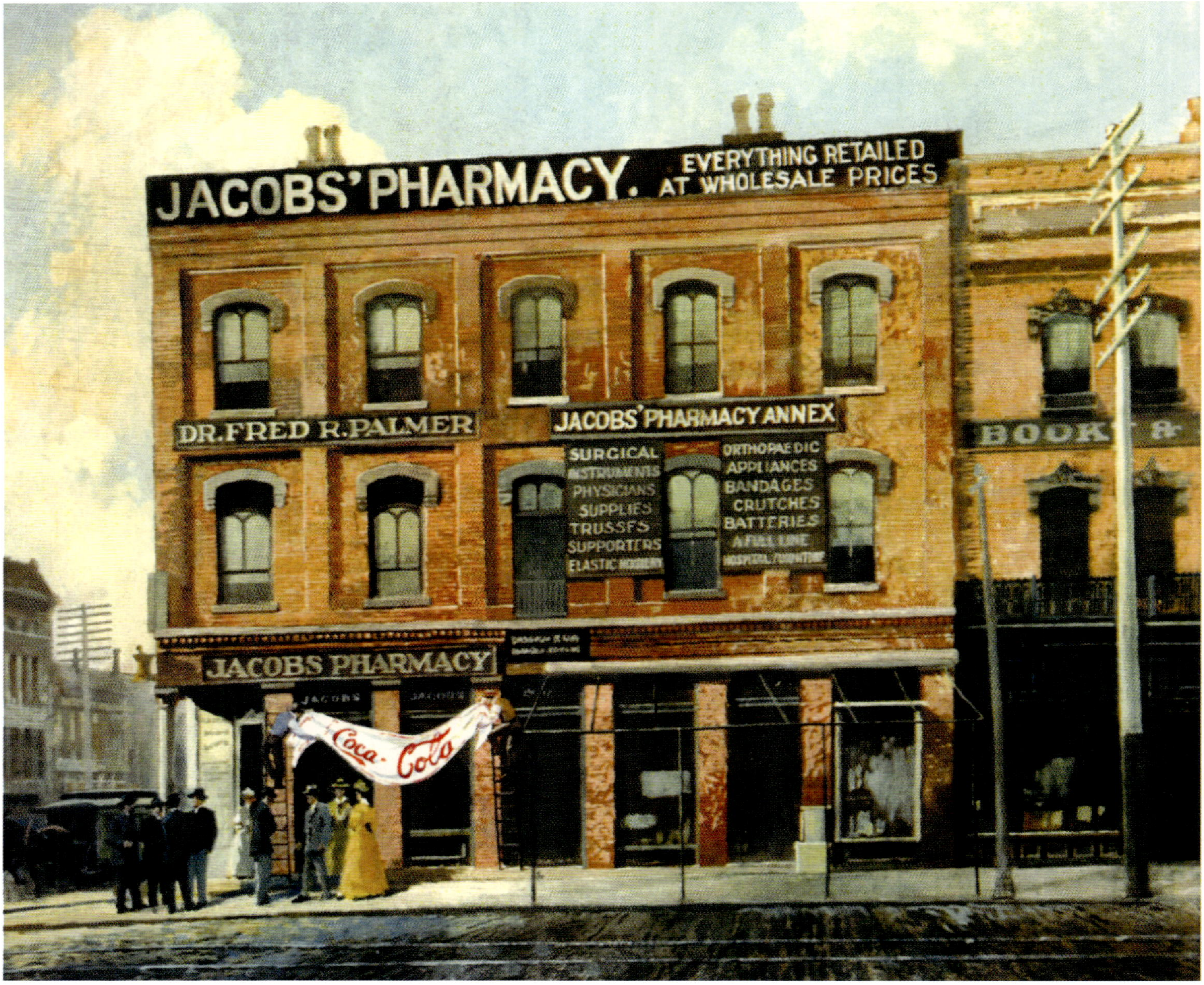
JACOBS' PHARMACY.
EVERYTHING RETAILED AT WHOLESALE PRICES
DR. FRED R. PALMER
JACOBS' PHARMACY ANNEX
SURGICAL INSTRUMENTS PHYSICIANS SUPPLIES TRUSSFS SUPPORTERS ELASTIC HOSIERY
ORTHOPAEDIC APPLIANCES BANDAGES CRUTCHES BATTERIES A FULL LINE HOSPITAL FURNITURE
BOOK &
JACOBS PHARMACY
Coca-Cola

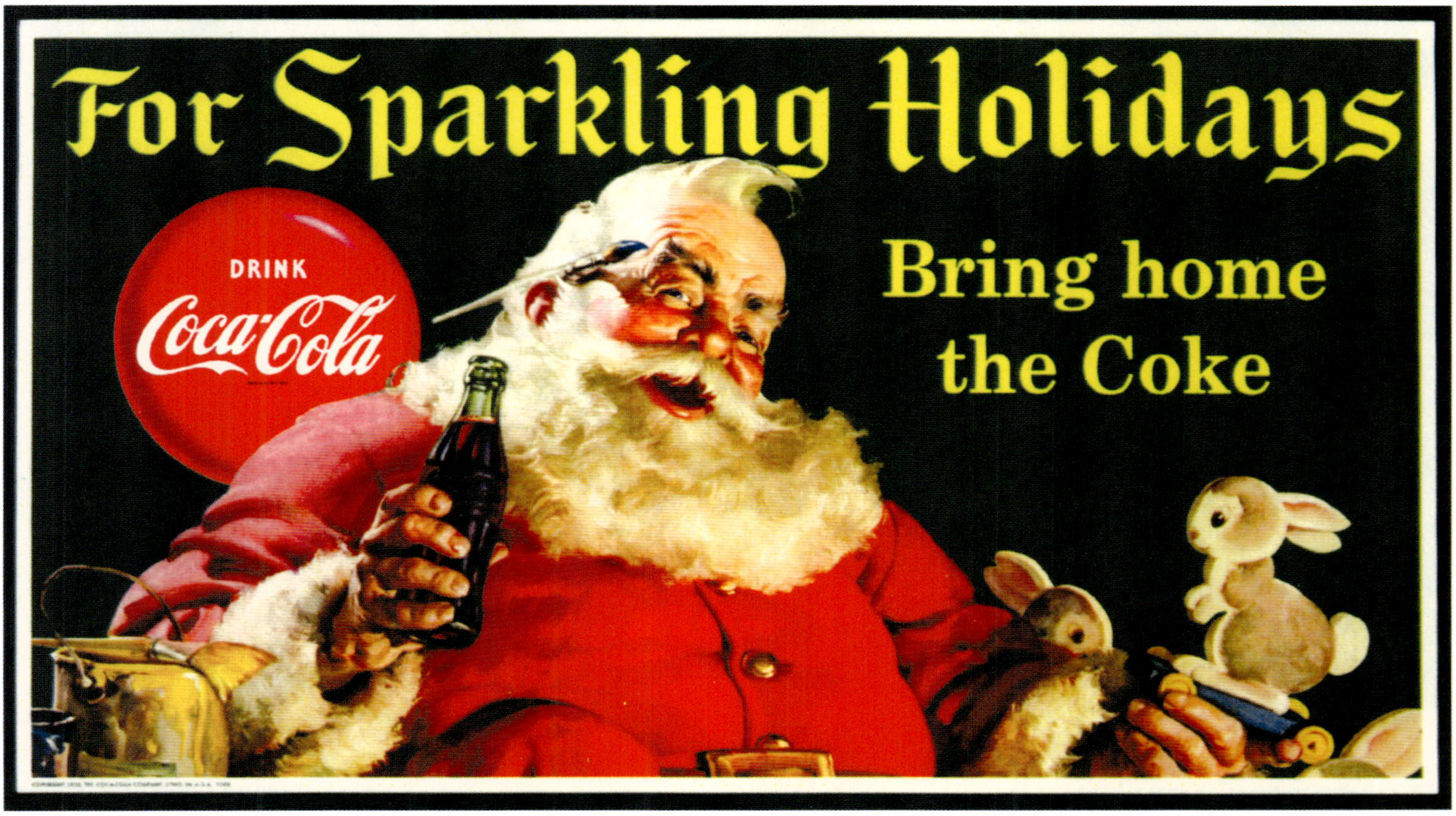
For Sparkling Holidays
DRINK
Coca-Cola
Bring home the Coke

The Coca-Cola Company: A Visual History

Graphis takes a look back at Coca-Cola's history and design evolution. Since its 1886 inception, this icon has seen its share of changes. Just consider the company's logo, bottles, advertisements, and even its recipes (the popular Cherry Coca-Cola, Diet Coke, and the ill-fated New Coke of the 1980s). Some things have been consistent throughout its first 120-plus years, though. As you'll see on the following pages, Coca-Cola began with a serious commitment to advertising and design, and that practice has rung true over the years, most recently evidenced by creative powerhouse Turner Duckworth's redesign work. Read on for Coke's story and the Turner Duckworth Q&A.

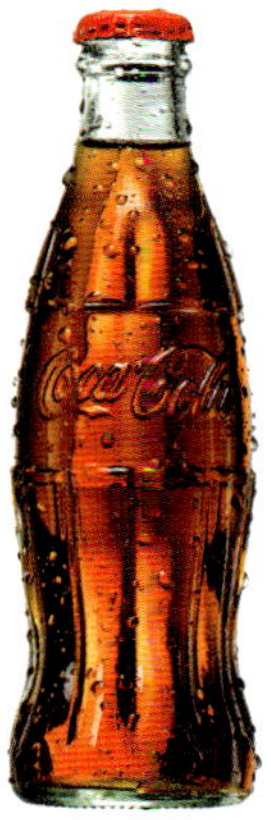

The Coca-Cola Story

Everyone has sampled the "Coke side of life." Its trademark scripted, bright red logo can be seen all over the world—from English pub umbrellas to football grounds, from Chinese shop signs to 20-feet-tall neon ads in Times Square, New York. It wouldn't be an exaggeration to say that The Coca-Cola Company is present in every country in the world, and arguably it was the world's first truly global brand. It has been declared both the world's most recognisable trademark and the world's most popular branded drink.

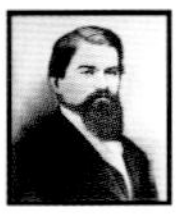
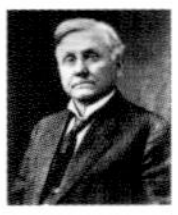
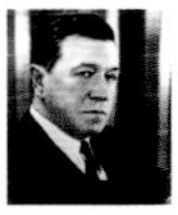
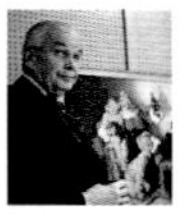

Medicine

Yet this amazing success story had very humble beginnings. A pharmacist named John Pemberton, who lived in Atlanta, Georgia, invented Coca-Cola. One afternoon in 1886, the year when workers were building the Statue of Liberty in New York harbour, he was experimenting with combinations of ingredients in a three-legged brass pot in his backyard to try to develop a new drink. He came up with a fragrant caramel-coloured liquid. Out of sheer curiosity, he took it to neighbouring Jacobs' Pharmacy, where he added carbonated water. After testing it on customers, who all thought this was something special, Jacobs' Pharmacy started selling it for five cents a glass.

In the first year, Pemberton sold just nine glasses of Coca-Cola a day, which made him around $50. It had cost Pemberton $70 to create and advertise the drink, so he made a loss. But he persevered; encouraged by the drink's popularity with customers, convinced that he would eventually make something of it.

The drink was named Coca-Cola by Pemberton's bookkeeper, Frank Robinson, who also wrote the name for the logo in the distinctive script that is still in use today.

Pemberton's young company started to grow sales of its drink by getting other pharmacies to sell Coca-Cola, too. It sold 25 gallons of syrup to drugstores, and ensured all the stores that sold the drink had hand-painted Coca-Cola signs to help promote it.

Coca-Cola's famous advertising campaigns have their roots right at the beginning of its history: soon after the drink had been created, Pemberton placed the first newspaper ad in The Atlanta Journal, inviting people to try "the new and popular soda fountain drink."

Sadly, Pemberton died in 1888, and so never saw his drink taken to the masses. The person to do this was Atlanta businessman Asa Griggs Candler, who bought the rights to the drink for $2,300.

Candler had a vision for the business, to turn the now-popular drink from a beverage into a business. He partnered with Pemberton's bookkeeper, Frank Robinson. Together they raised $100,000, then a very substantial sum, to kick-start the business.

In 1891, Candler had full control of the business, and within a year, he had increased the sale of Coca-Cola syrup tenfold. In 1892 the company was incorporated, and The Coca-Cola Company was officially born.

They began a huge marketing campaign, using new advertising techniques. To spread the word, he gave away coupons for free Coca-Cola tasters in newspapers, and offered pharmacists two gallons of the syrup, if they would agree to give away one gallon's worth as free samples when people produced his coupon. He fitted them with urns, clocks, calendars and scales all bearing the brand name. The combination of this strongly branded approach and a drink which almost everyone loves worked wonders, and sales grew fast. By 1895, just 4 years later, Candler had grown demand, enough that he needed to build syrup plants in Chicago, Dallas and Los Angeles, and declared to his shareholders that "Coca-Cola is now consumed in every state and territory in the United States " Today it is sufficiently easy to launch a product nationally, so it is easy to miss just what a major achievement this was. In an era when it took days to travel across the country, when there was no radio or television, to be available in every state so quickly was quite phenomenal.

Up until 1894, Coca-Cola was only sold by the glassful, until a Mississippi businessman named Joseph Biedenharn bottled Coca-Cola at his factory and sent a dozen to Candler. Candler didn't believe the idea of Coca-Cola in a bottle would be successful, hated the product, and quickly dismissed it. He again overlooked this crucial development in 1899, when two lawyers from Chattanooga, Tennessee, Benjamin F. Thomas and Joseph B. Whitehead, secured exclusive rights from Candler to bottle and sell the beverage in nearly all of the United States—for only one dollar. In fact, Candler was so sure that this idea wouldn't amount to anything that he didn't even bother collecting the dollar!

This was the start of an unusual corporate structure which continues to this day. The Coca-Cola Company supplies syrup, called concentrate, to customers all over the world. Some of these customers are restaurants and bars which sell the drink by the glass, as the original pharmacy customers, while the other group of customers are bottling companies, who add carbonated water to the syrup in a factory, and bottle it for sale in shops. Thomas and Whitehead began by opening bottling plants in Chattanooga and Atlanta, but soon realised that there was a better way for them to roll out bottled Coca-Cola across the country. The two Chattanooga lawyers were joined by another, and the trio split the USA into three territories, and began selling the bottling rights to local entrepreneurs; not only did this reduce the amount of capital the lawyers needed, as each local entrepreneur used his own money, but it also provided local knowledge and the commitment of business owners which would have been very hard to set up any other way. The first sub-licensed bottler began in 1900, and by 1909, there were 400 Coca-Cola bottling plants in the country.

By the turn of the century, Candler had increased Coca-Cola's sales to 40 times their 1890 level, and his continuing advertising campaign and his free samples had spread the word of Coca-Cola across America.

Bubbling overseas

The drink was first taken overseas by Candler's son, Charles. On a trip to London, Charles took a jug of syrup with him, and totted up modest orders for five gallons. Coca-Cola was first sold in England on 31 August 1900, and gradually built enough momentum to be sold in Selfridges and The London Coliseum. After seeing the success of the bottled drinks, The Coca-Cola Company decided to license out bottling rights to overseas territories itself. The first international bottling plants began in 1906 in Canada, Cuba and Panama, with others, including the Philippines and Guam, following shortly afterwards in 1912 and 1917, respectively. As he had done so effectively in the United States, Candler supported the new supplies of drinks with a thorough marketing campaign, to ensure the bright red logo was seen in shops and cafés everywhere. Most of the companies granted the rights to bottle Coca-Cola in different countries were brewers. This worked well, as the brewers already had bottling plants and expertise, so it was relatively easy and quick for them to add the new drink to their range. The brewers also already had distribution through their own existing customer base, which meant that Coke got access to shops, bars and restaurants far faster than it would have done had it set up a brand new business from scratch in a new country.

The drink had become very well known, and was clearly successful, so inevitably a number of competitors appeared, though of course none knew the precise recipe, which was kept utterly secret. The Coca-Cola Company started to get concerned that it was too easy for customers to be given a different drink and mistakenly think that it was The Real Thing, which not only meant that Coca-Cola lost out on the sale, but also potentially that customers would not enjoy it as much and might not buy it next time. Something needed to be done. So the company decided to come up with a distinctive bottle to ensure their product stood out. It was in 1916, following a design contest, that the now-famous bottle was first used, designed by the Root Glass Company of Terre Haute, Indiana. The winning design was chosen for its attractive appearance, original design, and because, even in the dark, people could easily identify it as the genuine article.

New leadership, new vision

After nearly three decades of turning the drink into a substantial and successful business, Candler eventually sold the business in 1919 to Ernest Woodruff for $25 million; his son Robert became president in 1923. The company was reincorporated as a Delaware corporation and listed on the New York Stock Exchange, selling 500,000 shares to the general public for $40 per share. Coca-Cola was now firmly established in the USA; Woodruff's mission was to go global, and his vision: to create a brand that was "in arm's reach of desire."

During the 1920s and 1930s, Woodruff set his sights on international expansion. By the time Woodruff took over in 1923, Coca-Cola was strongly established in North America, had some bottling arrangements in South America, and had just opened its first European bottling plant in France. From this base, Woodruff's Coca-Cola went on in the 1920s to open plants in France, Guatemala, Honduras, Mexico, Belgium, and Italy. In 1926, Coca-Cola set up a Foreign Department, which became the Coca-Cola Export Corporation in 1930. In all countries where Coca-

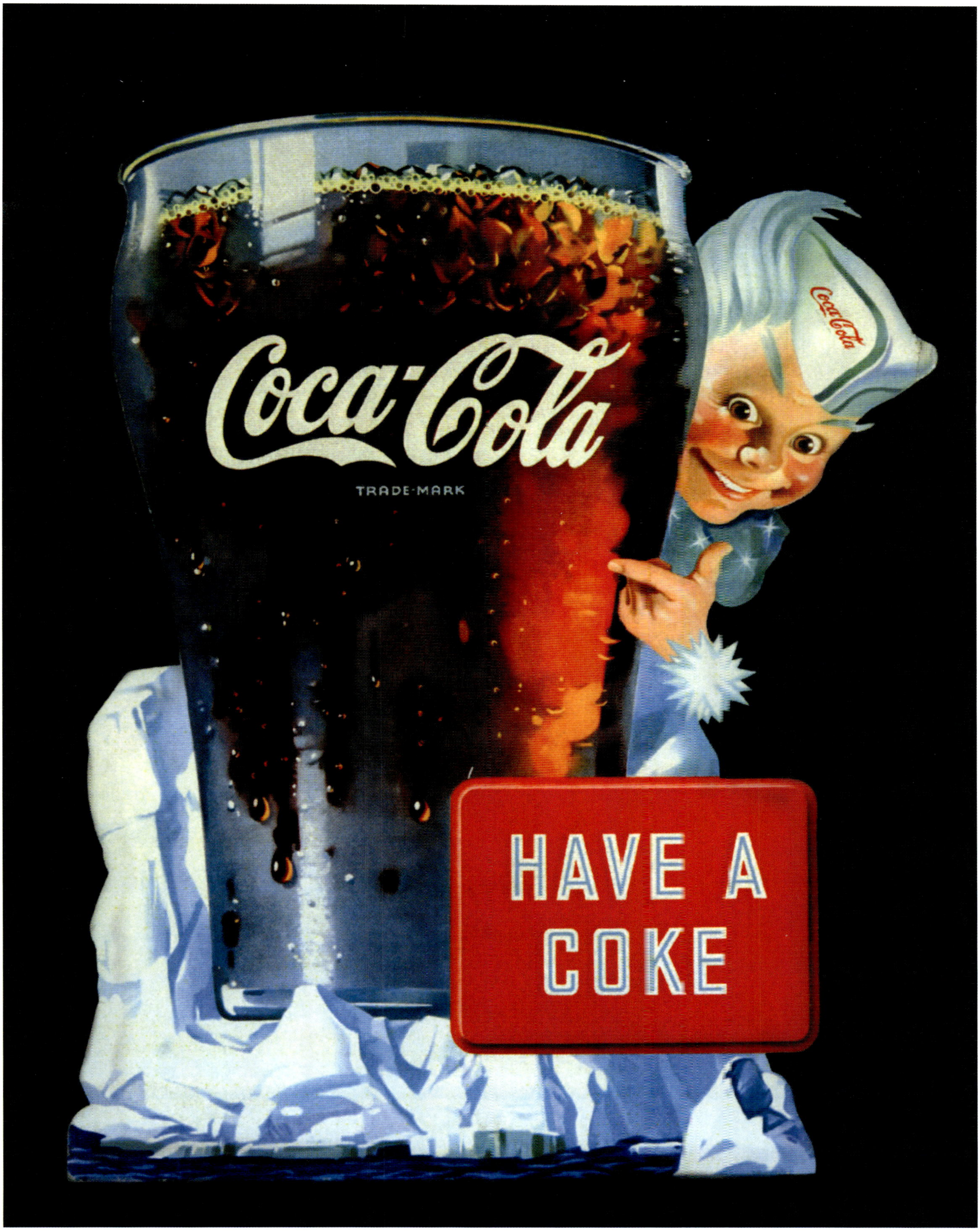
Coca-Cola
TRADE-MARK
Coca-Cola
HAVE A
COKE

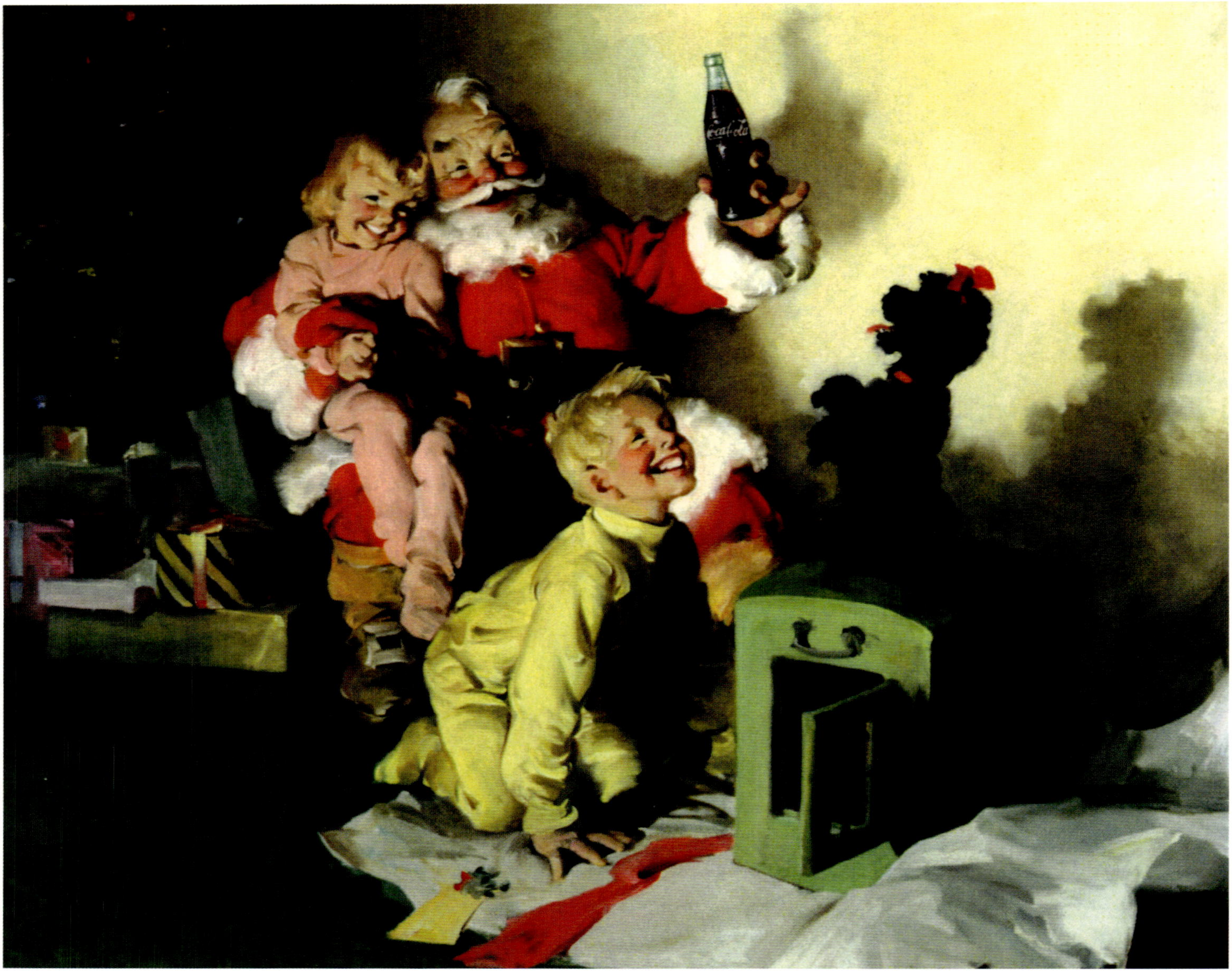

Cola sprung up, a creative, vibrant and culturally relevant advertising campaign followed.

A significant international move occurred in 1928, when Woodruff began a partnership with the Olympic Games in Amsterdam. A thousand bottles of Coca-Cola accompanied the U.S. team, and the drink was on sale in the Olympic stadium. Vendors were adorned with caps and coats emblazoned with the Coca-Cola logo, and the drink was also sold at surrounding cafés, restaurants and shops. By the start of the Second World War, Coca-Cola was present in 44 countries.

A marketing genius, Woodruff developed the company's successful but limited line, introducing the six-pack (making the drinks more transportable and encouraging people to buy in bulk) and the open-top cooler. Coca-Cola was available in vending machines from 1929 and advertised on the new medium of radio. In 1932, bottlers hired women to act as door-to-door salespeople for the drink, with a target of 125 calls per day. At Christmas 1931, Coca-Cola's famous red, human Santa Claus made his debut, banishing the long-established and scary, elf-like Santa into the mists of time.

Coke's wartime effort

Throughout the Second World War, Coca-Cola continued to manufacture, even offering the drink for five cents to any serviceperson, whatever country they were in, no matter the cost to the company. Bottling plants were opened to supply troops with the drink, following a request from General Eisenhower himself on 29 June, 1943, requesting the shipment of materials for 10 bottling plants, along with 3 million bottles of Coca-Cola and enough supplies to make the same amount twice a month. All supplies were to be sent to North Africa. Coca-Cola responded within six months, and set up a bottling plant in Algiers. In all, 64 bottling plants opened during the war, and more than 5 billion bottles of Coca-Cola were consumed by service people. Mobile service stations were also taken to the battlefields, and people throughout Europe and the Pacific had their first taste of the drink. These war-time bottling plants were later converted and run by local civilians, who continued to produce and sell the drink even after the Americans had left.

Promoting global happiness

Post-war America was the perfect place for Coca-Cola to expand—people were embracing a carefree lifestyle, and Coca-Cola's advertising mirrored this desire, with images of loved-up couples at the drive-in, and happy families driving round in shiny cars. Coca-Cola continued to be served at soda fountains, and now was added to the menu at ice cream parlours. The company still had just one product, albeit an extraordinarily successful one, and it began experimenting with new flavours, and introduced Fanta in the 1950s (which was originally concocted in Germany), followed by Sprite in 1961, TAB in 1963 and Fresca in 1966. The company acquired the Minute Maid Company in 1960, branching out into juices. New lines of Coca-Cola were also rolled out, including bigger bottles and metal cans in 1960.

The 1950s and 1960s saw bottling plants built in more countries, includ-

The Coca-Cola Company
Founders: John Pemberton (creator), Asa Griggs Candler (business founder)
Year of foundation: 1886
Country of foundation: USA
Countries now trading in: Over 200
Current turnover and profit: Net income $1.2 billion, Revenue $7.3 billion

Image Credits
(page 66 top) Jacobs Pharmacy, the first store to sell Coca-Cola.
(page 66 bottom) 1956 Santa Claus advertisement by Haddon Sundblom.
(page 67 top) Coca-Cola logo designed by Frank Robinson in the 1800s.
(page 67 bottom) 1916 Coca-Cola glass bottle designed by the Root Glass Company.
(page 68 from left to right) John Pemberton, Coca-Cola founder and creator; Asa Candler, Coca-Cola owner in 1891; Robert Woodruff, Coca-Cola president for six decades; Artist Haddon Sundblom pictured with a 1964 Santa Claus advertisement he created.
(page 69) 1945 "Sprite Boy" advertisement.
(page 70) 1964 Santa Claus advertisement by Haddon Sundblom.
(page 71) Coca-Cola Classic can created in the 1970s, based on original Coca-Cola logo design by Frank Robinson in the 1800s; Coke Zero released in March 2005, Diet Coke with Splenda, Diet Coke Lime, and Diet Coke Cherry created in 2004.
All images courtesy of The Coca-Cola Company.

ing Cambodia, Montserrat, Paraguay, Macau and Turkey. During the global economic boom of the 1970s and 1980s, many of Coca-Cola's small and medium-sized bottlers joined forces to better serve their growing international customer base. By 1969, for the first time, Coca-Cola sales in international markets exceeded those in the U.S.

In 1971 Coca-Cola created a particularly special television advertisement that saw young people from all over the world gather on a hilltop in Italy to sing "I'd Like to Buy the World a Coke." Coca-Cola had made its mark on the international market, and for a time was seen as an icon of unity in an era that had not yet grasped the consequences of globalisation. Significantly, in 1978, the People's Republic of China declared The Coca-Cola Company as the only company allowed to sell packaged cold drinks in China.

Intelligent risk taking

In 1981, Roberto C. Goizueta became Chairman of The Board of Directors and CEO of The Coca-Cola Company, and decided to take the company forward with a strategy he called "intelligent risk taking." This began with the introduction of Diet Coke in July 1982, the very first extension of the Coca-Cola trademark. Coke's arch rival, Pepsi, had released their diet version in 1963 with great success. Diet Coke's inception was quickly followed with a range of alternatives, including caffeine-free, Cherry Coke and Diet Coke. Within two years, Diet Coke had become the top low-calorie drink in the world.

Goizueta's riskiest initiative began in 1985, when he released a new tasting Coca-Cola, the first change in formula for 99 years. Why fix something that isn't broken? Well, it was breaking: Coke's share of the soft drinks market had decreased since the end of the Second World War. Its share price had also decreased. Pepsi had directly challenged Coke's success in the marketplace by conducting blind taste testing on the streets of America, with many people opting for the sweeter Pepsi. This saw Pepsi overtake Coke in supermarket sales.

"New Coke" passed taste testers' approval in extensive testing before launch, being preferred to Pepsi by most, but didn't succeed in the marketplace. In an unprecedented expression of brand loyalty, people demanded their old Coke back, Coca-Cola received over 40,000 pleading letters and their phone lines were continually blocked with customers desperate to have their old drink back again. Critics named the initiative the biggest marketing blunder ever, and Pepsi declared themselves the victor of the "Cola wars." The company listened, and after 79 days of New Coke, they started supplying the original Coca-Cola again, labelled Coca-Cola Classic, alongside its younger relation.

Its return was momentous: ABC News's Peter Jennings interrupted regular programming to share the news with viewers, and speaking to the senate, U.S. Senator David Pryor called the reintroduction "a meaningful moment in U.S. history." More importantly, its sales leaped up, reclaiming top spot, which it has never lost since. New Coke was slowly discontinued, and the original recipe is still used today.

Flying high

During the 1990s, Coke made its presence known in the sporting world, sponsoring the Olympic Games, FIFA World Cup, Rugby World Cup and the National Basketball Association. 1993 saw the introduction of the incredibly catchy "Always Coca-Cola" advertising campaign, and by 1997, the company was selling [illegible] billion servings of its products every day. One of the last companies to have the pleasure of Coca-Cola's presence was India; as Indian law forbade companies to trade if they withheld trade-secret information, something Coca-Cola insisted upon to protect their formula. In 1993, India changed its laws regarding trademarks, and Coca-Cola went on sale. The growth of Coca-Cola was aided by the acquisition of Indian brands Limca, Maaza and Thums Up. The company followed this pattern of growth by acquisition in other countries, too, and acquired Barq's Root Beer in the USA and Inca Kola in Peru. In 1999 The Coca-Cola Company purchased the soft drinks brands of Cadbury Schweppes plc in various countries, including Great Britain. This expanded the existing product range of beverages such as Coca-Cola, Diet Coke, Cherry Coca-Cola, Fanta, Sprite, Lilt and Five Alive to include the Schweppes' range, Dr Pepper, Oasis, Kia-Ora and Malvern water.

Where are they now?

The Coca-Cola Company now owns more than 400 brands and sells more than 1.5 billion beverage servings each day. Over its lifespan, it has produced more than 10 billion gallons of syrup. Out of all countries Coca-Cola does business in, among those with the highest per capita consumption are Mexico and Iceland. The company employs over 90,000 people and is headed up by Muhtar Kent, President and CEO. To celebrate its heritage, The New World of Coca-Cola opened in 2007, an attraction dedicated to the brand, and one of Atlanta's main tourist attractions. Now a major global corporation already mature in many of its markets, Coca-Cola faces new challenges, from changing patterns of demand for soft drinks in many developed countries to enormous and fast growing potential in increasingly affluent countries such as China. Coca-Cola continues to add to its extensive brand list, including the launch of Coke Zero in 2005, and other acquisitions including water and tea companies. Recently, Coca-Cola launched its first ever clothing range of sustainable apparel. Sold in Wal-Mart, the t-shirts are made of recycled plastic Coke bottles. Today, 72% of Coca-Cola is sold outside the USA, and Coca-Cola's share price continues to rise, based on expectations of continued profitable growth to come.

The Coca-Cola Company now owns more than 400 brands and sells more than 1.5 billion beverage servings each day.

The Coca-Cola Series 1970s-2005

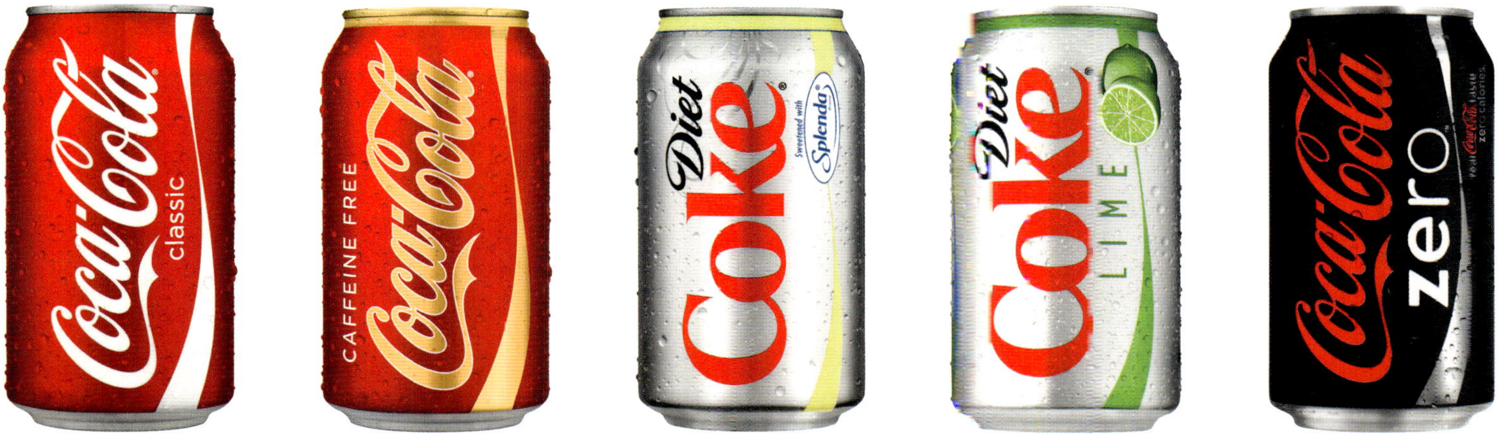

"Like the packaging, the focus of the overall visual identity was to create a system that was pure and simple and referenced back to the original core brand elements in a modern and honest way."

"The goal was to use just a few simple elements to create a wide spectrum of designs that are consistent, yet surprising."

Comments by David Turner & Bruce Duckworth, *Heads of Design, Turner Duckworth: London & San Francisco*

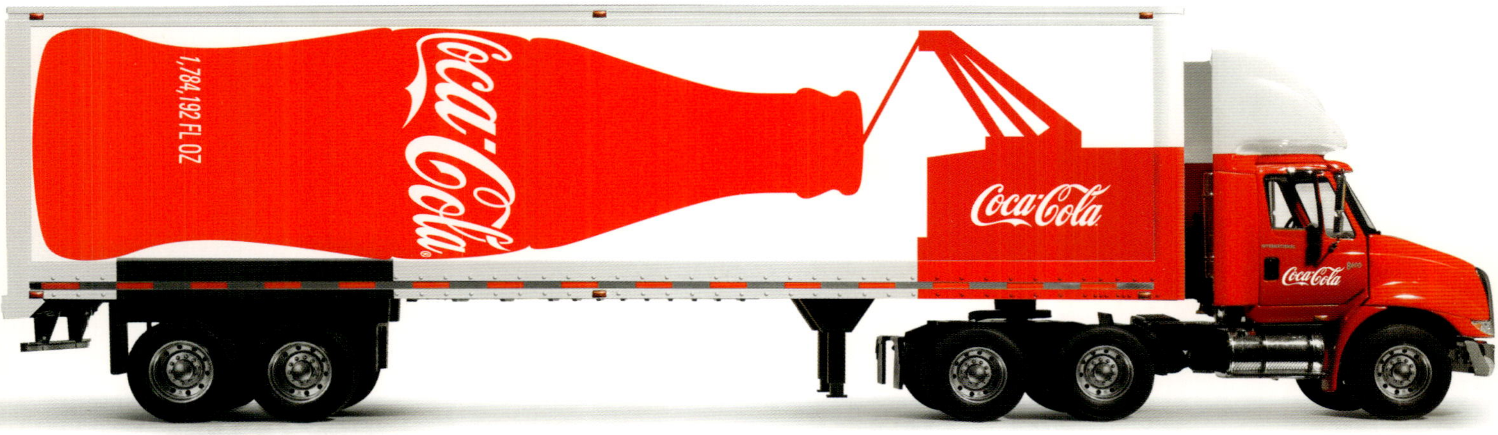

Q&A: David Turner & Bruce Duckworth

Before Turner Duckworth's award winning redesign, Coca-Cola's image was much like other leading beverage companies: heavily painted with graphics. Aiming to return to the classic Coca-Cola look, Turner Duckworth went back to basics—literally. Drawing from Coke's latest idea, "Coke brings joy" (developed hand in hand with Wieden + Kennedy), they eliminated the extra ribbons and bubbles from the cans and brightened the white and red colors. The new designs are simple and clean, rid of unnecessary design noise, and potent in their simplicity. And though they've been out in the marketplace less than a year, Turner Duckworth has already been honored by the Cannes Grand Prix, and recognized by BrandWeek *and* Creative Review. *Plus, Coke's presence at the 2008 Summer Olympics promises even more exposure for the project. Graphis spoke to David Turner and Bruce Duckworth about their redesign work for one of the world's most iconic brands.*

Tell us a bit about the Coca-Cola rebranding project.

Coca-Cola determined that over the years, the brand's visual identity had become cluttered and uninspiring, diluting the brand's iconic status. Coca-Cola developed a new creative idea to refocus the brand: 'Coke brings joy,' a simple statement about the happiness the product brings. Moira Cullen, Design Director for Coca-Cola North America, challenged Turner Duckworth to use the idea to design a new visual identity and packaging system that would spotlight the brand's powerful equities. The design team at Coca-Cola North America wanted a new direction for the brand's visual identity that would make Coca-Cola feel happy, fresh and honest.

What was the Turner Duckworth solution?

With global and North American initiatives designed to simplify the brand already in place, Turner Duckworth was able to focus on Coca-Cola's distinctive equities—the color red, the Spencerian script, the iconic contour bottle and the dynamic ribbon device—and how to present them in a dramatic and unexpected way.

What do you think your design brings to the product and company?

Developed through a collaborative relationship with Coca-Cola North America, this program has helped re-assert the company's reputation for design leadership.

What brought about the idea to strip the Coca-Cola packaging designs and return to a very basic format? What message or idea were you trying to convey?

Coca-Cola packaging had become covered in drips and bubbles graphics, meant to emulate the fizzy refreshment inside. As part of the visual identity program, Moira Cullen asked Turner Duckworth to align packaging with the '21st century refreshment' strategy that was being implemented across Coca-Cola North America's portfolio of brands. By eliminating extraneous design elements to reveal the proprietary equities of Coca-Cola—the Spencerian script and the ribbon design—a new visual identity offering emotional resonance with the fewest possible elements was created.

How did Turner Duckworth interact with Coca-Cola to achieve the company's desired vision?

Coca-Cola provided a comprehensive brief that outlined internal strategy and initiatives focused on building a new identity for the brand. The brief served as a guide to help develop a new design strategy based on essential principles that could be applied to everything from cups to delivery trucks.

To help the Coca-Cola design team achieve internal approval, recommendations were presented in the context of best practices in design—a message they are particularly skilled in communicating—and an accompanying design guideline was produced for the company, the bottlers and their suppliers.

Turner Duckworth has received numerous awards already for the Coca-Cola redesign project. Did you anticipate this type of recognition?

Two of the most prestigious prizes, the Cannes Grand Prix and Agency of the Year from International Food and Beverage Awards, are the first ever wins by a design company, not an advertising firm. It's a big accomplishment for both Coca-Cola and Turner Duckworth.

Any final thoughts?

This design, which was initially developed for Coca-Cola North America, has influenced the Coca-Cola visual identity on a global basis.

For more information on Turner Duckworth, see page 76 or visit their website, www.turnerduckworth.com.

Images on this spread courtesy of Turner Duckworth.

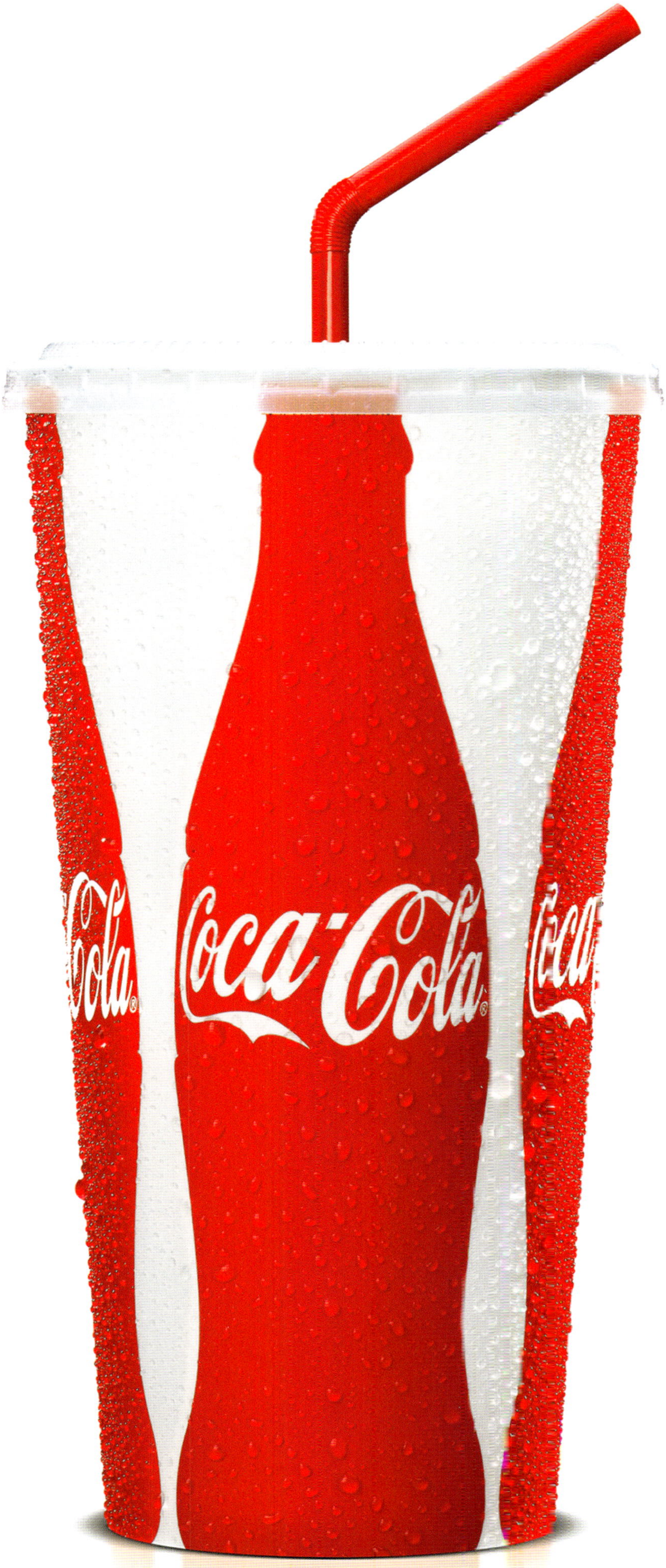
Coca-Cola

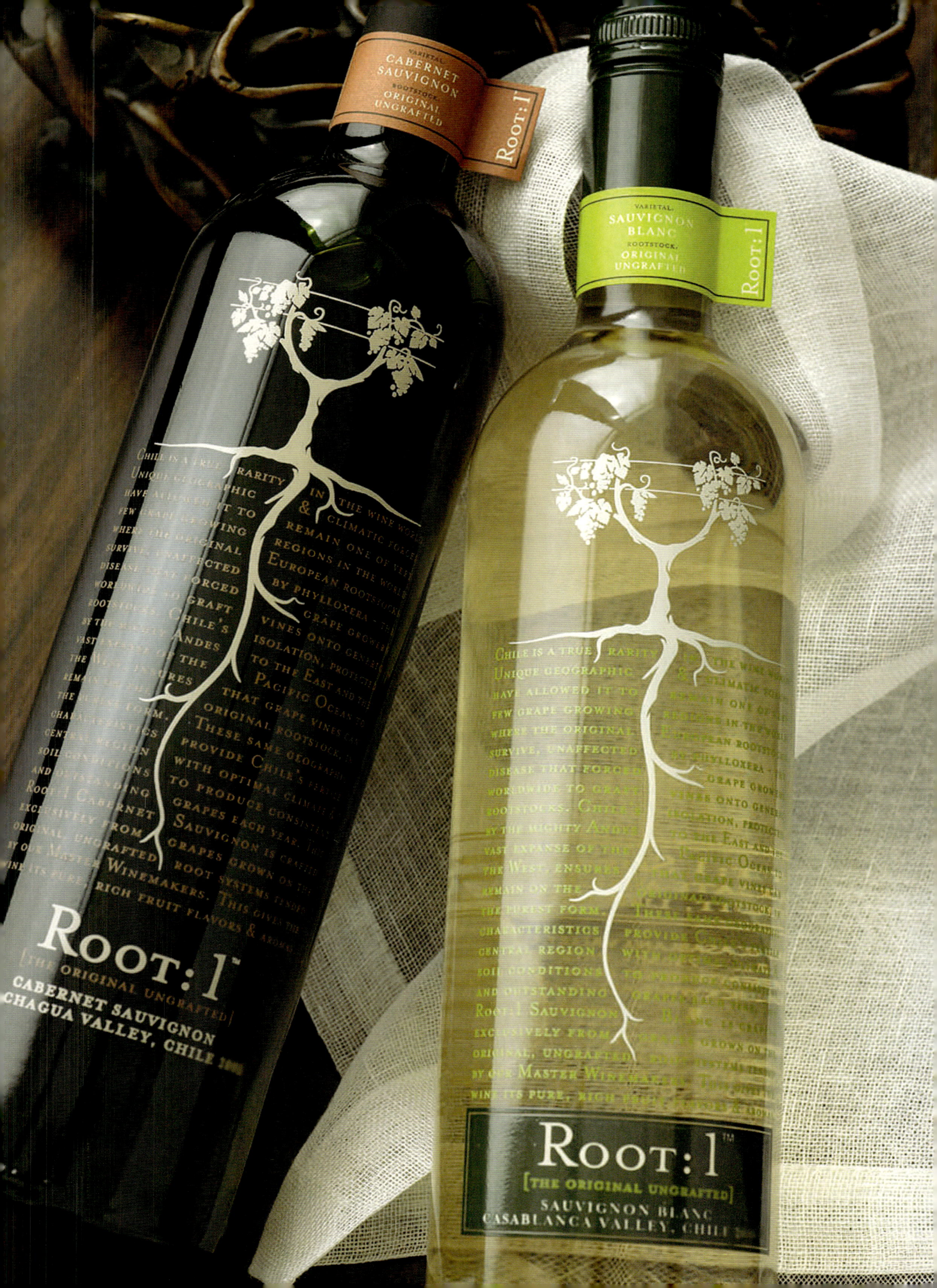
VARIETAL: CABERNET SAUVIGNON
ROOTSTOCK: ORIGINAL UNGRAFTED
Root:1
Root:1
[THE ORIGINAL UNGRAFTED]
CABERNET SAUVIGNON
VARIETAL: SAUVIGNON BLANC
ROOTSTOCK: ORIGINAL UNGRAFTED
Root:1
Root:1™
[THE ORIGINAL UNGRAFTED]
SAUVIGNON BLANC
CASABLANCA VALLEY, CHILE

Root: 1 is the latest collaboration by Turner Duckworth and Click Wine Group, who creates and sells wines across the globe. Their previous projects have included redesigns for the wines Fat bastard and Flying Fish, plus brand creations for 2 Up, Clean Slate, and High Note, now launching in U.S. channels. Last year, Click Wine Group sold over six million bottles. As of March 2008, their latest venture, Root: 1 Cabernet, was the fastest-growing imported Cabernet (750ml) at all price points. Beyond the quality of the wine itself, Click Wine Group gives Turner Duckworth much of the credit. ■ According to Alan MacDonald, Click Wine Group's VP of Marketing, "We separate ourselves from thousands of competitors because we spend so much time thinking about package design and how consumers visually relate to wine. There may be six hundred bottles on a store shelf, and many of them have very good wine inside. If we can't stand out on that shelf with a design that is both obvious and elegant, we will not have a chance to prove just how good our wine is." ■ "I think the results of TD's work can be seen in the success of Root: 1. Every year, about 250 new brands and 2,000 new items are launched in the wine category, and most will fail. In a very short period of time, Root: 1 has become the leading Chilean super-premium wine (over $10). This can only happen if the packaging causes consumers to put the wine in their carts and the wine is good enough to get them to return to the store to buy it again." ■ We spoke with Turner Duckworth creatives and founders David Turner and Bruce Duckworth about their latest Click Wine Group venture.

Root: 1™

"Click uses Turner Duckworth for the thing we do best: creating simple, emotive concepts that cut through with clarity and wit."

David Turner & Bruce Duckworth

Q&A with Bruce Duckworth and David Turner

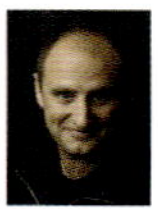

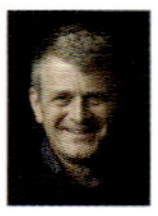

What has it been like to work with Click? Since you've worked together so many times before, is there an established approach to all projects?
We love to work with Peter Click and his company because their typical brief says, 'Give us something that disrupts the category.' What they give us is free reign, relying on the good judgment and experience of their people, who know definitively what works and what doesn't in the industry. Click is willing to shoulder expenses (like screenprinting, a gardener's tab or hangtags) to get a project done nicely.

How did Click Wine Group present the Root: 1 Cabernet project to you?
With shelves cluttered with wines begging for attention, Turner Duckworth's assignment was to create an eye-catching, memorable, premium brand.

What were your specific goals for the Root: 1 branding campaign?
To name and design a unique offering for the growing new category of Chilean wines.

What was the Turner Duckworth solution?
We told the story unique to this wine: ungrafted rootstock, untainted by phylloxera, found only in Chile. Root:1 refers to the Route 1 road to South America (and ties in nicely with the wine's sales performance).

Tell us more about the bottle design. What did you wish to convey to the consumer?
Root:1 tells the story of the original, ungrafted Cabernet Sauvignon rootstock, extinct in Europe and now found only in Chile. The rich history of this rootstock is visually linked to a glass of wine hidden in the vine. As you read the story, the root leads you down to where it all begins—beneath the soil. A gardener's tab creates a unique neck label.

How did the idea for the gardener's tab emerge? Is its purpose significant?
Winemaking is horticulture. Unexpected detail gives the bottle a premium feel.

Explain your decision to incorporate the story into your bottle design.
Even if consumers don't read the copy, its presence suggests this wine has a story to tell. Together, story and graphics explain the wine's uniqueness.

Beyond the actual bottle design, what other elements were integral to the Root: 1 Cabernet Sauvignon campaign?
The shipping carton doubles as a point of sale device. As cartons stack, a long root extends to the floor. Click uses Turner Duckworth for the thing we do best: creating simple, emotive concepts that cut through with clarity and wit.

What was the most interesting aspect of this project to you both as designers? What was the most challenging aspect?
From a product standpoint, the most exciting aspect of the assignment was the differentiating story of the wine's original, ungrafted rootstock – which is extremely rare in Europe, but thrives in Chile.
From a designer's point of view, the coolest aspect was the tightness of the brief—Root:1 was to be a Cabernet only. We did not have to consider the color needs of other varietals in our design. The challenge, of course, came not in this project, but thanks to the product's commercial success, in line extensions to follow.

How successful has your branding solution been for Click?
We must have done something right because in early March, according to AC Nielsen (12 weeks ending 3/8/08, U.S. Food), Root:1 was the fastest-growing imported Cabernet (750ml) at all price points and the number-one imported super premium cabernet ($10-15/bottle). Click has since launched a Sauvignon Blanc and is now developing two additional Root:1 varietals, all with our help.
For more information on Root: 1, visit www.root1wine.com. To learn more about Click Wine Group, check out www.clickwinegroup.com.

Alan MacDonald, VP of Marketing, Click Wine Group

"We have worked with TD for four years, and decided to begin using them when we made a strategic company decision that product packaging was of critical importance to the successful launch and sometimes relaunch of our wines. Turner was one of several companies we interviewed, and they were chosen because we felt they consistently showed us the widest range of work. We have gone back to them because we have always been happy with the end results. We think they understand what we are looking for, which is often complicated."

Turner Duckworth

Founded in 1992, Turner Duckworth: London & San Francisco is an award-winning brand design consultancy with studios in San Francisco and London. We help clients convey complex ideas with simple, emotive solutions. Consumers are bombarded by thousands of commercial messages every day. Our brand identity and packaging designs cut through with clarity and wit. David Turner is Head of Design in our USA studio. Bruce Duckworth is Head of Design in the UK.
We have a total of 40 employees. Turner Duckworth maintains constant collaboration between our two studios. Our designers swap places for one-month exchanges every year. David and Bruce speak to review work daily (we often say it's harder to get work past our partners than our clients). Transatlantic cross-pollination mixes British style and irony with American toughness and pragmatism. Clients and staff benefit from a design perspective broader than that of most agencies grown through acquisition.
Turner Duckworth's collaborative critique encourages excellence. 75 percent of our business is repeat clients. We are selective about new work because relationships tend to last. We teach clients principles of good design.
For 16 years, we've remained nimble, producing award-winning work through design excellence. From two offices we serve cultural icons like Amazon, Motorola, Waitrose, Superdrug and Royal Mail and entrepreneurial "brands on the rise" like Palm, Virgin Atlantic, Shaklee and Jamba Juice. Examine our portfolio. Judge our success yourself.

San Francisco Office: 831 Montgomery Street, San Francisco, CA 94133, (415) 675 7777 / London Office: Voysey House, Barley Mow Passage, London W4 4PH, +44 (0)208 994 7190
www.turnerduckworth.com

Bruce Duckworth, Turner Duckworth Head of Design, UK: Bruce Duckworth, who graduated with an honors degree in graphic design from Kingston University, has worked for some of the most respected design groups, including Minale Tattersfield and Lewis Moberly. Bruce's critical acclaim in design is evident in his many speaking engagements and awards, including D&AD for outstanding packaging and two Design Effectiveness Awards. He has judged a number of awards competitions and has lectured as part of the British Council's delegation to promote the effective use of design. Bruce is jointly responsible for the creative output of the company.
David Turner, Turner Duckworth Head of Design, USA: David graduated at the top of his class at St. Martin's School of Art London in 1984. He is widely respected in the design arena, and his work has received critical acclaim and awards, including Gold and Silver Clios and the prestigious Art Directors Club of Europe Gold Award. David has served as the Chairman for the Clio Design Awards Jury and as a juror for the I.D. Design Awards. David worked as a director of the international design consultancy Minale Tattersfield on major projects in the UK, Europe and Asia before establishing Turner Duckworth in 1993.

Image Credits
(page 74) photograph by Armstrong Studios (page 75) Root: 1 logo by Turner Duckworth (page 76) portrait of David Turner (left) and Bruce Duckworth (right) by Paul Elledge (page 77 top) Root: 1 CS Stack and Root: 1 SB Stack photos by Brent Whiting, Whiting Design; Root: 1 SB 07 label photograph courtesy of Turner Duckworth, photo by Lloyd Hryciw (page 77 bottom) Colchagua at sunset photograph by Manuel Kojchen.

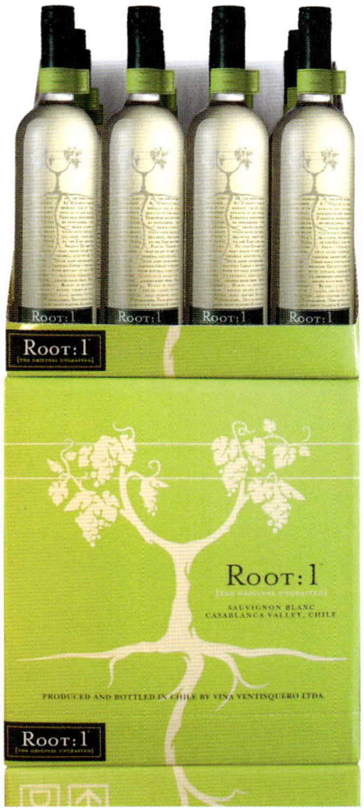
Root: 1
Root: 1
Sauvignon Blanc
Casablanca Valley, Chile
Root: 1

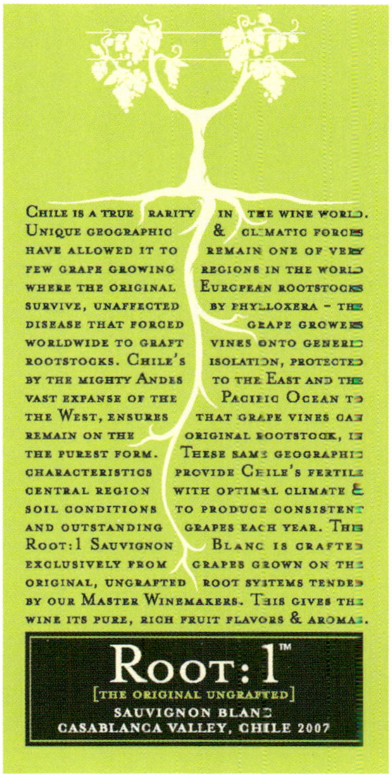
Chile is a true rarity in the wine world. Unique geographic & climatic forces have allowed it to remain one of very few grape growing regions in the world where the original European rootstocks survive, unaffected by phylloxera – the disease that forced grape growers worldwide to graft vines onto generic rootstocks. Chile's isolation, protected by the mighty Andes to the East and the vast expanse of the Pacific Ocean to the West, ensures that grape vines can remain on the original rootstock, in the purest form. These same geographic characteristics provide Chile's fertile central region with optimal climate & soil conditions to produce consistent and outstanding grapes each year. This Root:1 Sauvignon Blanc is crafted exclusively from grapes grown on the original, ungrafted root systems tended by our Master Winemakers. This gives the wine its pure, rich fruit flavors & aromas.
Root: 1™
[The Original Ungrafted]
Sauvignon Blanc
Casablanca Valley, Chile 2007

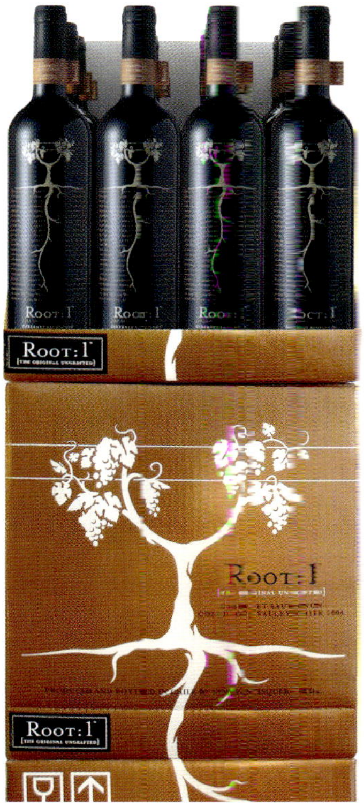
Root: 1
Root: 1
Root: 1

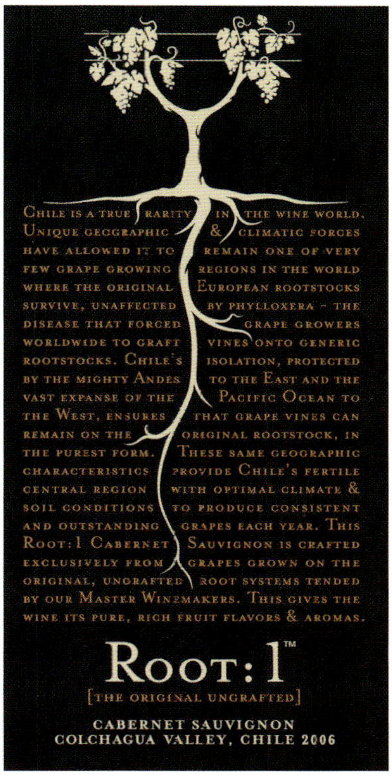
Chile is a true rarity in the wine world. Unique geographic & climatic forces have allowed it to remain one of very few grape growing regions in the world where the original European rootstocks survive, unaffected by phylloxera – the disease that forced grape growers worldwide to graft vines onto generic rootstocks. Chile's isolation, protected by the mighty Andes to the East and the vast expanse of the Pacific Ocean to the West, ensures that grape vines can remain on the original rootstock, in the purest form. These same geographic characteristics provide Chile's fertile central region with optimal climate & soil conditions to produce consistent and outstanding grapes each year. This Root:1 Cabernet Sauvignon is crafted exclusively from grapes grown on the original, ungrafted root systems tended by our Master Winemakers. This gives the wine its pure, rich fruit flavors & aromas.
Root: 1™
[The Original Ungrafted]
Cabernet Sauvignon
Colchagua Valley, Chile 2006

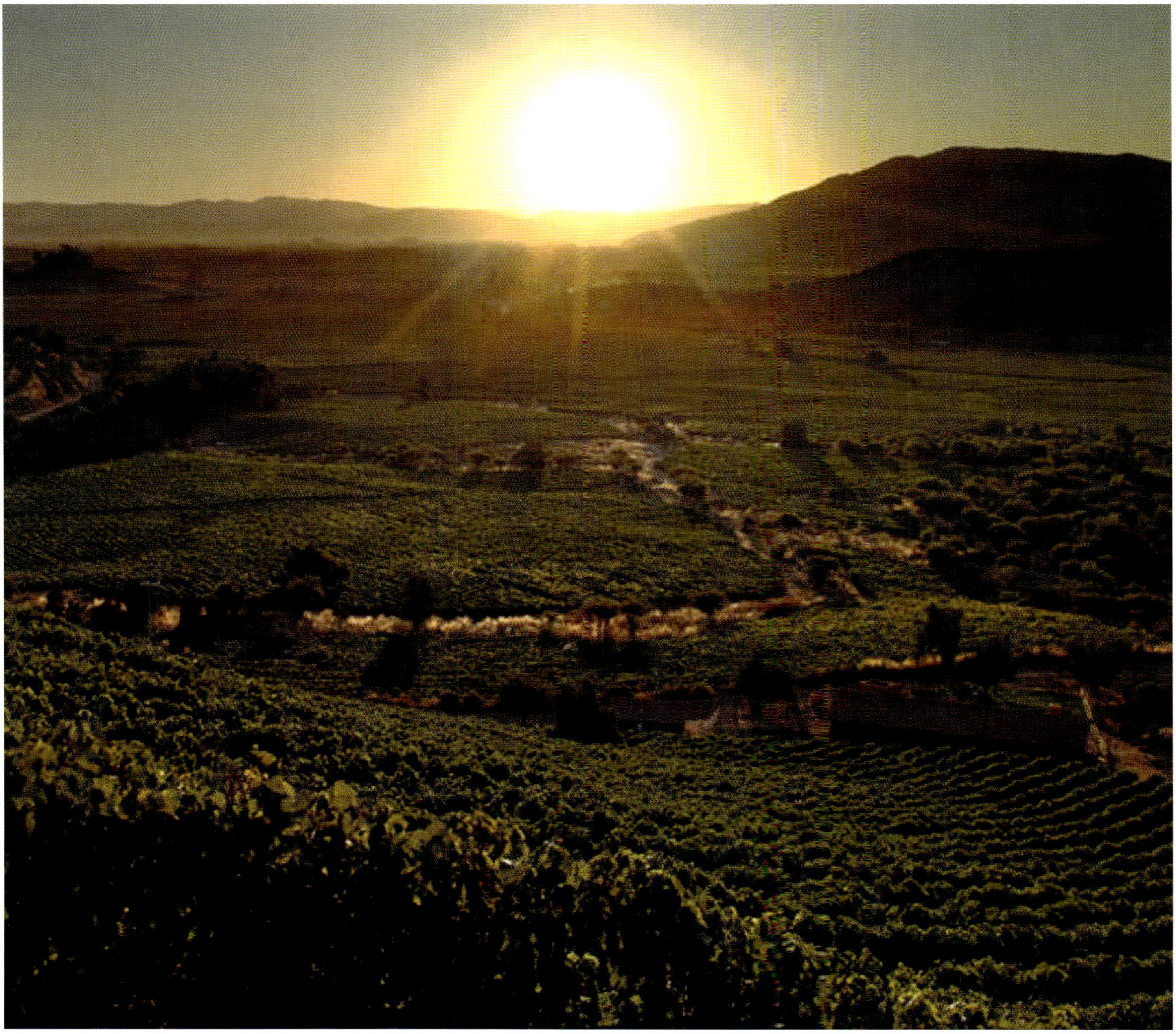

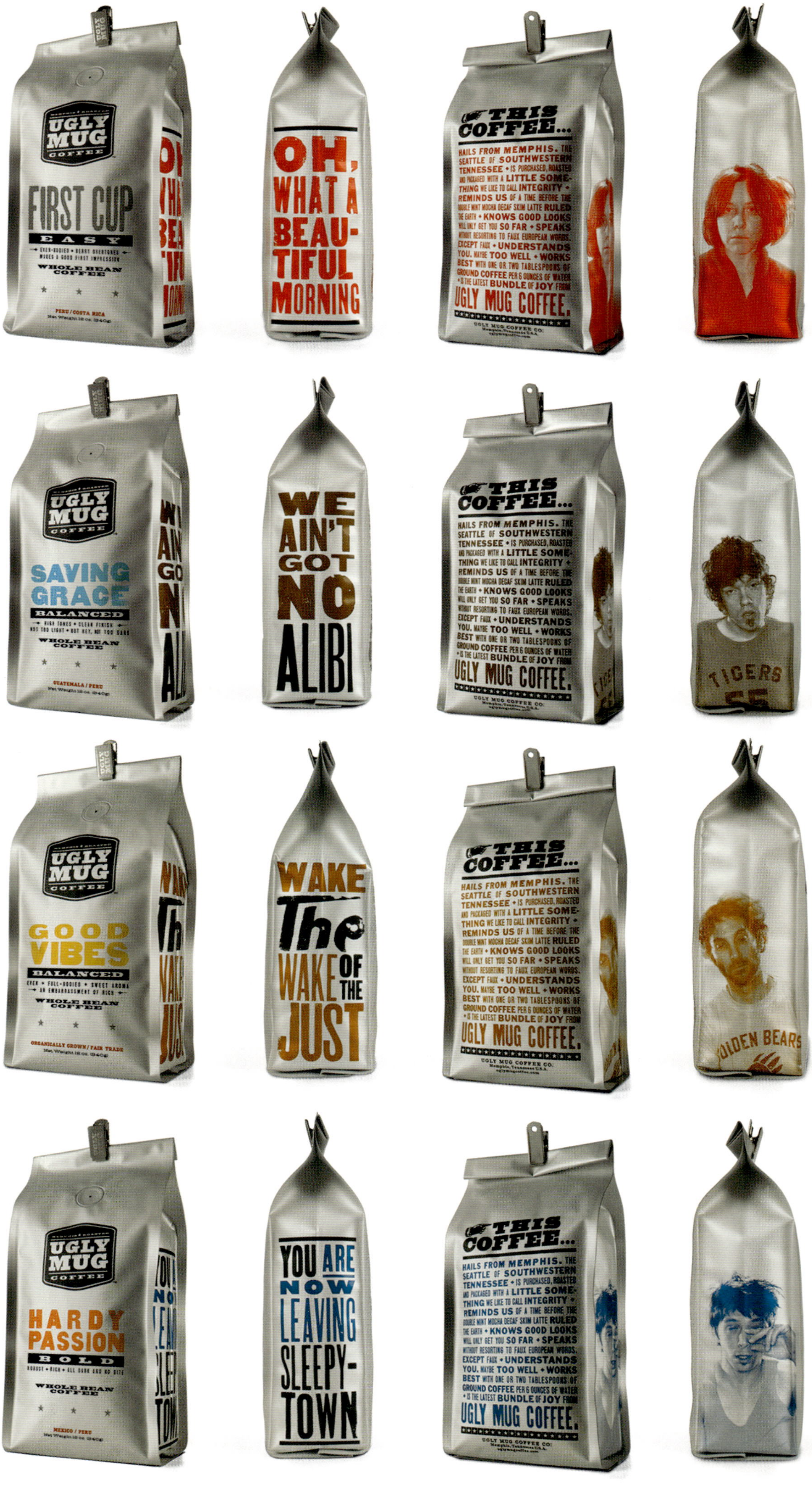
UGLY MUG COFFEE
FIRST CUP
EASY
EVEN-BODIED • BERRY OVERTONES MAKES A GOOD FIRST IMPRESSION
WHOLE BEAN COFFEE
PERU / COSTA RICA
Net Weight 12 oz. (340g)
OH, WHAT A BEAU-TIFUL MORNING
THIS COFFEE...
HAILS FROM MEMPHIS. THE SEATTLE OF SOUTHWESTERN TENNESSEE • IS PURCHASED, ROASTED AND PACKAGED WITH A LITTLE SOMETHING WE LIKE TO CALL INTEGRITY • REMINDS US OF A TIME BEFORE THE DOUBLE MINT MOCHA DECAF SKIM LATTE RULED THE EARTH • KNOWS GOOD LOOKS WILL ONLY GET YOU SO FAR • SPEAKS WITHOUT RESORTING TO FAUX EUROPEAN WORDS. EXCEPT FAUX • UNDERSTANDS YOU. MAYBE TOO WELL • WORKS BEST WITH ONE OR TWO TABLESPOONS OF GROUND COFFEE PER 6 OUNCES OF WATER • IS THE LATEST BUNDLE OF JOY FROM
UGLY MUG COFFEE.
UGLY MUG COFFEE CO.
UGLY MUG COFFEE
SAVING GRACE
BALANCED
HIGH TONES • CLEAN FINISH NOT TOO LIGHT • BUT HEY, NOT TOO DARK
WHOLE BEAN COFFEE
GUATEMALA / PERU
Net Weight 12 oz. (340g)
WE AIN'T GOT NO ALIBI
THIS COFFEE...
UGLY MUG COFFEE.
UGLY MUG COFFEE CO.
TIGERS
55
UGLY MUG COFFEE
GOOD VIBES
BALANCED
WHOLE BEAN COFFEE
ORGANICALLY GROWN / FAIR TRADE
Net Weight 12 oz. (340g)
WAKE The WAKE OF THE JUST
THIS COFFEE...
UGLY MUG COFFEE.
UGLY MUG COFFEE CO.
GOLDEN BEARS
UGLY MUG COFFEE
HARDY PASSION
BOLD
WHOLE BEAN COFFEE
MEXICO / PERU
YOU ARE NOW LEAVING SLEEPY-TOWN
THIS COFFEE...
UGLY MUG COFFEE.
UGLY MUG COFFEE CO.

Ugly Mug Coffee approached Young & Laramore to create branding that would differentiate them from the rest of the big-name coffee competitors. The result? Now, the best part of waking up is clever, engaging packaging with an irreverent, winking voice that leaves no room for confusion on coffee shop and grocery store shelves. Young & Laramore's Creative Director, Charlie Hopper, talks to Graphis about the pretty side of ugly.

A Q&A with Young & Laramore's Charlie Hopper

Give us the broad strokes. How did Y&L approach the Ugly Mug campaign?

As a chance to help a company that's spent a lot of time learning the best way to make a great product in the most ethical way charm customers into investing time and interest in a brand they'd never heard of.

What were the limitations of Ugly Mug Coffee's original branding?

Ugly Mug's previous branding did manage to indicate higher standards but wasn't true to the name. As we studied the situation, we realized two things: 1. The design and branding did not fully leverage the power of the name nor, we felt, did it adequately express the company's intense-yet-unceremonious approach; 2. On crowded grocery shelves, consumers were relying completely on the packaging to notice and learn about the brand. Capturing the tone from the get-go through whatever medium you encounter it—advertising, website, or, most importantly, packaging—was our only chance to communicate the essence of Ugly Mug: unpretentious premium coffee.

How did you resolve these issues?

We decided to use the package as our main vehicle for brand communications, and as the keystone to the voice and sensibility that extends through advertising and other materials. For the package, we examined everything, including the logo, and considered the messages sent by the typography, color choices, tone, paper and label material selection, along with the overall attention to detail, right down to the design on the metal clip that every bag has to help keep it tightly shut and fresh. We ended up treating every panel of the bag as an opportunity—including the photography of people in their most needy, pre-coffee Ugly Moments, the manifesto on the back, the 'ugly' remarks at every turn, and designed a system of randomization to give all the bags a slightly unique, hand-crafted feel.

What were your main goals?

To catch people's attention in a crowded arena (even outside the grocery, there are so many voices competing for your premium coffee interest) and keep it, and to get them to sample the beans. Then, as they get drawn in closer, to continually reward their interest with great design and provocative thinking. To communicate, at both the basest and most refined levels of communication, that this is a lively bunch of people roasting premium coffee. And our main clients, CEO Mark Ottinger and COO Tim Burleson, told us, 'Thank you for letting us be ourselves.'

Our primary goal was to get across effectively that Ugly Mug is an independent, willful, interesting company with a great product, something of an attitude, and the courtesy to provide an intellectual reward for sticking around long enough to hear us out. We think the graphic choice of dominant typography conveys, even to someone who can't read English, that this is a company with a strong point of view and a willingness to say interesting things boldly. So our primary goal was to make sure people didn't ignore this little company with the great attitude.

We hope people notice, whether they can articulate it, that a lot of coffee brands rely on hype, faux elitism, breathy earnestness or simple-but-in-the-end meaningless pretty pictures. Maybe the customer can't say why they chose Ugly Mug, but they feel good with it in the cart. And then, because this is a company that actually delivers on its promise of a premium product, the consumer is treated to a great cup of coffee.

What convinced you to go with a typographic approach?

Obviously, a package has a certain amount of raw factual info to convey through type. The painstaking art of letterpress, however, creates a signature graphic tone—first and foremost because letterpress is both unpretentious and hand-crafted. Ugly and beautiful, both. We worked with Yee-Haw Industries in Knoxville (which made a nice Tennessee connection to the Memphis-based Ugly Mug) to create the effect.

How does your branding work reflect Ugly Mug as a company?

They approach the category of premium coffee with enough intensity and seriousness to compete with other high-end specialty coffees, and also with the irreverence and good humor implied by the Ugly Mug Coffee name. We feel that there is a seriousness of intent in the sleek, well-proportioned design, and a whole lot of irreverence and good humor in the language and imagery.

Do you think this campaign speaks to a wide audience?

Yes. What's interesting is how disarming the humor is when set against the upscale feeling the highly designed typography conveys—both in packaging and advertising. Sophisticates feel they've encountered someone who understands premium coffee but has a refreshing lack of pretension; to the less sophisticated coffee drinkers who find themselves in the premium section, they sense kindred spirits.

It catches every sensibility, in a way. Though it seems aggressive, it's obviously being handled by people with refined tastes. Though the people handling it have refined tastes, their humor is obviously down-to-earth, and they recognize common truths about aspects of morning, coffee ritual, and personal moments where coffee plays a part.

How did you develop the text?

We chose topics that were in some way relevant to people who were in need of coffee: morning scenarios, sub-standard office coffee, etc. Then we simply considered how best to capture the views of a brand of coffee that's outspoken, thoughtful, unceremonious, seriously dedicated to getting the best product, and willing to speak irreverently.

Does the humor carry over to other areas of Ugly Mug's identity?

Yes. For example, every employee's business card features a set of descriptors that mirror the flavor descriptors on the bag—useful and funny, surprising and unconventional. As always, our goal is for every consumer touch point to further the brand.

Describe the other elements of your campaign.

We maintain the letterpress and tone of voice on everything from website to letterhead, from the magazine ad to the hot chocolate can.

How involved was the client?

We worked closely with them throughout. They were very trusting, and went through the process of discovery and research with us, then let us work. They were very gracious and very helpful and specific in their feedback when they had concerns.

Were there any other factors that helped shape your design?

Prior to making any creative decisions, we put this client through a process we call The Unlearning Curve. During that process, we work very hard to shed any preconceived notions by talking to various groups of consumers, employees, brokers and grocers, and by studying the competition. Learning the habits and behaviors first hand of the people we want to influence led us to conclude there was a niche available that Ugly Mug filled naturally.

What do you think your design brings to the product and the company?

We think it gives the company permission to be itself, and acknowledges that there is a market for people approaching the business the way they do. They needn't pretend to be artificially highbrow to appeal to the premium customer, nor fail to capture people's interest by being responsible and reserved. We think that the world is ready for a sincerely unpretentious, truly premium coffee.

Anything more we should know?

Few consumers really understand what makes a coffee roast better, or how fair trade operates (Ugly Mug has rejected conventional fair trade approaches and designed their own system, which they feel is much more fair, but it's extremely difficult to explain quickly). Consumers tend to operate on a combination of superstition, habit, and a belief in a brand's promise. We believe that communicating a lively sensibility with an attention to detail and very high standards gets across more than any lecture-sounding copy about how the roast is performed; it gets across more than any promise of freshness or description of taste. The belief on which the new Ugly Mug campaign rests is that a company that has high standards yet an unpretentious approach will keep those standards and that approach no matter what activity they're doing—roasting coffee, or doing ads.

For more information on Ugly Mug, visit www.uglymugcoffee.com.

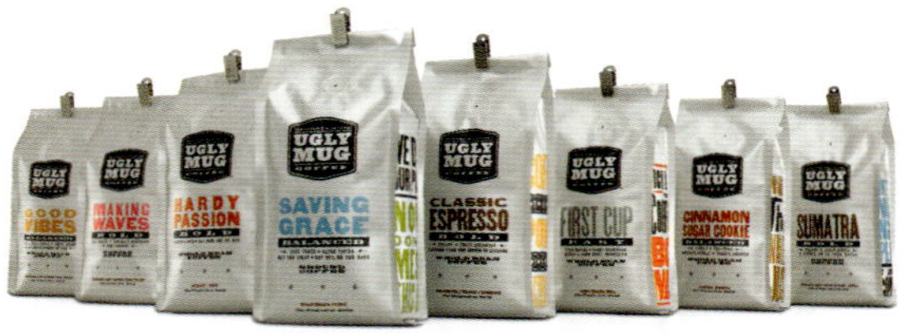

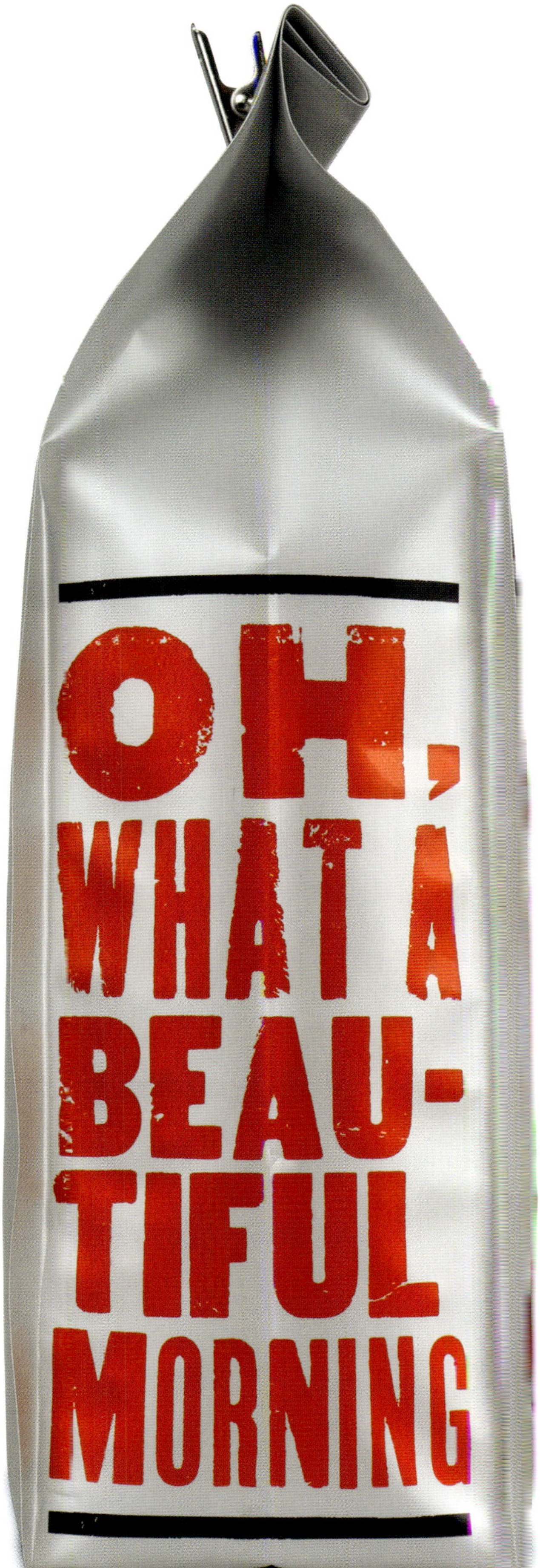
OH,
WHAT A
BEAU-
TIFUL
MORNING

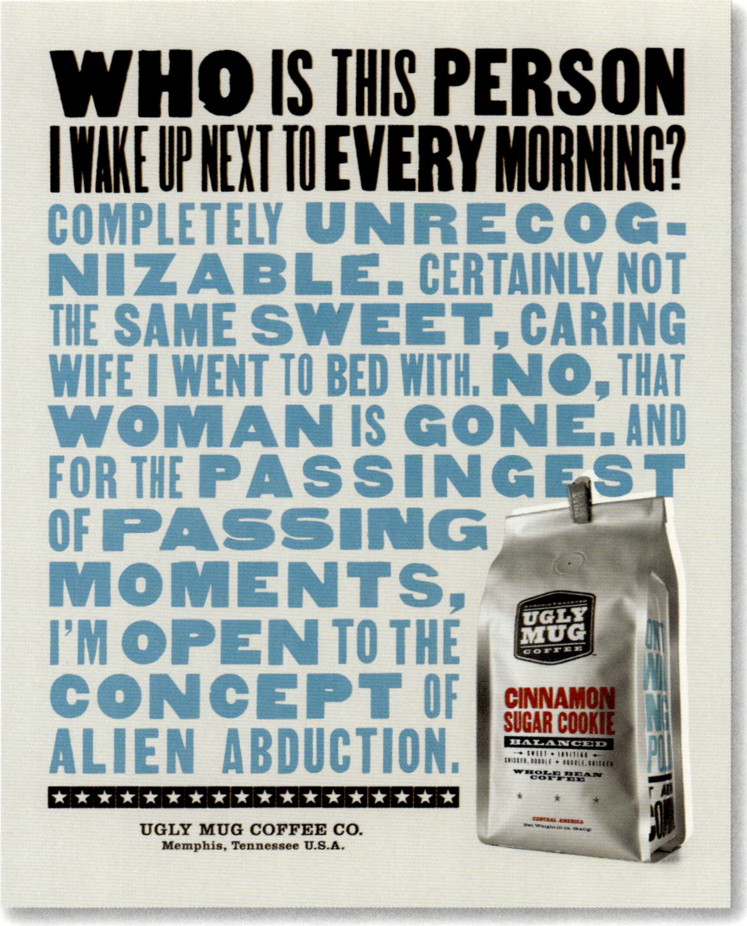

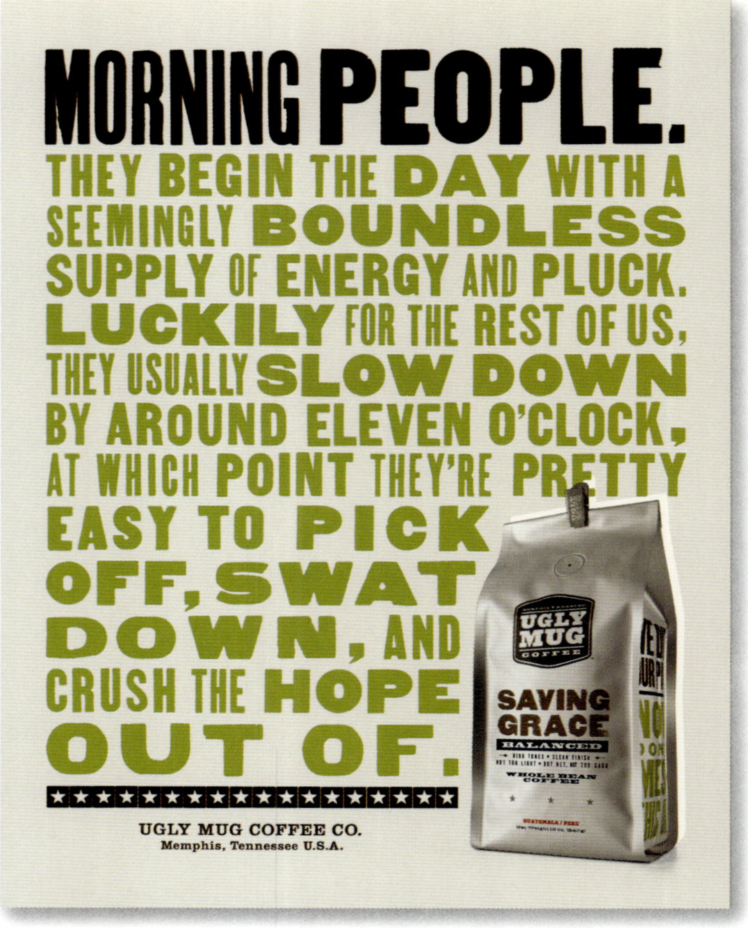

"Thanks to Y&L's branding work, we are forecasted to double our sales over last year, and our Q3 and Q4 forecast has us roasting more than we did all last year."

Tim Burleson, *Chief Operating Officer, Ugly Mug Coffee*

Young & Laramore Advertising

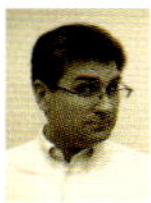

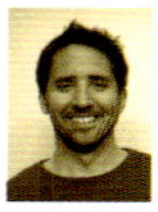

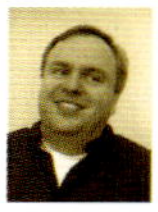

Founded by creatives, Young & Laramore is an independent, full-service advertising agency based in Indianapolis.
407 Fulton Street, Indianapolis, IN 46202
317.264.8000 / www.youngandlaramore.com

Charlie Hopper, Principal & Creative Director (pictured left): Confusion on the part of a small Midwestern ad agency president in 1984 led to Charlie's career in advertising, when he was mistakenly approved for an internship he had not applied for. Now a Principal and Creative Director at Young & Laramore, Charlie Hopper has worked there for 16 years—though not continuously, having interrupted his tenure for stints at TBWA Chiat/Day and Martin/Williams.

His work has appeared multiple times over two decades in various publications (*Graphis*, *Communication Arts*, *Lurzer's International Archive*) and shows (One Club, New York Art Director's). He's led advertising classes, judged shows such as the New England Hatch Awards, won national awards for songwriting, and had so-called humor published in *Creativity*, in the collection *Mountain Man Dance Moves* and on *McSweeneys.net*.

Trevor Williams, Associate Creative Director & Art Director (center): Born to excel in a career that combines discipline, insight and junkets, Trevor began his career working on a number of iconic brands first at Valentine Radford, and later at the fabled erstwhile D'Arcy. Since arriving at Young & Laramore in 2002, he's helped create more iconic brands—some from scratch. Recently he has led the development and launch of Here There Be Monsters, a design/digital division of Young & Laramore. His work has been honored by *Graphis*, The One Show, *Communication Arts*, Effies, *Lurzer's International Archive*, Mobius, London International and New York Festivals. When not at work he travels nationally to compete in volleyball tournaments, compensating for a genetically determined 5'8" stature with strategy and cunning.

Bryan Judkins, Associate Creative Director & Writer (right): Bryan first began writing around the age of five. Years later, he dropped out of college to perform improv comedy at an event across the street from the final exam he was supposed to be at, and eventually he found work creating advertising. Lured away from his natural habitat of Wisconsin, Bryan began working at Young & Laramore Advertising in 2005. Recently, he has led the development and launch of Here There Be Monsters, a design/digital division of Young & Laramore. His work has appeared in *Graphis*, *Communication Arts*, The One Show, *Lurzer's International Archive*, and Effies, among many other award shows and publications. Bryan is pleasant to be around and smells faintly of fresh photocopies.

Credits
Client: Ugly Mug Coffee
Agency: Young & Laramore Advertising
Creative Director: Charlie Hopper
ACD / Copywriter: Bryan Judkins
ACD / Art Director: Trevor Williams
Designer: Yee-Haw Industries
Strategy: Tom Denari, Margit Fawbush, Christian Mehall
Photographers: Harold Lee, Miller, Gary Sparks

****Additional Credits for Identity:***
Designers: Jonathan McGlothin, Elijah Schroeder, Yee-Haw Industries
(page 82-83) Ugly Mug Coffee images photographed by Uriaha Foust.
(page 82) From left, headshots of Charlie Hopper, Trevor Williams and Bryan Judkins photographed by Uriaha Foust.
All Ugly Mug Coffee images courtesy of Young & Laramore.

THIS COFFEE...

HAILS FROM MEMPHIS, THE SEATTLE OF SOUTHWESTERN TENNESSEE ◆ SHOOTS STRAIGHT, BUT KNOWS HOW TO TALK ITS WAY OUT OF A FIGHT ◆ CAN PROP TIRED EYES OPEN BETTER THAN TOOTHPICKS ◆ TASTES LIKE COFFEE, NOT SOME KIND OF CANDY CORN VANILLA FANTASY WORLD ◆ HELPS YOU GROW BIG AND STRONG ◆ WILL TOUGHEN UP YOUR SELF-IMAGE ◆ CAVES TO NO MAN ◆ CAME FROM MEMPHIS WITH A DOLLAR AND A DREAM ◆ IS RICH ENOUGH TO PLANT FLOWERS IN ◆ REMINDS US OF A TIME BEFORE THE DOUBLE MINT MOCHA DECAF SKIM LATTE RULED THE EARTH ◆ IS ROASTED IN THE CRADLE OF ROCK 'N ROLL, WHERE OTIS AND ELVIS GOT THEIR START ◆ ISN'T PICKED BY SOME GUY NAMED JUAN WITH A SOMBRERO AND A DONKEY...IT'S PICKED BY RAUL. RAUL DRIVES A SECOND-HAND PLYMOUTH AND UNDERSTANDS YOUR NEED FOR FINE COFFEE ◆ IS MEANT TO BE DRANK, NOT "EXPERIENCED" ◆ HAS KNOWN MORAL INDIGNATION ◆ IS THE ORIGINAL ENERGY DRINK ◆ NOT ONLY WAKES YOU UP, BUT SLAPS YOU AROUND A BIT, JUST TO MAKE SURE YOU DON'T SNEAK BACK TO BED ◆ IS READY TO HEAR YOUR CONFESSION ◆ KNOWS GOOD LOOKS WILL ONLY GET YOU SO FAR ◆ IS OUR GIFT TO YOU ◆ WAS PURCHASED, ROASTED AND PACKAGED WITH A LITTLE SOMETHING WE LIKE TO CALL INTEGRITY ◆ SPEAKS WITHOUT RESORTING TO FAUX EUROPEAN WORDS. EXCEPT FAUX ◆ IS AT THE FOREFRONT OF THE MUTINY ◆ BREWS DARK AND RICH LIKE THE FERTILE SOIL OF THE MISSISSIPPI RIVER ◆ IS MORE ROCKABILLY THAN POP ◆ CAN FLY A CROP DUSTER LOWER AND FASTER THAN ANYONE HERE ◆ IS ROASTED WITH AN EYE TOWARDS GREATNESS ◆ MUST NEVER FALL INTO THE WRONG HANDS ◆ DOESN'T SO MUCH PERCOLATE AS IT DOES RABBLE-ROUSE ◆ LEAVES BEHIND A TRAIL OF BLACK GROUNDS AND BROKEN DREAMS ◆ INSPIRES PRESIDENTS AND MADMEN ◆ IS LIKE A LULLABY IN REVERSE ◆ UNDERSTANDS YOU. MAYBE TOO WELL ◆ IS YOUR FAVORITE COFFEE'S FAVORITE COFFEE ◆ ◆ INFUSES THOSE WHO DRINK IT WITH SUPERHUMAN VIGILANCE ◆ TWANGS LIKE A STEEL GUITAR ◆ RIDES TALL IN THE SADDLE ◆ BRINGS STRENGTH TO THE WEAK OF SPIRIT AND HOPE TO THOSE WHO TRULY NEED IT.

★★★★★★★★★★★★★★★★★★★★★★★★★★★★★★★★★★★

UGLY MUG COFFEE CO. Memphis, Tennessee U.S.A.

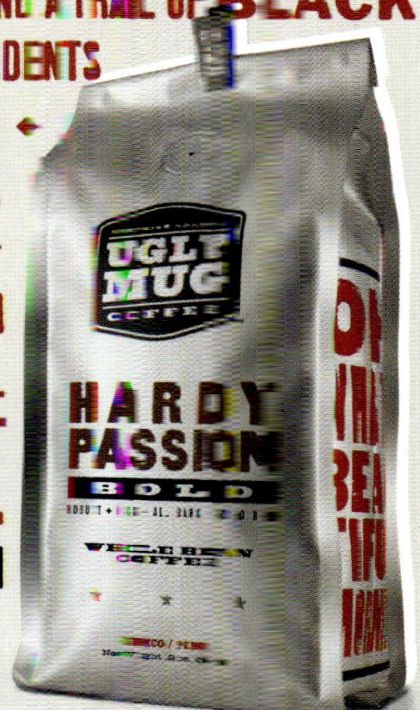

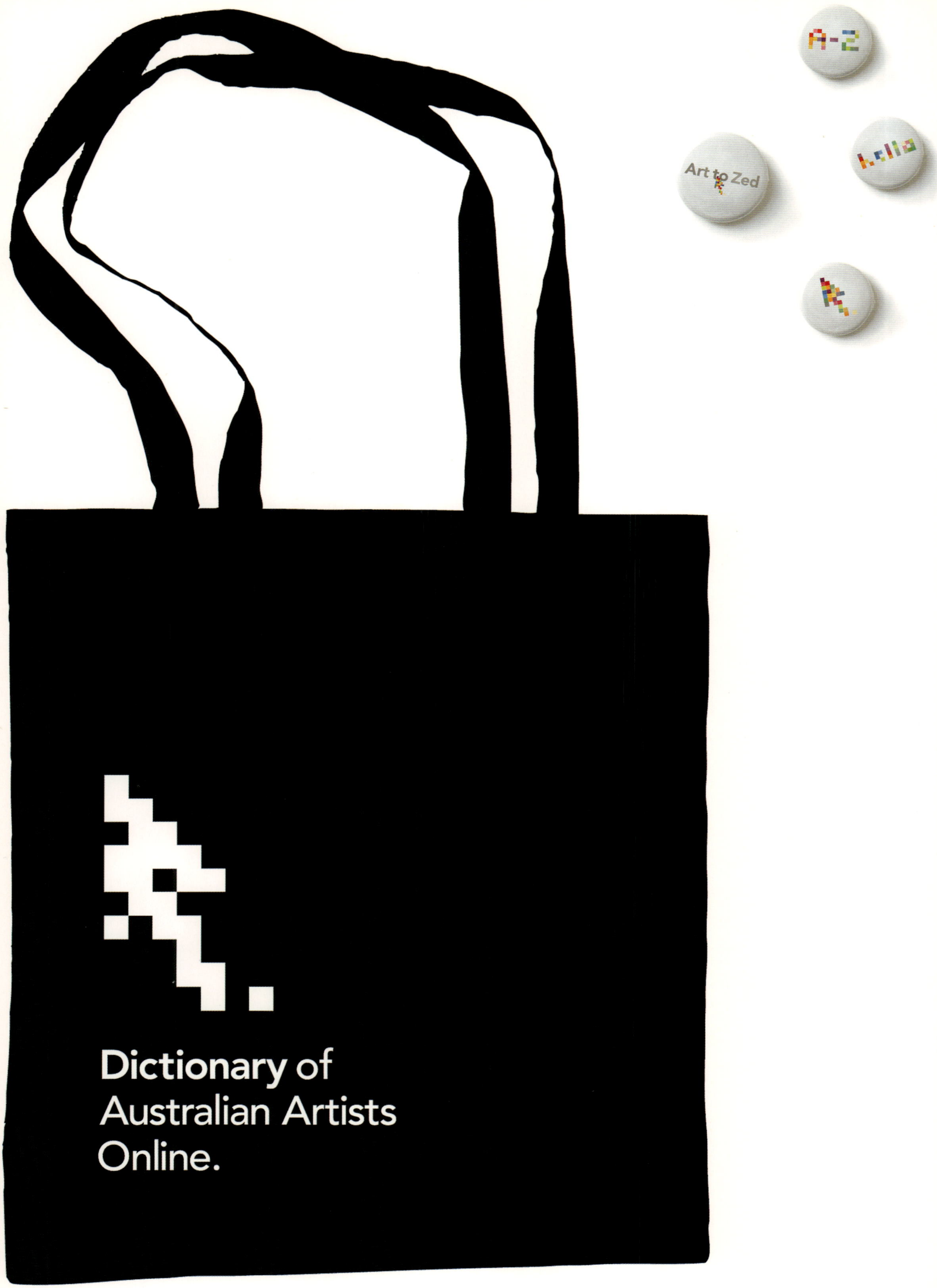
A-Z
Art to Zed
Dictionary of
Australian Artists
Online.

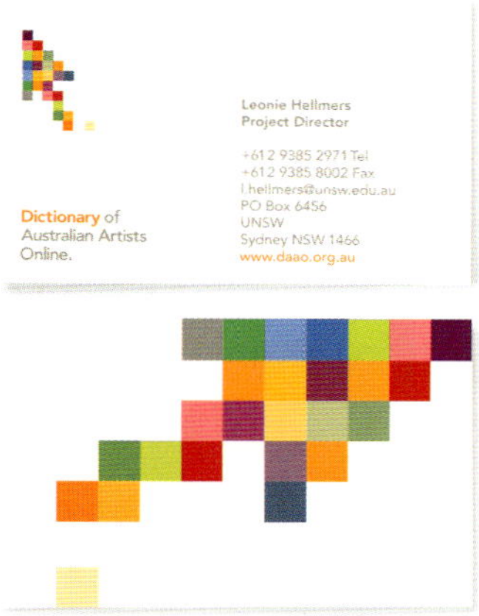
Leonie Hellmers
Project Director
+612 9385 2971 Tel
+612 9385 8002 Fax
l.hellmers@unsw.edu.au
PO Box 6456
UNSW
Sydney NSW 1466
www.daao.org.au
Dictionary of
Australian Artists
Online.

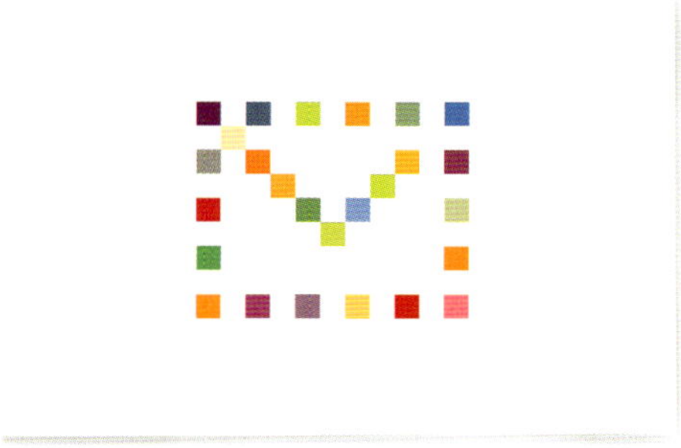

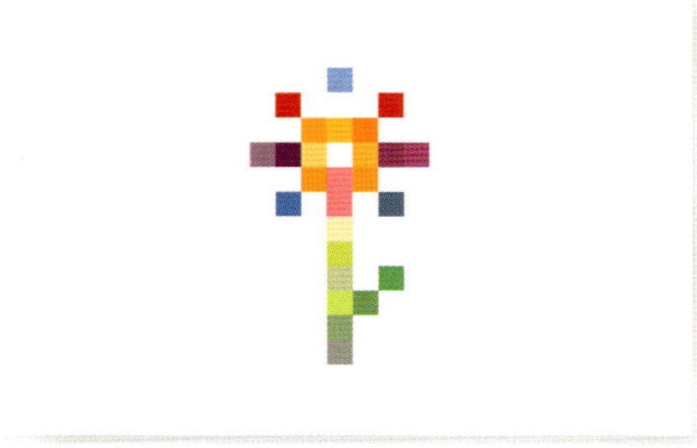

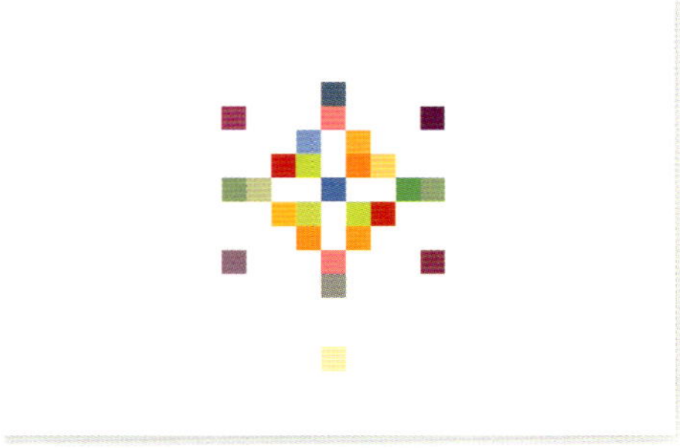

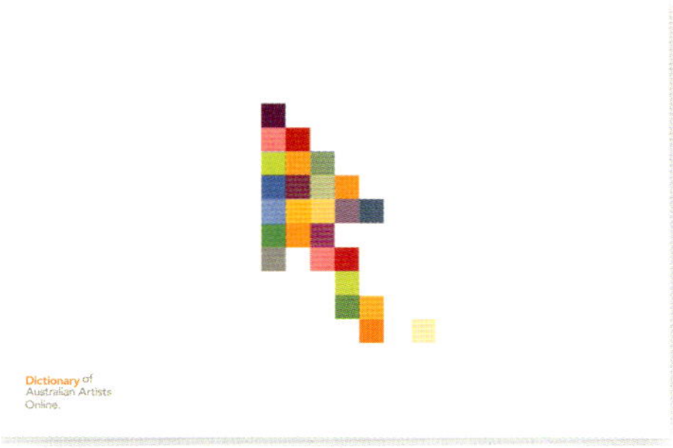
Dictionary of
Australian Artists
Online.

Dictionary of
Australian Artists
Online.
+612 9385 8256 Tel
+612 9385 8002 Fax
daao@unsw.edu.au
PO Box 6456
UNSW
Sydney NSW 1466
www.daao.org.au
Australian Government
Australian Research Council
Supported by the Australian
Research Council and led by UNSW

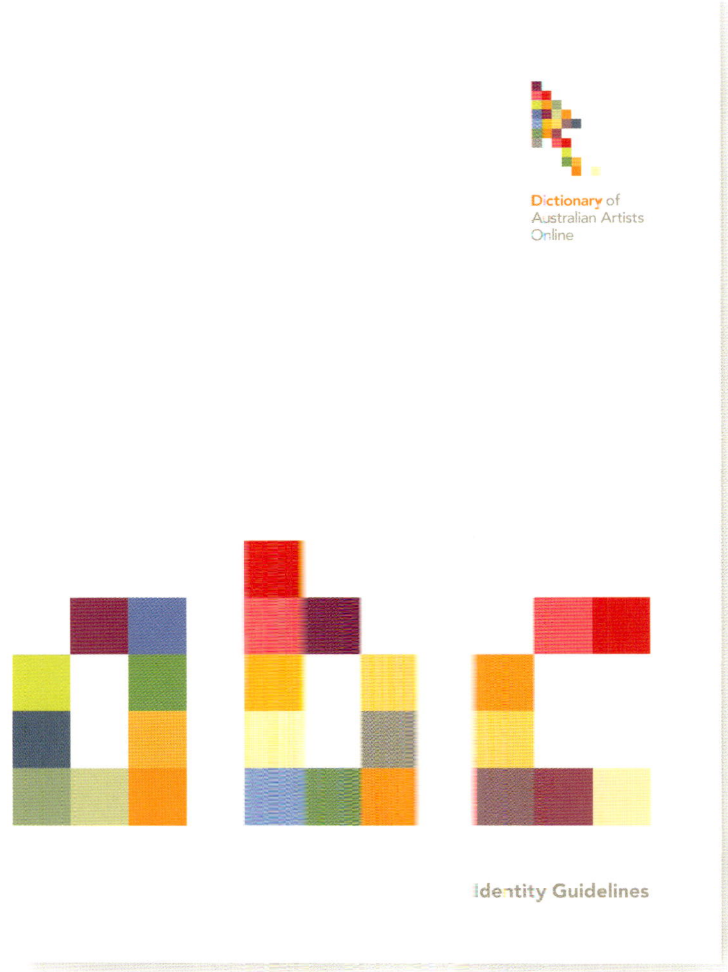
Dictionary of
Australian Artists
Online
Identity Guidelines

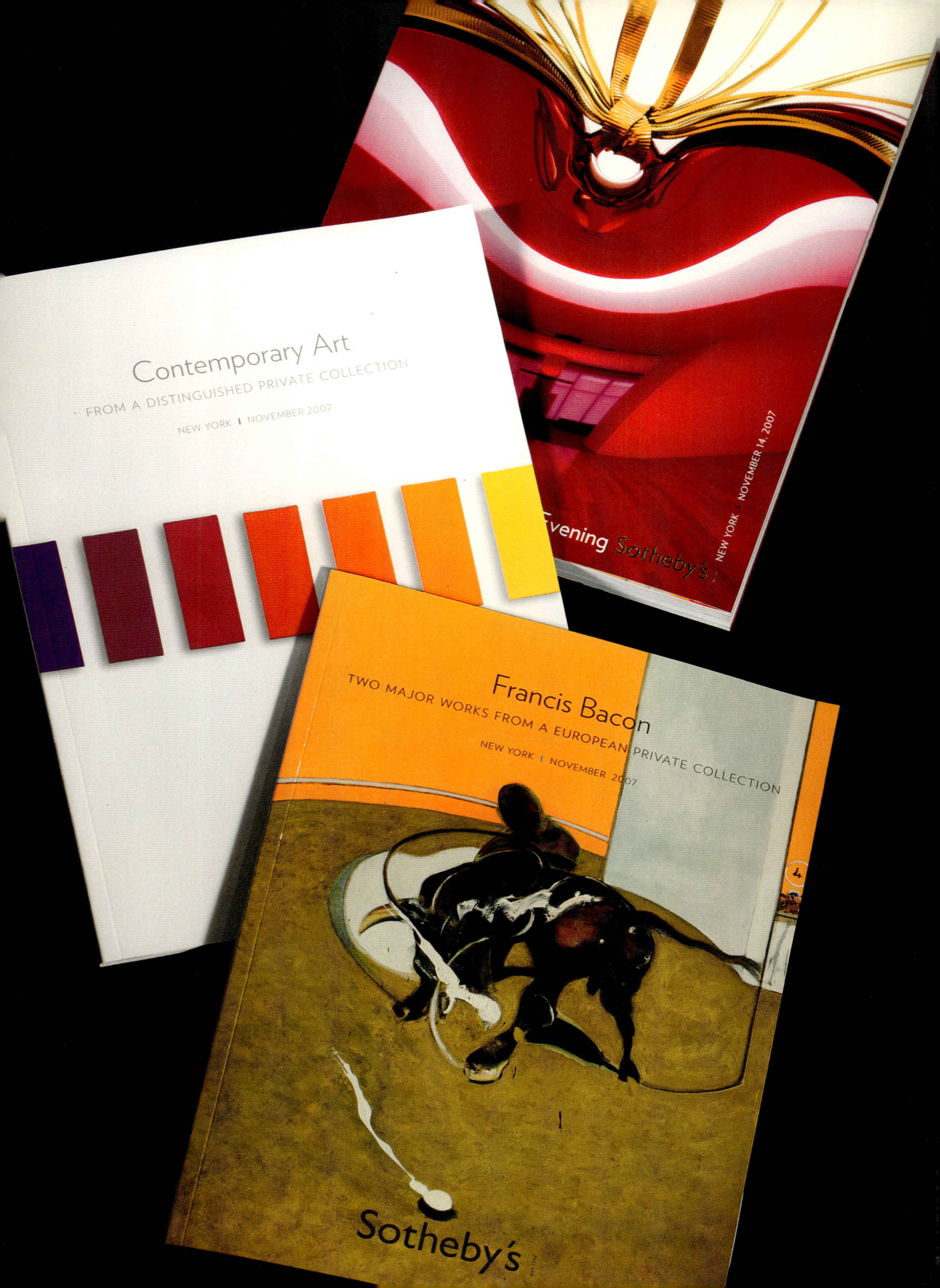

Contemporary Art
FROM A DISTINGUISHED PRIVATE COLLECTION
NEW YORK | NOVEMBER 2007
Evening Sotheby's
NEW YORK | NOVEMBER 14, 2007
Francis Bacon
TWO MAJOR WORKS FROM A EUROPEAN PRIVATE COLLECTION
NEW YORK | NOVEMBER 2007
Sotheby's

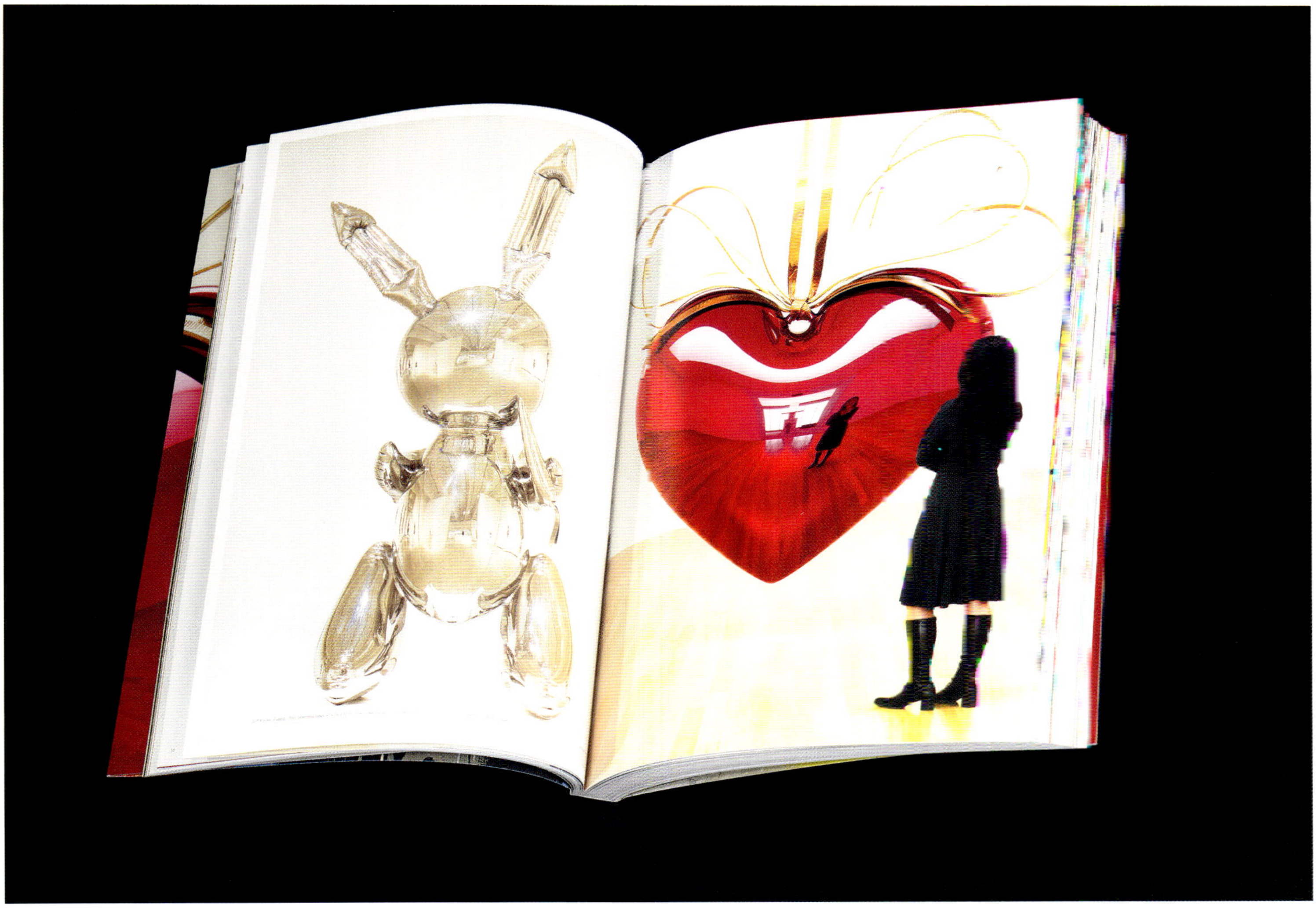

Sample page of Sotheby's Branding Guide

Standard size catalogue 210 x 270mm / 8.25 x 10.625″

15mm
.591″

Terry O'Neill
Brigitte Bardot, 1971
ESTIMATE £4,000-6,000

12mm
.472″

Caption can move freely for maximum legibility according to the featured art.

12mm
.472″

Background colour.
If image is squared up the background colour to the page can be
Black
White
Sotheby's Super Black (c100, m0, y0, k100)
Sotheby's Dove Grey (c3, m0, y0, k7)
No other colours allowed

External ads only.
Copyright line can move up and down or to the right trim. Try to stay away from logo and text at foot of ad.

68mm
2.68″

Sotheby's EST. 1744

14mm
.551″

DISTANCE REMAINS LOCKED

Photographs

AUCTION IN LONDON 13 MAY 2008 | ENQUIRIES +44 (0)20 7293 5137 | SOTHEBYS.COM

40mm
1.575″

8mm
.315″

Logo is locked in position.
Always centres S to s.
Prints 15%, 35%, 50%, 65%, 75% or 85% black.
Use whichever is most appropriate, but never black or white.
Logo never same colour as text beneath it.

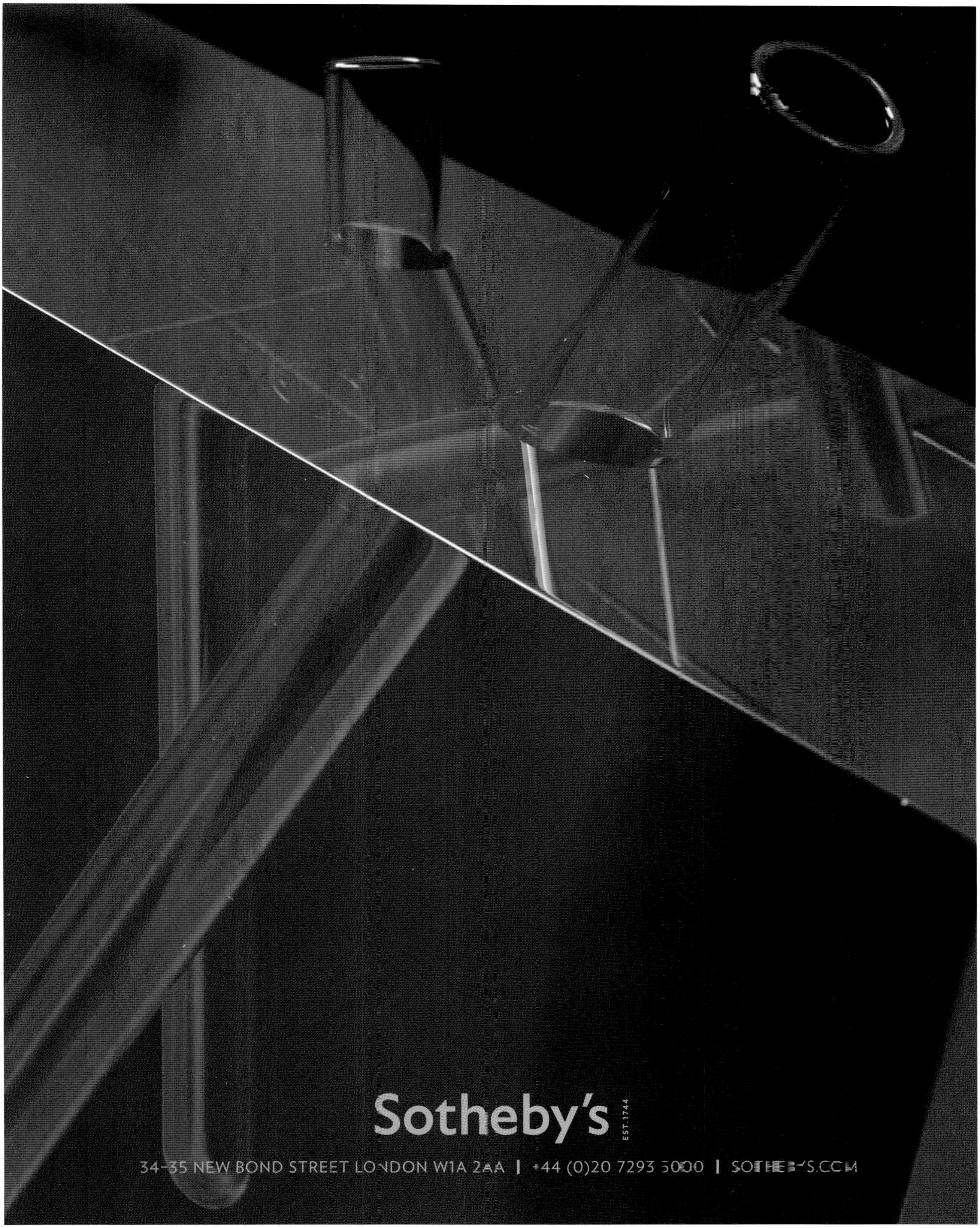

Sotheby's (this spread)

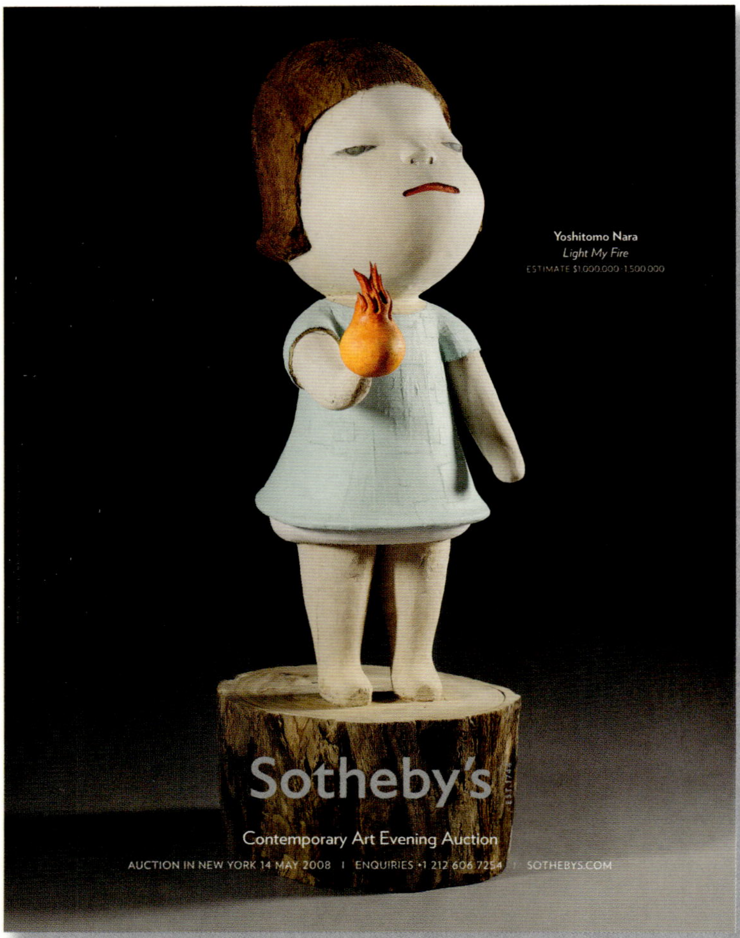

Yoshitomo Nara
Light My Fire
ESTIMATE $1,000,000-1,500,000
Sotheby's
EST 1744
Contemporary Art Evening Auction
AUCTION IN NEW YORK 14 MAY 2008 | ENQUIRIES +1 212 606 7254 | SOTHEBYS.COM

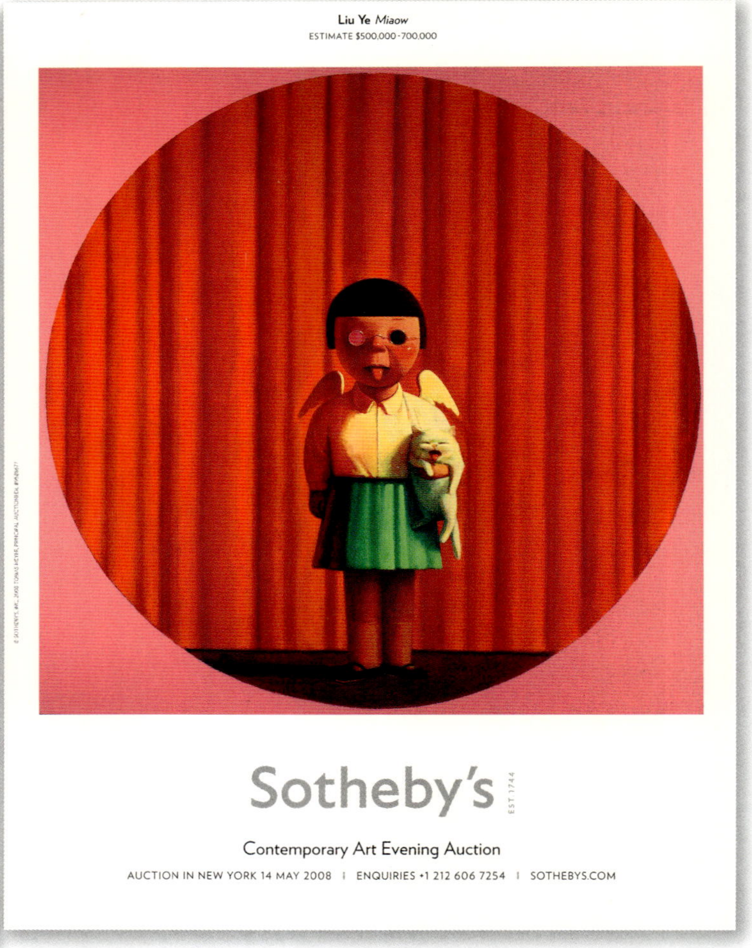

Liu Ye Miaow
ESTIMATE $500,000-700,000
Sotheby's
EST 1744
Contemporary Art Evening Auction
AUCTION IN NEW YORK 14 MAY 2008 | ENQUIRIES +1 212 606 7254 | SOTHEBYS.COM

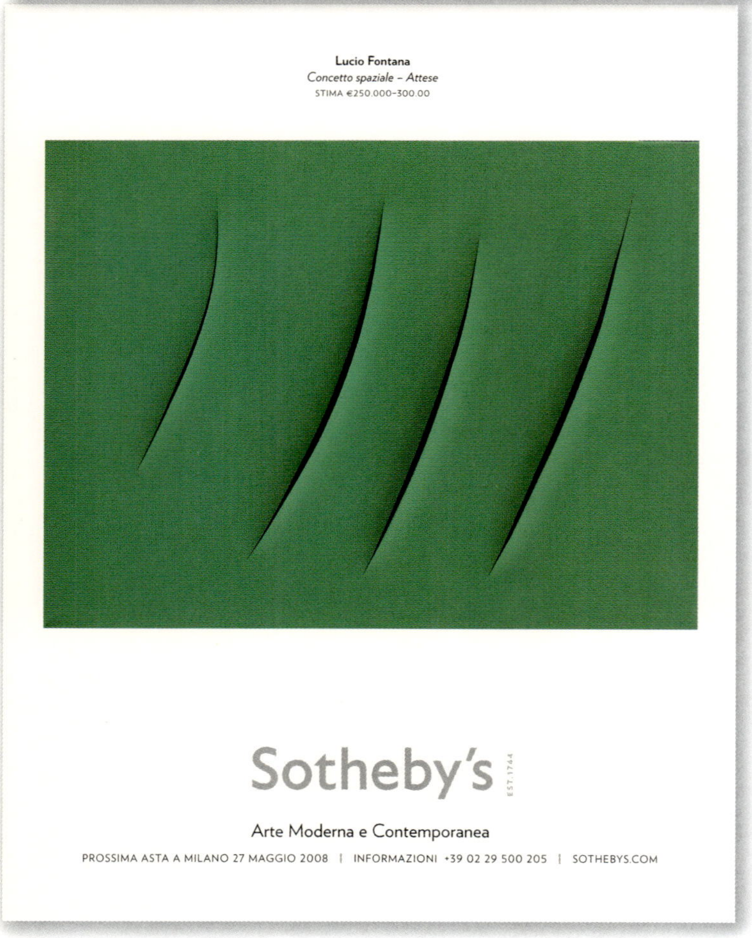

Lucio Fontana
Concetto spaziale – Attese
STIMA €250.000-300.00
Sotheby's
EST 1744
Arte Moderna e Contemporanea
PROSSIMA ASTA A MILANO 27 MAGGIO 2008 | INFORMAZIONI +39 02 29 500 205 | SOTHEBYS.COM

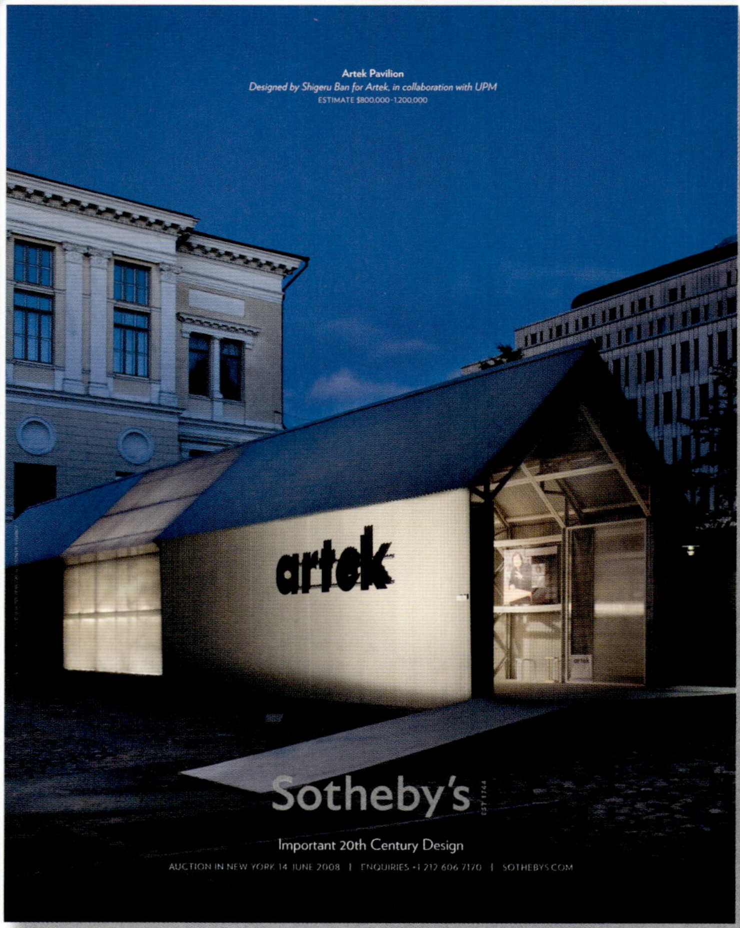

Artek Pavilion
Designed by Shigeru Ban for Artek, in collaboration with UPM
ESTIMATE $800,000-1,200,000
artek
Sotheby's
EST 1744
Important 20th Century Design
AUCTION IN NEW YORK 14 JUNE 2008 | ENQUIRIES +1 212 606 7170 | SOTHEBYS.COM

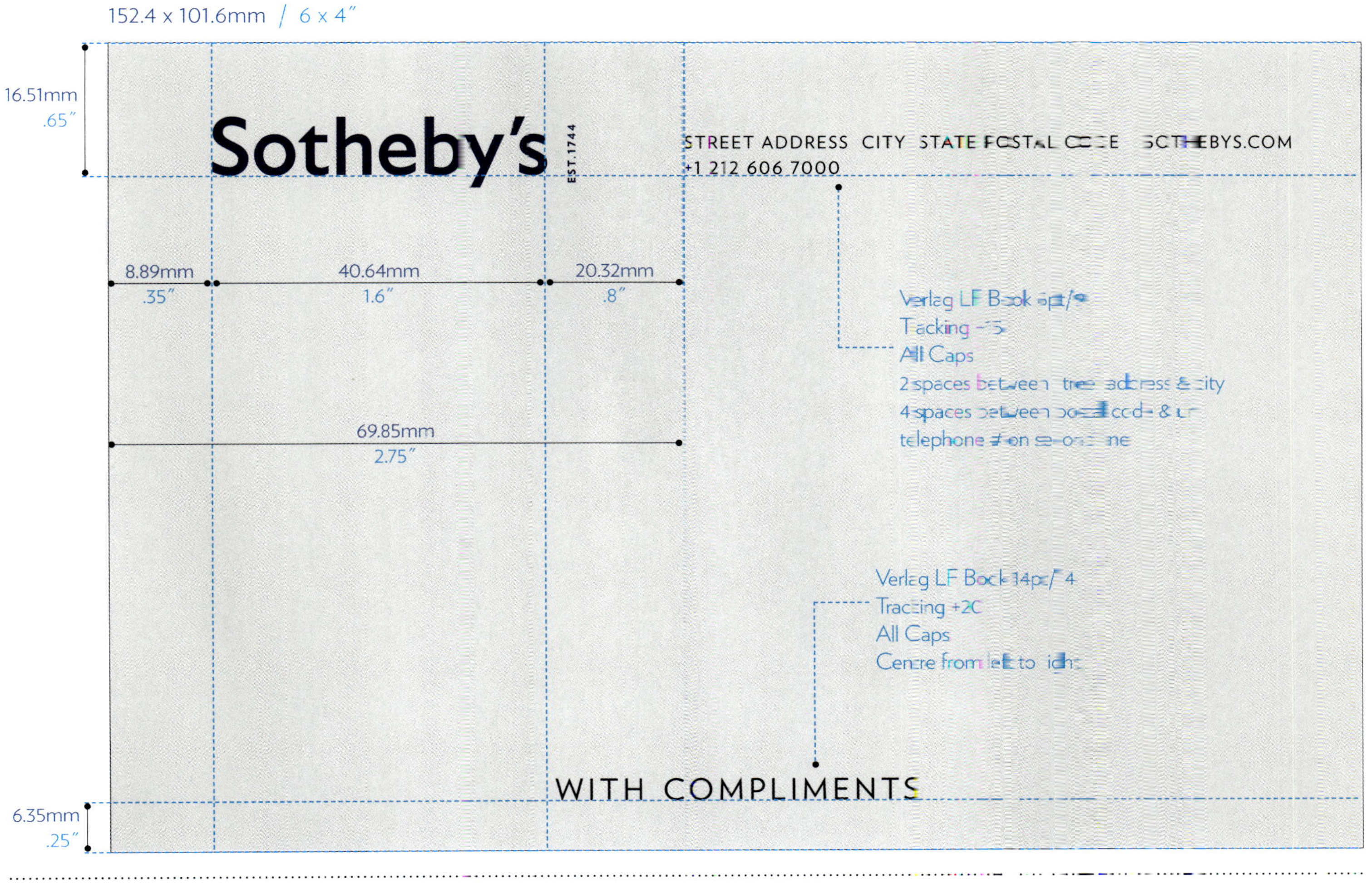

Part of Sotheby's Branding Manual Text

Sotheby's Advertising General Guidelines for all Adverts

All Sotheby's advertising must follow the same guidelines. This is essential in order to achieve consistency and a strong corporate look.

Logo

- Always to be positioned Centred S to s.
- On catalogue ad templates the logo is locked in place and must never be moved. This is to ensure absolute brand consistency and accurate alignment across a series of ads in the back of the same catalogue.
- Space between logo and information below is also locked to ensure consistency.

Text

- Must follow typographic guidelines at all times. Please see typefaces used. Type faces used.
- The aim is for the ads to look beautiful, and "premium" through their simplicity. Therefore the information needs to be kept to the absolute minimum.
- IMPORTANT – No expert names are to be included in Enquiries-phone number only. No personal emails – however a departmental email is acceptable.
- No + before phone numbers.
- No addresses for London or NY ads.
- Title and auction information copy always remain together grouped and centred beneath the logo never separated. This means the information is very clearly conveyed to the reader.
- Caption can be positioned where appropriate for maximum legibility. If image squares up logo should centre above it.

Images

- Ideally should bleed, but all text must be clearly legible.
- Can square up. If so then position under caption and align centre. See specs for acceptable page background colours.
- Can be cut out. If so, may benefit from the addition of a drop shadow.
- As these adverts, particularly those in external publications, have compete with many others, the photography must be simply fantastic. Please use glamorous shots for all three dimensional objects, ensuring great lighting, atmosphere and a premium feel. Also try to use a dynamic crop.
- The preference is for each ad to feature a single image created a stunning visual corporate look. However, if there is a strong business need for an advert to feature more than one image the pieces must work well together and the advert still look beautifully designed.

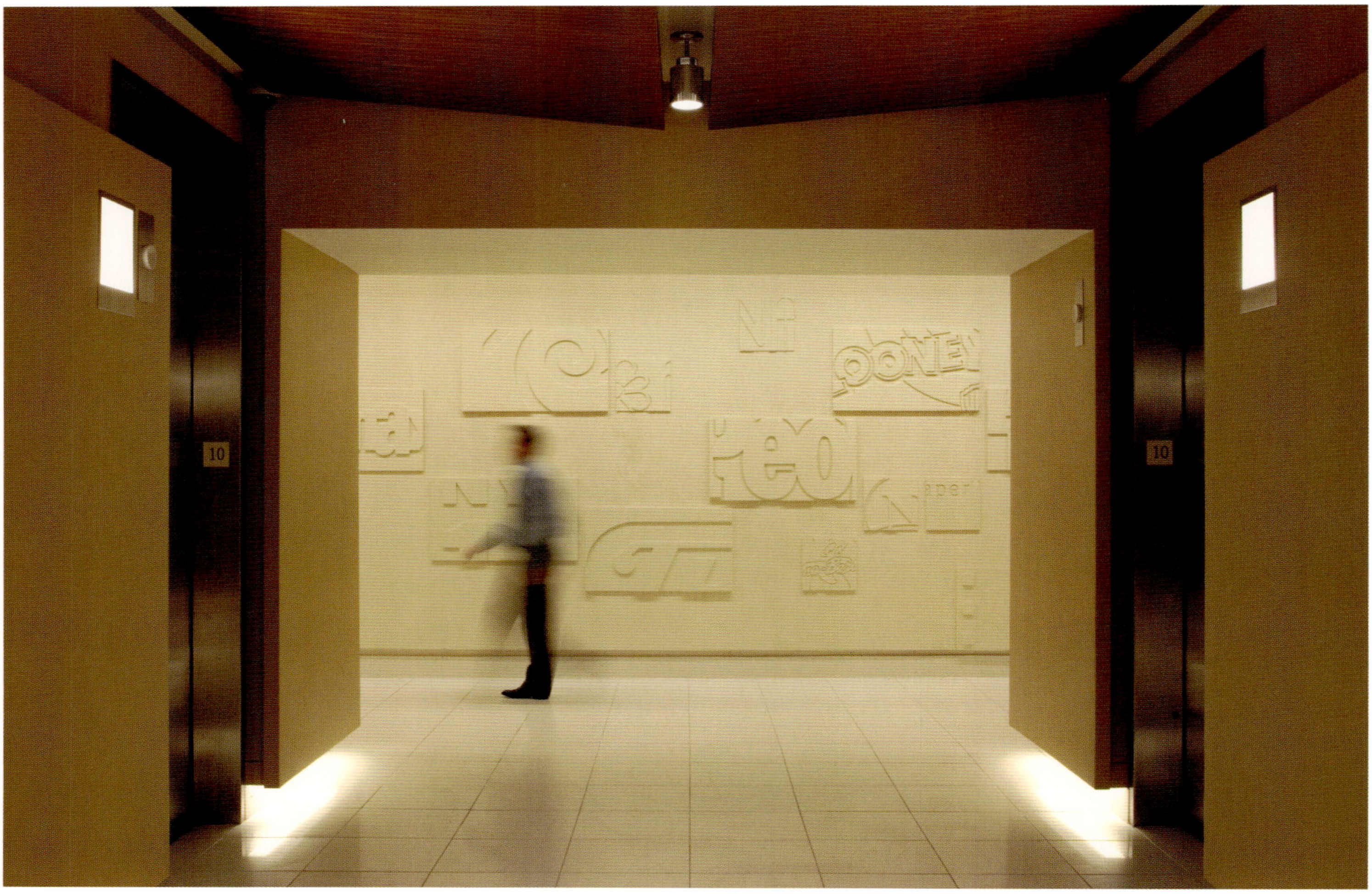

inside CNN

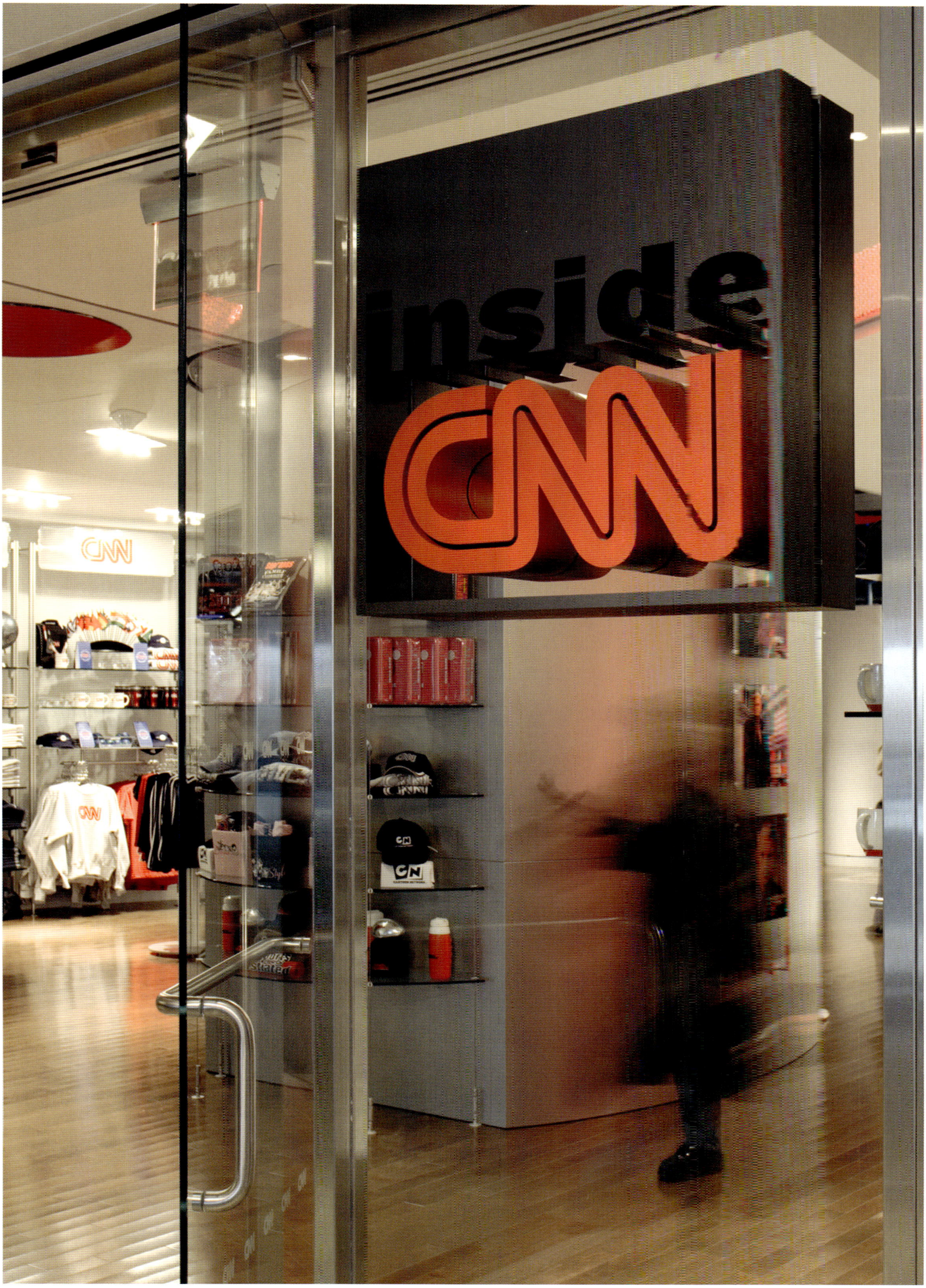
inside
CNN

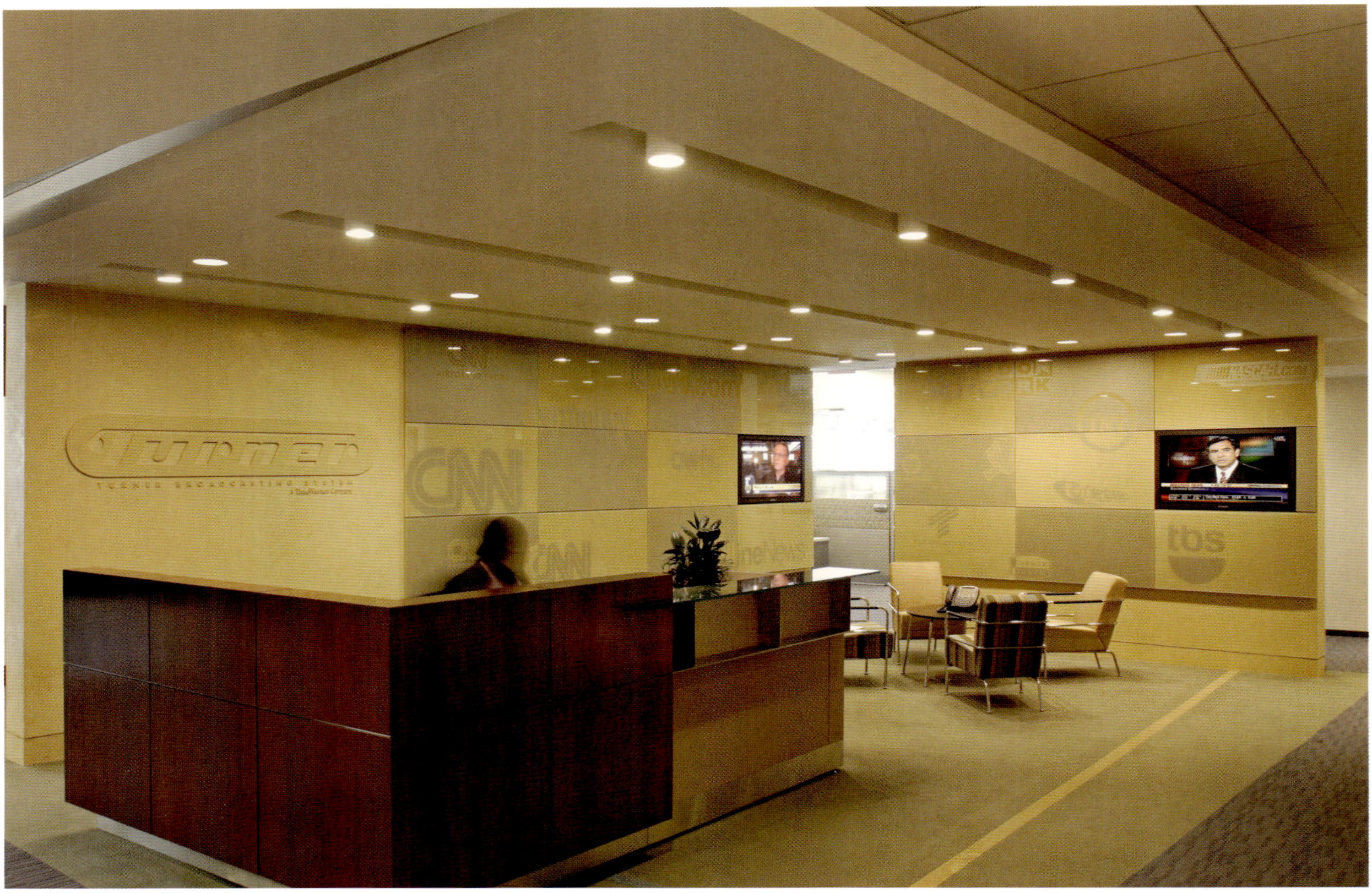
Turner
CNN
tbs

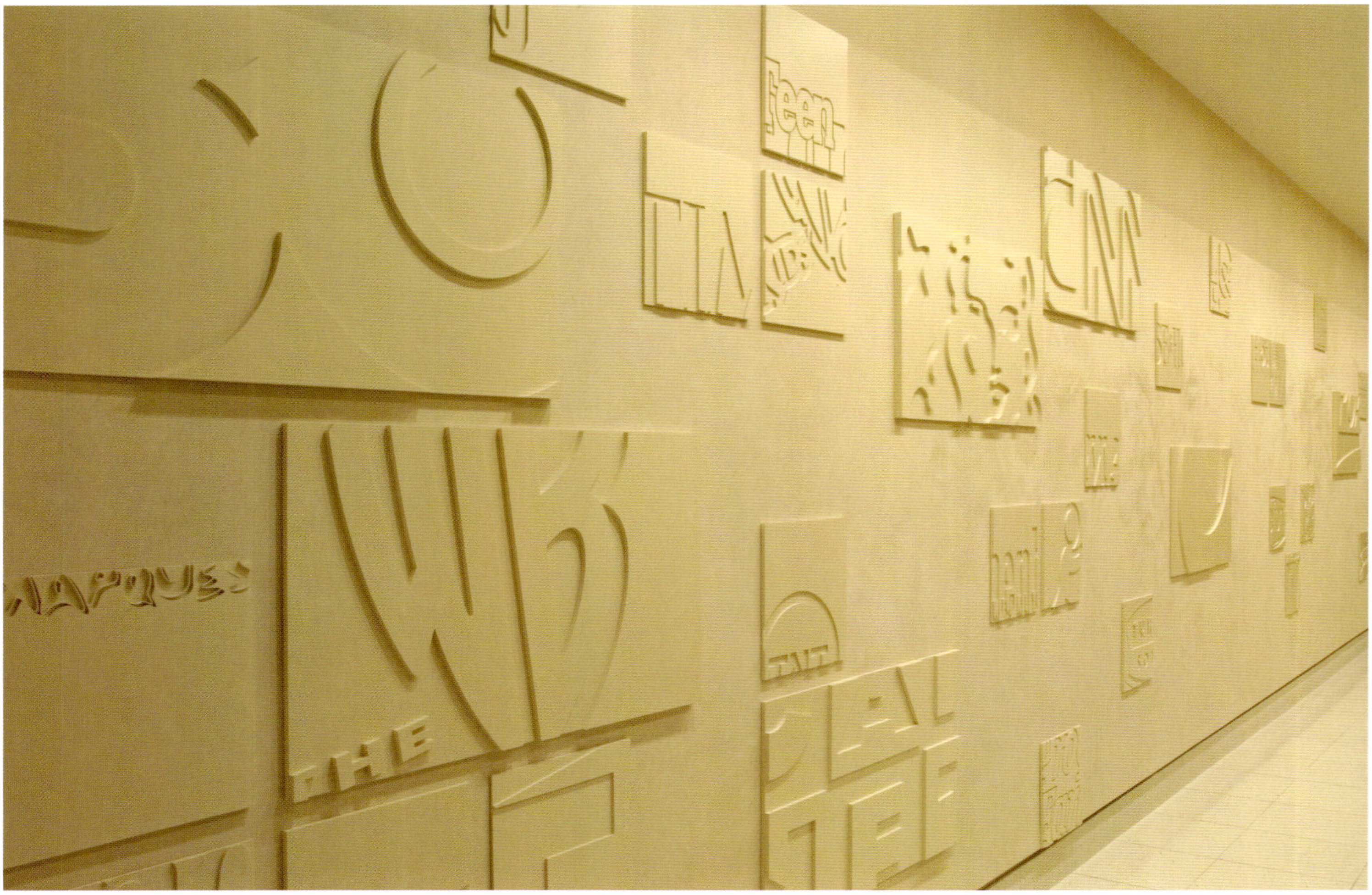
THE WB
CNN

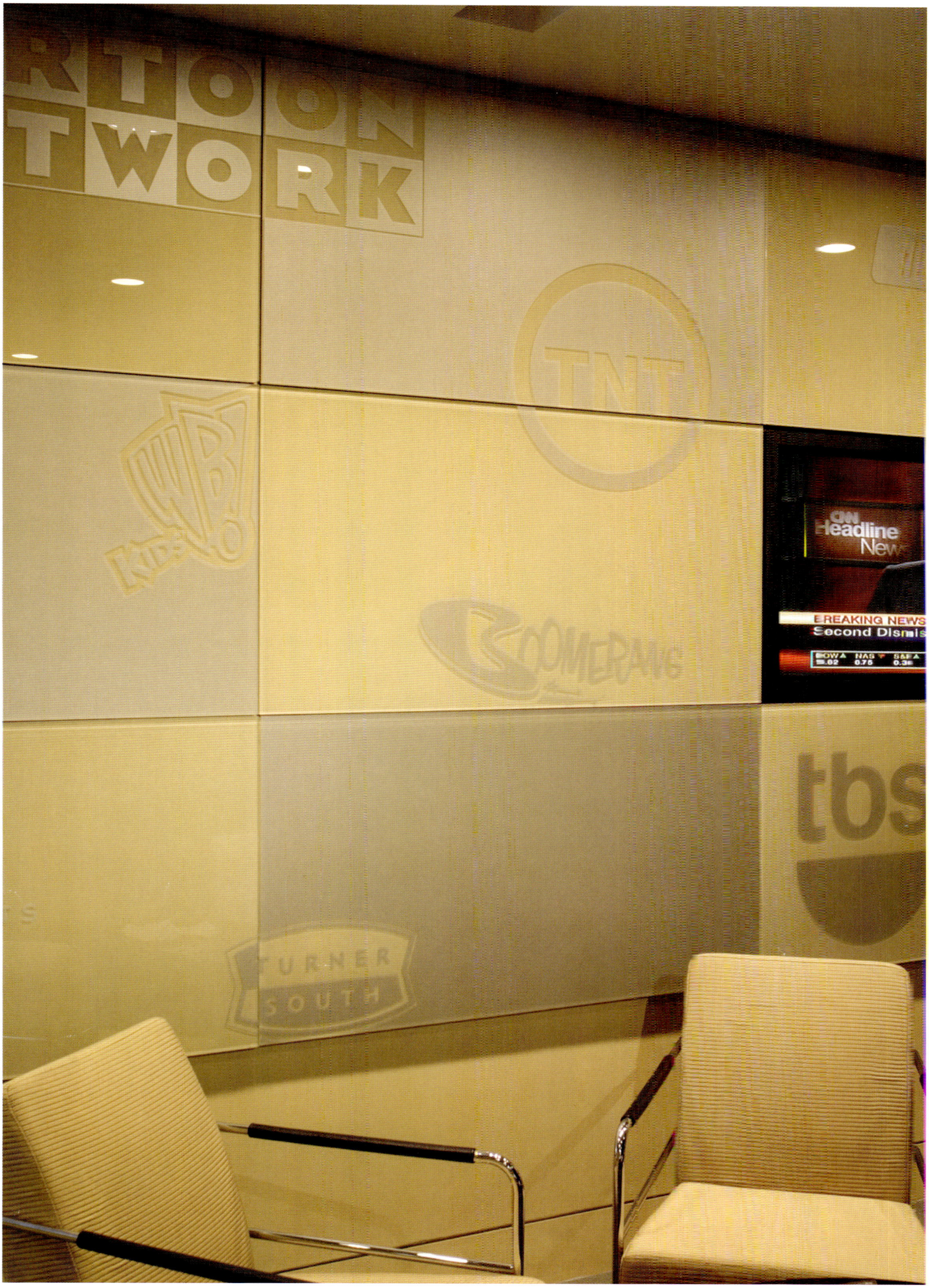
TWORK
TNT
KIDS
Headline News
BREAKING NEWS
Second Dismis
BOOMERANG
tbs
TURNER SOUTH

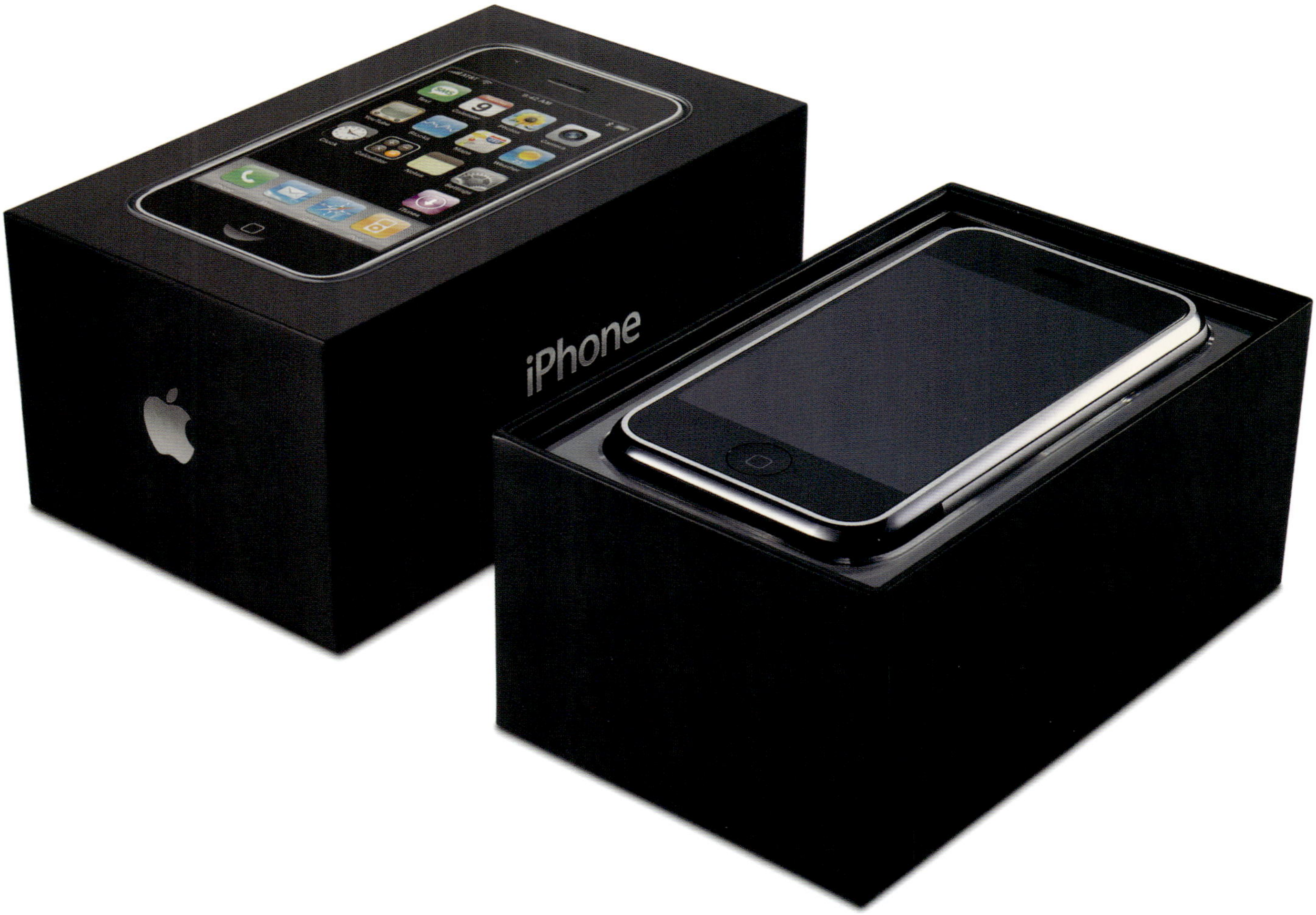
iPhone

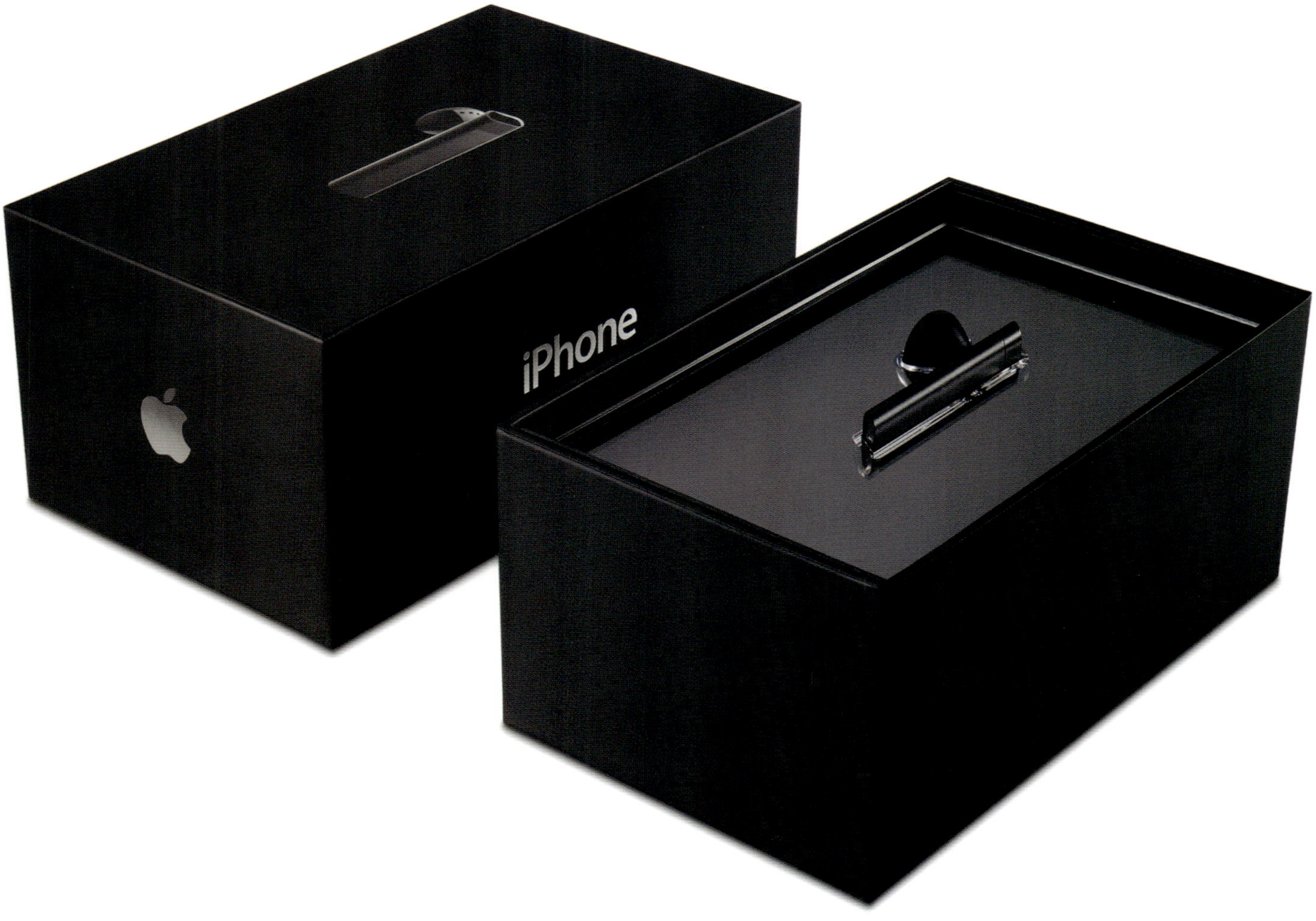
iPhone

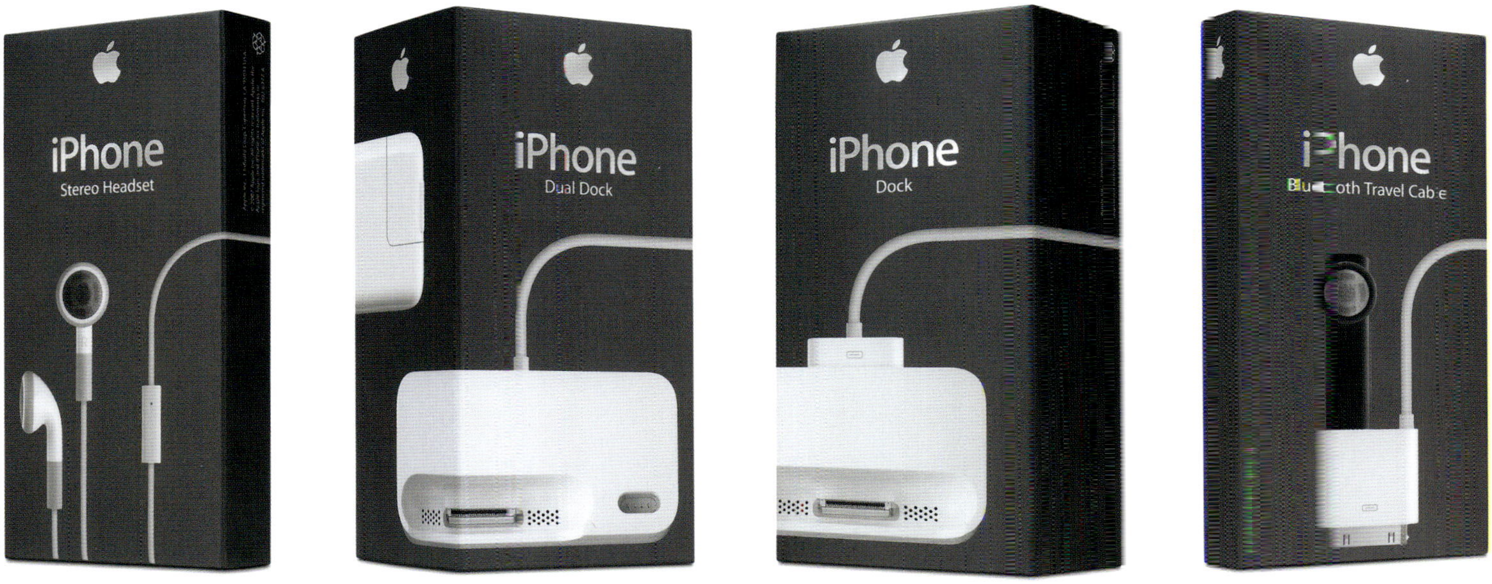
iPhone
Stereo Headset
iPhone
Dual Dock
iPhone
Dock
iPhone

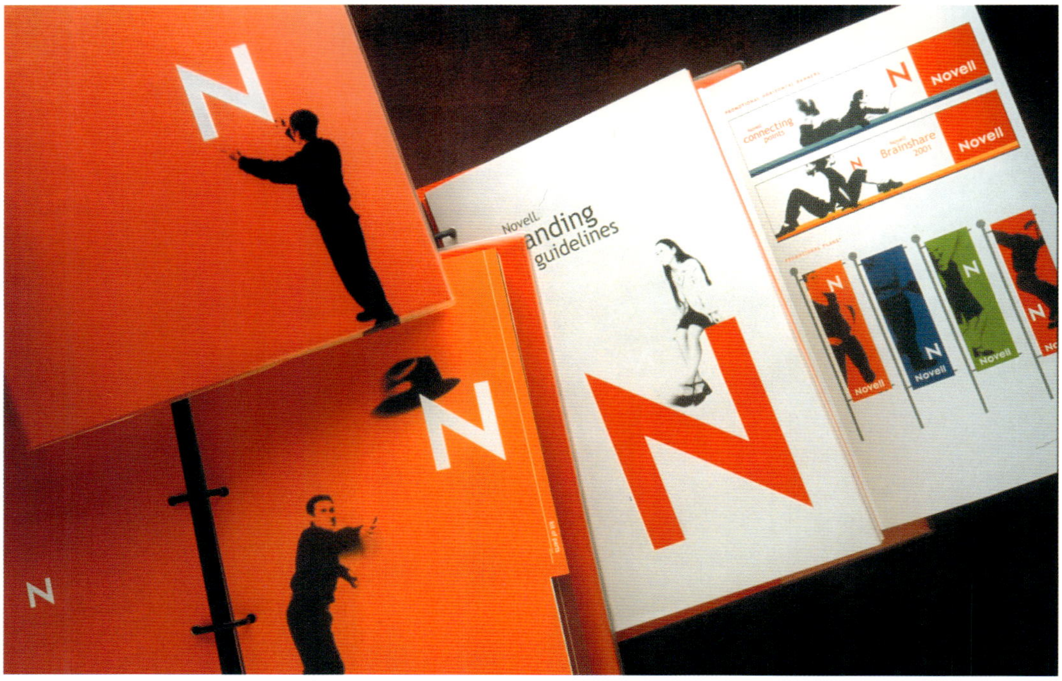
Novell
anding
guidelines
Novell
connecting
points
Brainshare
2001
Novell
Novell
Novell
Novell

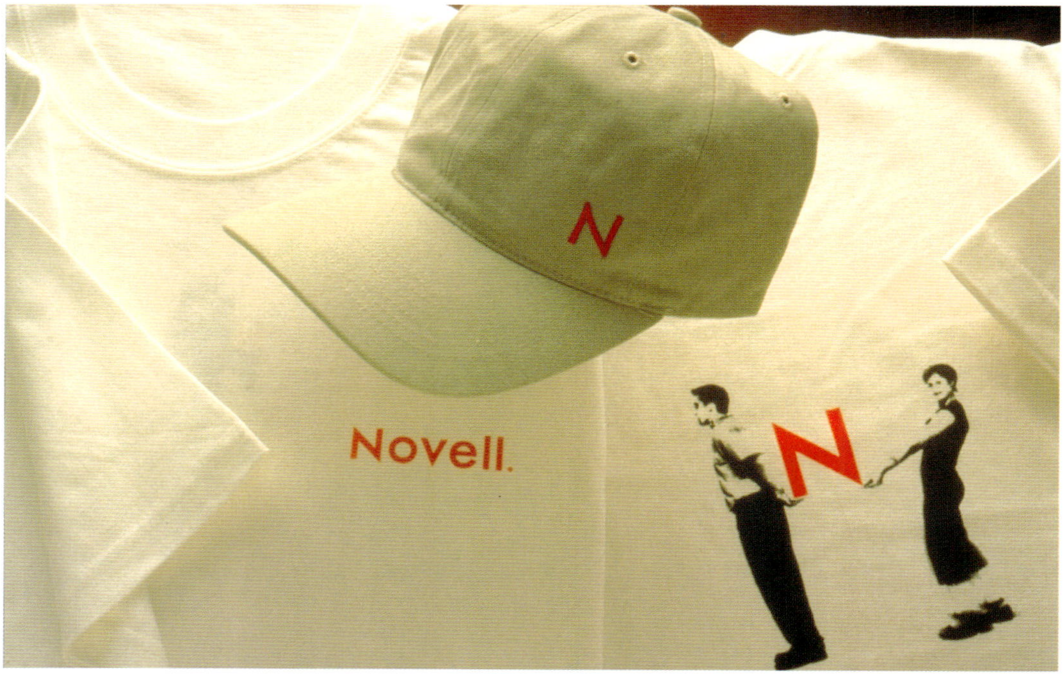
Novell

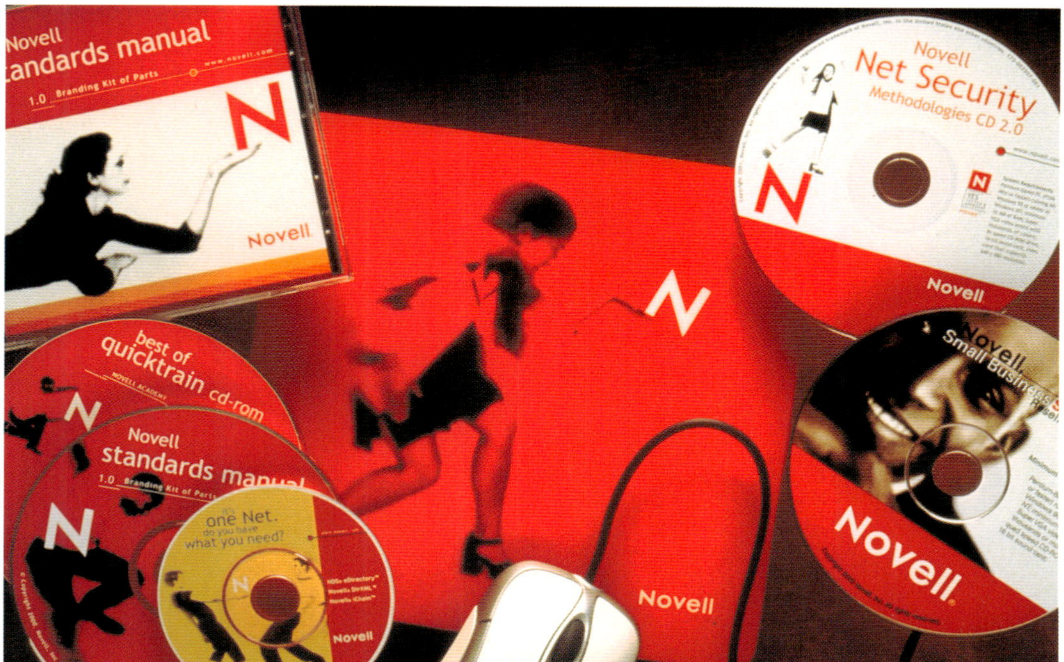
Novell
tandards manual
1.0 Branding Kit of Parts
Novell
Novell
Net Security
Methodologies CD 2.0
Novell
Novell
Small Business
best of
quicktrain cd-rom
Novell
standards manual
1.0 Branding Kit of Parts
one Net.
do you have
what you need?
Novell
Novell
Novell

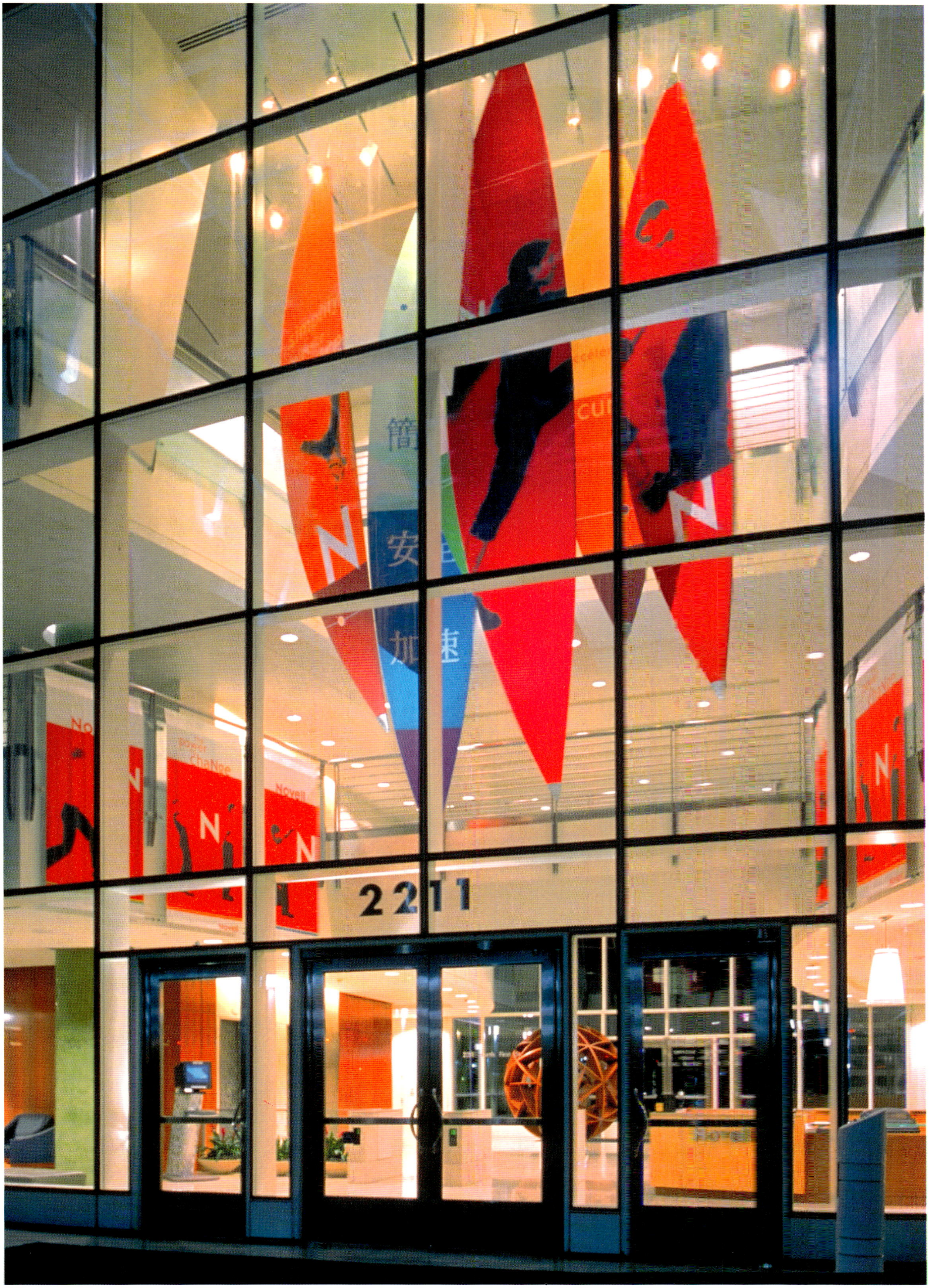

Hornall Anderson Design Works (this spread) | Novell, Inc. | Computers/Software

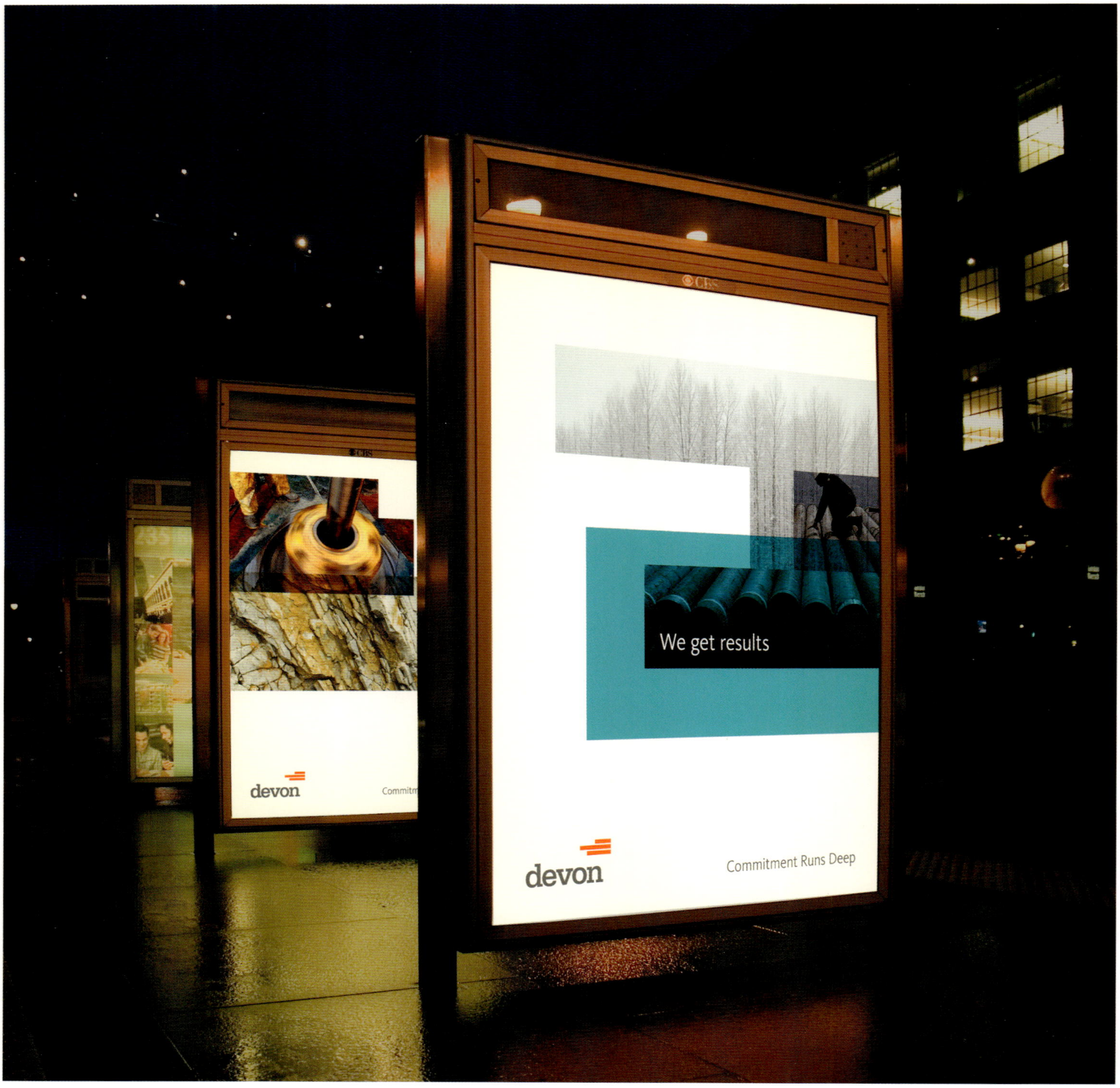
We get results
devon
Commitment Runs Deep

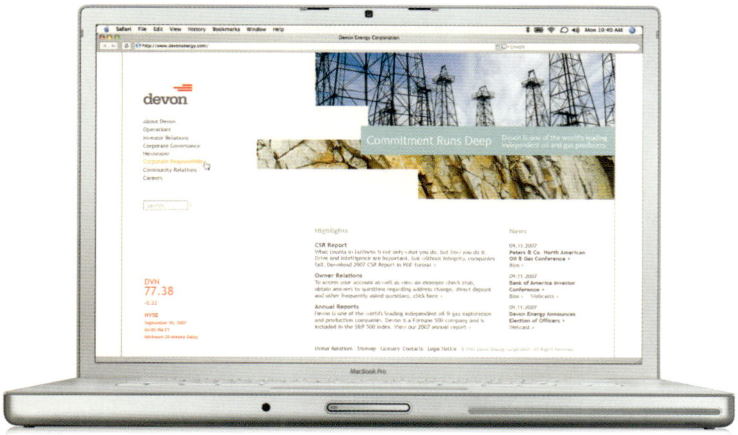
devon
Commitment Runs Deep
DVN
77.38

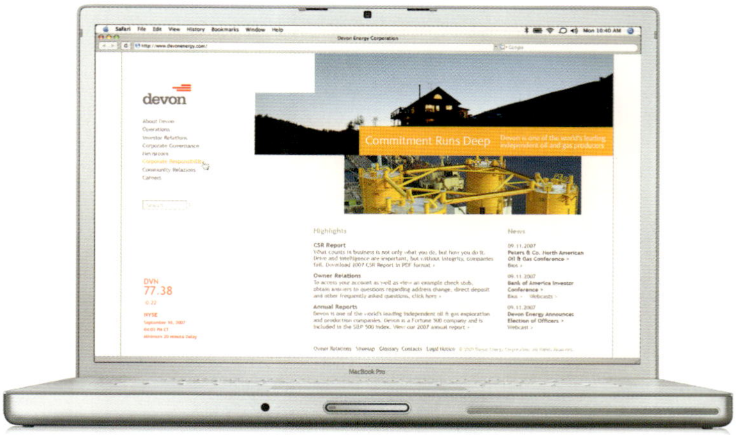
devon
Commitment Runs Deep
DVN
77.38

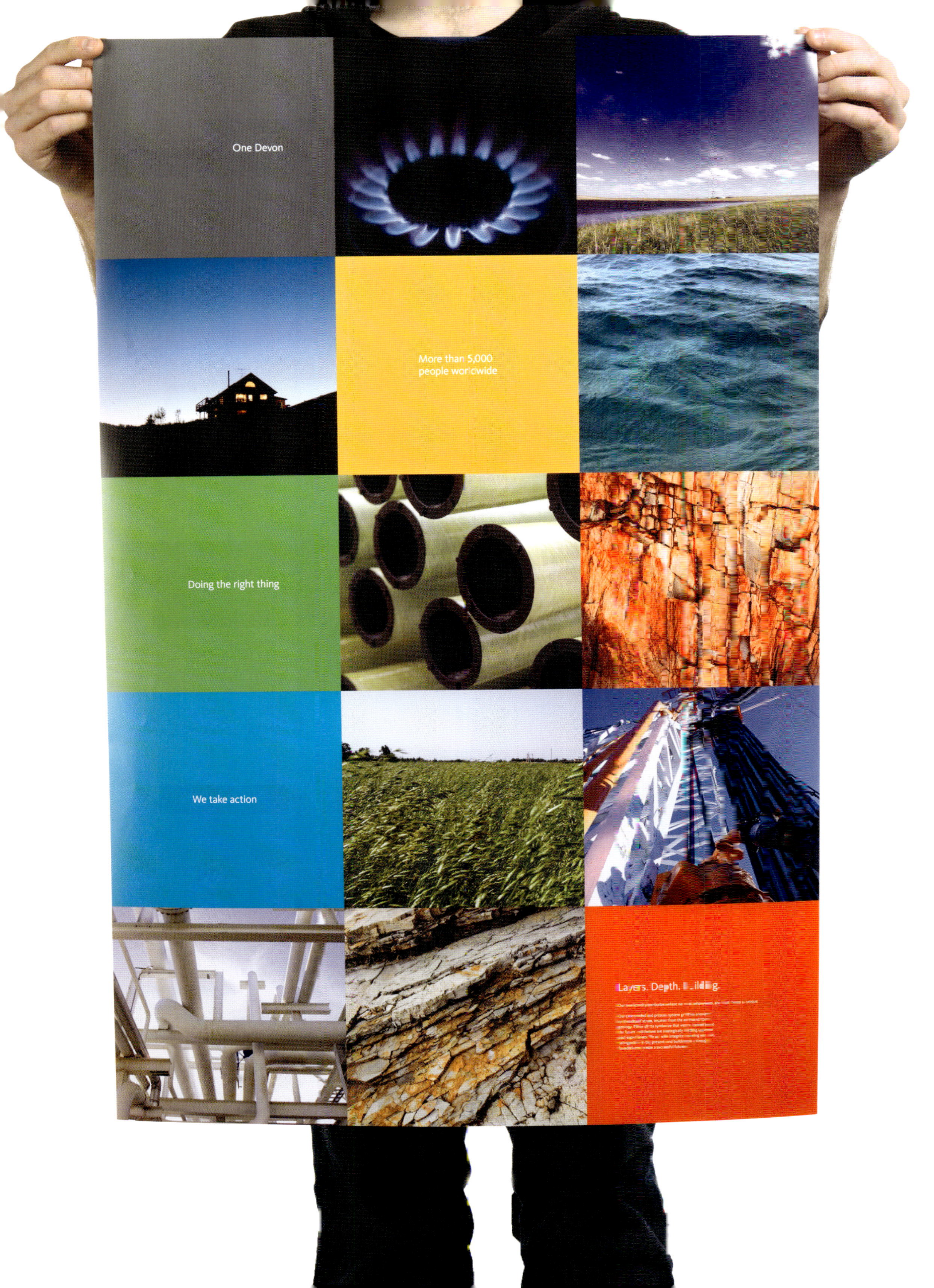

One Devon
More than 5,000
people worldwide
Doing the right thing
We take action
Layers. Depth.

ASTACURE

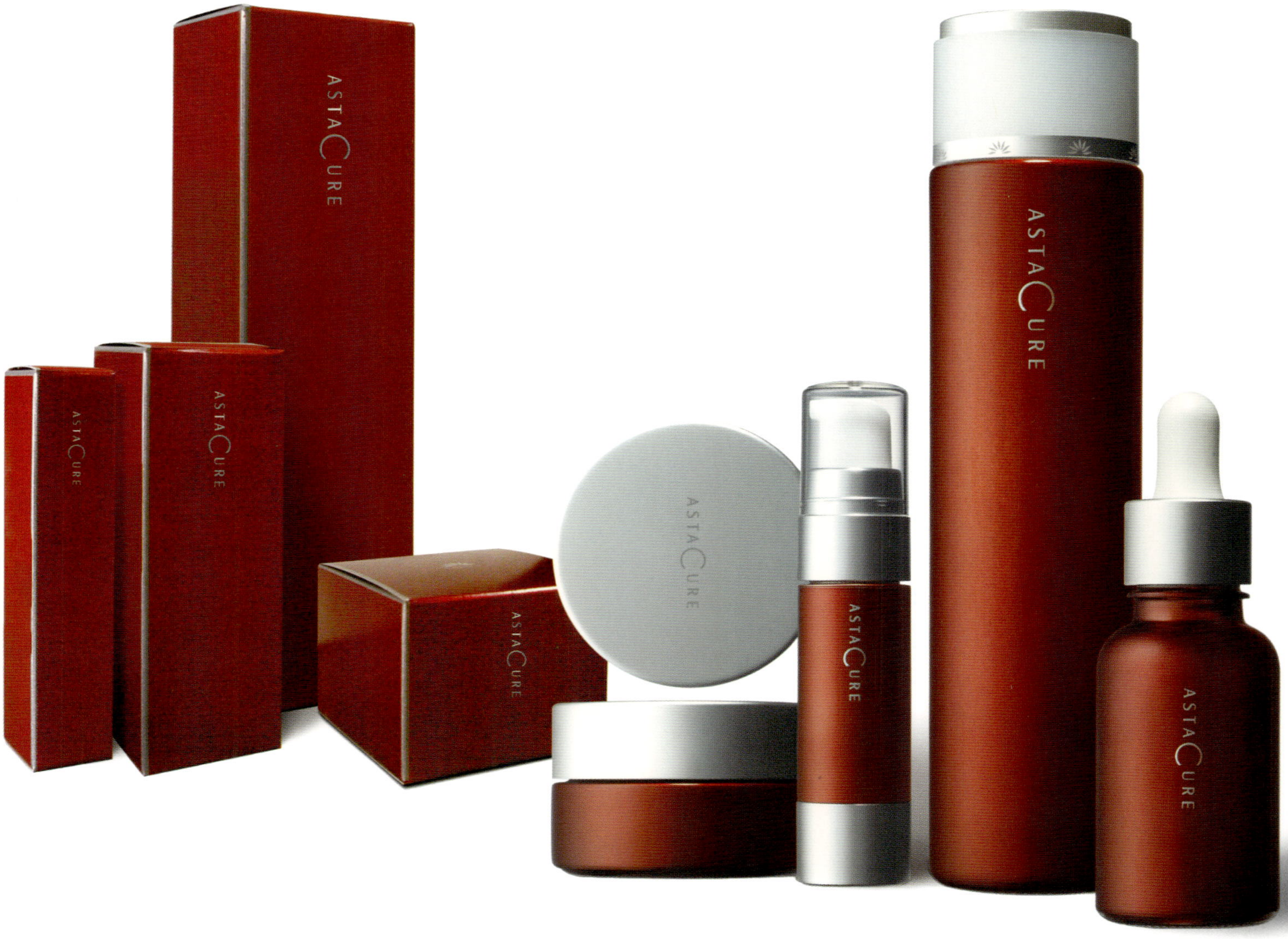

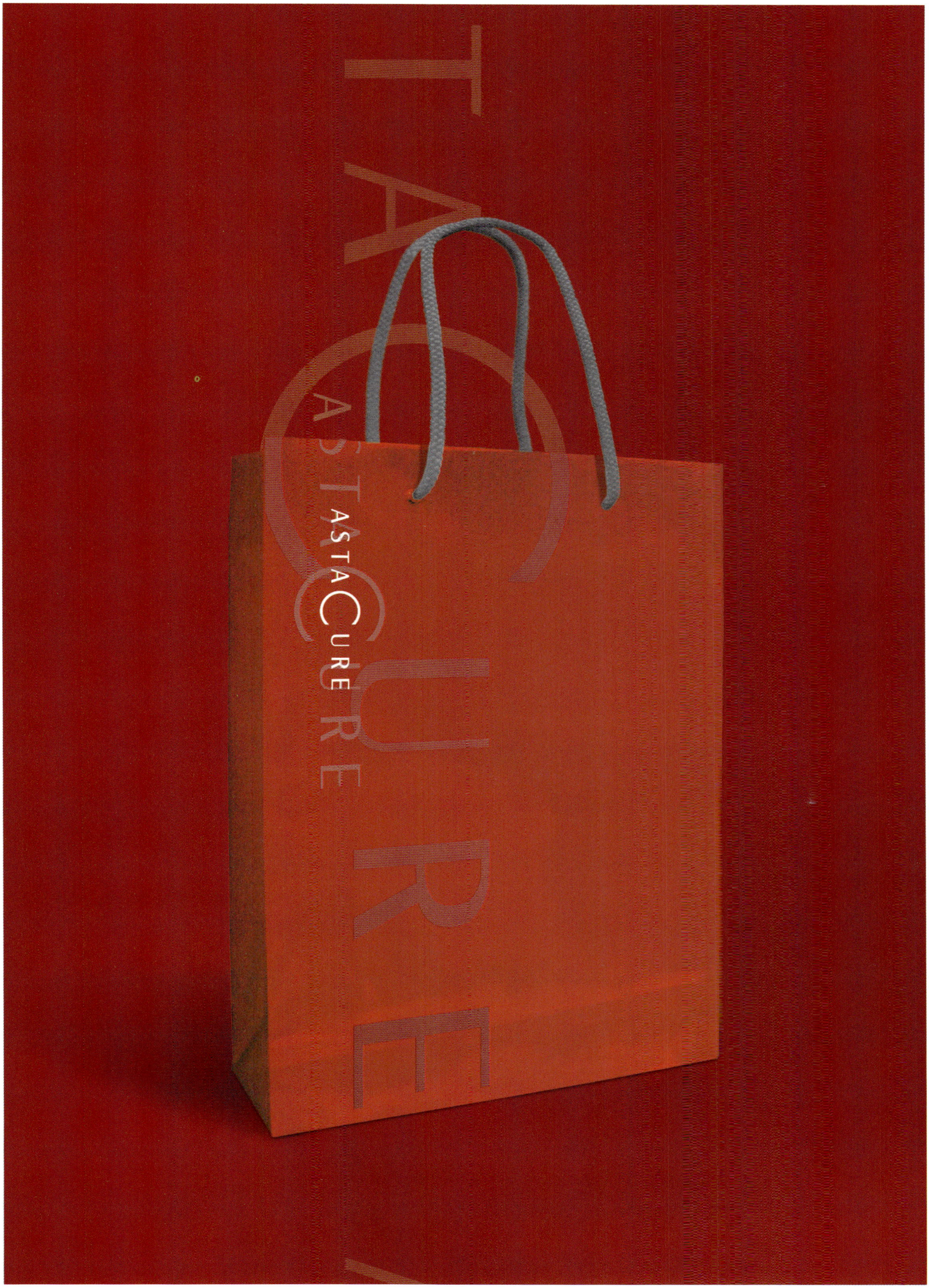
ASTACURE

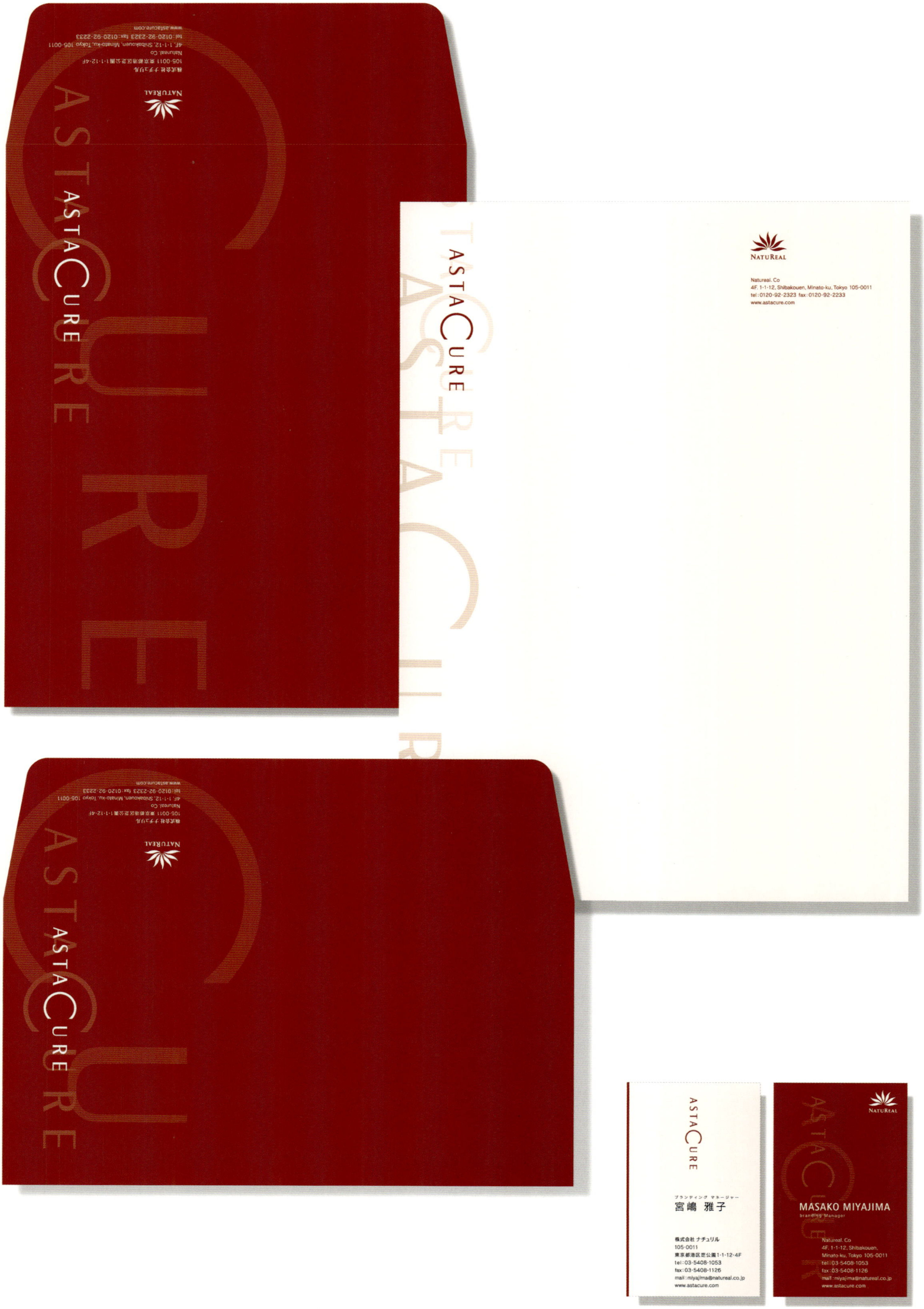
ASTACURE
NATUREAL
Natureal. Co
4F. 1-1-12, Shibakouen, Minato-ku, Tokyo 105-0011
tel:0120-92-2323 fax:0120-92-2233
www.astacure.com
ブランディング マネージャー
宮嶋 雅子
株式会社 ナチュリル
105-0011
東京都港区芝公園1-1-12-4F
tel:03-5408-1053
fax:03-5408-1126
mail:miyajima@natureal.co.jp
www.astacure.com
MASAKO MIYAJIMA
branding Manager
Natureal. Co
4F. 1-1-12, Shibakouen,
Minato-ku, Tokyo 105-0011
tel:03-5408-1053
fax:03-5408-1126
mail:miyajima@natureal.co.jp
www.astacure.com

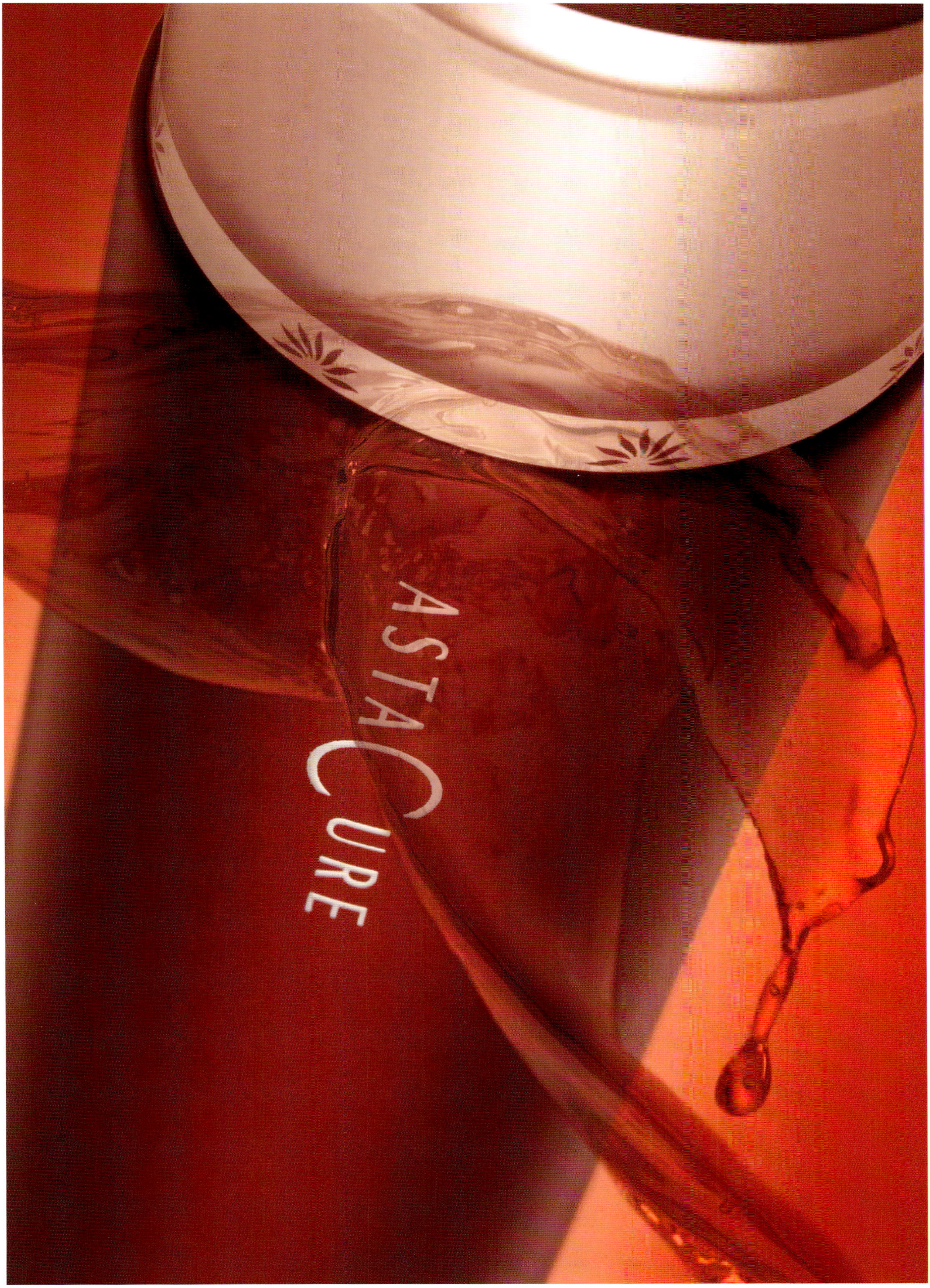
ASTACURE

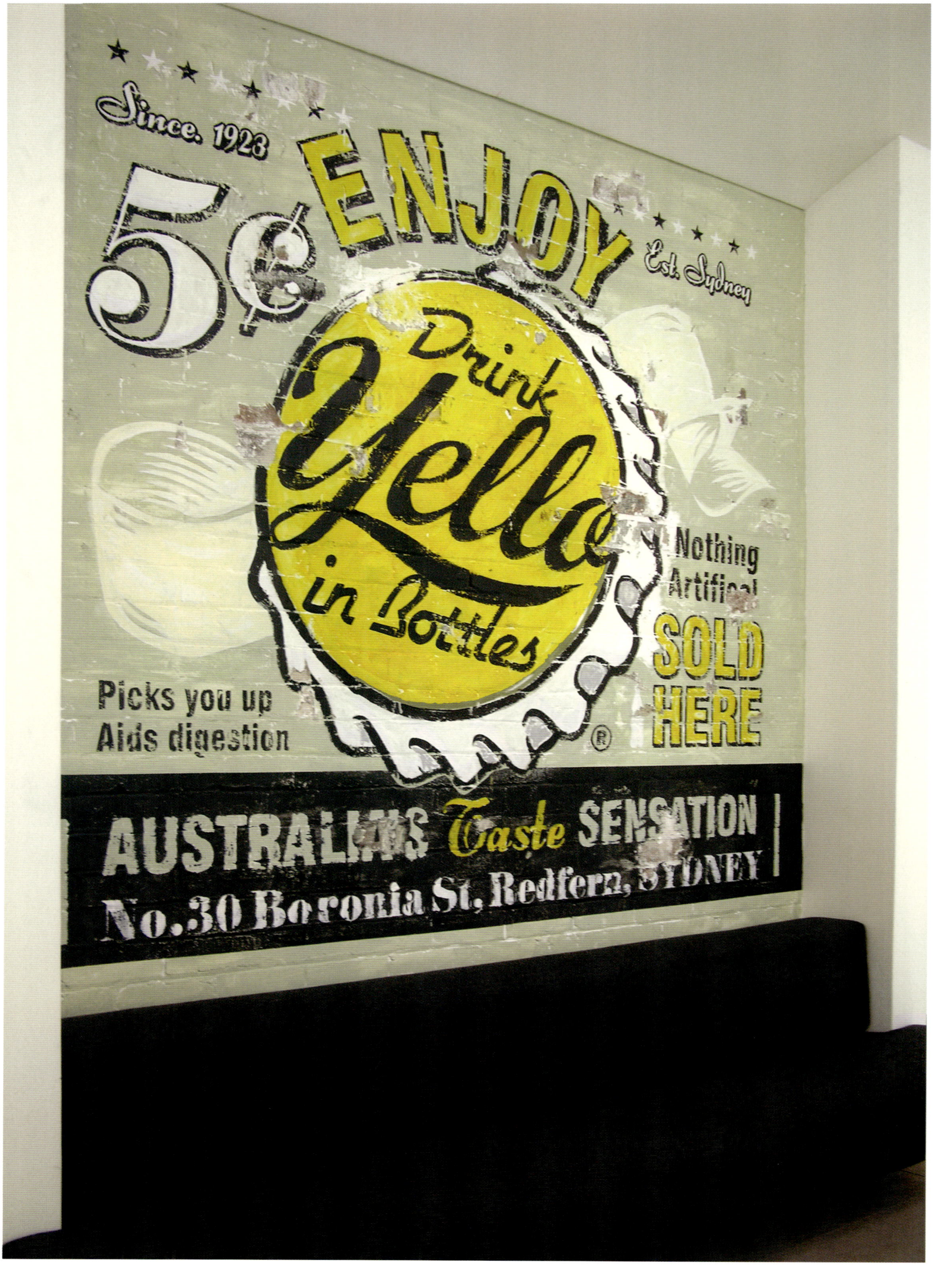
Since. 1923
5¢
ENJOY
Est. Sydney
Drink
Yello
in Bottles
Nothing
Artificial
SOLD
HERE
Picks you up
Aids digestion
AUSTRALIA'S Taste SENSATION
No.30 Boronia St, Redfern, SYDNEY

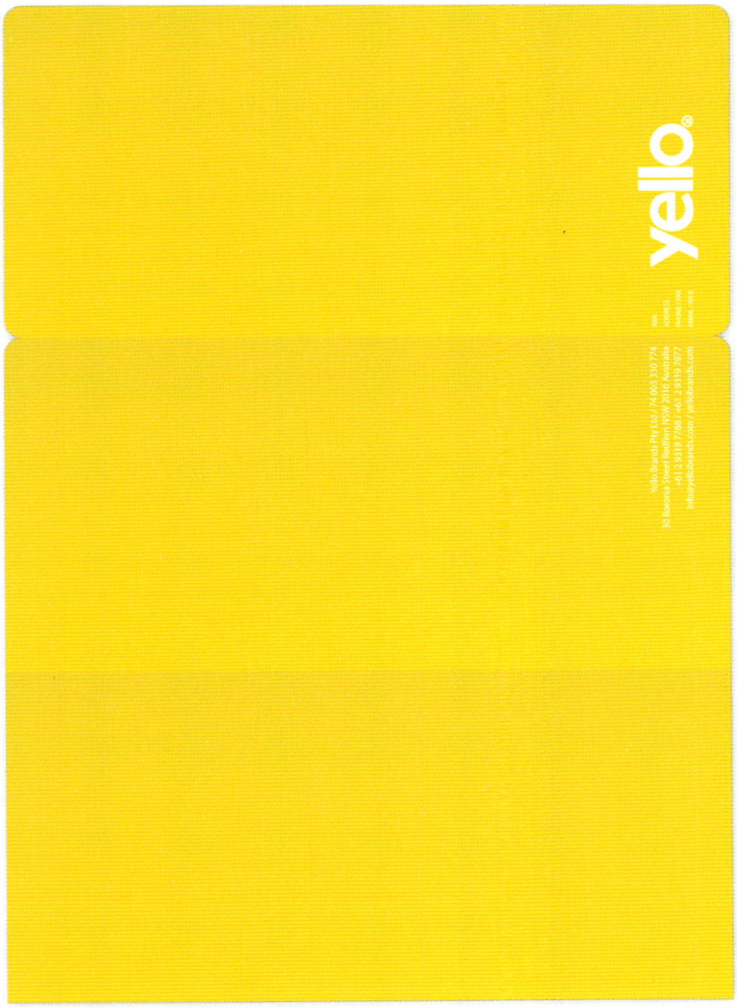
yello

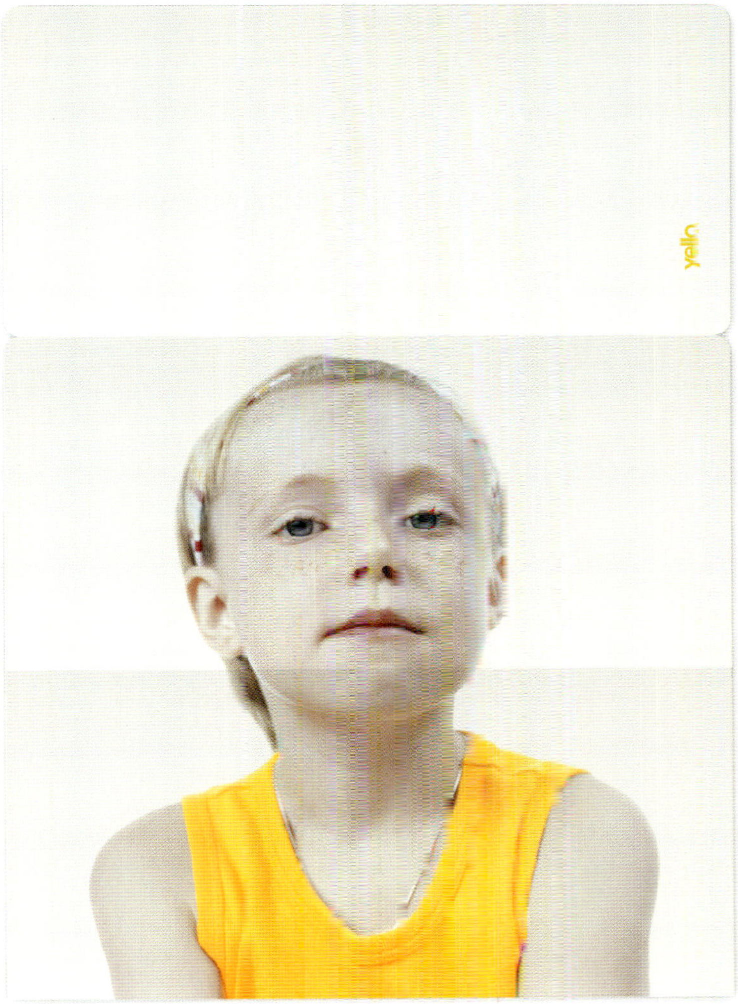
yello

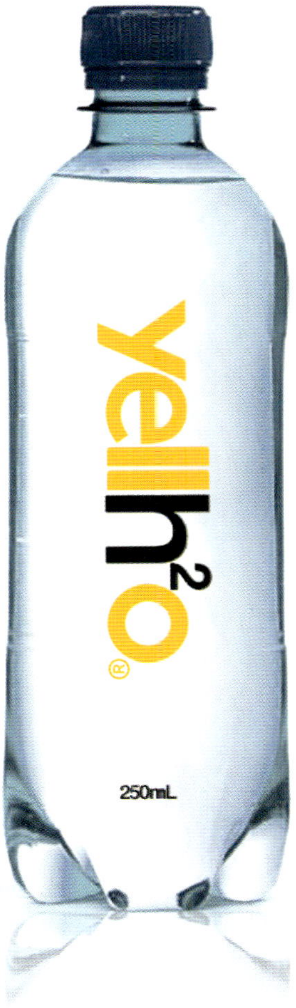
yellh2o
250mL

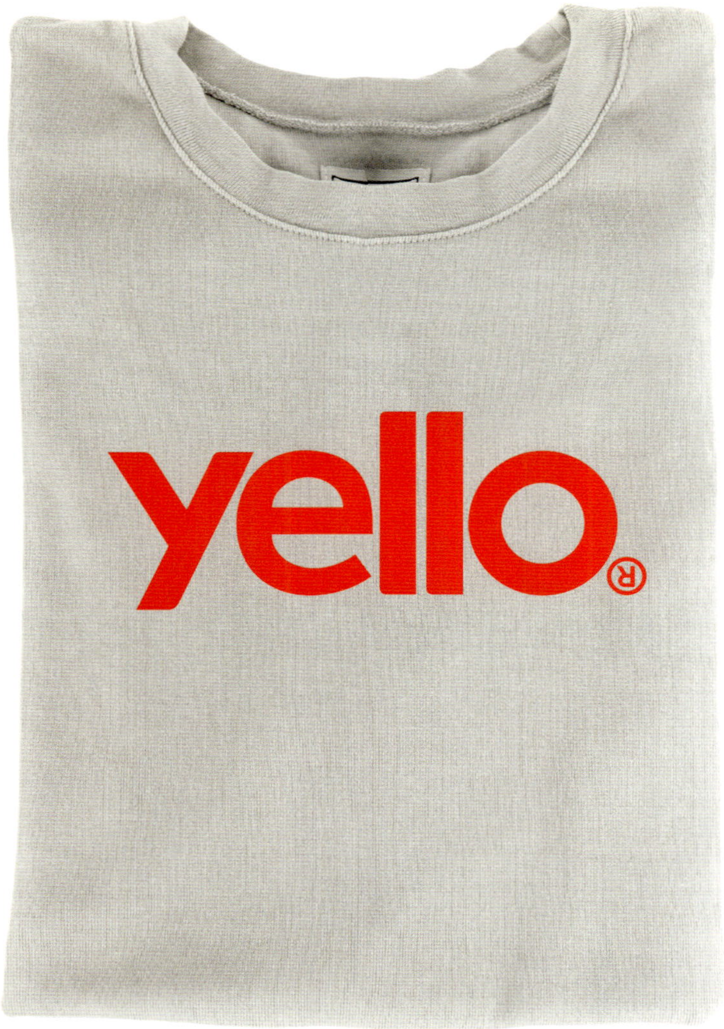
yello

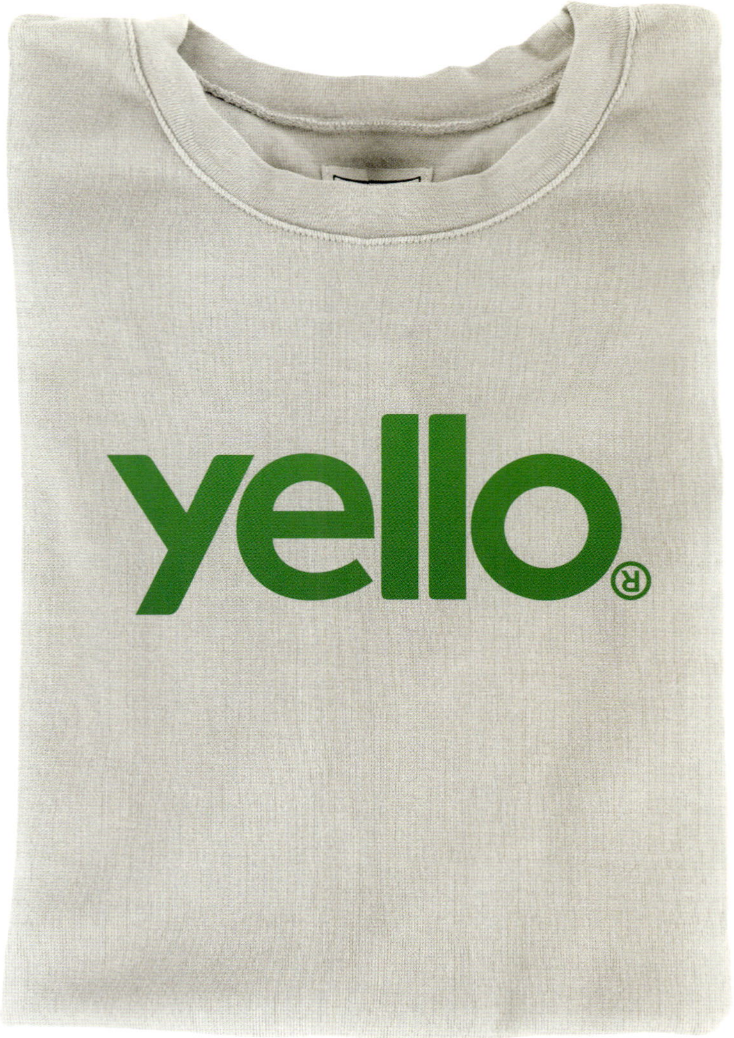
yello

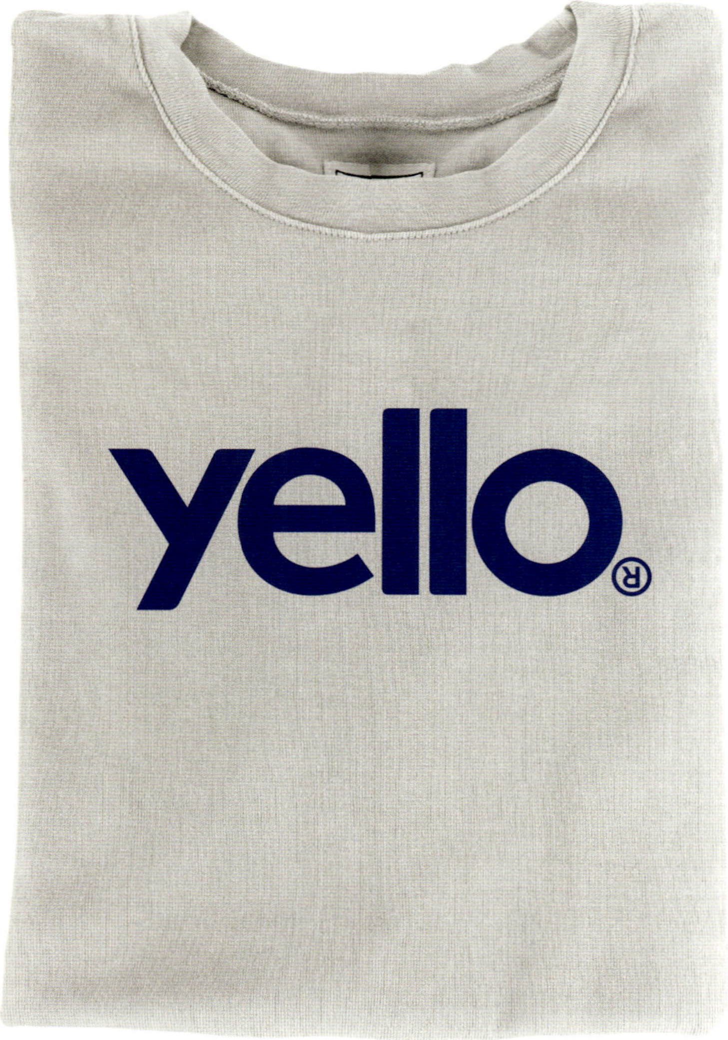
yello

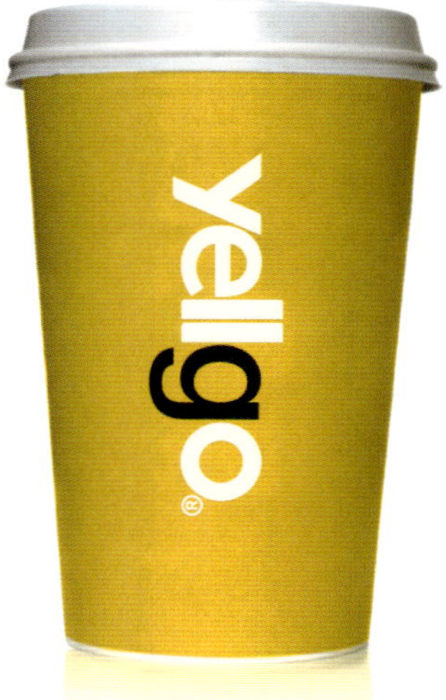
yellgo

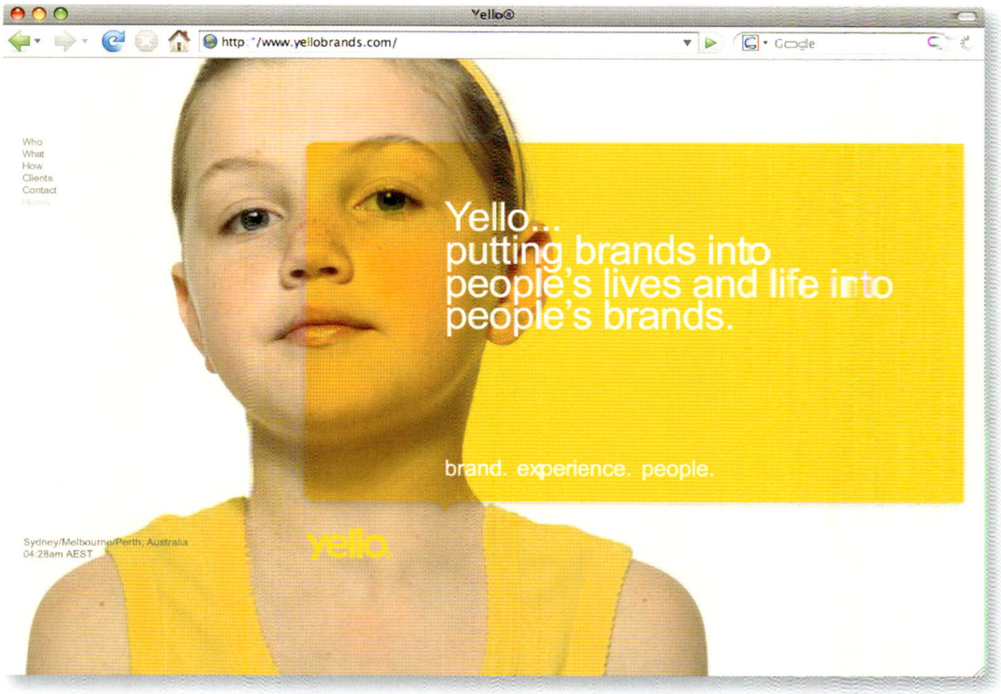

Yello®
http://www.yellobrands.com/
Who
What
How
Clients
Contact
Yello...
putting brands into
people's lives and life into
people's brands.
brand. experience. people.
Sydney/Melbourne/Perth, Australia
04:28am AEST
yello

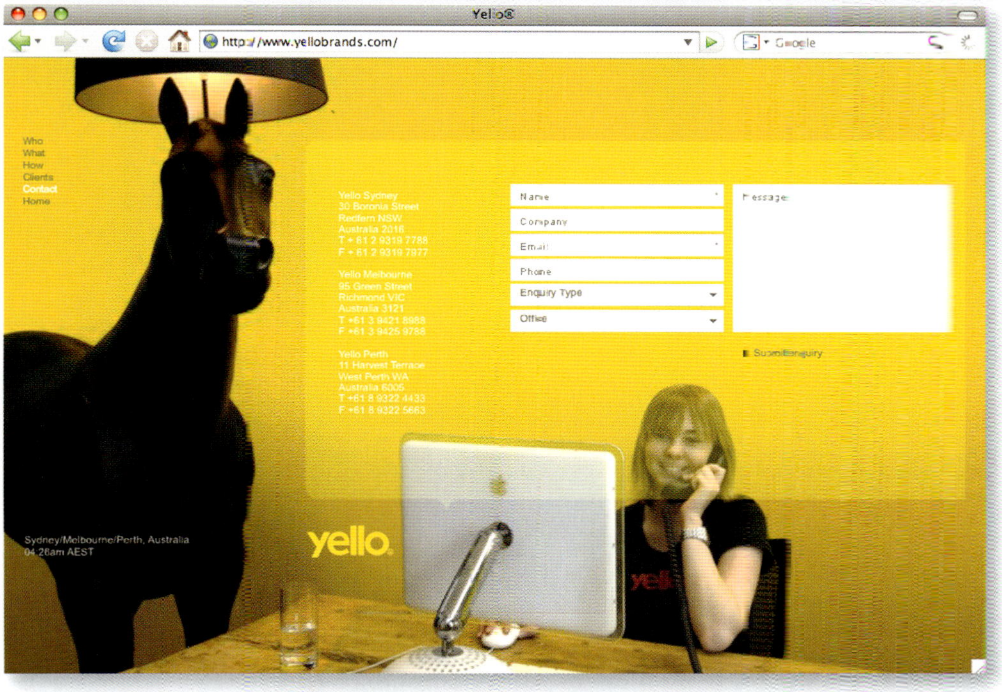

Yello®
http://www.yellobrands.com/
Who
What
How
Clients
Contact
Home
Yello Sydney
30 Boronia Street
Redfern NSW
Australia 2016
T + 61 2 9319 7788
F + 61 2 9319 7977
Yello Melbourne
95 Green Street
Richmond VIC
Australia 3121
T +61 3 9421 8988
F +61 3 9425 9788
Yello Perth
11 Harvest Terrace
West Perth WA
Australia 6005
T +61 8 9322 4433
F +61 8 9322 5663
Name
Company
Email
Phone
Enquiry Type
Office
Message
Sydney/Melbourne/Perth, Australia
04:28am AEST
yello

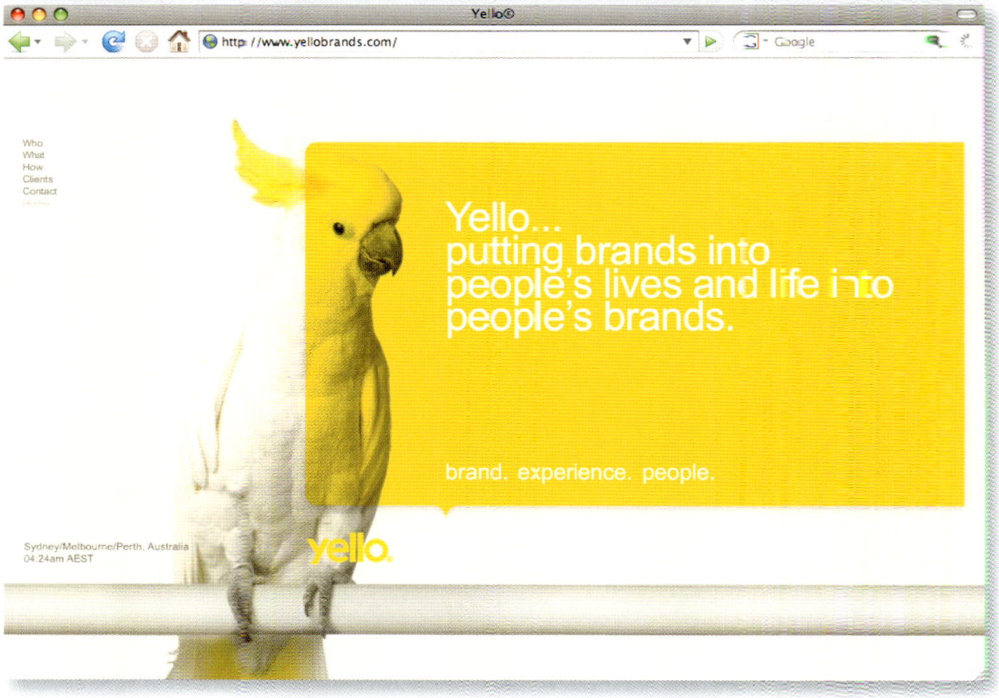

Yello®
http://www.yellobrands.com/
Who
What
How
Clients
Contact
Yello...
putting brands into
people's lives and life into
people's brands.
brand. experience. people.
Sydney/Melbourne/Perth, Australia
04:24am AEST
yello

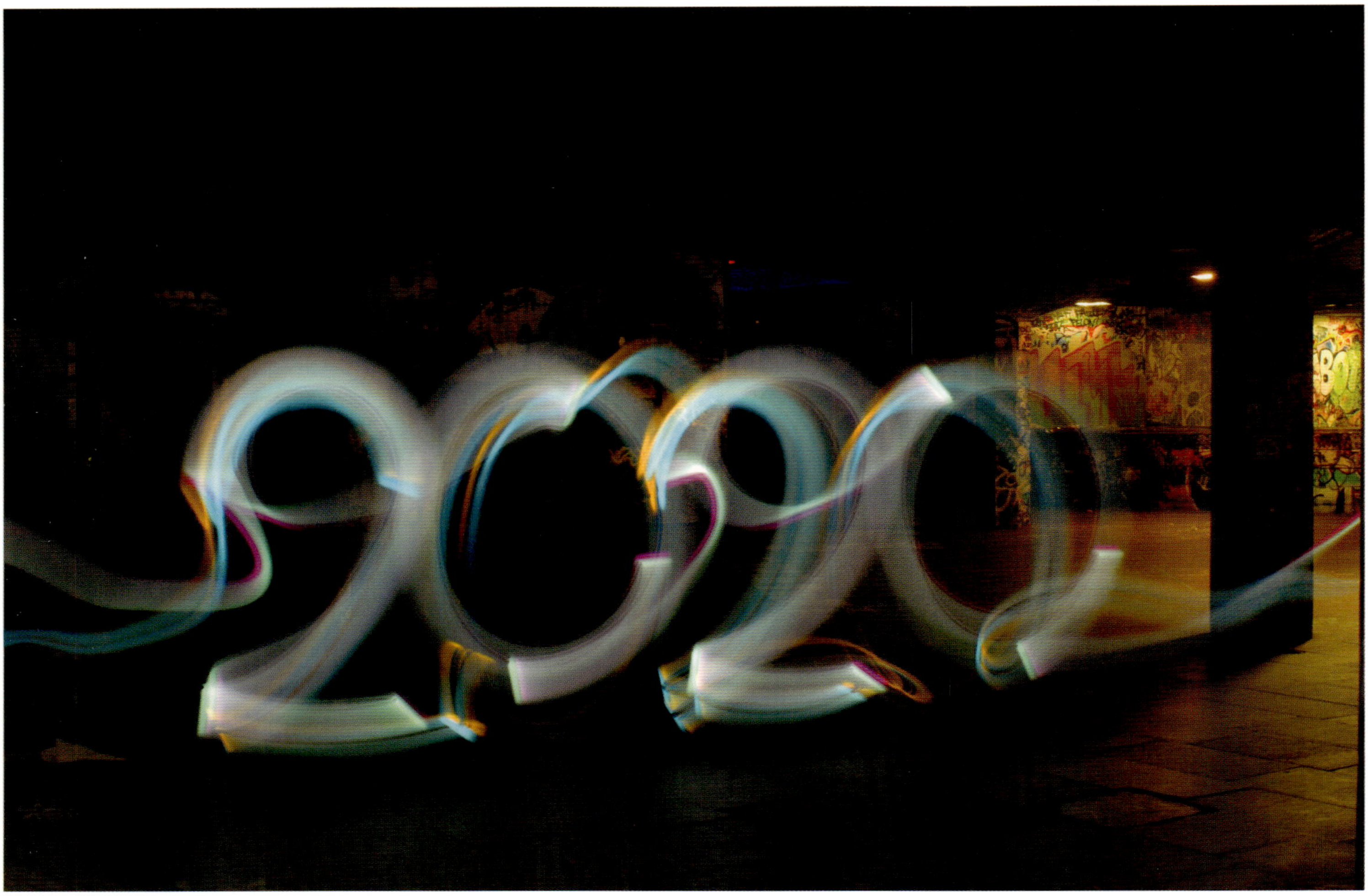
2020

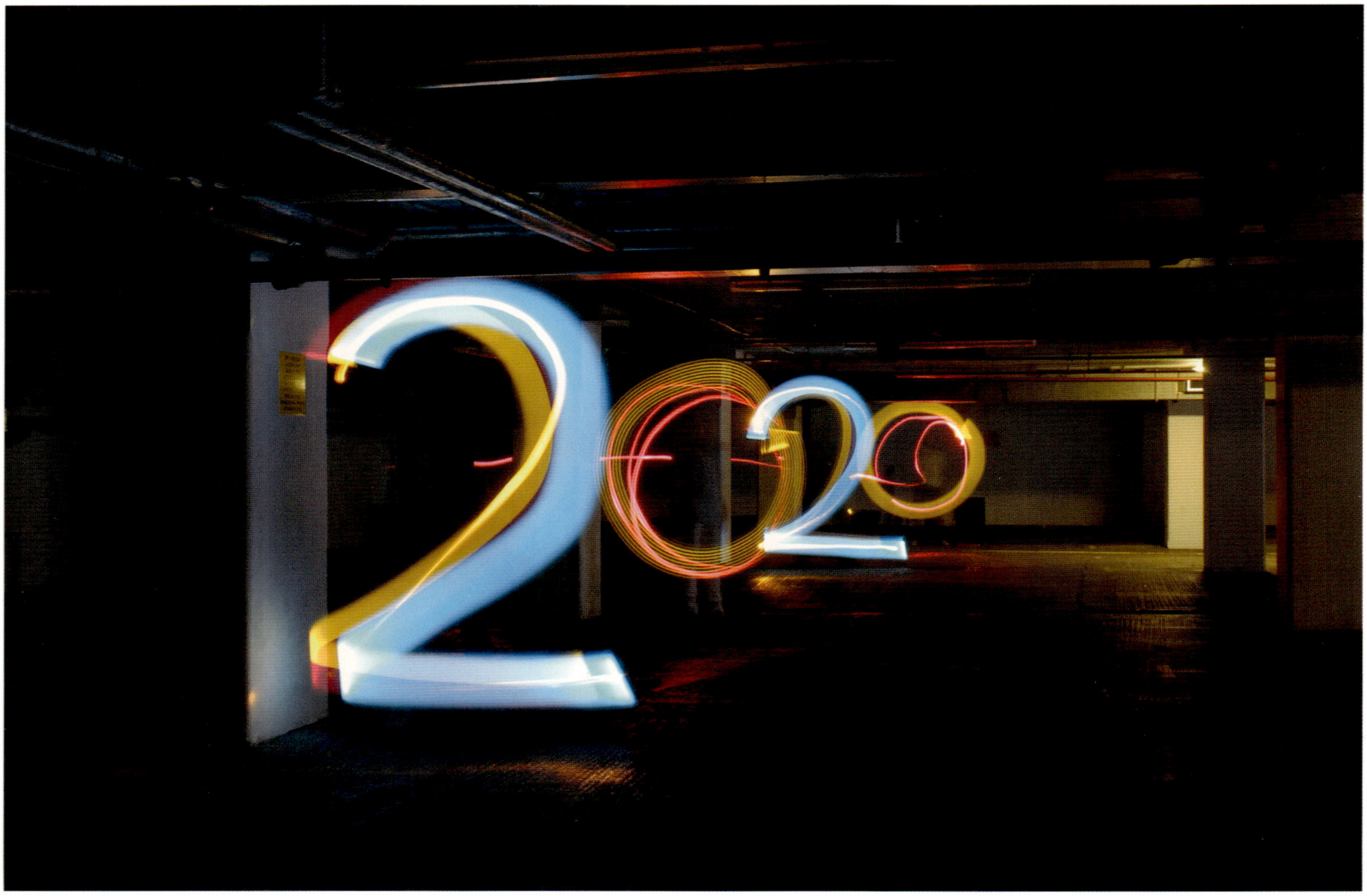
2020

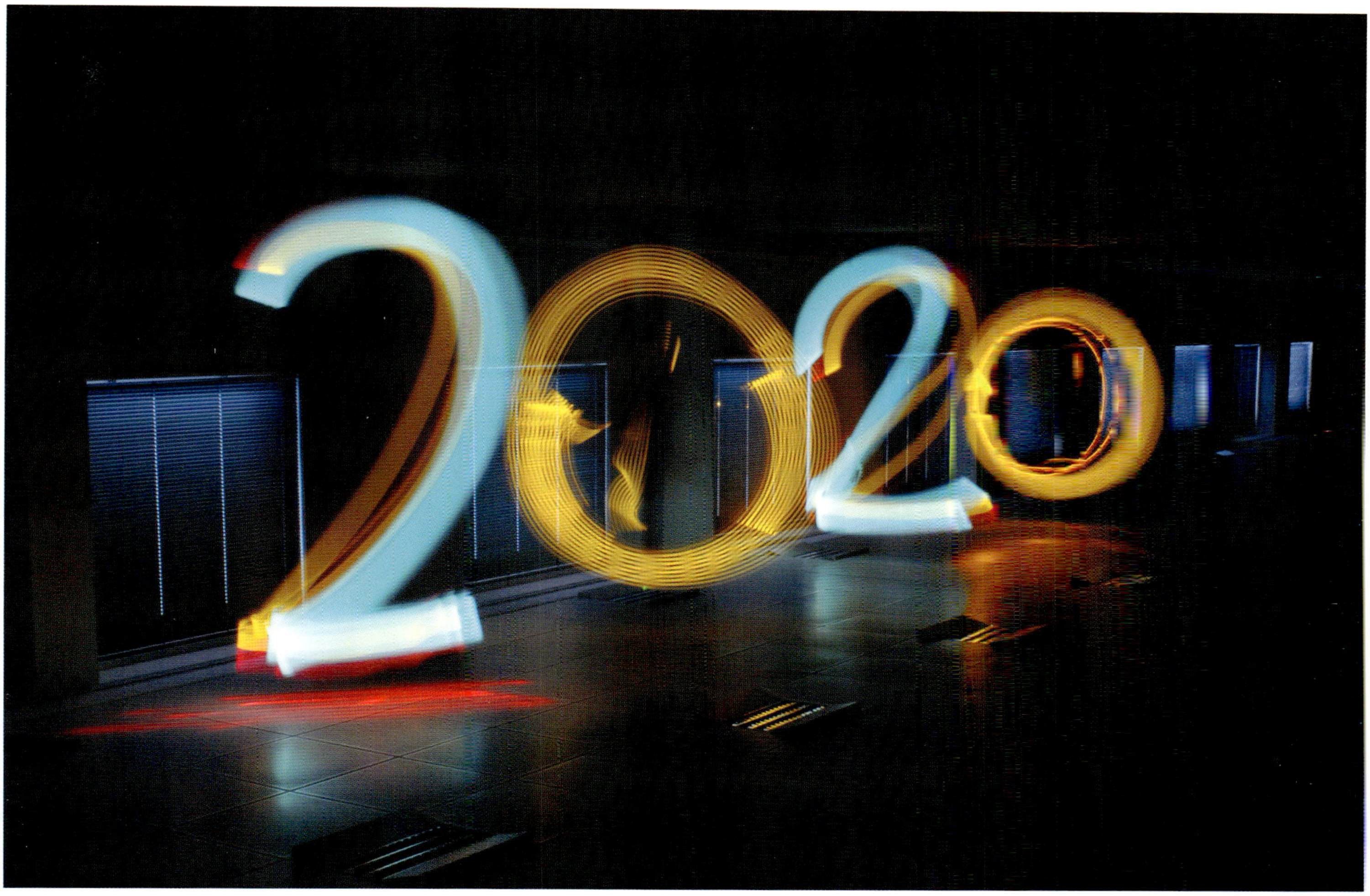
2020

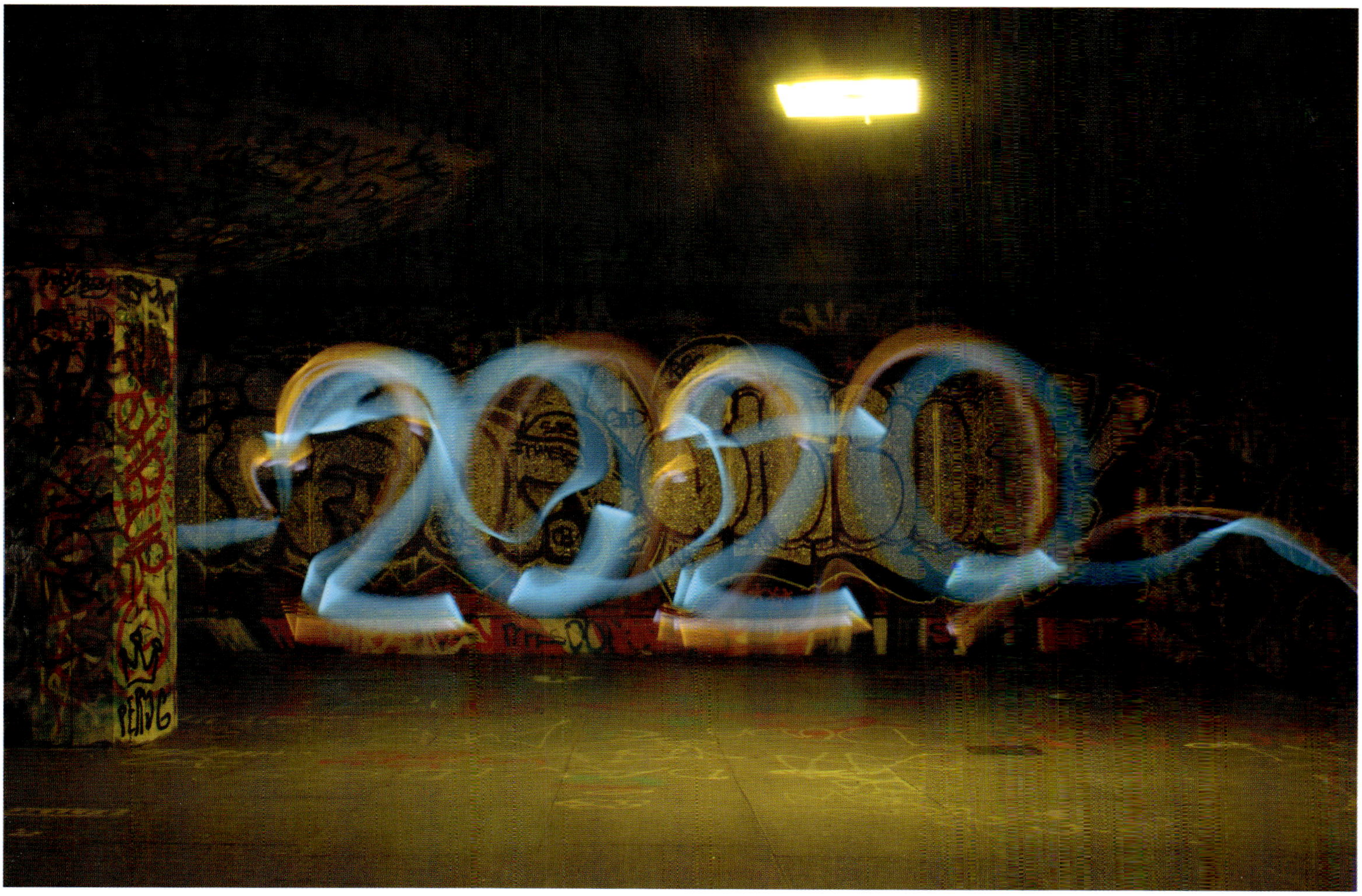
2020

THE ROASTED BEAN

CAFE

FIRE

AND

ICE

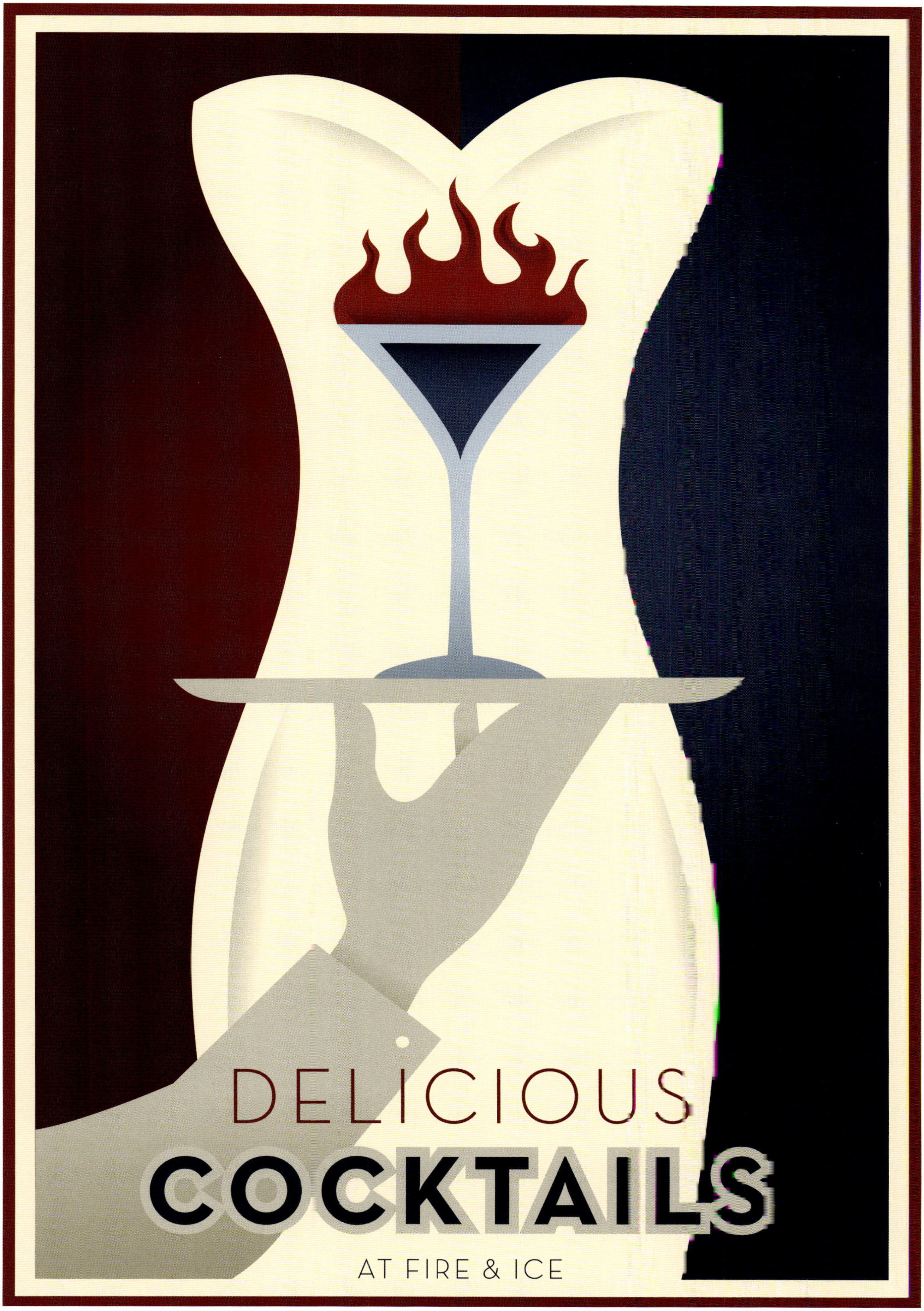
DELICIOUS
COCKTAILS
AT FIRE & ICE

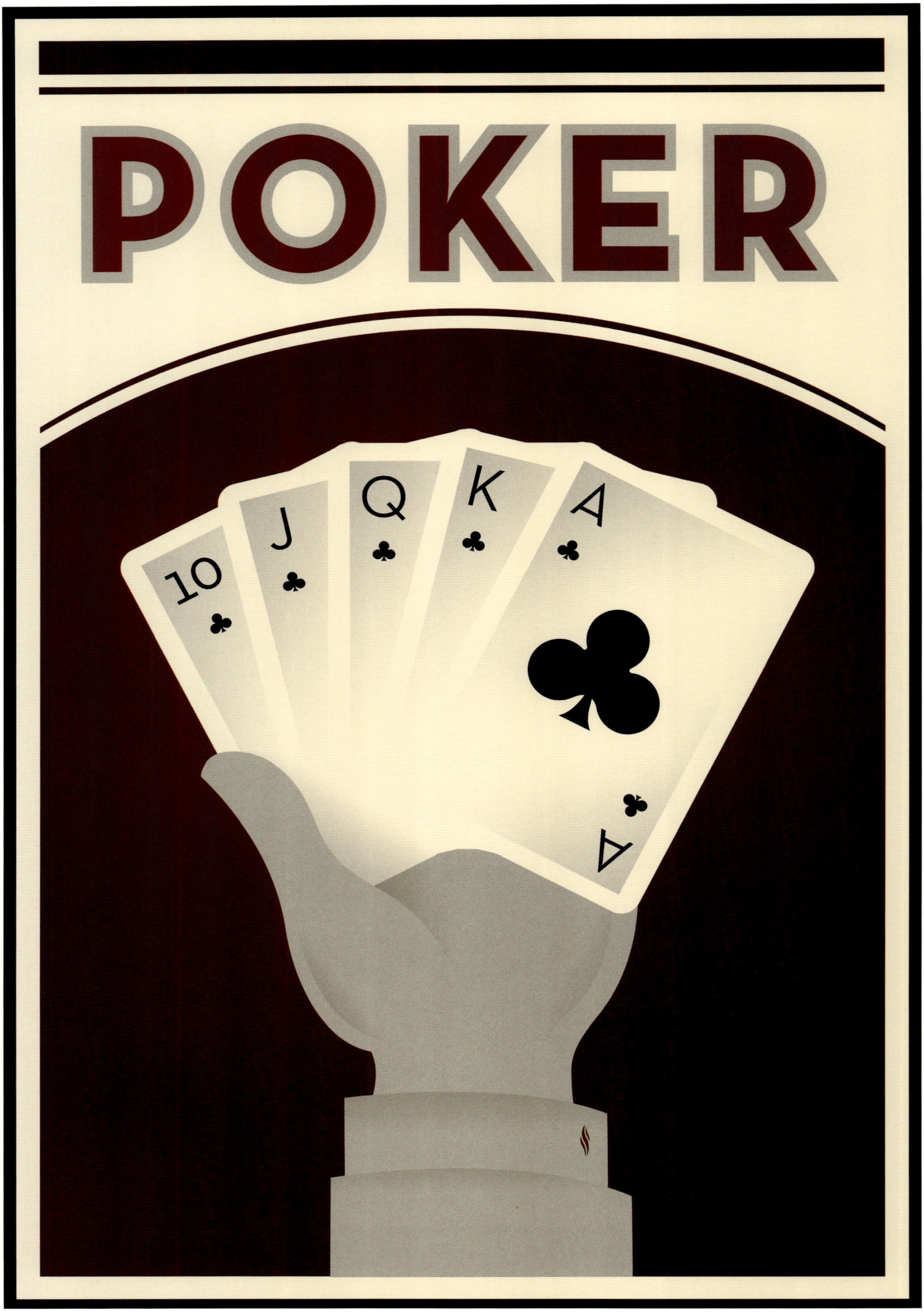
POKER
10
J
Q
K
A

FIRELAKE
GRAND
CASINO

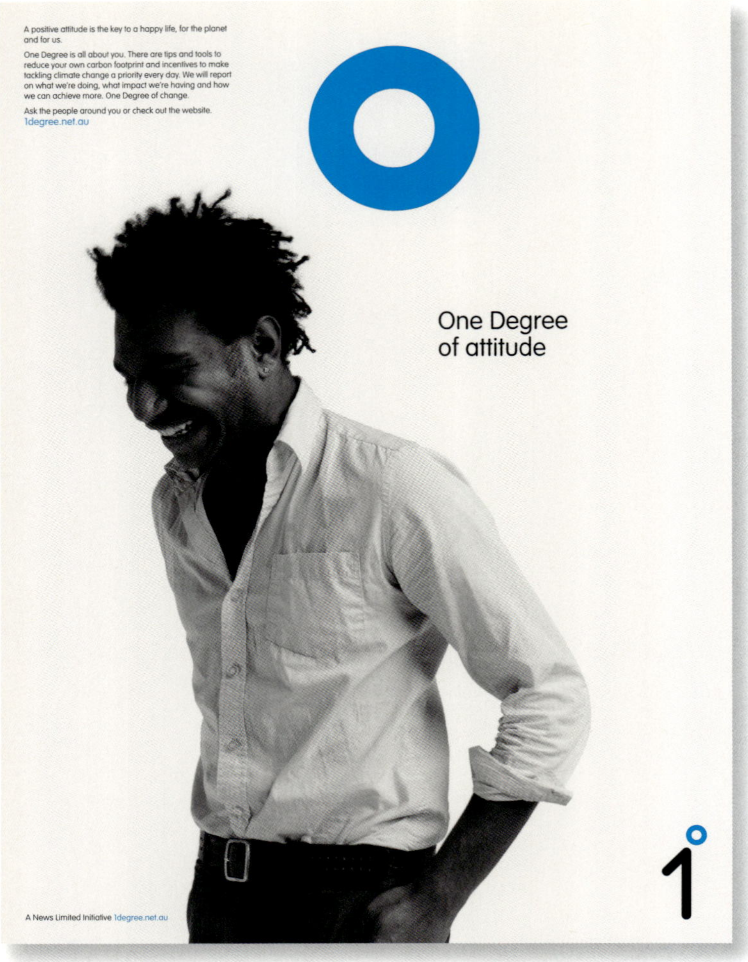
A positive attitude is the key to a happy life, for the planet and for us.
One Degree is all about you. There are tips and tools to reduce your own carbon footprint and incentives to make tackling climate change a priority every day. We will report on what we're doing, what impact we're having and how we can achieve more. One Degree of change.
Ask the people around you or check out the website.
1degree.net.au
One Degree of attitude
A News Limited Initiative 1degree.net.au

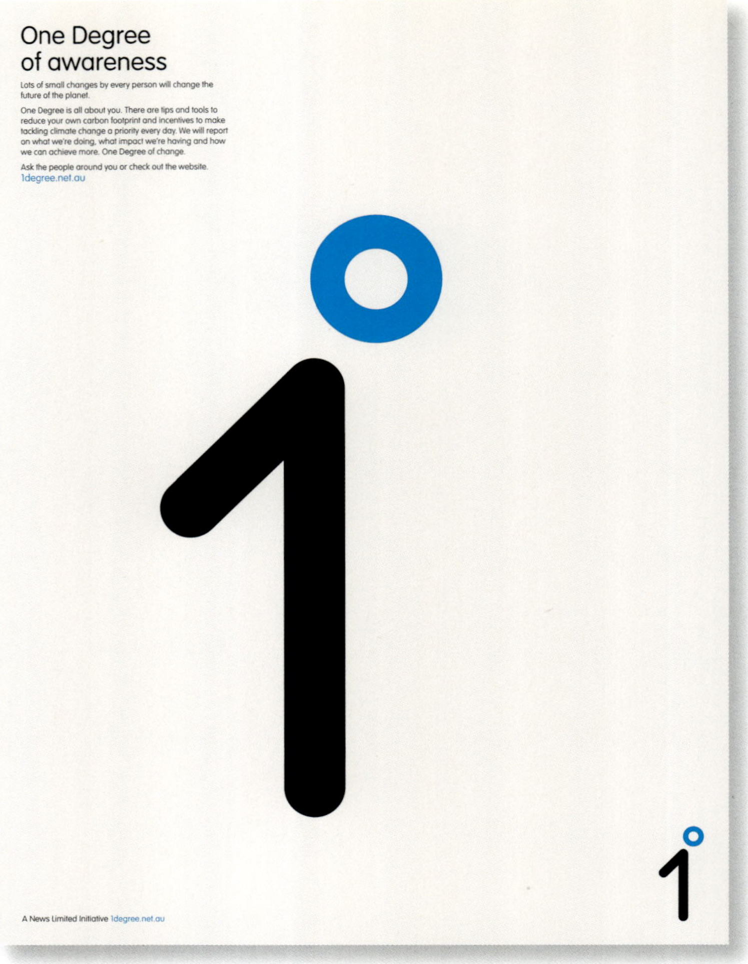
One Degree of awareness
Lots of small changes by every person will change the future of the planet.
One Degree is all about you. There are tips and tools to reduce your own carbon footprint and incentives to make tackling climate change a priority every day. We will report on what we're doing, what impact we're having and how we can achieve more. One Degree of change.
Ask the people around you or check out the website.
1degree.net.au
A News Limited Initiative 1degree.net.au

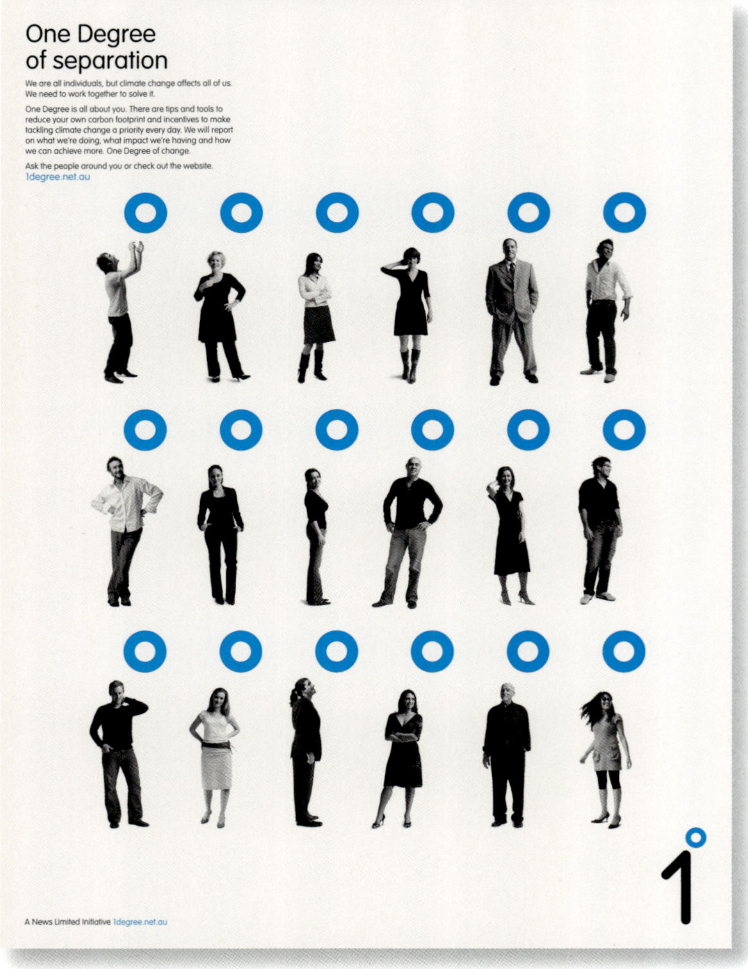
One Degree of separation
We are all individuals, but climate change affects all of us. We need to work together to solve it.
One Degree is all about you. There are tips and tools to reduce your own carbon footprint and incentives to make tackling climate change a priority every day. We will report on what we're doing, what impact we're having and how we can achieve more. One Degree of change.
Ask the people around you or check out the website.
1degree.net.au
A News Limited Initiative 1degree.net.au

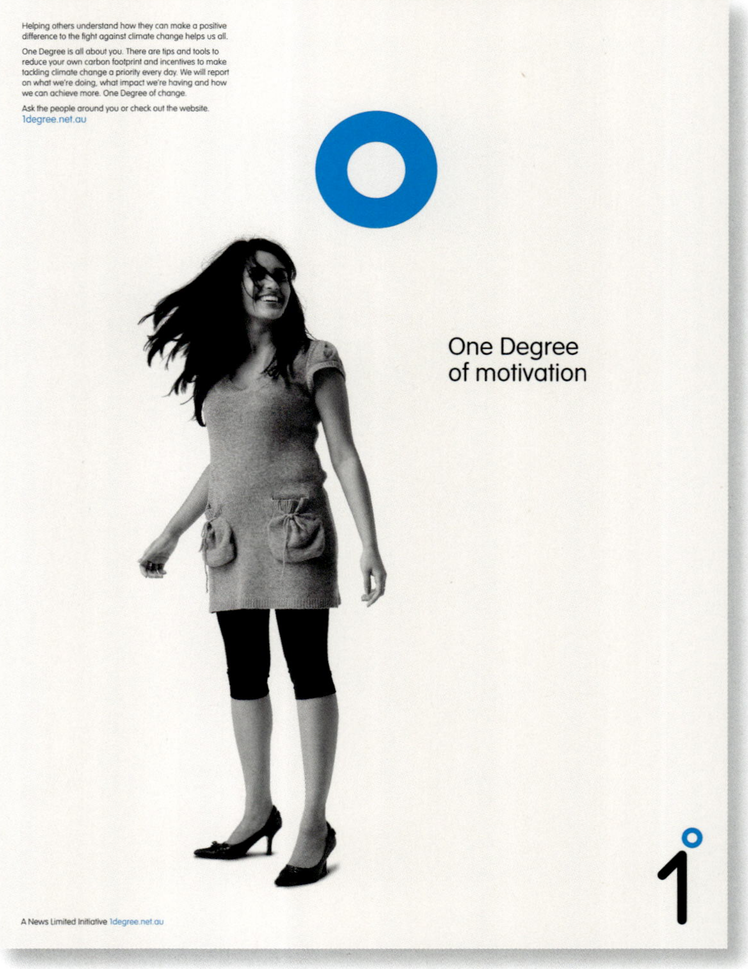
Helping others understand how they can make a positive difference to the fight against climate change helps us all.
One Degree is all about you. There are tips and tools to reduce your own carbon footprint and incentives to make tackling climate change a priority every day. We will report on what we're doing, what impact we're having and how we can achieve more. One Degree of change.
Ask the people around you or check out the website.
1degree.net.au
One Degree of motivation
A News Limited Initiative 1degree.net.au

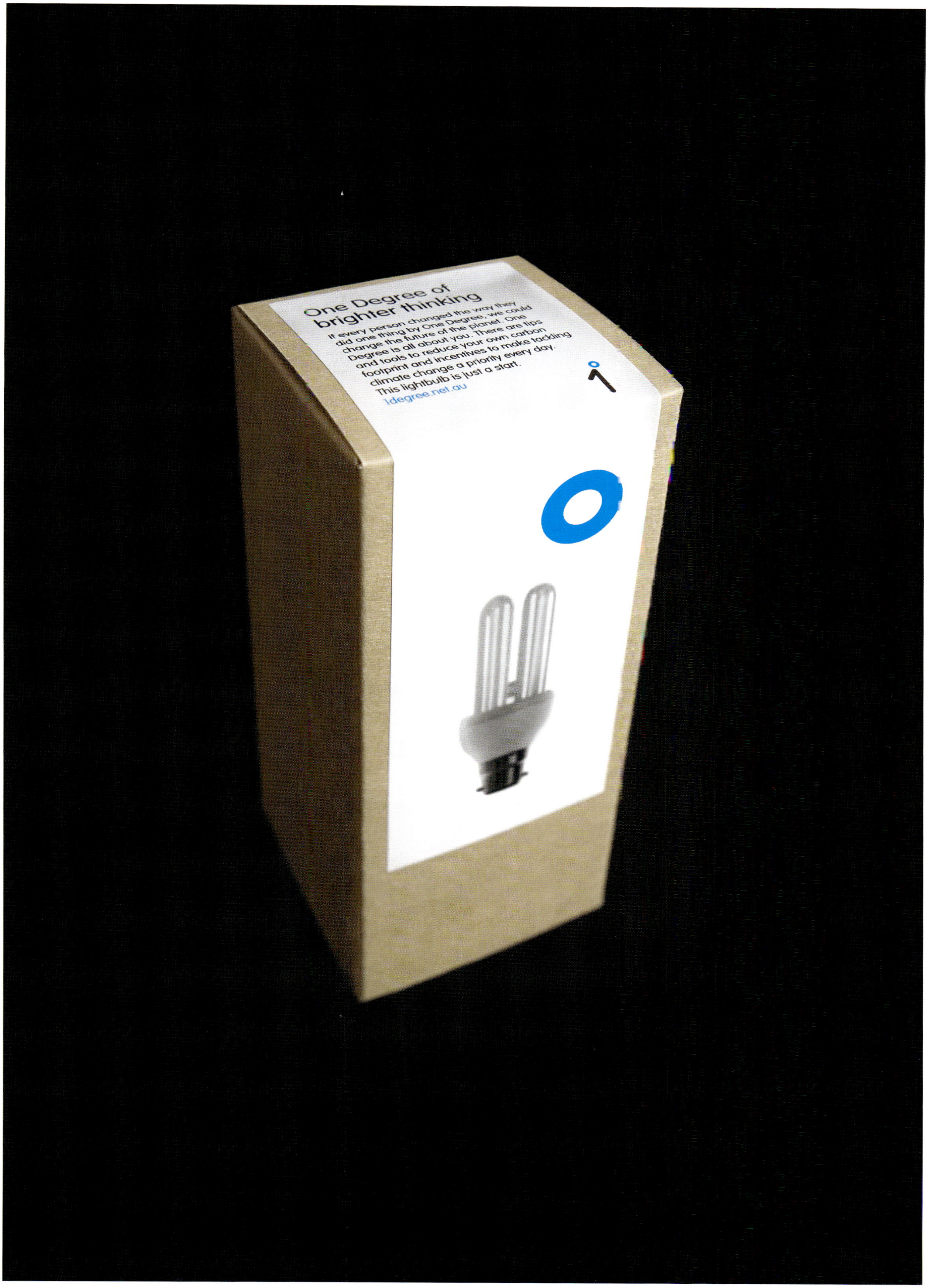

Landor Associates, Australia (this spread) | News Limited | Environmental

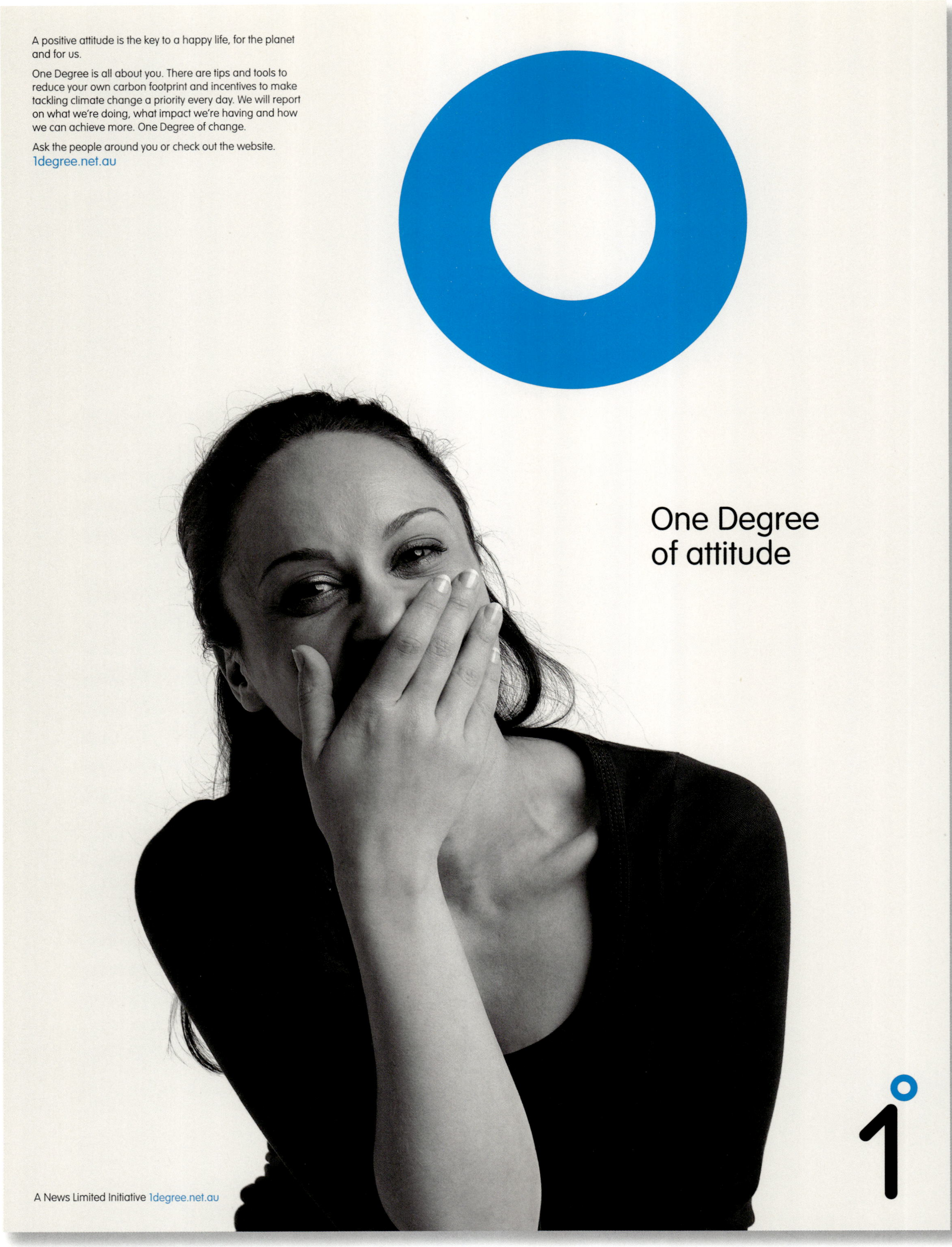

 Environmental | News Limited | (this spread) **Landor Associates, Australia**

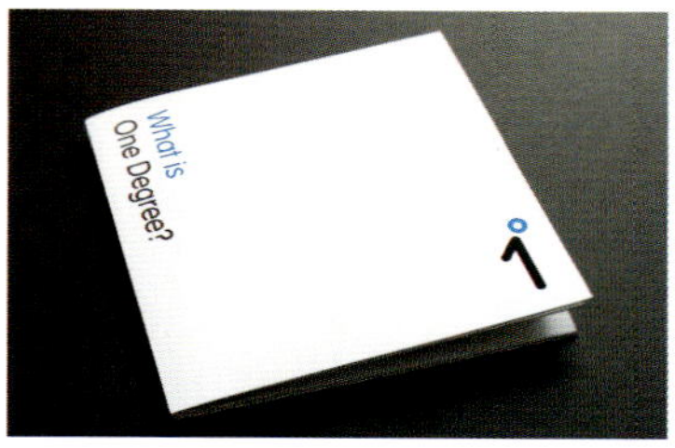
What is
One Degree?

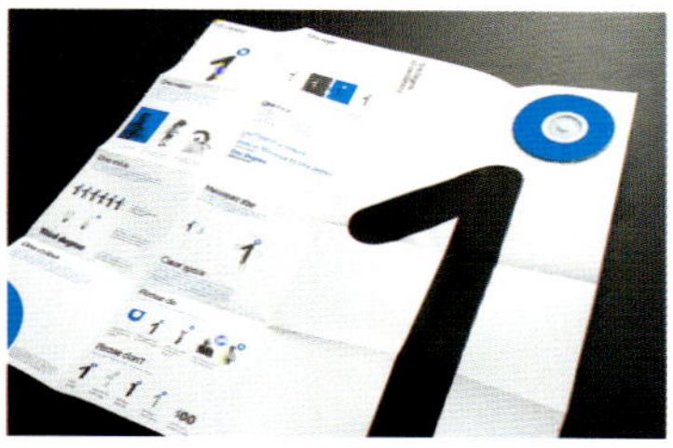

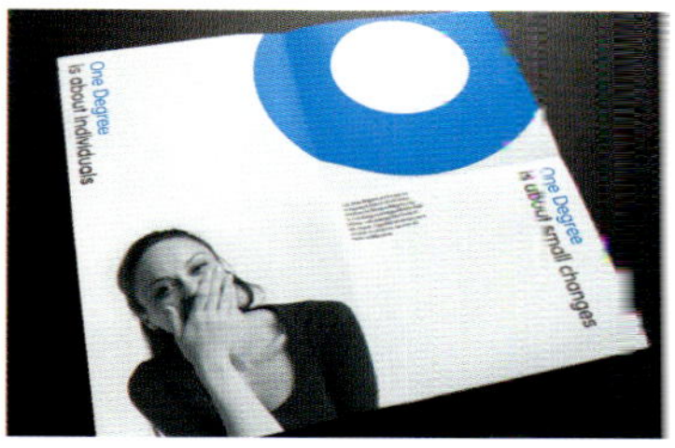
One Degree
is about individuals
One Degree
is about small changes

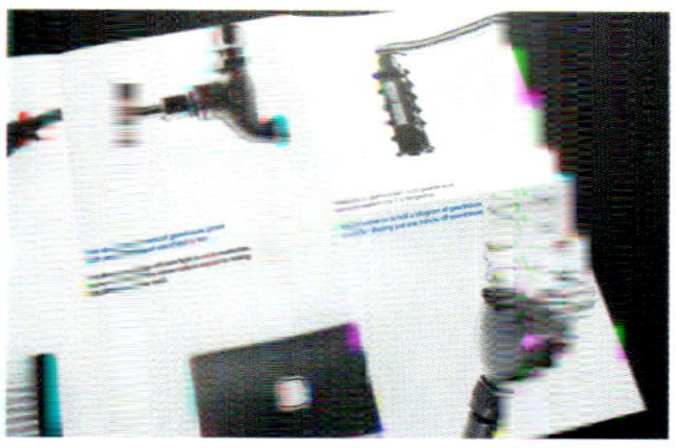

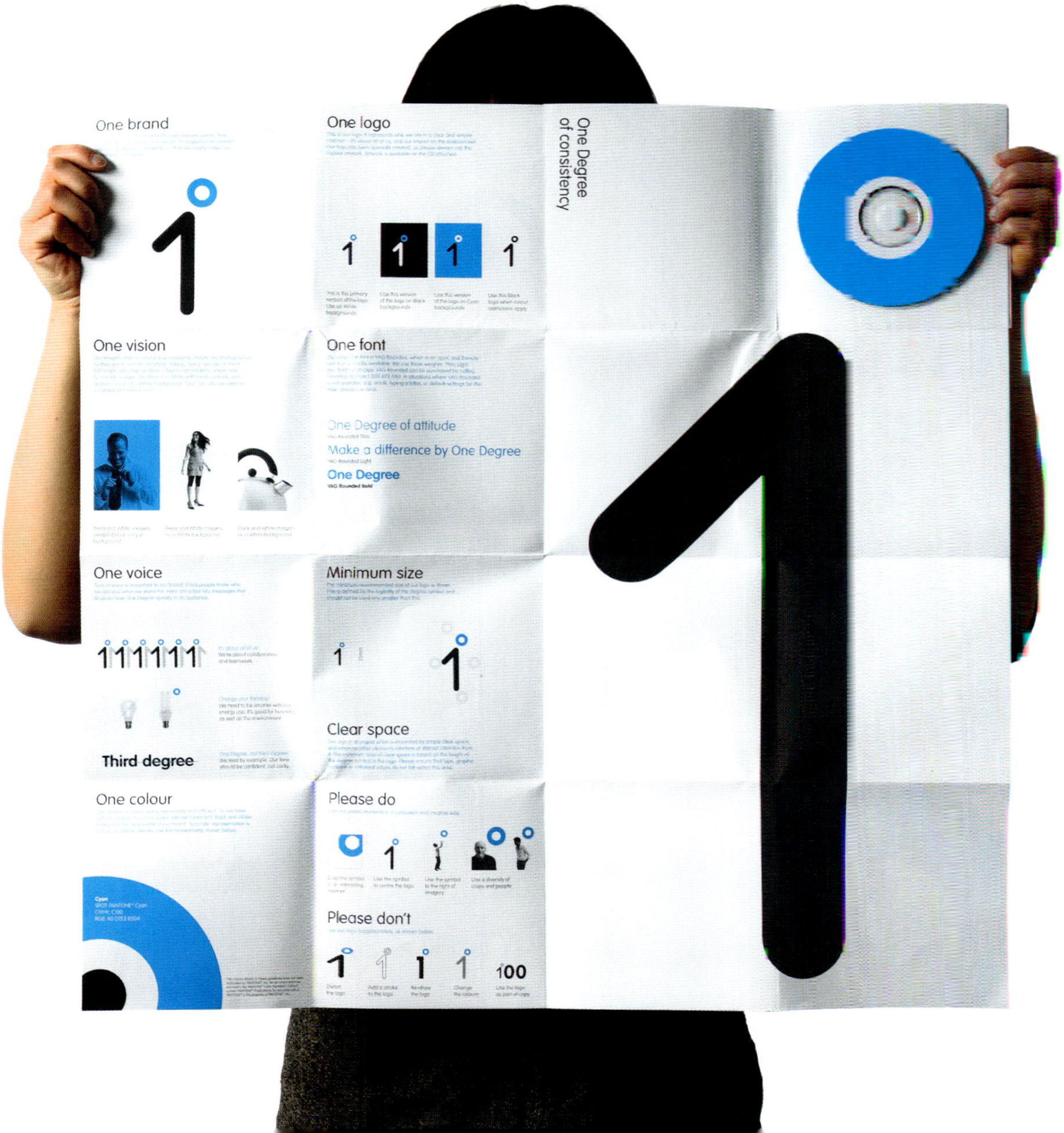
One brand
One logo
One Degree
of consistency
One vision
One font
One Degree of attitude
Make a difference by One Degree
One Degree
One voice
Third degree
Minimum size
Clear space
One colour
Please do
Please don't
100

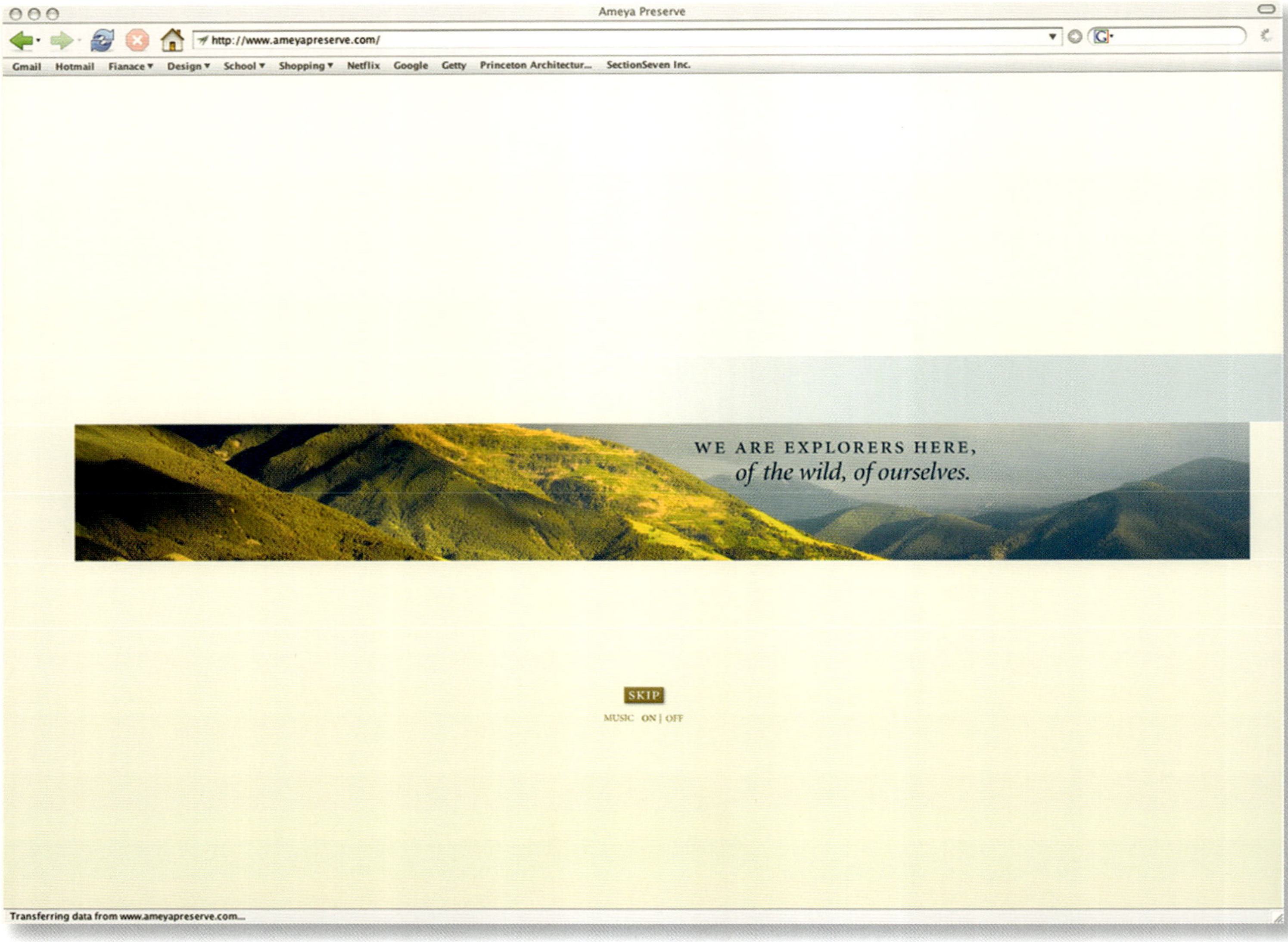

AMEYA
PRESERVE

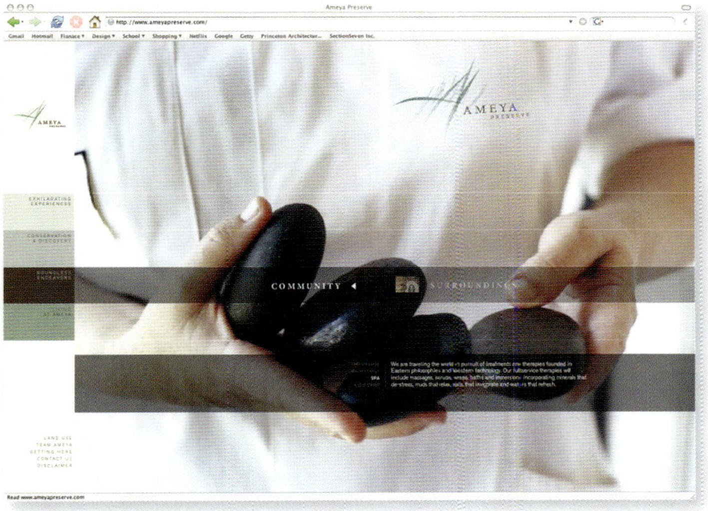
Ameya Preserve
http://www.ameyapreserve.com/
AMEYA PRESERVE
COMMUNITY
SURROUNDINGS

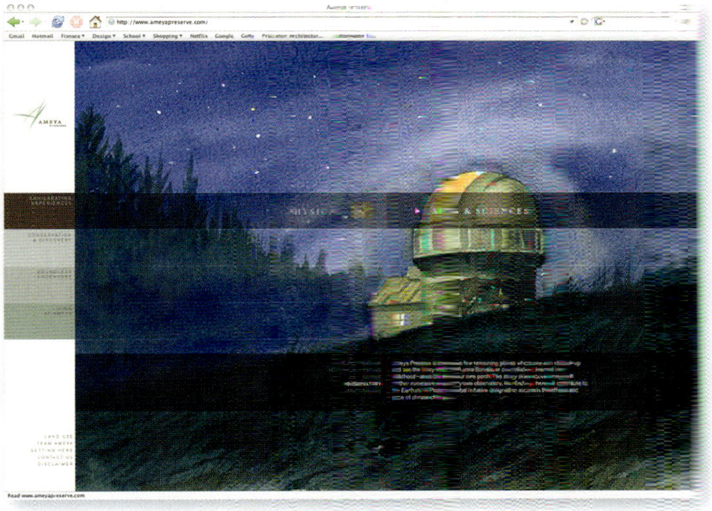
http://www.ameyapreserve.com/

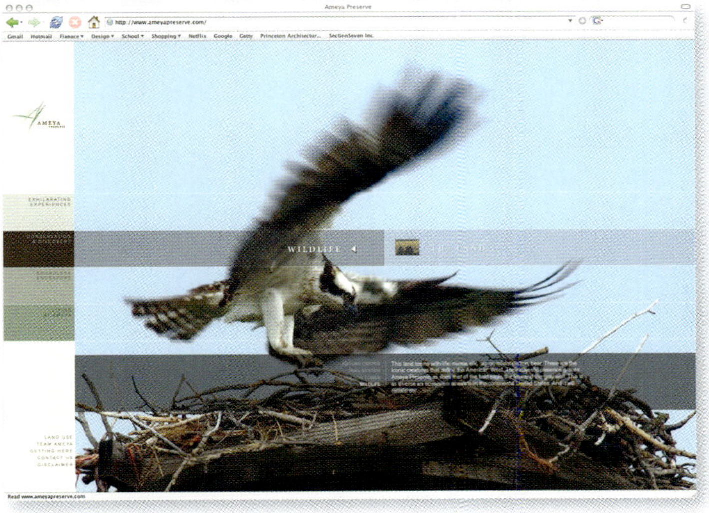
Ameya Preserve
http://www.ameyapreserve.com/
WILDLIFE

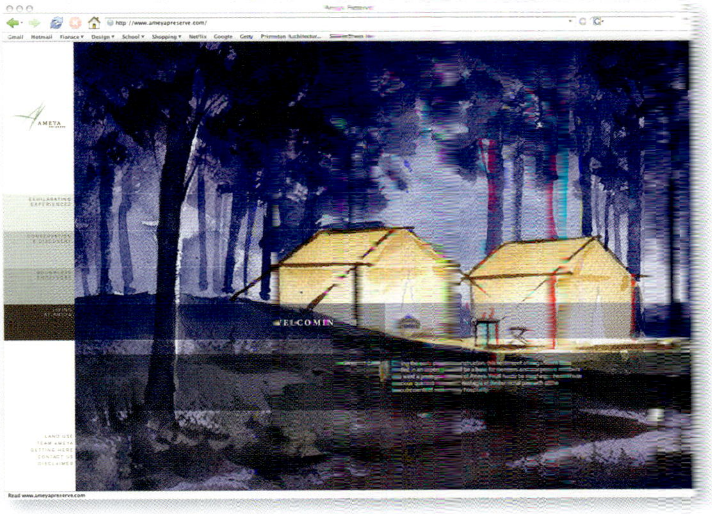
http://www.ameyapreserve.com/

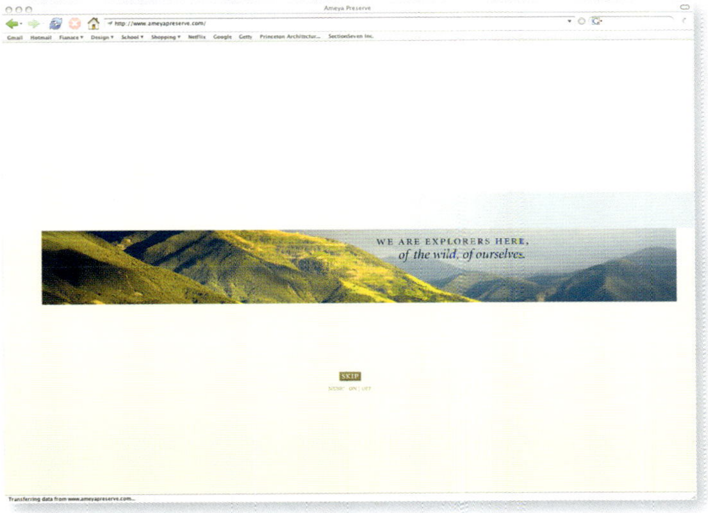
Ameya Preserve
http://www.ameyapreserve.com/
WE ARE EXPLORERS HERE,
of the wild, of ourselves.
SKIP

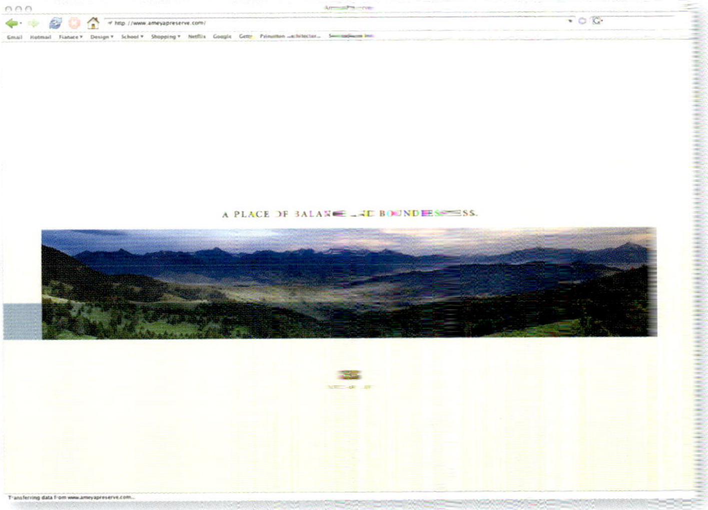
http://www.ameyapreserve.com/

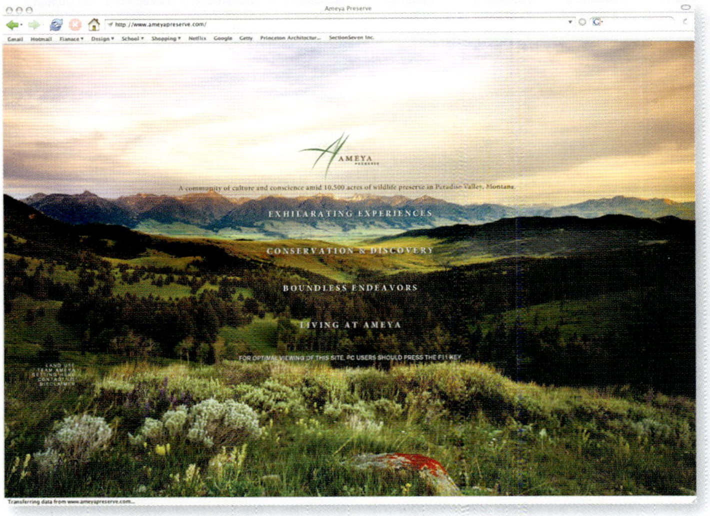
Ameya Preserve
http://www.ameyapreserve.com/
AMEYA
A community of culture and conscience amid 10,500 acres of wildlife preserve in Paradise Valley, Montana
EXHILARATING EXPERIENCES
CONSERVATION & DISCOVERY
BOUNDLESS ENDEAVORS
LIVING AT AMEYA
FOR OPTIMAL VIEWING OF THIS SITE, PC USERS SHOULD PRESS THE F11 KEY

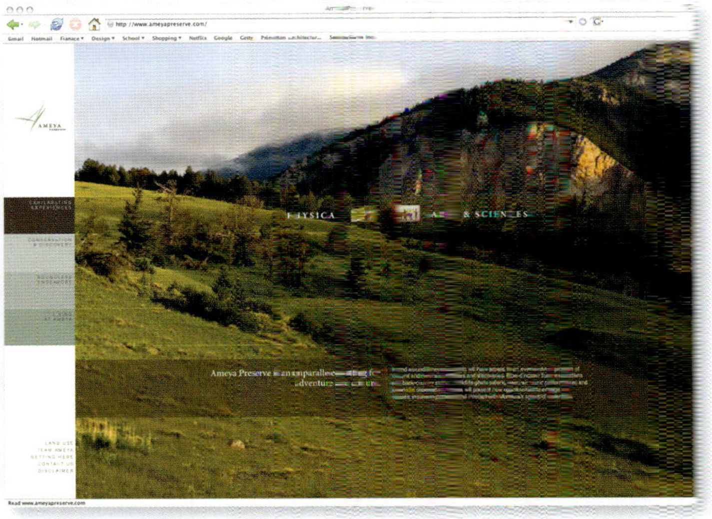
http://www.ameyapreserve.com/

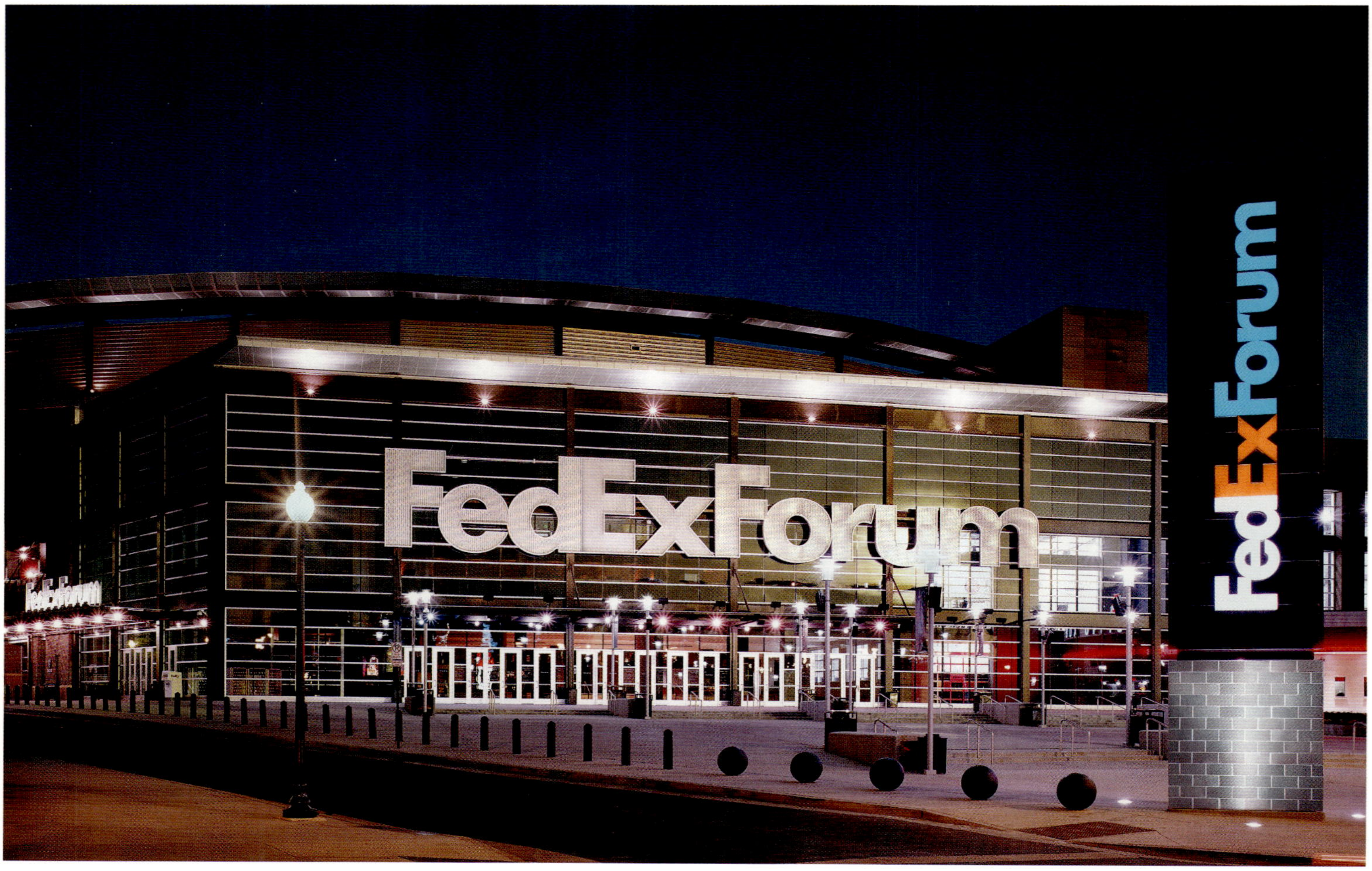
FedExForum
FedExForum
FedExForum

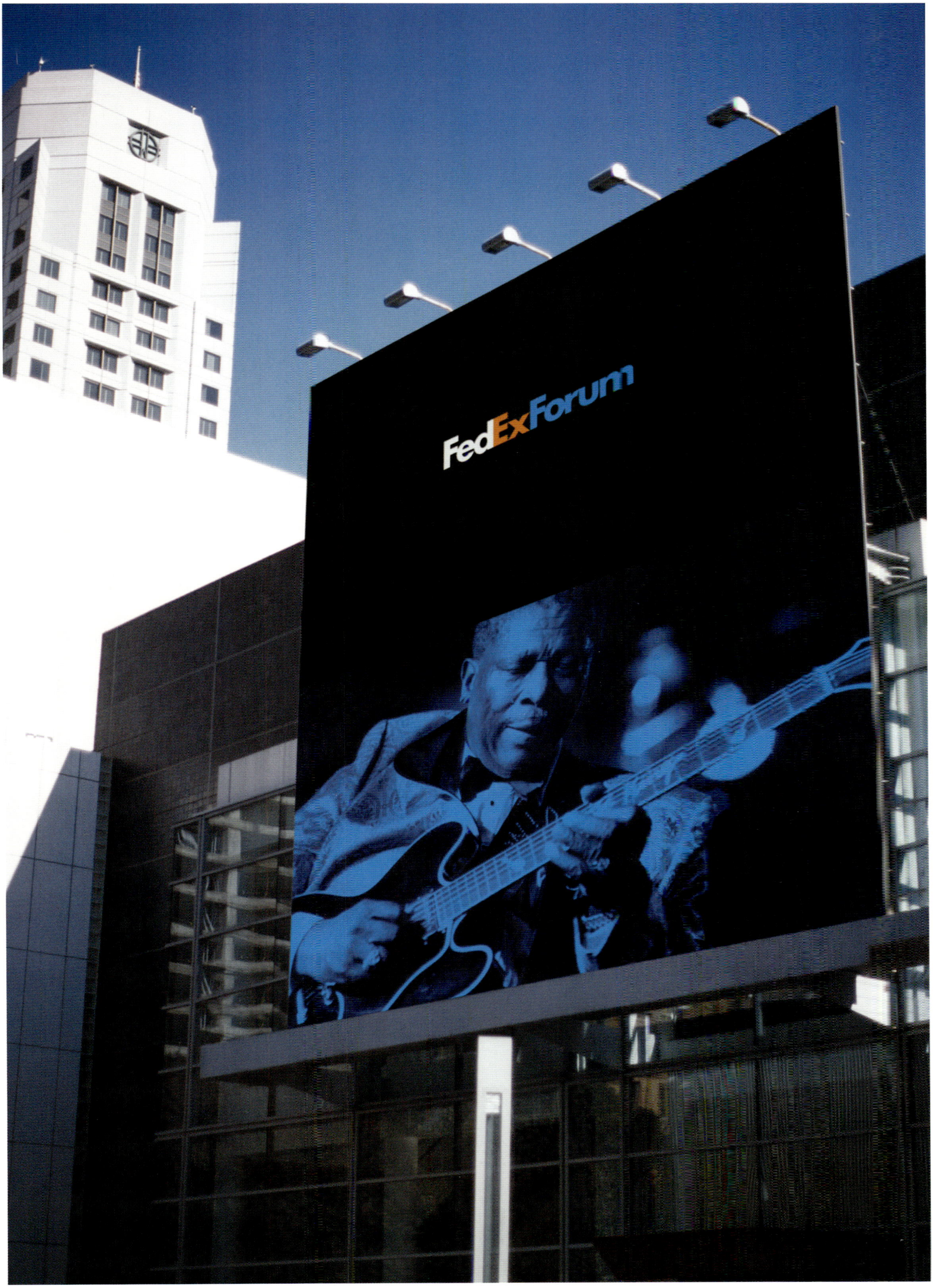
FedExForum

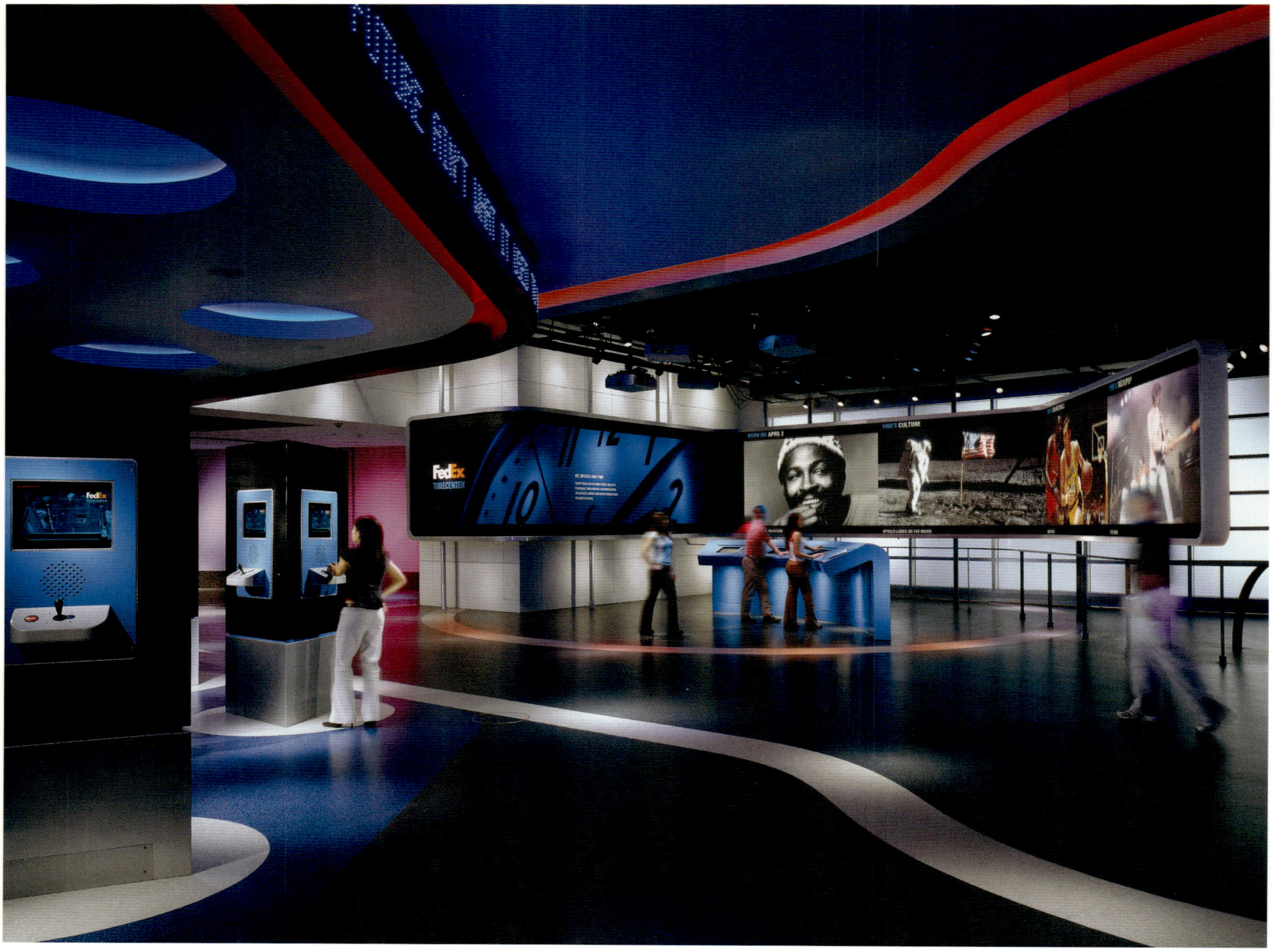
FedEx
TIMECENTER
1960'S CULTURE
APOLLO LANDS ON THE MOON

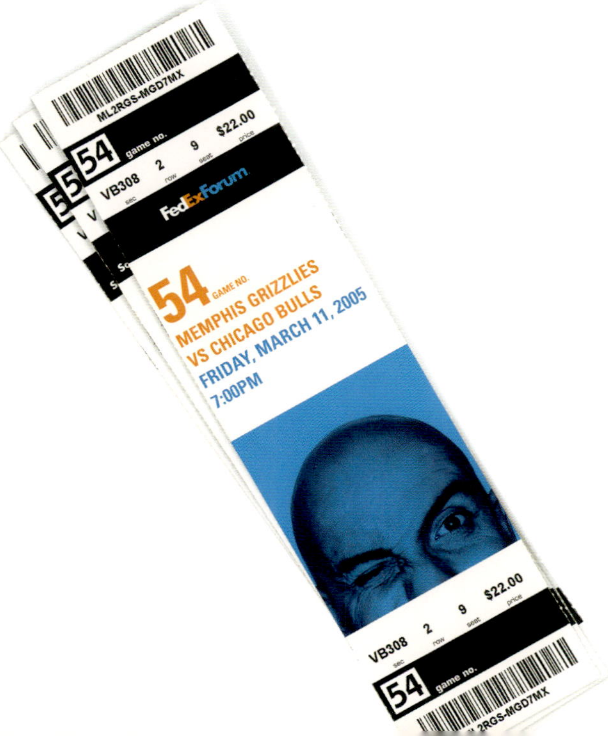
ML2RGS-MGD7MX
54 game no.
VB308 sec
2 row
9 seat
$22.00 price
FedExForum
54 GAME NO.
MEMPHIS GRIZZLIES
VS CHICAGO BULLS
FRIDAY, MARCH 11, 2005
7:00PM
VB308 sec
2 row
9 seat
$22.00 price
54 game no.

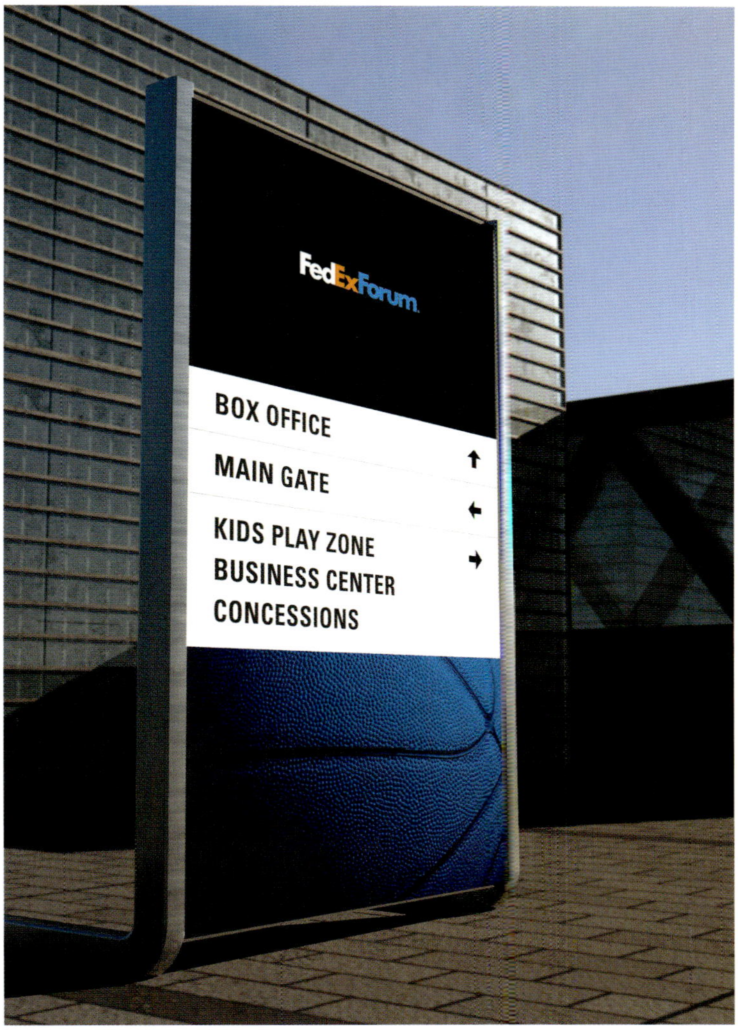
FedExForum
BOX OFFICE
MAIN GATE
KIDS PLAY ZONE
BUSINESS CENTER
CONCESSIONS

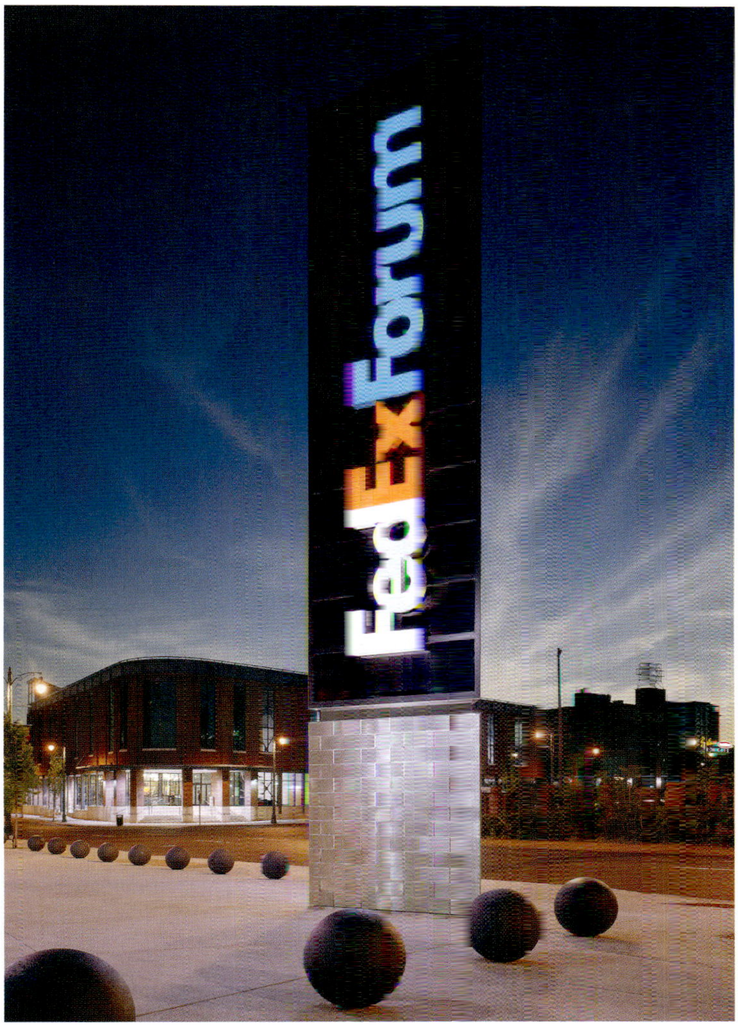
FedExForum

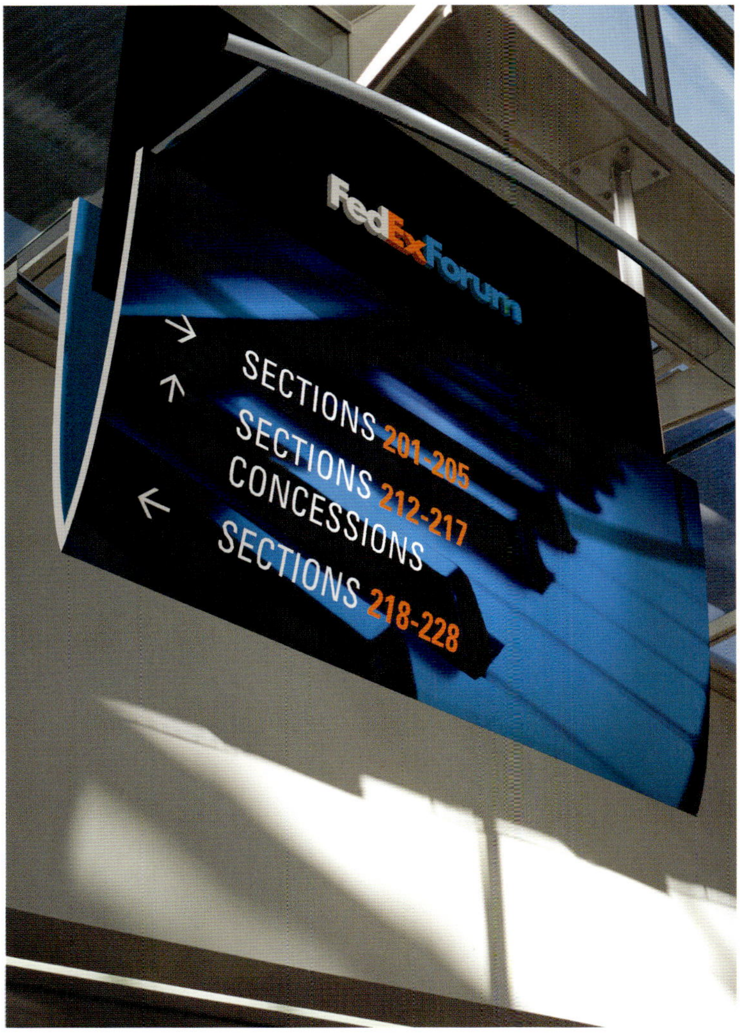
FedExForum
SECTIONS 201-205
SECTIONS 212-217
CONCESSIONS
SECTIONS 218-228

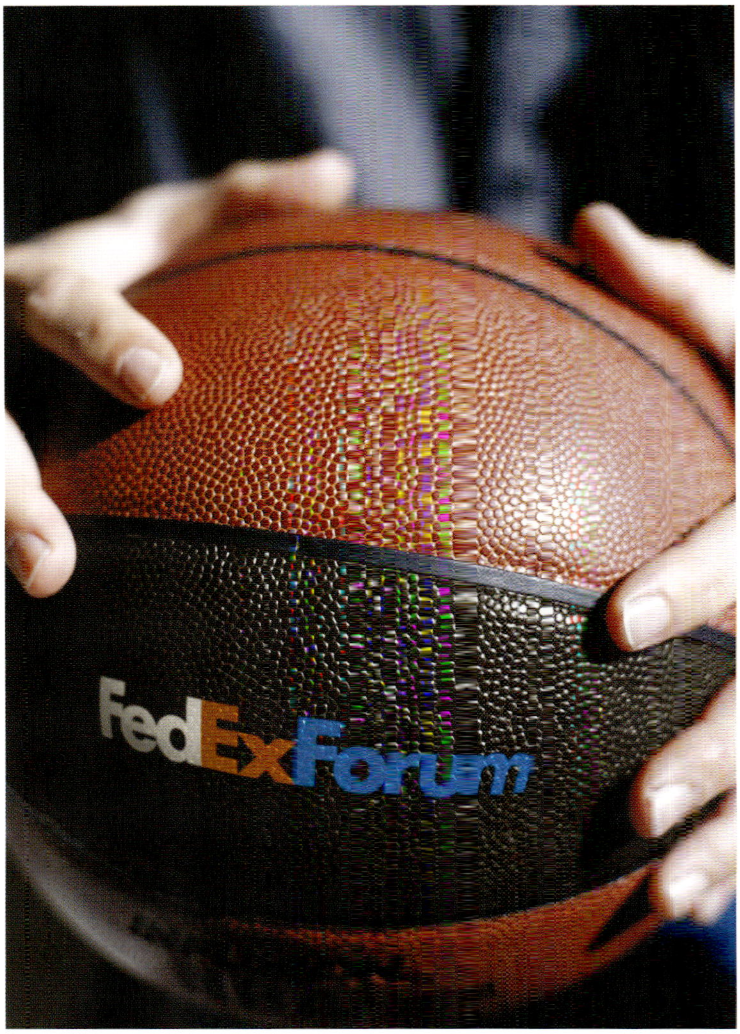
FedExForum

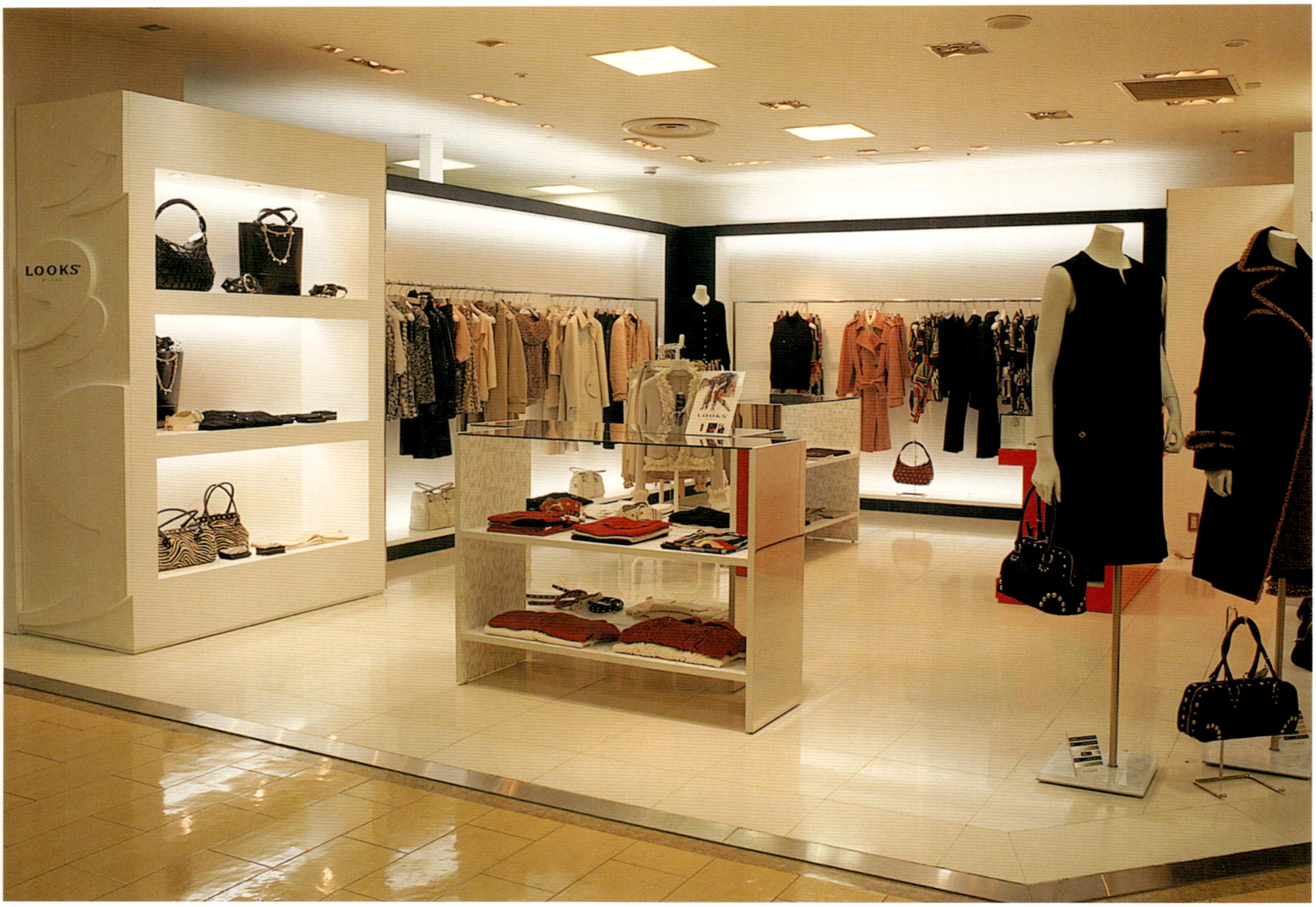

LOOKS'
MILANO

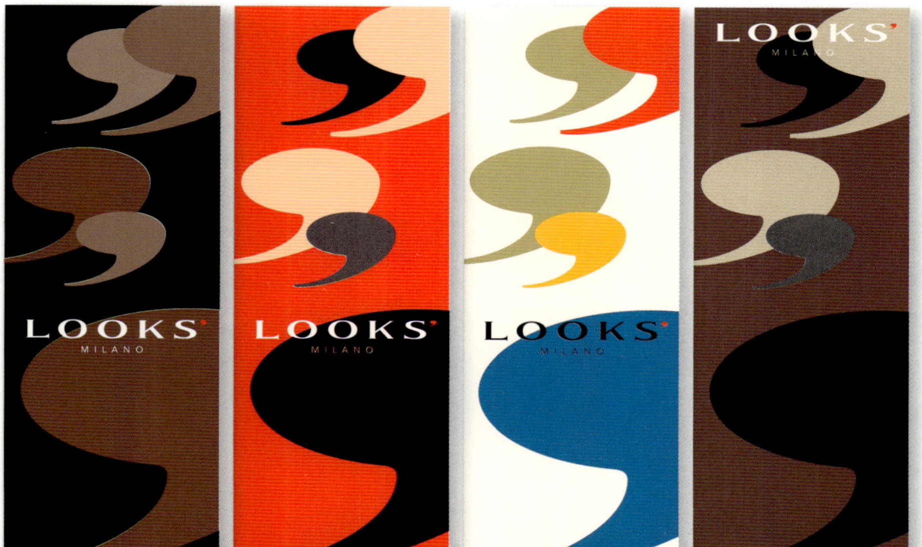

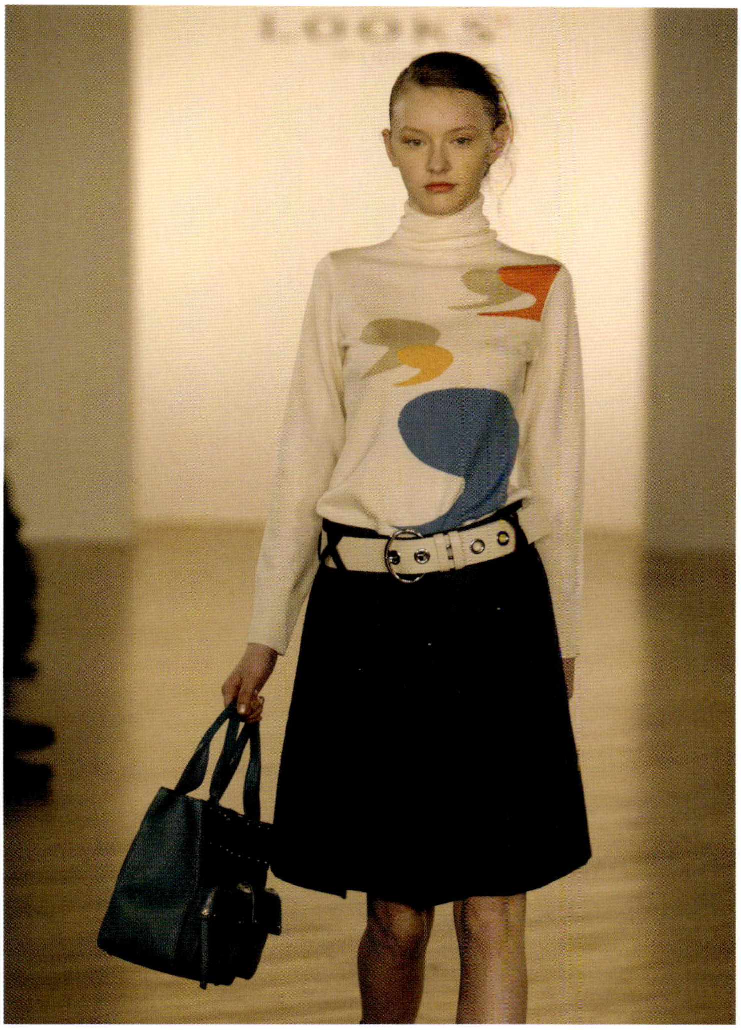
LOOKS'
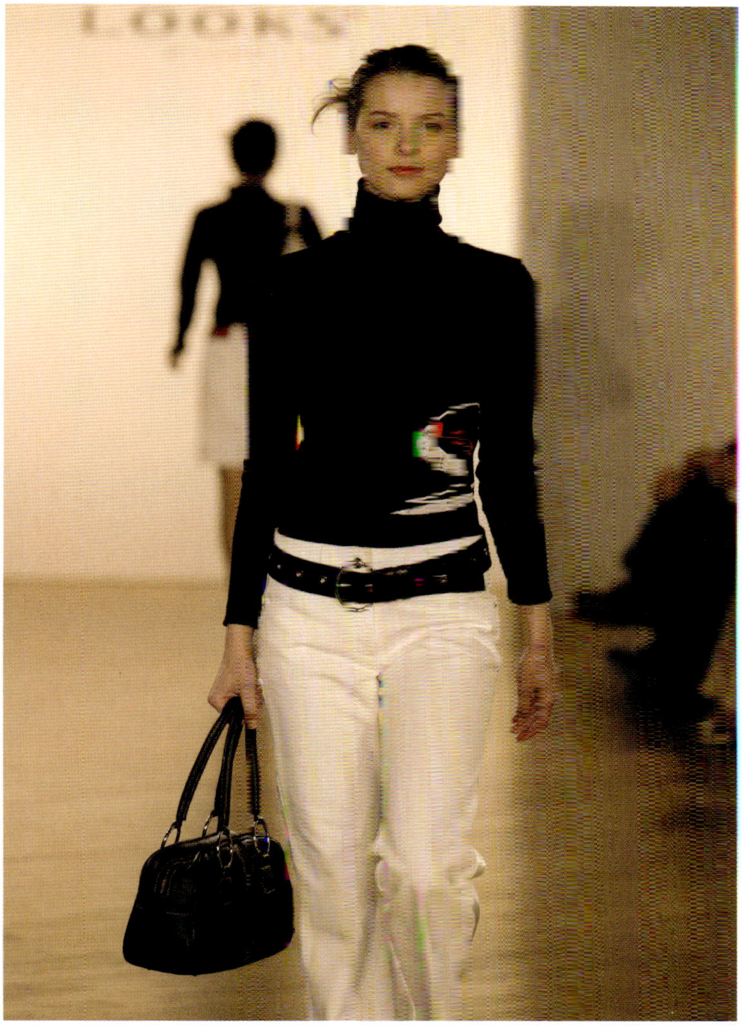
LOOKS'
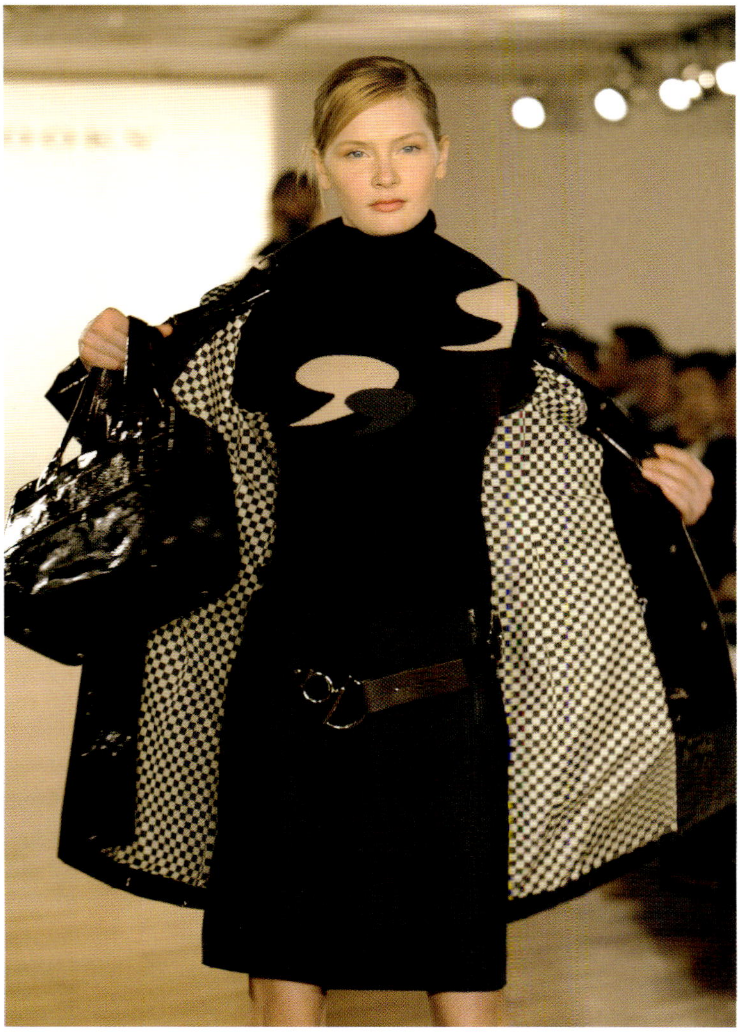
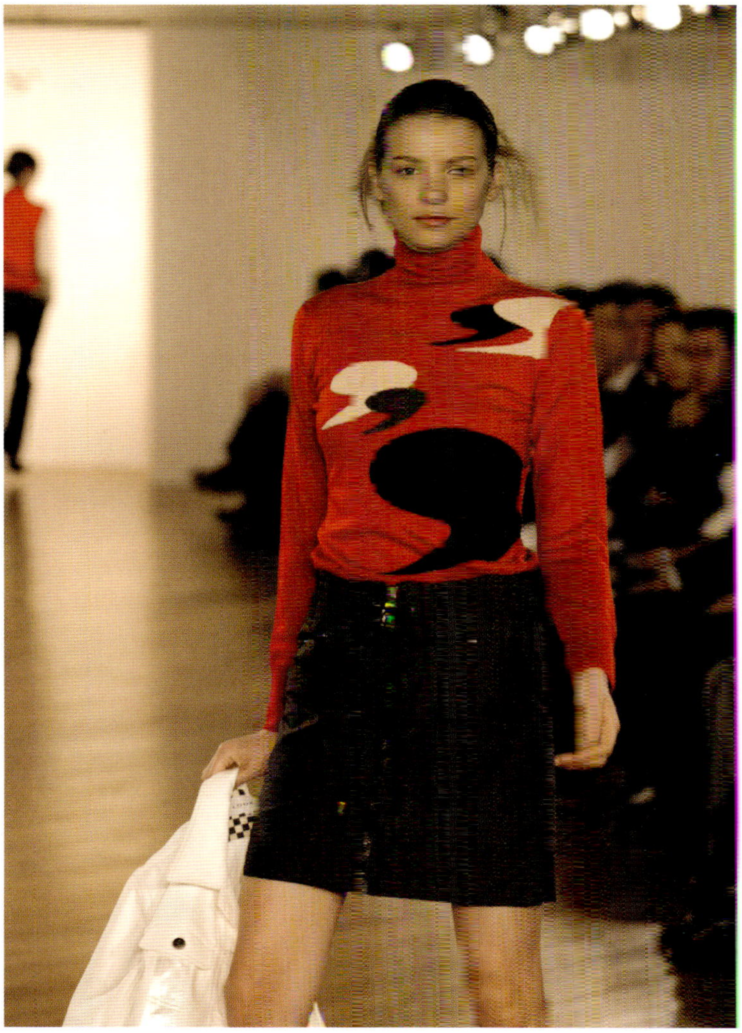

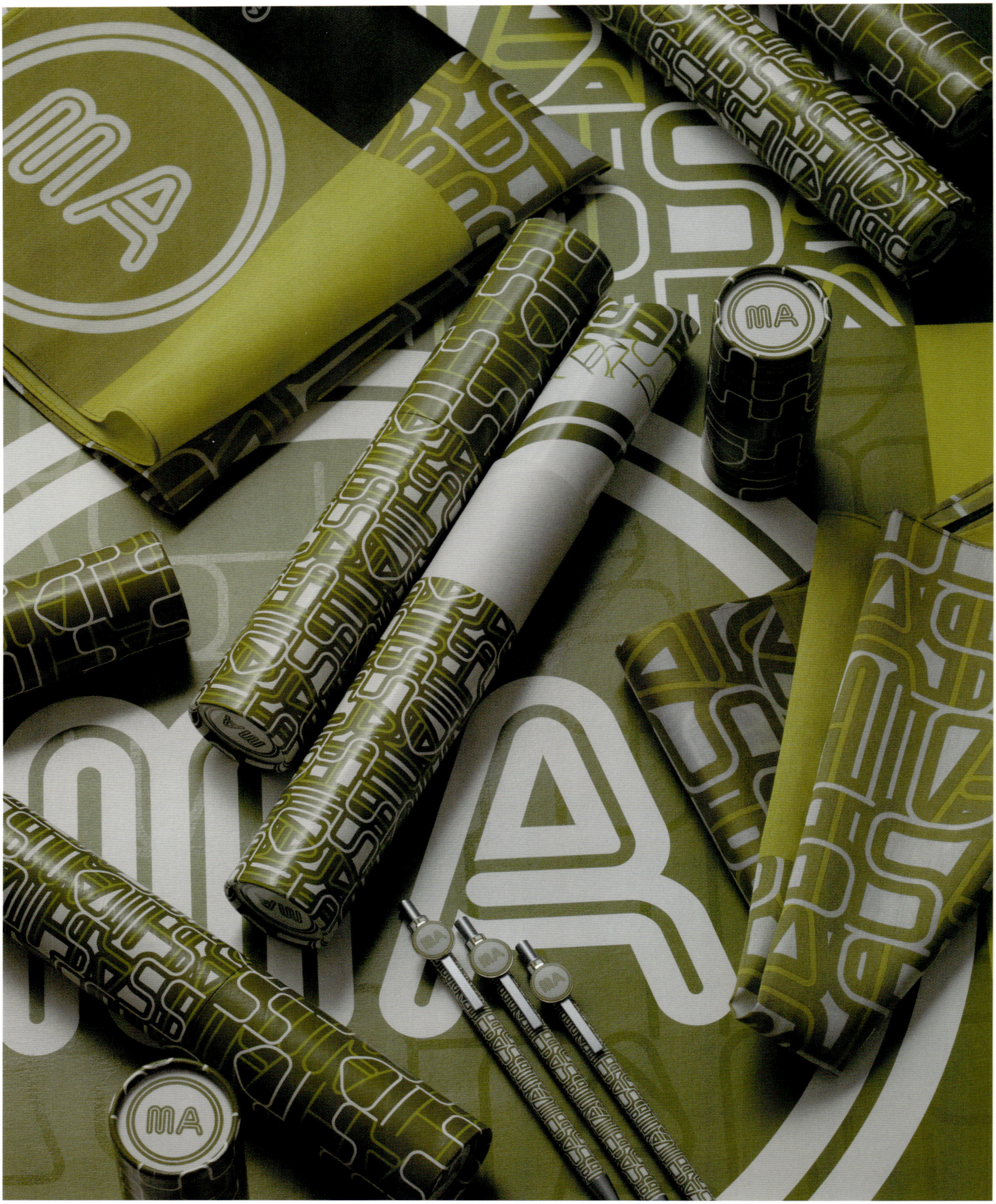

MISSASHIDA

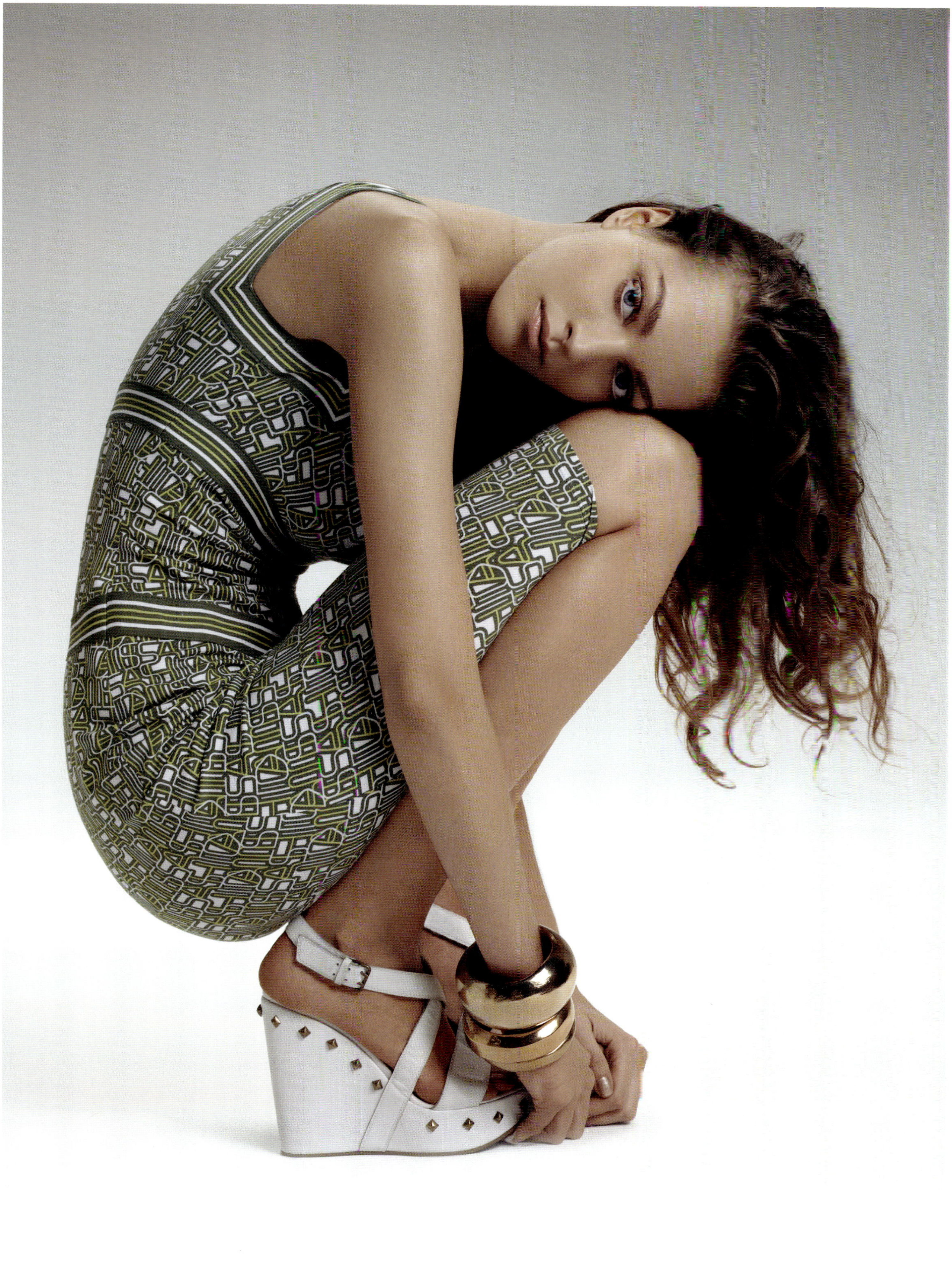

Graphics & Designing Inc. (this spread) | Jun Ashida Co., Ltd |

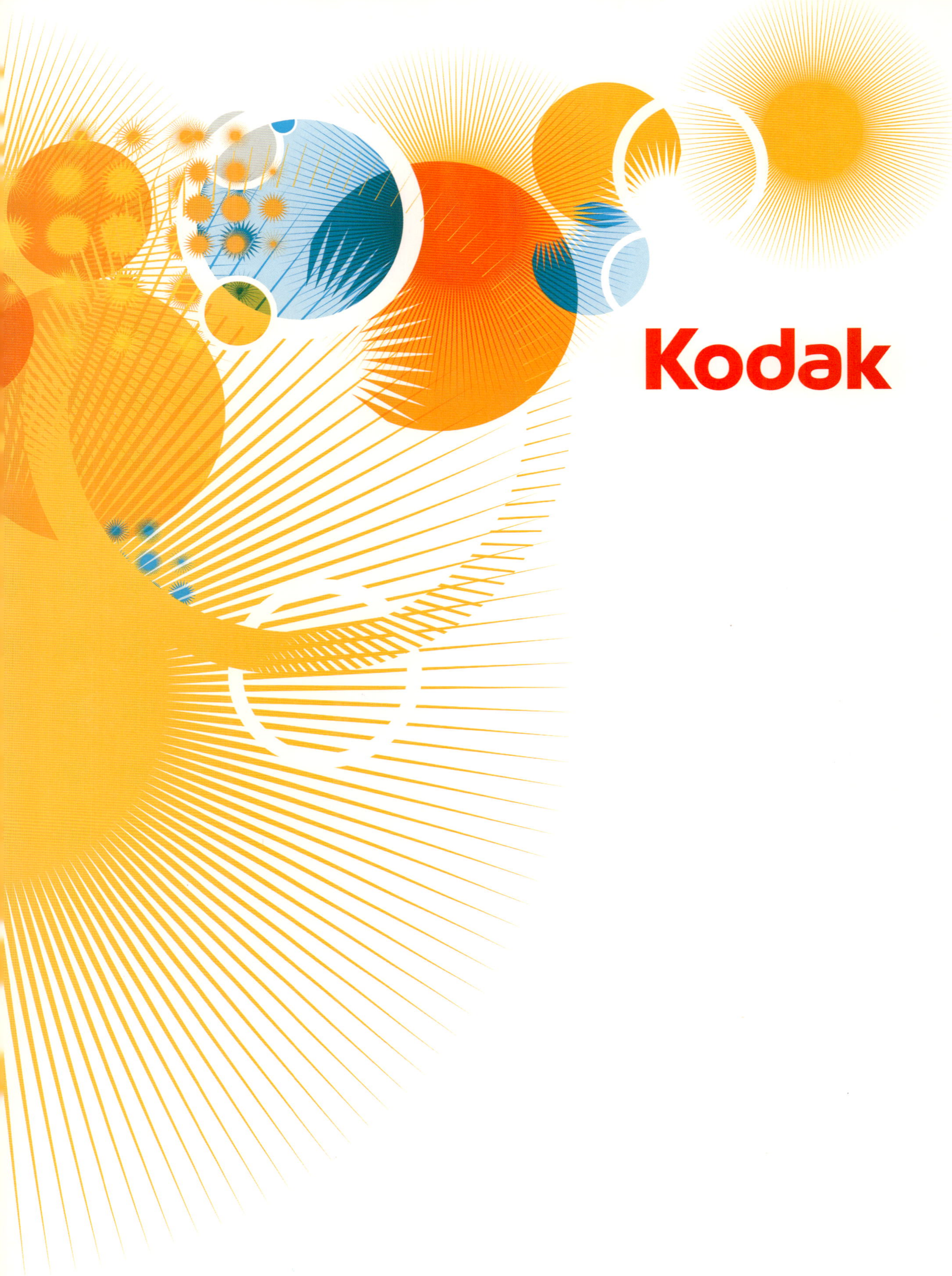

1907

1935

1960

1971

1987

san serif letters

streamlined letterforms

idiosyncratic a

COLOR PALETTE

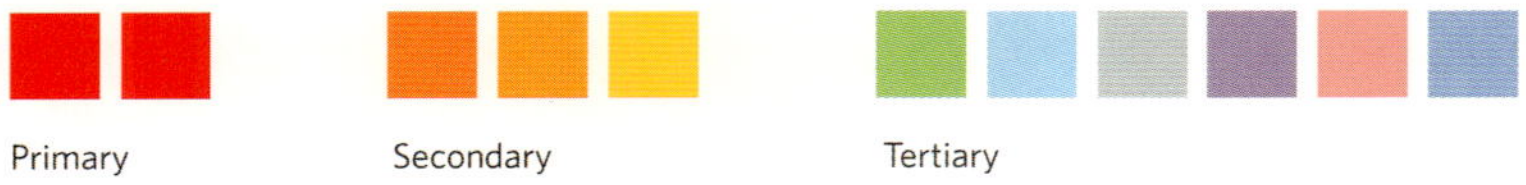

BASIC SHAPES

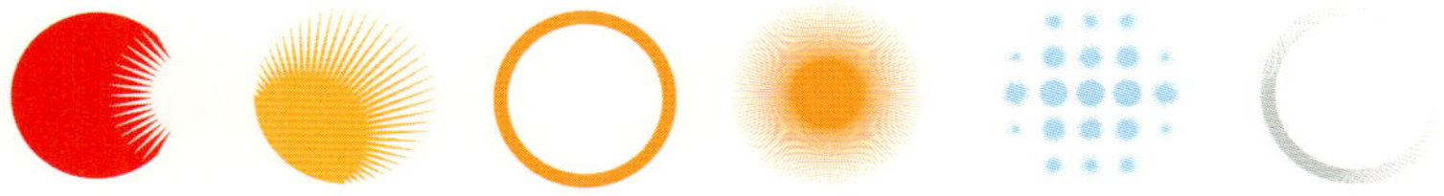

LANGUAGE SHAPE COMBINATIONS

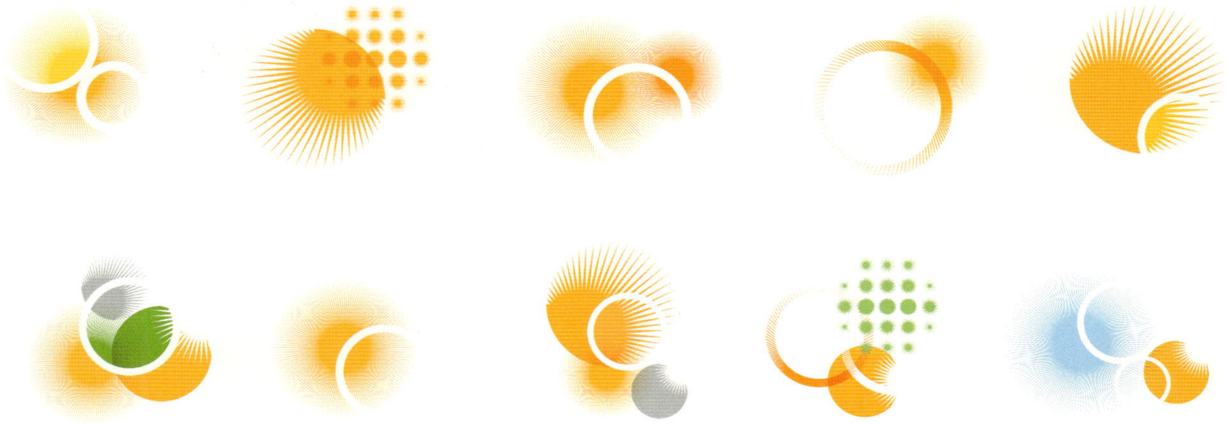

VOLUME INTENSITY CHART

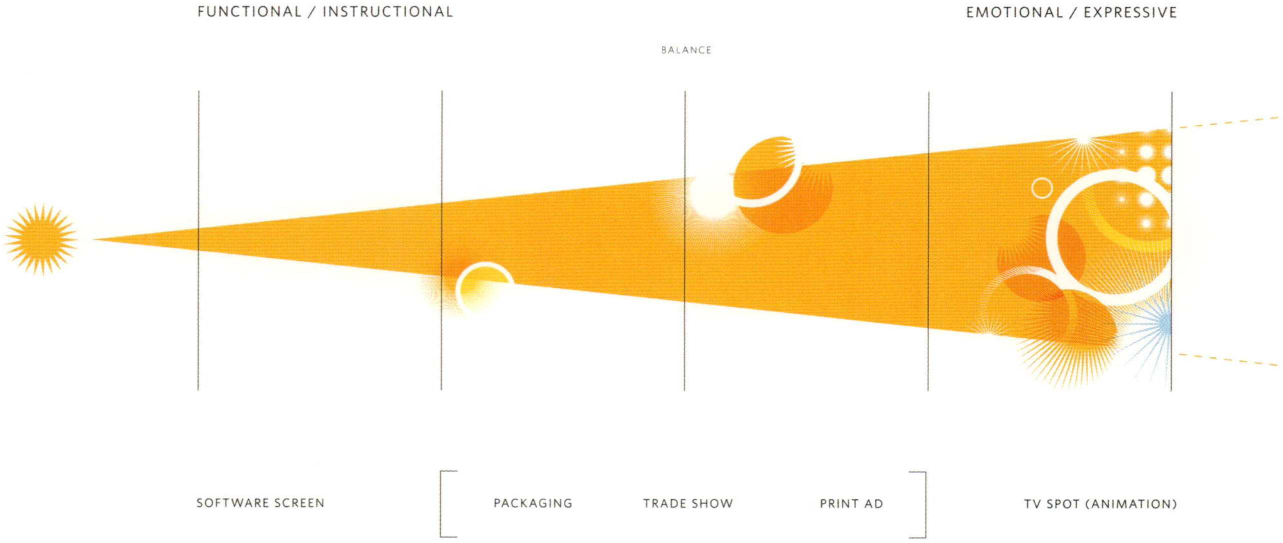

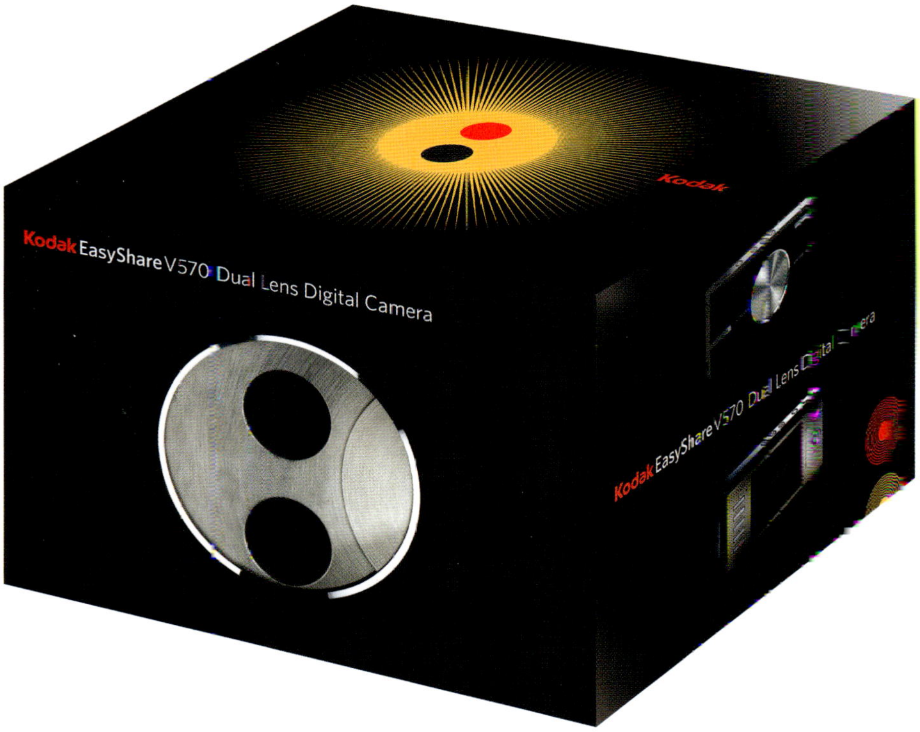
Kodak
Kodak EasyShare V570 Dual Lens Digital Camera

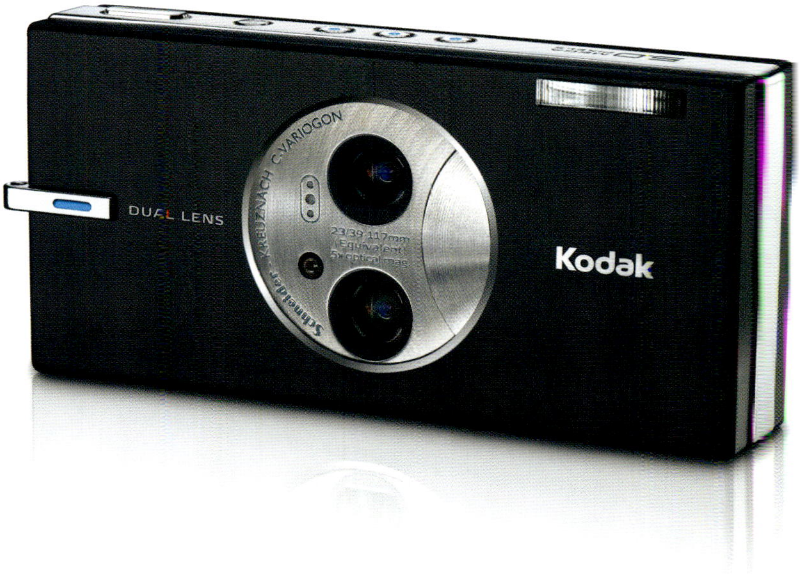
DUAL LENS
Schneider KREUZNACH C-VARIOGON
Kodak

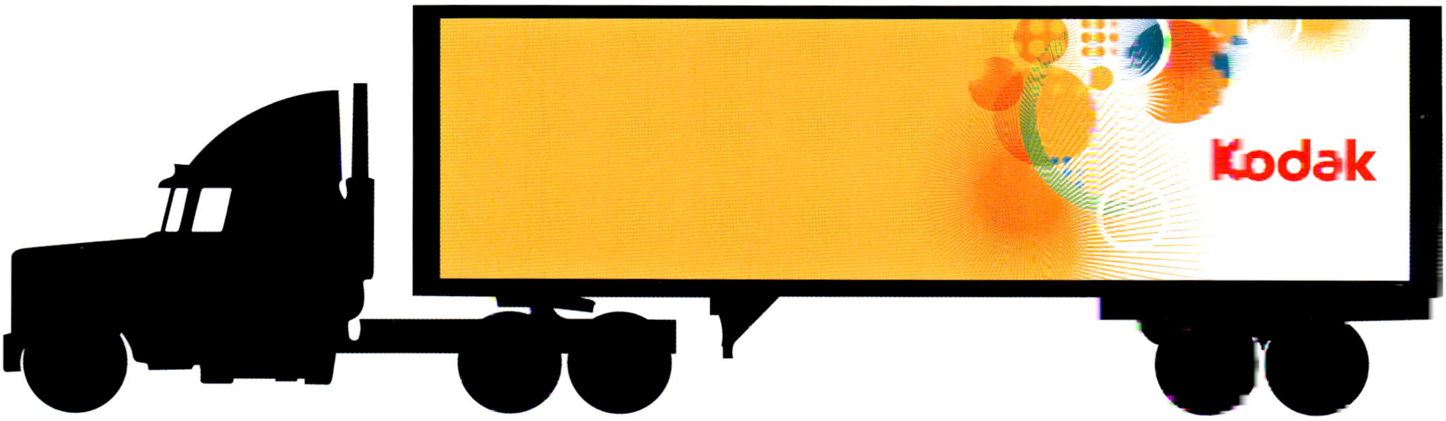
Kodak

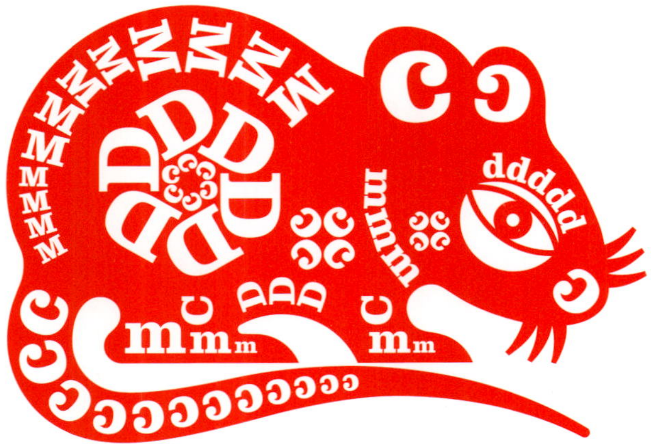

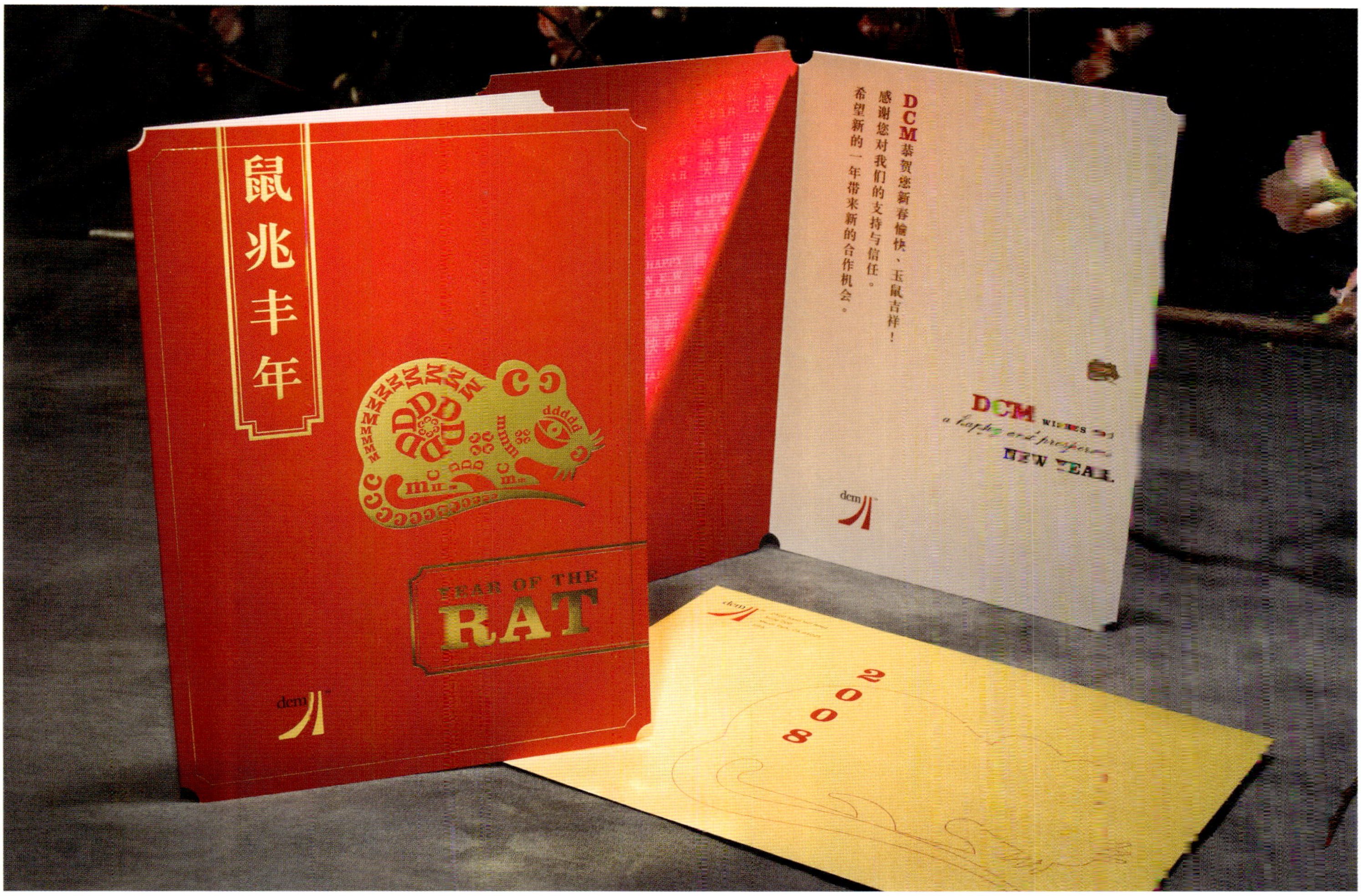
鼠兆丰年
YEAR OF THE
RAT
dcm
DCM恭贺您新春愉快，玉鼠吉祥！
感谢您对我们的支持与信任。
希望新的一年带来新的合作机会。
NEW YEAR
2008

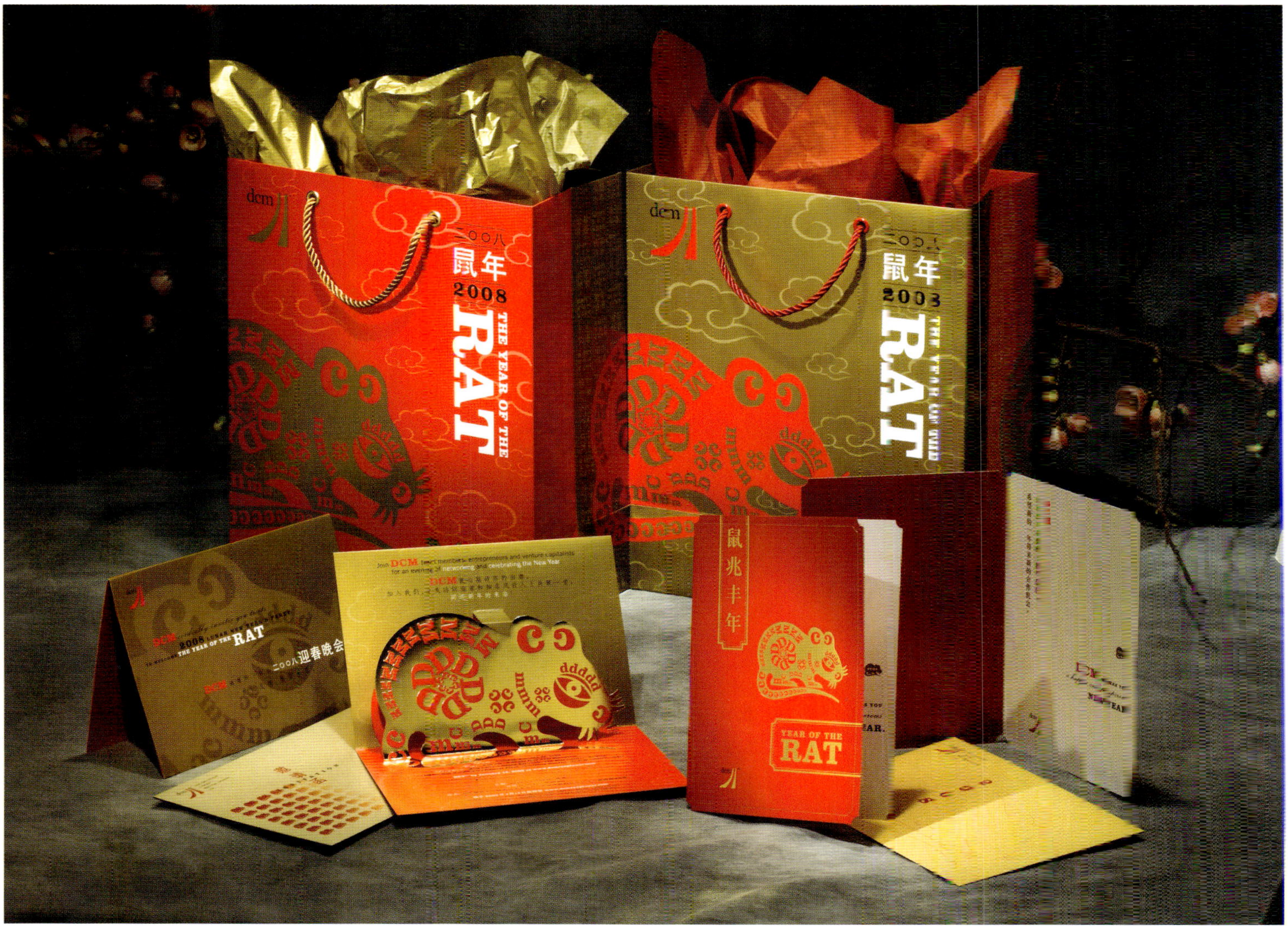
dcm
二OO八
鼠年
2008
THE YEAR OF THE
RAT
迎春晚会
鼠兆丰年
YEAR OF THE
RAT

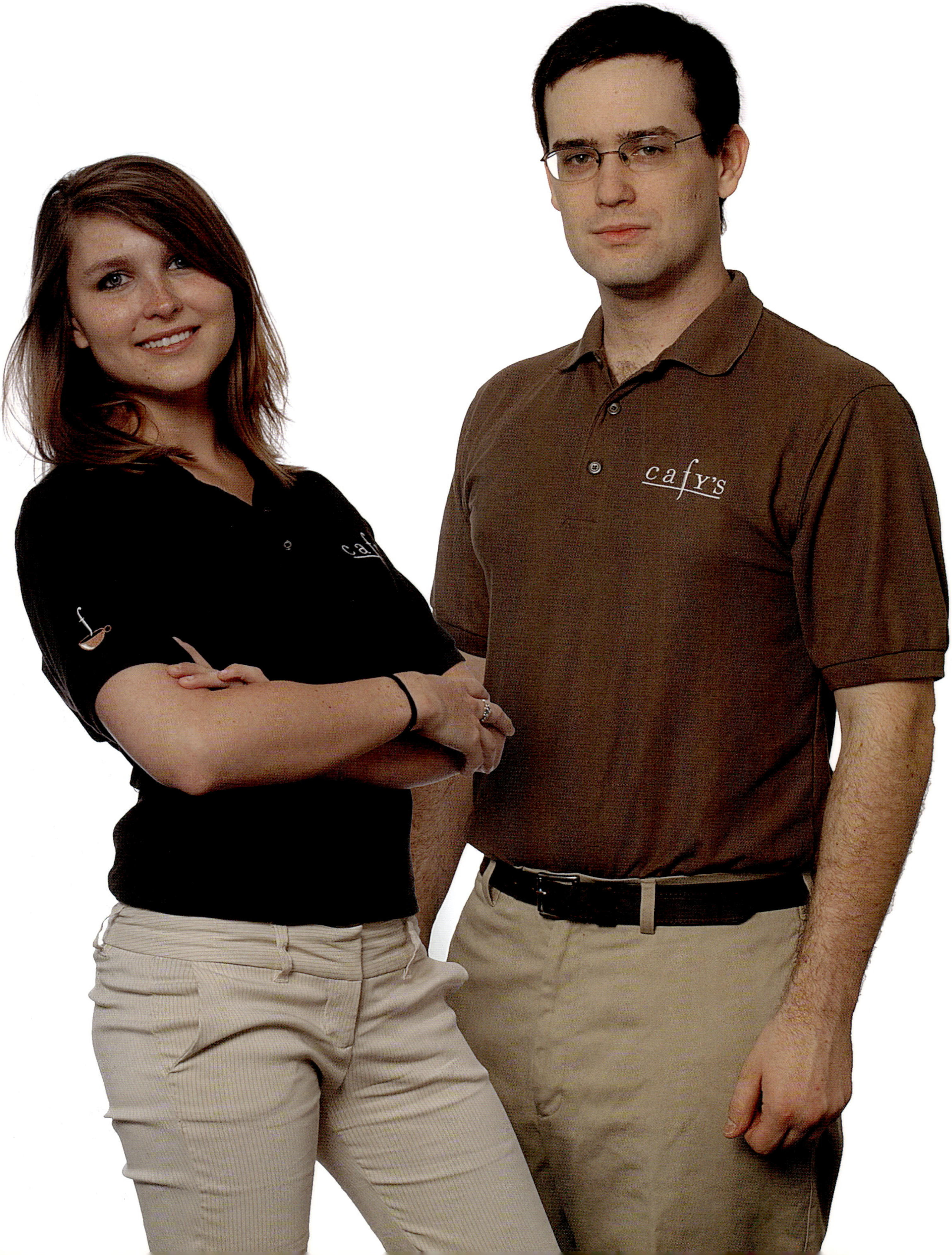
cafy's

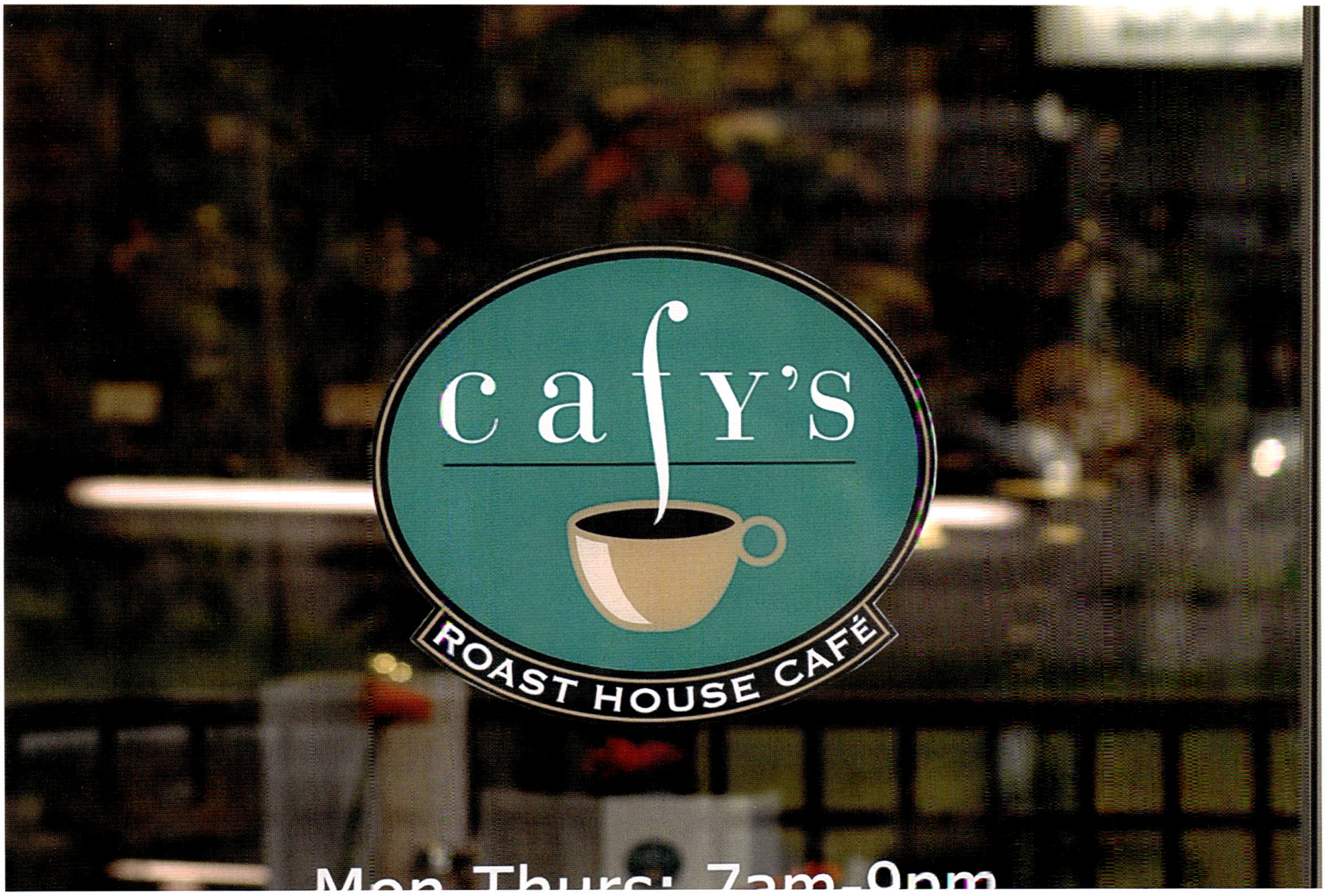

cafy's™
ROAST HOUSE CAFÉ

cafy's™
ROASTED COFFEE

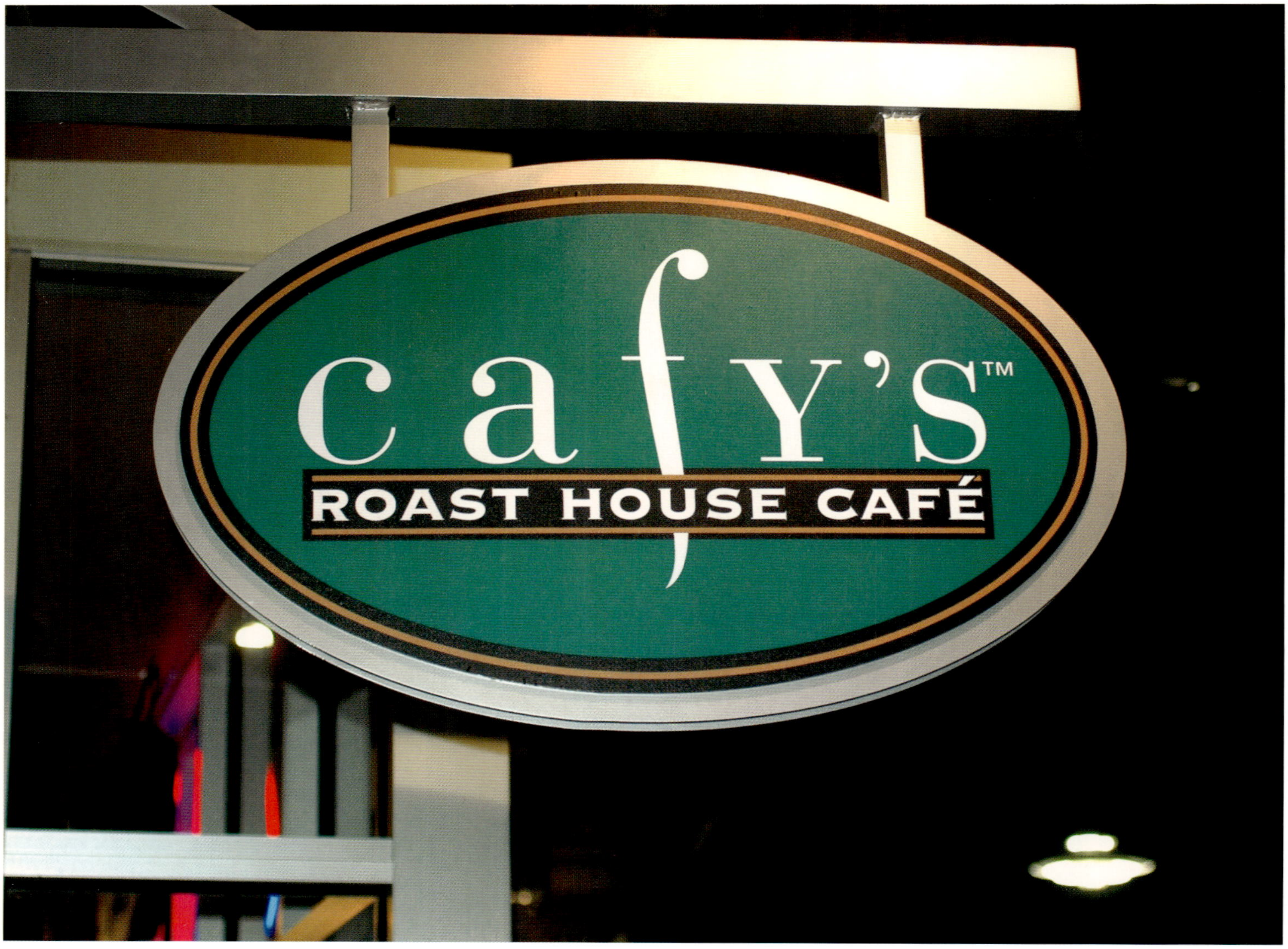
cafy's™
ROAST HOUSE CAFÉ

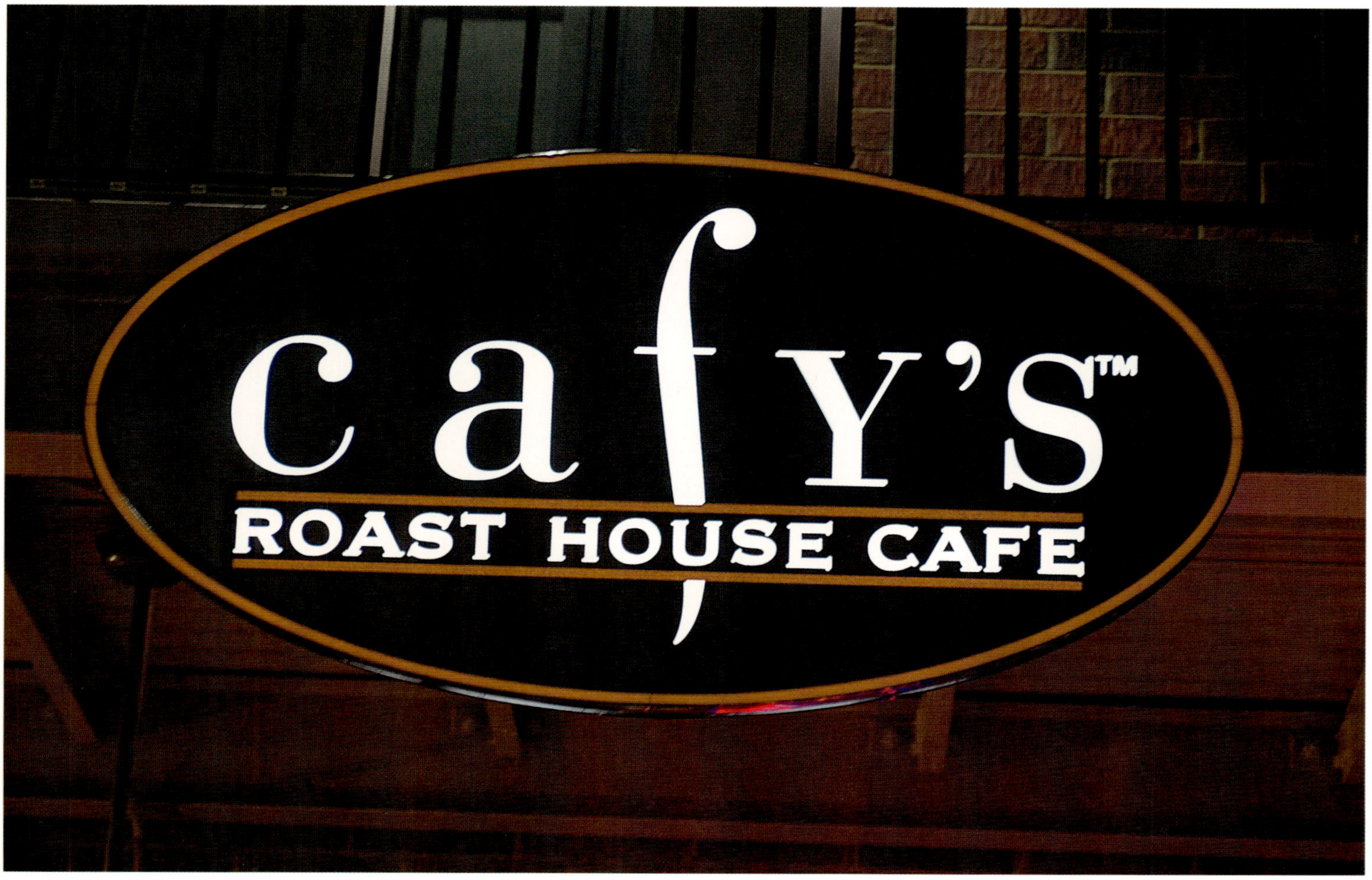
cafy's™
ROAST HOUSE CAFE

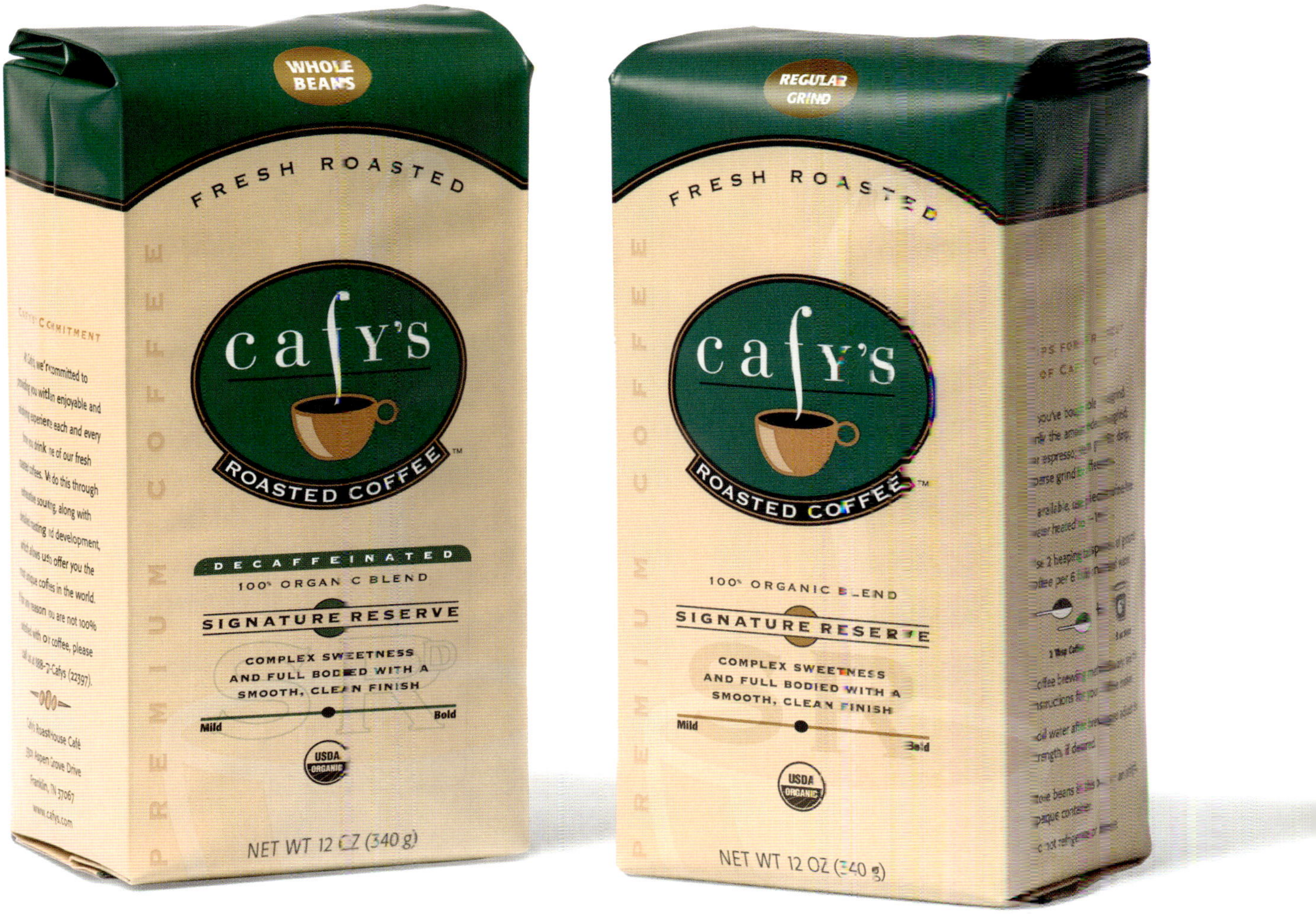
WHOLE BEANS
FRESH ROASTED
PREMIUM COFFEE
cafy's
ROASTED COFFEE
DECAFFEINATED
100% ORGANIC BLEND
SIGNATURE RESERVE
COMPLEX SWEETNESS AND FULL BODIED WITH A SMOOTH, CLEAN FINISH
Mild
Bold
USDA ORGANIC
NET WT 12 OZ (340 g)
REGULAR GRIND
FRESH ROASTED
PREMIUM COFFEE
cafy's
ROASTED COFFEE
100% ORGANIC BLEND
SIGNATURE RESERVE
COMPLEX SWEETNESS AND FULL BODIED WITH A SMOOTH, CLEAN FINISH
Mild
Bold
USDA ORGANIC
NET WT 12 OZ (340 g)

GLOBAL FOOD
FUNATICS

GLOBAL FOOD
FUNATICS

GLOBAL FOOD
FUNATICS

GLOBAL FOOD
FUNATICS

Amy Barclay
Restauranteur Journal
4 Denbigh Mews
London SW1V 2HQ

20 January 2007

Dear Amy

A new dawn for food-service-industry buyers

Global Food Funatics is a dynamic, forward thinking organisation that is passionate about good food. It is vital that our brand's values and activities are reflected in a high quality corporate image.

As suppliers, we know only too well just how important appearances are for organisations as well as individuals. Every piece of publicity we produce - every press release, e-newsletter and brochure sends a strong visual message about the brand. This message needs to be strong, consistent and clear at all times.

The following documents are intended to introduce our new brand and explain our ethos. We believe that Global Food Funatics offers a unique balance of value, availability and fun

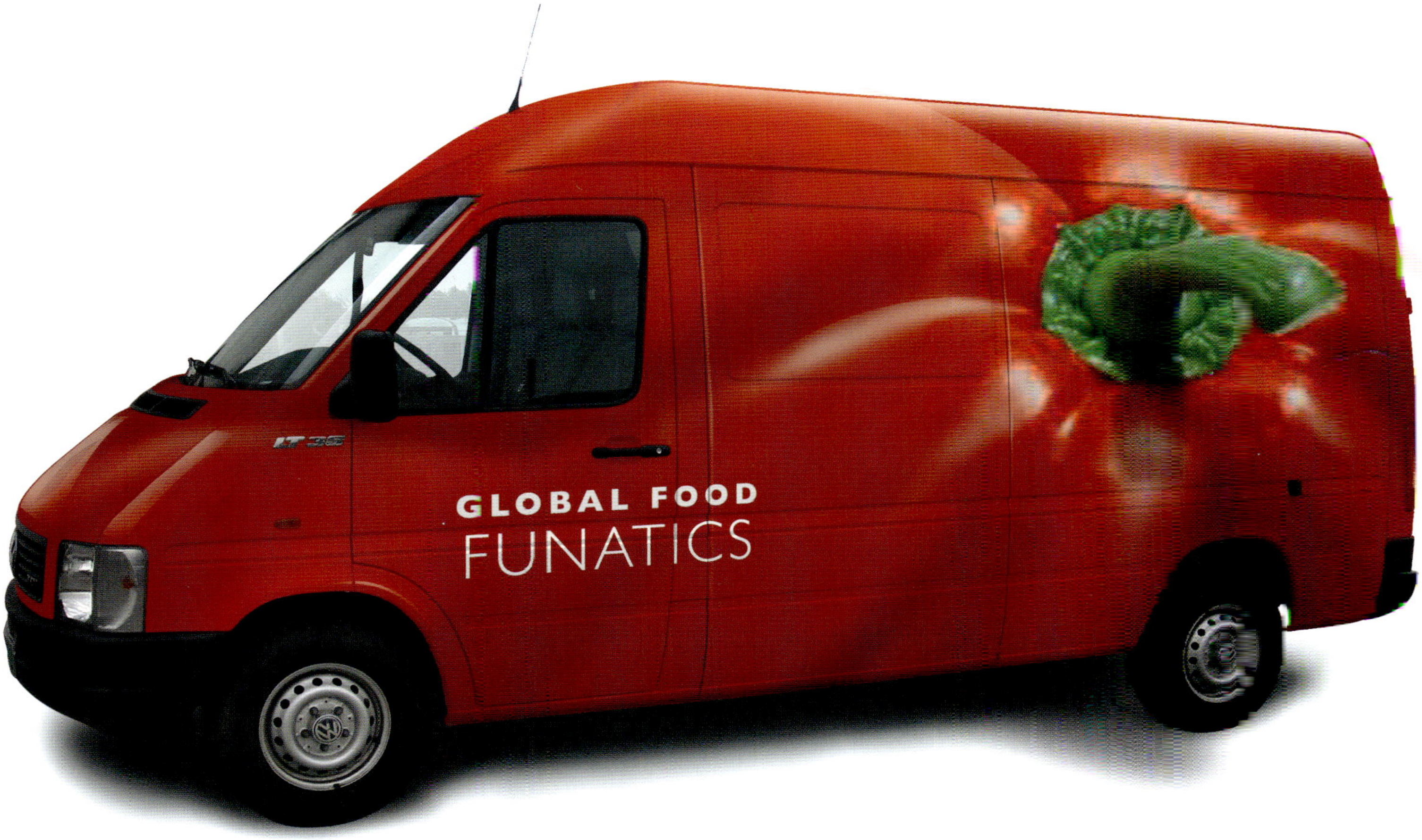
GLOBAL FOOD
FUNATICS

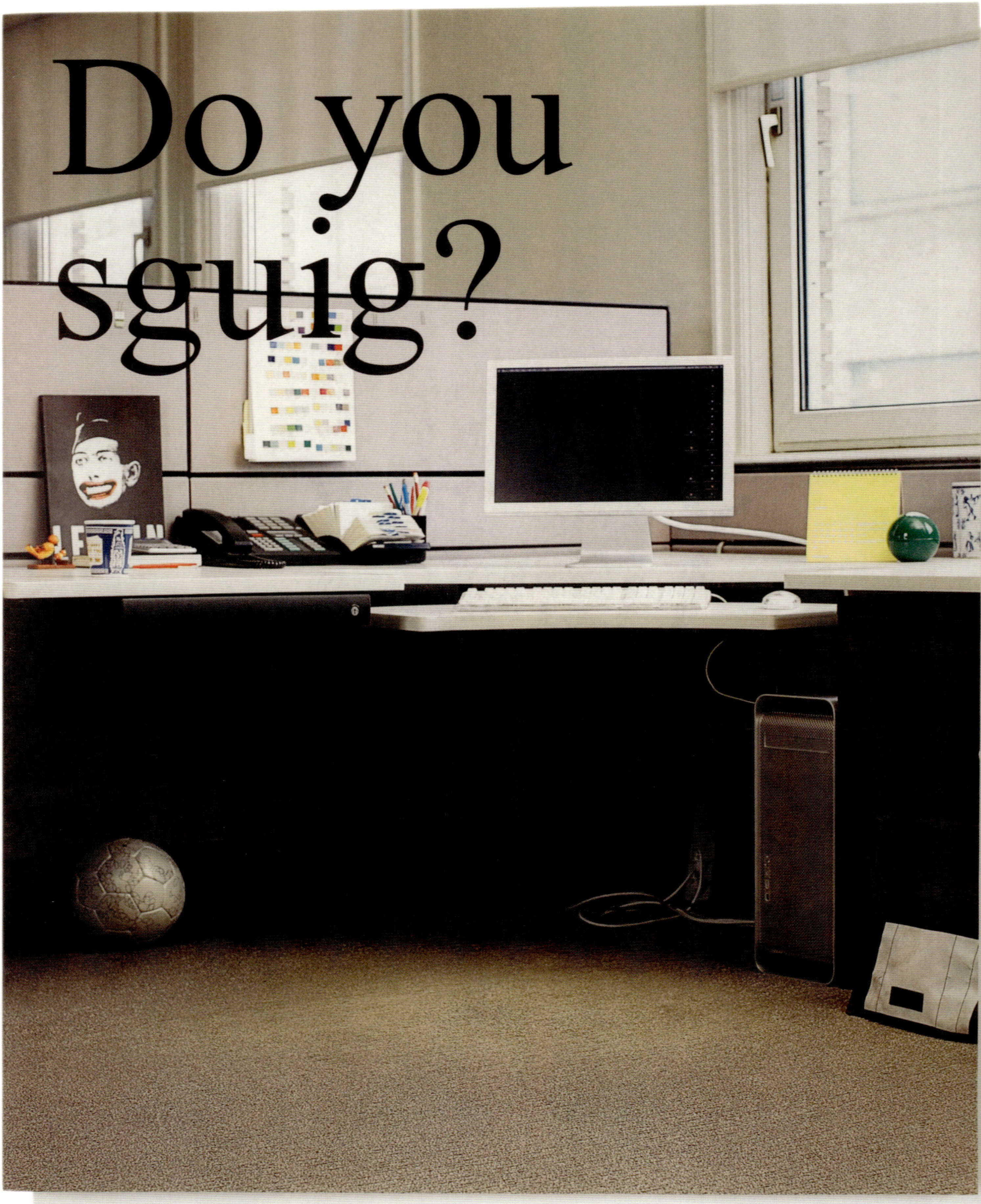
Do you
sguig?

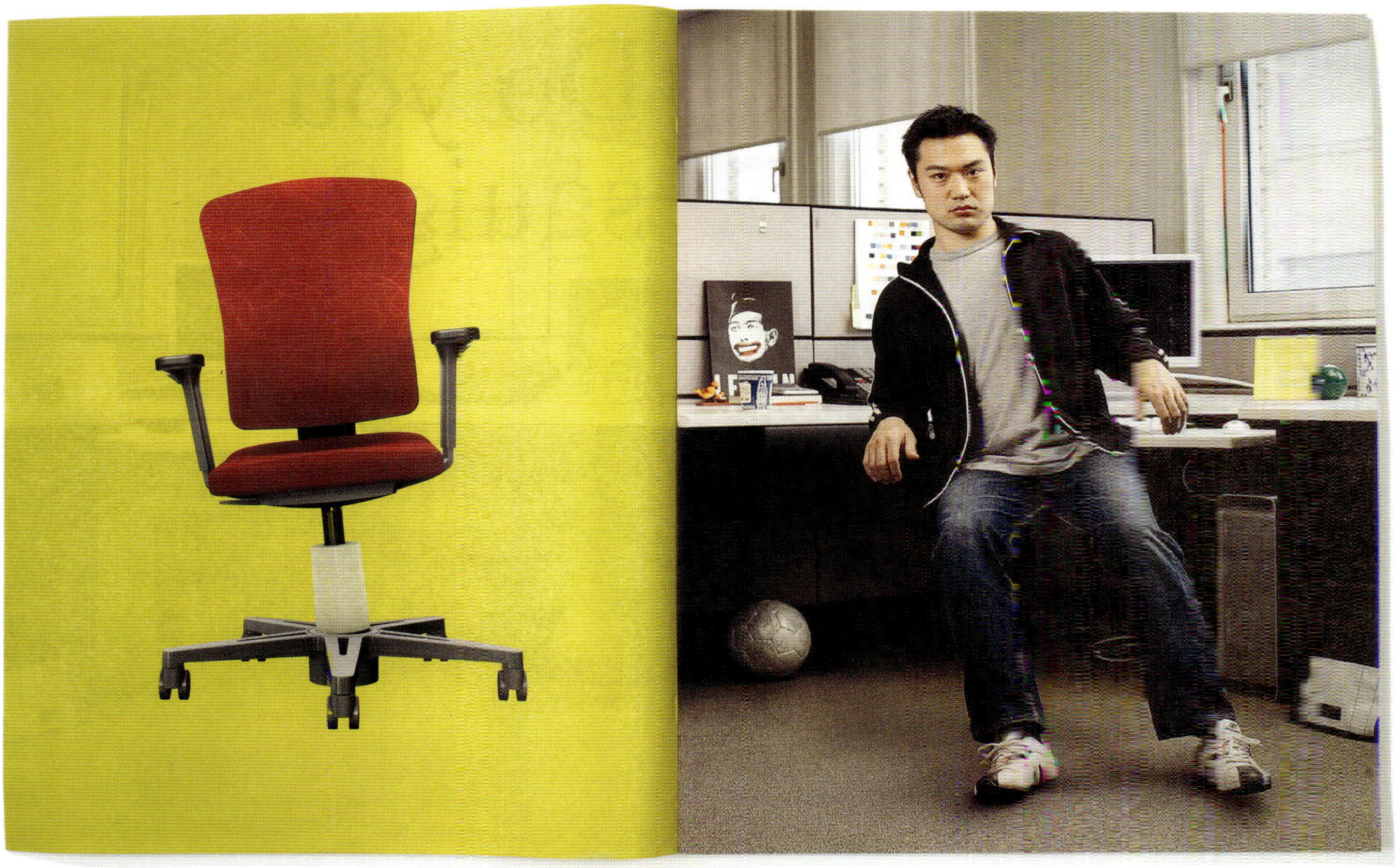

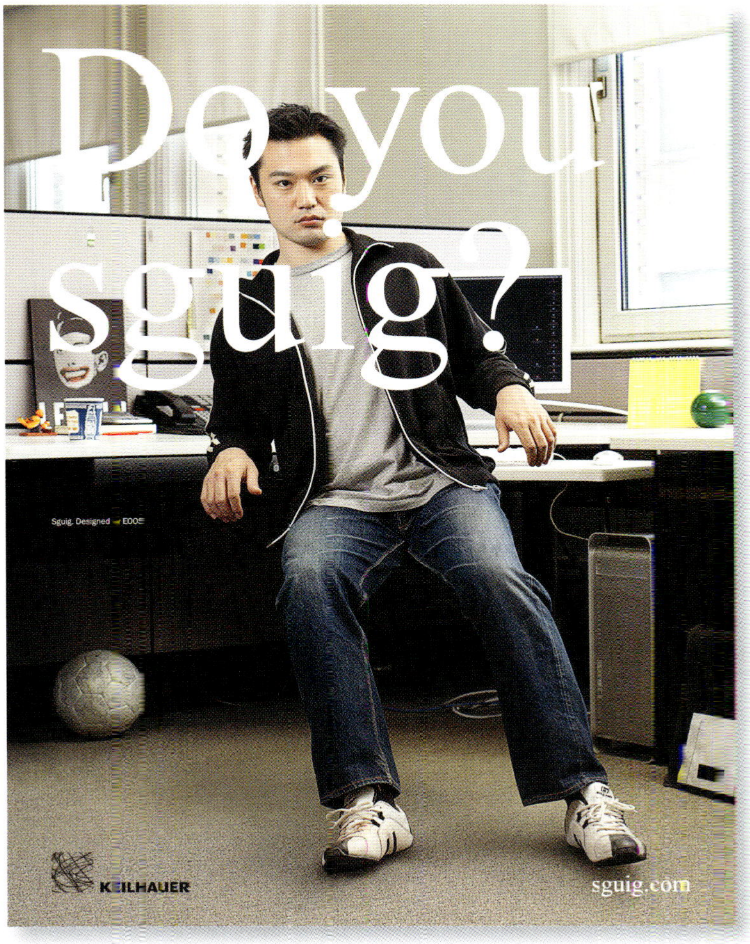
Do you
sguig?
Sguig. Designed EOOS
KEILHAUER
sguig.com

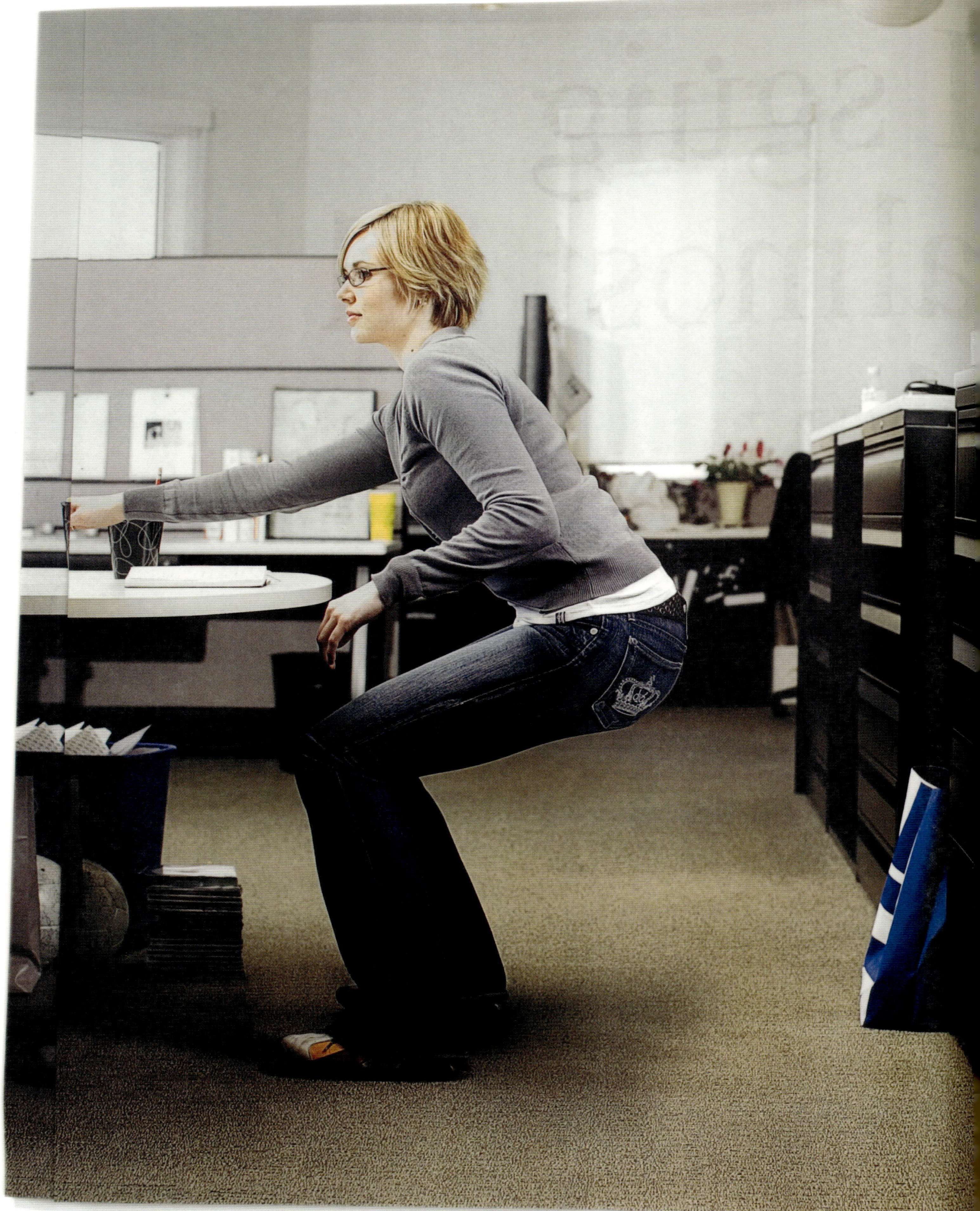

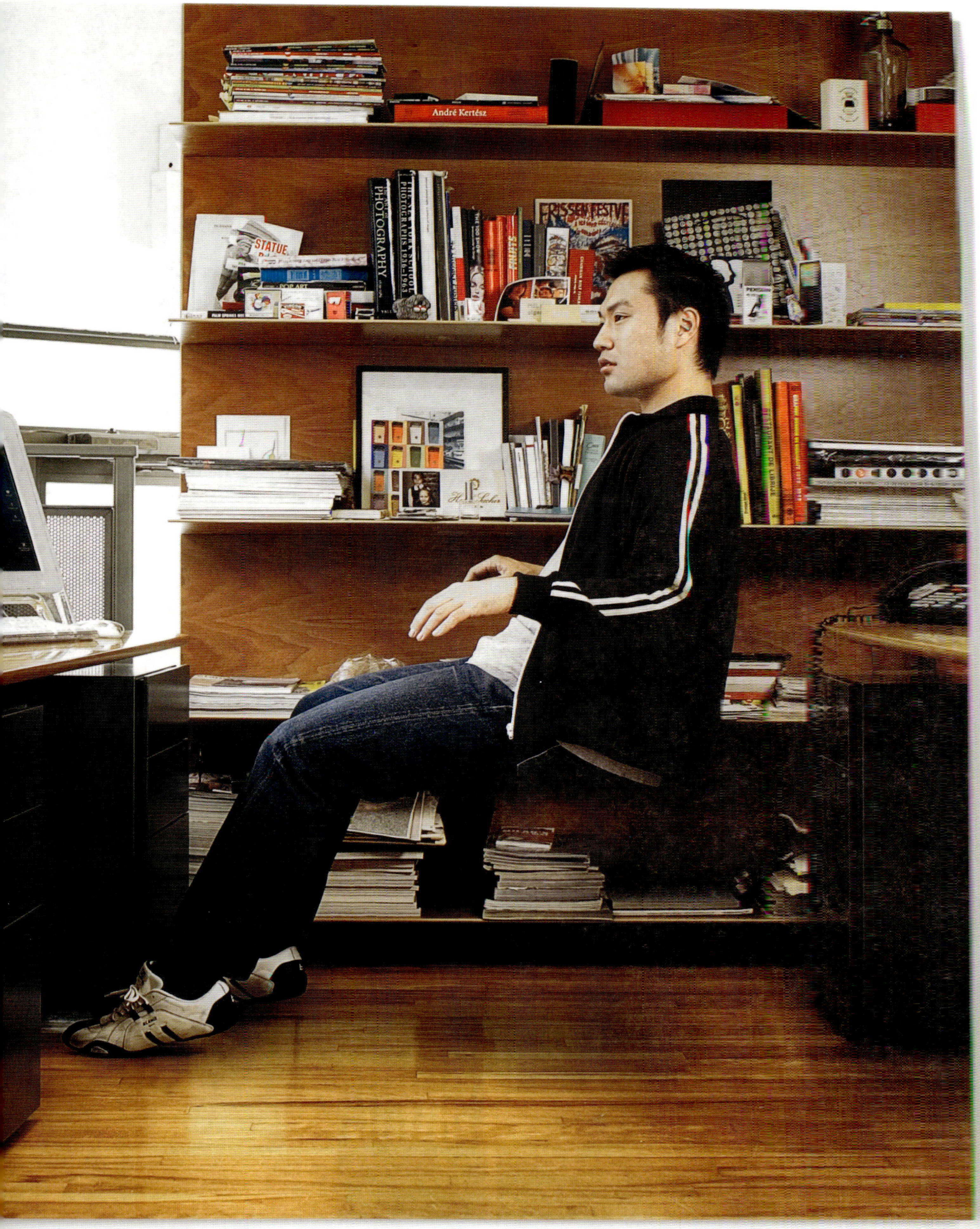
André Kertész
PHOTOGRAPHY
STATUE
POP ART

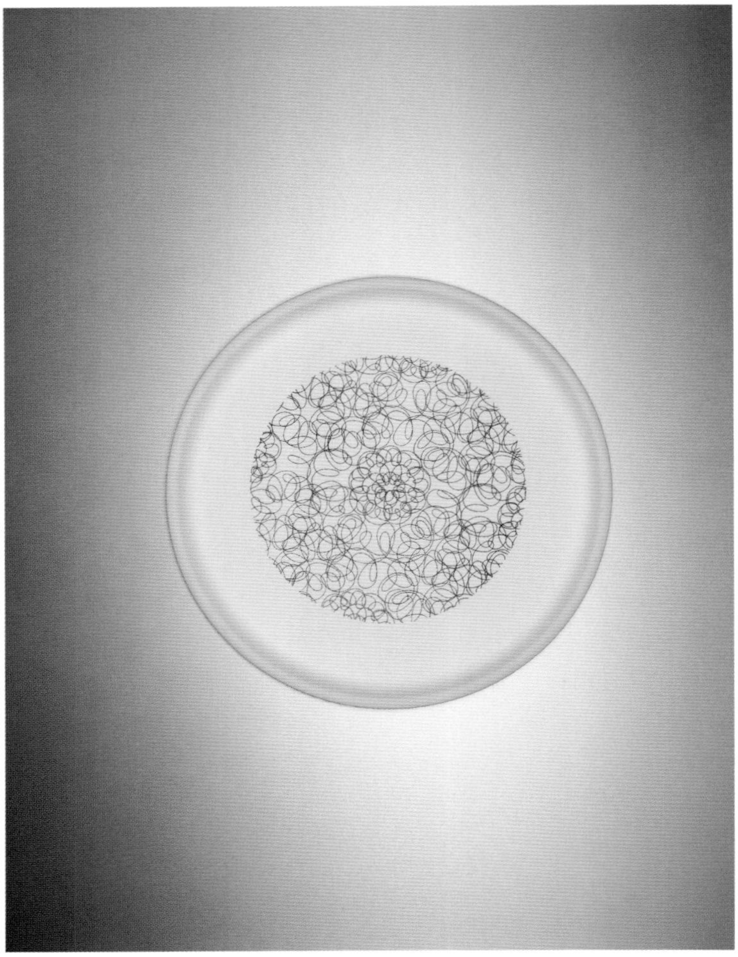

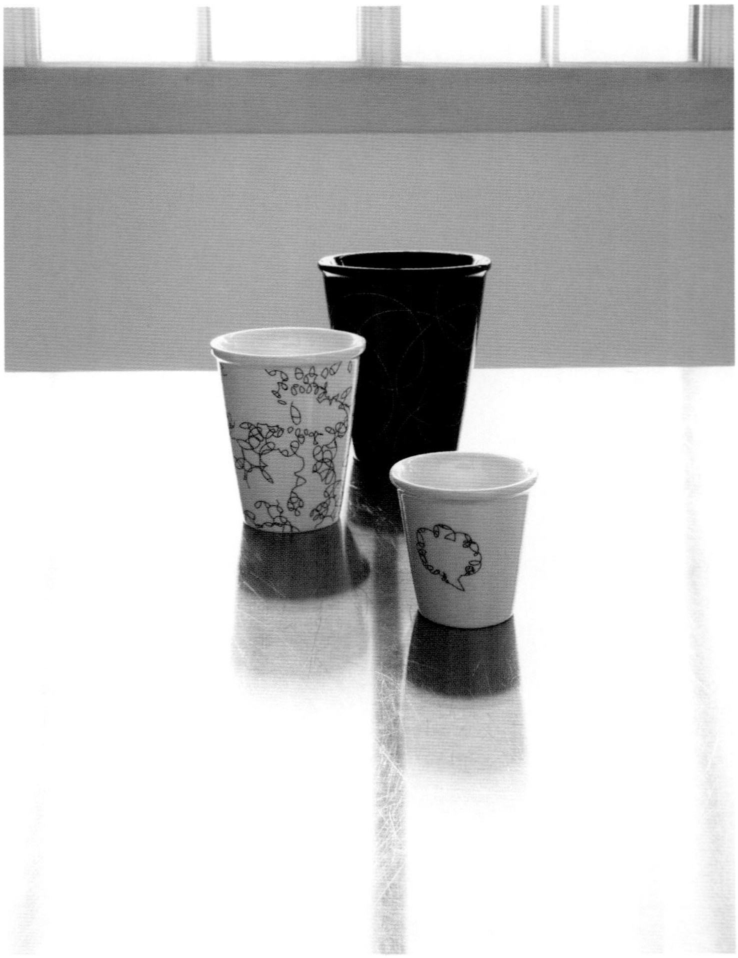

SGUIG

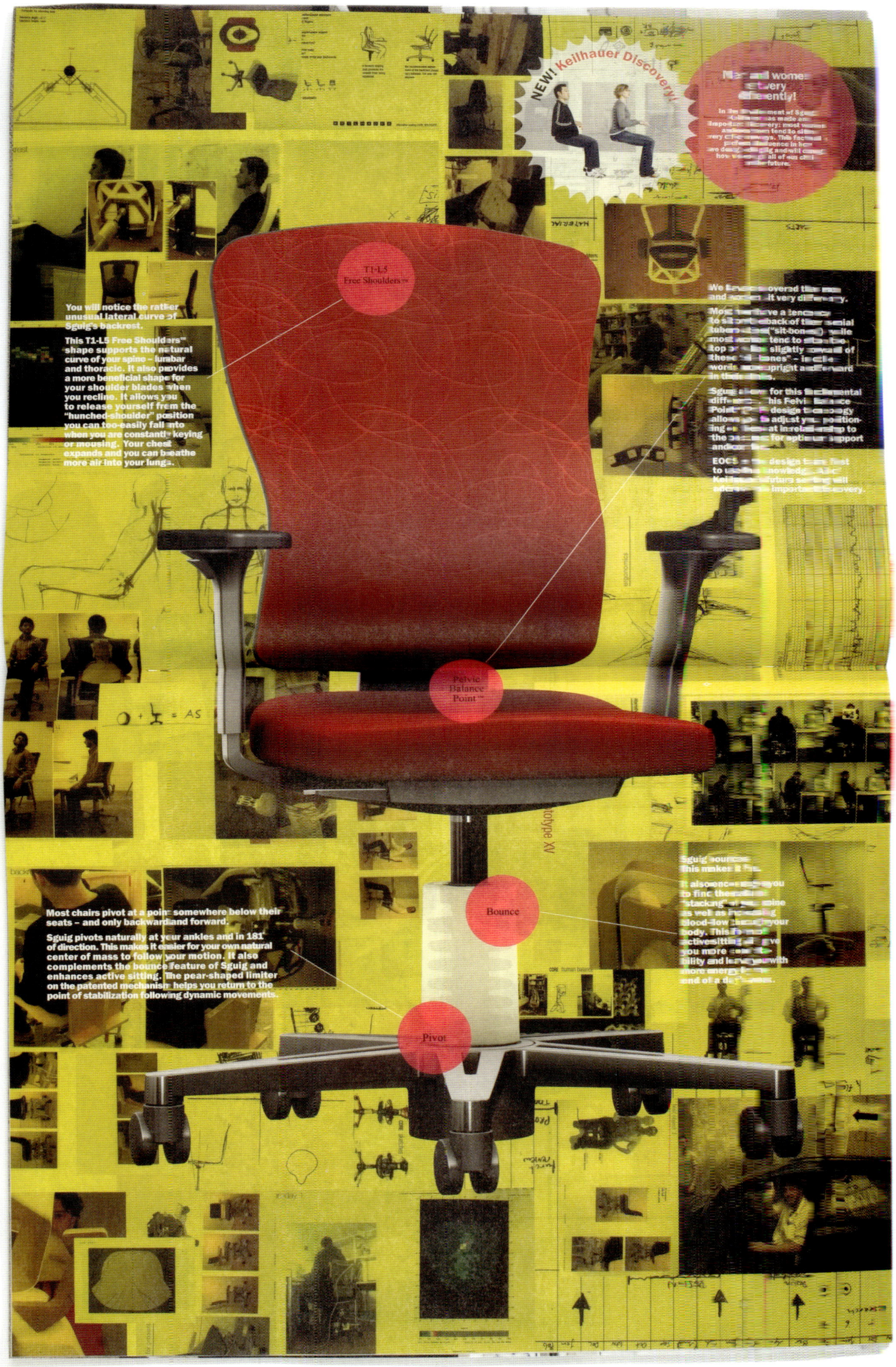
NEW! Keilhauer Discovery!
T1-L5 Free Shoulders™
You will notice the rather unusual lateral curve of Sguig's backrest.
This T1-L5 Free Shoulders™ shape supports the natural curve of your spine – lumbar and thoracic. It also provides a more beneficial shape for your shoulder blades when you recline. It allows you to release yourself from the "hunched-shoulder" position you can too easily fall into when you are constantly keying or mousing. Your chest expands and you can breathe more air into your lungs.
Pelvic Balance Point™
Bounce
Pivot
Most chairs pivot at a point somewhere below their seats – and only backward and forward.
Sguig pivots naturally at your ankles and in 181° of direction. This makes it easier for your own natural center of mass to follow your motion. It also complements the bounce feature of Sguig and enhances active sitting. The pear-shaped limiter on the patented mechanism helps you return to the point of stabilization following dynamic movements.

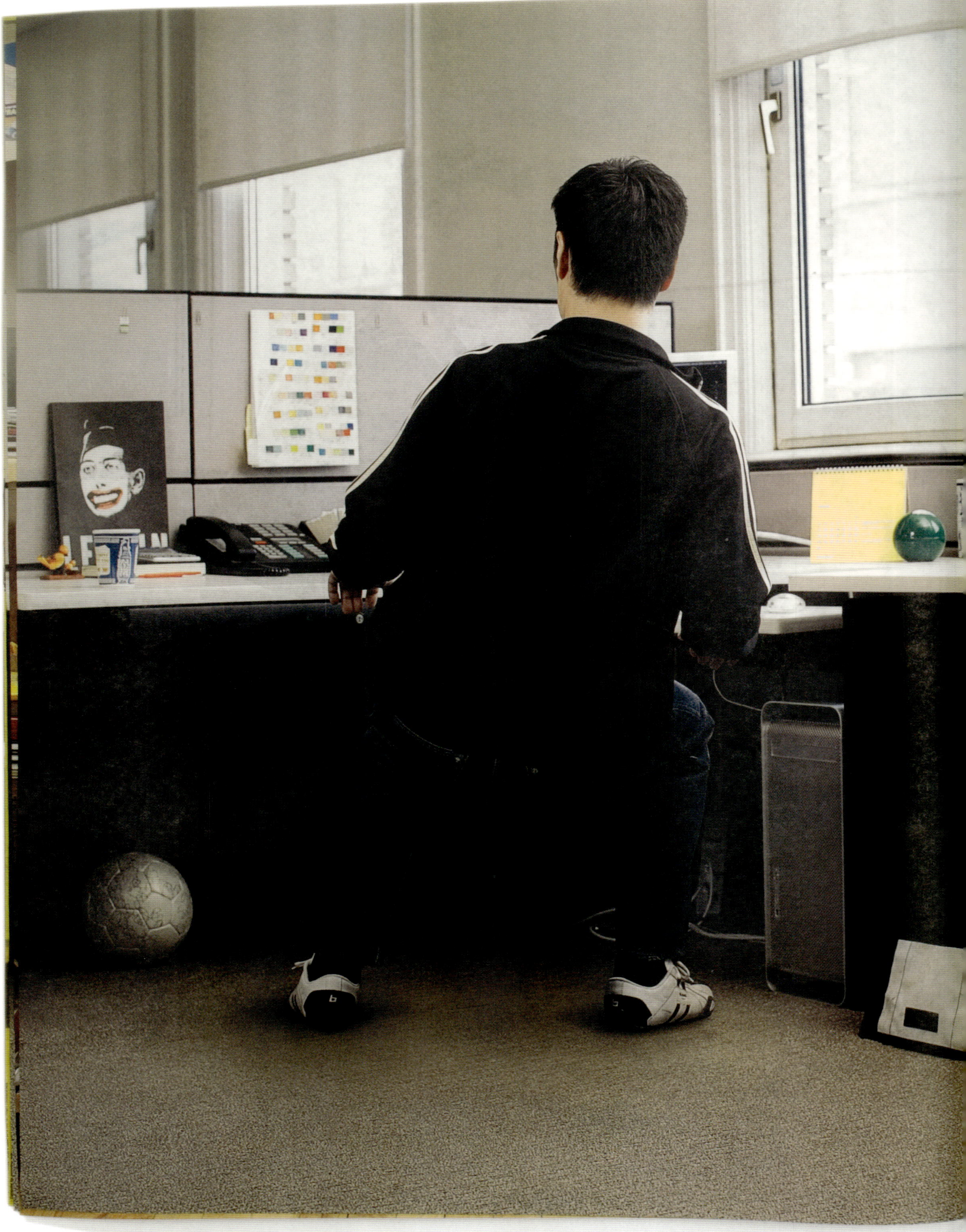

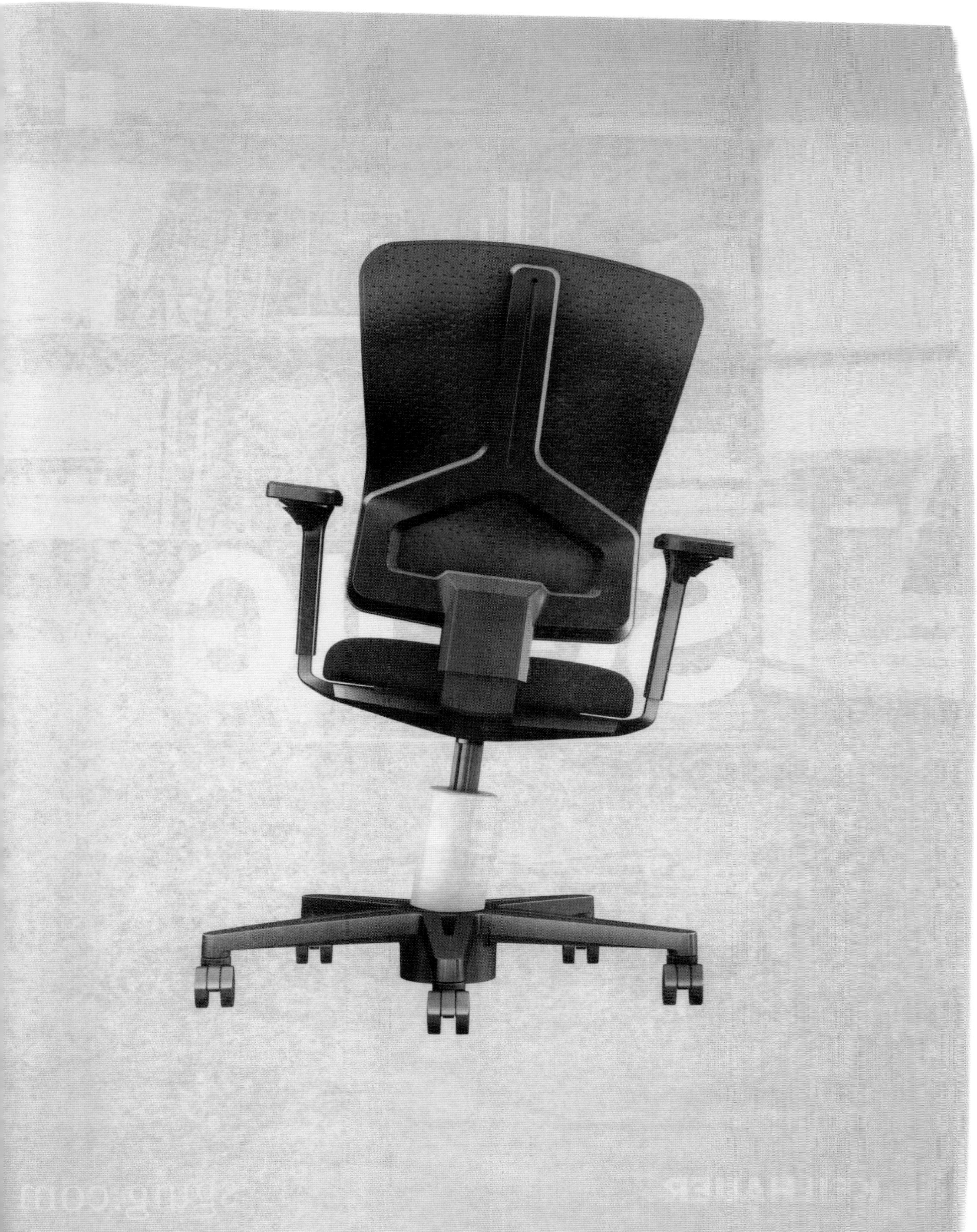

Lovelace

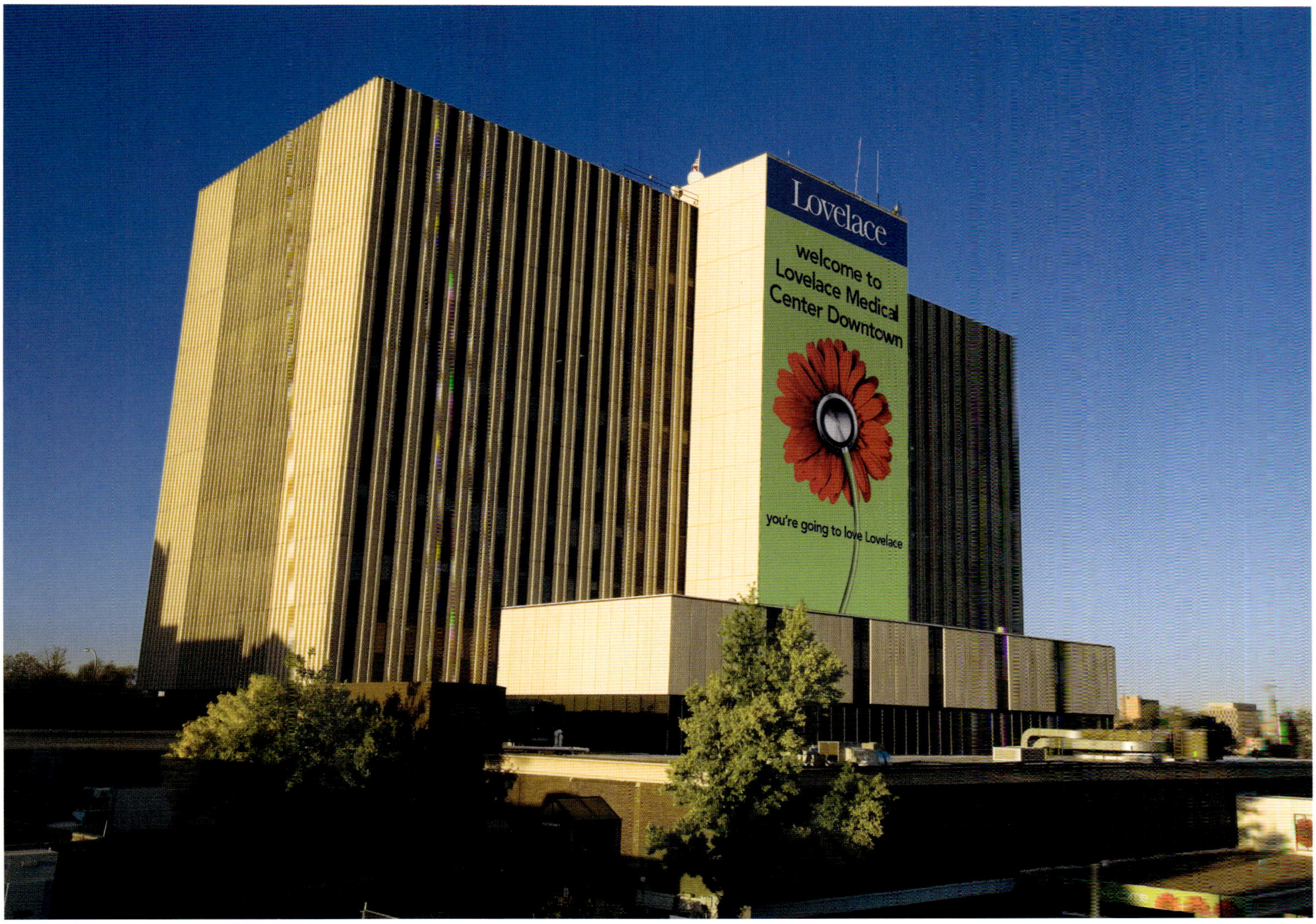
Lovelace
welcome to
Lovelace Medical
Center Downtown
you're going to love Lovelace

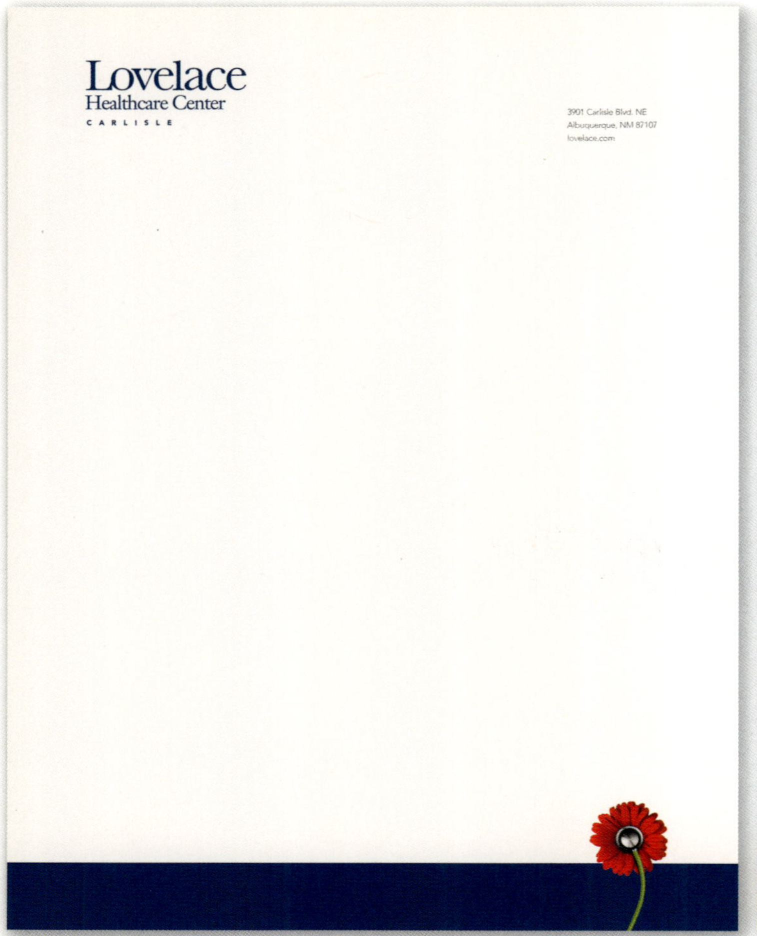
Lovelace
Healthcare Center
CARLISLE
3901 Carlisle Blvd. NE
Albuquerque, NM 87107
lovelace.com

Lovelace

Lovelace

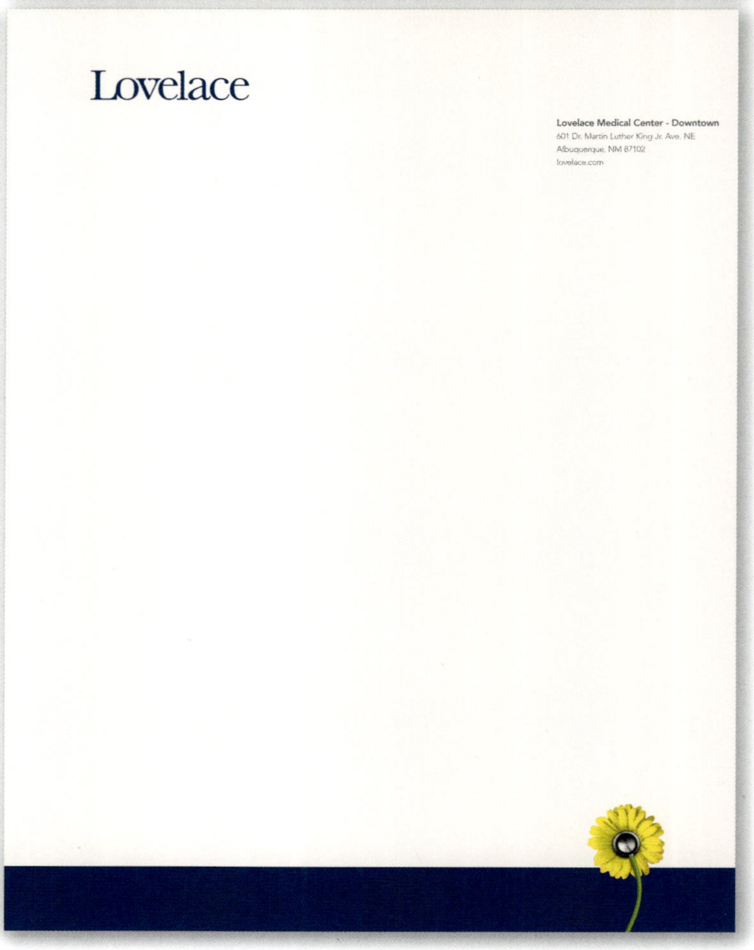
Lovelace
Lovelace Medical Center - Downtown
601 Dr. Martin Luther King Jr. Ave. NE
Albuquerque, NM 87102
lovelace.com

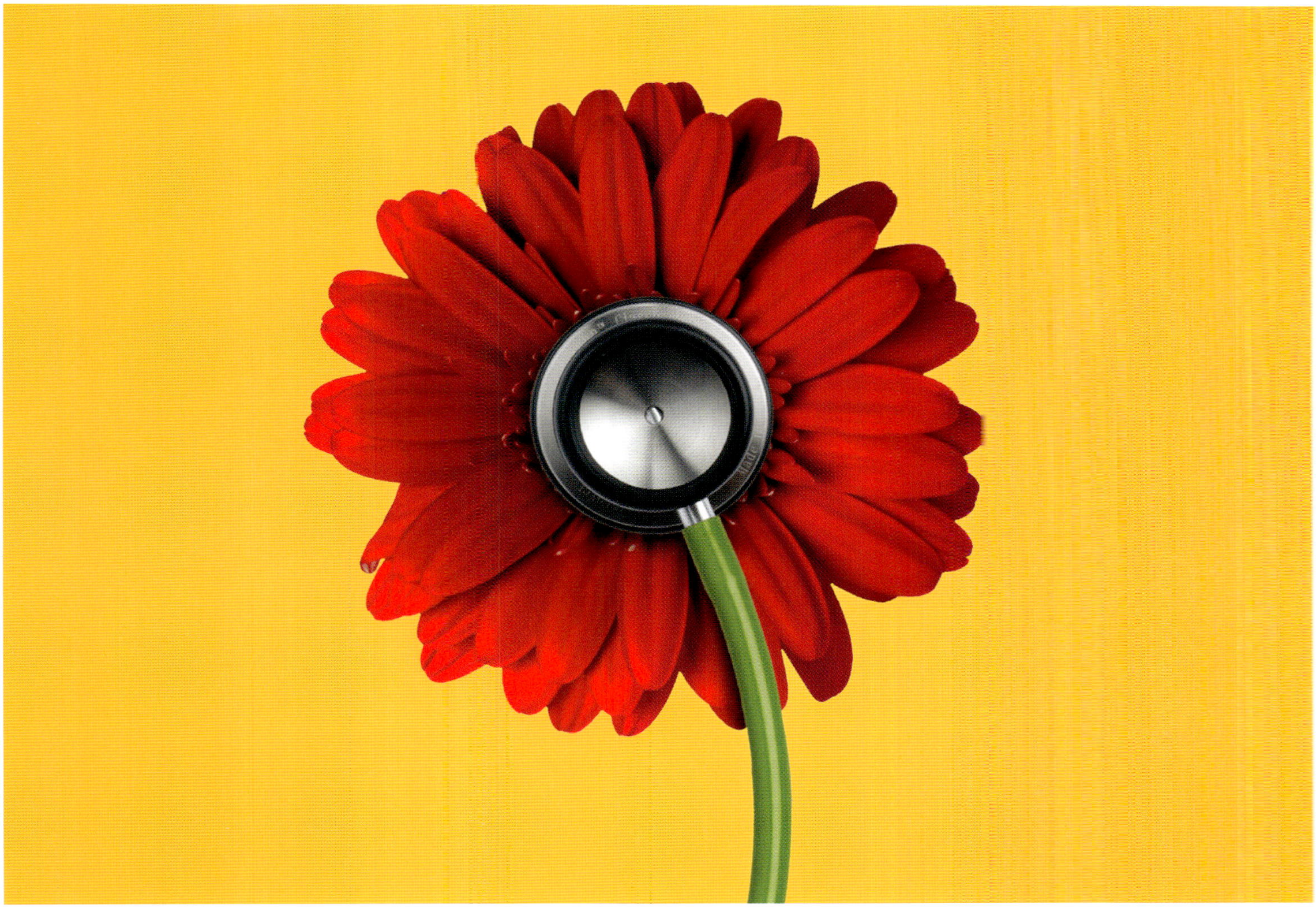

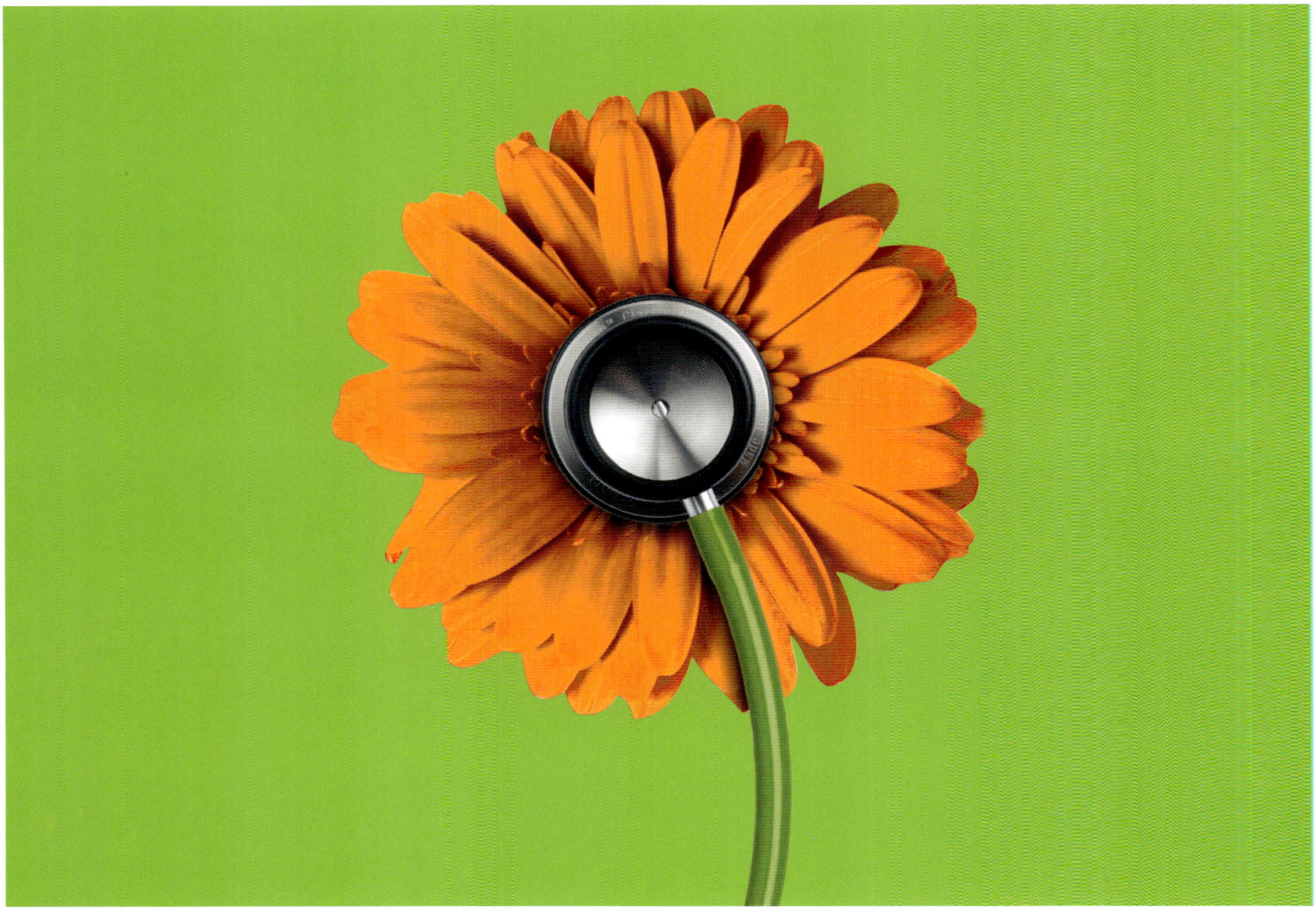

F1RST GRADUATE

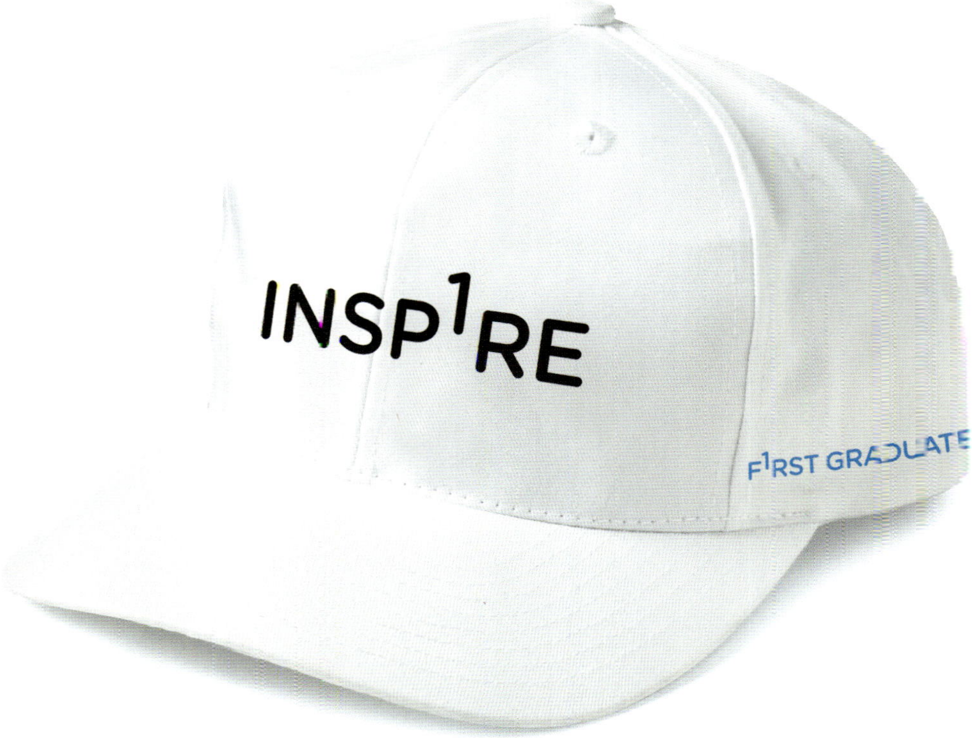
INSP1RE
F1RST GRADUATE

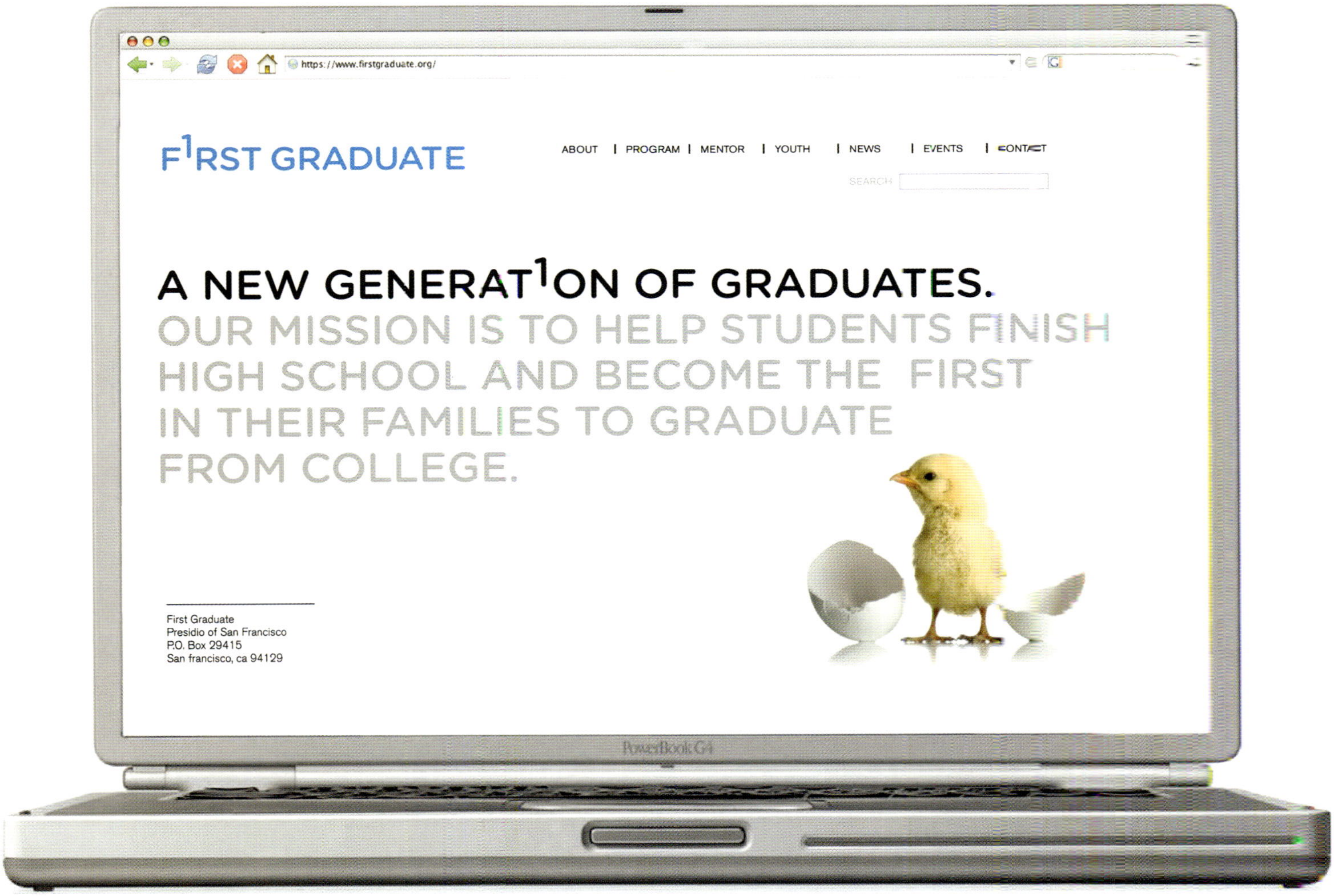
https://www.firstgraduate.org/
F1RST GRADUATE
ABOUT | PROGRAM | MENTOR | YOUTH | NEWS | EVENTS | CONTACT
SEARCH
A NEW GENERAT1ON OF GRADUATES.
OUR MISSION IS TO HELP STUDENTS FINISH HIGH SCHOOL AND BECOME THE FIRST IN THEIR FAMILIES TO GRADUATE FROM COLLEGE.
First Graduate
Presidio of San Francisco
P.O. Box 29415
San francisco, ca 94129
PowerBook G4

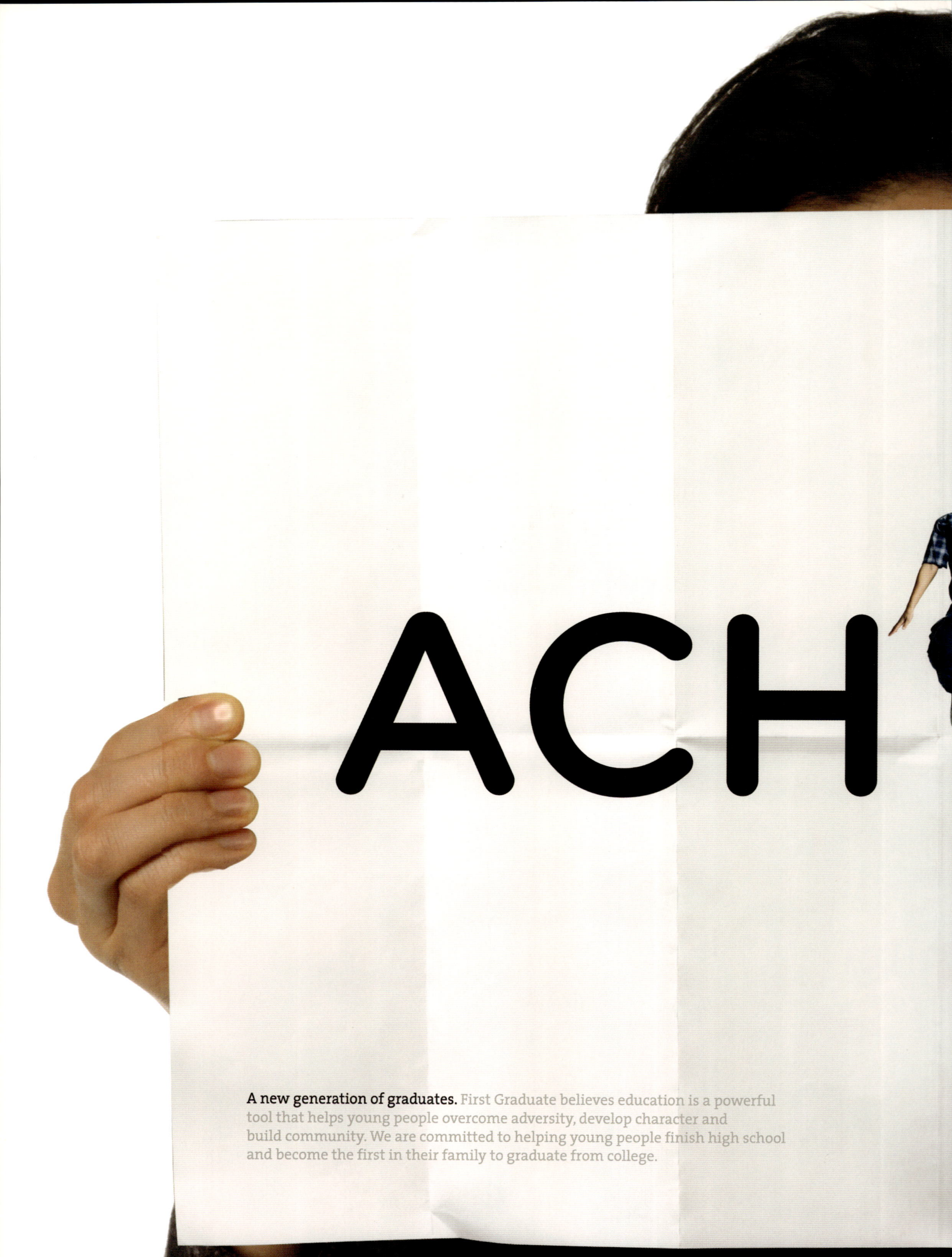

A new generation of graduates. First Graduate believes education is a powerful tool that helps young people overcome adversity, develop character and build community. We are committed to helping young people finish high school and become the first in their family to graduate from college.

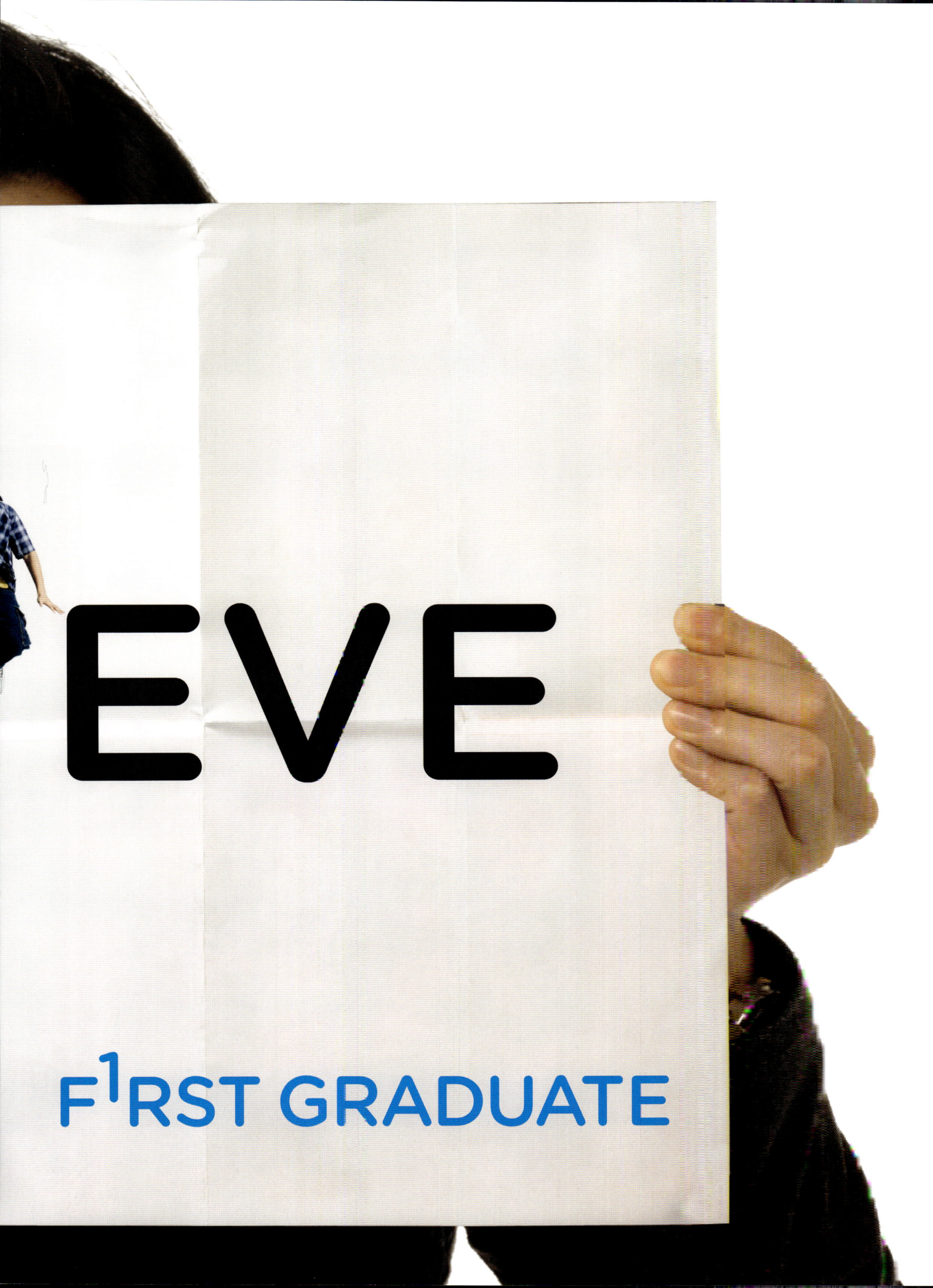
EVE
F1RST GRADUATE

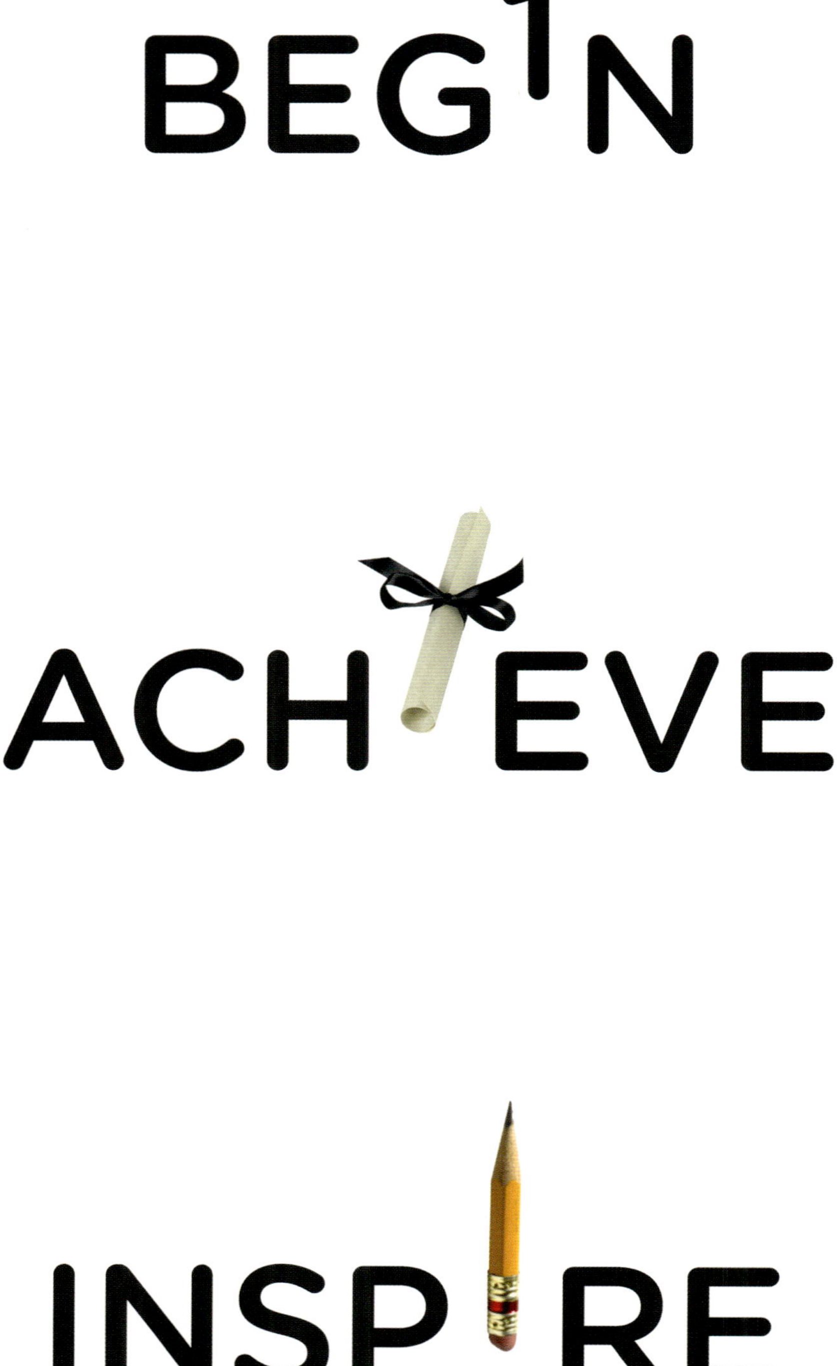

158 Non-Profit | First Graduate | (this spread) **Landor Associates, San Francisco**

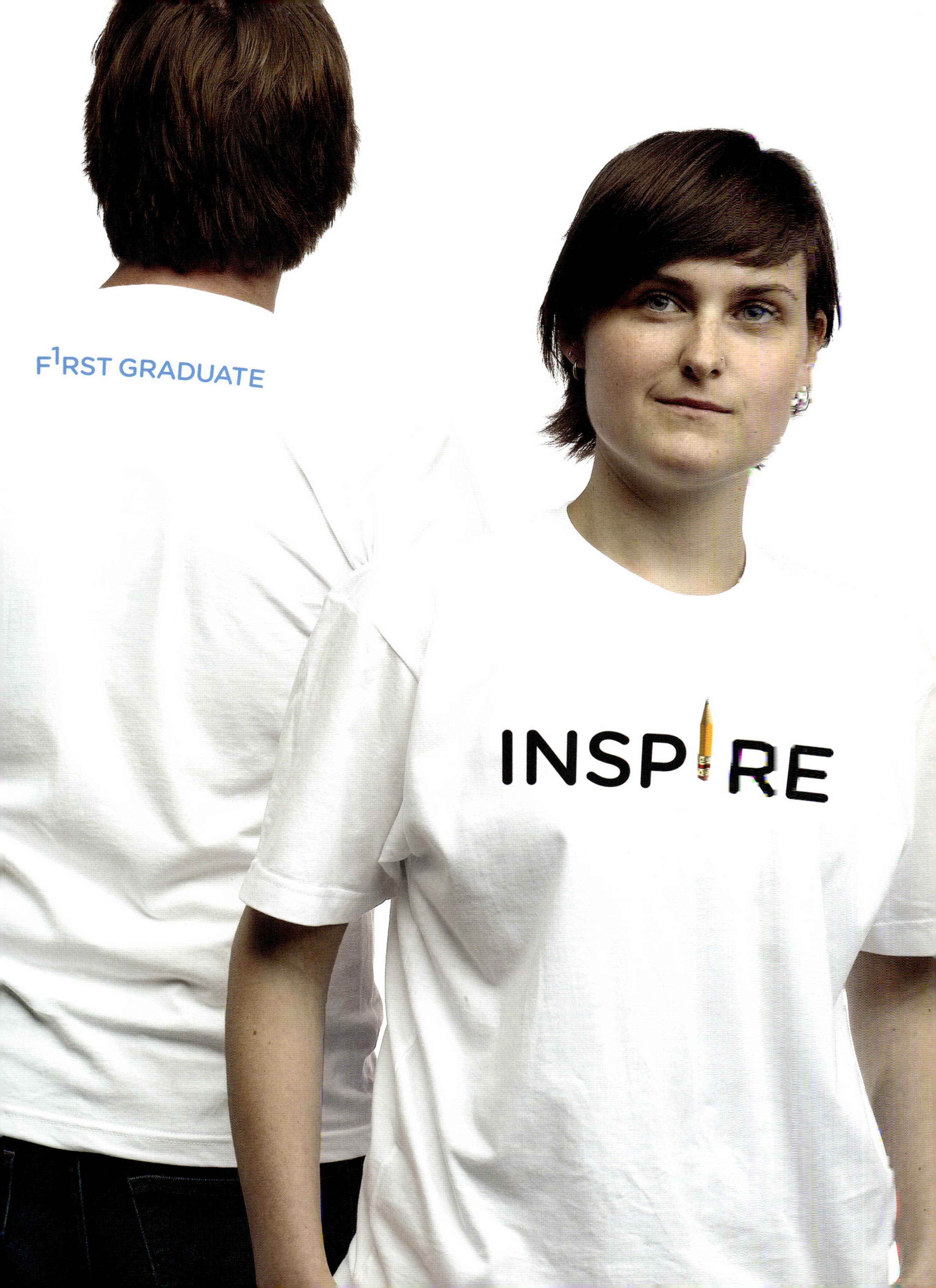
F1RST GRADUATE
INSPIRE

THE
PINK DOOR
PAPER COMPANY

THE

PINK DOOR

PAPER COMPANY

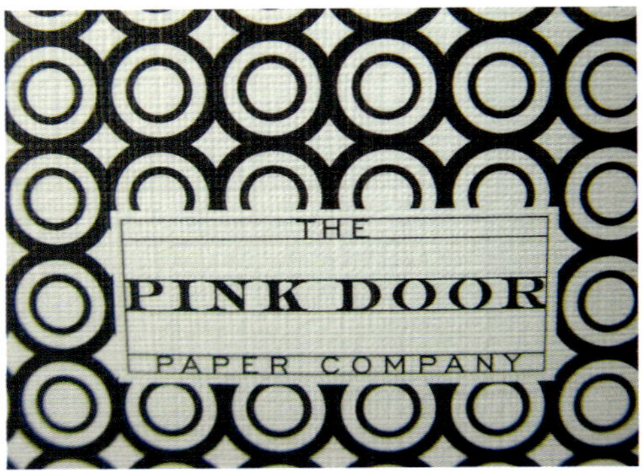
THE
PINK DOOR
PAPER COMPANY

THE
PINK DOOR
PAPER COMPANY

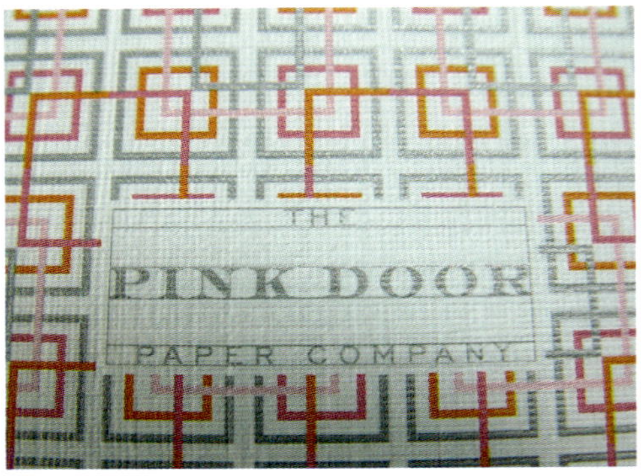
THE
PINK DOOR
PAPER COMPANY

THE
PINK DOOR
PAPER COMPANY

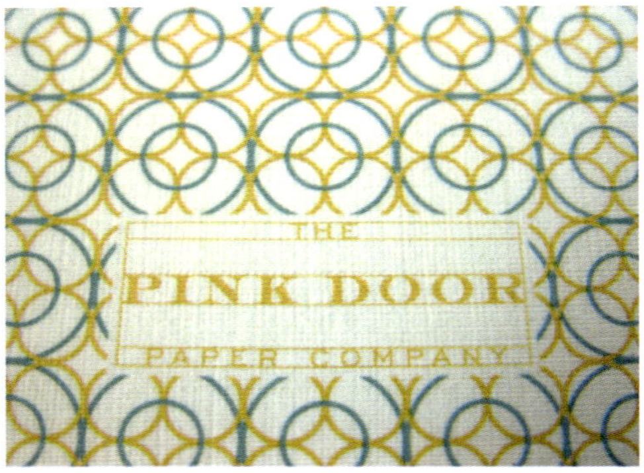
THE
PINK DOOR
PAPER COMPANY

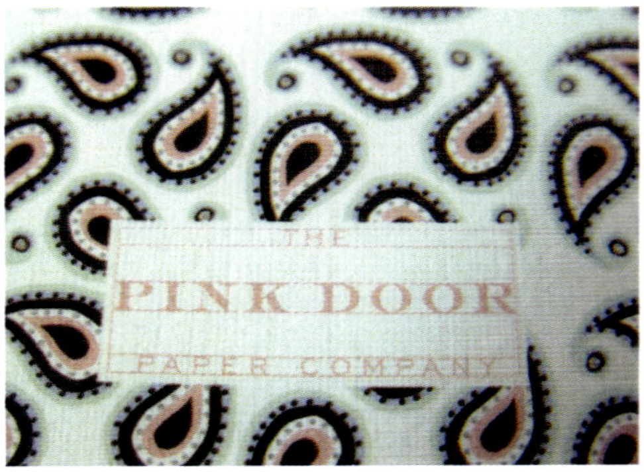
THE
PINK DOOR
PAPER COMPANY

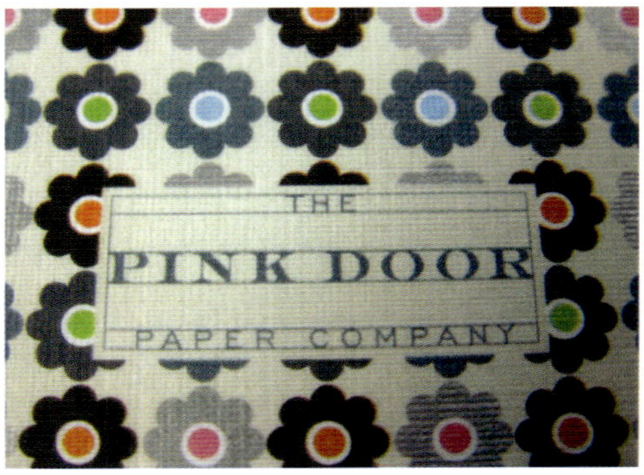
THE
PINK DOOR
PAPER COMPANY

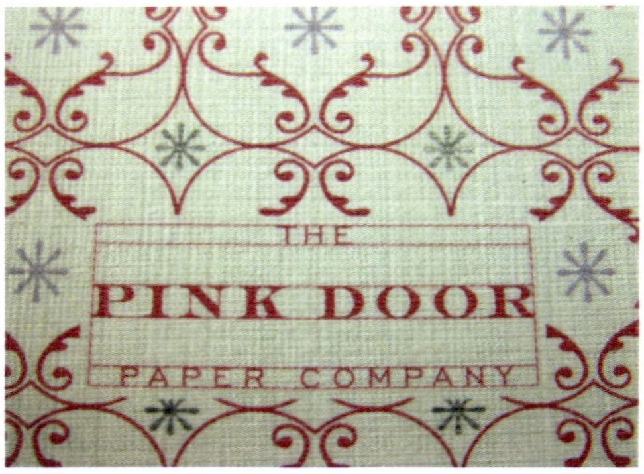
THE
PINK DOOR
PAPER COMPANY

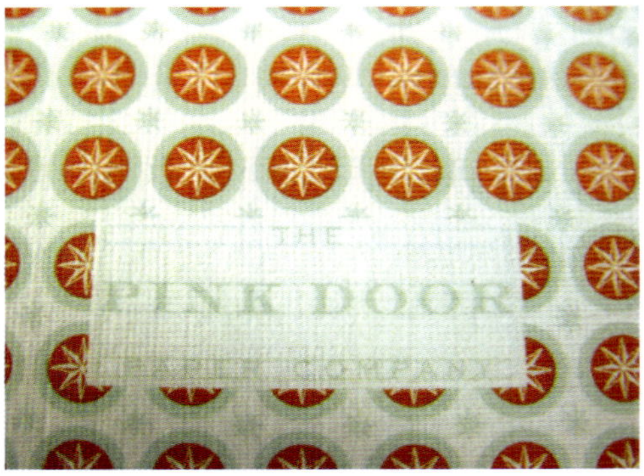
THE
PINK DOOR

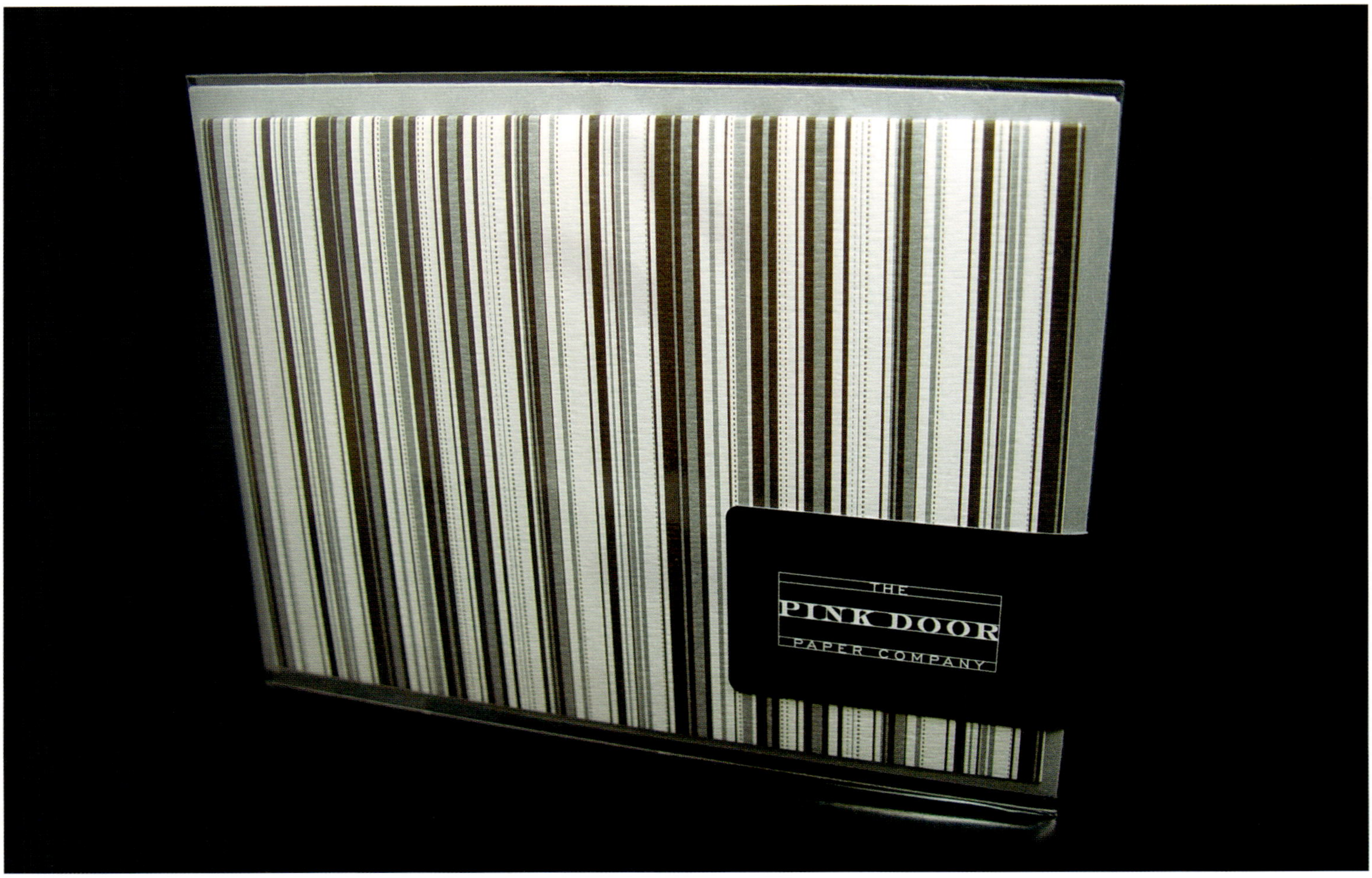
THE
PINK DOOR
PAPER COMPANY

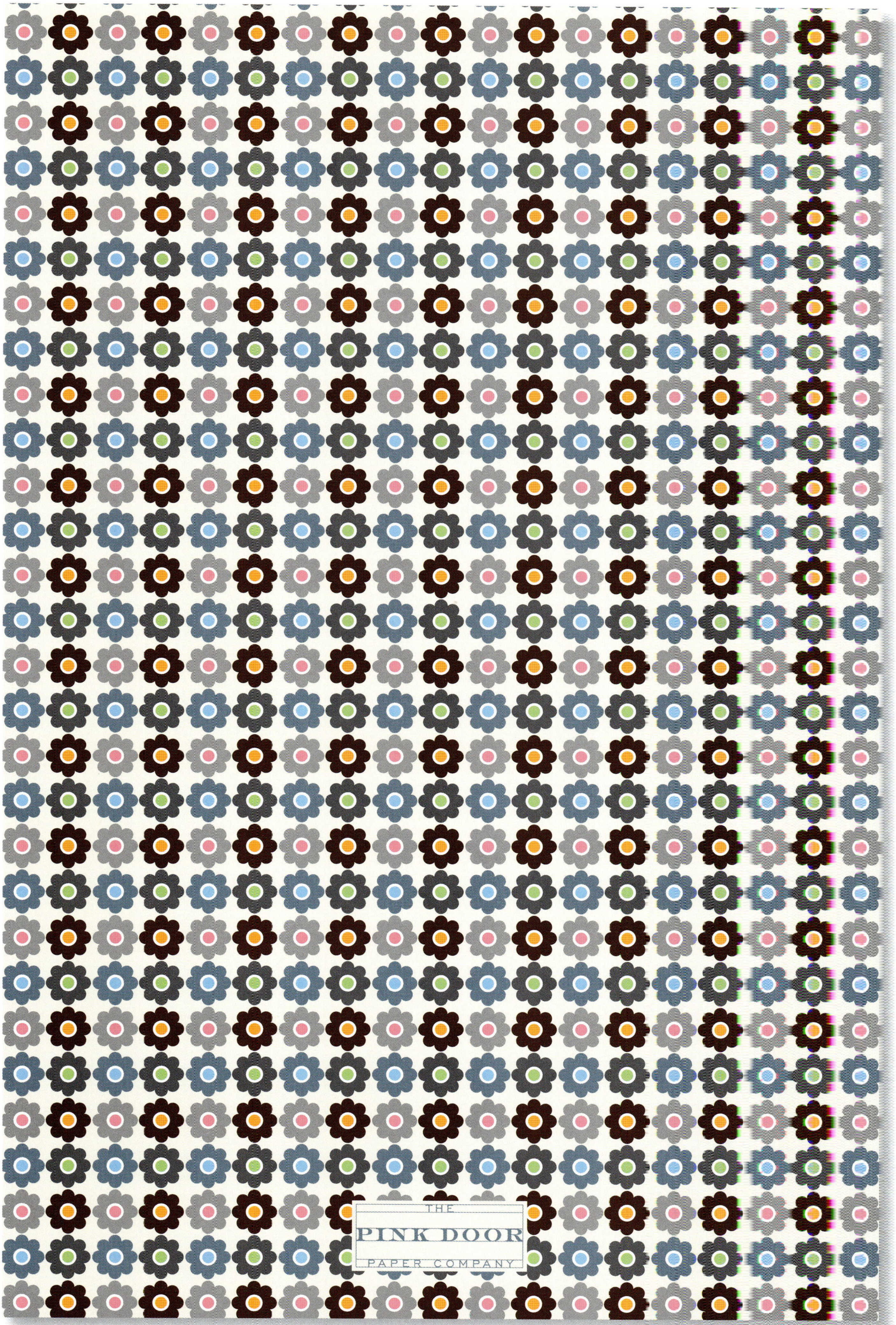
THE
PINK DOOR
PAPER COMPANY

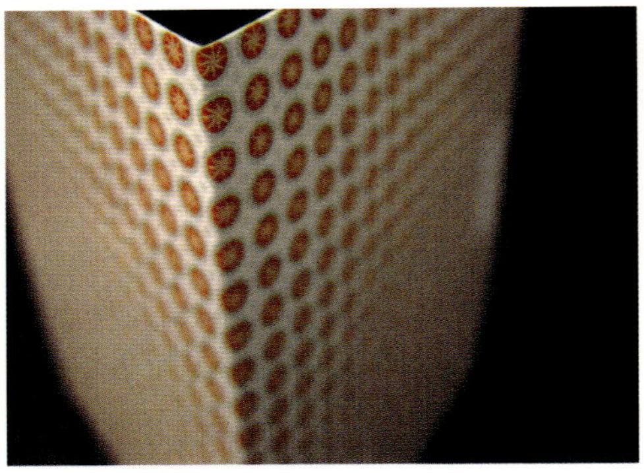
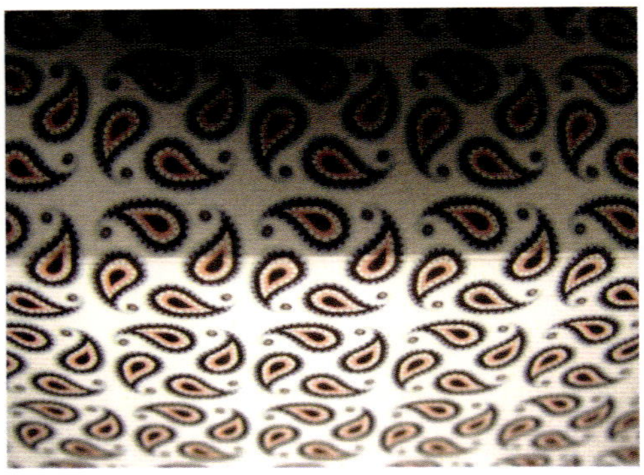
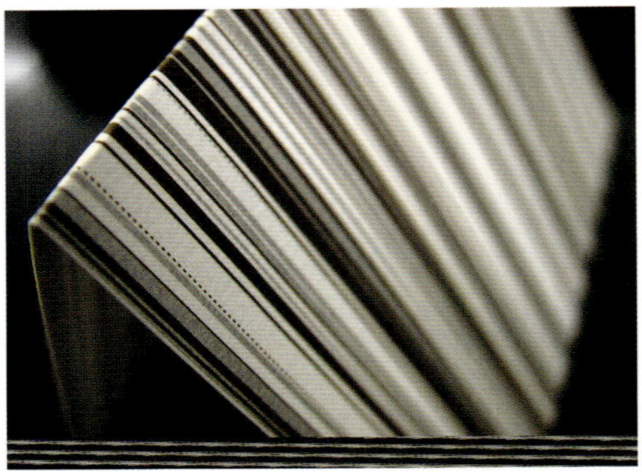
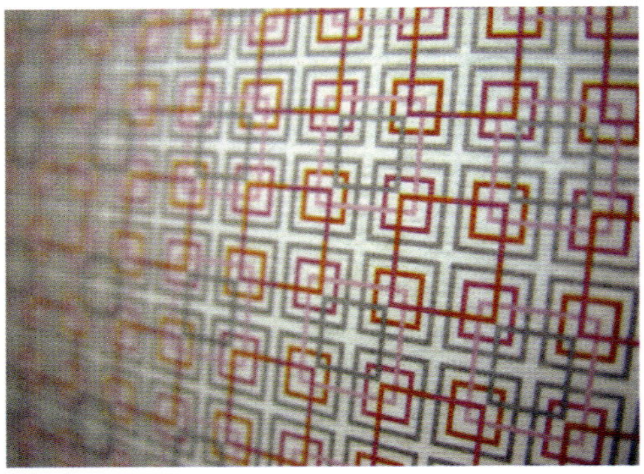
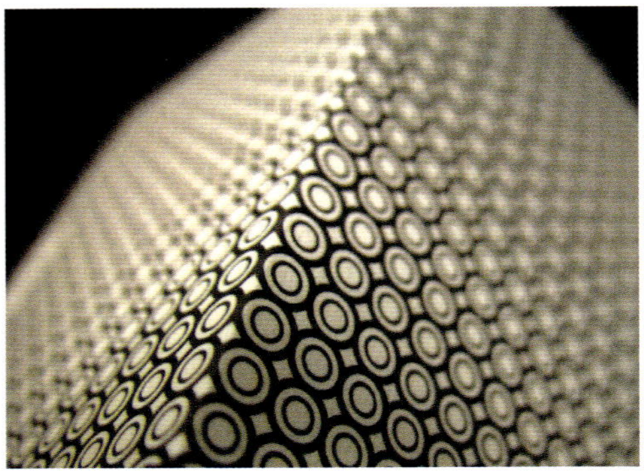
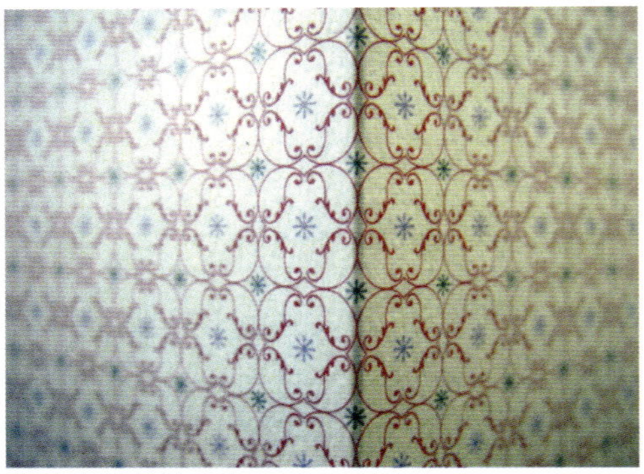
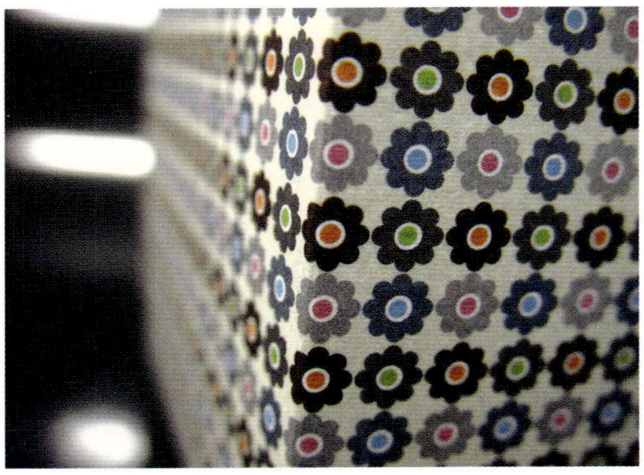
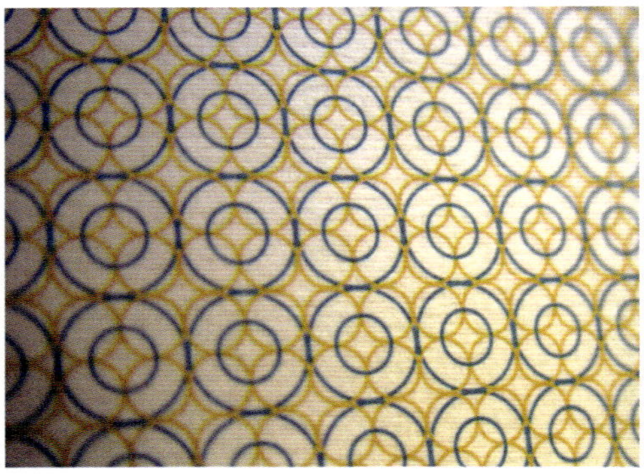
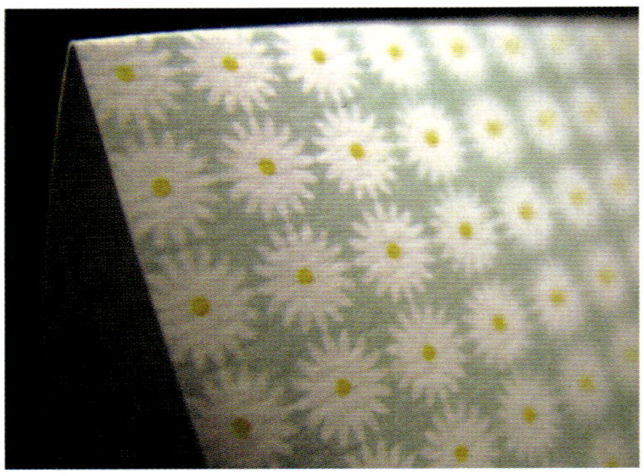
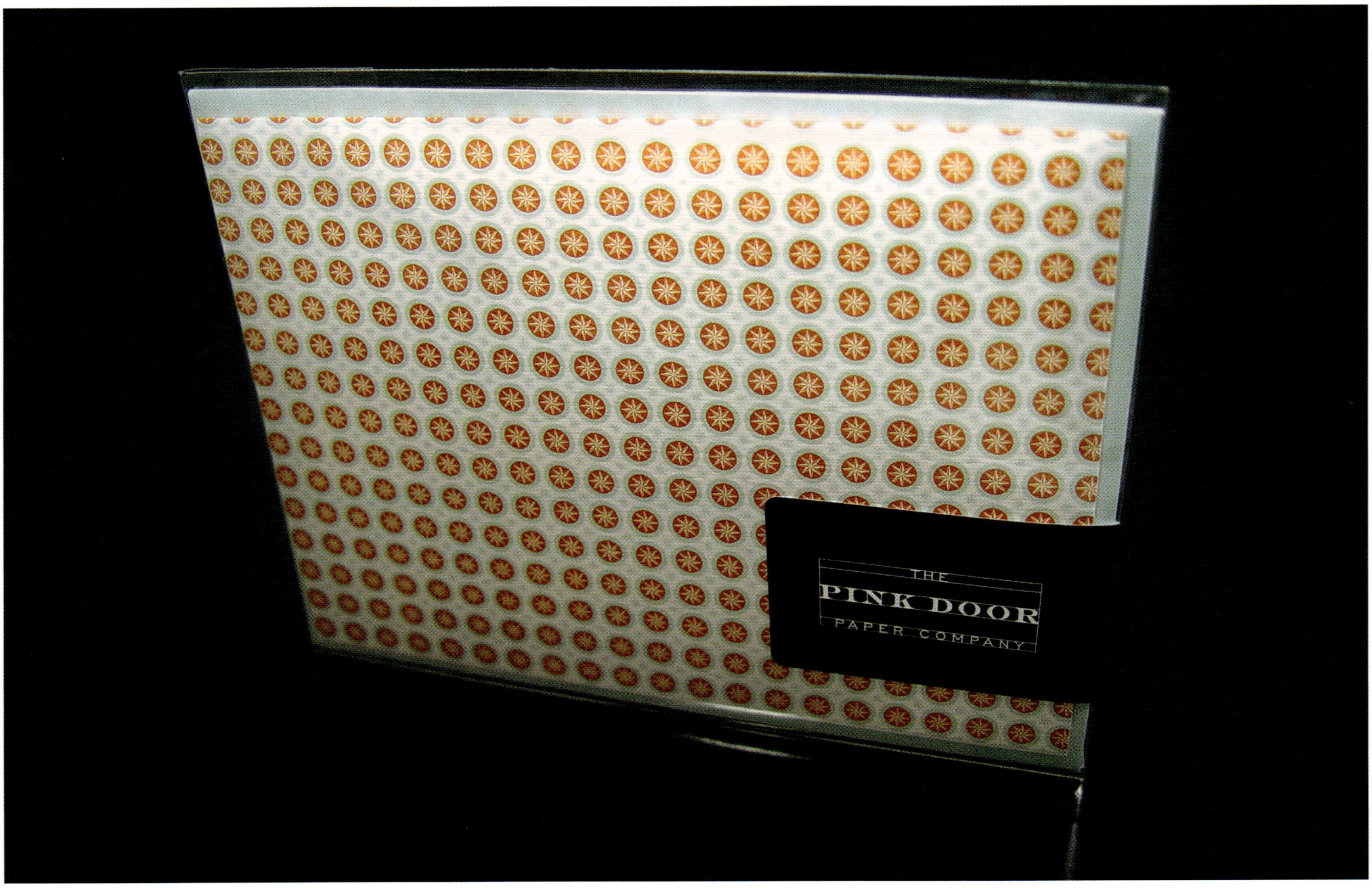
THE
PINK DOOR
PAPER COMPANY

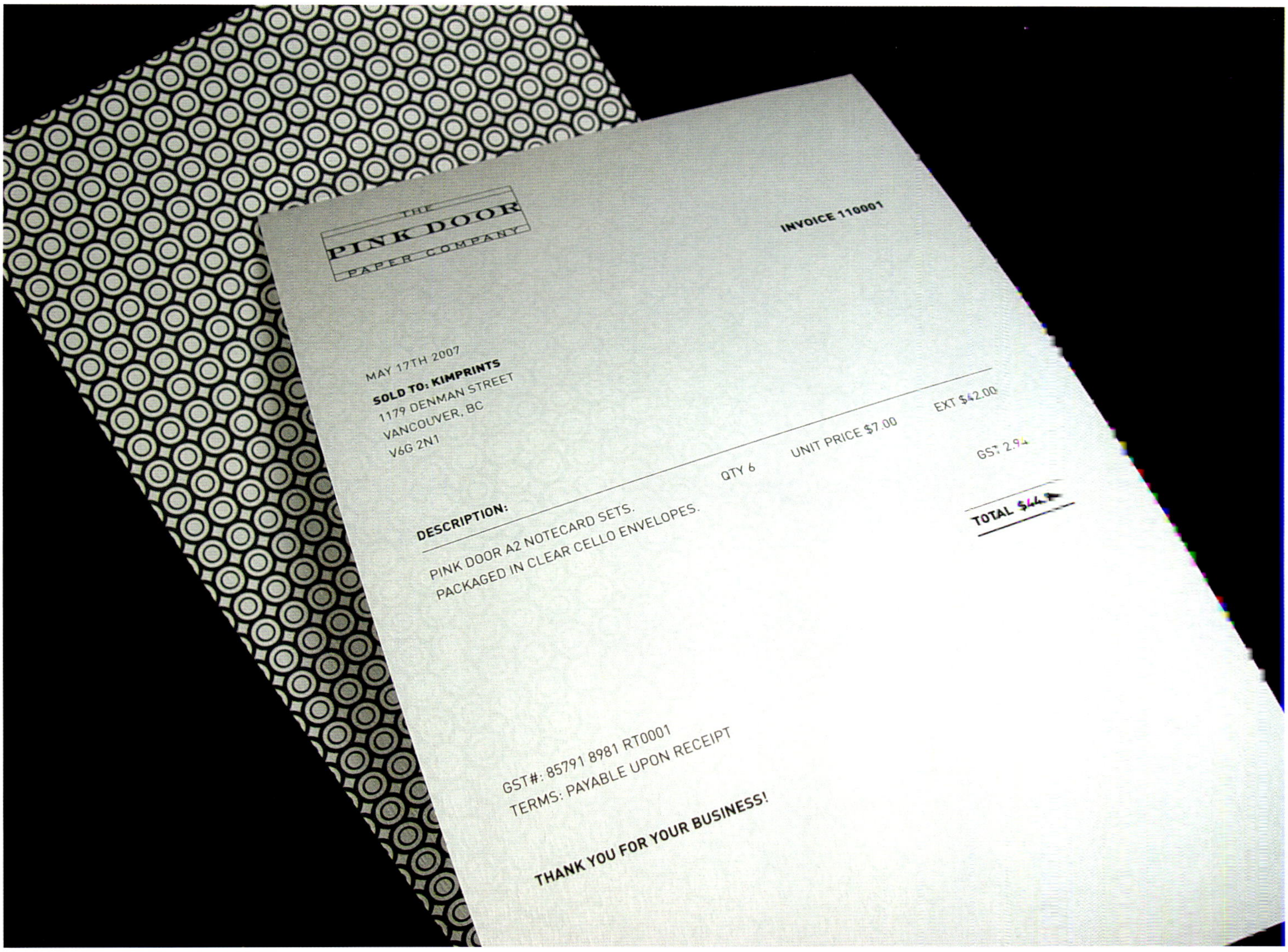
THE PINK DOOR PAPER COMPANY
INVOICE 110001
MAY 17TH 2007
SOLD TO: KIMPRINTS
1179 DENMAN STREET
VANCOUVER, BC
V6G 2N1
DESCRIPTION:
QTY 6
UNIT PRICE $7.00
EXT $42.00
GST 2.94
TOTAL
PINK DOOR A2 NOTECARD SETS.
PACKAGED IN CLEAR CELLO ENVELOPES.
GST#: 85791 8981 RT0001
TERMS: PAYABLE UPON RECEIPT
THANK YOU FOR YOUR BUSINESS!

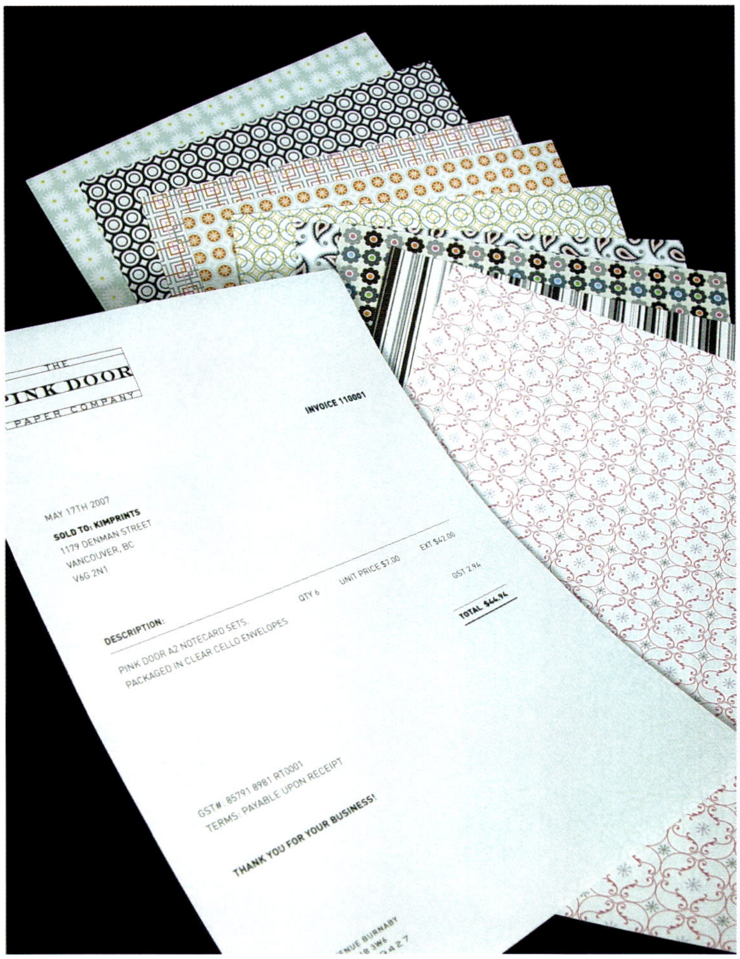

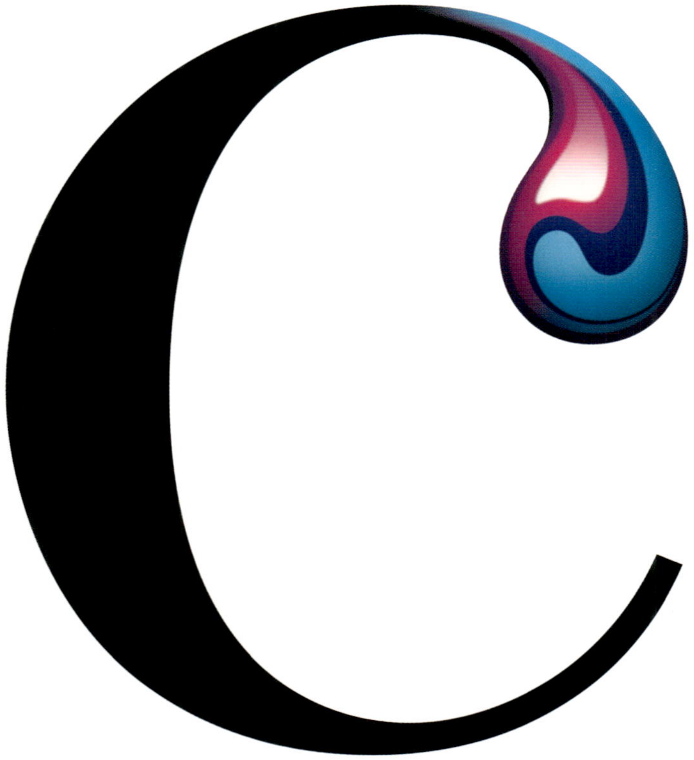

The Colournet Ltd
Unit 1
1 Dace Road
London E3 2NG

T +44 (0)20 8985 0805
F +44 (0)20 8985 0849

info@thecolournet.co.uk
www.thecolournet.co.uk

Directors: Mark Cameron, Simon Arnall
Registered office: The Colournet Ltd, Unit 1, 1 Dace Road, London E3 2NG
Registered office in England number: 3925074 VAT registration number: 802 5071 70

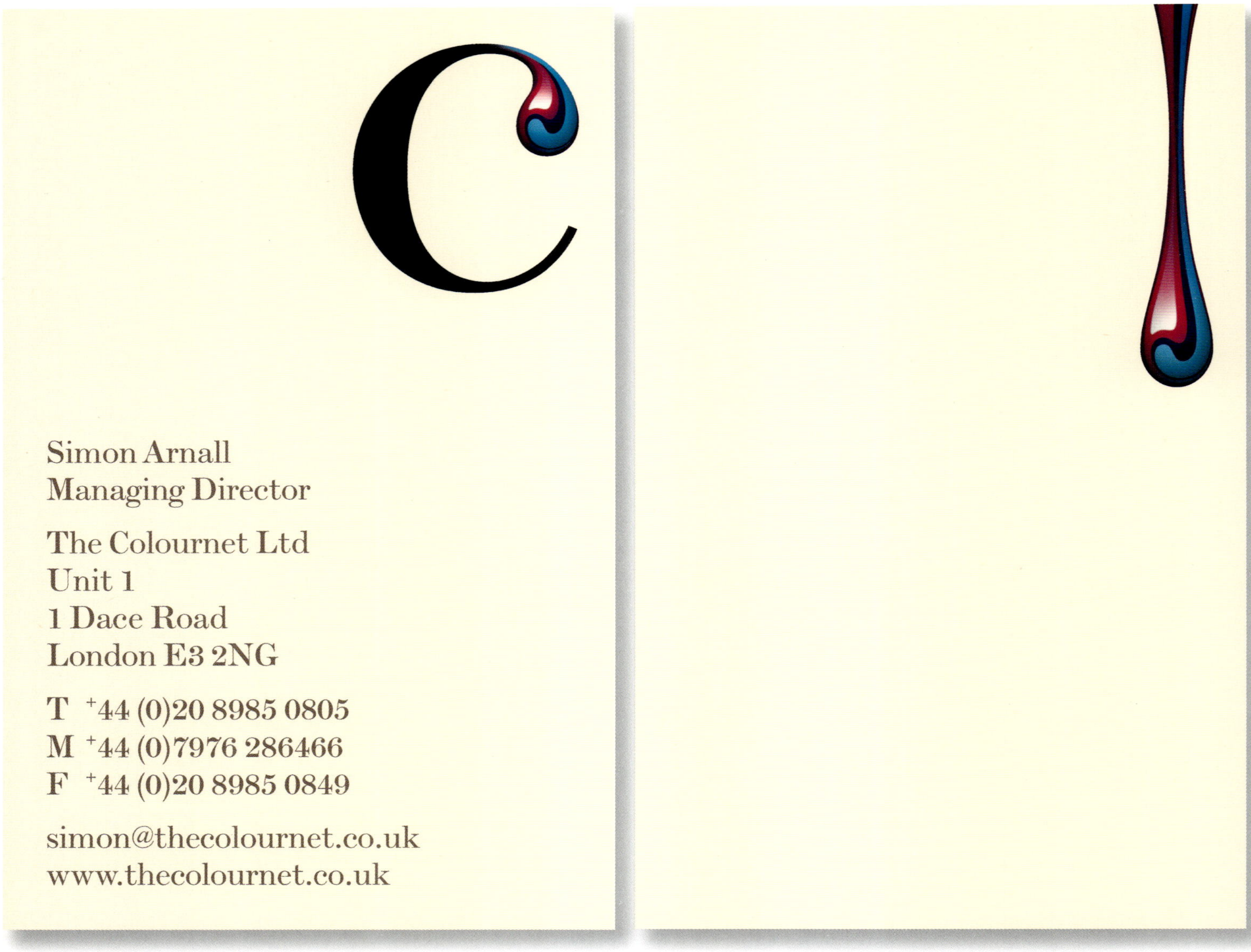
Simon Arnall
Managing Director
The Colournet Ltd
Unit 1
1 Dace Road
London E3 2NG
T +44 (0)20 8985 0805
M +44 (0)7976 286466
F +44 (0)20 8985 0849
simon@thecolournet.co.uk
www.thecolournet.co.uk

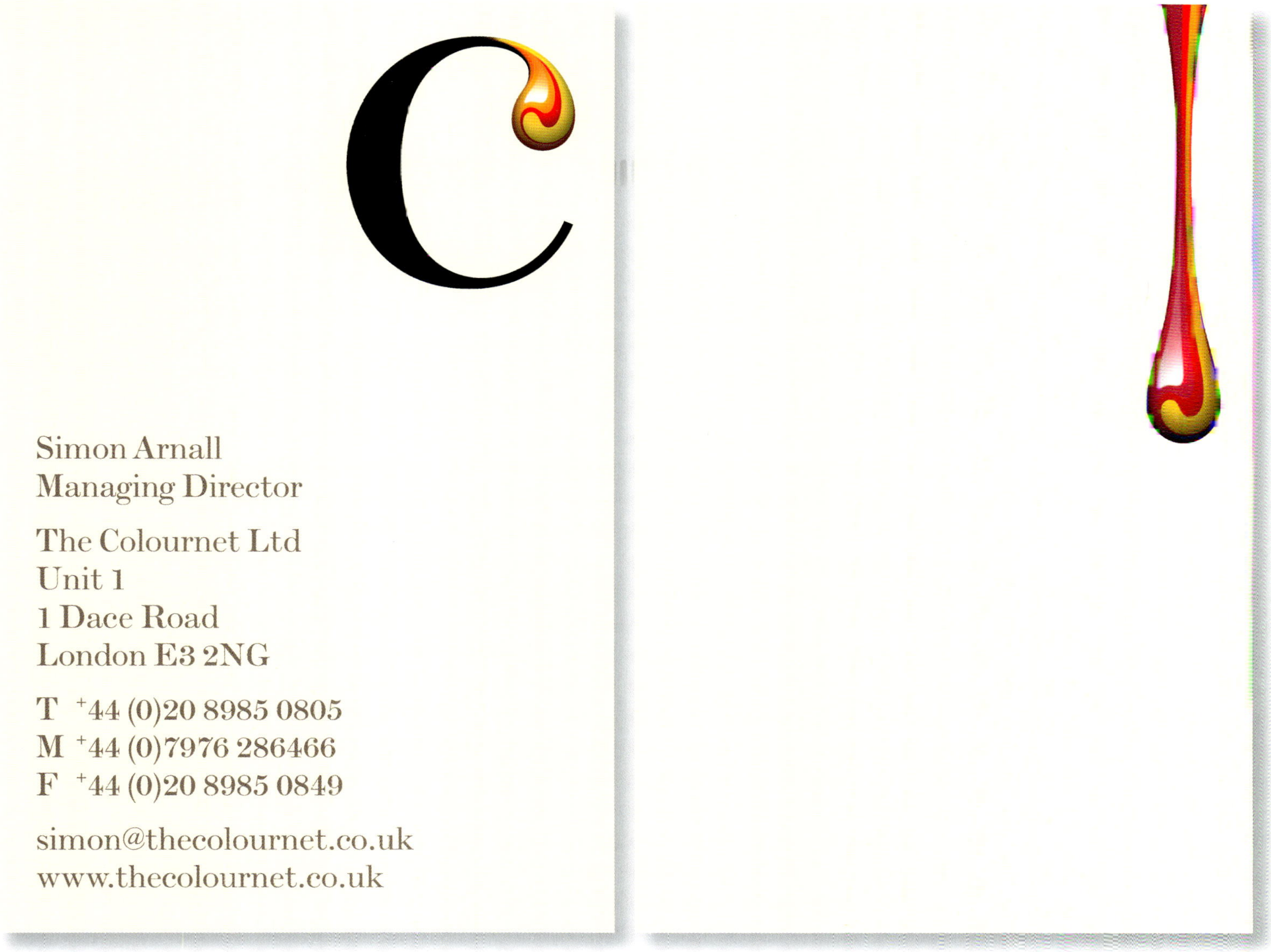
Simon Arnall
Managing Director
The Colournet Ltd
Unit 1
1 Dace Road
London E3 2NG
T +44 (0)20 8985 0805
M +44 (0)7976 286466
F +44 (0)20 8985 0849
simon@thecolournet.co.uk
www.thecolournet.co.uk

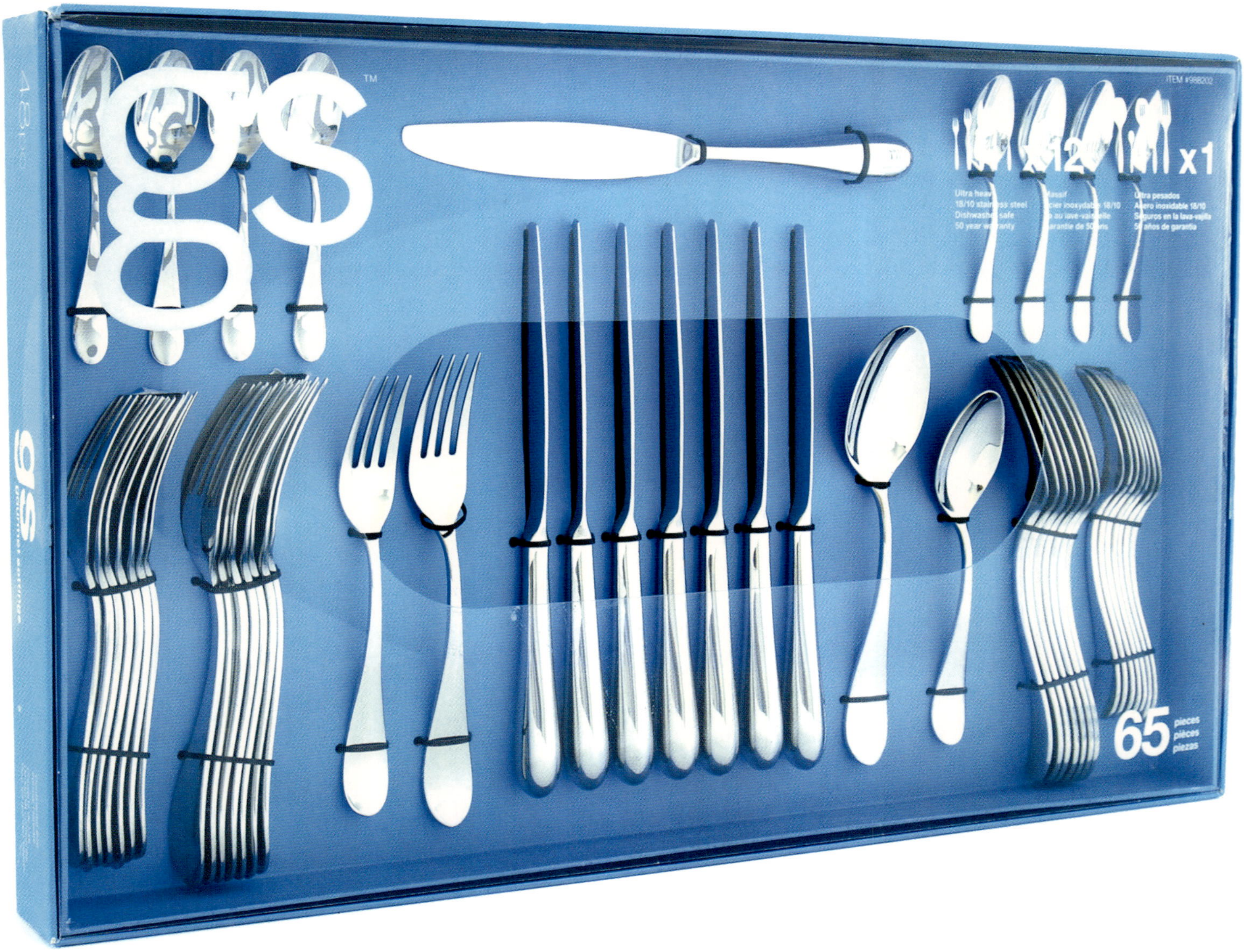
gs
x1
Ultra pesados
65
pieces
pièces
piezas

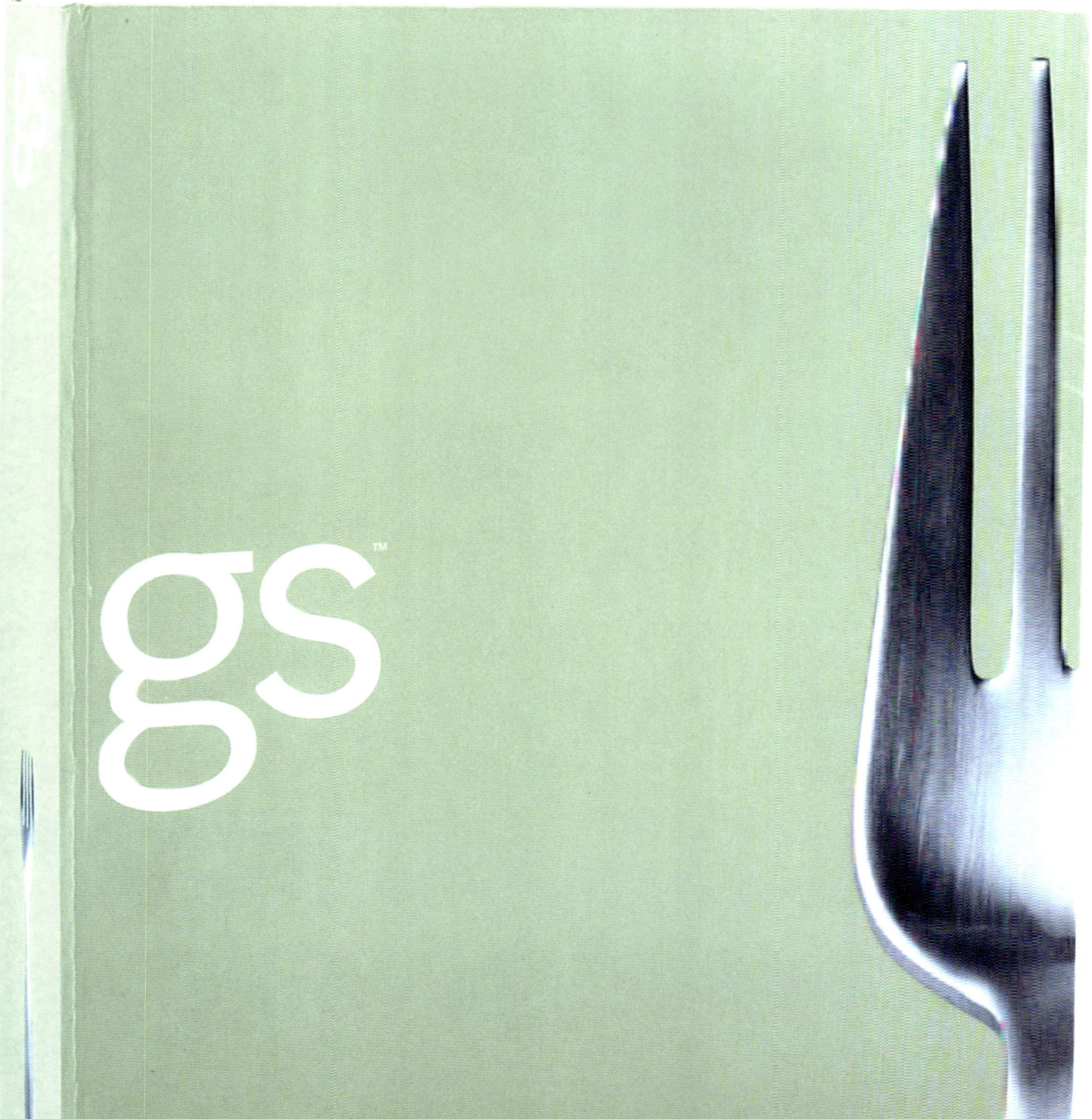
gs™
The Collection

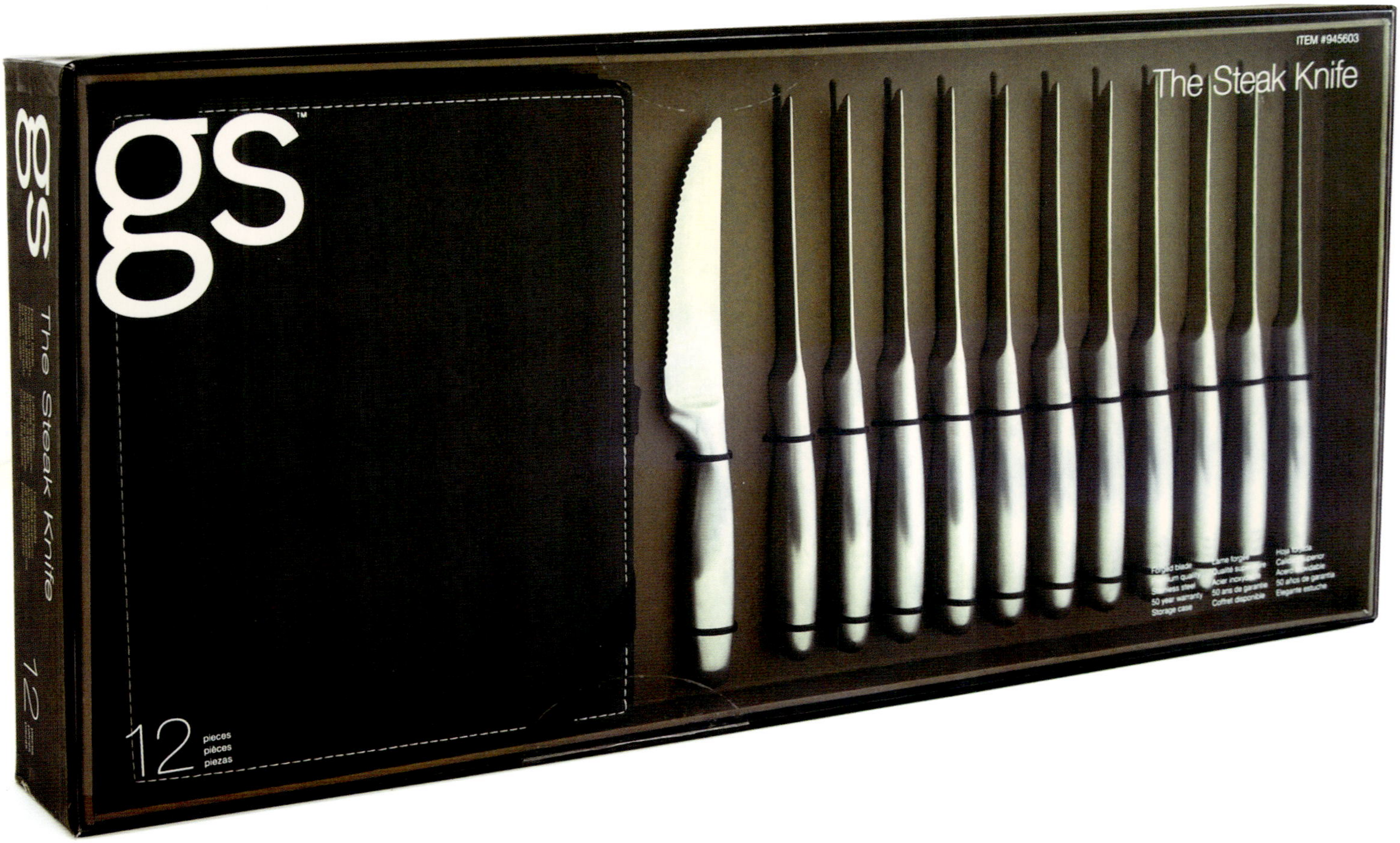
gs
The Steak Knife
12
ITEM #945603
The Steak Knife
gs™
12 pieces
pièces
piezas

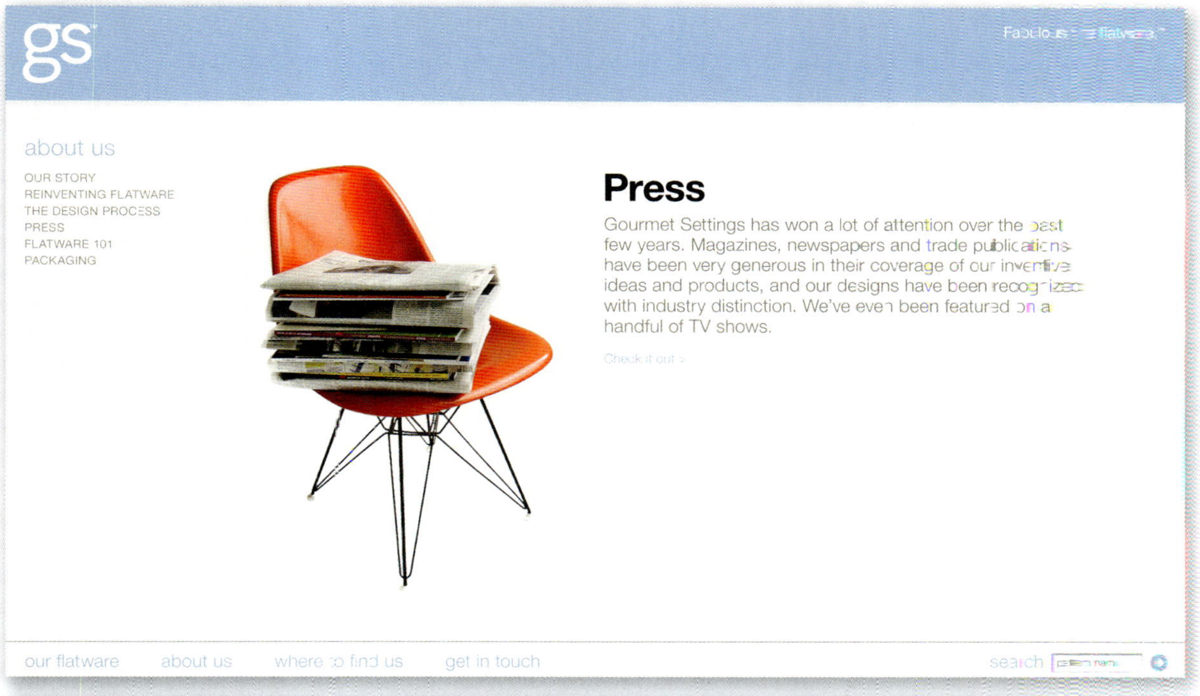

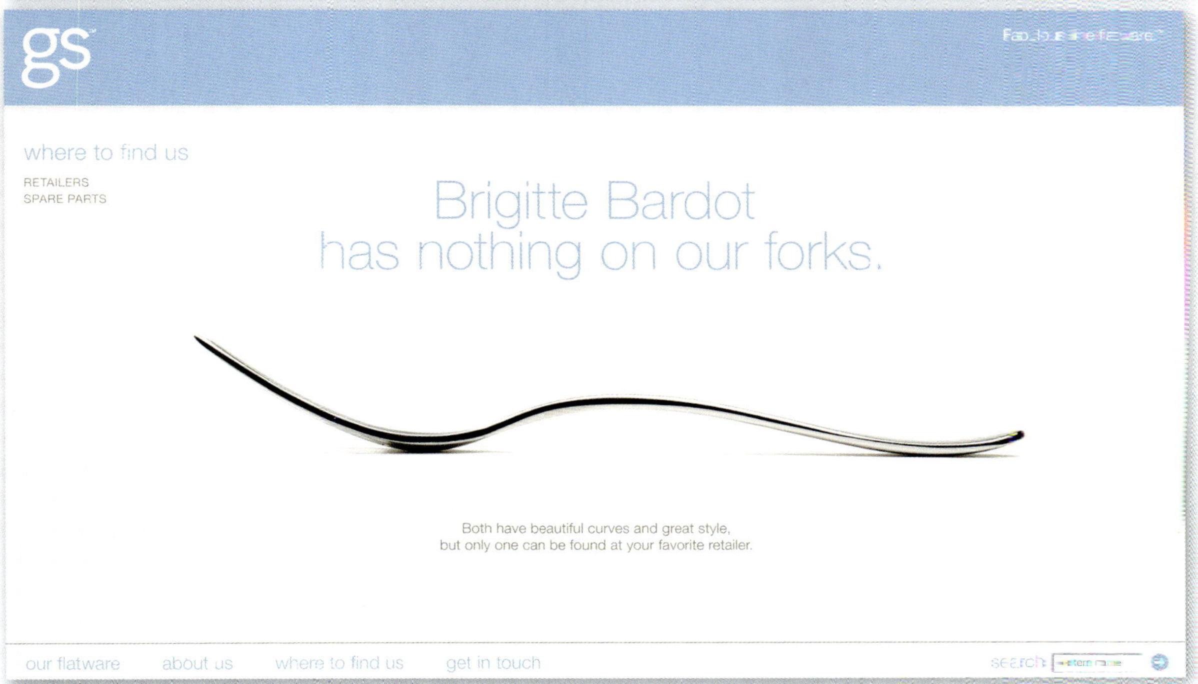

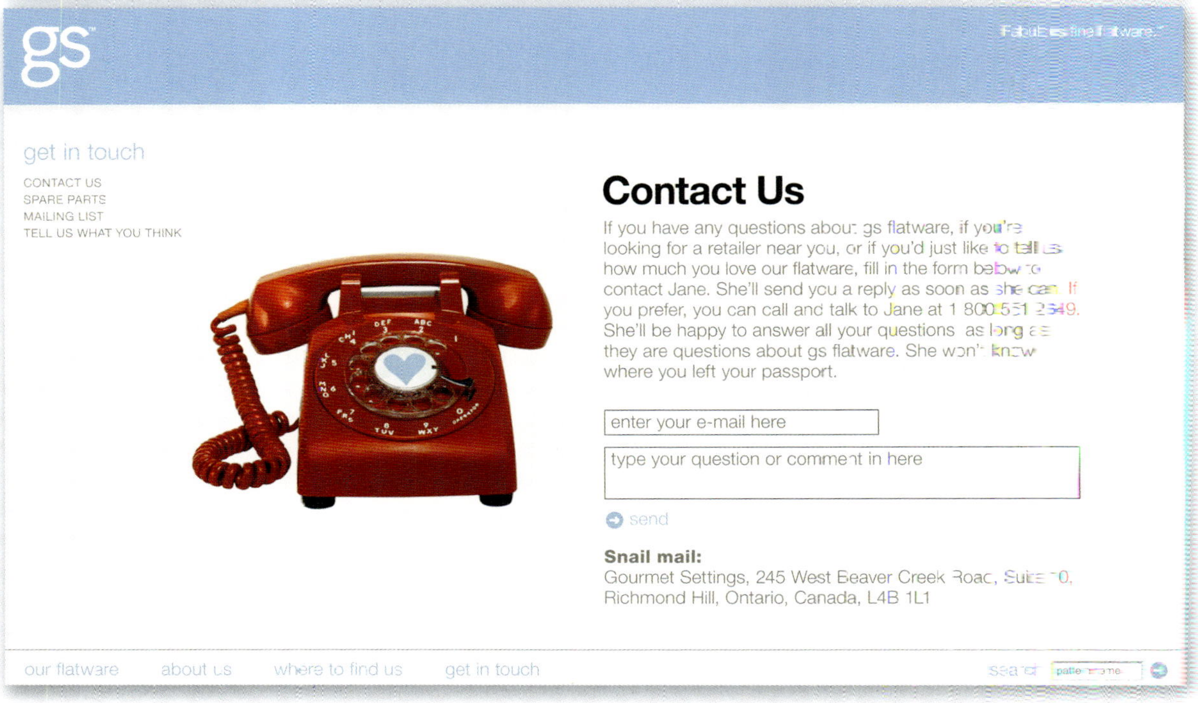

Hahn Smith Design Inc. (this spread) | Gourmet Settings (Hildy Abrams) | Products

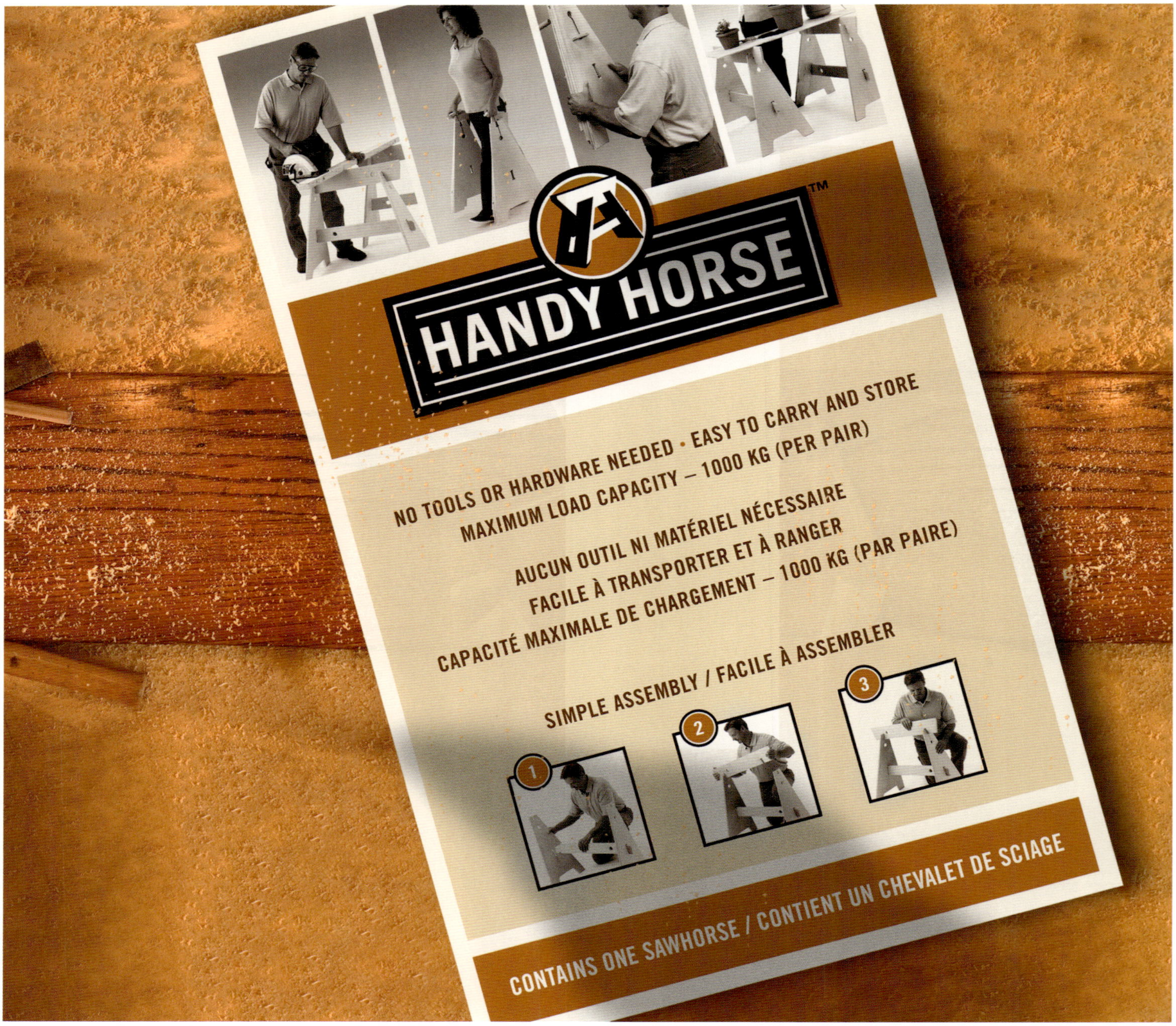
HANDY HORSE™
NO TOOLS OR HARDWARE NEEDED • EASY TO CARRY AND STORE
MAXIMUM LOAD CAPACITY – 1000 KG (PER PAIR)
AUCUN OUTIL NI MATÉRIEL NÉCESSAIRE
FACILE À TRANSPORTER ET À RANGER
CAPACITÉ MAXIMALE DE CHARGEMENT – 1000 KG (PAR PAIRE)
SIMPLE ASSEMBLY / FACILE À ASSEMBLER
1
2
3
CONTAINS ONE SAWHORSE / CONTIENT UN CHEVALET DE SCIAGE

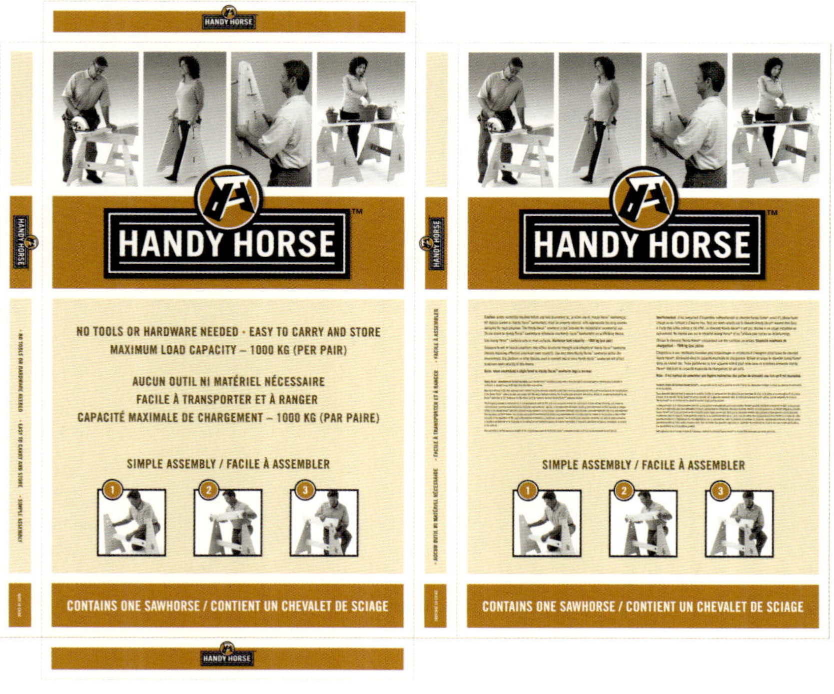
HANDY HORSE
HANDY HORSE™
NO TOOLS OR HARDWARE NEEDED • EASY TO CARRY AND STORE
MAXIMUM LOAD CAPACITY – 1000 KG (PER PAIR)
AUCUN OUTIL NI MATÉRIEL NÉCESSAIRE
FACILE À TRANSPORTER ET À RANGER
CAPACITÉ MAXIMALE DE CHARGEMENT – 1000 KG (PAR PAIRE)
SIMPLE ASSEMBLY / FACILE À ASSEMBLER
CONTAINS ONE SAWHORSE / CONTIENT UN CHEVALET DE SCIAGE
HANDY HORSE™
SIMPLE ASSEMBLY / FACILE À ASSEMBLER
CONTAINS ONE SAWHORSE / CONTIENT UN CHEVALET DE SCIAGE

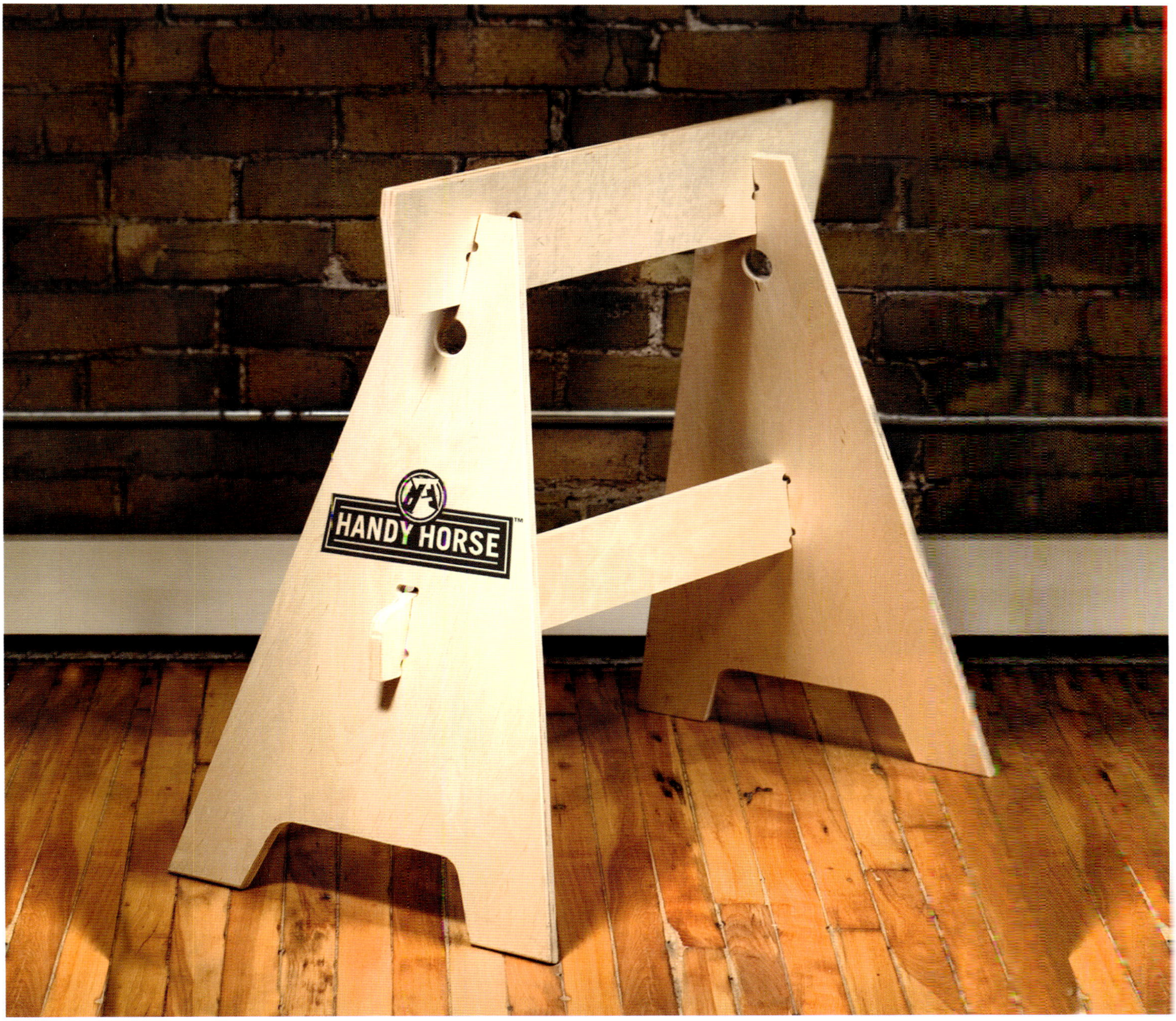
HANDY HORSE

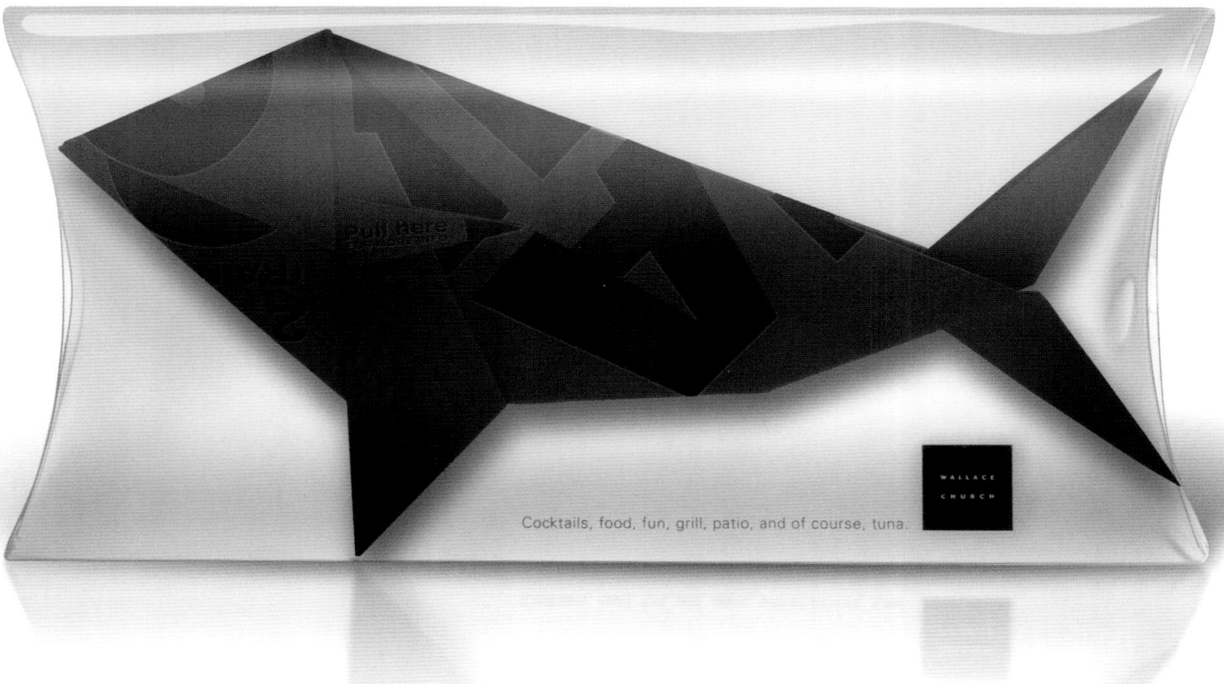
Pull here
Cocktails, food, fun, grill, patio, and of course, tuna.
WALLACE CHURCH

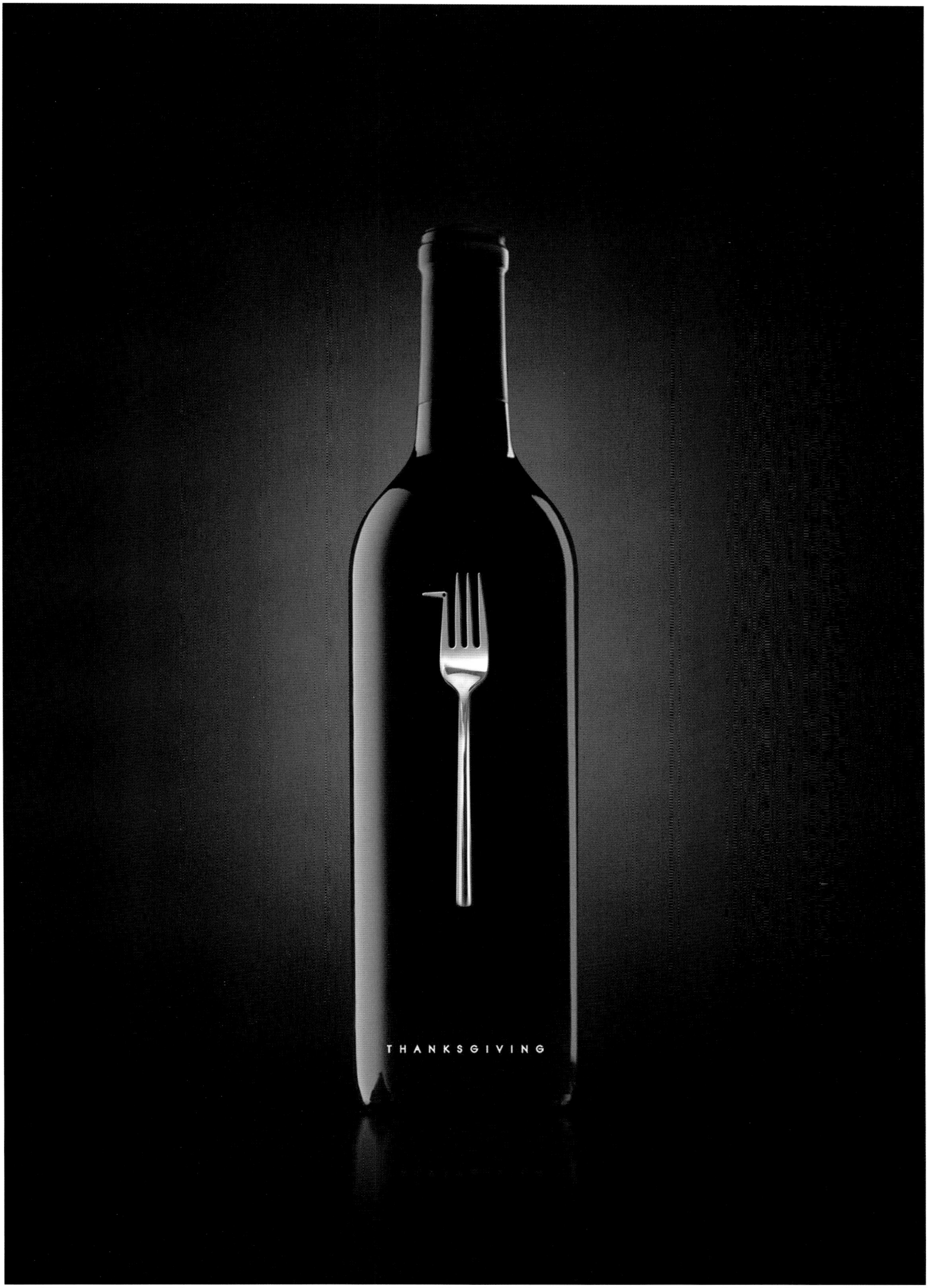
THANKSGIVING

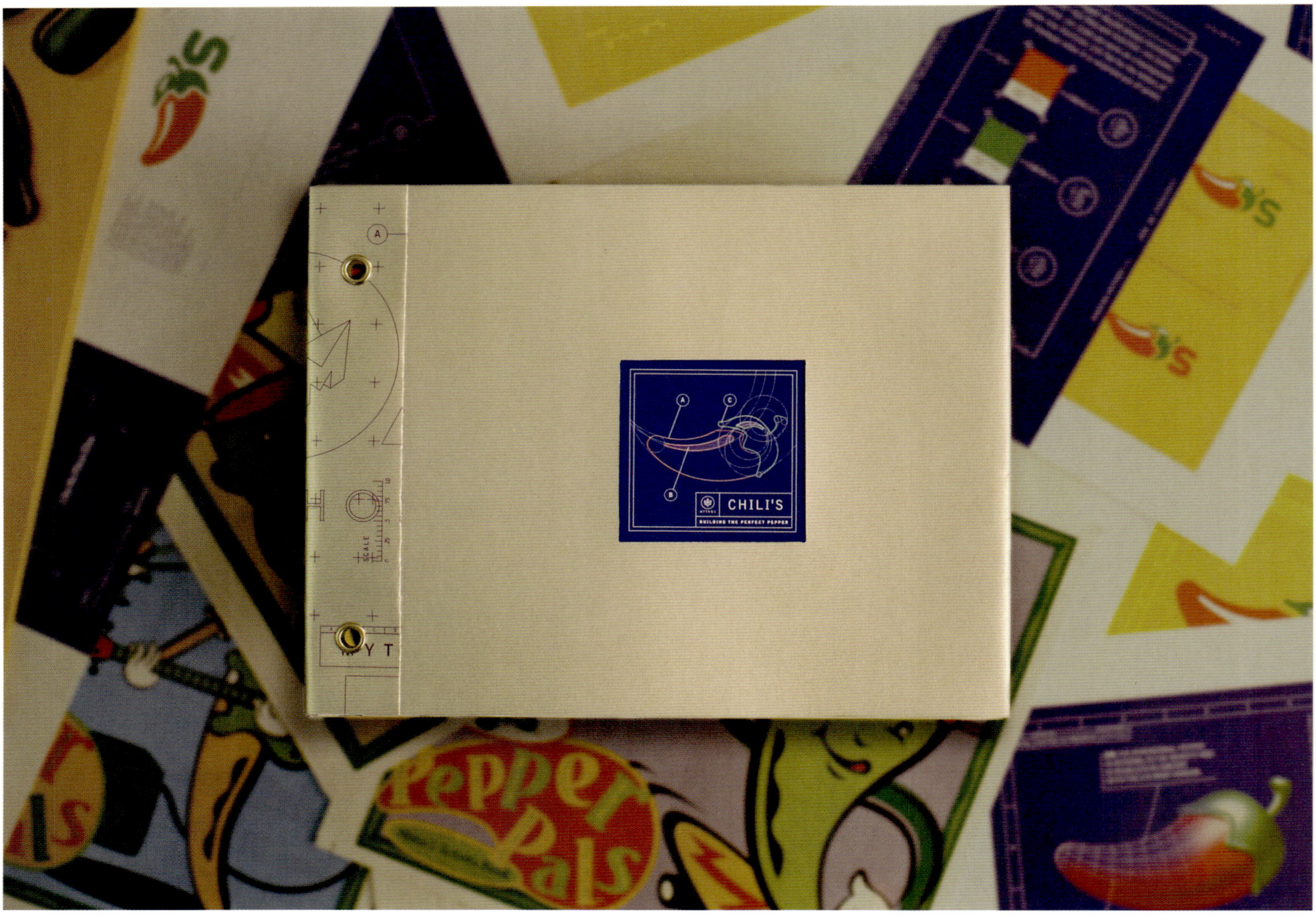
CHILI'S
BUILDING THE PERFECT PEPPER
Pepper Pals

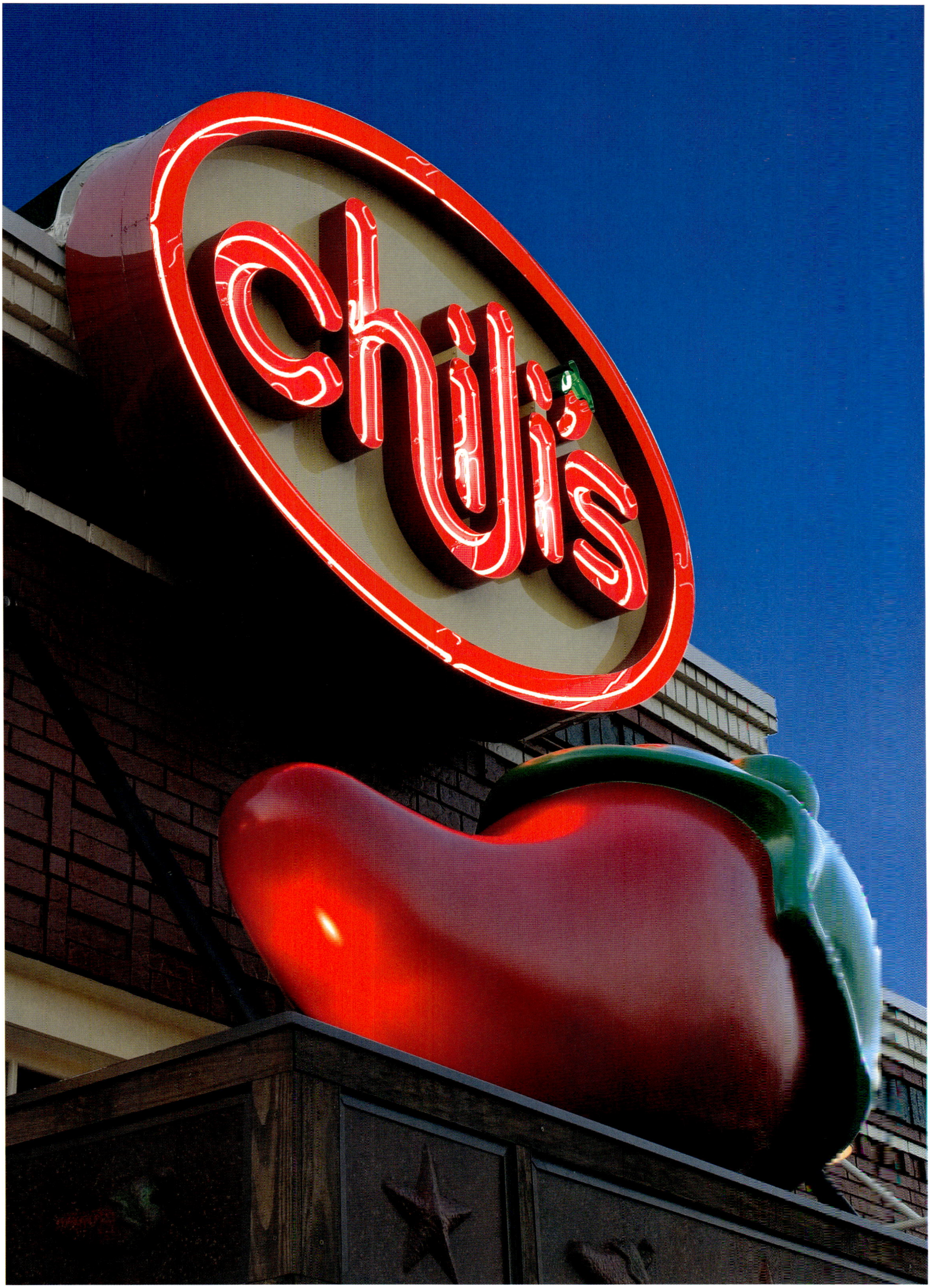
Chili's

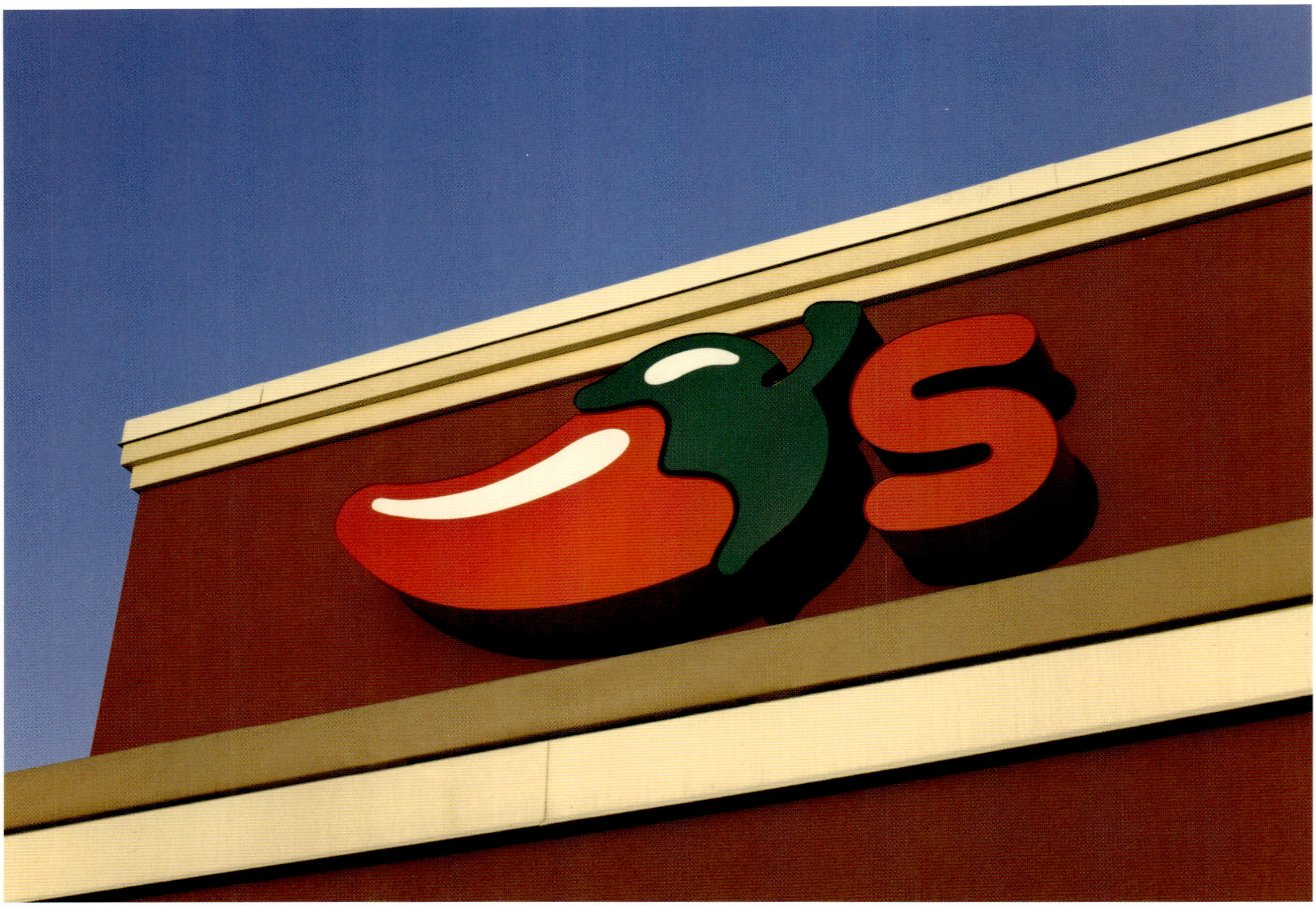

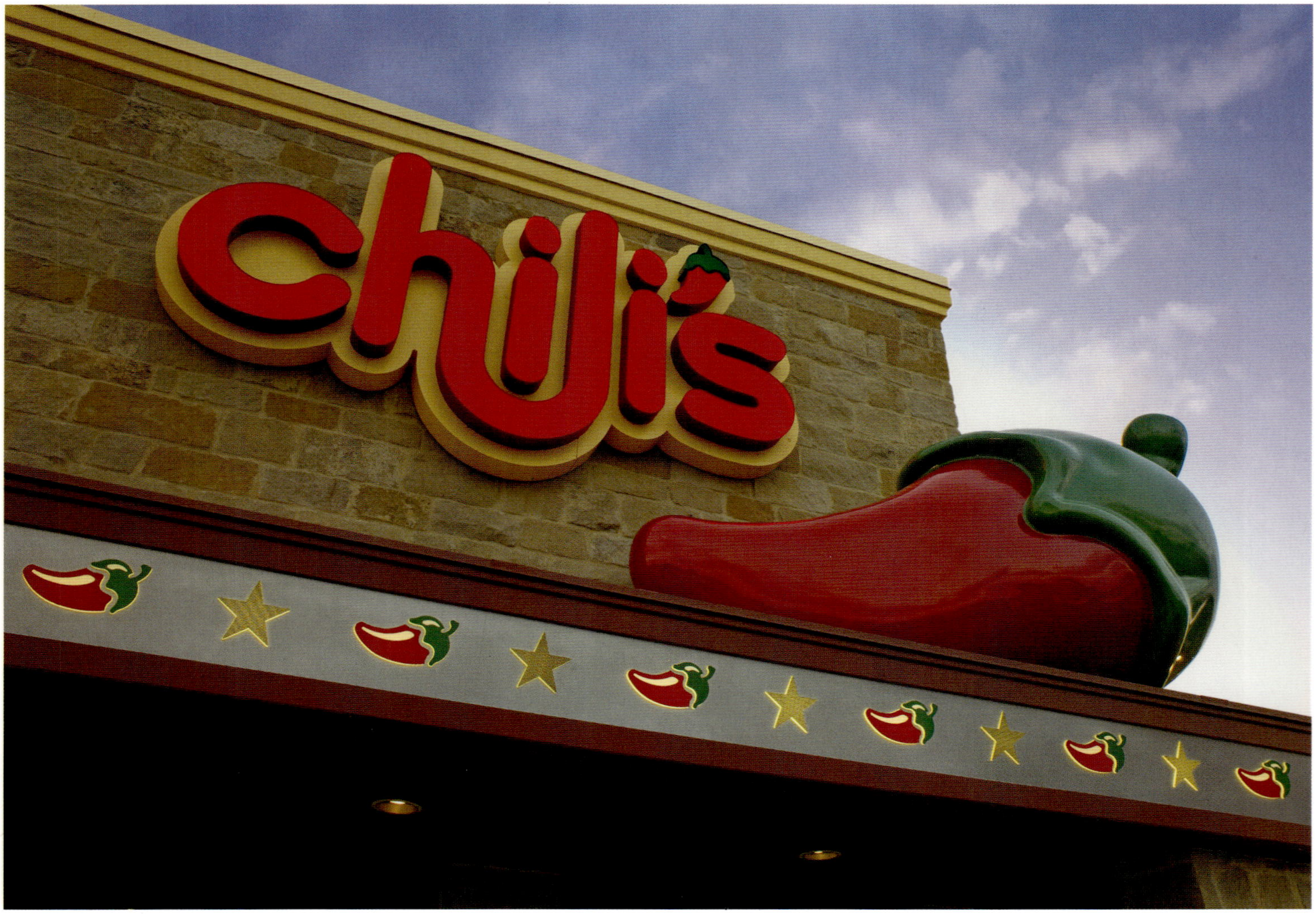
chili's

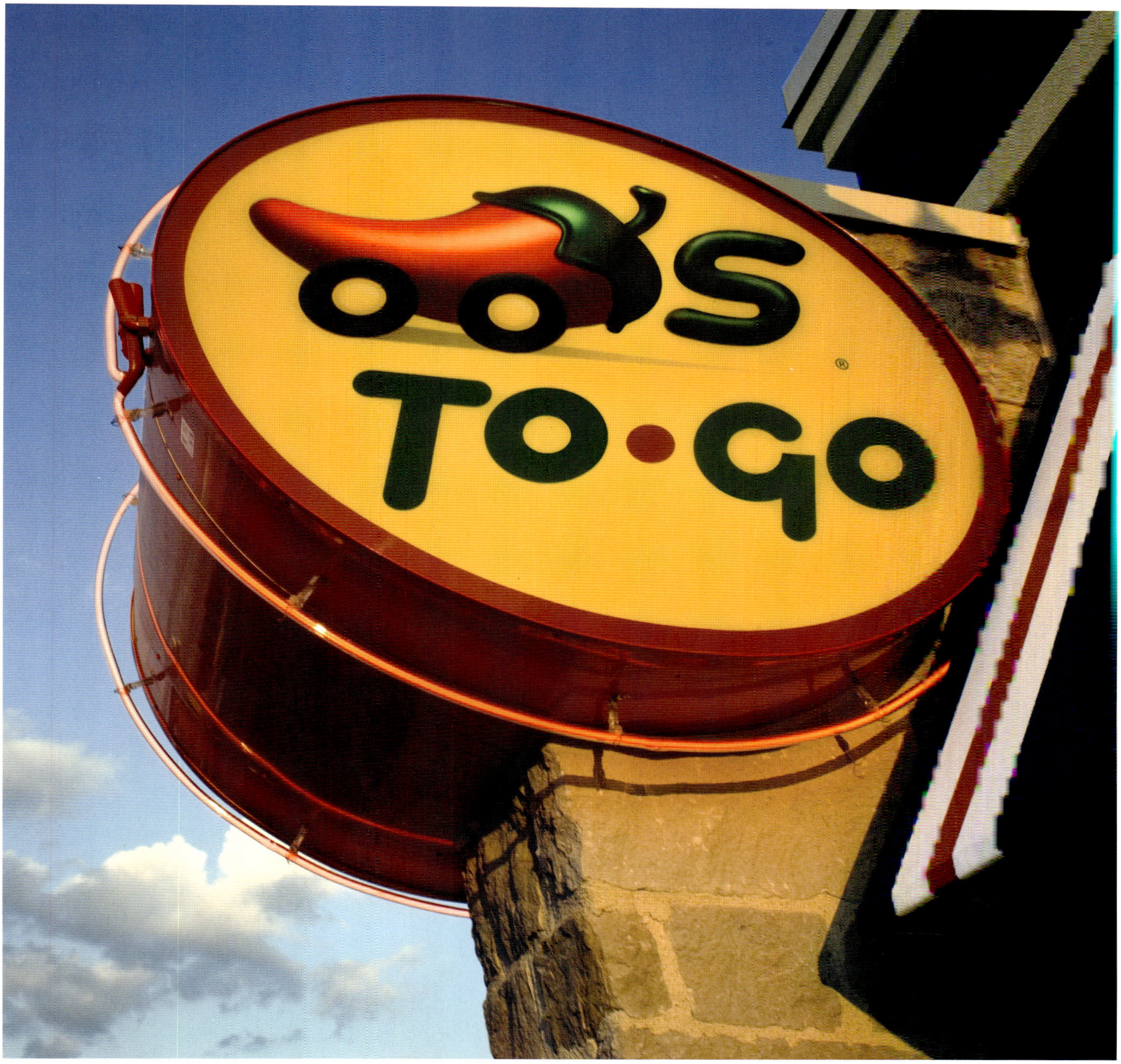
S
TO·GO

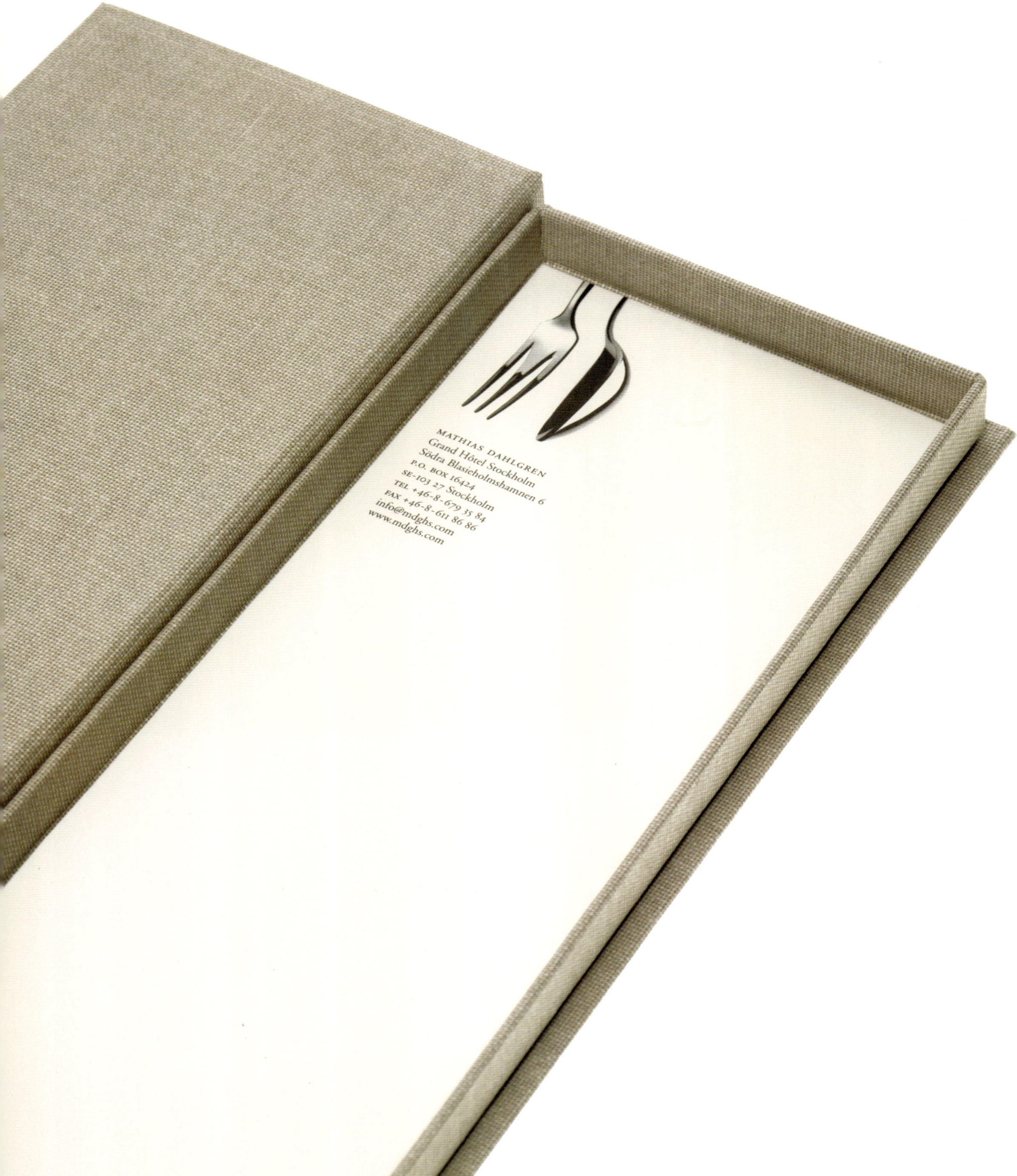
MATHIAS DAHLGREN
Grand Hôtel Stockholm
Södra Blasieholmshamnen 6
P.O. BOX 16424
SE-103 27 Stockholm
TEL +46-8-679 35 84
FAX +46-8-611 86 86
info@mdghs.com
www.mdghs.com

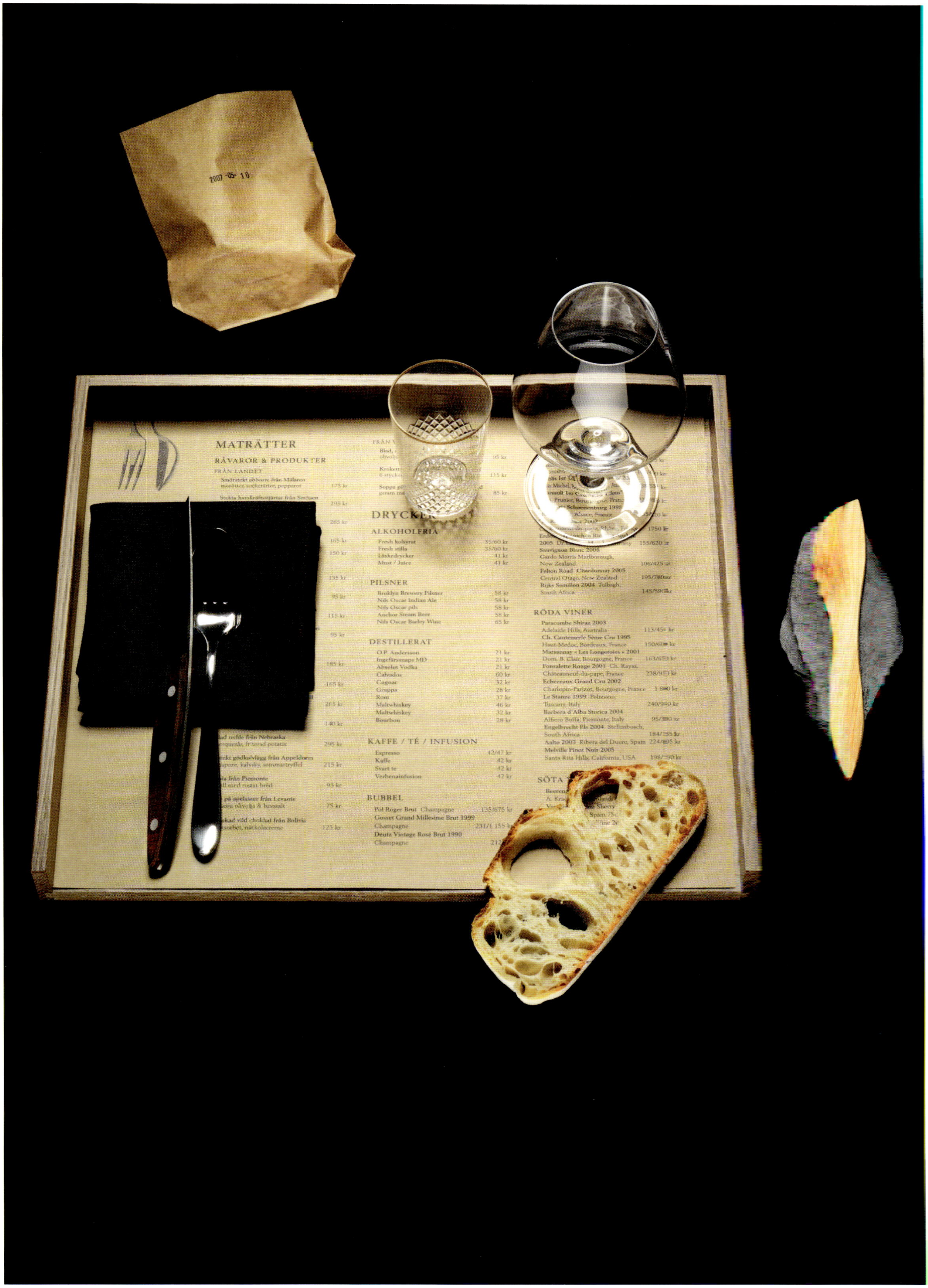
2007-05-10
MATRÄTTER
RÅVAROR & PRODUKTER
FRÅN LANDET
DRYCKER
ALKOHOLFRIA
Fresh kolsyrat 35/60 kr
Fresh stilla 35/60 kr
Läskedrycker 41 kr
Must / Juice 41 kr
PILSNER
Broklyn Brewery Pilsner 58 kr
Nils Oscar Indian Ale 58 kr
Nils Oscar pils 58 kr
Anchor Steam Beer 58 kr
Nils Oscar Barley Wine 65 kr
DESTILLERAT
O.P. Andersson 21 kr
Ingefärssnaps MD 21 kr
Absolut Vodka 21 kr
Calvados 60 kr
Cognac 32 kr
Grappa 28 kr
Rom 37 kr
Maltwhiskey 46 kr
Maltwhiskey 32 kr
Bourbon 28 kr
KAFFE / TÉ / INFUSION
Espresso 42/47 kr
Kaffe 42 kr
Svart te 42 kr
Verbenainfusion 42 kr
BUBBEL
Pol Roger Brut Champagne 135/675 kr
Gosset Grand Millesime Brut 1999
Deutz Vintage Rosé Brut 1990
Sauvignon Blanc 2006
Gardo Morris Marlborough,
New Zealand 106/425
Felton Road Chardonnay 2005
Central Otago, New Zealand 195/780
Rijks Semilion 2004 Tulbagh,
RÖDA VINER
Paracombe Shiraz 2003
Ch. Cantemerle 5ème Cru 1995
Haut-Medoc, Bordeaux, France
Marsannay « Les Longeroies » 2001
Dom. B. Clair, Bourgogne, France
Fonsalette Rouge 2001 Ch. Rayas,
Châteauneuf-du-pape, France
Echezeaux Grand Cru 2002
Charlopin-Parizot, Bourgogne, France
Le Stanze 1999 Poliziano,
Tuscany, Italy
Barbera d'Alba Storica 2004
Alfiero Boffa, Piemonte, Italy
Engelbrecht Els 2004 Stellenbosch,
South Africa
Aalto 2003 Ribera del Duero, Spain
Melville Pinot Noir 2005
Santa Rita Hills, California, USA

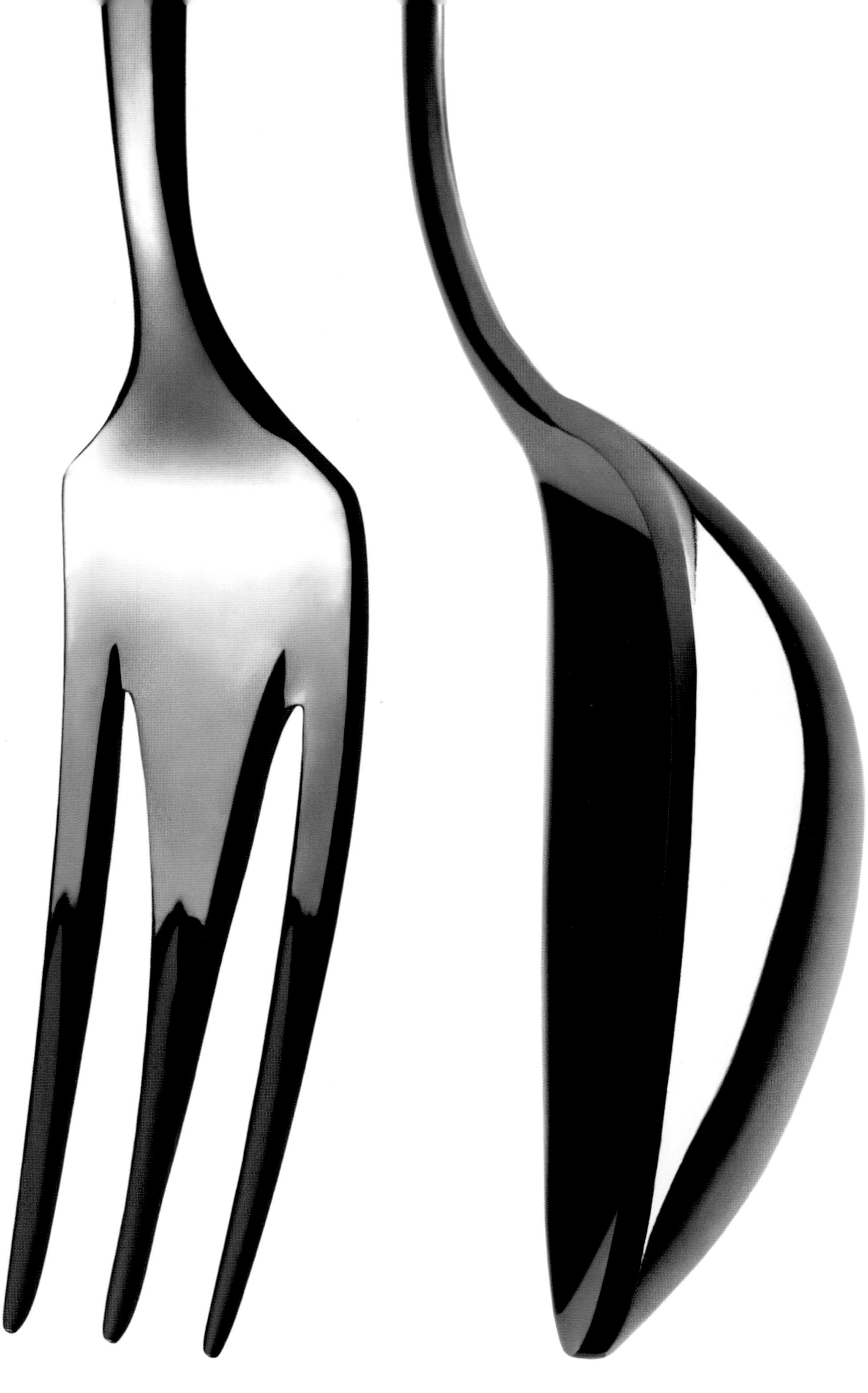

PLATINUM

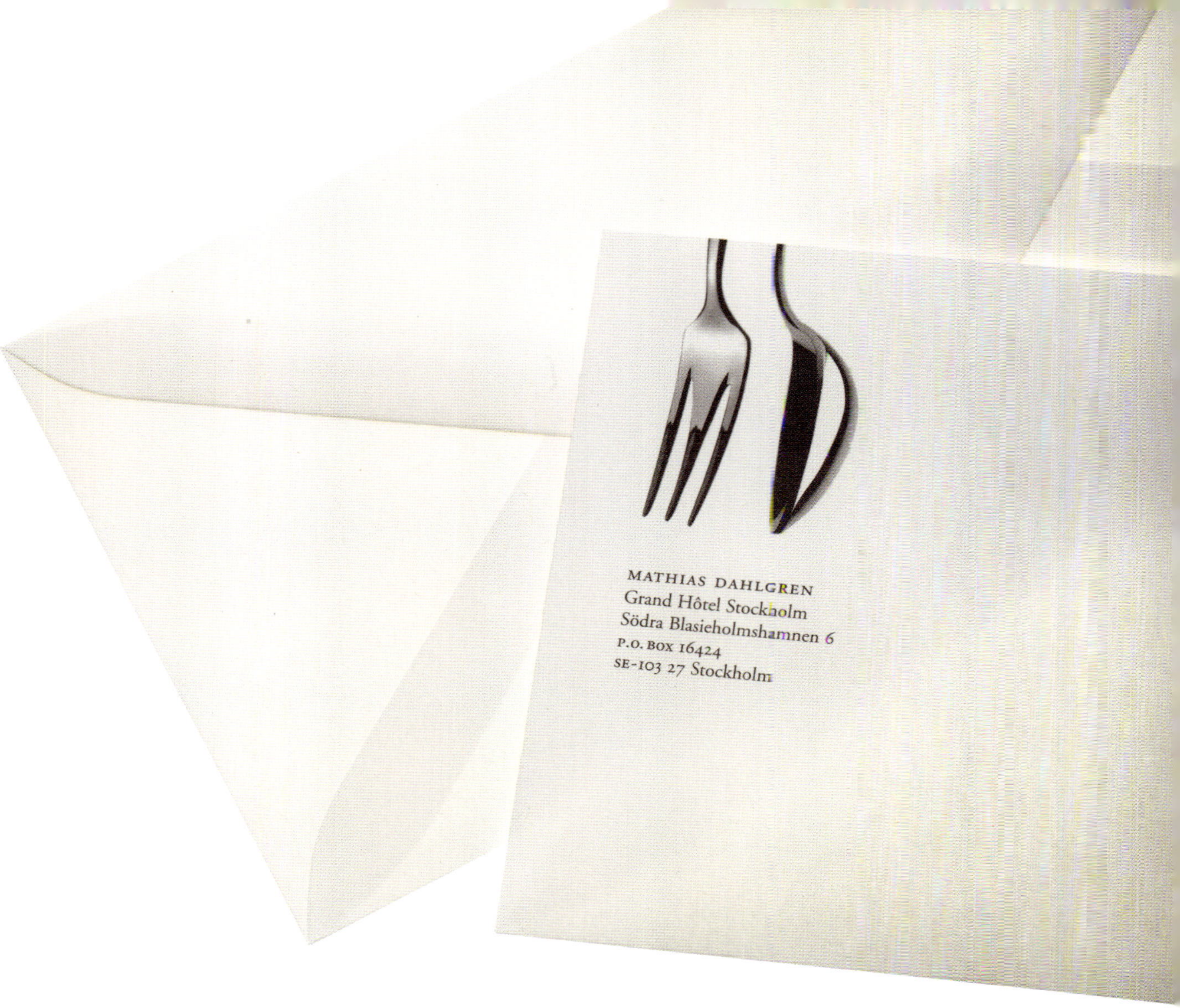
MATHIAS DAHLGREN
Grand Hôtel Stockholm
Södra Blasieholmshamnen 6
P.O. BOX 16424
SE-103 27 Stockholm

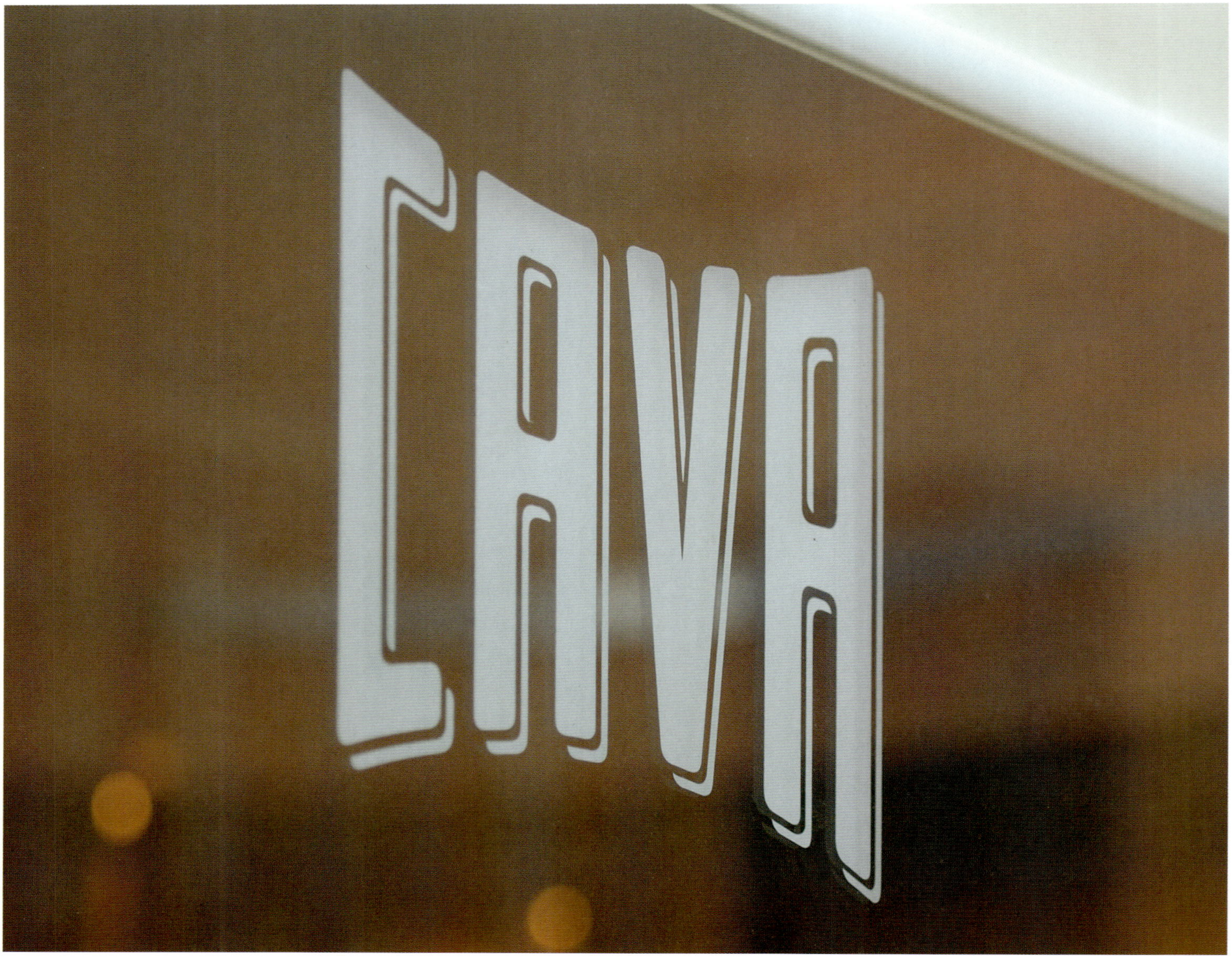
CAVA

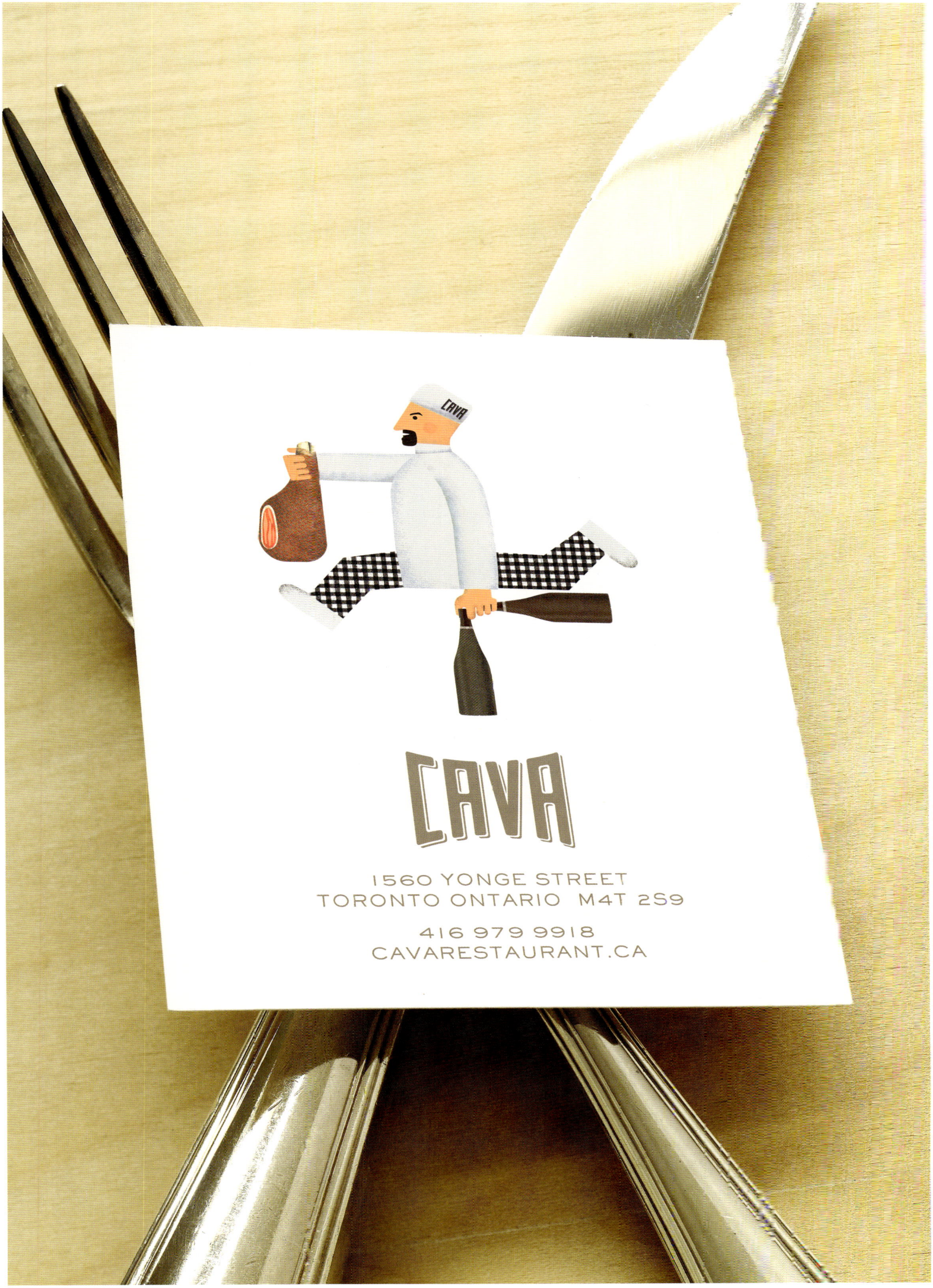
CAVA
CAVA
1560 YONGE STREET
TORONTO ONTARIO M4T 2S9
416 979 9918
CAVARESTAURANT.CA

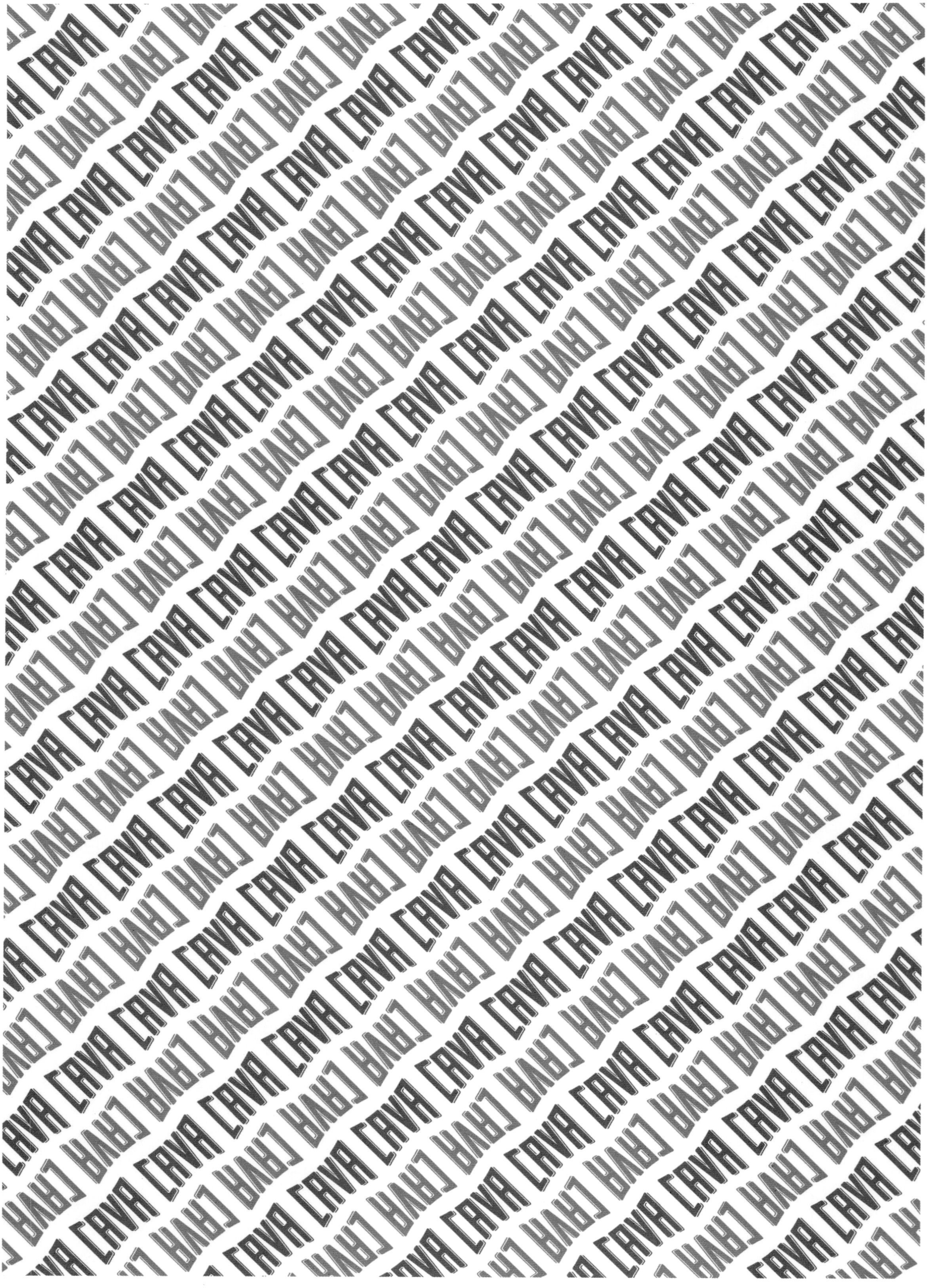

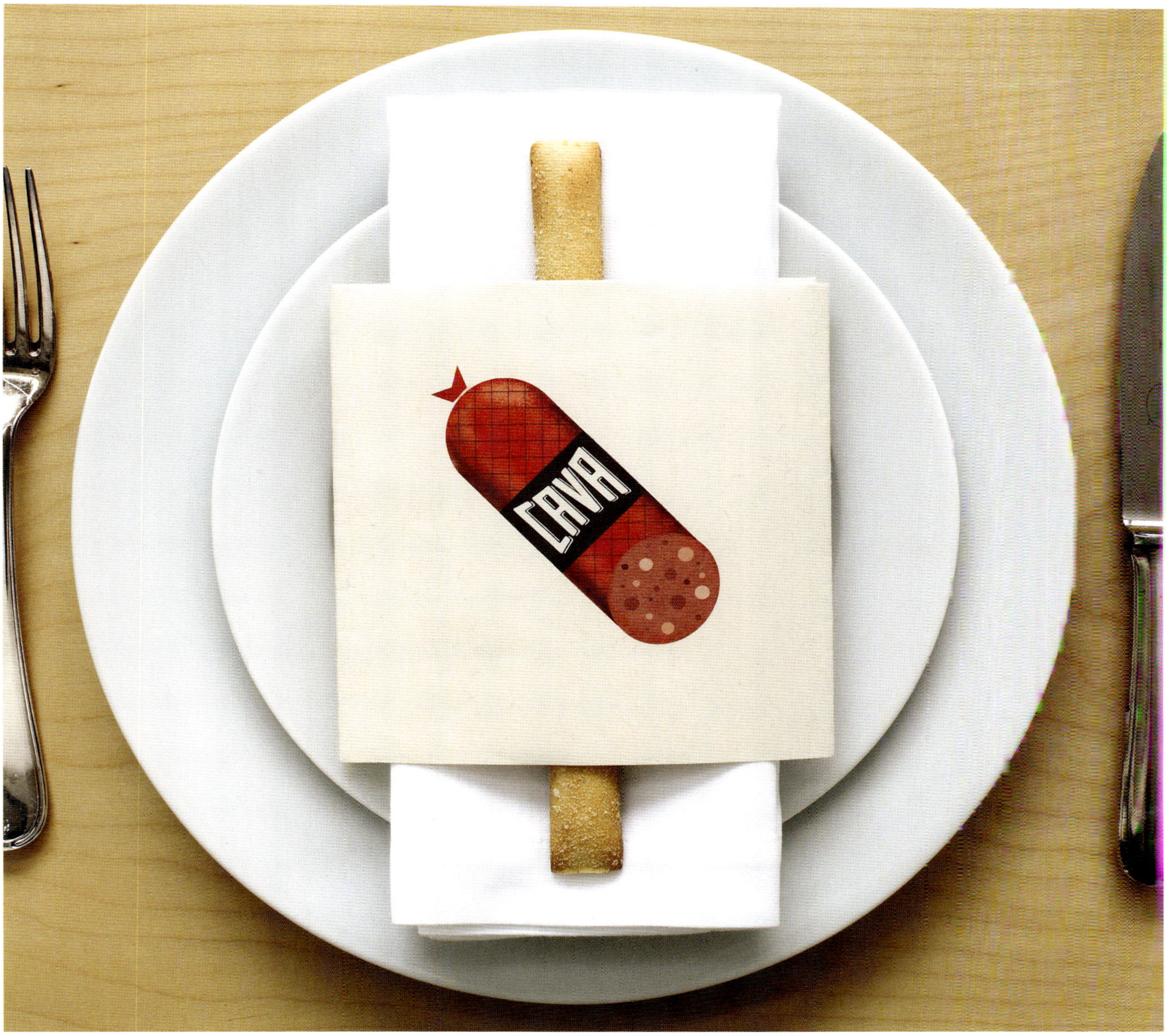
CAVA

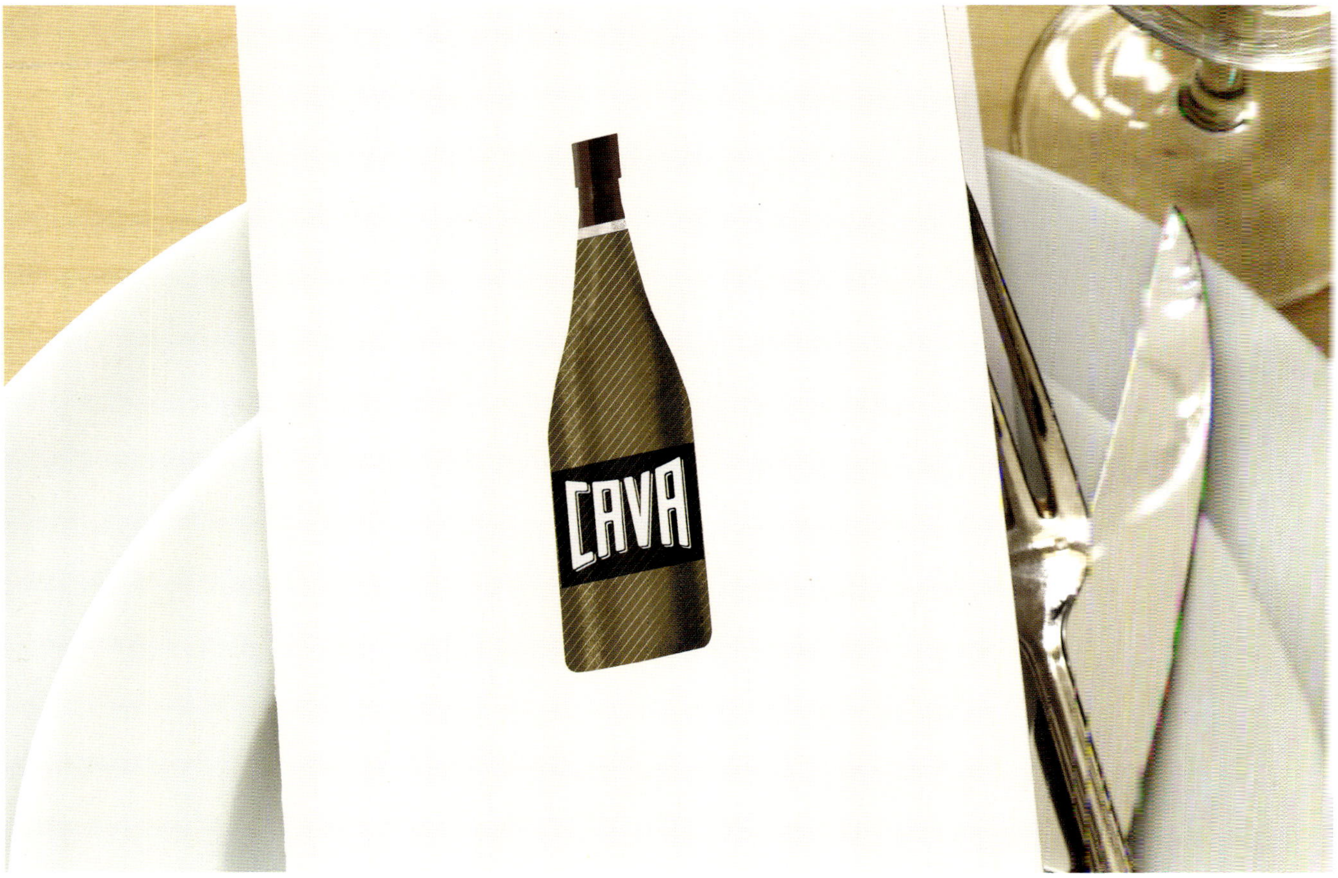
CAVA

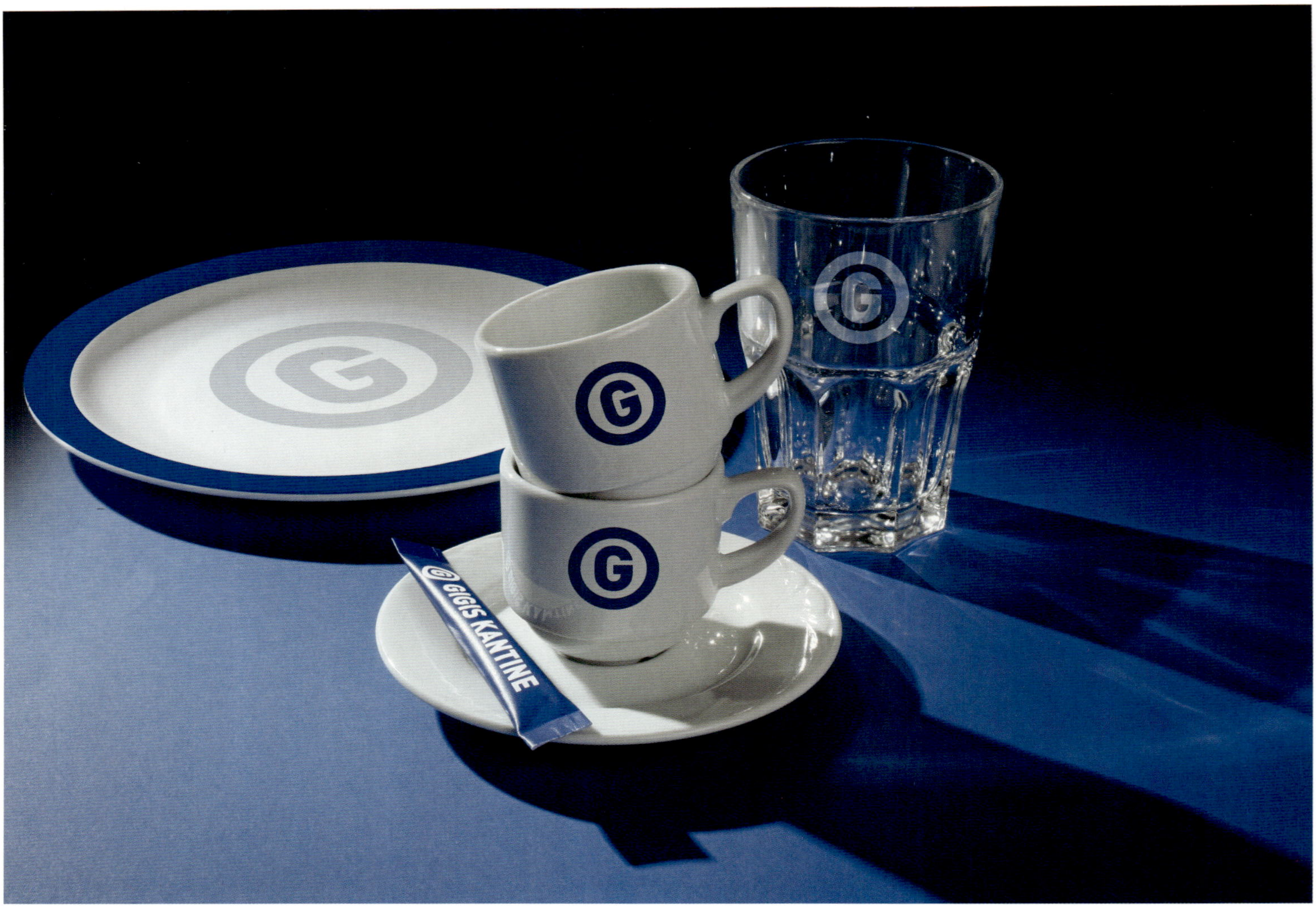
GIGIS KANTINE

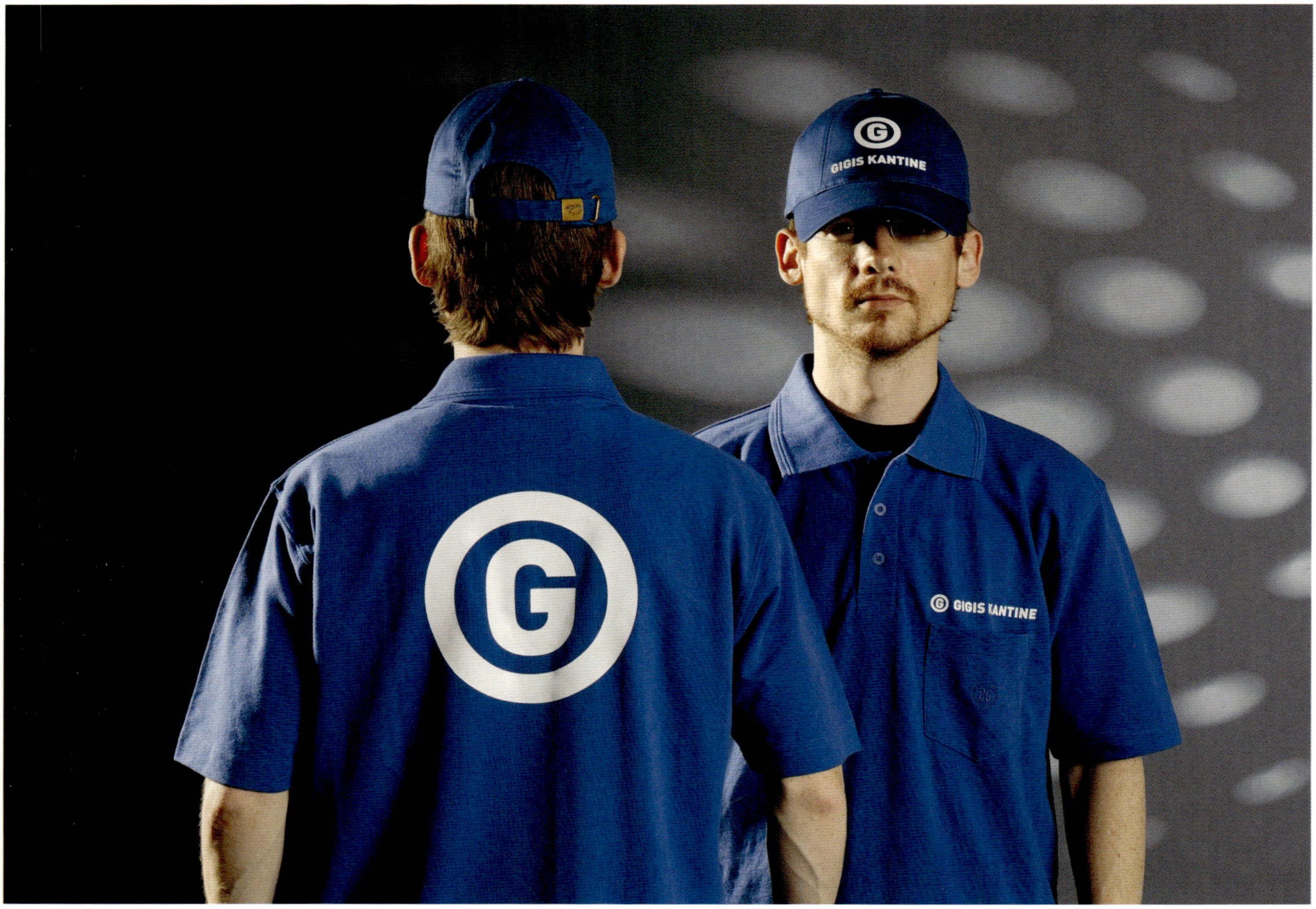
GIGIS KANTINE
GIGIS KANTINE

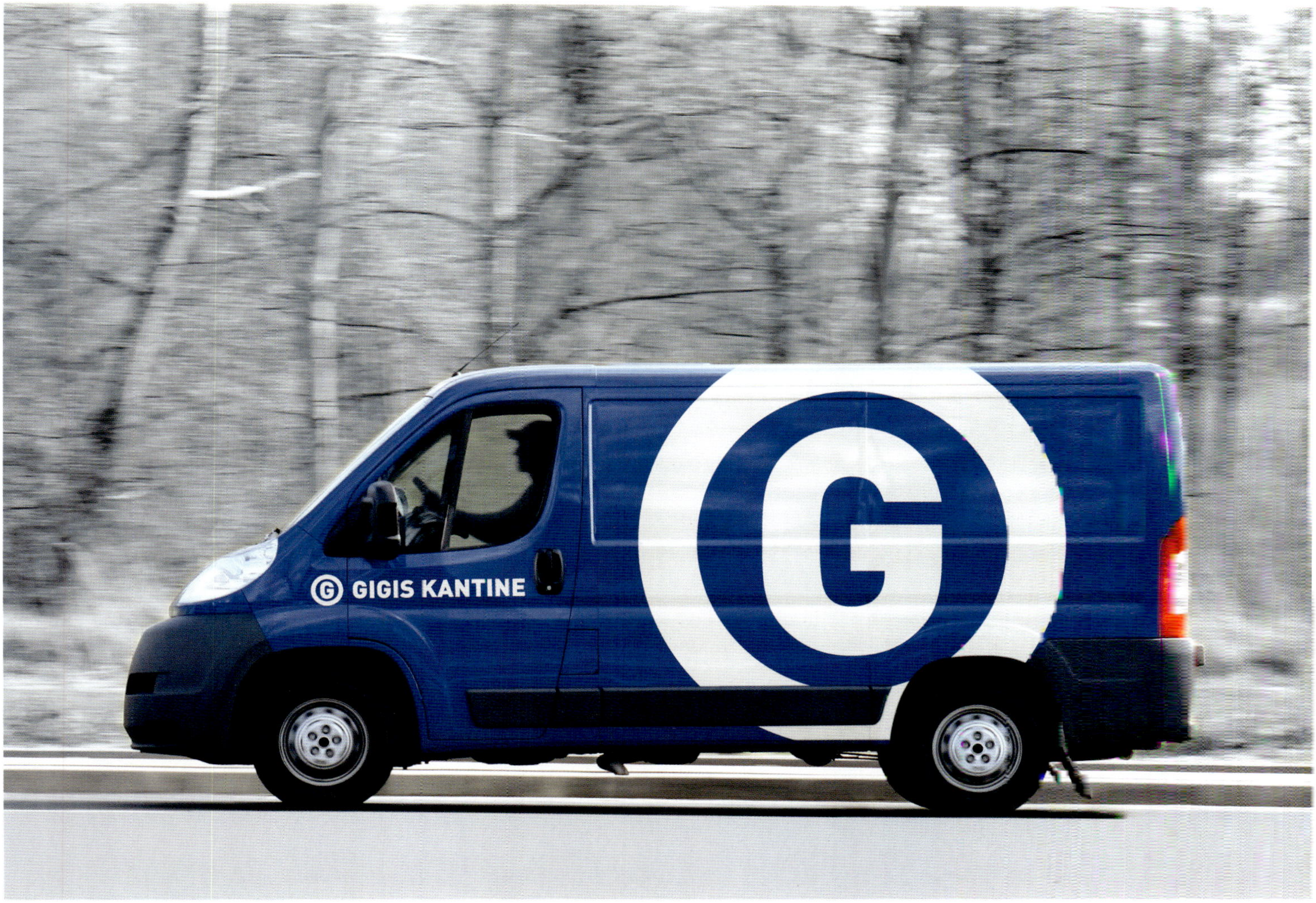
GIGIS KANTINE

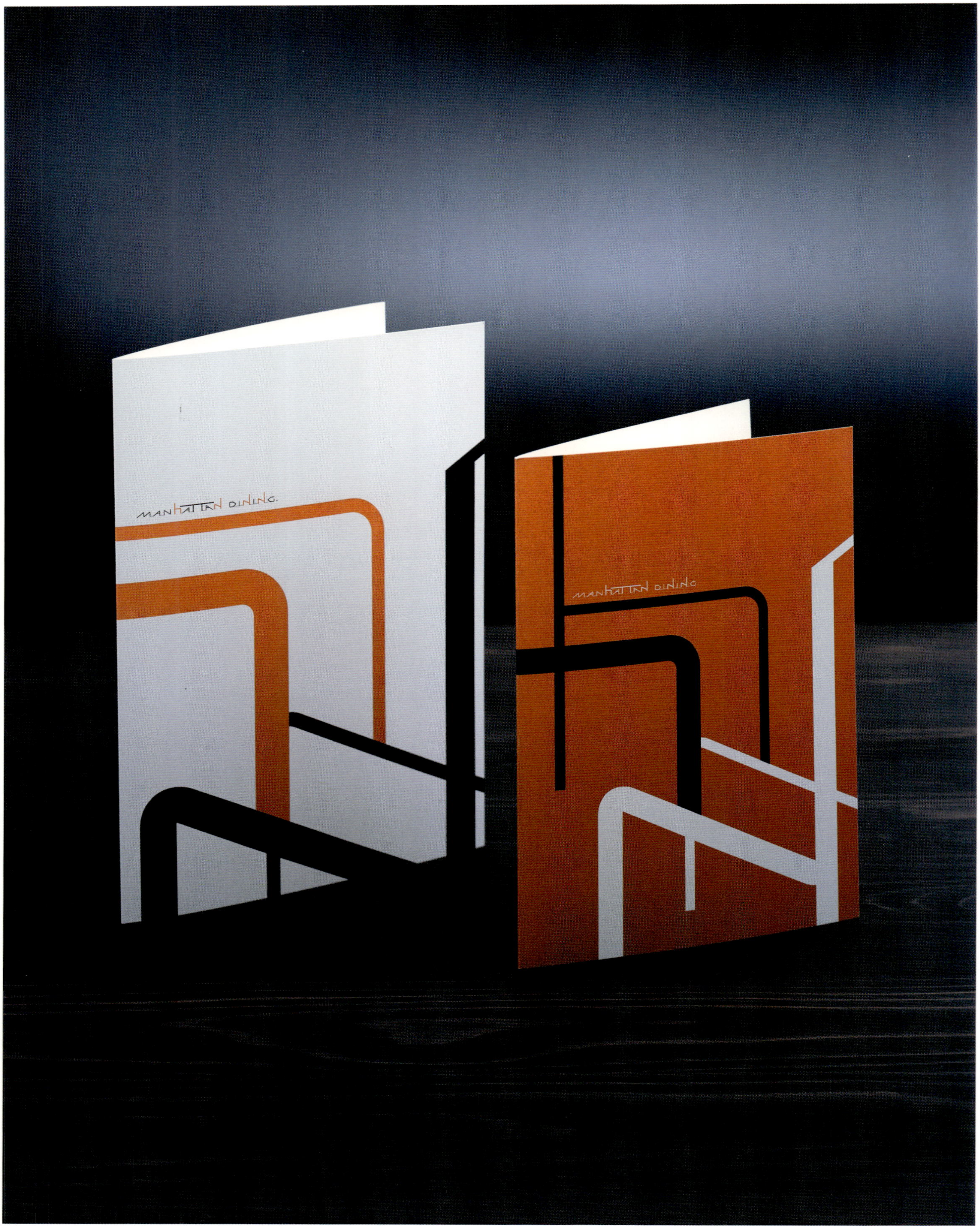
MANHATTAN DINING.
MANHATTAN DINING

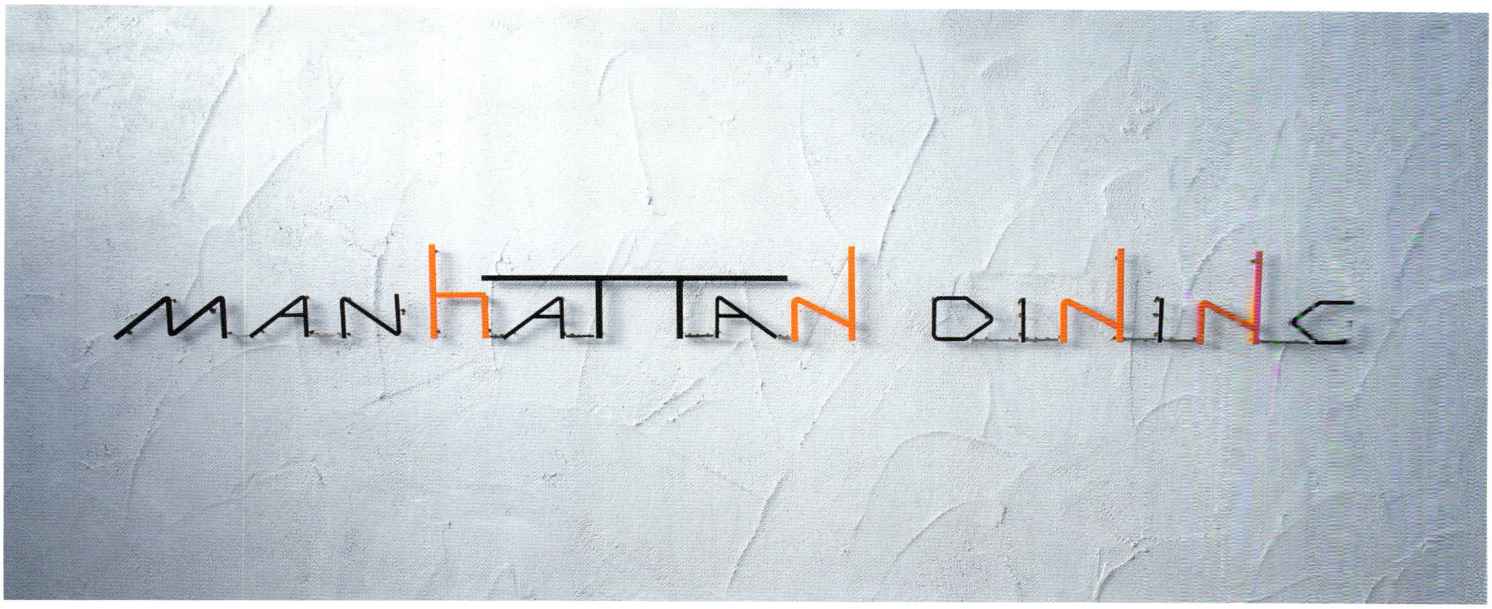

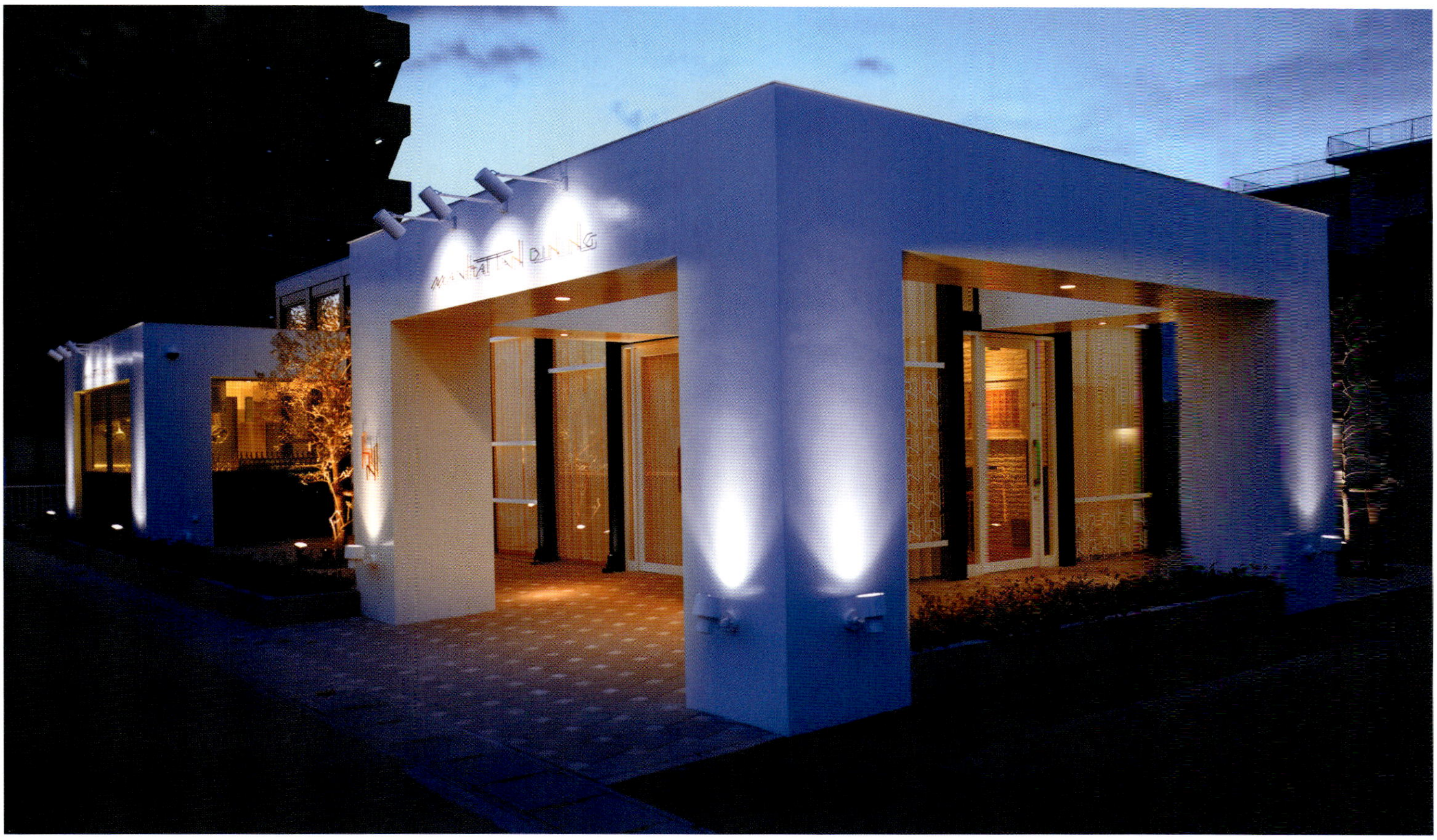

MANHATTAN DINING

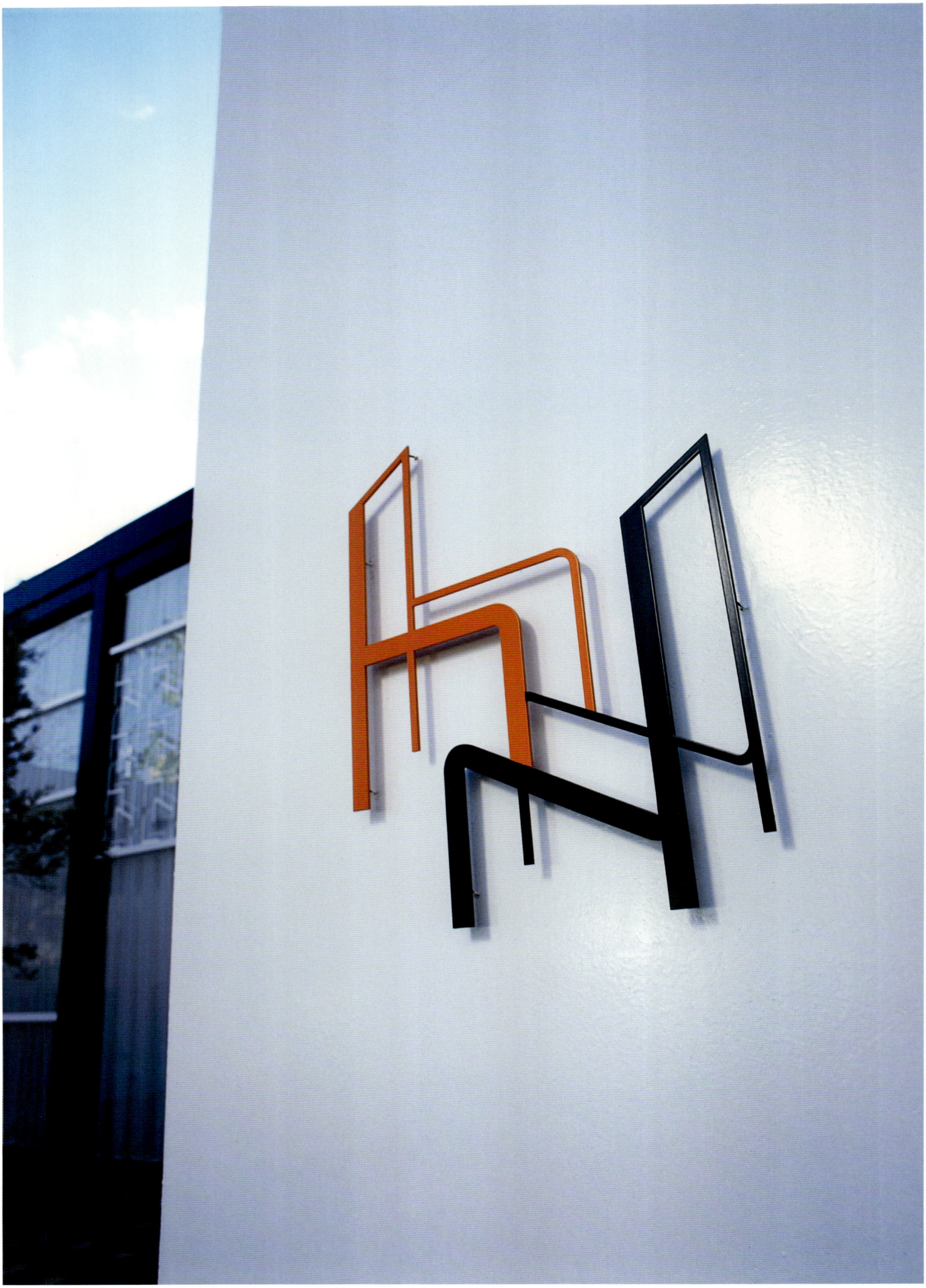

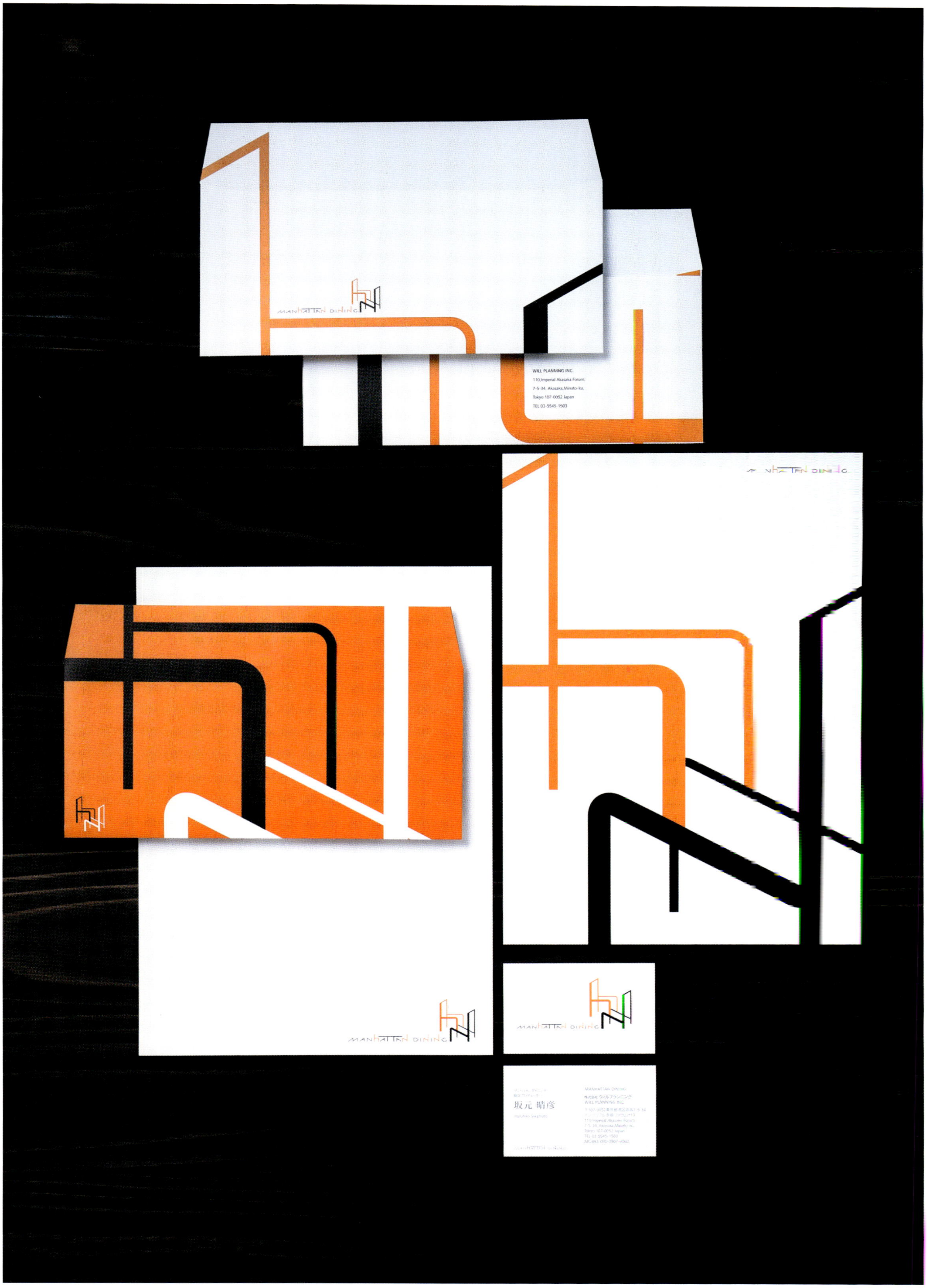
MANHATTAN DINING
WILL PLANNING INC.
110,Imperial Akasaka Forum.
7-5-34, Akasaka,Minato-ku,
Tokyo 107-0052 Japan
TEL 03-5545-1503
坂元 晴彦

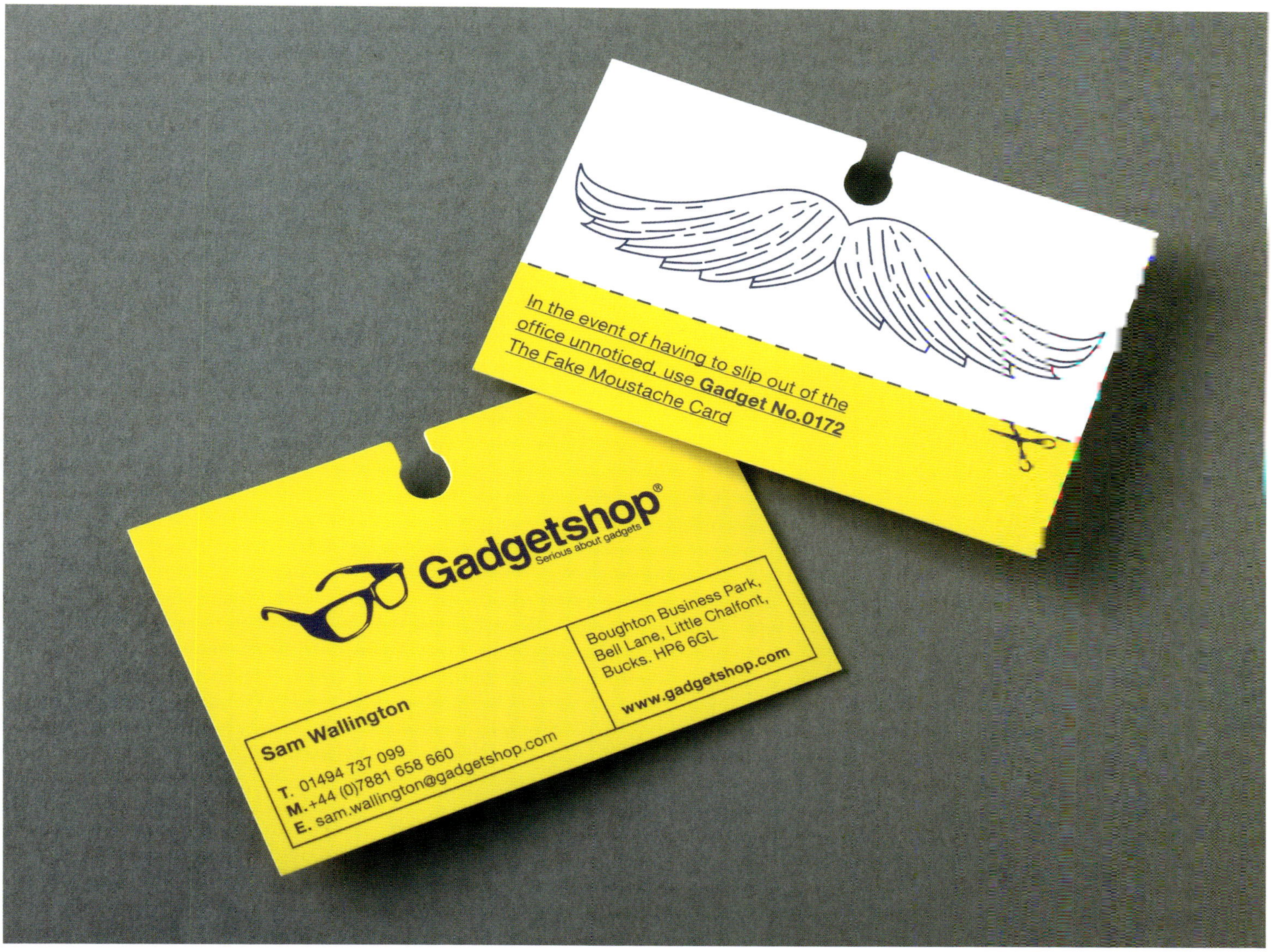
In the event of having to slip out of the
office unnoticed, use Gadget No.0172
The Fake Moustache Card
Gadgetshop®
Serious about gadgets
Boughton Business Park,
Bell Lane, Little Chalfont,
Bucks. HP6 6GL
www.gadgetshop.com
Sam Wallington
T. 01494 737 099
M. +44 (0)7881 658 660
E. sam.wallington@gadgetshop.com

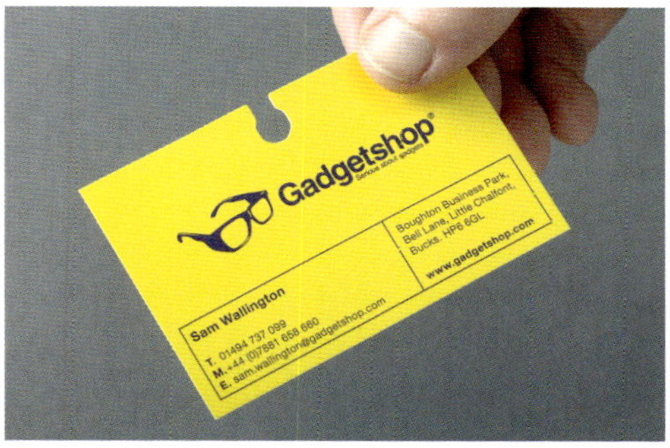
Gadgetshop
Sam Wallington

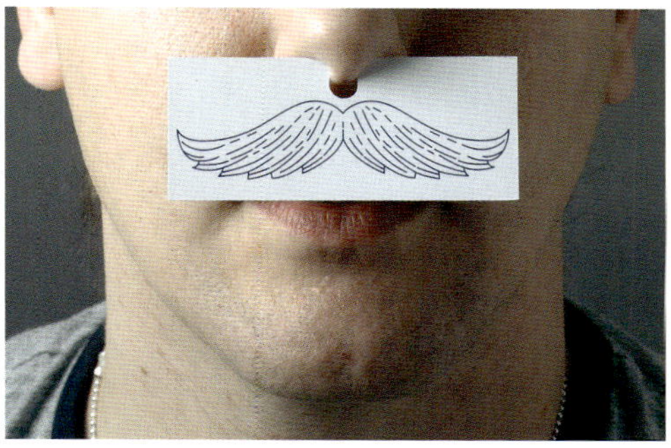

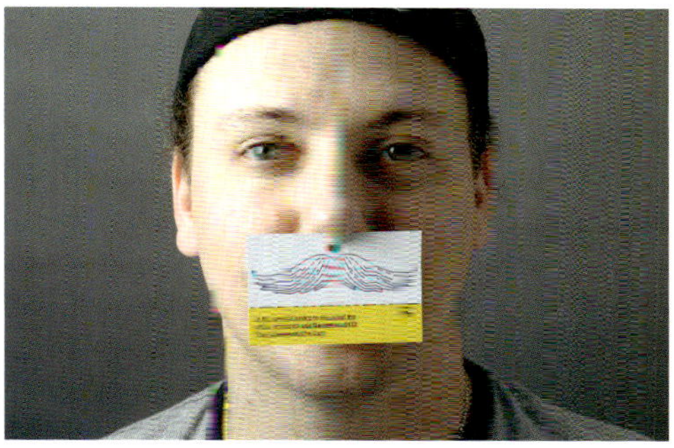

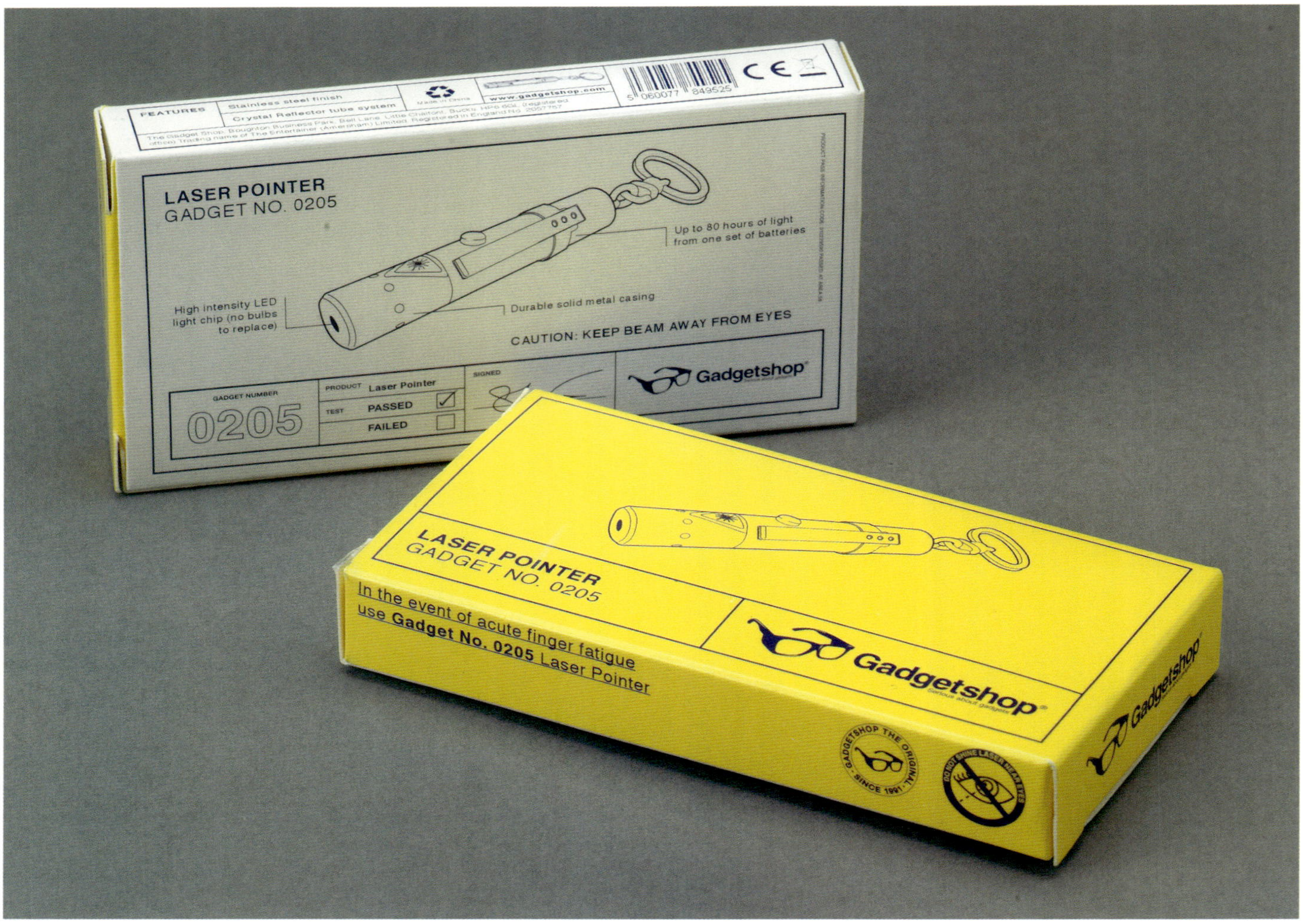
FEATURES
Stainless steel finish
Crystal Reflector tube system
www.gadgetshop.com
LASER POINTER
GADGET NO. 0205
Up to 80 hours of light from one set of batteries
High intensity LED light chip (no bulbs to replace)
Durable solid metal casing
CAUTION: KEEP BEAM AWAY FROM EYES
GADGET NUMBER
0205
PRODUCT Laser Pointer
TEST PASSED
FAILED
SIGNED
Gadgetshop
LASER POINTER
GADGET NO. 0205
In the event of acute finger fatigue use Gadget No. 0205 Laser Pointer
Gadgetshop
serious about gadgets
GADGETSHOP THE ORIGINAL SINCE 1991
Gadgetshop

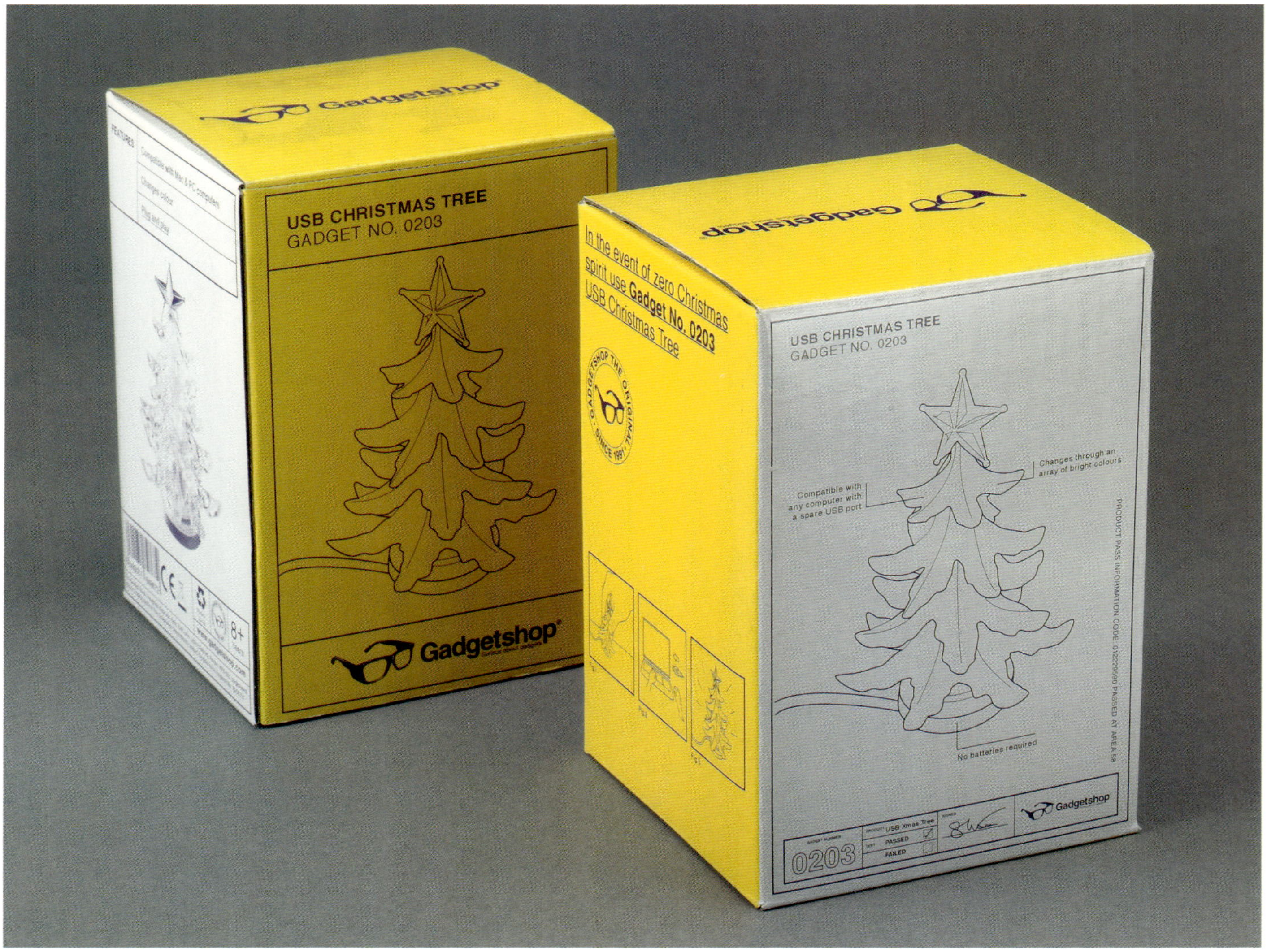
Gadgetshop
FEATURES
Compatible with Mac & PC computers
Changes colour
USB CHRISTMAS TREE
GADGET NO. 0203
Gadgetshop
serious about gadgets
Gadgetshop
In the event of zero Christmas spirit use Gadget No. 0203 USB Christmas Tree
GADGETSHOP THE ORIGINAL SINCE 1991
USB CHRISTMAS TREE
GADGET NO. 0203
Compatible with any computer with a spare USB port
Changes through an array of bright colours
No batteries required
PRODUCT PASS INFORMATION CODE: 01229590 PASSED AT AREA 58
0203
PRODUCT USB Xmas Tree
PASSED
FAILED
Gadgetshop

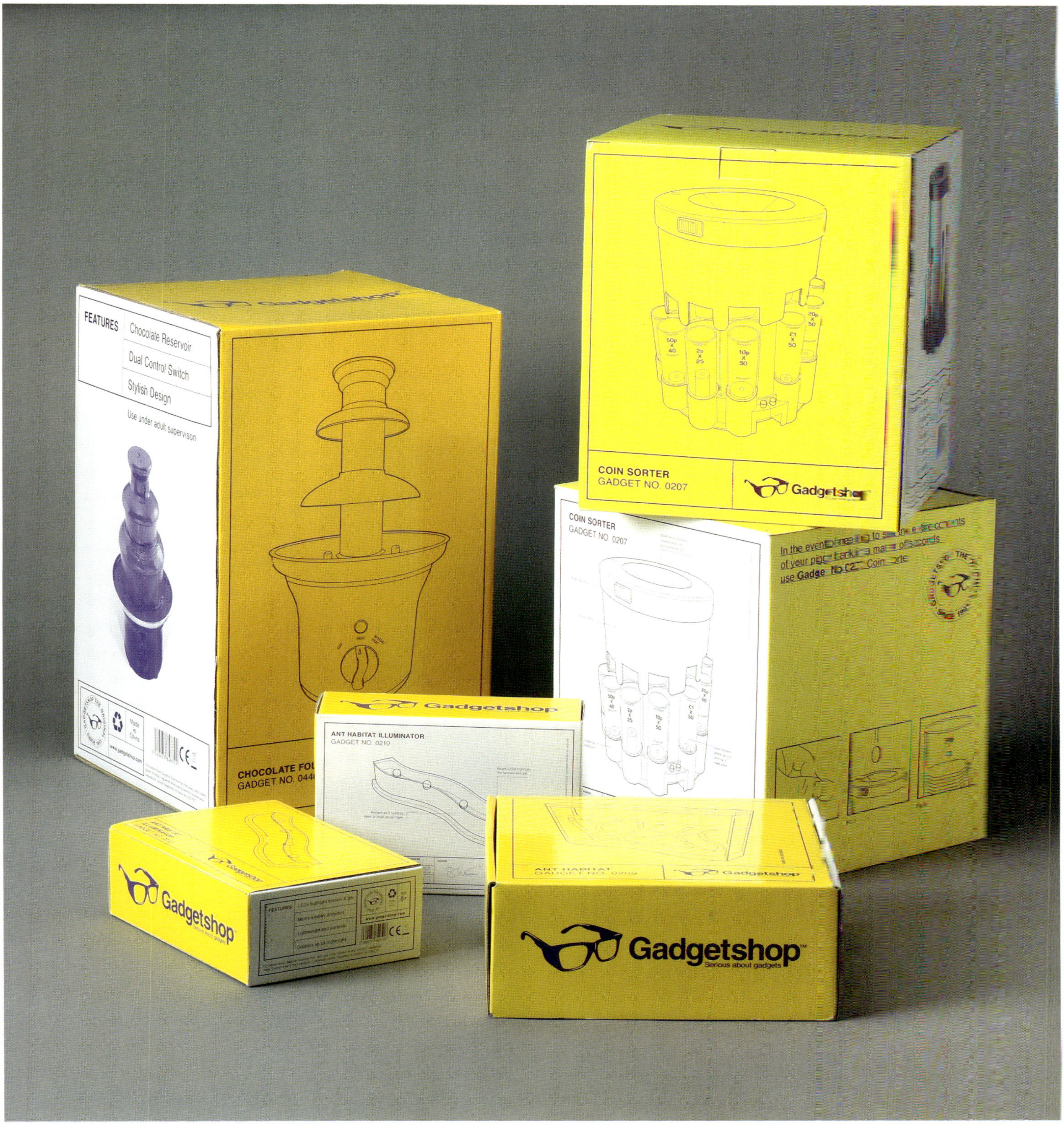
FEATURES
Chocolate Reservoir
Dual Control Switch
Stylish Design
Use under adult supervision
Gadgetshop
COIN SORTER
GADGET NO. 0207
ANT HABITAT ILLUMINATOR
GADGET NO. 0210
Gadgetshop
Serious about gadgets

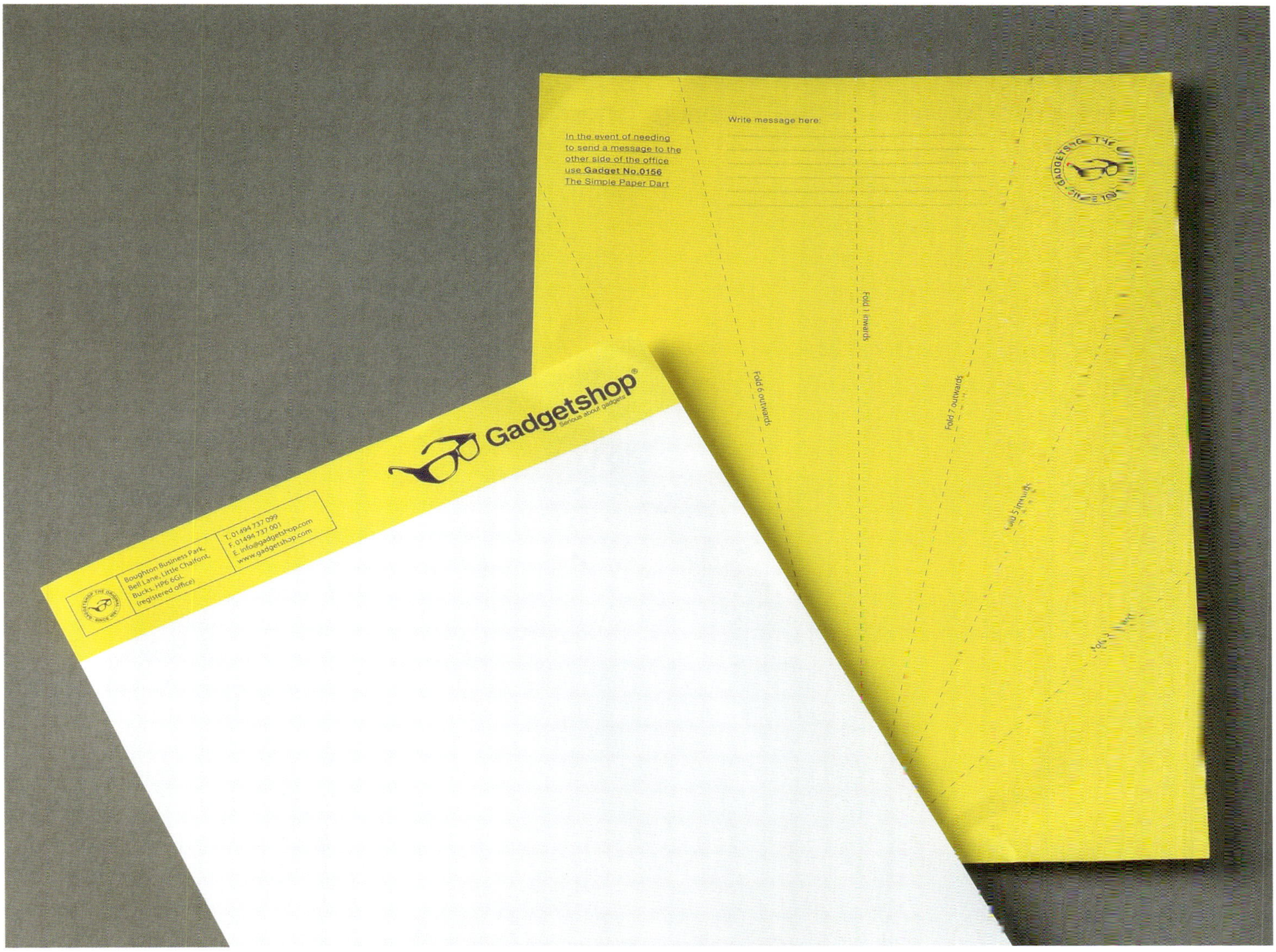
Write message here:
In the event of needing to send a message to the other side of the office use Gadget No.0156 The Simple Paper Dart
Fold 6 outwards
Fold 1 inwards
Fold 7 outwards
Gadgetshop®
Serious about gadgets
Boughton Business Park, Bell Lane, Little Chalfont, Bucks, HP6 6GL (registered office)
T. 01494 737 099 F. 01494 737 001 E. info@gadgetshop.com www.gadgetshop.com

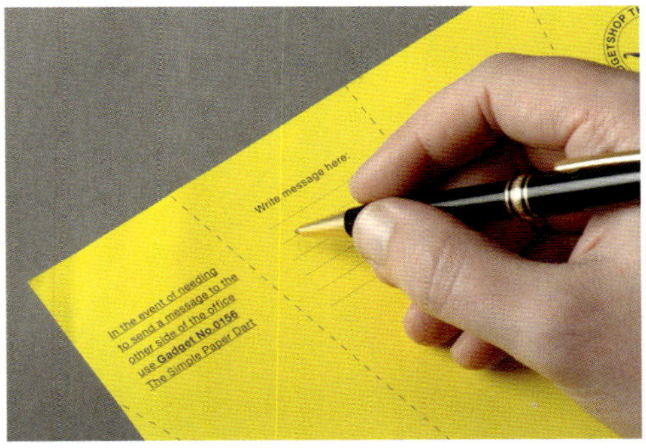
Write message here:
In the event of needing to send a message to the other side of the office use Gadget No.0156 The Simple Paper Dart

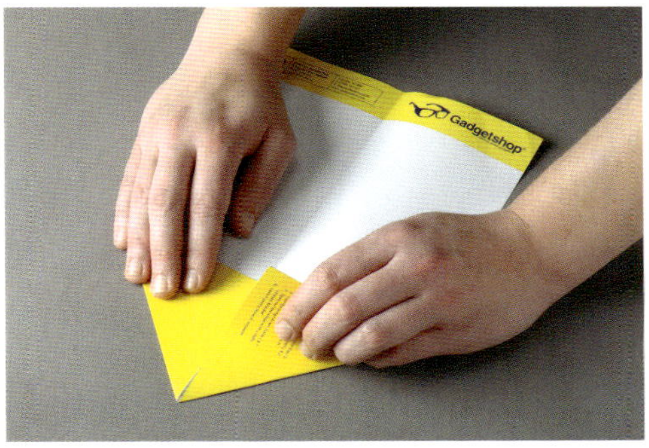
Gadgetshop

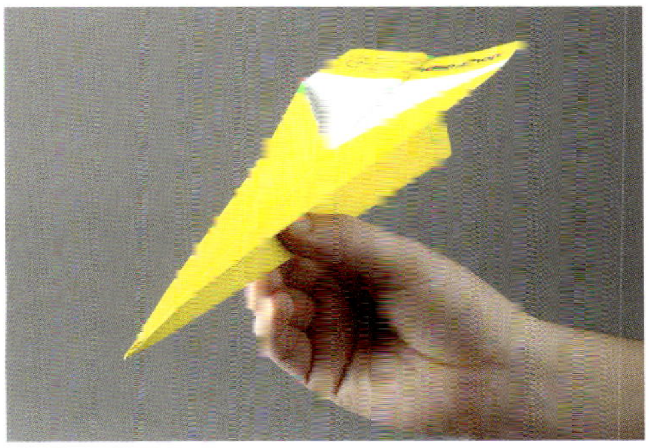

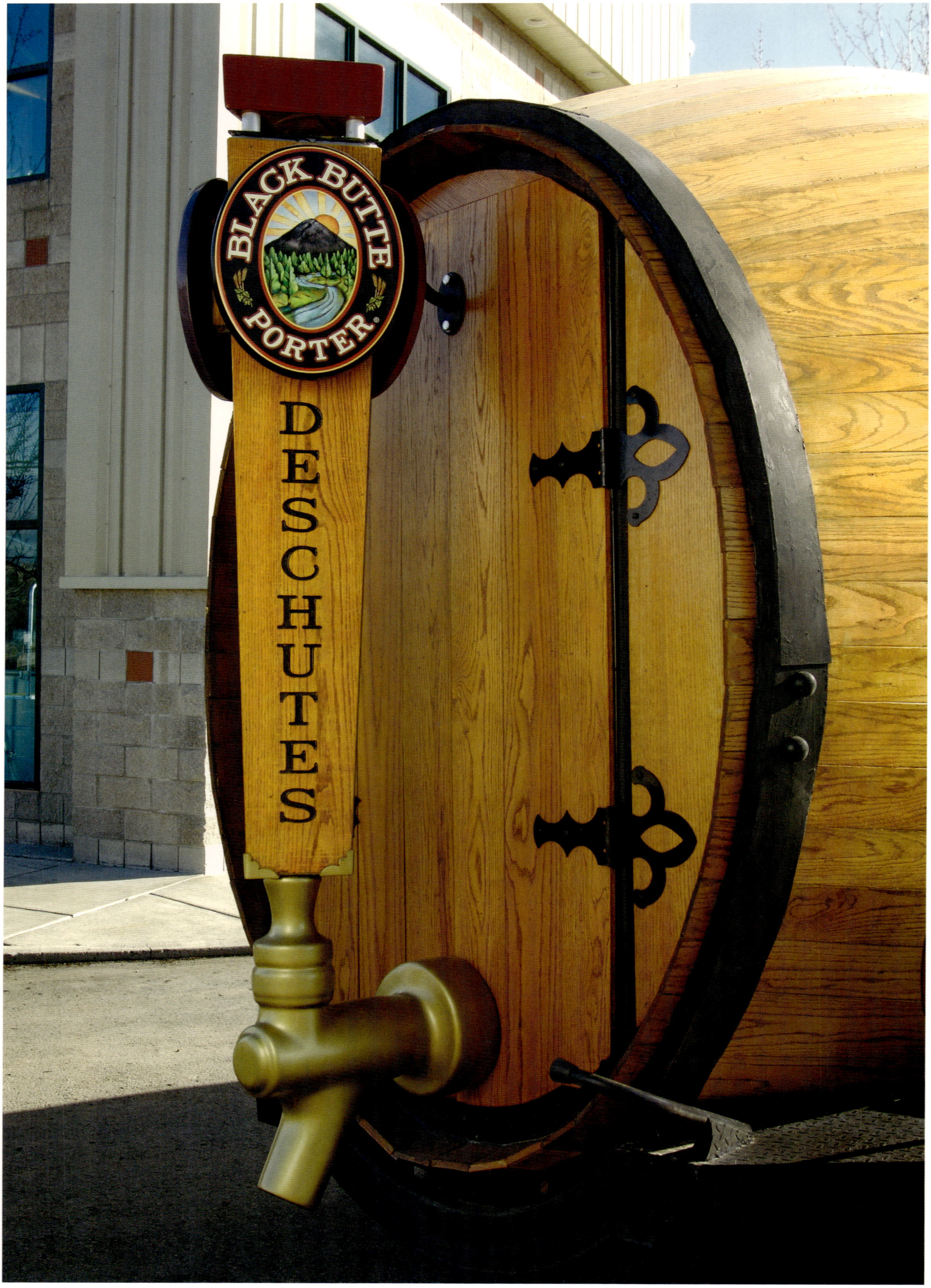
BLACK BUTTE PORTER
DESCHUTES

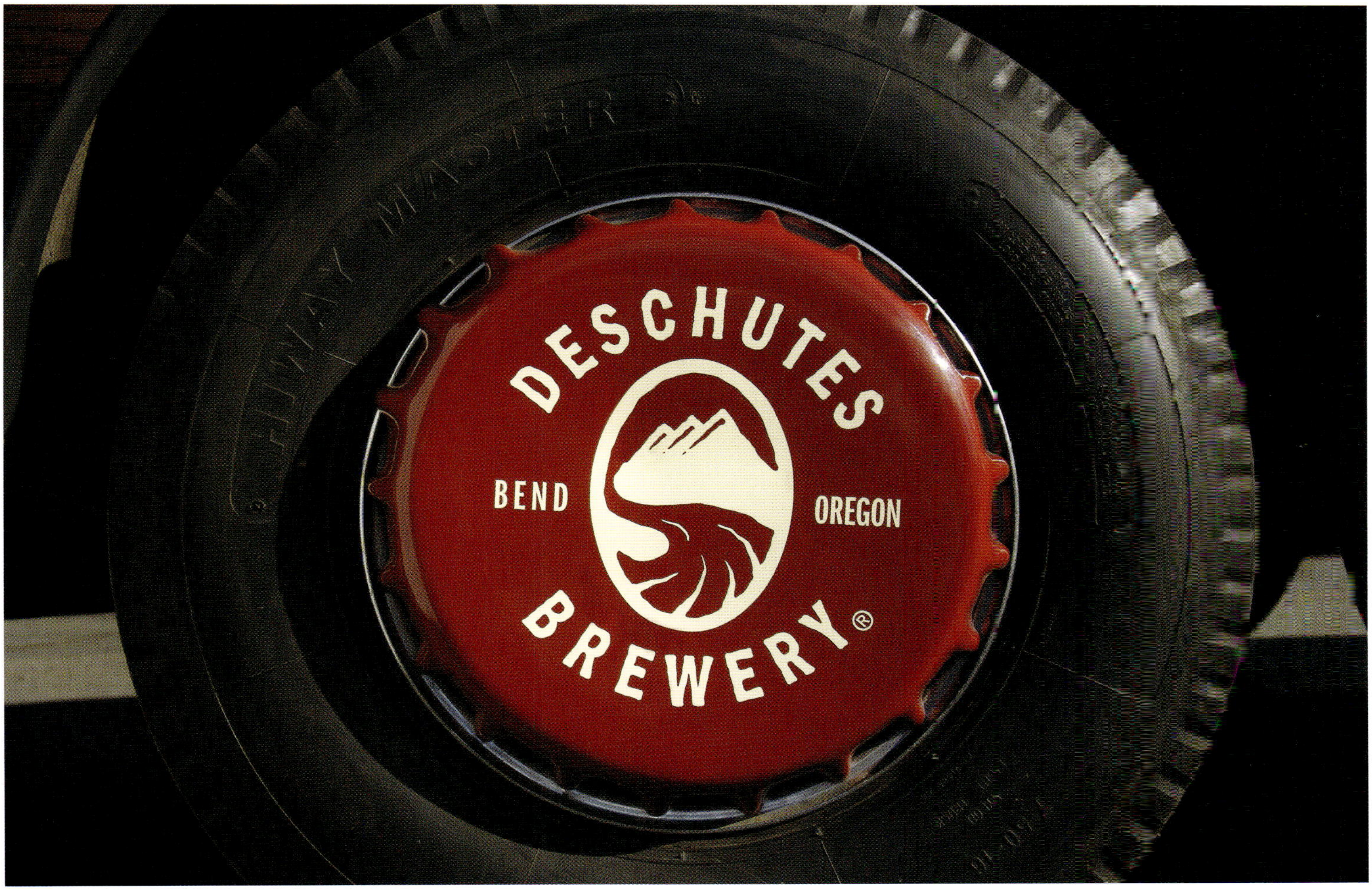
DESCHUTES
BEND
OREGON
BREWERY

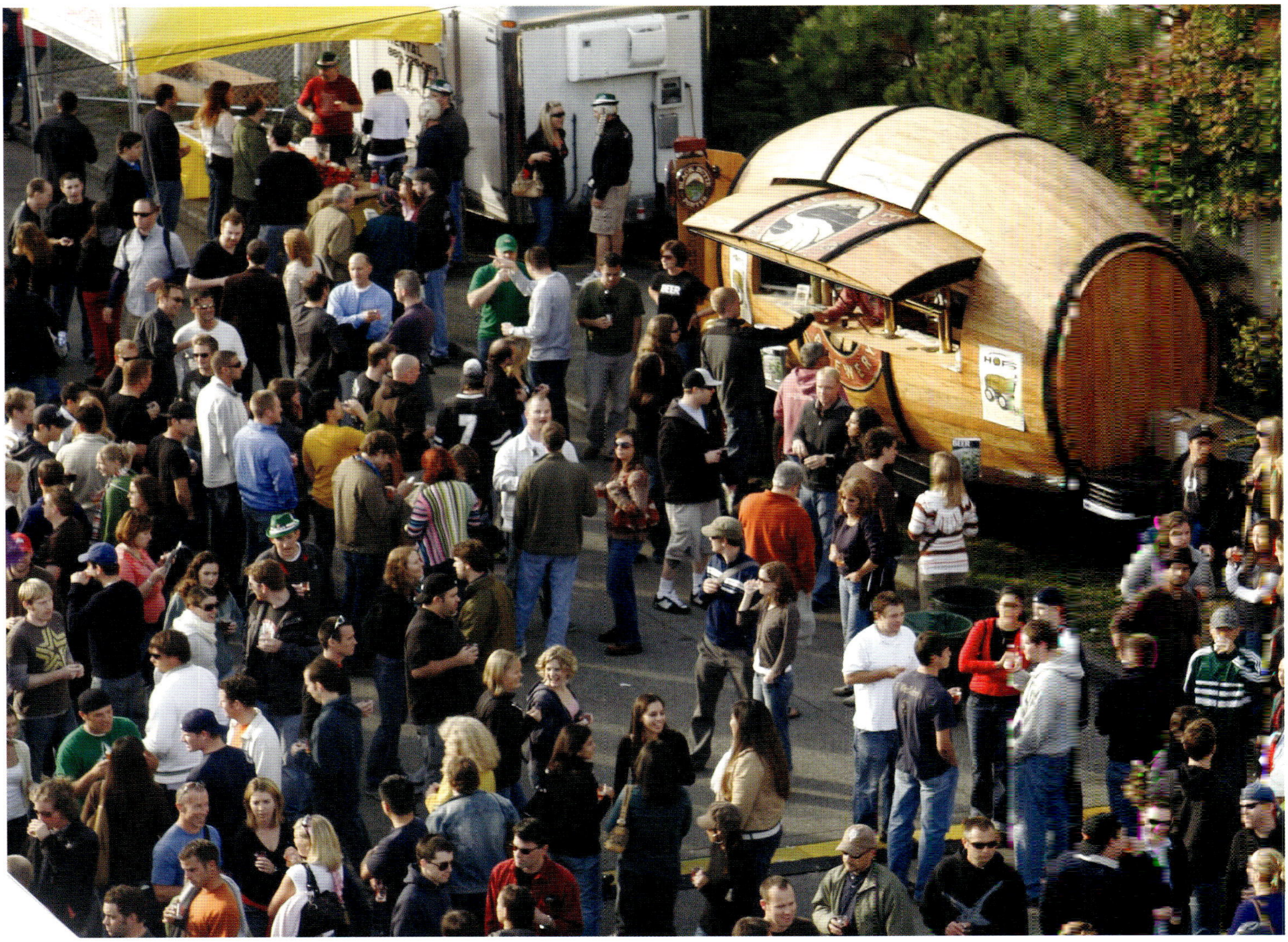

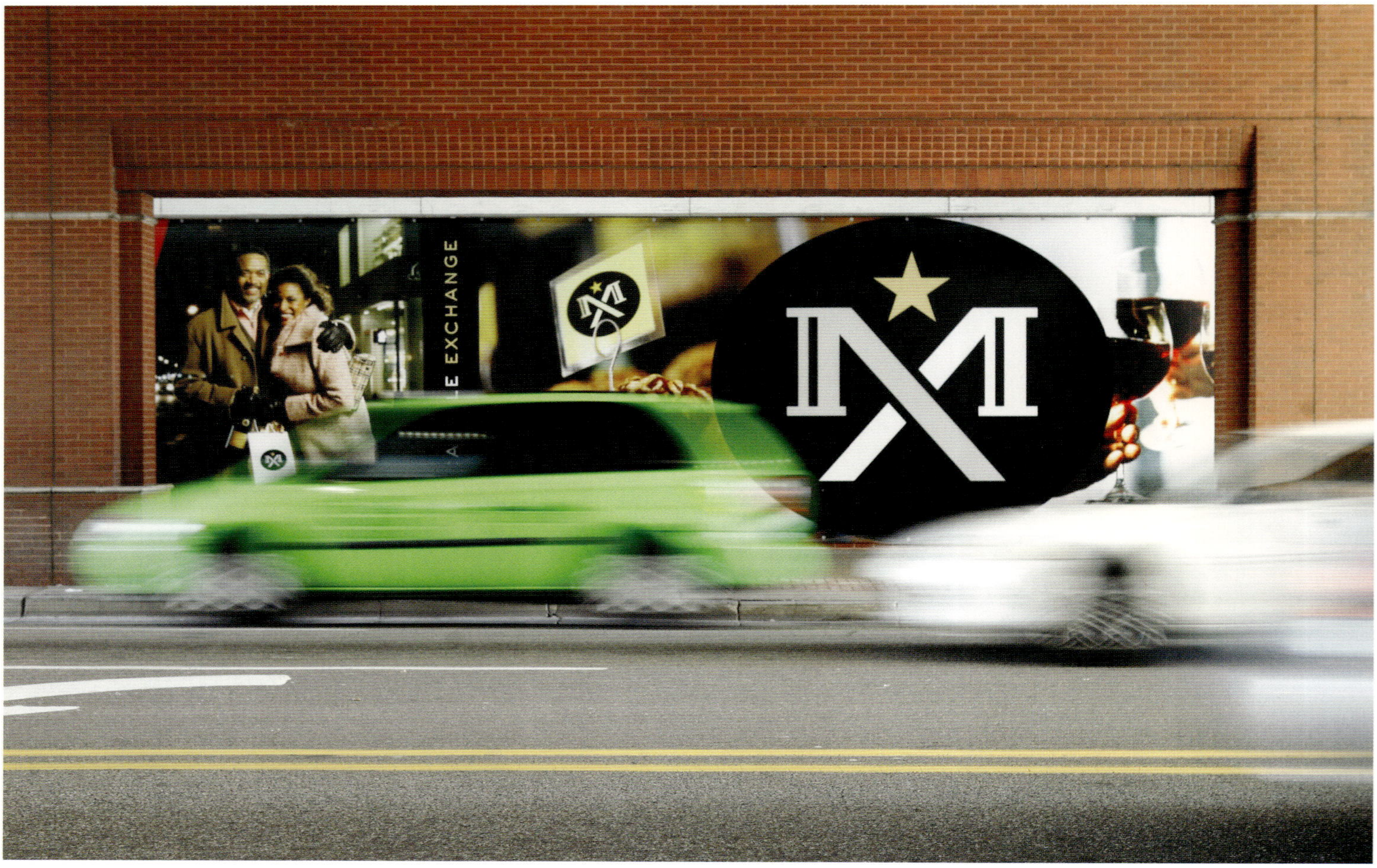

MERCANTILE EXCHANGE

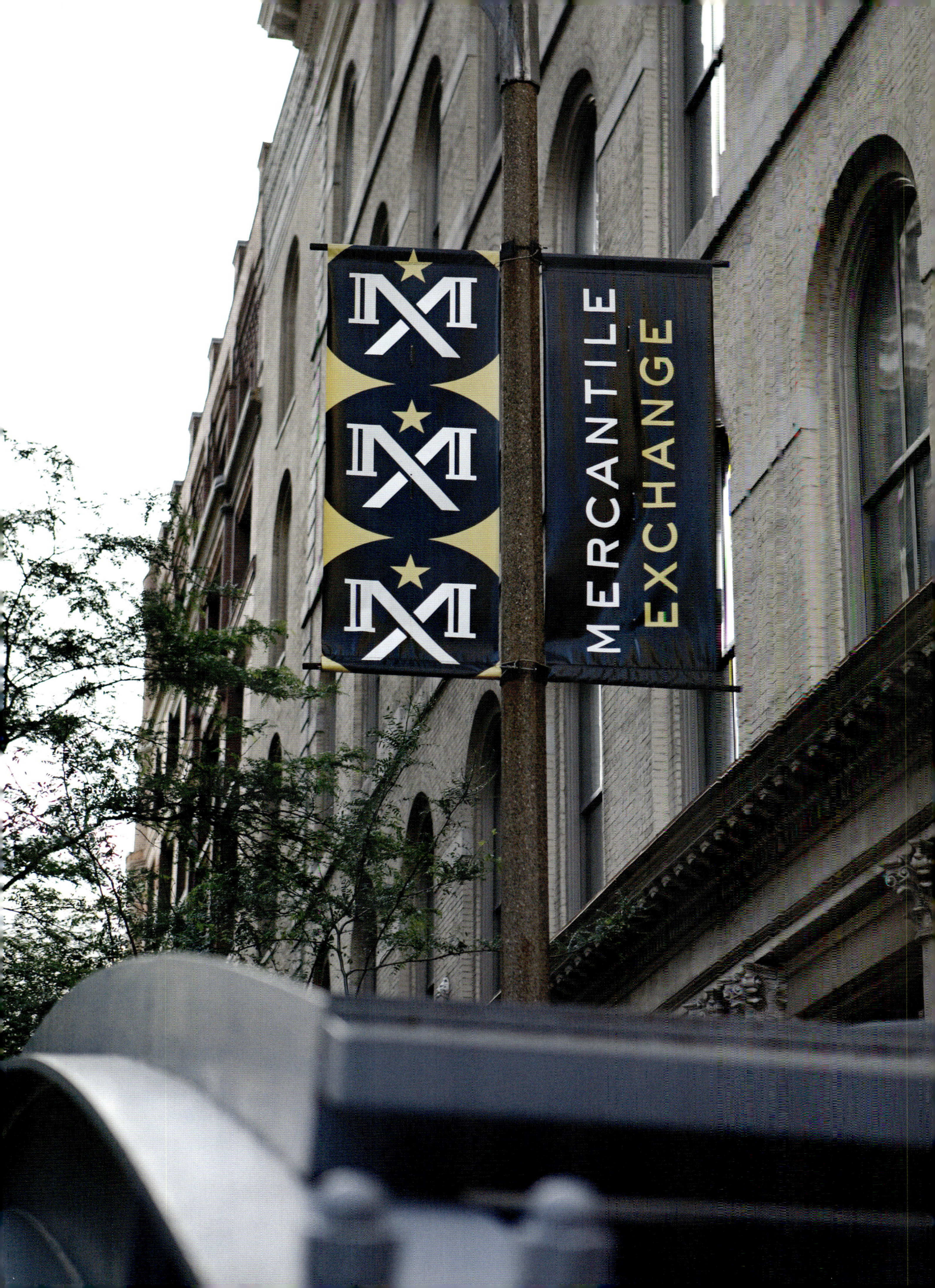
MERCANTILE
EXCHANGE

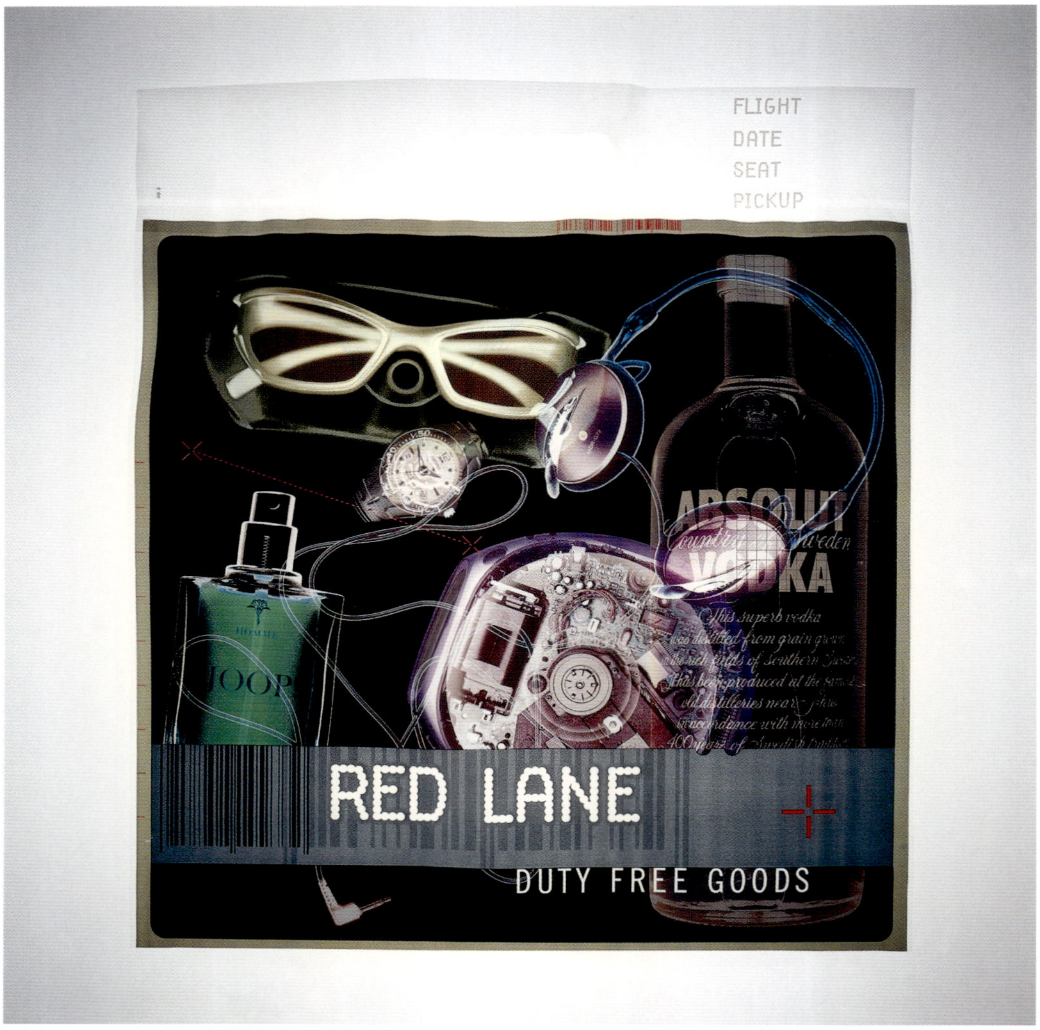
FLIGHT
DATE
SEAT
PICKUP
RED LANE
DUTY FREE GOODS

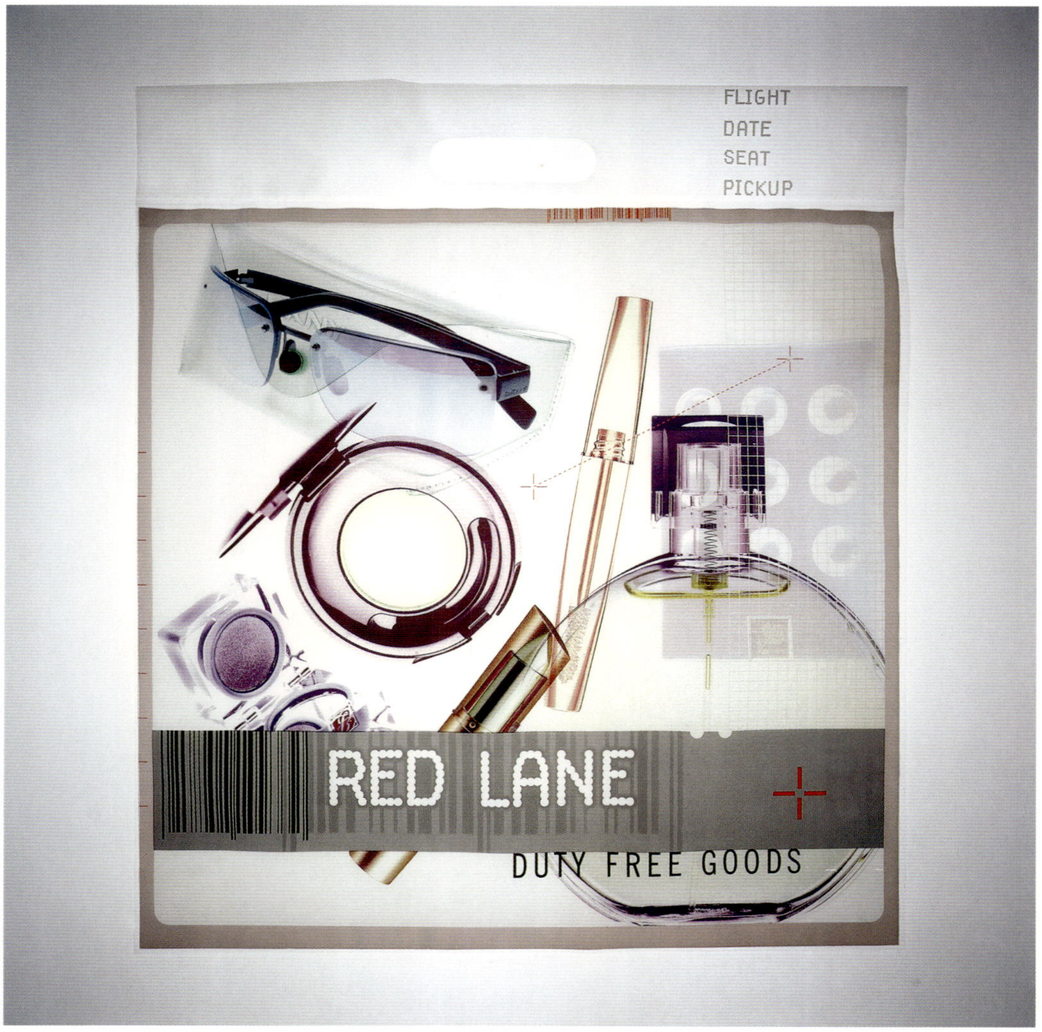
FLIGHT
DATE
SEAT
PICKUP
RED LANE
DUTY FREE GOODS

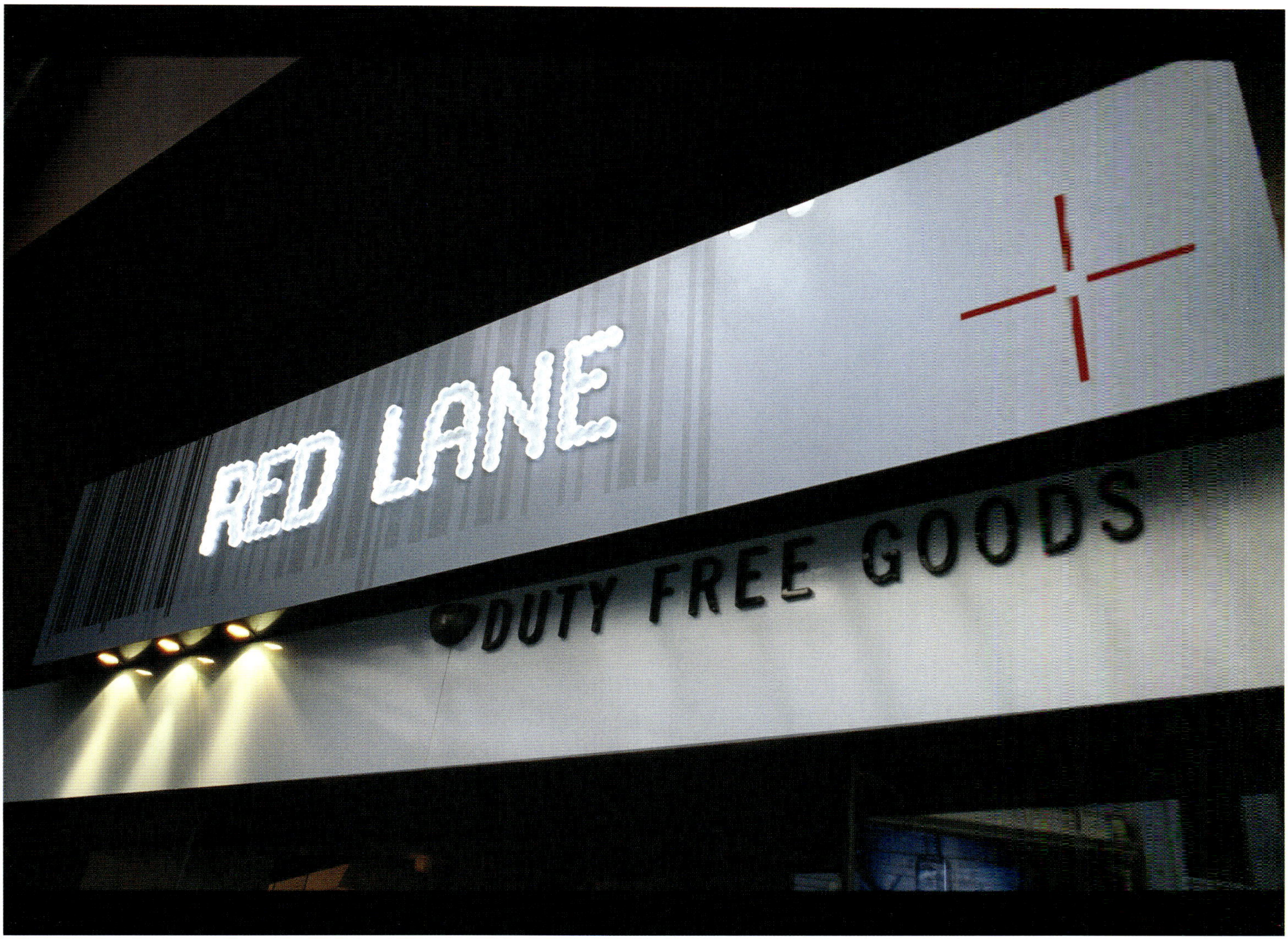
RED LANE
DUTY FREE GOODS

MILLER & GREEN

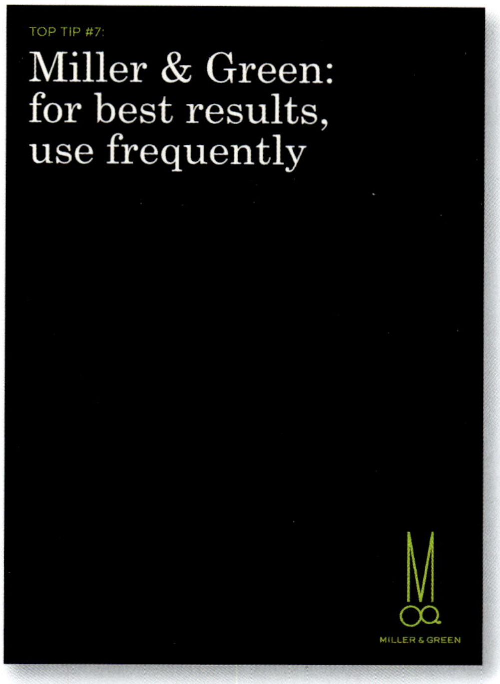
TOP TIP #7:
Miller & Green: for best results, use frequently
MILLER & GREEN

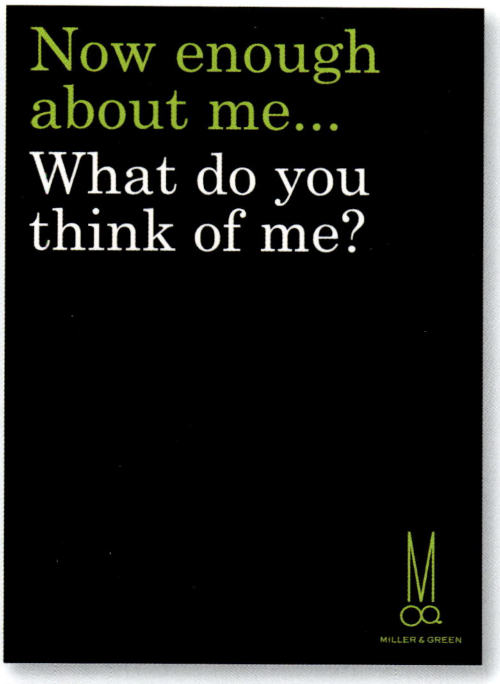
Now enough about me...
What do you think of me?
MILLER & GREEN

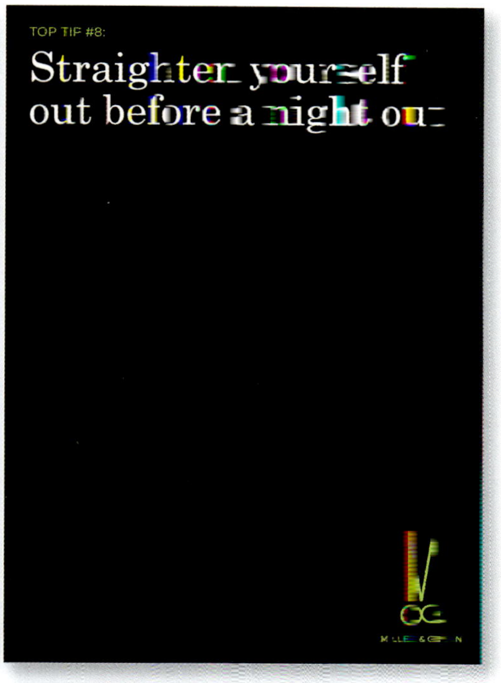
TOP TIP #8:
Straighten yourself out before a night out

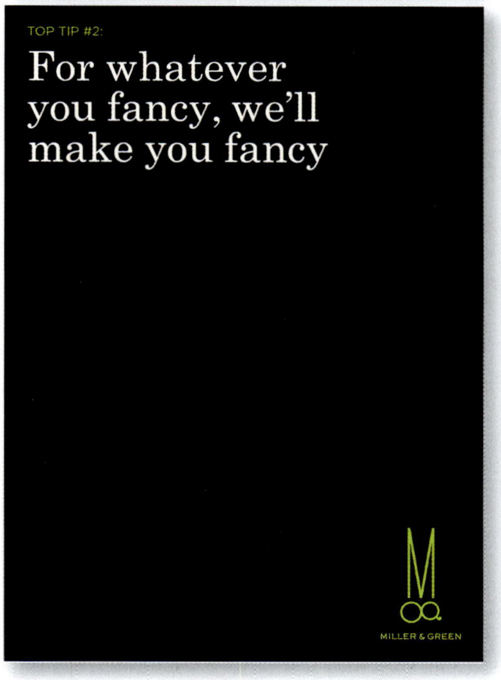
TOP TIP #2:
For whatever you fancy, we'll make you fancy
MILLER & GREEN

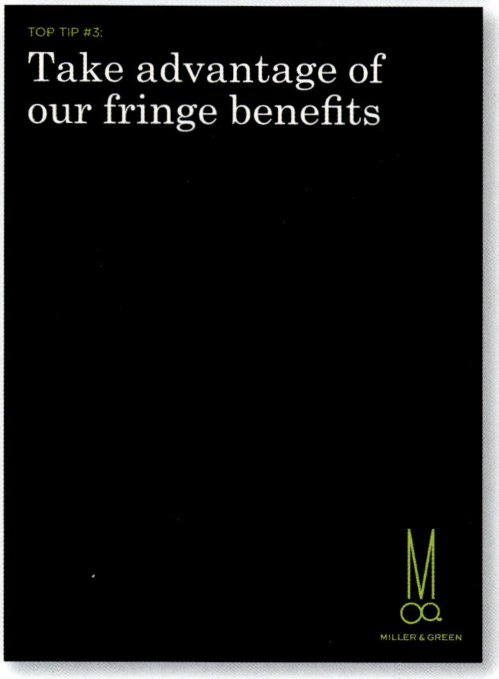
TOP TIP #3:
Take advantage of our fringe benefits
MILLER & GREEN

TOP TIP #4:
It's time to ditch Bob and go all Posh

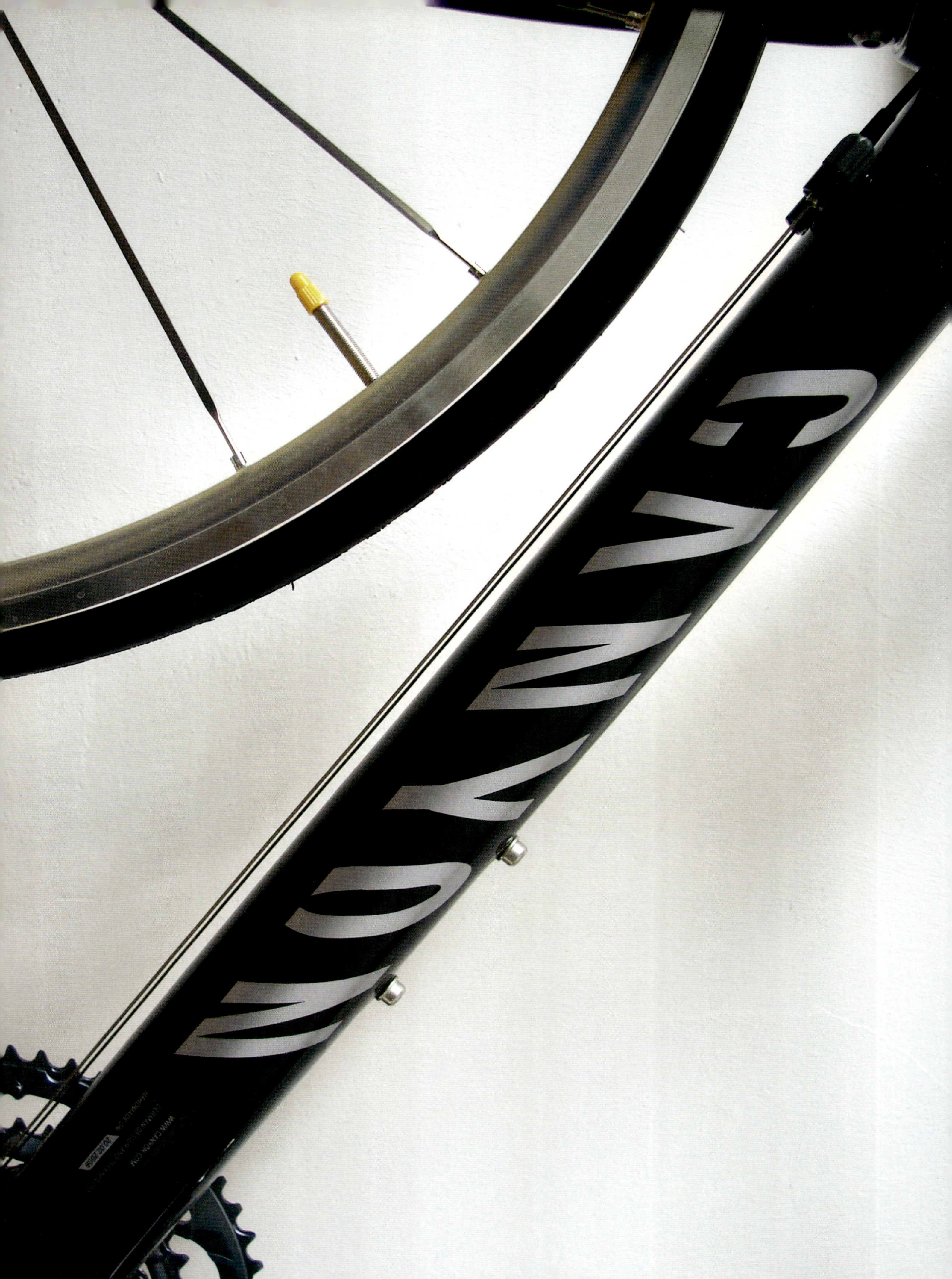

210 Sports | Canyon Bikes | (this spread) KMS TEAM GmbH

ABCDEFGHIJKLMNOPQ

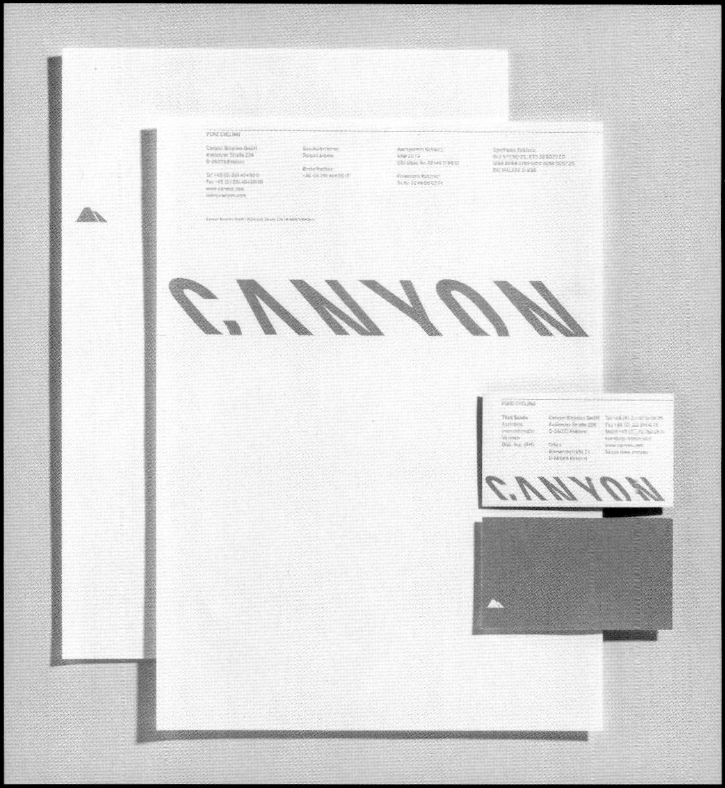

RSTUVWXYZ 0123456789

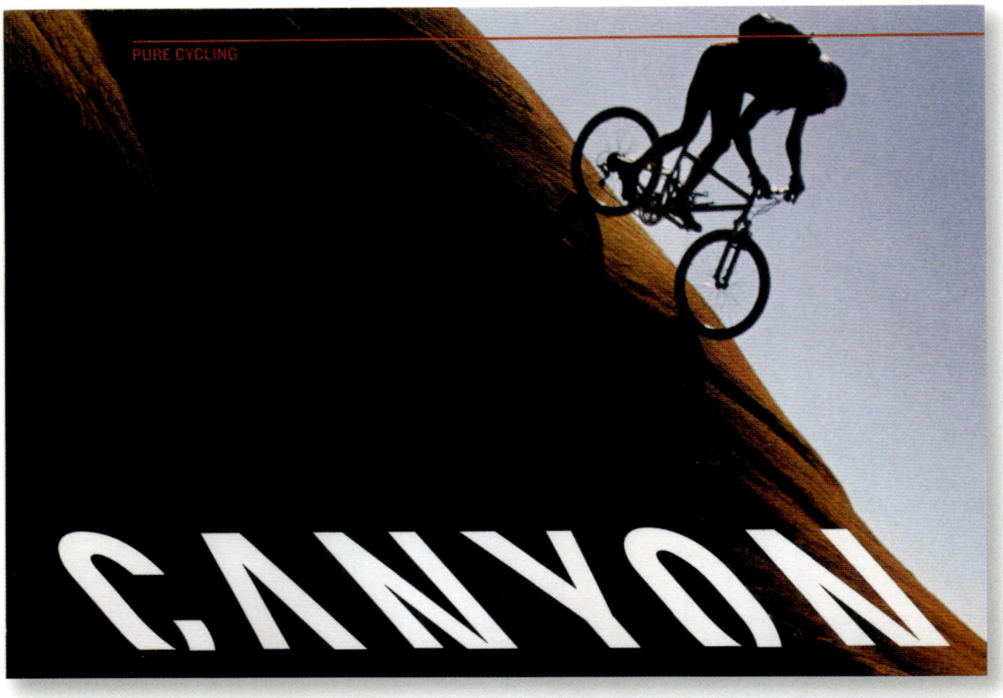
PURE CYCLING
CANYON

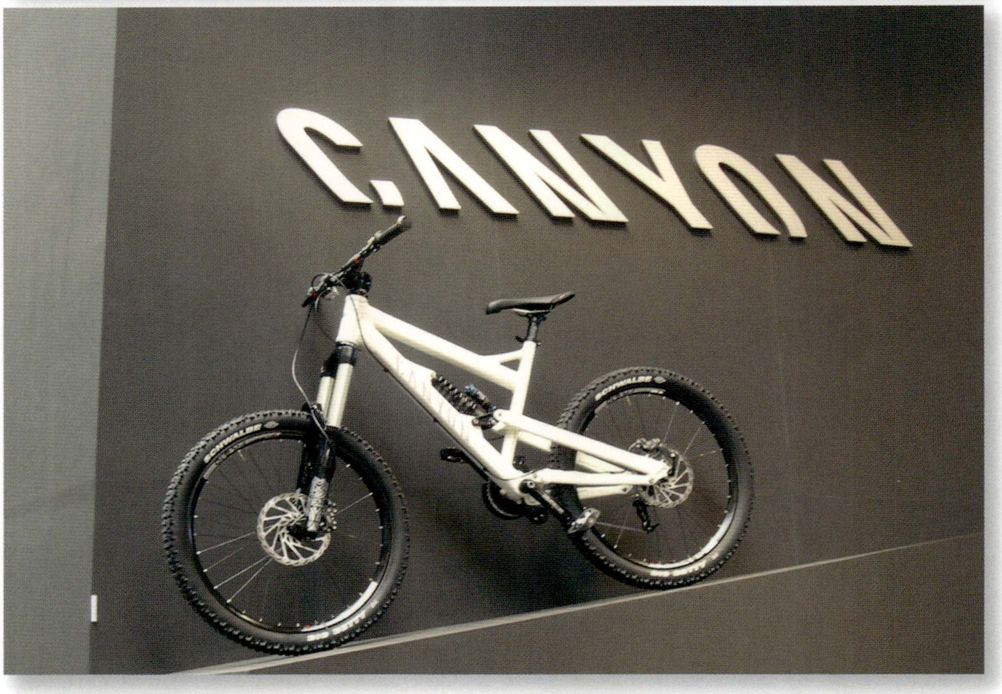
CANYON

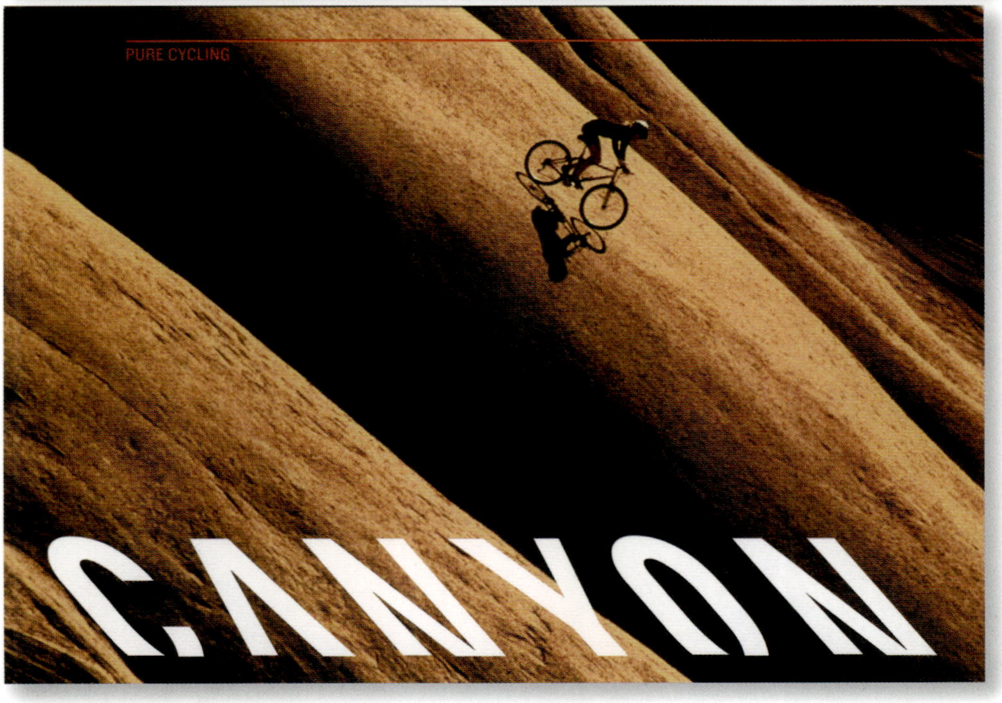
PURE CYCLING
CANYON

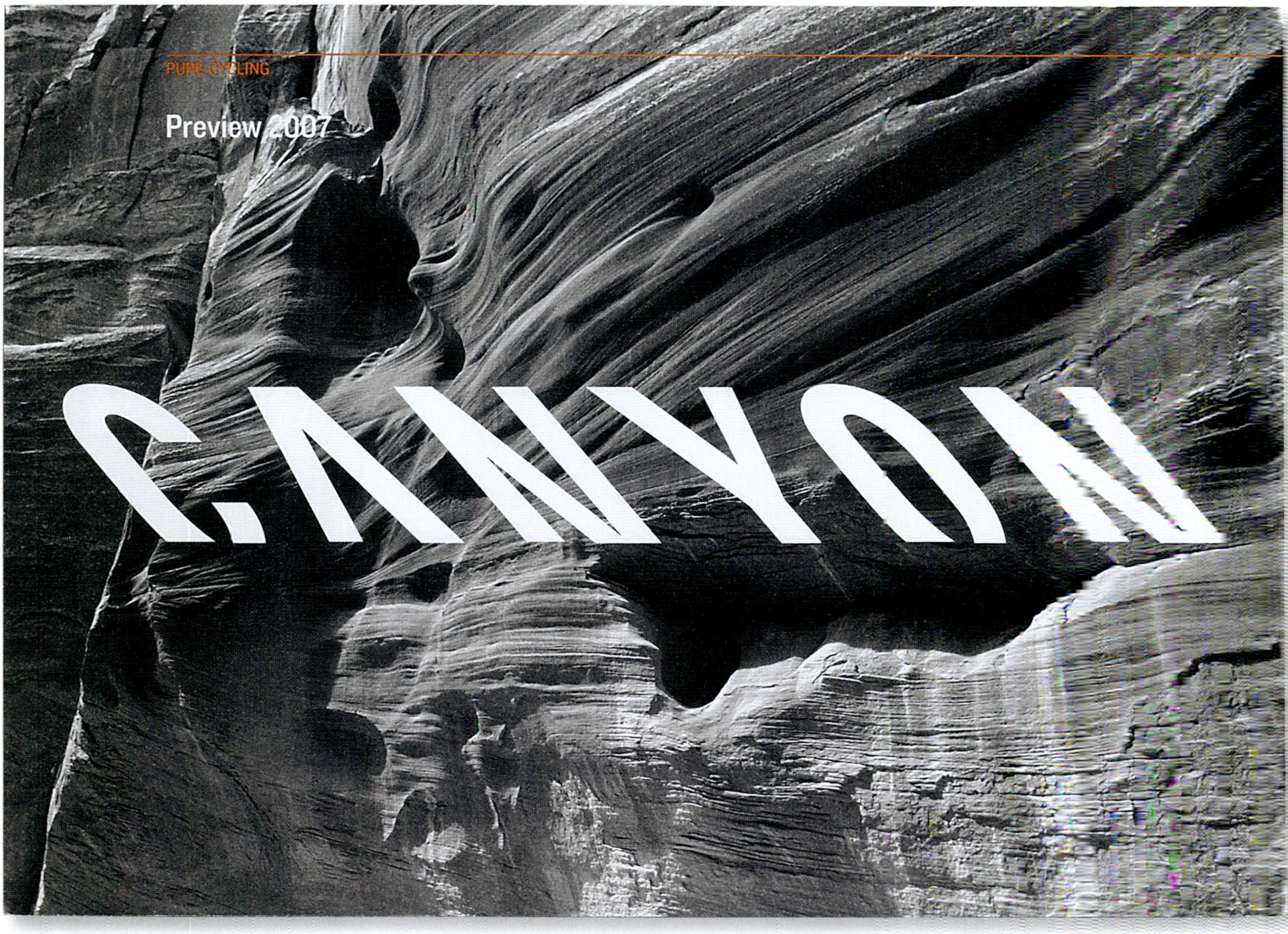
PURE CYCLING
Preview 2007
CANYON

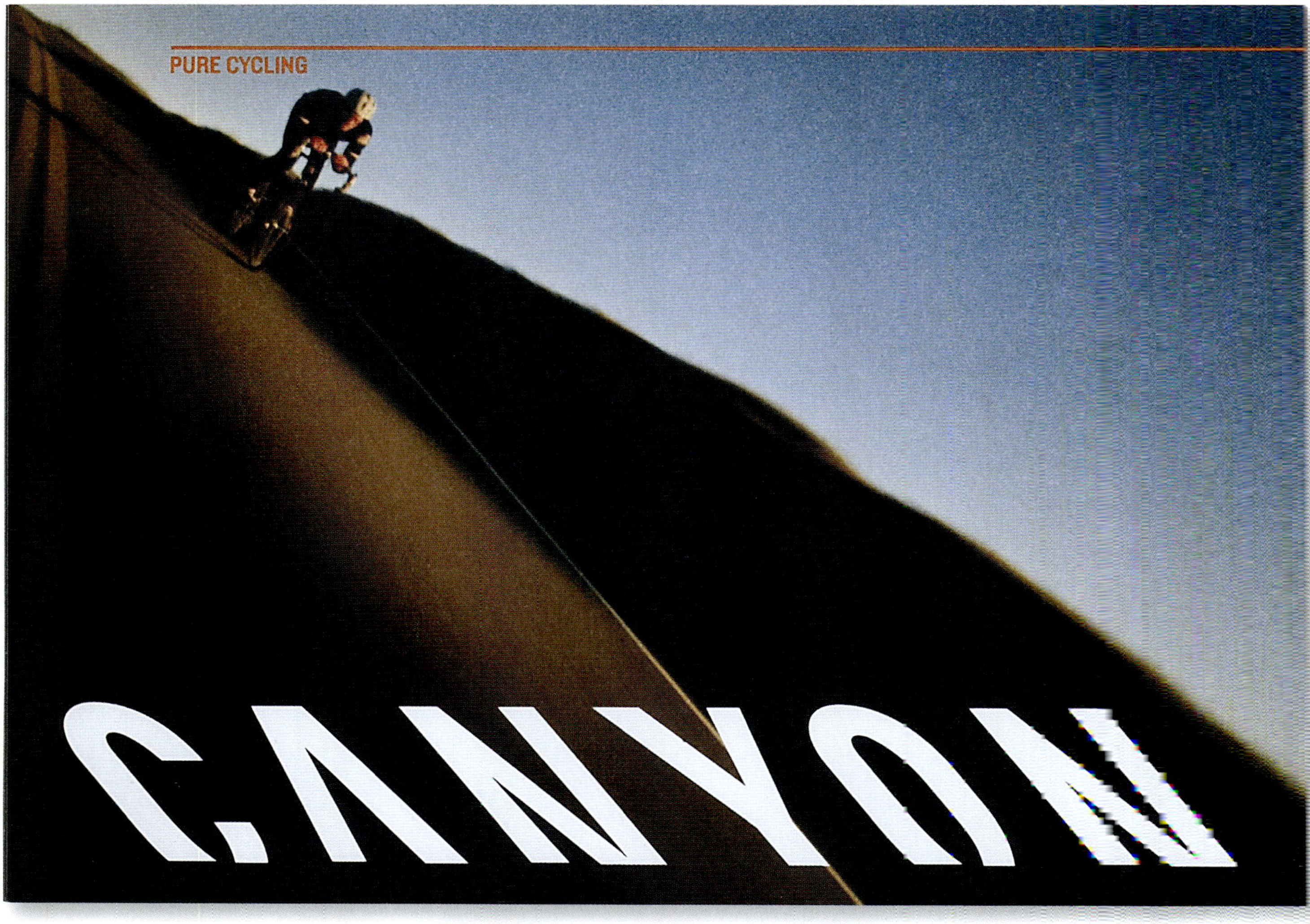
PURE CYCLING
CANYON

214Sports | V.I.O. | (this spread) Duffy & Partners LLC

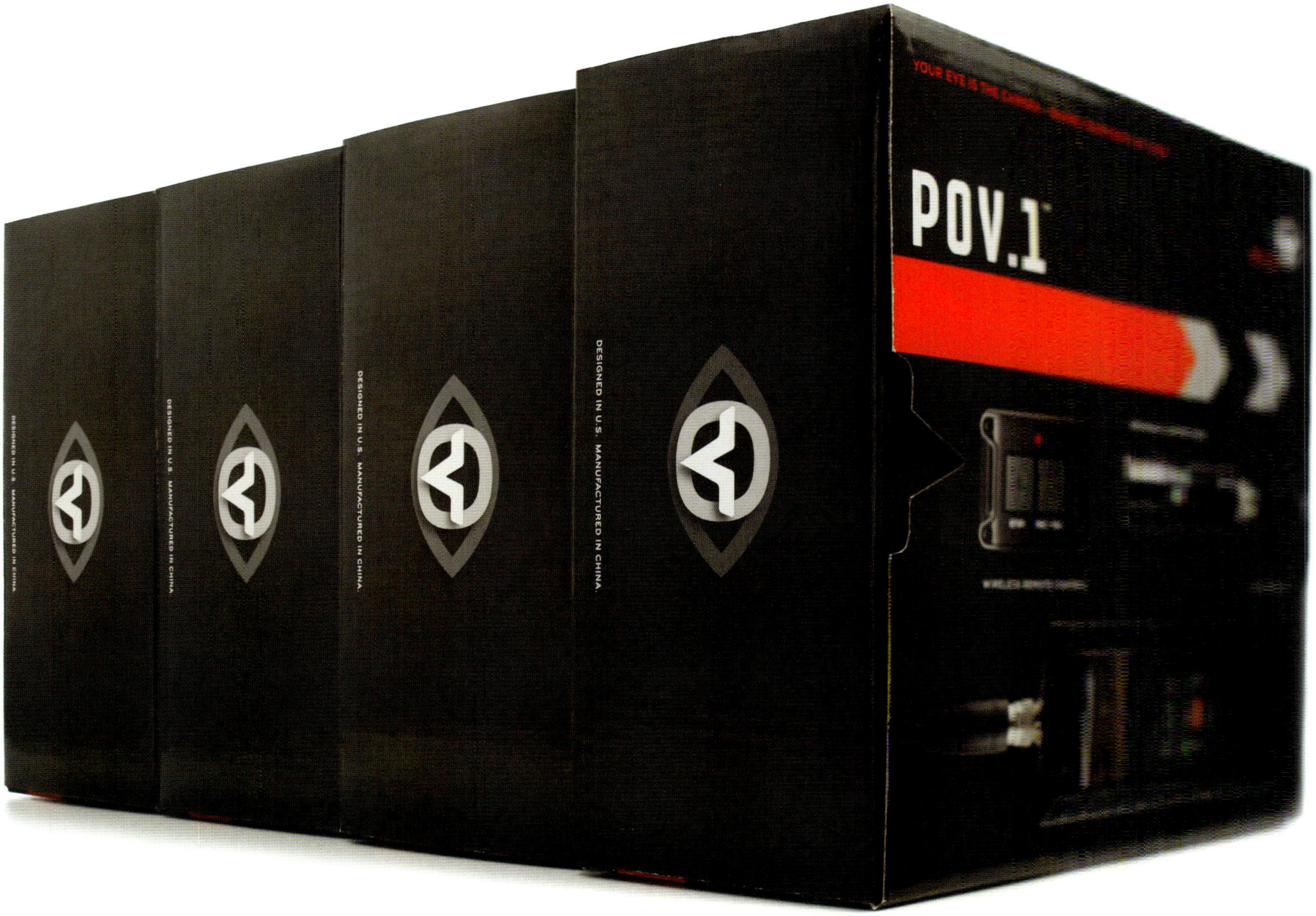
POV.1
DESIGNED IN U.S. MANUFACTURED IN CHINA.

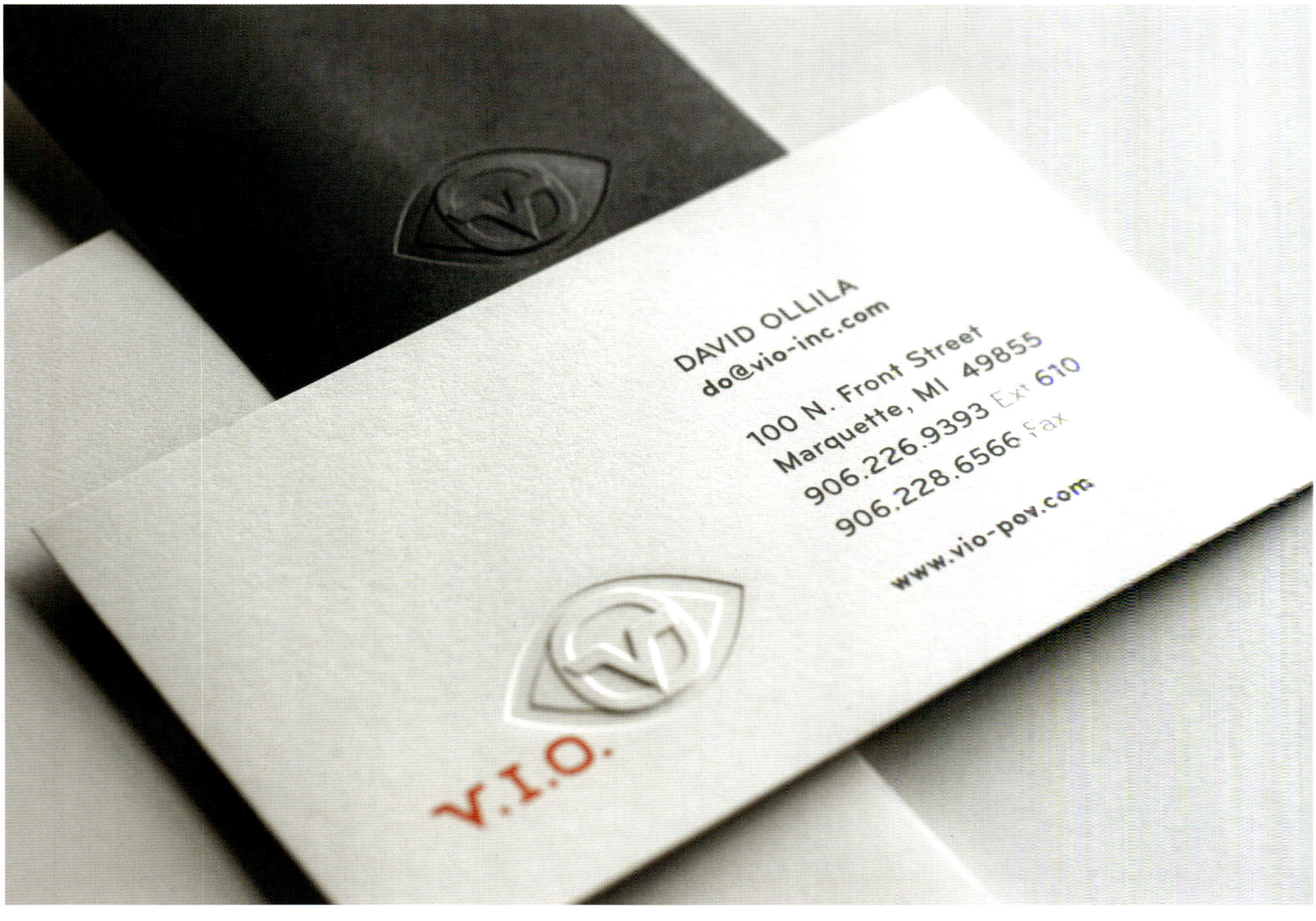
DAVID OLLILA
do@vio-inc.com
100 N. Front Street
Marquette, MI 49855
906.226.9393 Ext 610
906.228.6566 Fax
www.vio-pov.com
V.I.O.

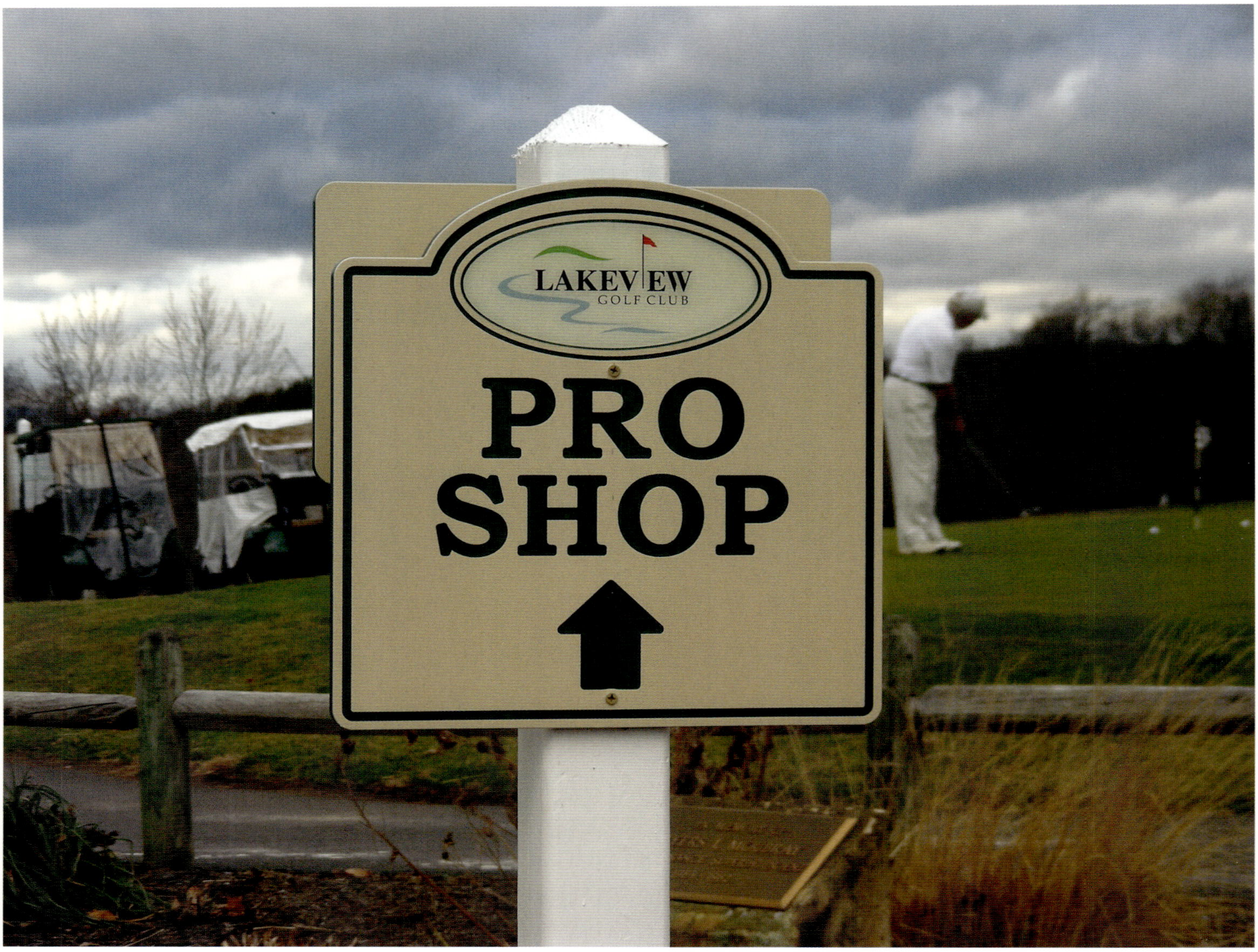
LAKEVIEW
GOLF CLUB
PRO
SHOP

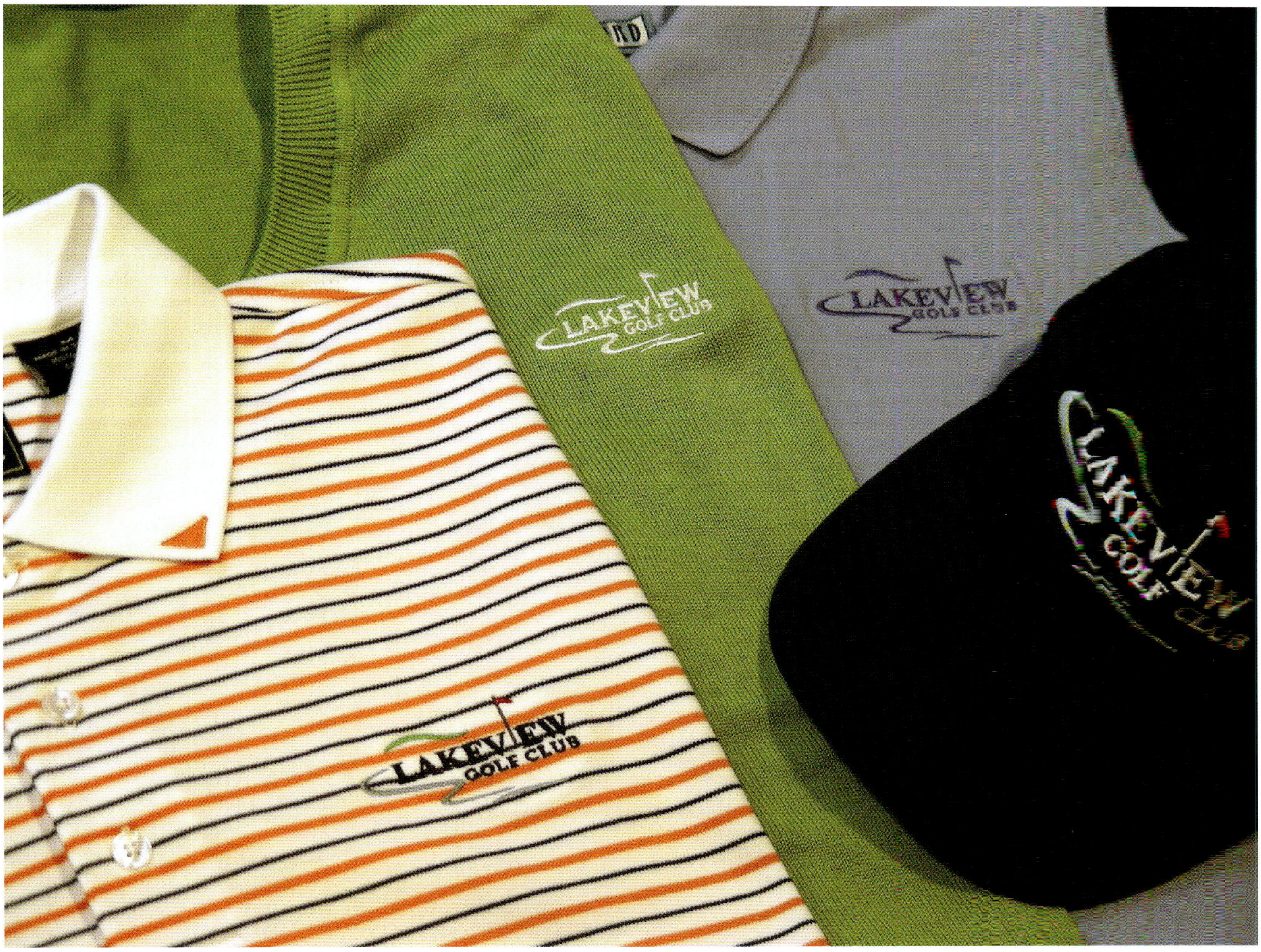
LAKEVIEW
GOLF CLUB
LAKEVIEW
GOLF CLUB
LAKEVIEW
GOLF CLUB
LAKEVIEW
GOLF CLUB

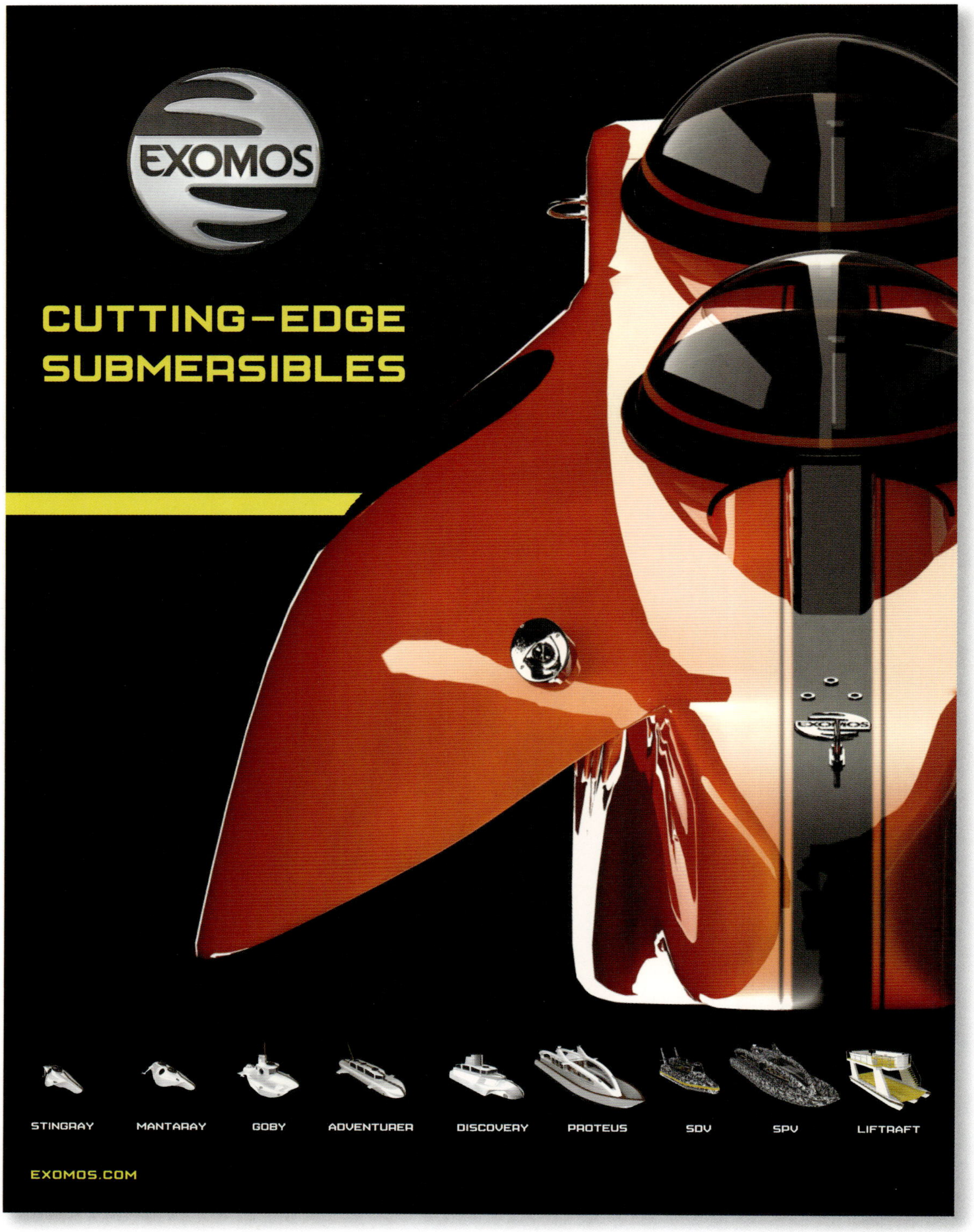
EXOMOS
CUTTING-EDGE
SUBMERSIBLES
STINGRAY
MANTARAY
GOBY
ADVENTURER
DISCOVERY
PROTEUS
SDV
SPV
LIFTRAFT
EXOMOS.COM

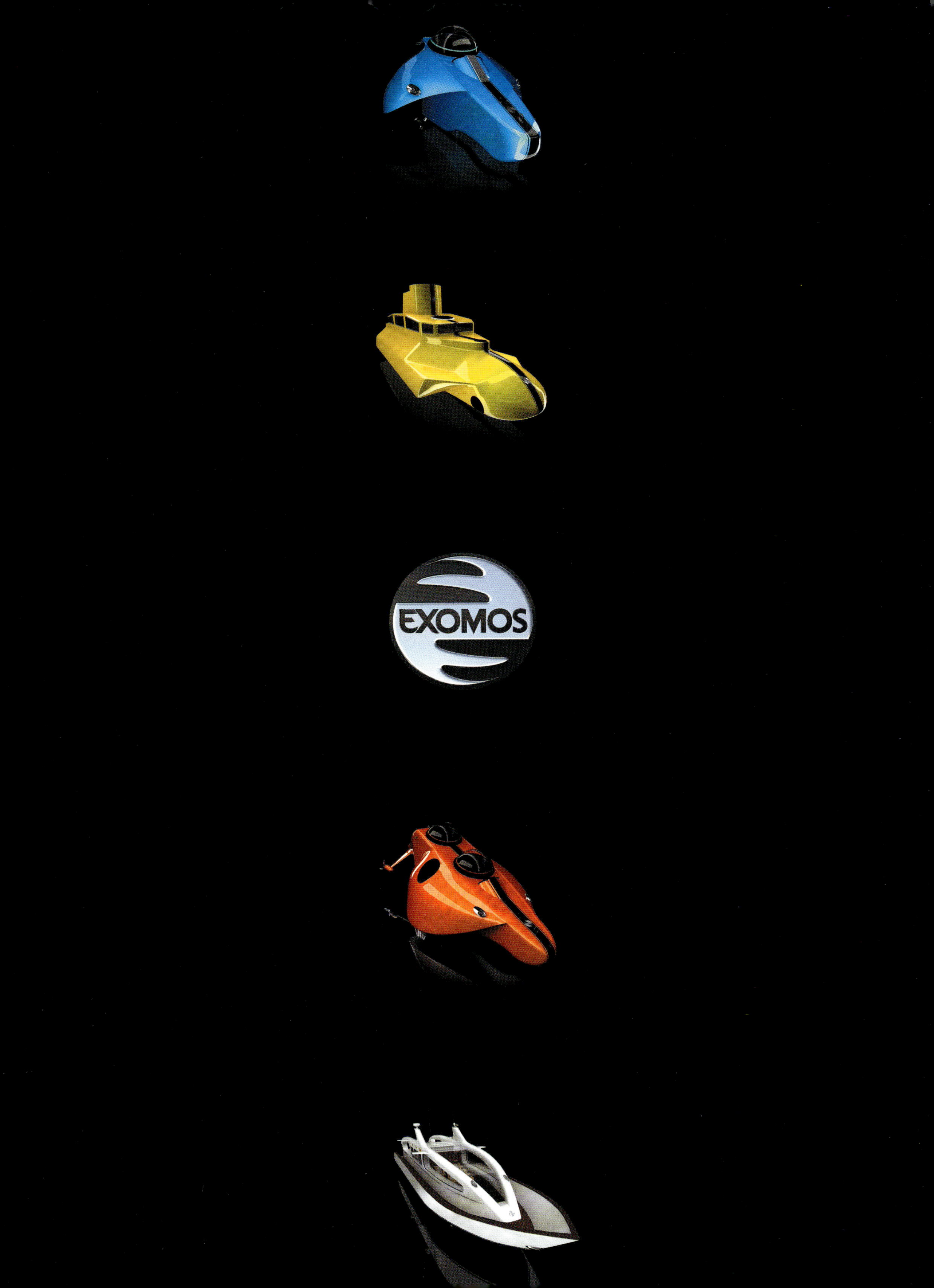
EXOMOS

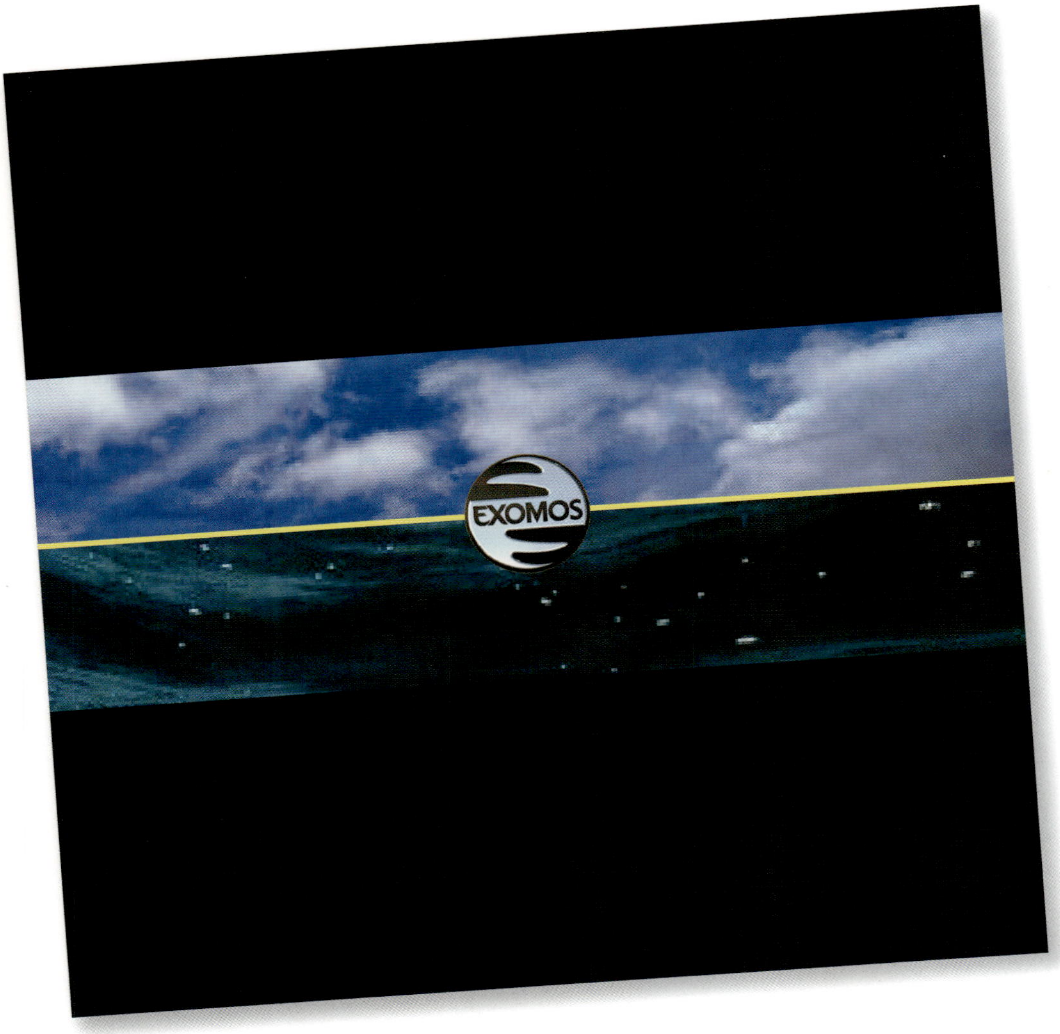
EXOMOS

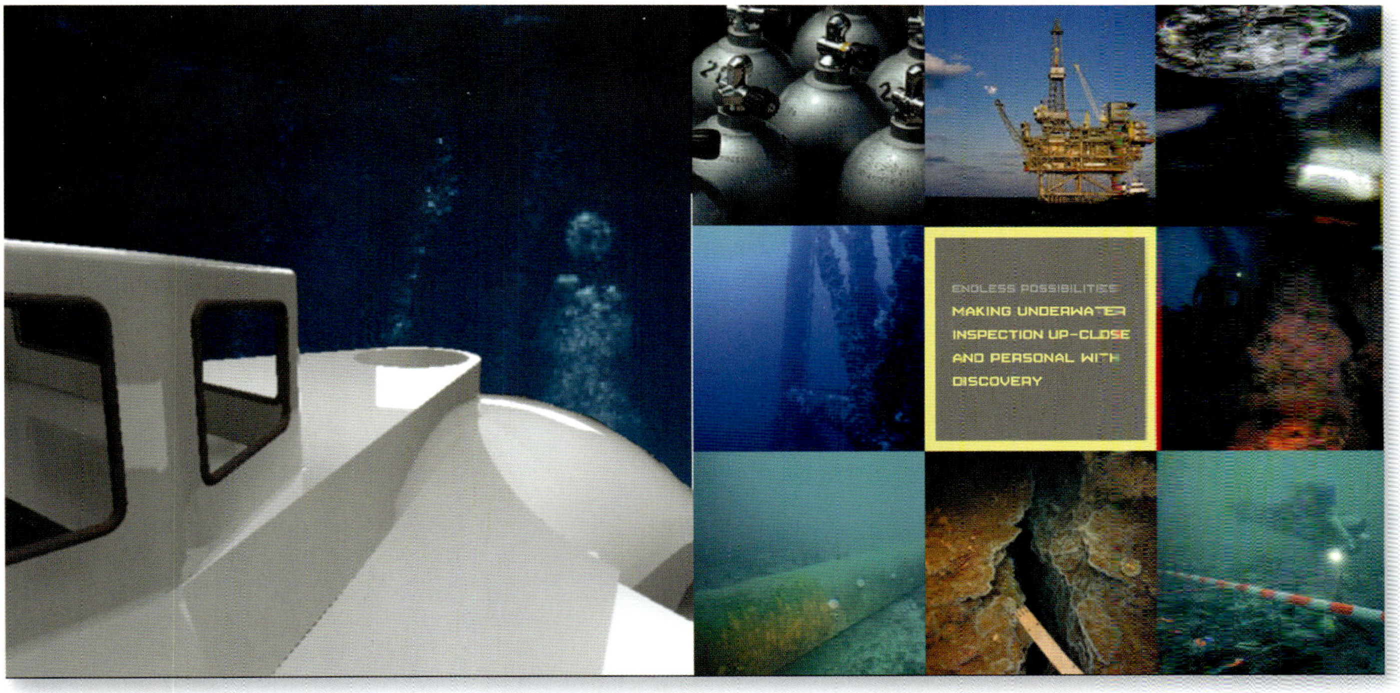
ENDLESS POSSIBILITIES
MAKING UNDERWATER INSPECTION UP-CLOSE AND PERSONAL WITH DISCOVERY

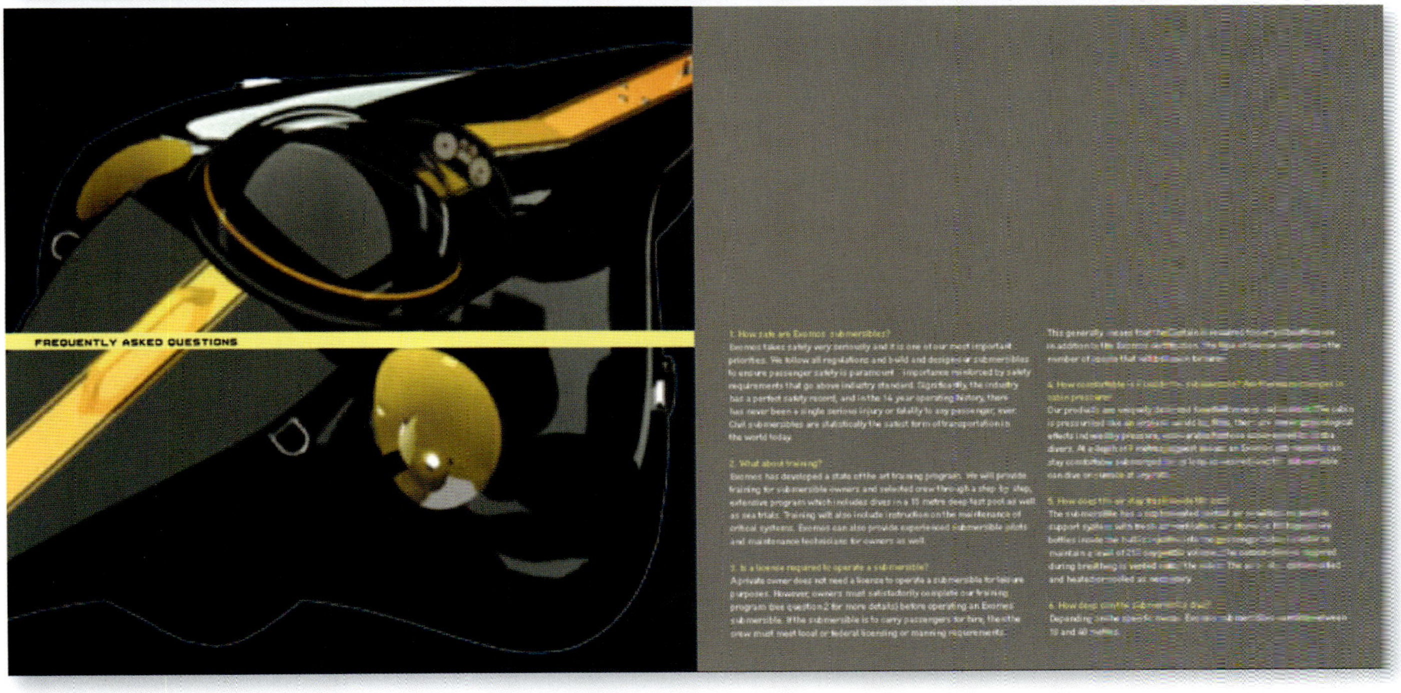
FREQUENTLY ASKED QUESTIONS
1. How safe are Exomos submersibles?
2. What about training?
3. Is a license required to operate a submersible?

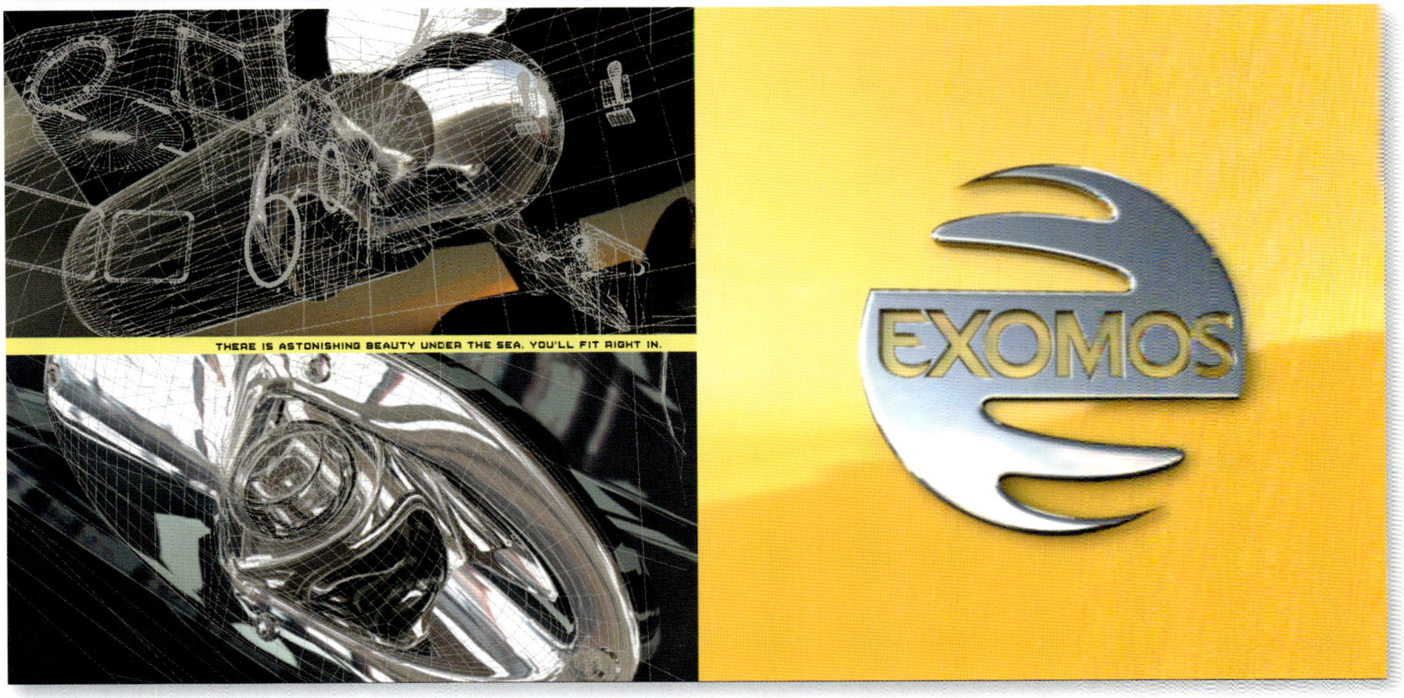
THERE IS ASTONISHING BEAUTY UNDER THE SEA. YOU'LL FIT RIGHT IN.
EXOMOS

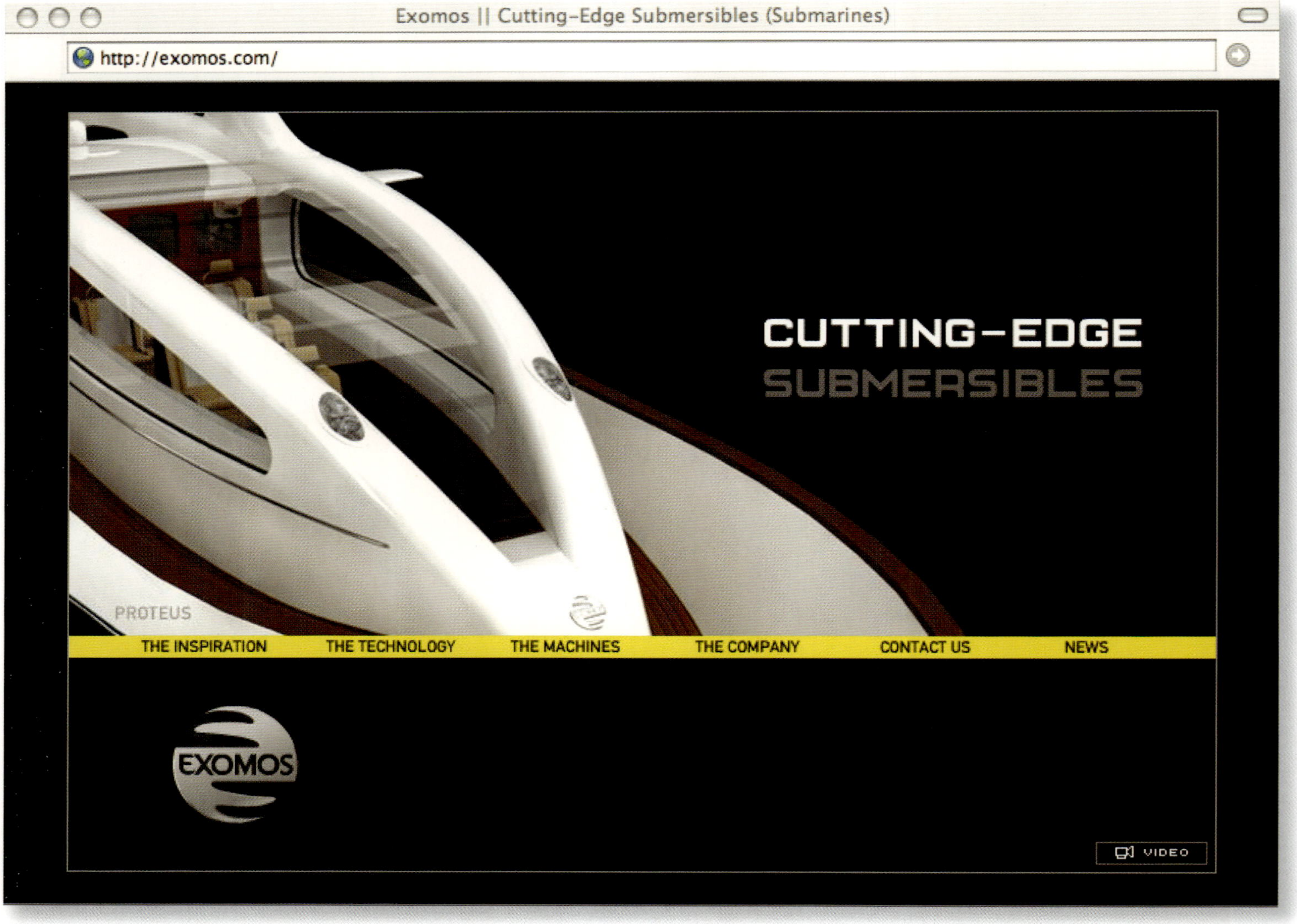
Exomos || Cutting-Edge Submersibles (Submarines)
http://exomos.com/
CUTTING-EDGE
SUBMERSIBLES
PROTEUS
THE INSPIRATION
THE TECHNOLOGY
THE MACHINES
THE COMPANY
CONTACT US
NEWS
EXOMOS
VIDEO

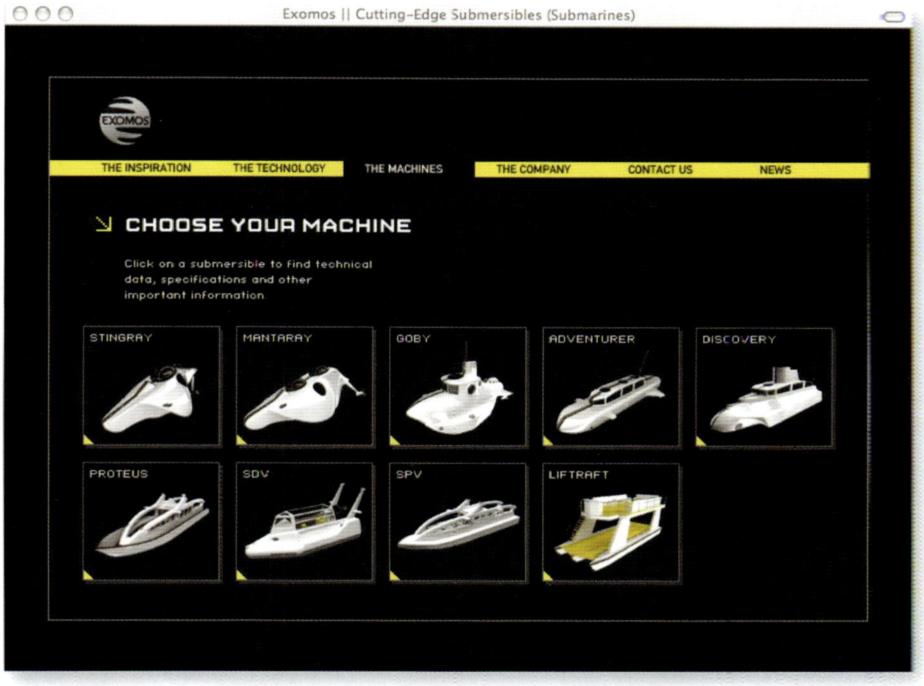
Exomos || Cutting-Edge Submersibles (Submarines)
EXOMOS
THE INSPIRATION
THE TECHNOLOGY
THE MACHINES
THE COMPANY
CONTACT US
NEWS
CHOOSE YOUR MACHINE
Click on a submersible to find technical data, specifications and other important information
STINGRAY
MANTARAY
GOBY
ADVENTURER
DISCOVERY
PROTEUS
SDV
SPV
LIFTRAFT

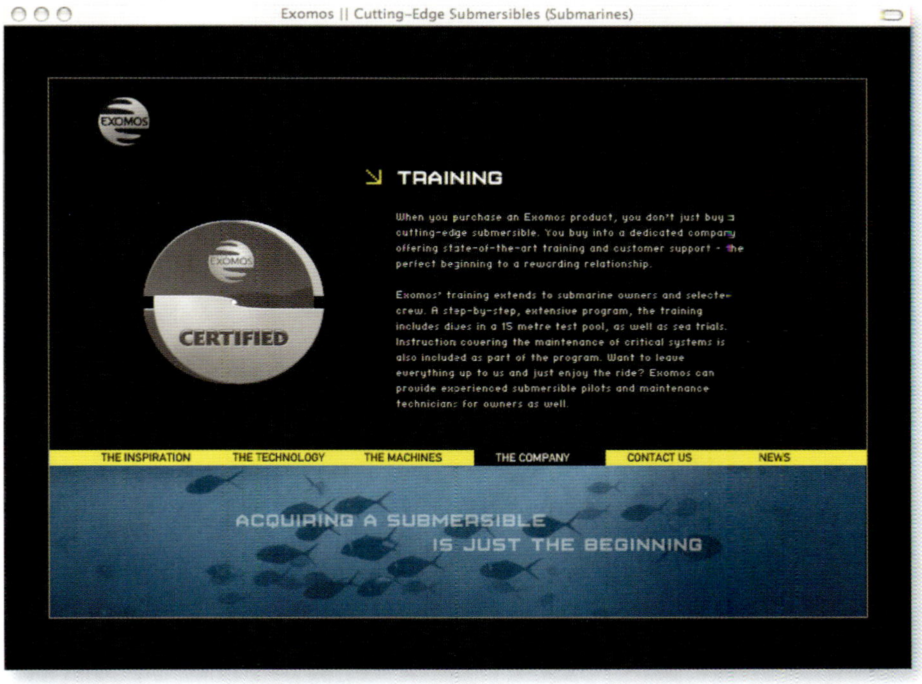
Exomos || Cutting-Edge Submersibles (Submarines)
EXOMOS
TRAINING
When you purchase an Exomos product, you don't just buy a cutting-edge submersible. You buy into a dedicated company offering state-of-the-art training and customer support - the perfect beginning to a rewarding relationship.
Exomos' training extends to submarine owners and selected crew. A step-by-step, extensive program, the training includes dives in a 15 metre test pool, as well as sea trials. Instruction covering the maintenance of critical systems is also included as part of the program. Want to leave everything up to us and just enjoy the ride? Exomos can provide experienced submersible pilots and maintenance technicians for owners as well.
CERTIFIED
THE INSPIRATION
THE TECHNOLOGY
THE MACHINES
THE COMPANY
CONTACT US
NEWS
ACQUIRING A SUBMERSIBLE
IS JUST THE BEGINNING

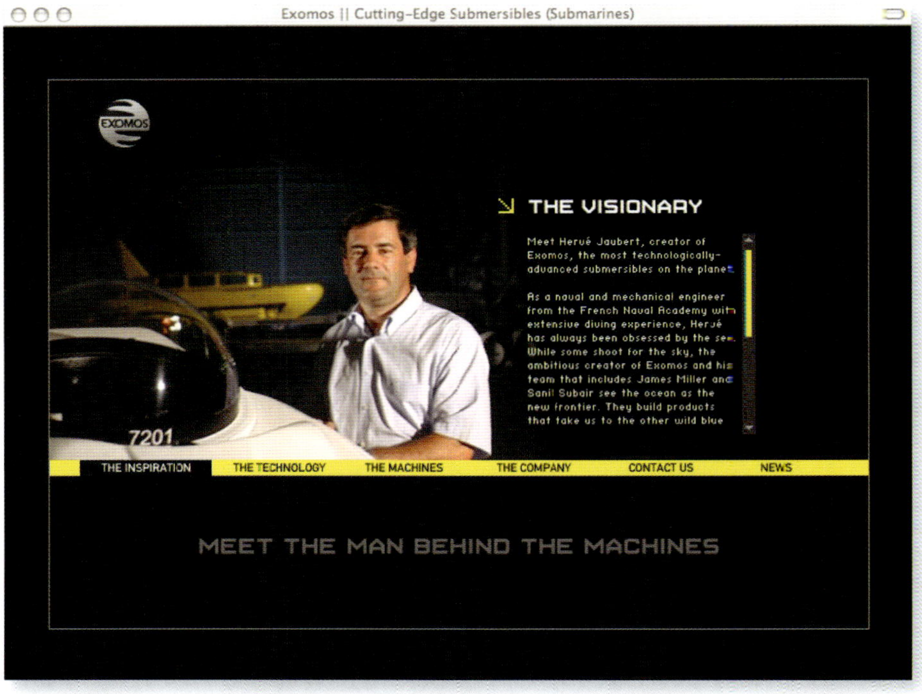
Exomos || Cutting-Edge Submersibles (Submarines)
EXOMOS
THE VISIONARY
Meet Hervé Jaubert, creator of Exomos, the most technologically-advanced submersibles on the planet.
As a naval and mechanical engineer from the French Naval Academy with extensive diving experience, Hervé has always been obsessed by the sea. While some shoot for the sky, the ambitious creator of Exomos and his team that includes James Miller and Sanil Subair see the ocean as the new frontier. They build products that take us to the other wild blue
7201
THE INSPIRATION
THE TECHNOLOGY
THE MACHINES
THE COMPANY
CONTACT US
NEWS
MEET THE MAN BEHIND THE MACHINES

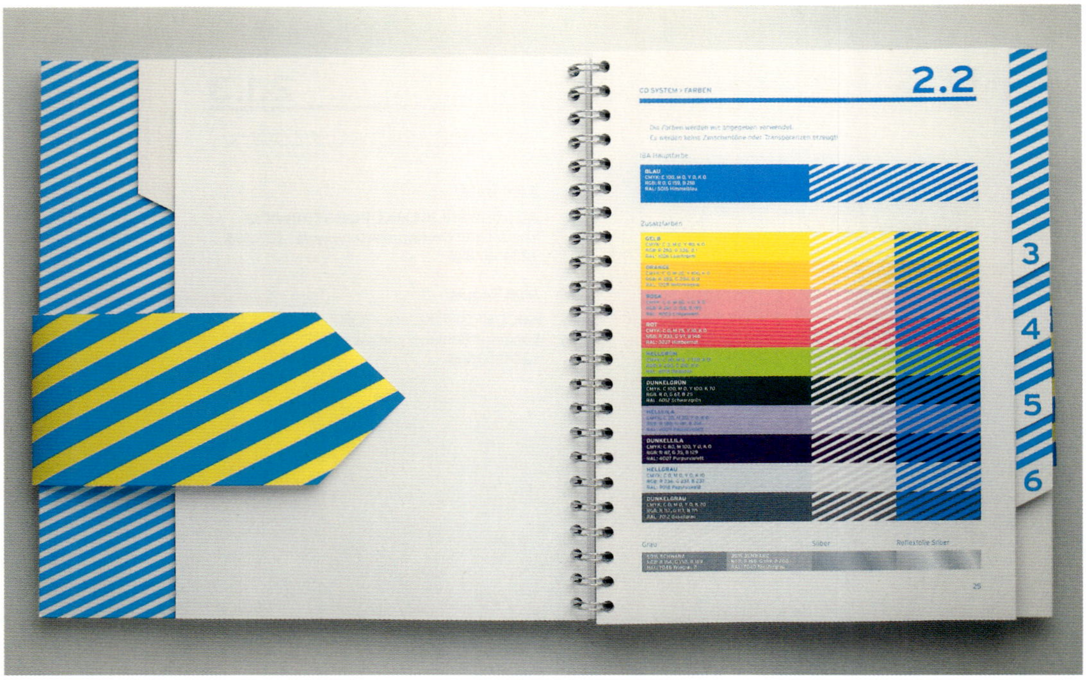
CD SYSTEM > FARBEN
2.2
3
4
5
6

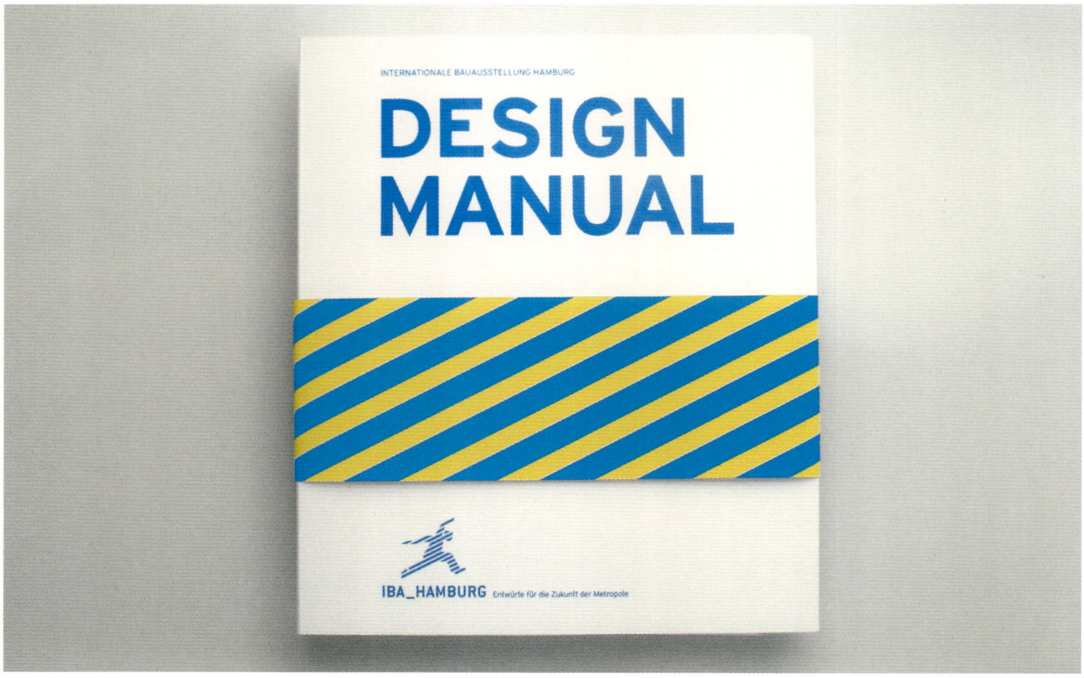
INTERNATIONALE BAUAUSSTELLUNG HAMBURG
DESIGN
MANUAL
IBA_HAMBURG Entwürfe für die Zukunft der Metropole

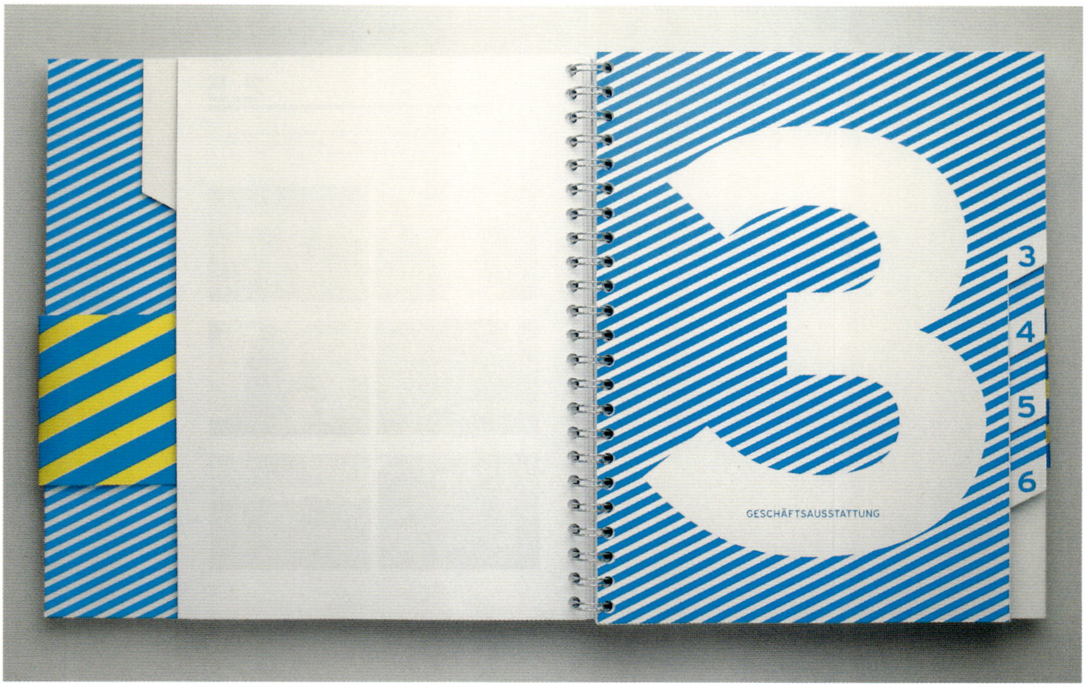
3
GESCHÄFTSAUSSTATTUNG
3
4
5
6

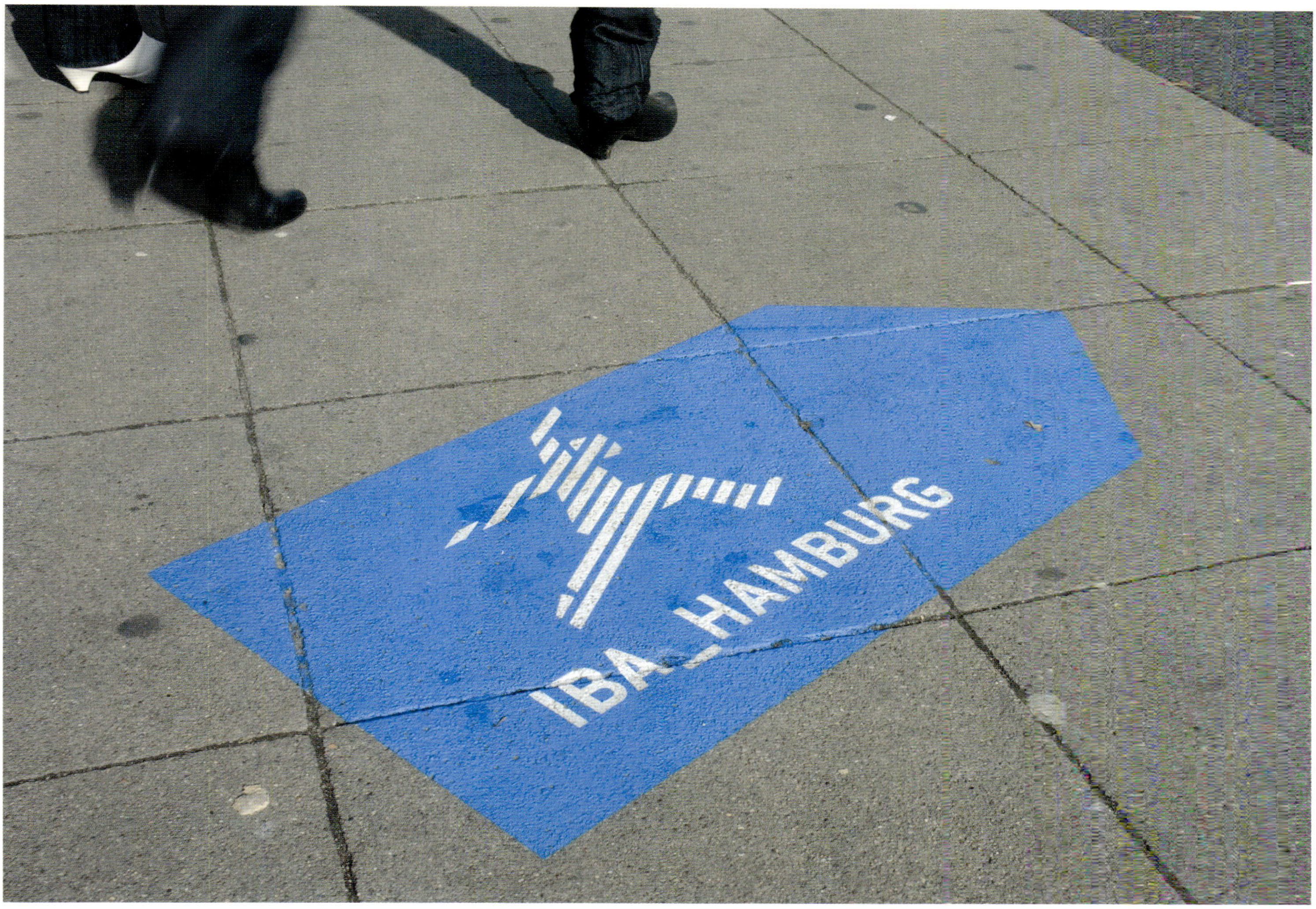
IBA_HAMBURG

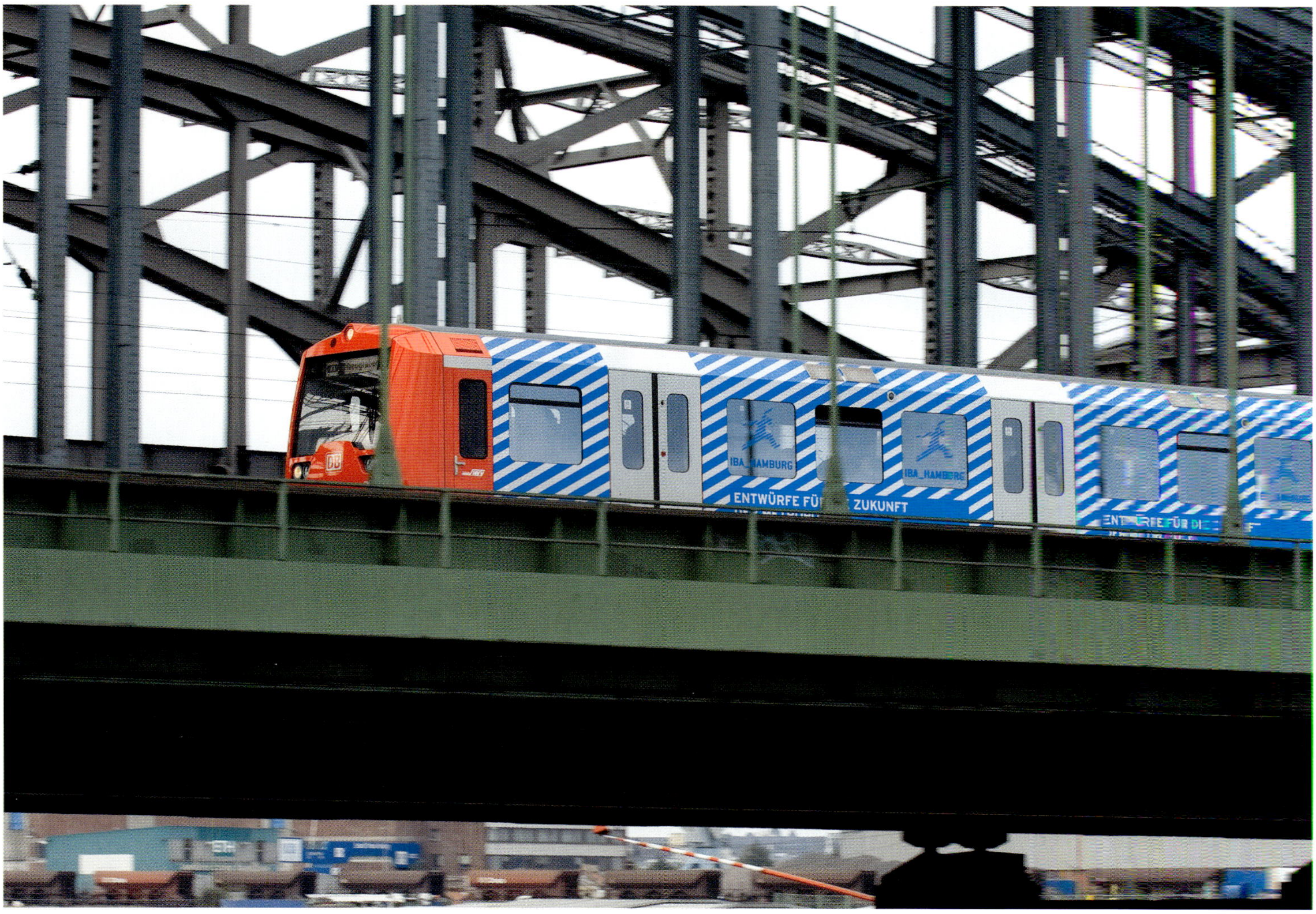
IBA_HAMBURG
IBA_HAMBURG
ENTWÜRFE FÜR
ZUKUNFT

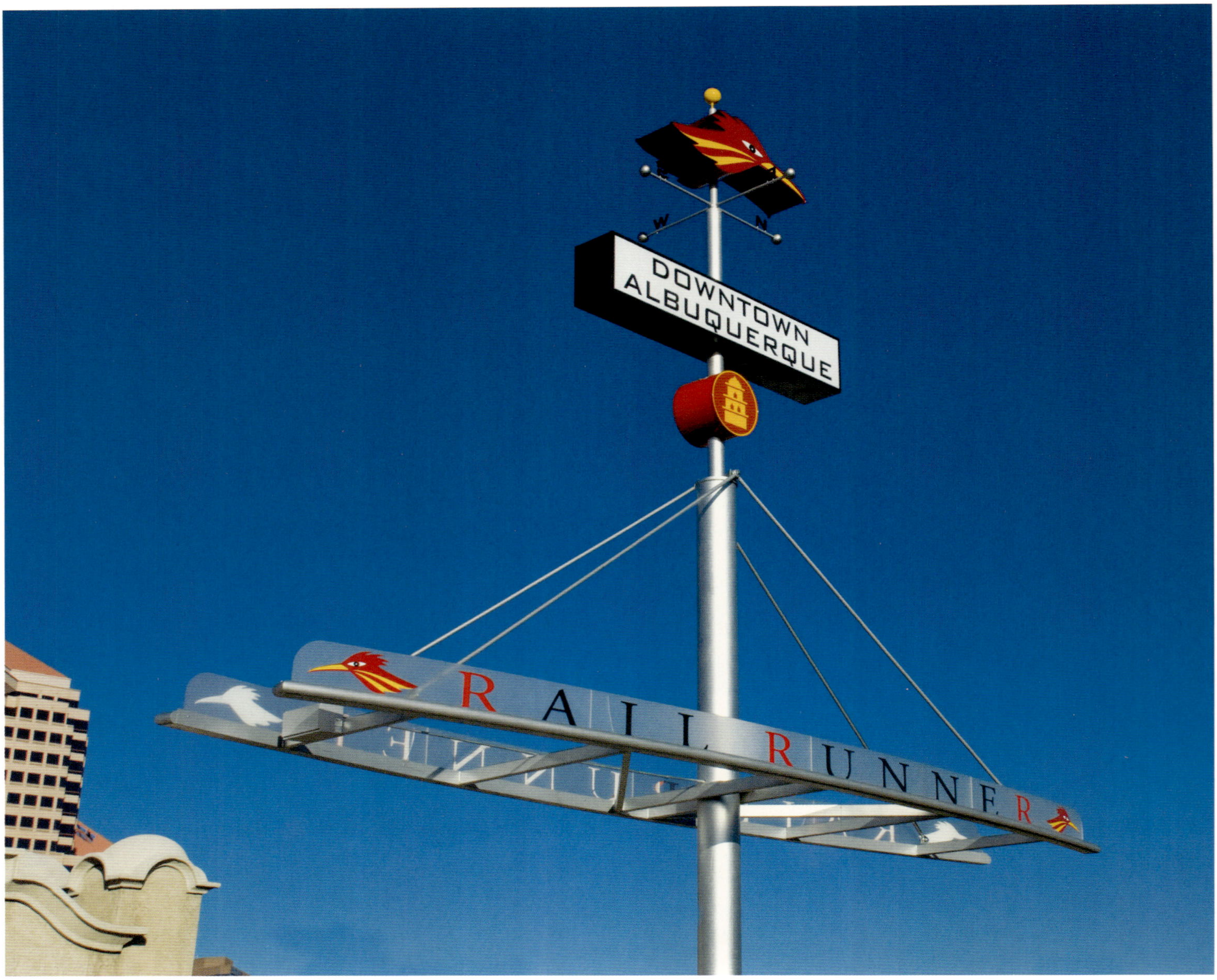
DOWNTOWN
ALBUQUERQUE
RAIL RUNNER

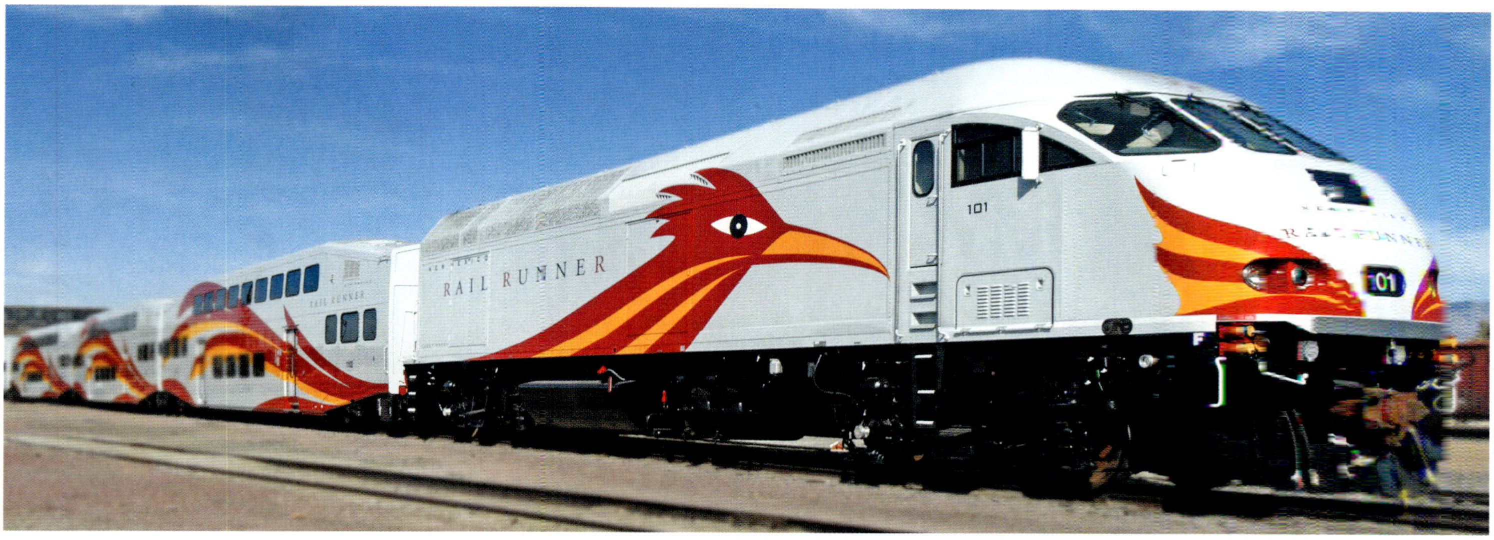
RAIL RUNNER
101

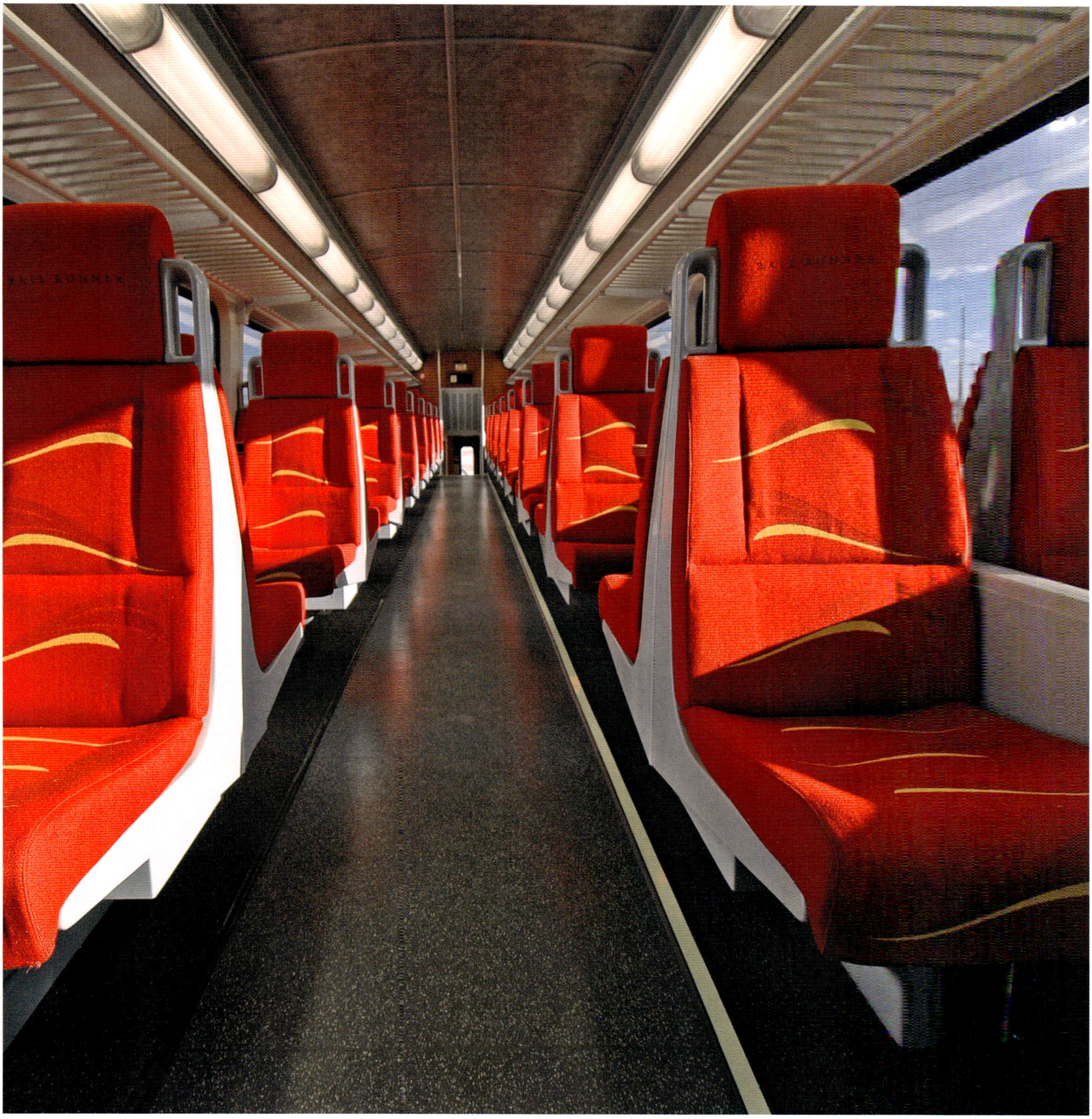

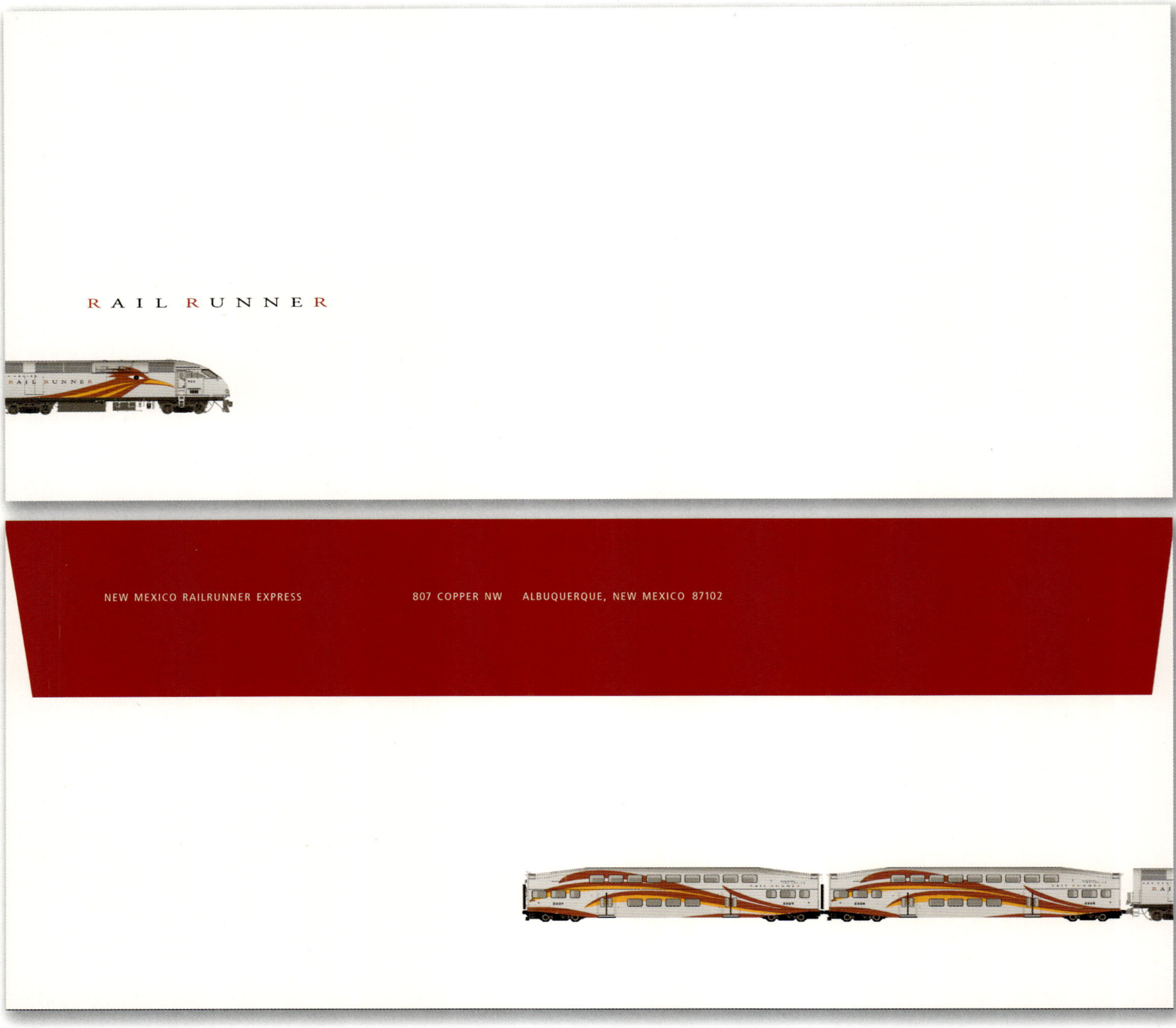
RAIL RUNNER
NEW MEXICO RAILRUNNER EXPRESS
807 COPPER NW ALBUQUERQUE, NEW MEXICO 87102

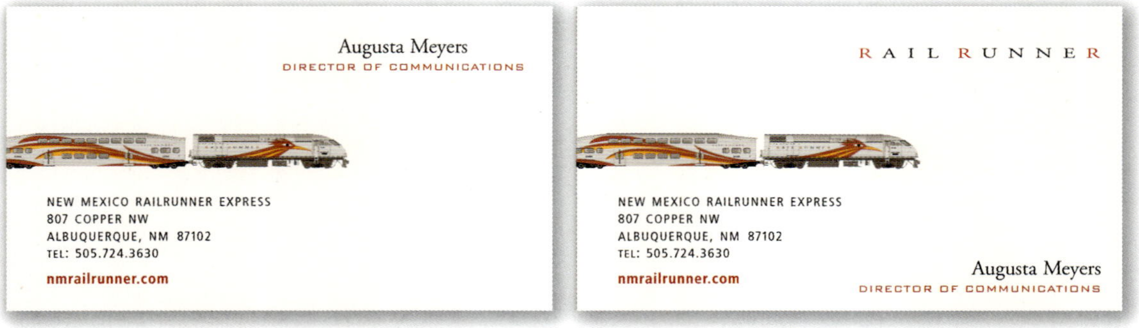
Augusta Meyers
DIRECTOR OF COMMUNICATIONS
NEW MEXICO RAILRUNNER EXPRESS
807 COPPER NW
ALBUQUERQUE, NM 87102
TEL: 505.724.3630
nmrailrunner.com
RAIL RUNNER
NEW MEXICO RAILRUNNER EXPRESS
807 COPPER NW
ALBUQUERQUE, NM 87102
TEL: 505.724.3630
nmrailrunner.com
Augusta Meyers
DIRECTOR OF COMMUNICATIONS

Credits&Comments

Credits&Comments

BrandingCaseStudies

10~17 Canyon | Design Firm: KMS TEAM GmbH, Munich | Client: Canyon Bicycles GmbH | Art Director: Helena Frühauf | Chief Creative Officer: Knut Maierhofer | Creative Director: Christoph Rohrer | Designer: Grace Chou | Project Manager: Sandra Ehm | Print Producer: Melanie Sauer

Description: Canyon Bicycles commissioned us to redesign its corporate appearance. In the context of a holistic corporate identity process, we advise the manufacturer of exclusive sports bicycles in the areas of brand development, corporate Design and communication in space. The central element is the striking, left-tilted lettering.

18~25 PLATINUM Corporate Design for KMS TEAM | Design Firm: KMS TEAM GmbH, Munich | Client: KMS TEAM | Creative Directors: Knut Maierhofer, Michael Keller | Creative Strategist: Christoph Rohrer | Design Director: Patrick Märki | Print Producer: Chrisina Baur | Web Developer: Bruno Marek

Description: KMS TEAM has a new corporate design. It highlights our role as Germany's largest independent design studio and visualizes the method of operation that helped us gain this position. The aim in developing the new design was to step out into public view in an assertive and concise manner, while at the same time remaining neutral with respect to the corporate designs of our clients. Thus, on the whole, we must be perspicuous, but in this perspicuousness we must display the objectivity that is a central component of our consulting service.

The Basic Idea – The corporate design is based on the concept of the "cloud of ideas." It visualizes thoughts, questions and ideas as fields encircling a head and is meant to indicate the method of operation of KMS TEAM. The "cloud of ideas" stands both for the diversity of the activities of the studio, on which we draw in developing a specific design, as well as for the concurrence of all the disciplines involved in the creative process.

The Implementation – The concept of the "cloud of ideas," which is implemented as a rotating bar animation in interactive applications, gives rise to the visual core of the design: an individual black bar. It constitutes the logo and is a clear branding element. At the same time it defines, in analogy to the navigational structure on the Internet, the graphical organizational structure (e.g. forms) and is a playful stylistic device for various applications (e.g. image-film show reel). The color scheme is limited to black and white. This conveys the neutrality and objectivity of KMS TEAM with respect to its clients. The visual language is exclusively derived from the color schemes of clients and is used as a contrastive background in all means of communication. As our font, we chose Universe Black, which is marked by a precise and clear style. The capitalization of the appendage "TEAM" alludes to the importance of our staff members.

26~31 Burj Dubai | Design Firm: Landor Associates, San Francisco | Client: Burj Dubai | Managing Director: Bengt Eriksson | General Manager: Olivier Auroy

32~37 PLATINUM Corporate ID | Design Firm: Landor Associates, San Francisco | Client: Wolfgang Puck | Creative Director: Nicolas Aparicio | Designers: Anastasia Laksmi, JJ Ha, Brian Green

Description: Wolfgang Puck is an icon.
Landor helped to make his brand iconic.
Wolfgang Puck, an indisputable icon in innovative California cuisine and the chef to the stars, wanted to gain back the control of his brand portfolio under one single vision and identity system. Mired in more than a decade of unmanaged license and franchise proliferation, Wolfgang Puck wanted to create a legacy he was proud of. Over the past years, Wolfgang had lost control over his brand due to an increasing number of licensing agreements that lacked any form of graphic and/or brand strategy guidelines. His name had been indiscriminately plastered on frozen pizza boxes, panini-making machines, cans of soup, airport restaurants, and other revenue-generating entities.

He hired Landor to help define the Wolfgang Puck brand strategy and to create an identity platform for the brand to live on well after he retires. Landor's work allowed Wolfgang Puck to examine the consumer holistically as a brand consumer, rather than a single category consumer, and leveraged cross-category offerings to maximize brand impact, and potentially revenues.

While the original task was simply to bring some consistency to the line, we identified the need to define a core idea for the brand and a brand architecture that would define a clear relationship between those business-to-consumer touch points like fine dining restaurants, casual dining and consumer products, and business-to-business touchpoints such as the catering business.

Informed by the brand idea, imagine, which reflects Wolfgang himself, always reinventing the future of food within a world of entertainment, we created a unified system we called a 'a peek into the world of Wolfgang.' The system is defined by a strong graphic panel on the top of any application, reserved for Wolfgang himself, where he is featured in an activity appropriate for the desired messaging. Product photography is never staged. It is photographed as if it was in the process of being made within the context of a restaurant. The new identity built upon the idea that the brand's products and dining venues were personally created by Puck, not a corporate food-processing brand. He alone could bring such innovative, freshly prepared food to the consumer. The identity system was designed to be flexible enough to apply to 3-star fine dining venues, casual dining venues, consumer products (frozen pizzas, soups, coffees, kitchen appliances, etc.) and catering outlets like kiosks, uniforms and trucks. The system impacted decisions not only on graphics and imagery but also environmental and spatial relationships, packaging materials, display formats, livery design, signage, billboard advertisements, corporate communications, training/guidelines materials and other elements that defined the Wolfgang Puck experience.

Through the use of consistent Typography, color palette and Photographic style, we have unified the various touch points of the brand. Keeping in mind the customer journey, a consumer will be able to go to a Wolfgang Gourmet Express and get a take out pizza, or go to a supermarket to purchase some soup, or tune into the Home Shopping Network to buy a blender, and understand that all those products come from the same brand.

Landor's work unearthed areas of opportunity for future business growth, including new categories and potential markets for the client, such as a Wolfgang Puck signature line of consumer products. Additionally, the cleanliness and flexibility of the creative system enabled Wolfgang Puck to appropriately brand a plethora of elements in its portfolio to create a holistic brand experience.

The system is slowly being rolled out across the various channels. Employees now understand the premise behind the brand and speak with a unified purpose. It has served as a filter to identify not only what types of food and price range will be offered at every tier, but also as a vehicle to understand strategic alliances and channels of distribution that will enhance the overall brand. We provided a unified voice and visual language for the Wolfgang Puck brand. Now the brand represents a promise, an experience. Licensees and franchisees now have specific production guidelines. Terms for brand management and veto power are being included into contracts currently being negotiated. Each line of business now can examine areas of business opportunity in a new light. It also brought key tenets of the brand to life: the elemental art of cooking, the charisma of Puck himself, an emphasis on freshness (both of ingredients and ideas) and the social nexus of the shared meal. The simplicity of the new system contrasts starkly with the overt, often garish and graphic standards of the commercial food industry. Defined by elegance and understated graphic elements, the system conveys an authority that resonates with consumers seeking a food experience that is both accessible and refined – a truly Wolfgang Puck experience.

Landor's team players worked with Wolfgang Puck for over a year to craft a complementary, cohesive and comprehensive brand. Landor's work for Wolfgang Puck was truly emblematic of helping the client think bigger and better - bigger than what the brand represents today, and better by being a strategic and creative partner in transforming the business through the brand.

About Landor: Landor believes in the power of ideas driven by consumer insight, and the need to align business strategy with marketing strategy to create brand-led business transformation. Wolfgang is a good example of ideas and creativity as our medium and our focus on impact, not input, as our purpose. Founded by Walter Landor in San Francisco in 1941, we are one company of 850 talented players, across 22 offices around the world.

Our work has been recognized by numerous organizations around the globe including: Communication Arts, AIGA, Graphis, Clio Awards, Print, Art Directors Club of San Francisco, and The Conference Board, among others.

38~47 Vespa | Design Firm: Piaggio & C. S.p.A. | Client: Vespa

48~57 PLATINUM Tazo Tea | Design Firm: Sandstrom Partners | Client: Tazo, Steve Smith | Creative Directors: Steve Sandoz, Steve Sandstrom, Steve Smith | Art Designer: Steve Sandstrom | Lead Designer: Steve Sandstrom | Photographers: Todd Eckelman, Mark Hooper, Polara Studio | Developers: Jud Holiday, Cole Peterson, J.C. Vieth | Information Architect: Susan Campbell | Support & Production Designers: Kristen Andersen, Shanin Andrews, Andrew Randall | Project Managers: Kristen Cassidy, Carol Johnson, Jill Raleigh (Sandstrom Design) & Whitney Zaring (Zaaz) | Writers: Palmer Pettersen, Steve Sandoz

58~65 St-Germain Integrated Campaign | Design Firm: Sandstrom Partners | Client: Cooper Spirits International | Creative Director: Steve Sandstrom | Design Director: Steve Sandstrom | Designers: Sarah Hollowood, Trevor Thrap | Illustrator: Antar Dayal | Photographers: Mark Hooper and various others | Print Producer: Prue Searles | Project Manager: Prue Searles | Web Developer: John Bohls | Writer: Mark Waggoner

66~71 Coca-Cola | Design Firm: The Coca-Cola Company | Client: Coca-Cola

72, 73 PLATINUM Coca-Cola | Design Firm: Turner Duckworth | Client: The Coca-Cola Company | Account Director: Jessica Rogers | Creative Directors: David Turner, Bruce Duckworth | Design Director: Sarah Moffat | Designers: Jonathan Warner, Radu Ranga, Josh Michels, Rebecca Williams, Chris Garvey

Description: Over the years, Coca-Cola's visual identity had become cluttered and uninspiring, diluting the brand's iconic status. The brand was losing its charm and cultural relevance. Working with Wieden + Kennedy, Coca-Cola developed a new creative idea with the goal of setting the brand back on track. This idea was "Coke brings joy," a simple statement about the happiness the product brings. Moira Cullen, Design Director at The Coca-Cola Company, challenged Turner Duckworth with taking this idea and designing a new visual identity and packaging system that would allow the brand to shine again. The first task was to take on the packaging. We redesigned the can as part of the complete overhaul of Coke's visual identity system, clarifying the design and using the latest printing techniques to produce a bright white and a rich red. We eliminated the extraneous ribbons and bubbles and focused on the simple joy of the classic trademark. The aluminum bottle design was a new creation. The classic contour bottle shape features an oversized Coke trademark and nothing more. The clean and confident design simplifies what it means to be Coke and makes the brand feel fresh and new again. Like the packaging, the focus of the overall visual identity was to create a system that was pure and simple and referenced back to the original core brand elements in a modern and honest way. The iconic bottle design we created combines the two most prominent trademarks of the Coca-Cola brand identity and creates a single mark that expresses the brand's positive attitude and reintroduces the brand to consumers in a new light. Together, the Spencerian Script and bottle icon designs can be used to create a multitude of layouts that serve a variety of functions. The goal was to use just a few simple elements to create a wide spectrum of designs that are consistent, yet surprising. In most cases, there is not a singular approach to how the bottle is used. Rather, it is more about the bottle's interaction with the subject that makes things visually interesting. Although the packaging has been out less than a year, it is already generating positive press in *BrandWeek* and *Creative Review*, as well as various design blogs, including UnderConsideration.com.

74~77 Root:1 Cabernet Sauvignon | Design Firm: Turner Duckworth | Client: Root:1 Cabernet Sauvignon | Creative Directors: David Turner, Bruce Duckworth

78~83 PLATINUM Ugly Mug Coffee Packaging | Design Firm: Young and Laramore, Indianapolis | Account Directors: Margit Fawbush, Christian Mehall | Art Director: Trevor Williams | Creative Director: Charlie Hopper | Designer: Yee-Haw Industries | Photographer: Harold Lee Miller | Writer: Bryan Judkins | Client: Ugly Mug Coffee

Description: Capturing the feel of a brand as unpretentious as Ugly Mug, yet retaining enough sophistication to reassure that this is indeed premium coffee (and confirm that the "ugly" joke is deliberate), a high-end silver background was combined with letterpress, actually-funny humor, and ugly mugshots of people right out of bed and in desperate need of good coffee.

Artists

84, 85 DAAO Brand Identity | Design Firm: Naughtyfish Design, Rushcutters Bay | Client: Dictionary of Australian Artists Online | Creative Director/Designer/Creative Strategist: Paul Garbett | Design Director: Danielle de Andrade

Description: The Dictionary of Australian Artists Online is a web-based search tool with links to data archives from Australia's major universities and art galleries. We used the metaphor of the dictionary to inform the design of the logo: not a traditional logo, but 26 dynamically arranged pixels, each representing a letter of the alphabet. The "pixels" can be rearranged in a multitude of configurations to suit the particular communication.

AuctionHouses

86~91 Sotheby's Visual Identity | Design Firm: Sotheby's | Client: Sotheby's | Account Director: Amy Todd Middleton | Content Strategists: Susan Casey, Amy Todd Middleton, Ann Jackson, Nicole Louis, Christina Lehmejian-Karaszewski | Copywriters: Susan Casey, Liz Thorp, Sandra Burch, Joshua Webster, Jonathan Wills | Creative Strategist: Susan Casey, Liz Thorp, Sandra Burch, Eri Koizumi | Design Directors: Sandra Burch, Liz Thorp, Joshua Webster | Designers: Eri Koizumi, Liz Thorp, Sandra Burch, Joshua Webster, Jonathan Wills, Christina Freyss | Project Manager: Joshua Webster | Typographer: Hoefler & Frere-Jones, Inc.

Description: What represents the Sotheby's-ness of Sotheby's? Beyond its logo, which design choices, visual elements, colour palettes and communication strategies brand Sotheby's?

The Sotheby's Visual Identity Guidelines have been created to ensure global consistency in the presentation of the Sotheby's brand, particularly through advertising, catalogues and marketing collateral. The Guidelines primarily focuse on Sotheby's new premium colour palette, the introduction of Verlag as the new Sotheby's corporate typeface, catalogue design, creative refresh and new advertising templates. Adhering to these guidelines and templates is essential to make sure all items have the same Sotheby's branded look and feel regardless of where in the world they are created. The new guidelines have been created with adequate flexibility so that projects can be diverse and exciting while still looking unmistakably "Sotheby's."

A company's "look" is the face of its brand.

Beginning with its logo, design choices represent the Sotheby's brand through thousands of publications, collateral materials, communications; in print, signage, and online. This Visual Identity Guidelines contain all the specifications necessary concerning Sotheby's logo, colour palette, typography and layout, and photography. These specifications may be applied to catalogues, advertising, postcards, invitations, brochures, shopping bags and other marketing collateral.

Broadcast

92~95 Time Warner Center | Design Firm: Poulin + Morris Inc., New York | Client: Time Warner | Designer: Douglas Morris

Communications

96, 97 iPhone Accessories | Design Firm: Graphic Design, Apple Computer, Cupertino | Client: Apple | Creative Director: Apple Graphic Design, Apple Industrial Design, Apple Packaging Engineering

Description: All of the packaging for the iPhone accessories were designed as a family—making it easier for customers to identify the difference between iPhone and iPod accessories.

Computer/Software

98, 99 Novell 2001 Campaign Identity Program | Design Firm: Hornall Anderson Design Works, Seattle | Client: Novell, Inc. | Creative Director: Jack Anderson | Art Director: Larry Anderson | Designers: James Tee, Holly Craven, Kaye Farmer, Jay Hilburn, Belinda Bowling, Cliff Chung (for signage) | Photographer: David Emmite

Corporate

100, 101 Devon Identity System | Design Firm: Landor Associates, San Francisco | Client: Devon Energy | Account Director: Bob Kersten | Designers: Ken Frederick, Grant Yagmourian, Joe Clarke, E. Gilliam | Executive Creative Director: Christopher Lehmann | Project Manager: Jennie Suchor | Writer: Cori Constantine

Description: Devon Energy is one of the world's leading independent oil and gas companies. Having grown exponentially over the past ten years through mergers and acquisitions, future growth will be organic. Historically shying away from branding efforts, Devon recognized that to better communicate with internal and external audiences—to engage its employees and build stronger relationships with communities, investors and regulators—it would need to more actively manage its brand. Landor developed positioning that focused on Devon's strength of acting with integrity—found throughout its organization, across cultures and geographies. Informed by the new positioning, Landor created a brandline, "Commitment Runs Deep" and an identity system that are inspired by the earth and geology—specifically, the idea of strata as a metaphor for building upon past experiences.

By knowing their past and taking action in the present, Devon builds on a strong foundation to create a successful future. Visually, this comes to life in various strata graphic shapes and a color palette that is inspired by energy and the earth. When combined to create layers of visual and verbal messages, each resulting communication piece is familiar yet becomes its own unique variation of elements.

Cosmetics

102~105 ASTACURE | Design Firm: BBI STUDIO INC., Tokyo | Client: Nakumura Co. | Art Director: Zempaku Suzuki | Creative Directors: Masako Miyajima, Shinobu Matsuoka | Creative Strategist: Nihon Keizai Advertising Co., Ltd. | Design Director: BBI STUDIO INC. | Designers: Zempaku Suzuki, Yoshihiro Sugimoto, Aki Hira

Description: A pharmaceutical company of Toyama prefecture in business for 60 years developed a series of skin-care products—ASTACURE—based on preventive medicine, and introduced a renewal branding for its logo and package. Since the prime antiaging ingredient, astaxanthin, was developed and has been produced in-house, it was also planned to raise the awareness of this ingredient. Translucent red was adopted as the brand color based on the color of antaxanthin and on the fact that it was a natural ingredient. The "C" in the logotype was designed and was based on the shape of a chemical machine used in the astaxanthin production process.

Designers

106~109 Yello | Design Firm: Yello, Sydney | Client: Yello Brands | Creative Director: Olivia Swinn | Design Directors: Adam Trunk, Troy Dagan | Designer: Taria Saeedi

Description: Yello is a brand experience company focused on building the best Australian brands and bringing global brands to life in the unique Australian market. The Yello brand has been designed more as a consumer brand in it's own right and over time will bring out merchandise and products that reflect our attitude and unique way of looking at the world from down under.

Education

110, 111 Futurism 2020 | Design Firm: FutureBrand, London | Client: FutureBrand | Creative Director: Tom Crew | Design Director: Tony Fox

Description: Futurism 2020—This mark was developed for a student award scheme. We wanted it to feel creative and alive—hence the use of light as a medium and the adaptive variations of the 2020 created.

Entertainment

112~114 FireLake Grand Casino Logo Family | Design Firm: Concussion, LLC, Fort Worth | Client: FireLake Grand Casino | Account Director: Amanda Gibson | Chief Creative Officer: Andrew Yanez

Description: The main logo takes cues from the Frank Lloyd Wright influenced architecture of the casino itself and integrates the core visual elements of fire and water inspired by its name. The logos are inspired by art deco design and allow the casino to embrace the style as a whole.

115 Casino Collateral | Design Firm: Concussion, LLC, Fort Worth | Client: FireLake Grand Casino | Account Director: Amanda Gibson | Chief Creative Officer: Andrew Yanez | Designer/Illustrator: Charlie Howlett

Description: These pieces take cues from the Frank Lloyd Wright influenced architecture of the casino itself.

Their individual "structures" and design aesthetic allow the simple messages to be delivered in a bold and expressive way.

Environmental

116~119 One Degree | Design Firm: Landor Associates, Sydney | Client: News Limited | Account Director: Richard Curtis | Art Director: Jason Little | Creative Strategists: Cable Daniel-Dreyfus, Richard Curtis | Design Directors: Jason Little, Tim Warren | Designers: Jason Little, Angela McCarthy, Michael Rigby, Tim Warren, Steve Clarke | Executive Creative Director: Mike Staniford | Executive Creative Strategist: Damian Borchok | Photographer: Stephen Ward | Project Manager: Eugenie Hung | Typographers: Jason Little, Steve Clarke, Michael Rigby | Writers: Jason Little, Richard Curtis

Description: News Limited's One Degree brand aims to drive employee, supplier and public action regarding climate change. It acts as an overarching banner that brings together all businesses within News Limited to reduce carbon emissions by inspiring thousands of employees and dozens of major companies to change their behaviour. Key goals included communicating News Limited's established environmental track record and providing employees with practical tools to reduce their own individual carbon footprint.

We created the One Degree brand, from strategic positioning and naming to identity design and implementation across launch collateral, guidelines, posters, advertisements and merchandise.

Credits&Comments

One Degree inspires and influences through its clear and engaging message and positive tone. Most individuals are already overloaded with work that the issue of climate change is too hard to think about. One Degree recognizes that every small action counts, and collectively these small actions can have a huge impact. The logo combines both the number and the degree symbol, which together represent a person. The visual language uses News Limited employees along with the degree symbol as the focus for communications, echoing the logo and implying a thought bubble with the intent to make one degree of change, one degree of effort, one degree of difference.

The brand adheres to strict environmental production variables, for example the posters printed on Mohawk Options (process-chlorine-free 100% post-consumer waste fiber, manufactured using non-polluting, wind-generated energy). A minimal colour palette of cyan and black retains 100% consistency across all materials, and keeps production costs to a minimum.

The recently launched One Degree brand now acts as a key driver for em ployees and stakeholders to help achieve News Limited's commitment to reduce greenhouse emissions by 20 percent and become carbon neutral by 2010.

120, 121 Ameya Preserve Identity | Design Firm: Siegel & Gale LLC, New York | Client: Ameya Preserve | Content Strategist: Aaron Frank | Creative Director: Sven Seger | Design Director: Fiona Blankenship | Designers: Monica Chai, Yumi lee

Description: The symbol, formed by blades of grass, literally roots the Ameya name in the spirit of the surroundings.

When an environmentally responsible real estate development in the Greater Yellowstone region of Montana needed a name, brand strategy, and visual identity, they turned to Siegel+Gale. Ameya Preserve was born.

Ameya. In a word the name embodies the vision and brand idea of "A Life of Balance." From Sanskrit for "boundless," Ameya evokes expansive terrain and open space. The symbol, comprised of blades of grass bending in the wind, captures the emotion and sensation of movement and discovery represented in the name. The idea of "boundless" captures the sense of exploration and activity that is central to the vision of Ameya Preserve. Implemented visually and verbally across a range of touchpoints, the identity continues to help the Preserve communicate its unique vision.

Events

122~125 FedEx Forum Identity Program | Design Firm: Landor Associates, San Francisco | Client: FedEx Services | Credit: Landor Associates

Fashion

126, 127 LOOKS | Design Firm: BBI STUDIO INC., Tokyo | Client: LOOKS | Art Director: Zempaku Suzuki | Creative Director: Kenji Onishi | Creative Strategist: DENTSU INC. | Design Director: BBI STUDIO INC. | Designers: Zempaku Suzuki, Yoshihiro Sugimoto, Aki Hirai

Description: The renewal of this cooperate brand image began with the development of a logotype emphasizing the image of Milan. Based on the concept to use the apostrophe of the brand name spelling "LOOKS'" as a motif every fashion season, the promotion was deployed throughout its items including price tags, shop entrances, buttons, knitwear and other items during the first season.

128, 129 Miss Ashida 2006SS | Design Firm: Graphics & Designing Inc., Tokyo | Client: Jun Ashida Co., Ltd | Art Director/Designer: Toshihiro Onimaru | Creative Director/Artist: Tae Ashida | Photographer: Hiromasa Sasaki

Description: Product Naming for the Global Fashion Brand, Miss Ashida. Graphic design for the 2006 Spring-summer collection of the Global Fashion Brand Miss Ashida.

Development of graphical designs to be used for logos, as well as collection outlines, posters, novelties, and products in apparel. Fashion is sourced through collaboration with Miss Ashida's designer, Tae Ashida.

Film

130~133 Re-design of Identity and Brand Language | Design Firm: BIG/Ogilvy & Mather, New York | Client: Kodak | Executive Creative Director: Brian Collins | Creative Directors: Weston Bingham, Allen Hori | Designers: Christian Cervantes, Satian Pengthasapon, Manual Miranda

Description: For the past 70 years, the company's logotype has changed, but the visual expression of the word Kodak has remained fairly constant. The concept behind the evolved wordmark reflects the duality of memories and technology. The K's suggest technology with their hard, solid letterforms while protecting the softer, rounder letterforms in between, representing memories. The wordmark is currently being applied to all Kodak communications, environments and products worldwide.

FinancialServices

134, 135 DCM "Year of the Rat" Lunar New Year Campaign | Design Firm: Gee + Chung Design, San Francisco | Client: DCM | Art Director/Creative Director/Design Director/Illustrator/Typographer: Earl Gee | Designers: Earl Gee, Fani Chung | Printers: Oscar Printing-Party Invitation and Greeting Card, Fong & Fong Printers and Lithographers- Gift Bag | Special Process: Foil Stamping, Die Cutting

Description: Objective – To create a Lunar New Year campaign to welcome the Year of the Rat for a venture capital firm with significant investments in China. Solution: The logo uses the company's initials to create the Chinese lunar calendar animal. The invitation uses a pop-up format to signify a bold, confident outlook for the firm's Chinese high technology ventures. The greeting card employs metallic gold foil to create a festive appeal. The gift bag conveys the concept of yin and yang through its wrap-around motif and alternating color scheme.

Food

136~139 Cafy's Identity | Design Firm: Ventress Design Group, Franklin | Client: Cafy's Roast House Cafe | Copywriters: Michelle Schwantes, Tom Ventress | Designer: Tom Ventress

140, 141 Revolving Identities and Application | Design Firm: Wren and Rowe Ltd, London | Client: Global Food Funatic | Art Director: Steve Younger | Creative Strategist: Paul Foulkes-Arellano

Description: Global Food Funatic is a new food company, which produces authentic Asian food for the European market. The company principals are larger than life, and we wanted to give the new company a personality to match. The identities can revolve depending on application, which matches the flexibility and humour of the company principals.

Furniture

142~149 Sguig Identity | Design Firm: Concrete Design Communications Inc., Toronto | Client: Keilhauer | Art Directors: Diti Katona, John Pylypczak | Designer: Tom Koukodimos | Photographers: Colin Faulkner, Finn O'Hara

Description: Keilhauer is a designer and manufacturer of office chairs and tables. To differentiate its products in a crowded North American market, Keilhauer's media products employ humor, simplicity and boldness – unusual brand characteristics in the industry.

This branding campaign introduces a new chair called Sguig, designed by Eoos. Sguig is the first Keilhauer chair to feature a new design technology that provides optimum comfort and support.

Health

150~153 Lovelace Health System Rebrand Launch | Design Firm: Kilmer & Kilmer Brand Consultants, Albuquerque | Client: Lovelace Health System | Art Directors: Richard Kilmer, Randall Marshall | Designers: Wayne Allen, Renee Innis | Photographer: Michael Barley

Description: The 85-year-old Lovelace Health System brand was in need of an overhaul. We reinvented their brand by capitalizing on the word "love" in their name, a powerful word that communicates care, passion, sensitivity and comfort. Our graphic solution features a versatile gerbera daisy with an aesthetic appeal, particularly to women, the primary decision makers in healthcare. We integrated this solution into a corporate identity system that now ties together a previously fragmented brand.

Non-Profit

154~159 Brand Development | Design Firm: Landor Associates, San Francisco | Client: First Graduate | Creative Director: Paul Chock | Designers: Henricus Kusbiantoro, JJ Ha, E Gilliam | Executive Creative Director: Nicolas Aparicio | Project Manager: Mignon Monroe

Description: Founded in 2000, the former Bay Area Youth Development Fund (b.a.y. fund) is a San Francisco non-profit that believes education is a powerful tool that helps young people overcome adversity, develop character and build community. Their mission is to help young people finish high school and become the first in their families to graduate from college.

The organization was challenged by the confusion and unfamiliarity of its name. Landor aided their rebranding efforts by first assisting in the early stages of the naming development, and later creating their new identity that unified the focus and inspiration they wanted to express in their new name, First Graduate.

Based on First Graduate's philosophy of using education to overcome adversity, develop character and build community, the new identity, consists of a wordmark with a superscripted number one. It clearly communicates the organization's mission to tutor and mentor children so they become the first college graduates in their families.

PaperCompanies

160~165 Brand Identity | Design Firm: Hangar18 Creative Group Ltd., Vancouver | Client: Pink Door Paper Company | Account Director/Designer: Sean Carter

Description: A complete design program and naming of an upstart stationery company that puts a focus on tight, modern patterns that appeal to a design-savvy consumer base. We wanted the patterns on the cards to be personal and almost wearable, so they vary between bold and masculine geometrics to feminine and soft florals. Absolutely no bamboo shoots or orchid branch designs here! The logo suggests a watermarking die, while the supporting components—the packaging, web site and sales kit—are designed to be bold yet flat to thrust the emphasis back on to the patterns and texture of the product.

Printers

166~169 Colournet | Design Firm: 300million, London | Client: Colournet | Art Directors: Matt Baxter, Martin Lawless | Designer: Katie Morgan

Description: Colournet is a print consultancy, specialising in quality litho work for the creative industry. Their clients include many of the UK's mostly highly regraded brand and design agencies, as well as high-end commercial clients.

Products

170~173 Branding | Design Firm: Hahn Smith Design Inc., Toronto | Client: Gourmet Settings (Hildy Abrams) | Art Directors: Alison Hahn, Nigel Smith | Designers: Stephane Monnet, Brian Kroekker, Leo Jung, Tearney McMurtry | Photographers: Brian Sano, Bob Gundo, Stephane Monnet, Foila Studios | Writers: Nigel Smith, Alison Hahn, Brian Kroekker, Stephane Monnet

Description: The Gourmet Settings brand proposition is to re-think the conventions of flatware design and production, and to produce beautiful, contemporary, fine quality products at great prices. So how does this small Canadian flatware company with a very limited marketing budget compete with housewares giants? Using bold graphics and playful, no-nonsense copywriting and talking directly to the consumer we tell them in plain language why the product is better. We also try to make an emotional connection with the copy such as: "Think about it. You use your utensils 365 days a year. Shouldn't they bring a smile to your lips?" Press folders, stationery, and compliments cards are easily identifiable as Gourmet Settings-esque. The business cards communicate at a glance what Gourmet Settings sells and the brand personality. The Gourmet Settings catalogue is an important marketing tool for buyers and retailers. Used to present the Gourmet Settings flatware to potential retailers, the catalogue stands at the forefront of Gourmet Settings identity and has been distributed to retailers internationally. The website, recently completed, is a primary Gourmet Settings branding, marketing and sales piece. (There wasn't enough room to add all of our contributors, and we must include an integral member of our team to the list—the programmer, Matt Burtch).

174, 175 Handy Horse Packaging | Design Firm: Zync Communications Inc., Toronto | Client: Weston Forest Group | Art Director: Michael Kasperski | Creative Director: Marko Zonta | Designer: Michael Kasperski

Description: When you have an "easy to use and store" product, like the Handy Horse, it's all about making sure that the consumer understands this at a glance when scouring the shelves of their local hardware store. Zync developed a simple, bilingual creative treatment on the package's external showing regular people handling and assembling the product.

Promotions

176 Origami Tuna Party Invite: "Tunagami" | Design Firm: Wallace Church, Inc., New York | Client: Wallace Church, Inc. | Creative Director: Stan Church | Designer: Chung-Tao Tu

Description: Every year Wallace Church throws a Tuna Party where we grill up fresh tuna for our clients and friends. For our 2007 party, we created a unique invitation: an origami fish. We printed our invitation as a small poster, black on black, and folded it into a fish. We then tucked the fish into a clear plastic pillow envelope and sent it "swimming" through the mail to its recipient. Upon receipt, the guest would tug at the designated fin to unfold the fish, revealing the invitation.

177 Wallace Church Thanksgiving Wine | Design Firm: Wallace Church, Inc., New York | Client: Wallace Church, Inc. | Creative Director: Stan Church | Designers: Bird Tubkam, Chung-Tao Tu

Description: Every year Wallace Church designs a Thanksgiving wine bottle as a gift for clients and friends. Here, a simple twist on a classic fork (creating a whimsical turkey) suggests all things Thanksgiving: a turkey feast with a good wine.

Restaurants

178~181 Chili's Restaurant Brand | Design Firm: Sibley/Peteet Design, Austin | Client: Chili's Restaurant | Art Director: Rex Peteet | Chief Creative Officer/Creative Director: Tim McClure /Mythos, GSD&M's Branding Group | Designers: Rex Peteet, Carrie Eco | Illustrator: Rex Peteet | Photographer: Matthew Wetzler

182~185 PLATINUM Mathias Dahlgren Restaurant | Design Firm: Dolhem Design, Stockholm | Client: Mathias Dahlgren | Art Director/Designer/Illustrator: Jan Vana | Creative Director: Christophe Dolhem | Photographer: Lennart Weibull | Project Manager: Sara Helmersson

Description: When the Bocuse d'Or winner Mathias Dahlgren opened his new restaurant at the Grand Hotel in Stockholm, Dolhem Designs job was to create a common language for the two dining halls in the reastaurant—the bar and the dining room.

The logotype is based on Mathias initialls MD, and are in the shape of a fork and a spoon. The graphic profile conveys the restaurants ambition of showcasing the typically Swedish in an innovative way in both food and shape.

186~189 Cava Identity | Design Firm: Concrete Design Communications Inc., Toronto | Client: Cava Tapas Restaurant | Art Directors: Diti Katona, John Pylypczak | Designer/Illustrator: Agnes Wong

Description: Cava is acclaimed chef/owner Chris McDonald's interpretation of rustic, modern dining – a wine and tapas bar featuring eclectic flavours from Spain, Italy and France with occasional Mexican flourishes. Concrete designed an identity program featuring a series of whimsical illustrations that capture the casual and playful dining experience as well as the restaurant's reputation for in-house cured meats.

190, 191 GIGIS KANTINE | Design Firm: Brandl & Schärer AG, Olten | Client: Luigi Lansini | Creative Director/Designer: Massimo Lansini

Description: Corporate identity for a canteen and catering company.

192~195 Manhattan Dining/CI | Design Firm: Graphics & Designing Inc., Tokyo | Client: Will Planning Inc. | Art Director: Toshihiro Onimaru | Creative Director: Takanori Aiba | Designer: Toshihiro Onimaru

Retail

196~201 Logo, Packaging, Stationery items for The GadgetShop | Design Firm: ArthurSteenHorneAdamson, Gloucestershire | Client: The GadgetShop | Account Director: Mike Horne | Associate Creative Director: Scott McGuffie | Copywriters: Marksteen Adamson, Mike Horne, Scott McGuffie, Richard Delingpole | Creative Director/Creative Strategist: Marksteen Adamson | Designer: Scott McGuffie | Illustrators: Robbie Graham, Russell Hancock, Richard Delingpole | Project Manager: Tanya Brookes

Description: The original Gadget Shop went into administration in 2002. The company name, trademarks and domain names were bought by the Entertainer group and re-launched in 2007. The positioning of the brand needed to make it stand out in an overcrowded market, something that hadn't been the case when the original Gadget Shop was started in 1991. With a target audience of predominantly male web-savvy 18-40 year olds and a certain amount of gift-buying girlfriends and mothers, the brand needed to stand out both in-store and on-line.

Corporate Identity – The Gadgetshop logo symbol is an illustration of a pair of old-school safety goggles and the gadget shop logo is set in simple Helvetica, in purple (thus retaining one of the original brand elements), on a bright yellow background, giving the company a geeky, scientific laboratory look to go with the new tone of voice. The line "Serious about gadgets" in the logo is intended to make The Gadgetshop stand apart from those who merely sell gimmicks.

Writing for Design/Packaging – Every application in the brand identity has a statement beginning with "In the event of...," an homage to Department "Q" of James Bond. This tone of voice is intended to give the products the feel of coming to you directly from the Quartermaster of a Secret Service Department, elevating otherwise trivial or silly items to the status of essential, potentially life-saving Gadgets.

Stationery – Every piece of corporate printed matter, from business card to letterhead, becomes a gadget in it's own right. For example, business cards also double up as Gadget No. 0172: the Fake Moustache card—which can be used, "in the event of having to slip out of the office unnoticed." The implication is: Gadgets are no laughing matter and Gadgetshop is serious about Gadgets.

Packaging – The intention is that every item in the Gadgetshop range is a vital piece of equipment that may, conceivably, save your life. Every Gadget has a Gadget Number and is signed off by the testing department. The no-nonsense line illustrations give instructions on the use of the Gadget inside, while the information panels give important statistics and vital data. A statement beginning "in the event of" makes it quite clear that even ostensibly trivial items are, in fact, Serious Gadgets.

202, 203 Neighborhood Hops Traveling Beer Festival | Design Firm: [illegible] advertising, B[illegible] | Client: Deschutes Brewery | Account Director: Kevin Smyth | Art Director: A[illegible] Moreno – Collateral/Ad | Chief Creative Officer: Paul Evers | Creative Director: [illegible] Jenkins | Designer: Sebastian Schroeder – Barrel | Illustrator: Corianton Hale - Collateral/Ad | Set Designer & Props: [illegible] - Paul - EP Industries - Barrel Fabricator | Writer: Frank Gjata - Collateral/Ad

Description: The challenge: How do you convey the passion of a craft brewery to markets outside the region?

Solution – Bring the brewery and pub experience to them. Execution: Create a one-of-a-kind giant traveling beer barrel (essentially a traveling pub) that holds 12 kegs and 16 taps. Create a series of traveling beer festivals that tour neighborhoods celebrating the craft of great beer making and the spirit of the local community with local music and fare. Spread the word using a mix of traditional media and non-traditional local grassroots event marketing. Wild postings and telephone pole postings, posters in coffee shops and bookstores, the barrel as a mobile billboard promoting the next event and 10,000 handbills distributed at other large public events all advertise the event series in a manner that is purposefully low-key and authentic to a neighborhood event. All proceeds benefited local charities."

204, 205 Mercantile Exchange | Design Firm: TOKY Branding + Design, St. Louis | Client: [illegible] Companies | Chief Creative Officer: Eric Thoelke | Designers: [illegible]

Description: Overall Branding of St. Louis' Downtown retail district

206, 207 Red Lane | Design Firm: Clemenger BBDO, Wellington | Client: Duty Free Stores | Art Director/Designer: Dianne Fuller | Creative Director: [illegible] | Photographer: [illegible]

Description: Re-branding Duty Free Stores New Zealand – Wellington

Objective – To create a new down town (out of Airport) duty free shopping brand that capitalised on the essence of duty free shopping as an extension of the travel experience and to reposition the competitors as just purveyors of luxury goods.

Idea – To bring the International Airport experience into the inner city

Solution – We used the language of the airport customs and the duty free shopping experience to create a new name—"Red Lane"—the path you take when you have purchased something to declare. This was visually supported with imagery of luxury and fashion goods shown as x-rays. We used the shopping bag as a branded badge that customers wear with pride on and beyond their journey.

Results – Sales In the first quarter of reopening sales were up 93% over the same period last year Promotional Efficacy Following a successful series of launch parties with local travel agents as well as the creation of a new Red Lane branded direct marketing material they have seen redemptions of vouchers triple in the last three months of operation.

Awards – Red Lane was awarded best new business in the Wellington Top Shop Awards in October 2003. Entrance into the Top Shop Awards is by customer nomination, and judging is carried out by [illegible] and a panel of retail experts. Stores are judged on service, shop fit and promotional execution.

Services

208, 209 Miller and Green Cards | Design Firm: [illegible] Associates, Australia | Client: Miller and Green | Account Director: Richard Curtis | Art Directors: Jason Little, Angela McCarthy | Design Director: Jason Little | Designers: Jason Little, Angela McCarthy, [illegible] | Executive Creative Director: Mike Staniford | Project Manager: Karan Savory | Writers: Angela McCarthy, Sam Moore

Description: We were asked to create an identity for the new Miller and Green salon, which would mirror their promise to be elegant, unique and experience-driven within a traditionally generic industry.

We advised Miller and Green to launch a strong brand from the outset that would drive their business and create impact in the market. A series of postcards were distributed to local and surrounding businesses revealing the new salons identity and location. The focal point of each card was the delivery of writing that illustrated the salons elegant yet vivacious character. This irreverent and playful attitude was maintained through all communications with the customer, including the return survey card.

Sports

210~213 Canyon | Design Firm: KMS Team GmbH, Bavaria | Client: Canyon Bikes | Art Director: Helena Frühauf | Chief Creative Officer: Knut Maierhofer | Creative Director: Christoph Rohrer | Designer: Grace Chou | Project Manager: Sandra Ehm | Print Producer: Melanie Sauer

Description: Canyon Bicycles commissioned us to redesign its corporate appearance. In the context of a holistic corporate identity process, we advise the manufacturer of exclusive sports bicycles in the areas of brand development, corporate design and communication in space. The central element is the striking, left-tilted lettering.

214, 215 V.I.O. | Design Firm: Duffy & Partners LLC, Minneapolis | Client: V.I.O. | Designers: Joseph Duffy IV, Alan Leusink | Project Manager: Bridget Schumacher | Creative Director: Dan Olson | Associate Creative Director: Alan Leusink

Description: V.I.O. – Video. In and Out – is a new company introducing portable and wearable video camera technology. This technology allows you to record digital video with hands free operation by attaching the camera lens head to a helmet, bike handle, firearm or any other device in motion. The charge was to communicate that V.I.O. is something new and unique. The stationery system's simplicity and color combination appeals to both of the company's target markets: the enthusiast sports participants (skiers, mountain bikers, surfers) and tactical (military, police, fire) customers.

216, 217 Identity for the Lakeview Golf Club | Design Firm: Sang Yoon/Freelancer, Keezletown | Client: Lakeview Golf Club | Account Director: Harold Teer | Art Director/Artist/Designer/Illustrator/Photographer: Sang Yoon

Transportation

218~223 Exomos Brand Identity | Design Firm: FutureBrand, New York | Client: Exomos | Creative Director: Avrom Tobias | Designers: Mike Williams, Tom Li, Brendan Oneill, Mike Sheehan, Tini chen, Phil Rojas | Illustrators: Antonio Baglione, Oliver de la Rama | Writer: Stephanie Carroll

Description: With unprecedented developments built on water (e.g.- The Palm—the world's largest man-made islands and The World- islands in the shape of continents), it is not surprising that a revolutionary submarine and submersible company emerged out of Dubai—a company that offers a unique range of products for consumer, military and commercial audiences. We were hired to rename the company (initially called Palm Submarines), create an identity and provide full marketing support. The brand was positioned as a bold new way to explore the new wild blue yonder (or blue under!). The new name, based on the idea of "exo-skeletal" suggests the submersibles becomes like a second skin to users under the water and brand identity effectively captures the interplay and reflection of movement above and below water.

Having created a high-tech, modern design system used across all Exomos marketing materials, the company truly stands out as an innovative leader in aquatic engineering. Deciding to let the brand speak for itself, we chose to highlight the submersibles as works of art and serious machines. We meticulously rendered each one using 3D programs, effectively communicating the scientific principles through diagrams and wireframes. A brochure reinforced the company's amazing achievements and advancements, while the use of neon and metallic inks and varnishes helped further suggest the unique boldness of the products. The entire Exomos package mirrored the visionary mission of the company and its inventor, and created a high-tech brand for those seeking new fields of discovery.

224, 225 IBA Hamburg Corporate Design | Design Firm: feldmann+schultchen design studios, Hamburg | Client: IBA Hamburg GmbH | Art Directors: Ekaterina Grizik, Eva Malawska, Julia Otten, Arne Schultchen, Andre Feldmann

Description: Leap across the Elbe, the motto of the 2006 – 2013 IBA - Internationale Bauausstellung [International Building Exhibition], captured within a logo that portrays the planning process and the objectives as well as the will and fortitude of the city and its inhabitants. "The leap" became the leading symbol for Hamburg's most significant building project, the progress and linking of the Elbe islands, the largest inner-city development area of all major cities. Slanted stripes which distinctively and architecturally formed the appearance of the IBA Hamburg will accompany and highlight all processes and results over the coming years.

226~228 New Mexico Rail Runner Express Corporate Indetity | Design Firm: Vaughn Wedeen Creative, Inc., Albuquerque | Client: The Mid-Region Council of Governments of New Mexico (MRCOG) | Account Director: Wendy Forbes | Art Directors/Creative Directors/Designers: Steve Wedeen, Rick Vaughn, Pamela Chang

ContributorsDirectory

300million www.300million.com
1 Rosoman Place, Exmouth Market, London, EC1R OJY, United Kingdom
Tel +44 020 7833 3838

ArthurSteenHorneAdamson www.ashawebsite.com
Suite 404 Eagle Tower, Montpellier Drive, Cheltenham, Gloucestershire, GL50 1TA, United Kingdom
Tel +44 01242 574111 | Fax +44 01242 574333

BBI STUDIO INC.
Oxson 3F, 1-2-13, Shintomi, Chuo-Ku, Tokyo, 104-0041 Japan
Tel +81 3 3552 6960 | Fax +81 3 3552 6950

BIG/Ogilvy & Mather www.ogilvy.com
309 West 49th Street, New York, NY 10019, United States
Tel 212 237 6621 | Fax 212 237 4106

Brandl & Schärer AG www.brandl.ch
Solothurnerstrasse 121, Postfach, Olten 4601, Switzerland
Tel +41 (0)62 205 90 40 | Fax +41 (0)62 205 90 45

Clemenger BBDO www.clemengerdesign.co.nz
8 Kent Terrace, Wellington, New Zealand
Tel/Fax 64 4 802 3362

The Coca-Cola Company www.coca-cola.com
1 Coca Cola Plz NW, Atlanta, GA 30313, United States
Tel 404 957 9899

Concrete Design Communications Inc. www.concrete.ca
2 Silver Avenue, Toronto, ON M6R 3A2, Canada
Tel 416 534 9960 | Fax 416 534 2184

Concussion, LLC www.concussion.net
707 W Vickery Boulevard, Suite 103, Fort Worth, TX 76104, United States
Tel 817 336 6824 | Fax 817 336 6823

Dolhem Design www.dolhemdesign.se
Nybrogatan 3, Stockholm, 114 34, Sweden
Tel +46 8 771 50 47 | Fax +46 8 771 50 48

Duffy & Partners LLC www.duffy.com
713 South Second Street, Suite 602, Minneapolis, MN 55401, United States
Tel 612 548 2333 | Fax 612 548 2334

feldmann+schultchen design studios www.fsdesign.de
Himmelstrasse 10-16, d-22299, Hamburg , Germany
Tel +49(0)40 51 00 00 | Fax +49(0)40 51 70 00

FutureBrand, London www.futurebrand.com
14 Gray's Inn Road, London, WC1X 8WS, United Kingdom
Tel +44 207 067 0010 | Fax +44 870 990 5473

FutureBrand, New York www.futurebrand.com
300 Park Avenue South, 5th Fl, New York, NY 10010, United States
Tel 212 931 6300 | Fax 212 931 6301

Gee + Chung Design www.geechungdesign.com
38 Bryant Street, Suite 100, San Francisco, CA 94105, United States
Tel 415 543 1192 | Fax 415 543 6088

Graphic Design, Apple Computer www.apple.com
1 Infinite Loop MS 83-PPS Cupertino, CA 95014, United States
Tel 408 974 5286 | Fax 408 974 9649

Graphics & Designing Inc. www.gandd.co.jpt
3-3-1 Shirokanedai, Minato-ku, Tokyo, Japan
Tel +81 3 3449 0651 | Fax +81 3 3449 0653

Hahn Smith Design Inc. www.hahnsmithdesign.com
398 Adelaide Street West, Suite #1007, Toronto, ON M5V1S7, Canada
Tel 416 504 8833 | Fax 416 504 8444

Hangar18 Creative Group Ltd. www.hangar18creative.com
220-1737 West. 3rd Avenue, Vancouver, BC V6J 1K7, Canada
Tel 604 737 7111 | Fax 604 737 7166

Hornall Anderson Design Works www.hadw.com
1008 Western Avenue, Suite 600 Seattle WA 98104, United States
Tel 206 467 5800 | Fax 206 467 6411

Kilmer & Kilmer Brand Consultants www.kilmer2.com
125 Truman NE, Albuquerque, NM 87108, United States
Tel 505 260 1175 | Fax 505 260 1155

KMS TEAM GmbH www.kms-team.de
Tölzer Str. 2c, D-81379 Munich, Germany
Tel +49 (0)89 490411-0 | Fax +49 (0)89 490411-109

Landor Associates, Australia www.landor.com
Level 11, 15 Blue Street, North Sydney, NSW 2060 Australia
Tel +61 2 8908 8700

Landor Associates, San Francisco www.landor.com
1001 Front Street, San Francisco, CA 94111, United States
Tel 415 365 1700 | Fax 415 365 3197

Naughtyfish Design www.naughtyfish.com.au
Level 3, 306B, Rushcutters Bay, NSW 2011 Australia
Tel 02 9357 5911 | Fax 02 9029 4062

Piaggio & C. S.p.A. www.piaggio.com
Viale Rinaldo Piaggio, 25, 56025 Pontedera (PISA), Italy
Tel +39 0587 272111 | Fax +39 0587 272344

Poulin + Morris Inc. www.piaggio.com
286 Spring Street, Sixth Floor, New York, NY 10013, United States
Tel 212 675 1332 | Fax 212 675 3027

Sandstrom Partners www.sandstromdesign.com
808 SW 3rd, No 610, Portland, OR 97204, United States
Tel 503 248 9466 | Fax 503 227 5035

Sang Yoon
4050 Walnut Hill Drive, Keezletown, VA 22832, United States
Tel 540 568 6833 | Fax 540 568 6598

Sibley/Peteet Design, Austin www.spdaustin.com
522 East 6th Street, Austin, TX 78701, United States
Tel 512 473 2333 | Fax 512 473 2431

Siegel & Gale LLC www.siegelgale.com
437 Madison Avenue, 12th Floor New York, NY 10022, United States
Tel 212 817 6650 | Fax 212 817 6680

Sotheby's www.sothebys.com
1334 York Avenue, New York, NY 10021, United States
Tel 212 894 1180 | Fax 212 894 1231

tbd advertising www.tbdadvertising.com
856 NW Bond Street, #2, Bend, OR 97701, United States
Tel 541 388 7558 | Fax 541 388 7532

TOKY Branding + Design www.toky.com
3001 Locust Street, St. Louis, MO 63103, United States
Tel 314 534 2000 | Fax 314 534 2001

Turner Duckworth www.turnerduckworth.com
831 Montgomery Street, San Francisco, CA 94133, United States
Tel 415 675 7777 | Fax 415 675 7778

Vaughn Wedeen Creative, Inc. www.vwc.com
116 Central Avenue, SW Suite #300, Albuquerque, NM 87102, United States
Tel 505 243 4000 | Fax 505 247 9856

Ventress Design Group www.ventress.com
3310 Aspen Grove Drive, Suite 303, Franklin, TN 37067, United States
Tel 615 727 0155 | Fax 615 727 0159

Wallace Church, Inc. www.wallacechurch.com
330 East 48th Street, New York, NY 10017, United States
Tel: 212 755 2903 | Fax: 212 355 6872

Wren and Rowe Ltd www.wrenrowe.co.uk
4-6 Denbigh Mews, Near Pimlico, London, SW1V 2HQ, United Kingdom
Tel +44 207 828 5333 | Fax +44 870 487 7035

Yello Brands www.yellobrands.com
30 Boronia Street, Redfern, NSW, 2016 Australia
Tel +61 2 9319 7788

Young and Laramore www.yandl.com
407 North Fulton Street, Indianapolis, IN 46202, United State
Tel 317 264 8000 | Fax 317 264 8001

Zync Communications Inc. www.zync.ca
282 Richmond Street East, Suite 200, Toronto, ON M5A 1PA, Canada
Tel 416 322 2865 | Fax 416 322 2864

DesignFirmsIndex

DesignersIndex

ClientsIndex

AccountDirectorsIndex

ArtDirectorsIndex

CreativeDirectorsIndex

DesignDirectorsIndex

CreativeStrategistsIndex

ProjectManagersIndex

PhotographersIndex

IllustratorsIndex

CopywritersIndex

WritersIndex

AdditionalContributorsIndex

Two ways to dramatically save on our Books!

Standing Orders:
50% off or $35 for a $70 book, plus $10 for shipping & handling
Get our new books at our best deal, long before they arrive in book stores! A Standing Order is a subscription commiment to the Graphis books of your choice.

Pre-Publication Sales:
35% off or $45 for a $70 book, plus $10 for shipping & handling
Our next best deal. Sign-up today at www.graphis.com to receive our pre-publication sale invitations! Order early and save!

Graphis Titles

DesignAnnual2009

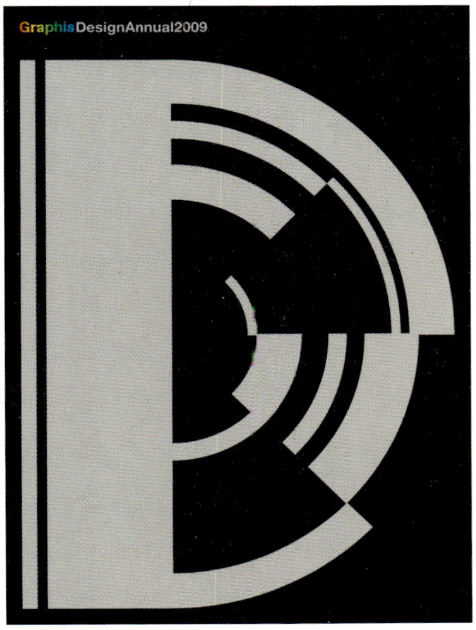

Summer 2008
Hardcover: 256 pages
200-plus color illustrations

Trim: 8.5 x 11.75"
ISBN: 1-932026-13-4
US $70

GraphisDesignAnnual2009 assembles an international trio of Designers as New York's **Stefan Sagmeister**, South Korea's **Ahn Sang-Soo**, and Pentagram London's **Harry Pearce** present their sagacious views on Design under the theme of "What's Personal Is Universal." Features over 300 award-winning designs in 30-plus categories by industry standouts like **Ogilvy, TAXI Canada, Frost Design, BBDO, Melchior Imboden, Turner Duckworth**, and **RBMM**, among many others.

NewTalentAnnual'07/'08

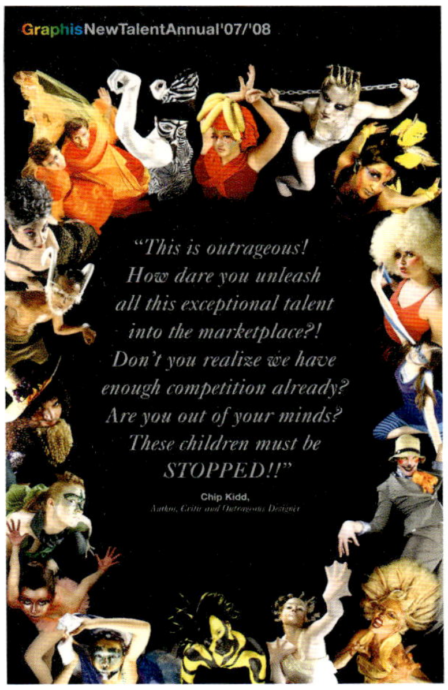

Fall 2007
Hardcover: 256 pages
300-plus color images

Trim: 7 x 11 3/4"
ISBN: 1-932026-42-8
US $70

GraphisNewTalentAnnual'07/'08 is a forum for the year's best internationally produced student work. It provides young talent a rare opportunity for exposure and recognition, and serves as an invaluable resource for firms seeking the best and brightest new professionals. This year, we honor two highly respected organizations and their chairs: Designer **Chris Hill** of the Creative Summit student design show and the School of Visual Arts' Department Chair, **Richard Wilde**.

AdvertisingAnnual2009

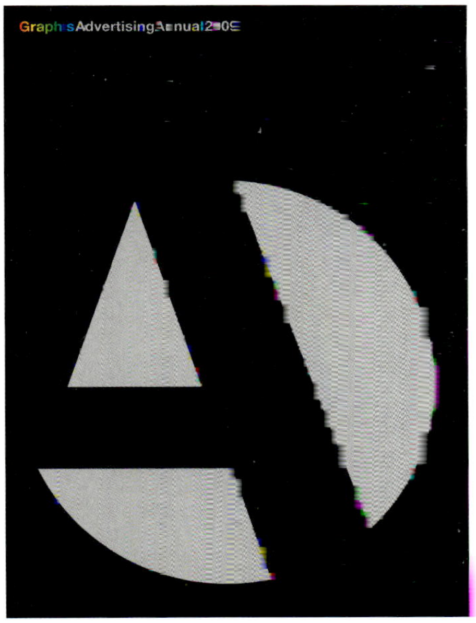

Fall 2008
Hardcover: 256 pages
300-plus color images

Trim: 8.5 x 11.75"
ISBN: 1-932026-52-5
US $70

GraphisAdvertisingAnnual2009 spotlights the year's best print ads from New York to New Delhi. This year, **Dangel Advertising** describes their latest Crate & Barrel campaign, **DeVito/Verdi** explains their Legal Sea Foods mock-newspaper ads, and **The Partners** discuss a unique outdoor exhibition for The National Gallery. Features 200+ Gold and Platinum winning ads from agencies like **The Martin Agency, MacLaren McCann, BVK** and **Goodby Silverstein & Partners**.

Letterhead7

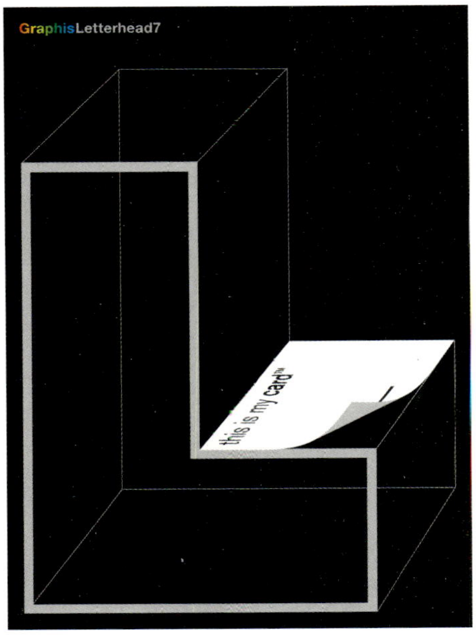

Fall 2007
Hardcover: 256 pages
300-plus color illustrations

Trim: 8.5 x 11.75"
ISBN: 1-932026-49-5
US $70

GraphisLetterhead7 is a comprehensive collection of the most innovative stationery designs of the last few years. Seamlessly combining art and function, each featured piece has been awarded a new Graphis Gold or Platinum Award for excellence. Selected from an extensive pool of entries, winning designs were created by internationally respected firms like **Catapult Strategic Design, Guy Villa Design, Graphics & Designing Inc., KNARF, Voicebox Creative**, and **The Moderns**.

LogoDesign7

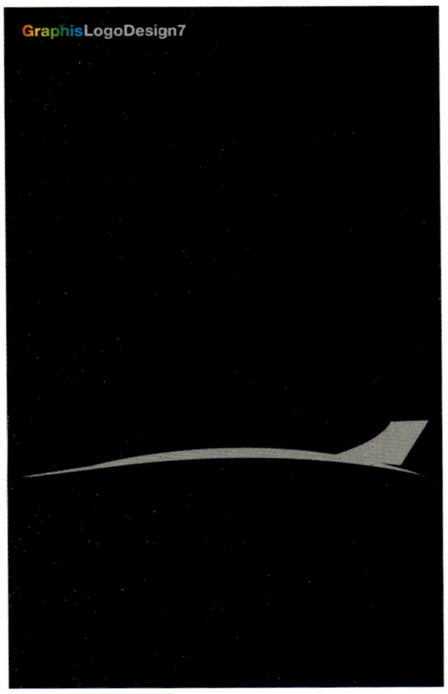

Spring 2008
Hardcover: 256 pages
500-plus color images

Trim: 7 x 11 3/4"
ISBN: 1-932026-03-7
US $70

GraphisLogoDesign7 features profiles and interviews with some of the world's most respected designers: **Steve Sandstrom** of Sandstrom Design, Pentagram New York's **Michael Bierut**, G+D's **Toshihiro Onimaru**, **Joe Duffy** of Duffy & Partners, **Don Sibley** and **Rex Peteet** of Sibley/Peteet Design, Catapult's **Art Lofgreen**, RBMM's **Brian Boyd**, and the creator of the world-famous Recycling logo, **Gary Anderson**. The solutions presented in here are the world's best.

PosterAnnual'08/'09

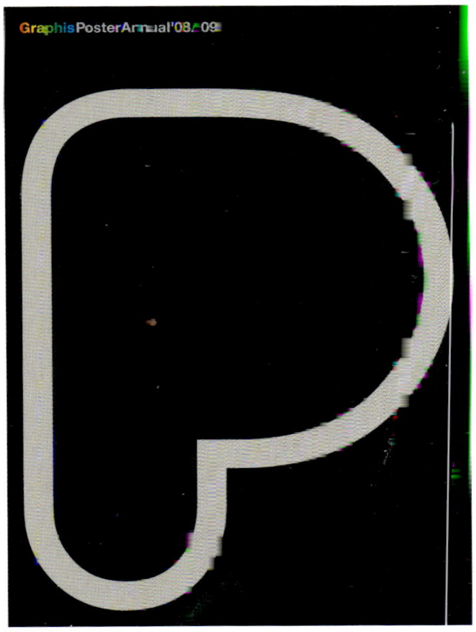

Summer 2008
Hardcover: 256 pages
300-plus color images

Trim: 8.5 x 11.75"
ISBN: 1-932026-12-5
US $70

GraphisPosterAnnual'08/'09 features a symposium of poster curators and collectors from MoMA, the German Poster Museum, Hong Kong Heritage Museum, Switzerland's Basler Afrika Bibliographien, Lahti Poster Museum, Cuba's Casa de las Americas, and Rene Wanner's Poster Page. Topics include selection criteria and current trends. Presenting over 300 of the year's best posters by Designers like **Milton Glaser**, **Niklaus Troxler**, and **Takashi Akiyama**, this is a must-have

Available at www.graphis.com

www.graphis.com